PAUL'S RHETORIC IN ITS CONTEXTS

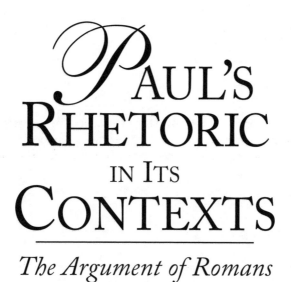

PAUL'S RHETORIC
IN ITS
CONTEXTS

The Argument of Romans

THOMAS H. TOBIN, SJ

HENDRICKSON PUBLISHERS

© 2004 by Thomas H. Tobin, SJ

Hendrickson Publishers, LLC
P. O. Box 3473
Peabody, Massachusetts 01961-3473

ISBN 1-56563-946-4

Printed in the United States of America

First Printing — October 2004

Cover Art: Detail of Saint Paul from the cupola mosaic located in the baptistry of the Arians, Ravenna, Italy. Photo used by permission of Scala / Art Resource, NY.

Imprimi potest: Very Rev. Edward W. Schmidt, SJ, Provincial, Chicago Province of the Society of Jesus, February 23, 2004.

Library of Congress Cataloging-in-Publication Data

Tobin, Thomas H., 1945–
    Paul's rhetoric in its contexts : the argument of Romans / Thomas H. Tobin.
      p. cm.
    Includes bibliographical references and indexes.
    ISBN 1-56563-946-4 (alk. paper)
    1. Bible. N.T. Romans—Criticism, interpretation, etc. I. Title.
    BS2665.52.T63 2004
    227′.1066—dc22
                         2004013739

In memory of
William G. Thompson, SJ
and James J. Doyle, SJ,
and for
Joseph A. Fitzmyer, SJ
and John Strugnell

Boni magistri
Optimi libri

Table of Contents

Preface   xi

Abbreviations   xiii

Introduction: Issues and Methodology   1

1. Situating Romans: Roman Jews and Roman Christians   16
   The Jewish Community of Rome   17
   The Christian Community of Rome   34
   Conclusions   44

2. Situating Romans: Paul and the Roman Christians   47
   The Immediate Circumstances of Romans   47
   Paul's Convictions and the Controversies Leading up to Romans   53
      Paul's Call   54
      Controversies and Consequences   58
   Paul and the Roman Christian Community at the Time of Romans   70
   Retrospective   76

3. The Structure, Genre, and Purposes of Romans   79
   The Overall Literary Structure of Romans   79
   Literary Cues in Romans   84
   The Diatribe and the Genre of Romans 1:16–11:36   88
   The Purposes of Romans   98

4. Jews, Gentiles, and the Impartiality of God   104
   Romans 1:18–32: The Subproposition and the Exposition   108
   Romans 2:1–3:20: Defense and Proofs   110
      Romans 2:1–11: Apostrophe to Someone Who Acts Hypocritically   110
      Romans 2:12–29: God's Impartiality and Its Consequences   113
         Romans 2:12–16: The Impartiality of God   113
         Romans 2:17–29: Apostrophe to a Jew Who Acts Hypocritically   115
      Romans 3:1–20: Objections and Replies   118
   Conclusions   122

5. The Paradox of Righteousness, Abraham, and Upholding the Law   124
   Romans 3:21–26: The Subproposition and the Exposition   130
   Romans 3:27–4:25: Argument Based on the Example of Abraham   143
     Romans 3:27–31: Rhetorical Questions and Replies   143
     Romans 4:1–25: The Example of Abraham's Faith apart from
      Observance of the Law   145
      Romans 4:1–8: Abraham's Faith Reckoned to Him as
       Righteousness   146
      Romans 4:9–12: Abraham's Righteousness prior to His
       Circumcision   148
      Romans 4:13–17a: The Promise through Faith to All Abra-
       ham's "Seed"   150
      Romans 4:17b–22: Abraham's Firm Faith in God's Promise   151
      Romans 4:23–25: Application to the Present of the Example
       of Abraham's Faith   152
   Conclusions   153

6. The Incompatibility of This Grace and Sin   155
   Romans 5:1–5: The Subproposition   158
   Romans 5:6–21: The Exposition—Christ's Death Is Incompatible
    with Sin   160
     Romans 5:6–11: The Significance of Christ's Death   163
     Romans 5:12–21: Comparison and Contrast of Christ and Adam   166
      Adam's Sin and Its Consequences in Judaism and Earliest
       Christianity   167
      Romans 5:12–14: Adams's Sin   177
      Romans 5:15–21: Comparison and Contrast with Christ   182
   Conclusions   186

7. Baptism and Ethics   188
   Romans 6:1–14: The Reinterpretation of Baptism   192
     Romans 6:1–2: Rhetorical Questions about Continuing in Sin   192
     Romans 6:3–4: Baptism into the Death of Christ   193
     Romans 6:5–11: Dying to Sin and Living to God in Christ Jesus   194
     Romans 6:12–14: Let Not Sin Reign in You but Offer Yourselves to God 196
   The Broader Context of Paul's Arguments in Romans 6:1–14   197
     Galatians 3:26–28   198
     First Corinthians   200
   Romans 6:15–23: Freed from Sin but Slaves to Righteousness   208
     Romans 6:16–19: Slaves Either to Sin or to Righteousness   208
     Romans 6:20–23: The Consequences   209
   The Broader Context of Paul's Arguments in Romans 6:15–23   210
   Conclusions   217

8. The Goodness of the Law and Human Limitations   219
   Romans 7:1–6: Freedom from the Law Compared to Marriage Law   220
   Romans 7:7–25: Speech-in-Character about the Goodness of the Law
    and Human Limitations   225

      The Identity of the Speaker in Romans 7:7–25 and Greco-Roman
        Philosophy   228
      A Detailed Analysis of the Speech-in-Character of Romans 7:7–25   238
   Conclusions   245

9. The Unity of Romans 8–11   251
   Recent Interpretations of Romans 8–11   251
   The Thematic and Rhetorical Structure of Romans 8–11   254
   The Eschatological Contexts of Romans 8–11   256
      Israel in Hellenistic Jewish Eschatology   256
      Israel and the Eschatology of Paul's Earlier Letters   262
   Conclusions   272

10. Eschatology and the Extent of Sonship   273
   Romans 8:1–17: The Spirit and the Reinterpretation of Its Role   274
      Romans 8:1–4: Now No Condemnation in Christ Jesus   279
      Romans 8:5–8: Contrast of Flesh and Spirit   284
      Romans 8:9–13: Those in Whom the Spirit Dwells   285
      Romans 8:14–17: Who Are the Sons and Heirs?   286
   Romans 8:18–30: The Framework of an Inclusive Eschatology   288
      Romans 8:18–22: The Eager Expectation of Creation   289
      Romans 8:23–28: Expectations of Those Who Have Received the Spirit   292
      Romans 8:29–30: Those Called and Destined for Glory   294
   Conclusions   297

11. Paul's Anguish and the Issue of Israel   299
   Important Aspects of Romans 8:31–11:36   300
   First-Person Singular Passages   302
      Romans 9:1–5 and 11:25–27   303
      Romans 10:1–4; 11:1–2; 11:11–14   308
      Romans 8:38–39   316
   Conclusions   317

12. Christ, Jews, and Gentiles   320
   Romans 8:31–9:5: Transition and Introduction   322
      Romans 8:31–39: Nothing Can Separate Us from the Love of God   323
      Romans 9:1–5: Paul's Personal Anguish over His Fellow Jews   324
   Romans 9:6–29: God's Promises Have Not Failed—the Choice of
      Israel and the Gentiles   326
      Romans 9:6–13: God's Promises to Israel Have Not Failed (Abraham,
        Isaac, and Jacob)   326
      Romans 9:14–18: God Is Not Unjust in His Choices (Moses and Pharaoh)   329
      Romans 9:19–29: The Example of the Potter and Its Application to
        God's Richness to Both Jews and Gentiles   331
      Conclusions   339
   Romans 9:30–10:21: The Present Situation of Jews in Relation to the
      Gentiles   339
      Romans 9:30–10:13: Jews, Gentiles, and Christ as the Goal of the Law   341

*Romans 10:14–21: God's Promises and the Present Responses of Israel
   and the Gentiles*   348
Conclusions   352

13. All Israel and the Full Number of the Gentiles   353
   Romans 11:1–10: Israel's Present Hardening Is Partial   354
   Romans 11:11–24: Israel's Disbelief, the Entry of the Gentiles, and the
      Salvation of Israel   358
   Romans 11:25–32: The Mystery of Israel and the Gentiles   368
   Romans 11:33–36: Concluding Praise and Doxology of God   377
   Conclusions   379

14. Issues of Christian Living: Love, Harmony, Accommodation, and the
   Greater Good   383
   The Structure of Romans 12:1–15:7   385
   Romans 12:1–21: Paul's Wisdom Instruction on Christian Ethics   386
      Romans 12:1–2: The Basis of Christian Living   387
      *Romans 12:3–8: Descriptive Section—the Christian Community as
         One Body in Christ*   390
      *Romans 12:9–21: Prescriptive Section—the Theme of Love and Social
         Responsibilities*   393
   Romans 13:1–7: Submission to Secular Authorities and the Payment
      of Taxes   395
   Romans 13:8–14: Love of Neighbor, the Law, and the Demands of
      Baptism   400
      Romans 13:8–10: Love of Neighbor and the Fulfillment of the Law   401
      *Romans 13:11–14: The Nearness of the End and Living Orderly
         Lives*   403
   Romans 14:1–15:7: Reconciling the Weak and the Strong   404
   Conclusions   415

Concluding Observations   417

Appendix: Outline of Romans   425

Bibliography   431

Indexes of Modern Authors   445

Indexes of Ancient Sources   449

Preface

THIS BOOK HAS TAKEN ME LONGER TO WRITE than I expected. I had hoped to complete the book two or three years ago. This delay was partially due to other, more immediate obligations. But it was due also to the nature of the project as it developed. I wanted to reinterpret Paul's letter to the Roman Christians in ways I thought were more closely connected with the circumstances in which Paul wrote the letter. These circumstances included the situation of the Roman Christian community, Paul's own situation in his missionary activities, and how those two situations affected one another. I also wanted to emphasize the arguments Paul was making in the course of the letter and why he made them as he did. But I did not want to write another commentary on Romans. The reason is that commentaries, by their very nature, are forced to concentrate on the text passage by passage. What gets lost is the force and flow of the argument. All of this forced me to rethink Romans in very different ways. This took time, more time than I expected. The result is, I think, a better book; but that is not for me to decide.

A number of people have aided me in the course of writing this book. They include the students in the graduate program in theology at Loyola University of Chicago who, over the past decade, have taken my doctoral course on Romans. They have read much of the book in draft form and have habitually provided helpful and critical assessments of its arguments. A number of them have also been my research assistants: Drs. Susan (Elli) Elliott and Paul Hartog, Hans Svebbaken, Lawrence DiPaolo, Jeffrey Hubing, Sara Massey-Gillispie, Joseph Latham, Robert Garrett, David Creech, and Patricia Walters. They have provided invaluable bibliographical and editorial assistance. Thanks are also due to the members of the Midwest Patristic Seminar, who were kind enough to listen to and critique several chapters of the this book. I want particularly to thank Prof. Frans Jozef van Beeck, S.J., of Loyola University of Chicago, who was kind enough to read the manuscript and offer a number of important suggestions, and Prof. Sarah J. Tanzer of McCormick Theological Seminary, with whom I have discussed this project over the years and who was kind enough to read several chapters of the book and to make invaluable suggestions.

I want to thank both Loyola University of Chicago and the Jesuit Community of Loyola University. Both generously supported me during yearlong academic leaves from Loyola to do much of the research and writing of the book. I also want to thank several journals for their kind permission to use revised versions of articles that first appeared in their pages: the *Catholic Biblical Quarterly* for the use of material in chapter 4; the *Harvard Theological Review* for the use of material in chapter 5. The material in chapters 6 and 12 from *Studia philonica* is used with the permission of Brown Judaic Studies, Brown University.

Quotations of the Bible are from the Revised Standard Version, and quotations from Greek and Latin sources are from the Loeb Classical Library. In the case of translations of Paul from the Revised Standard Version, however, I have consistently changed "justification" and "justify" to "righteousness" and "to make righteous."

Finally, I want to say something about the use of primary and secondary literature. The secondary literature on Romans is virtually infinite, and no one can be expected to have read it all. I certainly have not. I have read much of it; but in order to keep this book in bounds, I have confined the citation of secondary literature to places where I think it is directly relevant to the arguments I am making. I have not tried to enter into all of the different debates about the interpretation of Romans over the centuries. That would have made the book unbearably long. I have, however, generously cited primary sources, from Greek and Latin literature, from Jewish literature of different sorts, and from other early Christian literature. I hope that such citations will allow the reader to understand more clearly and readily Paul's letter to the Roman Christians and the complex worlds of which both Paul and his letter were an integral part.

Abbreviations

GENERAL

ca.	circa
ch(s).	chapter(s)
col(s).	column(s)
ed(s).	editor(s), edited by
e.g.	*exempli gratia*, for example
esp.	especially
fl.	*floruit*, flourished
frg(s).	fragment(s)
HB	Hebrew Bible
Heb.	Hebrew
ibid.	*ibidem*, in the same place
i.e.	*id est*, that is
lit.	literally
LXX	Septuagint (the Greek OT)
MS(S)	manuscript(s)
MT	Masoretic Text (of the OT)
NF	Neue Folge
n(n).	note(s)
no(s).	number(s)
NS	new series
NT	New Testament
OT	Old Testament
p(p).	page(s)
par.	parallel (use to indicate textual parallels, e.g., Matt 25:14–30 par. Luke 19:11–27)
pl.	plate
praef.	*praefatio*
s.v.	*sub verbo*, under the word
trans.	translated by
vol(s).	volume(s)

PRIMARY SOURCES

Apocrypha and Septuagint

Bar	Baruch
Sus	Susanna
1 Esd	1 Esdras
2 Esd	2 Esdras
Add Esth	Additions to Esther
Jdt	Judith
1 Macc	1 Maccabees
2 Macc	2 Maccabees
3 Macc	3 Maccabees
4 Macc	4 Maccabees
Sir	Sirach
Tob	Tobit
Wis	Wisdom of Solomon

Old Testament Pseudepigrapha

Apoc. Ab.	Apocalypse of Abraham
Apoc. Mos.	Apocalypse of Moses
As. Mos.	Assumption of Moses
2 Bar.	2 Baruch (Syriac Apocalypse)
3 Bar.	3 Baruch
4 Bar.	4 Baruch (Paraleipomena Jeremiou)
1 En.	1 Enoch (Ethiopic Apocalypse)
2 En.	2 Enoch (Slavonic Apocalypse)
4 Ezra	4 Ezra
Jos. Asen.	Joseph and Aseneth
Jub.	Jubilees
L.A.B.	Liber antiquitatum biblicarum (Pseudo-Philo)
L.A.E.	Life of Adam and Eve
Let. Aris.	Letter of Aristeas
Odes Sol.	Odes of Solomon
Ps.-Phoc.	Pseudo-Phocylides
Pss. Sol.	Psalms of Solomon
Sib. Or.	Sibylline Oracles
T. Ab.	Testament of Abraham
T. Ash.	Testament of Asher
T. Benj.	Testament of Benjamin
T. Gad	Testament of Gad
T. Iss.	Testament of Issachar
T. Jos.	Testament of Joseph
T. Jud.	Testament of Judah
T. Levi	Testament of Levi

T. Mos.	*Testament of Moses*
T. Naph.	*Testament of Naphtali*
T. Reu.	*Testament of Reuben*
T. Sim.	*Testament of Simeon*
T. Zeb.	*Testament of Zebulun*

Dead Sea Scrolls and Related Texts

1QapGen	Genesis Apocryphon
1QH[a]	*Thanksgiving Hymns[a]*
1QpHab	*Pesher Habakkuk*
1QM	*Milḥamah* or *War Scroll*
1QS	*Serek Hayaḥad* or *Rule of the Community*
4Q285	*Sefer ha-Milḥamah*
4QDibHam[a]	Words of the Luminaries[a]
4QpNah	*Pesher of Nahum*
11QT[a]	*Temple Scroll*
CD	Cairo Genizah copy of the *Damascus Document*

Philo

Abr.	*De Abrahamo*
Aet.	*De aeternitate mundi*
Agr.	*De agricultura*
Cher.	*De cherubim*
Conf.	*De confusione linguarum*
Contempl.	*De vita contemplativa*
Decal.	*De decalogo*
Deus	*Quod Deus sit immutabilis*
Ebr.	*De ebrietate*
Fug.	*De fuga et inventione*
Her.	*Quis rerum divinarum heres sit*
Ios.	*De Iosepho*
Leg. 1, 2, 3	*Legum allegoriae* I, II, III
Legat.	*Legatio ad Gaium*
Migr.	*De migratione Abrahami*
Mos. 1, 2	*De vita Mosis* I, II
Mut.	*De mutatione nominum*
Opif.	*De opificio mundi*
Plant.	*De plantatione*
Post.	*De posteritate Caini*
Praem.	*De praemiis et poenis*
Prob.	*Quod omnis probus liber sit*
QE 1, 2	*Quaestiones et solutiones in Exodum* I, II
QG 1, 2, 3, 4	*Quaestiones et solutiones in Genesin* I, II, III, IV
Sacr.	*De sacrificiis Abelis et Caini*
Sobr.	*De sobrietate*

Somn. 1, 2	*De somniis* I, II
Spec. 1, 2, 3, 4	*De specialibus legibus* I, II, III, IV
Virt.	*De virtutibus*

Josephus

Ag. Ap.	*Against Apion*
Ant.	*Jewish Antiquities*
J.W.	*Jewish War*
Life	*The Life*

Mishnah, Talmud, and Related Literature

b.	Babylonian Talmud
m.	Midrash
t.	Tosefta
y.	Jerusalem Talmud
ᶜAbod. Zar.	*ᶜAbodah Zarah*
Nid.	*Niddah*
Qidd.	*Qiddušin*
Sanh.	*Sanhedrin*
Šabb.	*Šabbat*
Soṭah	*Soṭah*

Targumic Texts and Other Rabbinic Works

ᵓAbot R. Nat.	*ᵓAbot de Rabbi Nathan*
Tg. Neof.	*Targum Neofiti*
Tg. Ps.-J.	*Targum Pseudo-Jonathan*
Tg. Yer. I	*Targum Yerušalmi*

Apostolic Fathers

Barn.	*Barnabas*
1 Clem.	*1 Clement*
Diogn.	*Diognetus*

Ancient Christian Writings

Augustine
| *Civ.* | *De civitate Dei* |

Clement of Alexandria
| *Strom.* | *Stromata* |

Eusebius
| *Hist. eccl.* | *Historia ecclesiastica* |
| *Praep. ev.* | *Preaparatio evangelica* |

Orosius
| *Adv. pag.* | *Adversus paganos* |

Ancient Non-Christian Writings

Aelius Aristides
    Or.   *Orationes*

Aeschylus
    Sept.   *Septem contra Thebas*

Appian
    Hist. rom.   *Historia Romana*

Apuleius
    Metam.   *Metamorphoses*

Aristotle
    Eth. nic.   *Ethica nicomachea*
    Rhet.   *Rhetorica*
    Top.   *Topica*

Arrian
    Ep.   *Epistulae*

Athenaeus
    Deipn.   *Deipnosophistae*

Cicero
    Cat.   *In Catilinam*
    Flac.   *Pro Flacco*
    Inv.   *De inventione rhetorica*
    Lig.   *Pro Ligario*
    Off.   *De officiis*
    De or.   *De oratore*
    Or. Brut.   *Orator ad M. Brutum*
    Part. or.   *Partitiones oratoriae*
    Top.   *Topica*

Columella
    Rust.   *De re rustica*

Demetrius
    Eloc.   *De elocutione (Peri hermēneias)*

Demosthenes
    2 Aristog.   *In Aristogitonem ii*
    Mid.   *In Midiam*

Dio Cassius
    Hist. rom.   *Historia romana*

Dio Chrysostom
    Or.   *Orationes*

Diodorus Siculus
    Bibl. hist.   *Bibliotheca historica*

Diogenes Laertius
    D.L.   Diogenes Laertius, *De clarorum philosophorum vitis*

Pseudo-Diogenes
    Ep.   *Epistulae*

Dionysius of Halicarnassus
    Ant. rom.   *Antiquitates romanae*

Epictetus
 Diatr.   *Diatribae (Dissertationes)*
Euripides
 Andr.   *Andromache*
 Hec.   *Hecuba*
 Hipp.   *Hippolytus*
 Iph. aul.   *Iphigenia aulidensis*
 Med.   *Medea*
 Phoen.   *Phoenissae*
Galen
 Plac. Hip. et
 Plat.   *De placitis Hippocratis et Platonis*
Heraclitus
 All.   *Allegoriae (Quaestiones homericae)*
 Ep.   *Epistulae*
Hermias Alexandrinus
 Plat. Phdr. *In Platonis Phaedrum*
Hermogenes
 Prog.   *Progymnasmata*
Herodotus
 Hist.   *Historiae*
Homer
 Il.   *Ilias*
Horace
 Carm.   *Carmina*
 Serm.   *Sermones*
Isocrates
 Ad Nic.   *Ad Nicoclem*
Juvenal
 Sat.   *Satirae*
Livy
 Urbe cond. *Ab urbe condita libri*
Macrobius
 Sat.   *Saturnalia*
Martial
 Epigr.   *Epigrammata*
Menander
 Mon.   *Monostichoi*
Nepos
 Pel.   *Pelopidas*
Ovid
 Metam.   *Metamorphoses*
Persius
 Sat.   *Satirae*
Petronius
 Sat.   *Satyricon*

Phalaris
    Ep.   *Epistulae*
Plato
    Apol.   *Apologia*
    Leg.   *Leges*
    Phaedr.   *Phaedrus*
    Resp.   *Res publica*
    Symp.   *Symposium*
Plutarch
    Alex.   *Alexander*
    Arat.   *Aratus*
    Cic.   *Cicero*
    Cim.   *Cimon*
    Curios.   *De curiositate*
    Is. Os.   *De Iside et Osiride*
    Pel.   *Pelopidas*
    Stoic. rep.   *De Stoicorum repugnantiis*
Polybius
    Hist.   *Historiae*
Quintilian
    Inst.   *Institutio oratoria*
    Rhet. Her.   *Rhetorica ad Herennium*
Rutilius Lupus
    Fig. sent.   *De figuris sententiarum et elocutionis*
Sallust
    Bell. cat.   *Bellum Catalinae*
Seneca
    Ep.   *Epistulae morales*
    Ira   *De ira*
    Med.   *Medea*
    Tro.   *Troades*
Pseudo-Socrates
    Ep.   *Epistulae*
Sophocles
    Aj.   *Ajax*
    Ant.   *Antigone*
    Oed. col.   *Oedipus coloneus*
    Phil.   *Philoctetes*
Stobaeus
    Ecl.   *Eclogae*
Strabo
    Geogr.   *Geographica*
Suetonius
    Claud.   *Divus Claudius*
    Dom.   *Domitianus*
    Jul.   *Divus Julius*
    Tib.   *Tiberius*

Tacitus
  Agr.   *Agricola*
  Ann.   *Annales*
  Hist.   *Historiae*
Theon of Alexandria
  Prog.   *Progymnasmata*
Thucydides
  Hist.   *Historiae*
Tibullus
  Carm.   *Carmina*
Valerius Maximus
  Fact. et dict.   *Factorum et dictorum memorabilia*
Xenophon
  Anab.   *Anabasis*
  Mem.   *Memorabilia*
  Oec.   *Oeconomicus*

SECONDARY SOURCES

AB   Anchor Bible
ABD   *Anchor Bible Dictionary*. Edited by D. N. Freedman. 6 vols. New York: Doubleday, 1992
ABRL   Anchor Bible Reference Library
AGJU   Arbeiten zur Geschichte des Spätjudentums und Urchristentums
AnBib   Analecta biblica
ANRW   *Aufstieg und Niedergang der römischen Welt: Geschichte und Kultur Roms im Spiegel der neueren Forschung*. Edited by H. Temporini and W. Haase. Berlin, 1972–
AOT   *The Apocryphal Old Testament*. Edited by H. F. D. Sparks. Oxford: Clarendon, 1984.
BDAG   Bauer, Walter, Frederick W. Danker, W. F. Arndt, and F. W. Gingrich. *Greek-English Lexicon of the New Testament and Other Early Christian Literature*. 3d ed. Chicago: University of Chicago Press, 2000
BDF   Blass, F., A. Debrunner, and R. W. Funk. *A Greek Grammar of the New Testament and Other Early Christian Literature*. Chicago: University of Chicago Press, 1961
BECNT   Baker Exegetical Commentary on the New Testament
BEvT   Beiträge zur evangelischen Theologie
Bib   *Biblica*
BJS   Brown Judaic Studies
BNTC   Black's New Testament Commentaries
BZNW   Beihefte zur Zeitschrift für die neutestamentliche Wissenschaft
CBQ   *Catholic Biblical Quarterly*
CBQMS   Catholic Biblical Quarterly Monograph Series
CIJ   *Corpus inscriptionum judaicarum*

Corinth	Corinth: Results of Excavations Conducted by the American School of Classical Studies at Athens
CRINT	Compendia rerum iudaicarum ad Novum Testamentum
CSEL	Corpus scriptorum ecclesiasticorum latinorum
EKKNT	Evangelisch-katholischer Kommentar zum Neuen Testament
FBBS	Facet Books, Biblical Series
FF	Foundations and Facets
FRLANT	Forschungen zur Religion und Literatur des Alten und Neuen Testaments
GLAJJ	*Greek and Latin Authors on Jews and Judaism.* Edited and translated by Menahem Stern. 3 vols. Jerusalem: Israel Academy of Sciences and Humanities, 1974–1984
HDR	Harvard Dissertations in Religion
HTKNT	Herders theologischer Kommentar zum Neuen Testament
HTR	*Harvard Theological Review*
HTS	Harvard Theological Studies
IB	*Interpreter's Bible.* Edited by G. A. Buttrick et al. 12 vols. New York: Abingdon, 1951–1957
ICC	International Critical Commentary
JBL	*Journal of Biblical Literature*
JIWE	*Jewish Inscriptions of Western Europe.* David Noy. 2 vols. Cambridge: Cambridge University Press, 1993–1995
JJS	*Journal of Jewish Studies*
JQR	*Jewish Quarterly Review*
JSJSup	Supplements to the Journal for the Study of Judaism
JSNTSup	Journal for the Study of the New Testament: Supplement Series
JSPSup	Journal for the Study of the Pseudepigrapha: Supplement Series
LD	Lectio divina
LEC	Library of Early Christianity
LSJ	Liddell, H. G., R. Scott, H. S. Jones. *A Greek-English Lexicon.* 9th ed. with revised supplement. Oxford: Clarendon, 1996
MBS	Message of Biblical Spirituality
MNTC	Moffatt New Testament Commentary
NEchtB	Neue Echter Bibel
NICNT	New International Commentary on the New Testament
NJBC	*The New Jerome Biblical Commentary.* Edited by R. E. Brown et al. Englewood Cliffs: Prentice-Hall, 1990
NovT	*Novum Testamentum*
NTAbh	Neutestamentliche Abhandlungen
NTS	*New Testament Studies*
NumenSup	Supplements to Numen
OCD	*Oxford Classical Dictionary.* Edited by S. Hornblower and A. Spawforth. 3d ed. Oxford: Oxford University Press, 1996.
OTP	*Old Testament Pseudepigrapha.* Edited by J. H. Charlesworth. 2 vols. New York: Doubleday, 1983–1985
PNTC	Pillar New Testament Commentary

SBLDS	Society of Biblical Literature Dissertation Series
SBLEJL	Society of Biblical Literature Early Judaism and Its Literature
SBLSBS	Society of Biblical Literature Sources for Biblical Study
SBLSymS	Society of Biblical Literature Symposium Series
SBT	Studies in Biblical Theology
SC	Sources chrétiennes. Paris: Cerf, 1943–
SD	Studies and Documents
SE	*Studia evangelica I, II, III* (= TU 73 [1959], 87 [1964], 88 [1964], etc.)
SNT	Studien zum Neuen Testament
SNTIW	Studies of the New Testament and Its World
SNTSMS	Society for New Testament Studies Monograph Series
SP	Sacra pagina
SPhA	*Studia philonica Annual*
SPIB	Scripta Pontificii Instituti Biblici
SVF	*Stoicorum veterum fragmenta.* H. von Arnim. 4 vols. Leipzig: Teubner, 1903–1924
SVTP	Studia in Veteris Testamenti pseudepigraphica
TDNT	*Theological Dictionary of the New Testament.* Edited by G. Kittel and G. Friedrich. Translated by G. W. Bromiley. 10 vols. Grand Rapids: Eerdmans, 1964–1976
TNTC	Tyndale New Testament Commentaries
TU	Texte und Untersuchungen
WBC	Word Biblical Commentaries
WMANT	Wissenshaftliche Monographien zum Alten und Neuen Testament
WUNT	Wissenschaftliche Untersuchungen zum Neuen Testament
ZNW	*Zeitschrift für die neutestamentliche Wissenschaft und die Kunde der älteren Kirche*
ZTK	*Zeitschrift für Theologie und Kirche*

Introduction: Issues
and Methodology

*T*HIS BOOK BEGAN WITH DISSATISFACTION. My dissatisfaction originated in reading a number of excellent commentaries on Paul's letter to the Romans that have appeared over the past twenty-five years.[1] This may sound odd, but let me explain. Although I learned a great deal about Romans from reading these commentaries, I still came away feeling dissatisfied with them for several reasons.

One reason for this dissatisfaction is the commentary format itself. Commentaries are both necessary and valuable. But they also force an interpreter to concentrate on individual passages and details rather than on the movement of an argument or narrative across passages. One comes away with a detailed knowledge of passages taken individually but much less about how the passages form an articulated whole. Introductions can obviate this to some extent but not altogether. Once the commentary proper begins, the interpretation of individual passages takes precedence.

In addition to this rather general reason for my dissatisfaction, there are also reasons peculiar to the interpretation of Romans. The first concerns the contexts necessary for understanding what Paul was about when he wrote or, more likely, dictated Romans. Most modern interpreters of Paul agree that Romans was not a theological treatise in any conventional sense but a real letter written to a specific Christian community for specific purposes. To understand Romans, one needs to

---

[1] Some of the more significant commentaries are the following: Brendan Byrne, *Romans* (SP 6; Collegeville, Minn.: Liturgical Press, 1996); C. E. B. Cranfield, *A Critical and Exegetical Commentary on the Epistle to the Romans* (2 vols.; ICC; Edinburgh: T&T Clark, 1975–1979); James D. G. Dunn, *Romans* (2 vols.; WBC 38A, 38B; Dallas: Word, 1988); Joseph A. Fitzmyer, *Romans: A New Translation with Introduction and Commentary* (AB 33; New York: Doubleday, 1993); Douglas J. Moo, *The Epistle to the Romans* (NICNT; Grand Rapids: Eerdmans, 1996); Leon Morris, *The Epistle to the Romans* (PNTC; Grand Rapids: Eerdmans, 1988); Heinrich Schlier, *Der Römerbrief: Kommentar* (HTKNT 6; Freiburg im Breisgau: Herder, 1977); Walter Schmithals, *Der Römerbrief: Ein Kommentar* (Gütersloh: Mohn, 1988); Thomas R. Schreiner, *Romans* (BECNT 6; Grand Rapids: Baker, 1998); Ulrich Wilckens, *Der Brief an die Römer* (3 vols.; EKKNT 6; Zurich: Benziger, 1978–1982).

understand the character and makeup of the Roman Christian community. One also needs to understand Paul's situation when he wrote the letter and his relationship to the Roman Christians at that time. What did they know about him, and what did he know about them? What difference did this make to what Paul wrote in Romans? Although most interpreters on Romans recognize the importance of these multiple contexts, they do not act on this recognition persistently or consistently enough. For example, most interpreters note that, for all Romans and Galatians have in common, they seem to take radically different positions at certain points. Interpreters tend to attribute these differences to the different audiences Paul was addressing in Romans and Galatians. But they do not adequately press the implications of the differences. They continue to interpret Romans through "parallel" passages in Galatians and vice versa. The result is that consistently the radical differences between Galatians and Romans are often overlooked or underestimated. For example, in Gal 3:15–18, Paul wrote about the promises that God made to Abraham and "to his seed" in Gen 12:7, 13:5, 17:7, and 24:7. He insisted, however, that "to his seed" was singular and so was referring only to Christ and, by implication, not to the Jewish people. In Rom 4:13, 16, Paul again appealed to these promises to Abraham and "to his seed." But here he took "seed" as a collective noun referring to Abraham as the father of "many nations." In the context of Romans 4, Paul clearly meant by "many nations" both Jews and Gentiles. There is a radical difference between excluding the Jewish people from God's promises to Abraham and including them in those promises. Much more is happening here than a change of audience. This example is emblematic of the way interpreters treat the often radical differences between Galatians and Romans. To account for these radical differences, we need to pay much more attention to the specific contexts in which Paul was writing both Galatians and Romans than has been the case.

Again, virtually all interpreters of Romans agree that Romans is not a theological treatise. Context is important if one is ever to understand Romans properly. Nevertheless, there is still a tendency to treat what Paul wrote in Romans as topics rather than as issues. What I mean is that interpreters tend to be interested primarily in *what* Paul wrote and pay too little attention to *how* and *why* he wrote as he did. What were the issues Paul thought were at stake that led him to write as he did to the Roman Christians? Here again more persistent attention to specific contexts is called for. But something more is also called for, a more careful reading of Romans as an argument or as an articulated series of arguments meant to *persuade* the Roman Christians of certain things. For example, the tendency is to think of much of Romans as Paul's explanations of justification (Rom 1–4), salvation (5–8), and the fate of Israel (9–11). But if Romans was something other than a theological treatise, why did Paul choose these topics? What was at stake for Paul? How and why were these topics also issues between Paul and the Roman Christian community? Romans was more than the explanation of topics. It was an articulated series of arguments about important differences between Paul and the Roman Christians.

A further problem in the interpretation of Romans is a literary one. What is the structure of Romans, especially the structure of the main body of Romans 1–11? Because of their emphasis on the topics of Romans just mentioned, interpreters tend to overlook or, at least, undervalue the specifically literary clues to the structure of the letter. For example, as one reads Rom 1:16–11:36, one cannot help but be struck by the differences in style and tone between different sections of the letter. One the one hand, some sections of Romans read like expositions or explanations. Their tone is calm and not argumentative. Romans 1:18–32, 3:21–26, 5:1–21, and 8:1–30 are of this sort. On the other hand, other sections of Romans are quite argumentative or polemical in style and tone. Romans 2:1–3:20, 3:27–4:25, 6:1–7:25, and 8:31–11:36 are of this sort, and they are marked by various rhetorical devices that create a much livelier, more engaged, and argumentative tone. These devices include rhetorical questions, apostrophes (addresses to imaginary interlocutors), dialogues with imaginary interlocutors, refutations of objections and false conclusions, speeches-in-character, comparisons of various sorts, and examples. Paul's use of these devices in these sections of Romans creates a very different tone from that found in the expository or explanatory sections. I will argue that these literary cues are surer guides to the structure of Romans than the theologically oriented "topics" are.

More broadly, but connected with this: what was the genre of the main body of Romans? When the Roman Christian community heard Paul's letter read to them, what did they think they were hearing? Again, because most interpreters are concerned primarily with the topics or the contents of the letter, they do not pay enough attention to the question of genre. All the rhetorical devices mentioned above as well as the argumentative, polemic tone of much of the letter suggest that when the Roman Christian community heard it read to them, they probably would have understood it as a diatribe. As we shall see, this has implications not only for how one interprets the arguments of the letter but also for how Paul understood his relationship to the Roman Christian community.

These, then, are the immediate reasons for my dissatisfaction. A broader and less obvious reason is, I think, at the root of the others. Why is there almost an inevitable tendency, especially in the interpretation of Romans, to gravitate toward concentrating on the contents or the topics of the letter to the detriment of its contexts, issues, literary structure, and genre? The reason is rooted in history. Over the centuries Paul has been a controversial writer. His letters, especially Galatians and Romans, have been the subject of almost endless interpretations and reinterpretations. This has especially been the case in the wake of the Reformation in the sixteenth century. The interpretation of Paul was at the center of many of the theological conflicts not only between Catholics and Protestants but also between Catholics and Catholics and Protestants and Protestants. These conflicts dominated the interpretations of Paul, especially of his letters to the Galatians and the Romans, well into the last century.

In recent decades, we have come to live in a more ecumenical age. For the most part, this ecumenism is reflected in the best recent commentaries on Paul's letters, even those on Galatians and Romans. Most try to move across denominational boundaries and take seriously interpreters from other denominations and of no denomination. But this task is more difficult than it first appears. While most interpreters have moved beyond specifically denominational interpretations of Paul, it has been much more difficult to move beyond the framework itself of these interpretations. For example, while most interpreters have moved beyond taking denominational positions in the interpretation of Romans on such topics as justification by faith, salvation, or the "works of the law," the belief has remained that these topics are indeed what Paul's letter to the Romans is about. Positions on these topics vary greatly, but the belief persists that, for the most part, these topics lie at the heart of Romans.[2] The result has been that the same traditional topics continue to dominate the interpretation of Romans. It has been very difficult to get below the varnish of these topics to the grain of the letter itself.[3]

This reality lies at the root of my dissatisfaction. It is also what led me to write this book. The result is an interpretation of Romans that, for the most part, satisfies my own search to understand what Paul was about and what he hoped to achieve in writing to the Roman Christian community. Whether it satisfies anyone else is not for me to say. At this point, however, I want to describe the broad contours of the argument this study will be making. I hope they will provide the reader with some orientation for the more detailed arguments that follow.

This book's primary interest is the arguments of Paul in Romans. It is not a commentary on Romans. It thus is not concerned with a detailed, verse-by-verse interpretation of Romans such as is proper to a commentary but with these details only insofar as they contribute to an understanding of Paul's arguments. In addition, it is not concerned with issues that came to be of great importance in the later theological controversies about Paul's theology but were not Paul's primary concerns in Romans. Such issues include justification, original sin, and the contrast between faith and works.

This study insists on the importance of the multiple contexts within which Romans must be interpreted. This is especially the case for three closely related contexts that are explicitly the subjects of chapters 1 and 2 but also play a role again and again in the course of this study. The first is the context of the Roman Christian community. Our knowledge of the history and character of this community is quite limited. But there is enough evidence to indicate that, though largely Gentile in background, the roots of the Roman Christian community were in the Roman Jewish community. This was the case even for most of the Gentile members of the community. This background continued to influence the outlooks and practices of the Roman Christian community even after its separation from the Roman Jewish community around A.D. 49 because of its belief in Christ. Its members continued to see themselves as part of Judaism. More specifically, although they no longer practiced circumcision, most still insisted on the continued observance of the ethical commandments of the Mosaic law. For most of them, both belief in Jesus as the Christ and observance of the ethical commandment of the law obviously belonged together.

---

[2] An admirable exception to this is Krister Stendahl's marvelous essay "The Apostle Paul and the Introspective Conscience of the West," in *Paul among Jews and Gentiles* (Philadelphia: Fortress, 1976), 78–96. He correctly argued that Paul's concern was not with sin and guilt but with the relationship between Jews and Gentiles or between Jewish Christians and Gentiles Christians. Paul was not an example of an introspective conscience.

[3] Both Lloyd Gaston (*Paul and the Torah* [Vancouver: University of British Columbia Press, 1987]) and John G. Gager (*Reinventing Paul* [Oxford: Oxford University Press, 2000]) have also tried to do this. Their critiques of traditional interpretations of Paul are usually very much to the point. But I find their own interpretations of Paul too dominated by other, albeit admirable, concerns about the contemporary relationship between Jews and Christians.

Especially Jewish monotheism and observance of the law were what distinguished them from their Greco-Roman neighbors and grounded their orderly and ethically superior way of life. As part of Israel, they also shared in God's promises to Israel and looked forward to being part of the eschatological victory promised by God to Israel.

The second is the context of Paul himself. Paul wrote Romans in the light of his own past experiences and the controversies in which he had been involved. These influenced Paul's writing of Romans in complex ways. Roughly twenty years before Romans, Paul's life as a Jew was suddenly transformed by God's revelation to him of the risen Jesus and by God's call to him to preach faith in that risen Jesus to the Gentiles (Gal 1:15–16; Phil 3:3–11; 1 Cor 9:1; 15:8–9). Paul also became convinced that this faith in the risen Jesus no longer entailed observance of the Mosaic law, either for Jewish or for Gentile believers. These convictions involved Paul in a series of controversies, with both Peter and other Jewish believers (Gal 2:1–14) and with the Gentile believers of Galatia who wanted to be circumcised and observe the law in addition to believing in Jesus. Paul also advocated an ethical alternative to observance of the law. In place of observance of the law, believers were to live their lives by the practice of various virtues. In this they were to be guided by the Spirit of God, which they received in their baptism (Gal 5:1–6:10). Paul argued for these convictions especially in his letter to the Galatian believers. In his dismay and anger at the Galatians' desire to be circumcised and observe the law, Paul seems at points in the letter to have discounted almost completely the value of the law (Gal 3:6–14) and even to have excluded the Jewish people from the promises made by God to Abraham about them (Gal 3:15–18; 4:21–31). In Galatians, Paul contrasted faith in Christ and observance of the law so starkly that they seem opposed to one another almost in principle. I will insist throughout this book on interpreting Galatians both in its complexity and in the sharpness of its polemic. Interpreters have too often rubbed smooth the rough edges of Galatians. When Paul came to write Romans, he came to it as the heir of a legacy of sometimes bitter controversies. This needs to be taken very seriously, and so I will return again and again, in the course of this book, especially to Galatians to understand the controversial context within which Paul wrote to the Roman Christians.

The third is the immediate context in which Paul wrote Romans. Here I will argue that Paul and the Roman Christians knew a good deal about each other. On the one hand, through members who knew Paul, the Roman Christian community had come to know about Paul and what they thought he stood for. This was especially the case for what Paul had written to the Galatians. In addition, they knew of the ethical disarray of the Corinthian Christians to whom Paul had addressed 1 Corinthians. For most of the Roman Christians, Paul was not simply controversial but was also someone about whom they themselves had grave suspicions and misgivings. On the other hand, Paul also knew a good deal about the Roman Christians and was aware of their suspicions and misgivings about him and his controversial views. He wrote Romans, as we shall see, to overcome these suspicions and misgivings and to persuade them of the truth of his interpretation of the gospel.

I will also insist, much more than has previously been the case, on the importance of literary cues and genre for understanding the structure and argument of

Romans. As mentioned above, whereas some sections of Romans read like expositions or explanations, other sections are quite argumentative or polemical, marked
by various rhetorical devices that create a much livelier, more engaged tone. On the
basis of these literary cues, I will argue that the structure of Rom 1:18–11:36 is
made up of four major sections (1:18–3:20; 3:21–4:25; 5:1–7:25; 8:1–11:36). Each
major section begins with an expository or explanatory passage (1:18–32; 3:21–26;
5:1–21; 8:1–30) which is then followed by a longer and more argumentative or polemical passage (2:1–3:20; 3:27–4:25; 6:1–7:25; 8:31–11:36). These sections also
mark out the main stages in Paul's arguments. In addition, I will argue that the body
of Romans is best understood as an example of a diatribe. In the ancient world, diatribes were popular discourses or instructions usually of an ethical-religious nature
and also had a strong dialogical component. They originated in the setting of a
philosophical school, and their purpose was not simply to inform but also to transform the hearers ethically or religiously. All the rhetorical devices mentioned above
as well as the argumentative, polemic tone of much of the letter point in this direction. When the Roman Christian community heard Paul's letter read to them, they
probably would have understood it as a diatribe. As we shall see, this also has implications not only for how one interprets the arguments of the letter but also for how
Paul understood his relationship to the Roman Christian community. All of this is
the subject especially of chapter 3.

Chapters 4–14 of this study contain detailed analyses of Paul's arguments.
These arguments are Paul's attempts to respond to the deep misgivings the Roman
Christian community had about aspects of his interpretation of the gospel. Several
points need to be kept in mind throughout this analysis. First, the attitudes of the
Roman Christian community toward Paul were complex. Paul and the Roman
Christian community certainly had some basic convictions in common. Both saw
themselves within the context of Judaism, that is, the Jewish way of life. Both were
committed to Jewish monotheism, the belief in one God who was the God of Israel.
Both accepted the Jewish scriptures as a central source of authority. Both were committed to the centrality of Jesus as the Messiah, or Christ, within the context of Jewish belief. Both saw their faith in Jesus as the Messiah as the fulfillment of their
Jewish beliefs and expectations and not a rejection of them. Although they did so for
different reasons, both also agreed that circumcision was no longer necessary for full
membership in the community. Because of this, both would have agreed that
Gentile believers were now to have equal status with Jewish believers.

There were, however, significant differences between them. These differences
clustered around their different convictions about the basic value and continued observance of the Mosaic law. The Roman Christians, whether of Gentile or of Jewish
origin, for the most part continued to observe the ethical commandments of the law.
Because of the ethical superiority of its commandments, the law was what distinguished them from their non-believing fellow citizens. Given these convictions, they
looked with alarm at some of the things they thought Paul advocated. Paul's views
of the law called into question much that was integral to their identity. They were
scandalized by the sharp contrasts he continually drew in Galatians between the
Mosaic law and its observance, on the one hand, and faith and righteousness, on the
other. These contrasts were so stark that they found it difficult to imagine how Paul

could ever have considered the Mosaic law to have been of divine origin or its observance to have been divinely commanded. Paul was claiming that no one was ever made righteous through observance of the law. He was, in effect, calling into question not only the Roman Christians' present observance of the law; he was also calling into question observance of the law in the past by the Jewish people. He was, in fact, calling into question not only the status of the law but also the status of the Jewish people, whether present or past. There seemed to be no advantage, nor did it seem there had ever been an advantage, to being members of the Jewish people. Paul's account of things even called into question the future of the Jewish people. The promises God made to Abraham and to his "seed" were not to the Jewish people but to Christ and, through Christ, to believers in him. The Jewish people, Israel, could be neither sons nor heirs of God's promises to Abraham and so were excluded from the future, eschatological fulfillment of those promises. All of this seemed to them to annul the clear meaning of the Jewish scriptures. Finally, they were also troubled by what they saw as the practical consequences of Paul's views about the law. For them, observance of the law provided a framework for conducting their lives in an orderly, ethical fashion. The Roman Christians feared that Paul's conviction that believers, empowered by the Spirit, would be able to practice virtue and avoid vice without observing the law was wrongheaded. They saw the moral disarray of the Corinthian Christians as ample evidence that their fears were well founded. They viewed these problems as the predictable results of abandoning observance of the Mosaic law.

Second, Paul's responses to these misgivings were also complex. Paul consistently appeals to convictions and viewpoints he shares with the Roman Christians, and bases his arguments on them. This is especially the case in the expository sections of the letter. In 1:18–32, he bases his arguments on a Hellenistic Jewish critique—shared by him and the Roman Christians—of Gentile religiosity and morality. In the other three expository sections, he appeals to traditional Christian creedal formulas that both of them have in common. In three of the four major argumentative sections of the letter (2:1–3:20; 3:27–4:25; 8:31–11:36), Paul appeals extensively to the Jewish scriptures for support of his arguments. In the other major argumentative section (Rom 6–7), although Paul appeals only once to the Jewish scriptures for support (7:7, citing Exod 20:27; Deut 5:18), they play a major role in his argument in 7:7–25. The authority of the Jewish scriptures is something Paul shares with his Roman Christian audience.

Paul also consistently takes the concerns of his Roman Christian audience seriously. He often responds to them by significantly revising earlier controversial positions that he now acknowledges to have been misguided. This is true, for example, of his reinterpretation of the significance of Abraham in Romans 4. It is also true of his reinterpretation of the significance of baptism, the role of the Spirit, the place of freedom, and the value of the law in Romans 6–7. Finally, it is especially true of his reinterpretation of the ultimate fate of the Jewish people, Israel, and their relationship to the Gentiles in 8:31–11:36.

More important, however, Paul significantly revises the framework within which he places his arguments. As mentioned, his earlier arguments in Galatians were marked by stark contrasts between faith in Christ and observance of the

Mosaic law. Paul's perspective in Romans, however, is much more historically or temporally oriented. Paul pointedly distinguishes between the past (1:18–3:20), the present (3:21–4:25; 5:1–7:25), and the future (Rom 8–11). This very different perspective allows Paul to acknowledge the value and even the binding force of the law in the past (2:1–3:20), while at the same time claiming that believers are now no longer obligated to observe it (3:21–26). This historically oriented perspective allows Paul to interpret the history and the future of the Jewish people in such a way as ultimately to include them in the mystery of God's providence rather than exclude them as he seemed to do in parts of Galatians.

Third, for all of his willingness to rethink and significantly revise some of his earlier controversial views, Paul continues to insist on several of his earlier basic convictions. First, the righteousness of God is now revealed in Christ. Second, this righteousness is now appropriated through faith in Christ and apart from observance of the Mosaic law. And finally, Jews and Gentiles alike experience God's righteousness through faith in Christ and apart from observance of the law. All three of these convictions were rooted in Paul's own experience of God's revelation to him of the risen Jesus and in his call to preach this Jesus to the Gentiles (Gal 1:15–16; Phil 3:3–11; 1 Cor 9:1; 15:8–9). Paul is not willing to compromise on these convictions, and in Romans he tries to persuade the Roman Christians of their truth. All of Paul's arguments based on what they have in common are meant to persuade them of the truth of these convictions.

Finally, to understand Paul's convictions and those of his Roman Christian audience, we must keep in mind one further perspective they share. For both Paul and the Roman Christians, their convictions, both those on which they agree and those on which they disagree, are primarily concerned with the relationship between two groups, Jews and Gentiles. Neither Paul nor the Roman Christians are primarily concerned with individuals as such. This is crucial to keep in mind lest we fall back into the trap of thinking that Romans is primarily about the sin, guilt, justification, and salvation of the individual. To do so inevitably leads once again to the misinterpretation of Romans in the categories of the Reformation debates. This must be resisted clearly and consistently.[4]

Chapter 4 of this study treats the issues and arguments in the first major section of Romans (1:18–3:20). These issues concern the relationship between Jews and Gentiles. More specifically, given their convictions about the ethical superiority of the Mosaic law, the Roman Christians were profoundly troubled by Paul's belief that Jews and Gentiles as groups were in reality equally sinful. In addition, they thought that Paul was also implicitly challenging the value of the Mosaic law itself. After all, if the Mosaic law did not lead to the practice of that law, what was its value? The Mosaic law would be no more valuable than the legal systems of the Greeks and other peoples.

In the subproposition for this section, Paul begins by claiming that the wrath of God is being revealed against *all* human wickedness (1:18–20). He follows this up with an uncontroversial critique of specifically Gentile religiosity and conduct (1:21–32). Paul is clearly using standard Hellenistic-Jewish apologetic motifs that his

---

[4] This is something on which Stendahl ("The Apostle Paul") rightly insists.

Roman Christian audience would readily understand and agree with. In 2:1–3:20, he slowly turns to the issue of Jewish sinfulness. His tone here becomes much more argumentative. He argues that, as groups, Jews are as sinful as Gentiles, although for different reasons. Gentiles are sinful because of their adherence to idolatry and the practice of moral depravity. Jews, however, are sinful because of their lack of adherence to observance of the Mosaic law. Paul grounds this controversial conclusion in appeals to the Jewish scriptures and to traditionally Jewish viewpoints current in contemporary, especially Hellenistic, Judaism. Central to his argument is his appeal to the traditionally Jewish and scripturally grounded notion of God's impartiality. God judges everyone, both Jews and Gentiles, on an equal basis. On this basis, both Jews and Gentiles as groups are equally under the power of sin. Paul also claims that this reality does not at all demean the value of being a Jew or of the Mosaic law. Jews have been entrusted with the Mosaic law, and that alone is a great gift. The problem is that they have not observed the law. In fact, Paul claims, he is even upholding the value of the law because it is the law itself that brings about the knowledge of this sinfulness.

In 1:18–3:20, Paul crafts his rhetoric very carefully in order to persuade his Roman Christian audience that his apparently controversial position about the equal sinfulness of both Jews and Gentiles is rooted in the Jewish scriptures and in Jewish tradition, both of which he and the Roman Christian community have in common. His arguments are temporally or historically oriented: in the course of history both Jews and Gentiles have been equally sinful even though in different ways. This perspective is very different from that of Galatians, which was dominated by stark and virtually unresolvable contrasts. The difference will also play a crucial role in the rest of Romans, radically reshaping the stark and seemingly unresolvable contrasts of Galatians.

Chapter 5 of this study deals with the second major section of the letter (Rom 3:21–4:25). The structure of this section is similar to that of the first. As in 1:18–20, Paul begins with the statement of the subproposition in 3:21–22c. He claims that the righteousness of God has now been manifested apart from the Mosaic law. In addition, the Jewish scriptures witness to this righteousness, which is through faith in Jesus Christ for all who have faith, both Jews and Gentiles alike. Paul then explains the meaning of this subproposition in 3:22d–26 by citing and then commenting on a traditional Christian creedal formula that he shares with his Roman Christian audience. In 3:27–4:25, Paul's tone once again becomes argumentative. He claims that, in taking these positions, he is actually upholding the law (3:27–31). In support of this, he interprets the example of Abraham's faith (4:1–25).

Paul is especially dealing with two underlying issues in 3:21–4:25. Both are rooted in what he wrote earlier in his letter to the Galatian Christians. The first issue is the relationship of faith in Christ to observance of the Mosaic law. Because of its polemical intensity, Paul's arguments in Gal 3:1–4:31 consistently contrasted faith in Christ with observance of the Mosaic law, to the great detriment of the latter. His arguments were of an either-or sort, in which one alternative (faith in Christ) was accepted and the other (observance of the Mosaic law) rejected. The second issue is the significance of the patriarch Abraham. As mentioned earlier, Paul seemed at points in Galatians to exclude the Jewish people from the promises made by God to Abraham about them. Paul's positions on both of these issues deeply troubled the Roman Christians.

Paul argues very differently on both of these issues in Rom 3:21–4:25. In 3:21, the righteousness of God is now manifested apart from the law. This is very different from the position he took in Galatians in two significant ways. First, instead of the stark contrasts between faith in Christ and observance of the law so prominent in Galatians, Paul's perspective in this section of Romans is again temporal or historical. This allows Paul to maintain his basic conviction that, through faith in Christ, righteousness is *now* apart from observance of the law, without denigrating the divinely ordained role of the law in the past. Second, in 4:1–25, Paul uses the example of Abraham to show how righteousness through faith apart from observance of the law includes Jews as well as Gentiles. Abraham is the father, in faith, of both. More specifically, in 4:13, 16, Paul again appeals to the promises to Abraham and "to his seed." But he takes "seed" as a collective noun referring to Abraham as the father of "many nations." Here Paul clearly means both Jews and Gentiles. The Jewish people are now included in, rather than excluded from, the promises to Abraham.

Once again, as in 1:18–3:20, Paul crafts his arguments by appealing to what he and his Roman Christian audience have in common. In this case, the commonality is rooted in a traditional creedal formula they share and in the scriptural example of Abraham as the father in faith of both Jews and Gentiles. Paul maintains his basic convictions about the gospel. But the framework in which he places them and the arguments he uses to support them are very different from those he used in Galatians.

The next two sections of Paul's letter (Rom 5–7, 8–11) are much longer and more complex, and the same can be said of the issues that lie behind them. Chapters 6–8 of this study deal with Romans 5–7, whose structure is similar to that of the preceding two sections. Paul begins by stating the subproposition in 5:1–5. Made righteous through faith, believers should have peace with God through Jesus Christ, through whom they have access to "this grace" in which they now stand. In context, "this grace" obviously refers back to 3:21–26, to the righteousness made possible by Christ's death through faith apart from observance of the law for both Jews and Gentiles. In 5:6–21, Paul develops this view. First he again uses traditional creedal language that interprets Christ's death for sinners as bringing about a reconciliation with God (5:6–11). He then offers an elaborate comparison and contrast between Christ and Adam, the purpose of which is to show the incompatibility of this grace with sin (5:12–21). In Romans 6–7, his tone once again becomes argumentative. In Romans 6, Paul argues that believers cannot continue to live in sin. They have been baptized into the death of Christ and so have died to sin in order to live to God in Christ Jesus. Sin should have no power over them, but they should offer themselves to God in righteousness. Freed from sin, they are now slaves to God in righteousness. In Romans 7, Paul turns to the place of the law. He argues first that believers have now been freed from the law in order to serve God (7:1–6). In 7:7–25, he then uses the rhetorical device of speech-in-character, in which a seemingly unidentified person both defends the goodness and holiness of the law and, at the same time, confesses his inability to observe its commandments.

The issues behind Romans 5–7 are obviously ethical in nature. What Paul writes in these chapters can be understood only against the complex backgrounds of what he wrote earlier in Galatians and 1 Corinthians, the situation of ethical disarray in the Corinthian Christian community, and the reaction of the Roman Christian community. The Roman Christians were deeply troubled by Paul's insistence that believers were no longer obligated to observe the ethical commandments of the law. They found his alternate view in Gal 5:1–6:10, that Christians were to live ethical lives by the practice of various virtues under the guidance of the Spirit, misguided and troublesome. The law was not a yoke of slavery, as Paul claimed, but a way to live orderly, ethical lives pleasing to God. The ethical disarray of the Corinthian community, which Paul himself described in 1 Corinthians, was clear proof that their suspicions were fully justified.

Paul's response to these concerns is equally complex. Paul continues to insist that righteousness and salvation are apart from observance of the Mosaic law. He does this especially in Romans 5 on the basis of traditional creedal language that he shares with the Roman Christians. He interprets the language of Christ's death for sinners in such a way as to persuade his Roman Christian audience that "this grace" in which they all stand is incompatible with sin. This grace, which is apart from observance of the law, is a new and adequate basis for ethical living. But Paul also has come to recognize that some of his earlier views of ethics and the law expressed in Galatians were misguided and, to some extent, contributed to the ethical disarray of the Corinthian Christian community he himself was forced to deal with in 1 Corinthians. Because of this, he now significantly rethinks some of his earlier views in three significant ways. First, he changes the emphasis of his language about freedom and slavery. In Galatians, Paul claimed that believers were freed from the yoke of slavery to the law (Gal 5:1) and were to be guided by the Spirit in their practice of virtue (Gal 6:16–26). In Rom 6:15–23, however, believers are freed not from the law but from sin in order to become slaves to God in righteousness. The emphasis of his language has changed from freedom to slavery. Second, Paul reinterprets the meaning of baptism. In both Gal 3:26–28 and 1 Cor 12:12–13, he interpreted baptism as the ritual through which believers were united to the risen body of Christ through the power of the Spirit. Paul came to see that this interpretation of baptism, in which believers were united with the risen Christ, also unintentionally contributed to some Corinthian believers' views that they were no longer bound by normal ethical constraints. In Rom 6:1–14, Paul no longer interprets baptism as being united to the risen Christ but as dying with Christ to sin. He is very careful not to claim that in baptism believers have also risen with Christ. That remains in the future. It is also striking that in all of Romans 6 Paul never appeals to the Spirit as a guide to living ethically. Finally, in Romans 7, Paul turns to the role of the law. For the first time in his letters, he writes about the goodness and holiness of the law. This is very different from what he wrote about the law and its observance in Galatians. In 7:7–25, the speaker's problem with the law is not its goodness or holiness. He admits that it is both good and holy. The problem is with his incapacity to observe it. As we shall see, the speech-in-character in 7:7–25 is actually an appeal to the experience of the difficulties Paul thought the largely Gentile Christian community in Rome must have found when trying to observe the ethical commandments of the law. Paul intends the Roman Christians to see themselves in the speaker. In Romans 5–7, even more than in the previous two sections, Paul not only maintains some of his central convictions; he also significantly rethinks and revises some of his earlier views that he now understands as misguided.

Chapters 9–13 of this study treat the longest and by far the most complex of Paul's arguments, that in Romans 8–11. These chapters of Romans belong together for a variety of reasons. From a literary perspective, they reflect the same structure as the three earlier sections of the letter: an explanatory section (8:1–30) followed by a much longer argumentative section (8:31–11:36). They also belong together because they are all concerned with issues of eschatology.

The explanatory section is, for the most part, similar to the three preceding explanatory sections. In 8:3–4 Paul once again draws on traditional creedal language that he shares with the Roman Christians, and he builds on it in the course of 8:5–30. In addition, the style and tone are explanatory in the sense that Paul hopes his Roman Christian audience will recognize what he writes as a legitimate development of what they have in common. Paul is especially concerned here with the role of the Spirit and the question of who are "children," "sons," and "heirs" of God. The much longer argumentative section (8:31–11:36) is the most sustained, complex scriptural argument in any of Paul's letters. It is also one of the most misunderstood. Although Paul's arguments are extremely complex, the overall structure of the passage is fairly simple. After a transitional passage (8:31–9:5), Paul presents an elaborate scriptural interpretation of the promises made to Israel. He does this first by interpreting God's relation to Israel in the past (9:6–29), then by interpreting Israel's present situation of unbelief (9:30–10:21), and finally by expressing his firm convictions about Israel's ultimate inclusion along with the Gentiles in God's mysterious plan for the salvation of all (11:1–36).

To understand Romans 8–11 properly, one must always keep in mind two primary issues with which Paul is struggling. Both concern eschatology. The first issue again has to do with what Paul now considers some of the ill-conceived arguments he made in his letter to the Galatians. Especially in Gal 3:26–4:11, he seemed to argue that those who observe the law, Jews and those Galatians who wanted to observe it, are excluded from being either sons of God or heirs of God's promises. They are also excluded from the possession of the Spirit poured into their hearts in baptism, by which they would become sons and heirs. Paul even equated circumcision and observance of the Mosaic law with enslavement to the beggarly elemental principles of the universe in his exclusion of them. Given that their own eschatological hopes were deeply rooted in Judaism, the Romans Christians found Paul's seeming exclusion of Israel from believers' eschatological hopes incomprehensible. A second issue, broader and more personal, also concerns Paul in Romans 8–11: his own anguish over the present situation of most of his fellow Jews. This anguish may have been provoked by the misgivings of the Roman Christians, but it goes well beyond them. Romans 8–11 is the part of the letter in which Paul himself is most deeply invested and in which he is most clearly struggling to think through issues in significantly new and very different ways. In 9:3, he writes that he could wish himself accursed and cut off from Christ for the sake of his fellow Jews. And in 9:6, he claims, "it cannot be that the word of God has failed." But then how does one reconcile these promises with the reality that most of his fellow Jews have not come to believe in Jesus as he and a small number of his fellow Jewish Christians have? What does this say about the reliability of God's promises to Israel in the past? What does it say about the future fate of Israel? Especially in 8:31–11:36, this second issue is even more crucial for Paul than the first.

Paul's concentrates his attention in 8:1–30 on the first issue. In 8:1–17, he first builds on traditional creedal language shared with his Roman Christian audience and subtly reinterprets what he wrote especially in Gal 4:4–7, about the role of the Spirit and the meaning of sonship and inheritance, in such a way that the ultimate inclusion of Israel is no longer ruled out. Paul then develops this in Rom 8:18–30 into a universalizing eschatology that would make ample room for the inclusion not only of both Jews and Gentiles but also of all creation. He does this especially by developing the universalizing strains of eschatology he wrote about earlier in 1 Corinthians 15.

In Rom 8:31–11:36, Paul turns his attention to the second issue. This section is marked by several characteristics that need to be kept in mind if they are to be interpreted properly. First, here is the issue in which Paul himself is most personally invested and over which he struggles most. This is clear from the number of first-person-singular passages in this section (8:38–39; 9:1–5; 10:1–4; 11:1–2, 11–14, 25–27). Israel's fate and its relation to God's promises are far more than academic for Paul. Second, it becomes clear here how crucial Paul's change in framework is from the stark contrasts of Galatians to the historically or temporally oriented perspective of Romans. Paul struggles, by means of scriptural interpretations of God's promises to Israel in the past and of Israel's present situation of unbelief, toward an interpretation of a future in which "all Israel" is included along with the "full number of the Gentiles" in God's overall mysterious plan for salvation. Third, Paul does this, however, in such a way that he also integrates his basic convictions about the salvation of the Gentiles into his arguments. For Paul, the present situation and future fate of his fellow Jews cannot be understood apart from his basic conviction that salvation is now for all, Jews and Gentiles alike, through faith in Christ and apart from observance of the Mosaic law. Because of this, Paul's rethinking of the issues of the present situation and future fate of Israel also forces him to rethink how he understands the present situation and future fate of the Gentiles. For him, the two cannot be separated. Israel's present situation is due to its failure to recognize from the Scriptures that Christ is the goal of the law and that righteousness is now through faith rather than by observance of the Mosaic law and is meant for Jews and Gentiles alike. In addition, Israel's present failure is part of a larger, mysterious plan—to which the Scriptures again point—according to which the gospel comes to be preached to the Gentiles. Conversely, the ultimate inclusion of the "full number of the Gentiles" is what ultimately leads to the inclusion of "all Israel." Paul again develops his convictions about the inclusion of both "all Israel" and the "full number of the Gentiles" from the universalizing parts of his eschatology of 1 Corinthians 15. This emerges with particular clarity in Romans 11. The salvation of "all Israel" cannot but follow on the salvation of the "full number of the Gentiles."

Chapter 14 of this study treats the last major section of Romans, 12:1–15:7, an exhortation to the Roman Christian community. Although it is different in character from 1:16–11:36, Paul clearly intended 12:1–15:7 to be part of his overall argument. Only in 15:8–13, after the exhortation in 12:1–15:7, does Paul offer a summary of his overall argument. This is Paul's first opportunity to present more specifically his own views on ethical practice to the Roman Christian community.

Three issues underlay Paul's exhortation. The first is the issue of how believers are to live their everyday lives in a way pleasing to God apart from observance of the Mosaic law. The second issue is Paul himself or, more specifically, his reputation as a sower of discord and dissension. Both these issues are rooted in the Roman Christian community's misgivings about Paul and his ethical views. The third is an issue that caused division among the Roman Christians themselves. Apart from a minority, such as Priscilla and Aquila, who sided with Paul, most Roman Christians (the "strong"), whether of Jewish or Gentile origin, thought they should continue to observe the ethical commandments of the law but not its ritual and dietary laws. For them, "nothing is unclean" and "everything is clean." But there was also a minority (the "weak") of both Jewish and Gentile believers who thought they should also continue to observe the sabbath regulations and the Jewish dietary laws. The issue of observance of the Jewish dietary laws in particular was divisive because it affected how community gatherings were to be conducted. Did the food, particularly the meat served as such gatherings, have to be ritually pure?

Paul's response to the first two issues takes up most of 12:1–15:7. He tries to offer specific ways of living ethically and pleasing God without appealing to observance of the Mosaic law. He does this by drawing on the wider tradition of Jewish wisdom instructions, in which he emphasizes the moral obligations and responsibilities believers have to one another. He also draws on the specifically Christian image of believers all forming one body in Christ. In both ways, Paul emphasizes the values of love, harmony, orderliness, accommodation, and the common good of the community over the particular good of the individual. He does all of this without appealing to commandments of the Mosaic law. At the same time, he claims that believers, by loving their neighbor as themselves and doing no harm to their neighbor, "fulfills" the purpose of the law even though they are not as such "observing" it (13:8–10). Equally important for Paul, however, is the portrait he presents of himself to the Roman Christian community in advocating these practices. He wants to portray himself as someone who is not the sower of dissension and division, as they may think, but an advocate of love, harmony, orderliness, accommodation, and the common good of the whole community.

Based on these values, Paul then turns in 14:1–15:7 to the issue of the division between the strong and the weak over observance of Jewish dietary laws at community gatherings. In 14:1–12 Paul urges the Roman Christians to show each other mutual respect. He urges the strong not to despise the weak and the weak not to pass judgment on the strong. In 14:13–23, on the basis of this mutual respect, Paul turns to offer a more specific solution. Although his own position is that of the strong, Paul nevertheless takes the side of the weak. He urges the Roman Christians not to place stumbling blocks in each other's way. More specifically, if serving food and drink that the weak think are unclean becomes a stumbling block, then such food and drink should not be served at community gatherings. The good of these weak believers is more important than maintaining the admittedly correct principle that "nothing is unclean" and "everything is clean."

In taking this position, Paul is reacting very differently than he did in his earlier confrontation with Peter and the other Jewish Christians in Antioch in the fall of A.D. 49 (Gal 2:11–14). There he strongly opposed accommodation to Jewish dietary laws at community gatherings. Here he urges it. Yet this accommodation, as we shall see, is possible only because it does not affect his bedrock convictions. In his exhortation in Rom 12:1–15:7, Paul still maintains that believers, whether of Jewish or Gentile origin, are no longer obligated to observe the Mosaic law. Their ethical practice is rooted in their baptism and their love for their neighbor and not in observance of the law. What they do fulfills the purpose of the law, but it does not, at least in his mind, entail its observance. In this sense, Paul's exhortation in 12:1–15:7 is of a piece with the rest of his argument in Romans.

With this basic orientation in mind, one final introductory remark is called for. Paul's letter to the Roman Christians as well as the contexts in which he wrote it are complex. This also means that any interpretation of the letter will inevitably also be complex. My task is not to simplify this complexity but to clarify it insofar as possible. The persuasiveness of the interpretations that follow will depend on whether the complexities of the letter and its contexts are brought together in the most plausible way. The various strands of these arguments are inevitably interwoven, and their cogency depends on whether this interweaving forms a consistent and coherent portrait that seems to answer best the relevant questions about the text and its contexts.

Situating Romans: Roman Jews and Roman Christians

*P*LACING ANY TEXT IN ITS PROPER CONTEXT IS DIFFICULT. Placing ancient texts in their proper contexts, however, is even more so. Often the evidence for establishing their contexts is little more than the texts themselves. We are reduced to hints and clues provided by the text itself or to information preserved, usually accidentally, in other texts, inscriptions, archaeological remains, and so forth. All of this must be evaluated critically. In addition, any text has its own point of view, and that point of view includes the interpretation of its own context. This too must be evaluated critically. At first this sounds like a counsel of despair. Rather, it is a cautionary tale. Establishing the contexts of an ancient text remains crucial, but one must be aware of how difficult it is and how tentative one's conclusions remain.

All this is true of Paul's letter to the Roman Christians. Because Romans is also the only extant letter of Paul written to a Christian community that he had not founded or even visited, one needs to be even more cautious about the evidence of context found in it. Nevertheless, to understand Romans, we inevitably need to understand, as best we can, the letter's multiple contexts. First, there is the context of the Roman Christians themselves. Second, because Roman Christians were originally part of the larger Roman Jewish community, we also need to understand the context of Jews in Rome during the first century A.D. Third, there is the context of Paul at this time. Paul's personal experience, his experience as a missionary, and the controversies in which he was involved all contribute to the situation in which he found himself when he wrote Romans. Finally, we need to understand the relationship between the Roman Christians and Paul, or, more precisely, between what Roman Christians knew about him or thought they knew about him and what Paul knew about the Roman Christians and their misgivings about him. This chapter looks at the contexts of the Roman Jewish and the Roman Christian communities. The following chapter examines Paul's situation and his relationship to the Roman Christian community.

In his biography of the emperor Claudius (A.D. 41–54), the Roman historian and gossip Suetonius noted briefly that "he [Claudius] expelled from Rome Jews who were constantly making disturbances at the instigation of Chrestus."[1] The interpretation of this brief notice is the subject of much debate. There is general agreement, however, that the phrase "at the instigation of Chrestus" *(impulsore Chresto)* refers to Christ.[2] Since Christ was obviously never in Rome, the phrase means that during the reign of Claudius there were disturbances among Roman Jews over the significance of Christ. This led to some sort of expulsion of Jews from Rome. From the perspective of Suetonius or, more likely, his source, this was a dispute within the Roman Jewish community. This brief notice tells us that the Roman Christian community originated within the much larger Roman Jewish community. To understand the situation of the Roman Christians at the time of Romans, then, we also have to understand as clearly as possible important aspects of the Roman Jewish community during this period, that is, roughly during the first century. As we shall see, the Roman Christian community probably maintained a significant continuity of belief and practice with the Jewish way of life.[3] This continuity helps us understand both their reactions to Paul and his rhetorical strategy in his letter to them.

THE JEWISH COMMUNITY OF ROME

The origins of the Jewish community in Rome are obscure, but they may go back to the middle of the second century B.C.[4] The first contact between Jews and Rome we know of is the embassy sent to Rome in 161 B.C. by Judas Maccabeus to establish an alliance between Rome and the struggling Maccabean state (1 Macc 8:17–32). The Maccabees later sent two other embassies to Rome to renew the alliance, one in 143 B.C. (1 Macc 12:1–4) and the other a year later (1 Macc 14:24; 15:15–24).[5] First Maccabees itself gives no indication that the embassies came in contact with Jews who were already in Rome. We know, however, from Valerius Maximus, a first-century Roman writer, that Gnaeus Cornelius Hispalus, the *praetor peregrinus*, expelled Jews from Rome and "forced them to return to their homes" in 139 B.C. Because the decree came from the *praetor peregrinus* and they were forced to

---

[1] Suetonius, *Claud.* 25.4 *(GLAJJ* 2:307): *Iudaeos impulsore Chresto assidue tumultuantis Roma expulit.*

[2] Suetonius seems to have confused a common Greek name for slaves and freedmen, *Chrestus* (Χρηστός), meaning "useful" or "good," with *Christus* (Χριστός, "Christ"). By the time of Suetonius, *Chrestus* would have been pronounced the same as *Christus* through iotacism (a process in the Greek language by which several vowels and diphthongs came to be pronounced as *ē*). See Fitzmyer, *Romans,* 31.

[3] In general I have used the phrase "the Jewish way of life" rather than "Judaism." The former better catches the complex and concrete combination of items that went into being a Jew or part of the Jewish community in the ancient world.

[4] In general, see Emil Schürer, *The History of the Jewish People in the Age of Jesus Christ (175 B.C.–A.D. 135)* (rev. and ed. Geza Vermes, Fergus Millar, and Martin Goodman; 3 vols. in 4; Edinburgh: T&T Clark, 1973–1987), vol. 3, part 1, pp. 73–81; Harry J. Leon, *The Jews of Ancient Rome* (rev. ed.; Peabody, Mass.: Hendrickson, 1995), 1–45; and David Noy, *Foreigners at Rome: Citizens and Strangers* (London: Duckworth, 2000), 255–67.

[5] See Jonathan A. Goldstein, *I Maccabees* (AB 41; Garden City, N.Y.: Doubleday, 1976), 344–69, 444–62, 510–26.

return to their homes, the Jews living in Rome at this time may have been mer-chants and sojourners rather than either permanent residents or Roman citizens.[6] The details are obscure, but the reason for the expulsion seems to have been the Roman authorities' perception that Jews were trying to spread their Jewish way of life to non-Jews.[7] Although Valerius Maximus gives no further information, their number must have been large enough for the Roman authorities to take notice.

By the middle of the first century B.C., their numbers had grown significantly. This increase, although exaggerated for rhetorical purposes, is reflected in Cicero's *Pro Flacco* (28, 66), delivered in 59 B.C.[8] In the wake of Pompey's conquest of Pales-tine in 63 B.C., the Jewish population of Rome was also swelled by Jewish captives from the war. According to the Jewish writer Philo of Alexandria (*Legat.* 155), most of these captives were later manumitted and became Roman citizens. A good num-ber of them settled in the Trastevere district of Rome.[9]

The relationship between the Jews of Rome and both Julius Caesar and Au-gustus was quite amicable. A major reason for this was the support Jews from Pales-tine and Egypt provided to these men at crucial points in their careers.[10] In *Legat.* 156–158, Philo described in some detail Augustus's favorable treatment of Jews in Rome.[11] The relationship, however, between the Jews of Rome and the next two

---

[6] The praetors were occupied in the administration of justice. The *praetor peregrinus* dealt with lawsuits when either one or both parties were foreigners, in contrast to the *praetor urbanus*, who dealt with lawsuits between Roman citizens.

[7] Valerius Maximus, *Fact. et dict.* 1.3.3 (*GLAJJ* 1:147a–b). The text is preserved only in the epitomes of two later Latin writers (Januarius Nepotianus and Julius Paris). Both mention this kind of activity *(Romanis tradere sacra sua conati erant; Romanos inficere mores conati erant).* Valerius Maximus's source may have been the Roman historian Livy. Hispalus also expelled the Chaldean astrologers at the same time. Both expulsions reflect periodic Roman nervousness about the presence of foreign cults in Rome.

[8] "There follows the odium that is attached to Jewish gold. This is no doubt the reason why this case is being tried not far from the Aurelian Steps. You procured this place and that crowd, Laelius, for this trial. You know what a big crowd it is, how they stick together, how in-fluential they are in public meetings. So I will speak in a low voice so that only the jurors may hear; for those are not wanting who would incite them against me and against every respect-able man" (*GLAJJ* 1:68).

[9] Cicero also mentions Pompey's conquest of Palestine in *Flac.* 28, 67–68 (*GLAJJ* 1:68). It is not clear, however, whether Cicero's remarks on the Jewish crowd present at the trial also reflect the presence of these Jewish captives. Since most of the captives would not have been manumit-ted so quickly, it is unlikely that they would have been part of the crowd present at the trial.

[10] On the help provided to Julius Caesar by John Hyrcanus II and Antipater during his Egyptian compaign in 47 B.C., see Josephus, *Ant.* 14.127–139; *J.W.* 1.187–194. For the more complicated story of Herod the Great's help to Augustus, see Josephus, *Ant.* 15.183–218; *J.W.* 1.386–397, 431–434.

[11] "He knew therefore that they have houses of prayer and meet together in them, par-ticularly on the sacred sabbaths when they receive as a body a training in their ancestral philos-ophy. He knew that they collect money for sacred purposes from their firstfruits and send it to Jerusalem by persons who would offer the sacrifices. Yet nevertheless he neither ejected them from Rome nor deprived them of their Roman citizenship because they were careful to pre-serve their Jewish citizenship also, nor took any violent measures against the houses of prayer, nor prevented them from meeting to receive instructions in the laws, nor opposed their offer-ings of the firstfruits. Indeed so religiously did he respect our interests that supported by well-nigh his whole household he adorned our temple through the costliness of his dedications, and

emperors was rockier. In A.D. 19, the emperor Tiberius ordered four thousand Jews of military age deported to Sardinia to fight bandits, and the rest of the Jews and those who followed similar beliefs were banished from Rome. Josephus, Tacitus, Suetonius, and the Roman historian Dio Cassius all agree on the general outlines of the expulsion. Its causes, however, are less clear. Tacitus and Suetonius connect it with a wider attempt to suppress foreign cults, especially Egyptian and Jewish cults.[12] Dio Cassius connects it with Jews' success at converting non-Jews to their way of life.[13] Josephus, however, connects the expulsion with a particular incident. A Jew who fled from Palestine to Rome to avoid punishment had, along with three confederates, swindled a wealthy Roman matron, Fulvia, who had come to practice the Jewish way of life, out of money intended by her for the Jerusalem temple.[14] Josephus's explanation was probably meant to limit responsibility for the expulsion to the actions of a handful of rogue Jews. What is reflected in all four accounts, however, is Roman nervousness over, and distaste for, the influence of foreign cults on Romans.

The effects of the expulsion on Roman Jews are not clear. Certainly the deportation of four thousand men of military age to Sardinia would have been significant. Yet it is impossible to say what percentage of the other Jews actually left Rome at the time of the expulsion. One must remember that the Roman government, even in the city of Rome, was not bureaucratic in any modern sense; its means of seeing to it that decrees were carried out were limited. According to Philo (*Legat.* 159–161), for example, the effects of the expulsion were not long-lasting. After the death of Sejanus in 31, Tiberius seems to have restored the position of the Jews in Rome and elsewhere.[15] Philo's admittedly brief account of the restoration does not read as if thousands of Jews now returned to Rome after being away since A.D. 19. One suspects that many Jews had never left the city in the first place.

---

ordered that for all time continuous sacrifices of whole burnt offerings should be carried out every day at his own expense as a tribute to the most high God [τῷ ὑψίστῳ θεῷ]. And these sacrifices are maintained to the present day and will be maintained for ever to tell the story of a character truly imperial. Yet more, in the monthly doles in his own city when all the people each in turn receive money or grain, he never put the Jews at a disadvantage in sharing the bounty, but even if the distributions happened to come during the sabbath when no one is permitted to receive anything or to transact any part of the business of ordinary life, particularly of a lucrative kind, he ordered the dispensers to reserve for the Jews till the morrow the charity which fell to all." (Colson, LCL)

[12] Tacitus, *Ann.* 2.85.4 (*GLAJJ* 2:284); Suetonius, *Tib.* 36 (*GLAJJ* 2:306).

[13] Dio Cassius, *Hist. rom.* 57.18.5 (*GLAJJ* 2:419): Τῶν τε Ἰουδαίων πολλῶν ἐς τὴν Ῥώμην συνελθόντων καὶ συχνοὺς τῶν ἐπιχωρίων ἐς τὰ σφέτερα ἔθη μεθιστάντων, τοὺς πλείονας ἐξήλασεν ("As the Jews were flocking to Rome in great numbers and were converting many of the natives to their ways, he [Tiberius] expelled most of them.").

[14] Josephus, *Ant.* 18.81–84.

[15] Philo, writing sometime after 41 in *Legat.* 159–160, conveniently blamed the measures taken against the Jews on the influence of Sejanus, the *eminence grise* during Tiberius's reign up until his arrest and execution by the senate in 31 at Tiberius's behest. There is no evidence that Sejanus had a hand in the expulsion of A.D. 19. Sejanus is not mentioned in connection with the expulsion by any writer except Philo, but it served Philo's purposes in the *Legatio ad Gaium* well. Both of the emperors prior to Gaius Caligula, as well as Julius Caesar, could now be seen as positively disposed toward the Jews.

The reign of Gaius Caligula (37–41), although traumatic for Jews in Alexandria and Jerusalem, did not have a direct effect on the Roman Jewish community. Roman Jews must have been concerned about the anti-Jewish riots in Alexandria as well as Caligula's attempt to have a statue of himself set up in the Jerusalem temple. Their own position in Rome, however, was not affected.[16]

The reign of Claudius, in contrast, was more complex and troubling for the Roman Jewish community. It is also at this point that Roman Christians first emerge, as part of the Roman Jewish community in connection with the expulsion by Claudius. As mentioned above, Suetonius noted that Claudius "expelled from Rome Jews who were constantly making disturbances at the instigation of Chrestus."[17] This expulsion was probably the result of disturbances in the Roman Jewish community between the majority of Roman Jews and a minority who believed in Jesus as the Christ. Acts 18:1–2 seems to refer to the same expulsion: "After this he [Paul] left Athens and went to Corinth. There he found a Jew named Aquila, a native of Pontus, who had recently [προσφάτως] come from Italy with his wife Priscilla, because Claudius had ordered all Jews [πάντας Ἰουδαίους] to leave Rome." Since Paul arrived in Corinth probably early in 51 and there met Aquila and Priscilla/Prisca, who had recently (προσφάτως) arrived from Rome, the expulsion seems to have occurred in the late 40s. This is confirmed by an admittedly confused reference in the early-fifth-century Christian historian Orosius, who placed the expulsion in the ninth year of Claudius's reign, that is, in 49.[18] Once again, as with the expulsion in 19 under Tiberius, it is unclear who were actually expelled or who actually left Rome. Whereas Acts 18:2 refers to "all Jews" (πάντας Ἰουδαίους) being expelled, Suetonius's reference is ambiguous. The phrase "Jews who were constantly making disturbances" could refer to the expulsion of Jews in general or only to the expulsion of those who had been involved in the disturbances.[19] Given the limited ability of the Roman government to enforce its decrees, one suspects that the author of Acts 18:2 has exaggerated the extent of the expulsion. This is confirmed by the early-third-century Roman historian Dio Cassius, referring to events that he connected with Claudius's accession in 41: "As for the Jews, who had again increased so greatly that by reason of their multitude it would have been hard without raising a tumult to bar them from the city, he [Claudius] did not drive them out, but ordered

---

[16] For accounts of these events, see Philo, *Legatio ad Gaium,* and Josephus, *Ant.* 18.257–309; *J.W.* 2.184–203.

[17] Suetonius, *Claud.* 25.4 (*GLAJJ* 2:307).

[18] Orosius, *Adv. pag.* 7.6.15: *Anno eiusdem nono expulsos per Claudium urbe Iudaeos Iosephus refert. Sed me magis Suetonius movet, quo ait hoc modo* [the quotation from Suetonius follows]. The problem is that no such quotation is found in Josephus. We have no idea where Orosius obtained his information, which he wrongly attributed to Josephus. But there is no reason to think he obtained it from Acts 18:1–2. Only in this way does Orosius's remark tend to confirm the dating of the expulsion to the late 40s.

[19] In the phrase *Iudaeos impulsore Chresto assidue tumultuantis,* the participial phrase *assidue tumultuantis* could be taken either as expressing the cause of the expulsion or as specifying the meaning of the noun *Iudaeos.* In the former case, it would refer to all Roman Jews; in the latter, only to those who were involved in the disturbances. The second interpretation is more likely.

them, while continuing their traditional way of life, not to hold meetings."[20] Since there is no reason to think the situation in 41 described by Dio Cassius was any different at the end of the decade, the expulsion mentioned by Suetonius, Acts 18:2, and Orosius was probably limited to those involved in the disturbances. The situation of the Roman Jewish community under Claudius, then, was a troubled one. Soon after his accession, he ordered the Jews of Rome not to hold meetings. Then, toward the end of the decade, he expelled from Rome those who had been involved in disturbances within the Jewish community over belief in Jesus as the Christ.

As one looks over what we know of the history of the Jewish community of Rome through the middle of the first century, one is first struck by the extent to which its situation was affected by the decisions of the Roman government, whether under the republic or under the empire. Its status depended on the goodwill or ill will of the Roman authorities. This is hardly surprising, but it is important to keep in mind.

Three other aspects of the Roman Jewish community of the first century are also important, especially for understanding the Christian community in Rome. First, the Roman Jewish community was probably organized as independent voluntary associations. Although in some ways the status of the Jewish community of Rome was of a piece with that of other Hellenistic Jewish communities, there were also significant differences. In much of the Greek-speaking East, the status of Hellenistic Jewish communities had previously depended on the attitudes of their Hellenistic overlords. When the Romans achieved dominance in the East, they usually reaffirmed for the Hellenistic Jewish communities the status and privileges granted by the previous rulers. In most cases this meant that Jews lived in Hellenistic cities as groups of aliens (μέτοικοι, *peregrini*). The public recognition of these communities usually included the rights to live according to their ancestral customs, to regulate their own finances, and to have jurisdiction over their own members. This also meant some sort of centralized organization of the Jewish community in each city. These privileges, which gave Jewish communities in the East a quasi-civic status, were reaffirmed by the Roman authorities, often in the face of attempts by Greek cities to abolish them.[21]

---

[20] Dio Cassius, *Hist. rom.* 60.6.6 (*GLAJJ* 2:422): Τούς τε Ἰουδαίους πλεονάσαντας αὖθις, ὥστε χαλεπῶς ἂν ἄνευ ταραχῆς ὑπὸ τοῦ ὄχλου σφῶν τῆς πόλεως εἰρχθῆναι, οὐκ ἐξήλασε μέν, τῷ δὲ δὴ πατρίῳ βίῳ χρωμένους ἐκέλευσε μὴ συναθροίζεσθαι. Some scholars have suggested that this notice in Dio Cassius referred to the same events mentioned in Suetonius and Act 18:1–2, and then date all the events to either 41 or 49. The problem with this interpretation is that Suetonius and Acts clearly mention an expulsion but Dio Cassius explicitly denies there was an expulsion. In addition, Dio Cassius clearly dates Claudius's suppression of Jewish public meetings to 41, the first year of his reign; Acts 18:2 and Orosius date the expulsion to the end of the decade, that is, to around 49. From what follows immediately in Dio Cassius (τάς τε ἑταιρείας ἐπαναχθείσας ὑπὸ τοῦ Γαΐου διέλυσε), Claudius's suppression of Jewish meetings in 41 was part of a larger effort to suppress voluntary associations (ἑταιρεῖαι, *collegia*) in general. Claudius's actions in 49 were intended to rid Rome of what he thought were troublemakers in the Jewish community and not to expel all Jews from Rome.

[21] For examples of Roman decrees affirming Jewish privileges in Greek cities, see Josephus, *Ant.* 14.185–267; 16.160–178. See Schürer, *History*, vol. 3, part 1, pp. 107–25, for descriptions of the legal situations of different Jewish communities; also A. M. Rabello, "The Legal Condition of the Jews in the Roman Empire," *ANRW* 13.662–762.

The status of the Roman Jews, however, was different. It was not that of a group of aliens with quasi-civic standing but of a voluntary association or, more likely, associations. Voluntary associations were an integral part of both Greek and Roman culture. They were more or less permanently organized associations for a common purpose. Most had a religious component, but the specific purposes of the associations varied. Some were primarily religious, others were burial societies, and still others were composed of fellow workers in the same craft, industry, or trade.[22] Evidence indicates that the Jews of Rome were organized as voluntary associations. Josephus (*Ant.* 14.215–216) records a decree of Julius Caesar in which he banned religious associations (θιάσους) in Rome but excepted the Jews.[23] Similarly Dio Cassius connects the emperor Claudius's suppression of Jewish meetings in 41 with a larger effort to suppress voluntary associations (ἑταιρεῖαι) in general.[24]

There were a number of these Jewish associations in Rome, and they seem to have been independently organized local congregations or "synagogues," as the inscriptions refer to them.[25] Because almost all of the Roman Jewish inscriptions, which mention roughly thirteen of them, come from the third and fourth centuries, it is difficult to determine how many existed in the first century.[26] Peter Richardson has offered convincing evidence that at least three and perhaps as many as five go back to the reign of Augustus in the late first century B.C. and in the early first century A.D.[27] Given that the size of the Jewish community in Rome during the

---

[22] For associations in the ancient world, see the classic studies of Erich Ziebarth, *Das griechische Vereinswesen* (Stuttgart: S. Hirzel, 1896); Franz Poland, *Geschichte der griechischen Vereinswesens* (1909; repr., Leipzig: Zentral-Antiquariat der Deutschen Demokratischen Republik, 1967); Jean Pierre Waltzing, *Étude historique sur les corporations professionnelles chez les Romains depuis les origines jusqu'à la chute de l'Empire d'Occident* (4 vols.; 1895–1900; repr., Bologna: Forni, 1968). Most recently see John S. Kloppenborg and S. G. Wilson, eds., *Voluntary Associations in the Graeco-Roman World* (London: Routledge, 1996).

[23] On Julius Caesar's legislation to abolish various voluntary associations, see Suetonius, *Jul.* 42.3 where these associations are referred to with their Latin name *collegia*.

[24] Dio Cassius, *Hist. rom.* 60.6.6.

[25] Leon, *Jews*, 167–70. The term "synagogue" probably referred to the congregation. The building in which the congregation met was a "house of prayer [προσευχή]" (Philo, *Legat.* 156; *JIWE* 2:602 [*CIJ* 531]; Juvenal, *Sat.* 3.296). From *JIWE* 2:602 and Juvenal, it is clear that at least some of these houses of prayer were buildings publicly recognized as centers for Jewish congregations. On the complex question of the character of such buildings, see L. Michael White, "Synagogue and Society in Imperial Ostia: Archaeological and Epigraphic Evidence," in *Judaism and Christianity in First-Century Rome* (ed. Karl P. Donfried and Peter Richardson; Grand Rapids: Eerdmans, 1998), 30–68.

[26] For the collection of these inscriptions and their dating, see the new critical edition of all the inscriptions in *JIWE*, vol. 2.

[27] Peter Richardson, "Augustan-Era Synagogues in Rome," in *Judaism and Christianity in First-Century Rome* (ed. Karl P. Donfried and Peter Richardson; Grand Rapids: Eerdmans, 1998), 17–29. These synagogues are: (1) "Synagogue of the Hebrews" (*JIWE* 2:2 [*CIJ* 317], 2:33 [291], 2:578 [510], 2:579 [535]); (2) "Synagogue of the Augustesians" (2:96 [301], 2:169 [?] [338], 2:189 [368], 2:194 [416], 2:542 [496], 2:547 [284]); (3) "Synagogue of the Agrippans" (2:130[?] [425], 2:170 [365], 2:549 [503], 2:562); (4) "Synagogue of the Volumnians" (2:100 [402], 2:163 [417], 2:167 [343], 2:577 [523]); and (5) "Synagogue of the Herodians" (2:292 [173]). The evidence for the last two is considerably weaker than that for the first three.

first century A.D. has been estimated at between twenty thousand and forty or even fifty thousand, other synagogues probably also existed at that time, perhaps some of those attested in other Roman Jewish inscriptions.[28] An analysis of the synagogal offices mentioned in the inscriptions shows no evidence of a centralized organization beyond the level of the individual congregation.[29] Again, although these inscriptions are almost all from the third and fourth centuries, there is no reason to think that the situation was different in the first century. This is especially true given the Roman government's constant suspicion of voluntary associations. It is difficult to imagine that the Roman authorities would have countenanced a centralized organization of up to forty or fifty thousand members. This does not, of course, exclude more informal relationships among these communities. It would be naive to think that Jewish communities in Rome, given their common origins and interests, had no such informal relationships among themselves. They almost certainly did.

The second important aspect of the Roman Jewish community was its connection with the Jews of Palestine. The origins of most members of the Roman Jewish community had been in Palestine. According to Philo (*Legat.* 155), most Roman Jews were by his time Roman citizens, but they had originally been brought to Rome as slaves in the wake of Pompey's conquest of Palestine in 63 B.C. and had subsequently been emancipated. In addition, in the first century A.D., Herodian princes from Palestine were raised in Rome and became personal friends of future emperors. Between A.D. 37 and 44 Agrippa I became king of an area in Palestine that rivaled in size that of his grandfather Herod the Great, largely through his friendship with Gaius Caligula and Claudius.[30] The Roman Jewish community itself also took an active interest in the political affairs in Palestine. For example, after the death of Herod the Great in 4 B.C., it publicly sided with a Jewish embassy from Palestine against Archelaus and his efforts to obtain rule over all his father Herod's domains.[31] Because of the political centrality of Rome, contacts between the Roman Jewish community and Palestinian Jews were especially frequent and significant.

The third important aspect of the Roman Jewish community was the presence of Gentiles sympathetic to the Jewish way of life. The existence of such sympathetic Gentiles and their relationship to the Roman Jewish community is part of the larger and quite controversial issue of whether Judaism during this period was a "missionary" religion; that is, whether Jews during this period intentionally sought, as a group, to make converts to their way of life.[32] Stated in such broad terms, the issue

---

[28] The lower figure was suggested by R. Penna, "Les Juifs à Rome au temps de l'apôtre Paul," *NTS* 28 (1982): 328. The higher number was accepted by Leon, *Jews*, 135–36.

[29] Leon, *Jews*, 167–94. A recently discovered epitaph listing a Jew by the name of Anastasius as ἀρχιγερουσιάρχης (*JIWE* 2:521) probably refers to the leader of the gerousia of an individual synagogue.

[30] Raymond E. Brown, in Raymond E. Brown and John P. Meier, *Antioch and Rome: New Testament Cradles of Catholic Christianity* (New York: Paulist, 1983), 95–96. See also Schürer, *History*, 1:442–54.

[31] Josephus, *J. W.* 2.80–83; *Ant.* 17.299–303.

[32] Both Schürer (*History*, vol. 3, part 1, pp. 150–76) and Louis H. Feldman (*Jew and Gentile in the Ancient World: Attitudes and Interactions from Alexander to Justinian* [Princeton,

lies beyond the scope of this analysis, which is confined to what we can know or plausibly surmise about the presence of sympathetic Gentiles connected specifically with the Roman Jewish community.

Various Roman writers were clearly alarmed at the influence of the Jewish way of life on the non-Jewish inhabitants of Rome. This is especially the case for writers of late republican and early imperial Rome, such as Horace, Valerius Maximus, Seneca the Younger, Tacitus, and Juvenal.[33] For example, Seneca complained that "the way of life of this accursed race [the Jews] has gained such influence that it is now received throughout the world; the vanquished have given laws to their victors."[34] In the same vein, Tacitus lamented that "those who have gone over to their [the Jews'] way of life follow the same practice, and the earliest lesson they receive is to despise the gods, to disown their country, and to regard their parents, children, and brothers as of little account."[35] In addition, two of the expulsions of Jews from Rome mentioned above (in 139 B.C. and A.D. 19) were connected with the Roman authorities' alarm at a growing Jewish influence on the other inhabitants of Rome.[36] Both, it should be noted, were part of wider expulsions of devotees of foreign cults, of Chaldean astrology in 139 B.C. and of Egyptian cults in A.D. 19. This indicates that, at least to some extent, the stance of the Roman authorities toward the Jewish way of life was of a piece with their stance toward other foreign cults in Rome.

Does all this evidence lead to the conclusion that the Roman Jewish community had an intentional policy of proselytism during this period, especially during the late republican and early imperial periods? Probably not. The evidence of the expulsions attests to the attractiveness of Eastern religious traditions to some inhabitants in Rome but not necessarily to a sustained missionary effort on their part. The evidence of the Roman writers mentioned above also needs to be treated critically. All of them viewed with alarm the influence of the Jewish way of life (and of Eastern religions generally) on the inhabitants of Rome. All of them tended to reflect the disdain of the Roman upper classes for all things foreign, even though some of them were themselves parvenus. In their alarm they probably exaggerated the extent of the influence of these religions, particularly the Jewish way of life, on the Roman

---

N.J.: Princeton University Press, 1993], 288–415) think there was such an effort. Scot McKnight (*A Light among the Gentiles: Jewish Missionary Activity in the Second Temple Period* [Minneapolis: Fortress, 1991]) and Martin Goodman (*Mission and Conversion: Proselytizing in the Religious History of the Roman Empire* [Oxford: Clarendon, 1994]) think there was not. For an earlier defense of Jewish missionary activity and its place within the larger Greco-Roman context of religious competition, see Dieter Georgi, *The Opponents of Paul in Second Corinthians* (Philadelphia: Fortress, 1986), 83–228.

[33] Horace, *Serm.* 1.4.139–43 (*GLAJJ* 1:127); 1.9.60–78 (*GLAJJ* 1:129); Valerius Maximus, *Fact. et dict.* 1.3.3 (*GLAJJ* 1:147a–b); Seneca, *De superstitione*, in Augustine, *Civ.* 6.11 (*GLAJJ* 1:186); Tacitus, *Hist.* 5.5.2 (*GLAJJ* 2:281); Juvenal, *Sat.* 14.96–106 (*GLAJJ* 2:301).

[34] Seneca, *De superstitione*, in Augustine, *Civ.* 6.11 (*GLAJJ* 1:186): *Cum interim usque eo sceleratissimae gentis consuetudo convaluit, ut per omnes iam terras recepta sit; victi victoribus leges dederunt.* Translation by Green, LCL.

[35] Tacitus, *Hist.* 5.5.2 (*GLAJJ* 2:281): *Transgressi in morem eorum idem usurpant, nec quidquam prius imbuuntur quam contemnere deos, exuere patriam, parentes liberos fratres vilia habere.* Translation by Moore, LCL.

[36] See pp. 17–19.

populace. Again, because of their disdain, they saw this influence as the result of an intentional program of deception by the members of these religions. After all, what else could explain their attractiveness?

This being said, however, the fact remains that the Jewish way of life must have been attractive to a large enough body of inhabitants of Rome to be noticed both by the Roman authorities and these Roman writers. This seems especially to have been the case for the late republic and the early empire. We have no idea of how large this group was, and we may reasonably suspect that these writers exaggerated its size. Nevertheless, all the evidence points to the attractiveness of the Jewish way of life to some Romans.

We need to explore two issues further. First, can we tell what it was about the Jewish way of life that some non-Jews in Rome found attractive? Second, what were the responses among those who were sympathetic to the Jewish way of life? Were some more closely connected to the Jewish community than others? In answer to the first question, there were several aspects of the Jewish way of life that some non-Jews found attractive and that Roman writers mention, although they often interpret them negatively. Our discussion is based on what we can know or plausibly surmise specifically about the situation in Rome.

The first aspect is Jewish monotheism, which both Tacitus and Juvenal mention. They view Jewish rejection of the Roman gods negatively.[37] Still, in comparing Jewish monotheism with the Egyptian worship of animals, Tacitus writes favorably about the Jewish conception of God as supreme, eternal, and incapable of being represented in human form.[38] Monotheism, at least in the sense of belief in one god as supreme and the other gods as subordinate to, or as expressions of, this one god, had long been part of the Greco-Roman world, especially in Greek and Roman philosophy. During the imperial period it became more popular and widespread.[39] Interest in Jewish monotheism was part of a wider monotheistic trend during this period. From the *Letter of Aristeas* in the second century B.C. on, Hellenistic Jewish literature capitalized on this and made claims for the superiority of the Jewish way of life on the basis of its stark monotheism.

The second is the antiquity of the Jewish people, an antiquity widely conceded by Greek and Latin authors. Tacitus offers several possible explanations for the origins of the Jewish people and assumes that their origins were quite ancient, one tracing them back to the time of the expulsion of Saturn by Jove, another tracing them back to the reign of Isis in Egypt (*Hist.* 5.2.1–3). The same admission of antiquity is true for his explanation of the expulsion of the Jews from Egypt at the time of King Bocchoris and the establishment of the Jewish law by Moses (*Hist.* 5.3–4).

---

[37] Tacitus, *Hist.* 5.5.2 (*GLAJJ* 2:281) (see above); Juvenal, *Sat.* 14.97 (*GLAJJ* 2:301): "They worship nothing but the clouds and the divinity of the heavens." (Ramsay, LCL)

[38] Tacitus, *Hist.* 5.5.4 (*GLAJJ* 2:281).

[39] See *OCD*, s.v. monotheism; Martin P. Nilsson, *Geschichte der griechischen Religion* (2 vols.; 3d ed.; Munich: Beck, 1967–1974), 2.569–78; Mary Beard, John North, and Simon Price, *Religions of Rome* (2 vols.; Cambridge: Cambridge University Press, 1998), 1.286–87. All point out that "henotheism" (the worship of one god in particular or a special devotion to one god) may be a better term than "monotheism." The belief in the supremacy of one god over the other gods falls somewhere between the two.

The third is observance of the Sabbath rest, which Horace, Seneca, and Juvenal all mention.[40] Evidence indicates that by the first century the seven-day week as well as observance of the seventh day as a day of rest were becoming more widespread among non-Jews. The latter, however, was probably due less to the influence of the Jewish way of life than to the belief that Saturday, the "day of Saturn," was an unlucky day on which to do business.[41] Nevertheless, the coincidence of the two must have made the Jewish way of life attractive to at least some non-Jews.

Although it may at first seem odd, a fourth aspect was its prohibitions in matters of food. Both Tacitus and Juvenal mention this, again with disapproval.[42] The attraction of these prohibitions was connected with the ascetic aspects of Greco-Roman culture, especially Greco-Roman philosophy.[43] Seneca provides an indirect witness to this in *Ep.* 108.22. He describes how as a young man he had abstained from animal food under Pythagorean influence. But he stopped the practice at his father's request early in the reign of Tiberius because foreign cults were expelled from Rome at this time and abstinence from certain kinds of animal food was considered a sign of interest in them. This is almost certainly a reference to Tiberius's expulsion of Jews (and devotees of Egyptian cults) from Rome in 19. Indirectly, then, he attests to the attraction of Jewish abstinence from certain foods for some non-Jews in Rome.

A fifth aspect was its strong sense of community. On the one hand, many Romans found this inner Jewish cohesion offensive because it showed a hatred for the rest of the human race. Both Tacitus and Juvenal reflect this perception.[44] Tacitus in particular thought that Jews felt only hostility and hatred toward every other people and that those who went over to the Jewish way of life came to despise their own country and to regard their parents, children, and brothers as of little account, as mentioned earlier. On the other hand, even someone as hostile as Tacitus

---

[40] Horace, *Serm.* 1.9.68–72 (*GLAJJ* 1:129): "'Today is the thirtieth day, a Sabbath. Would you affront the circumcised Jews?' 'I have no scruples,' say I. 'But I have. I am a somewhat weaker brother, one of the many'" (Fairclough, LCL); Seneca, *De superstitione*, in Augustine, *Civ.* 6.11 (*GLAJJ* 1:186), after condemning observance of the Sabbath, writes, "The customs of this accursed race have gained such influence that they are now received throughout the world" (Green, LCL); Juvenal, *Sat.* 14.96, 105–106 (*GLAJJ* 2:301): "Some have a father who reveres the Sabbath. . . . For all this the father was to blame, who gave up every seventh day to idleness, keeping it apart from all the concerns of life." (Ramsay, LCL)

[41] Tibullus, *Carm.* 1.3.18; Elias J. Bickerman, *Chronology of the Ancient World* (2d ed.; Ithaca, N.Y.: Cornell University Press, 1980), 58–61; Nilsson, *Geschichte der griechischen Religion*, 2.487.

[42] Tacitus, *Hist.* 5.5.2 (*GLAJJ* 2:281): "They sit apart at meals"; Juvenal, *Sat.* 14.98–99 (*GLAJJ* 2:301): "They see no difference between eating swine's flesh, from which their father abstained, and human flesh." (Ramsay, LCL)

[43] Platonists, Stoics, Cynics, and Pythagoreans all had elements of asceticism connected with them. See *OCD*, s.v. asceticism; Martha C. Nussbaum, *The Therapy of Desire: Theory and Practice in Hellenistic Ethics* (Princeton, N.J.: Princeton University Press, 1994). Notions of asceticism are also found in ancient medical literature. See Gail Paterson Corrington, "The Defense of the Body and the Discourse of Appetite: Continence and Control in the Greco-Roman World," in *Discursive Formations, Ascetic Piety, and the Interpretation of Early Christian Literature* (ed. Vincent L. Wimbush; 2 vols.; Semeia 57–58. Atlanta: Scholars Press, 1992), 1:65–74.

[44] Tacitus, *Hist.* 5.5.1–2 (*GLAJJ* 2:281); Juvenal, *Sat.* 14.103–4 (*GLAJJ* 2:301).

commends Jews' loyalty to one another, their readiness to show each other compassion, and their care for the burial of their dead.[45] It is this community aspect that some non-Jews in Rome must have also found attractive. This was especially the case given how difficult life must have been for the vast majority of inhabitants of an ancient city such as Rome. This interest in a stronger sense of community was also part of a broader trend that made for the growing attractiveness of alternative cults.[46] The attractiveness of this aspect of the Jewish way of life should not be underestimated.

A sixth and crucial aspect of the Jewish way of life that some non-Jews in Rome found attractive was the Jewish claim for the ethical superiority of the Mosaic law. Once again Tacitus writes with grudging admiration about certain aspects of Jewish ethics, such as Jews' loyalty and compassion toward one another, their condemnation of infanticide, their care for burying their dead, and the willingness of the whole population of Jerusalem, both men and women, to fight on its behalf.[47] Certainly, Greco-Roman Jewish authors constantly claimed ethical superiority for the Jews. An emphasis on this superiority, as we shall see a bit later, was also an important element in the self-understanding of the Roman Christian community.

The Jewish historian Josephus, writing at the end of the first century, listed these same aspects and claimed that non-Jews found them attractive and widely imitated them (*Ag. Ap.* 2.281–284).[48] In fact, he emphasizes these aspects of the Jewish way of life throughout his own account, in *Ag. Ap.* 2.145–286, of the Jewish constitution (2.145–219) and his comparison of it with other constitutions (2.220–278): (1) monotheism (2.164–167; 190–192); (2) antiquity (2.154–156, 168, 256–257); (3) observance of the Sabbath rest (2.174, 234); (4) abstention from certain foods (2.174, 234); (5) density of community (2.146, 179–183, 257); (6) ethical superiority (2.146, 170–171, 199–211, 214). No doubt Josephus exaggerated the number of Gentiles for whom these aspects of the Jewish way of life were attractive. Nevertheless, both Josephus and various Roman writers did take note of these six characteristics. Often the Roman writers did so reluctantly, but this very reluctance points to the reality that they were attractive to some Gentile inhabitants of Rome. There is a significant overlap between what Josephus explains is central to the Jewish way of life and what was also attractive about the Jewish way of life to non-Jews.

---

[45] Tacitus, *Hist.* 5.5.1–3 (*GLAJJ* 2:281).

[46] Beard, *Religions of Rome,* 1:287–91.

[47] Tacitus, *Hist.* 5.5.1, 4; 5.13.3 (*GLAJJ* 2:281).

[48] "Our earliest imitators were the Greek philosophers, who, though ostensibly observing the laws of their own countries, yet in their conduct and philosophy were Moses' disciples, holding similar views about God, and advocating the simple life and friendly communion between man and man. But that is not all. The masses have long since shown a keen desire to adopt our religious observances; and there is not one city, Greek or barbarian, nor a single nation, to which our custom of abstaining from work on the seventh day has not spread and where the fast and the lighting of lamps and many of our prohibitions in the matter of food are not observed. Moreover, they attempt to imitate our unanimity, our liberal charities, our devoted labor in the crafts, our endurance under persecution on behalf of our laws. The greatest miracle of all is that our Law holds out no seductive bait of sensual pleasure, but has exercised this influence through its own inherent merits; and, as God permeates the universe, so the Law has found its way among all mankind." (Thackeray, LCL)

Josephus, however, also offers us something more, a glimpse into the self-understanding of the Roman Jewish community itself. Parts of Josephus's *Against Apion* (2.145–286) plausibly provide us with a more specific sense of how Roman Jews understood the superiority of the Jewish way of life and indirectly how that superiority would have been attractive to some non-Jewish inhabitants of Rome. In 71, after the end of the Jewish War, Josephus came to Rome with Titus, the Roman commander. He arrived in Rome about fifteen years after Paul wrote his letter to the Roman Christian community, and he lived in Rome from 71 until his death in about 100. At least through the reigns of Vespasian (69–79) and his son Titus (79–81), Josephus lived in quarters provided him by the emperors. His relationship with Titus's successor Domitian (81–96) is less clear. His patron during these later years seems to have been a man by the name of Marcus Vettius Epaphroditus rather than Domitian.[49] When Josephus arrived in Rome, he had some knowledge of Greek, but his real Greek "education" took place in Rome. He obtained most of his knowledge of Greek literature at Rome rather than earlier in Palestine.[50]

Josephus says virtually nothing about what his relationship to the Jewish community in Rome might have been.[51] No doubt that relationship was complex, but it is difficult to imagine that there was no relationship. The Jewish community in Rome could hardly have ignored a Jew so closely connected with the emperors. The most likely source for much of the extrabiblical Jewish material Josephus used in his writings would have been the Jewish community in Rome. For example, most of the arguments Josephus used in *Ag. Ap.* 2.145–286 to show the superiority of the Mosaic law have parallels in other Greco-Roman Jewish literature. It is highly unlikely that he gained this familiarity while in Palestine and much more likely that he gained it through contact with the Jewish community after his arrival in Rome. The educated stratum of the Roman Jewish community would have been the obvious source for such material.

The commonplace character of many of his arguments, however, should not lead us to think that there were no differences of outlook among different Jewish communities. Just as Philo was part of a larger intellectual tradition characteristic of the Judaism of Alexandria, Josephus's account of the Mosaic law—the Jewish constitution—and its superiority probably reflected outlooks and emphases at home in the Jewish community of Rome in the first century, or at least among its more educated members. To think otherwise would turn Josephus into a first-century Melchizedek.

---

[49] Harold W. Attridge, "Josephus and His Works," in *Jewish Writings of the Second Temple Period: Apocrypha, Pseudepigrapha, Qumran, Sectarian Writings, Philo, Josephus* (ed. Michael E. Stern; CRINT 2.2; Philadelphia: Fortress, 1984), 186–87.

[50] Even though written in Rome, the first edition of his *Jewish War* was written in Aramaic (Josephus, *J.W.* 1.3).

[51] We know very little else about his life in Rome. The short section of Josephus's *Life* (422–430) given to his time in Rome is devoted almost completely to showing how high his standing was with the Flavian emperors even in the face of numerous accusations against him. At least some of his accusers were Jewish (*Life* 424–425, 428–29), but it is not clear that all these Jewish accusers were Roman Jews. The only Jewish accuser he names (a certain Jonathan) was from Cyrene.

A striking characteristic of *Ag. Ap.* 2.145–286 is the extent and specificity of the comparisons—all intended to show the superiority of the Jewish constitution—that he makes between the Mosaic law and other, primarily Greek, constitutions.[52] It was certainly commonplace in Greco-Roman Jewish literature to speak of the Jewish way of life and the Mosaic law as superior to the laws and practices of non-Jews. But the comparisons were usually of a general sort. For example, Philo of Alexandria, in the beginning of *De opificio mundi* (1–3), asserts the superiority of the Mosaic law over the work of other lawgivers, but he does so in a very general way, without ever mentioning the names of those lawgivers. Josephus, however, is very explicit about who these other lawgivers are and about why the Mosaic law is superior to them. He devotes a whole section in his account of the Mosaic law to a comparison with the laws and practices of other peoples (*Ag. Ap.* 2.220–278). He shows the superiority of the Jewish constitution over those of the Spartans, the Athenians, the Scythians, and the Persians.

But these specific comparisons are not limited to this one section. They are quite extensive. At the beginning of his exposition (*Ag. Ap.* 2.150), he justifies these comparisons by claiming that he is only responding to anti-Jewish critics who have denied that Jews possessed these laws or that they were the most law-abiding of all the nations.[53] In 2.151–168, Josephus claims that the Jewish constitution is older than the laws of Lycurgus, Solon, Zaleucus, Minos, Pythagoras, Anaxagoras, Plato, and the Stoics. The superiority of the Mosaic law is also demonstrated by its combination of precept and practice (2.169–174). This is unlike the laws of the Spartans and the Cretans, who emphasize practice only, and unlike the laws of the Athenians and most others, who emphasize precepts only. Josephus also repeatedly emphasizes that, unlike other peoples, all the Jews observe their laws and educate their children in the knowledge and practice of them.[54] Likewise he emphasizes in various ways the ethical superiority of the Mosaic law over other laws.[55] The Mosaic law was established to promote the virtues of piety, friendly relations with each other, love of humanity, justice, perseverance, and contempt of death (2.145). Josephus especially emphasizes the superiority of Jewish sexual morality. Sexual relations are confined to marriage for the purpose of the procreation of children (2.199). Adultery, rape, homosexual practices, abortion, and incest are condemned.[56] This code of sexual morality is contrasted to the licentious Greek conception of the gods and the lax sexual morality that went with it.[57]

There is good reason to think that Josephus's extensive and specific comparisons of the Mosaic law with other codes of law did not originate with Josephus

---

[52] Josephus leaves Roman beliefs and practices and Roman traditions of law untouched. In one sense, the reason is clear: he did not want to anger his Roman benefactors. There may also, however, be another reason: the apologetic side of Jewish literature in Greek was aimed at Greeks and other people of the eastern Mediterranean rather than at the Romans. This may be another indication of how traditional the arguments made by Josephus were.

[53] Josephus repeats this justification in *Ag. Ap.* 2.236–238.

[54] Ibid., 2.175–178, 189, 204, 220–224, 225–231, 271–278.

[55] Ibid., 2.145, 199–214, 225–235, 250–254, 273.

[56] Ibid., 2.199–203, 215, 273–275, 276.

[57] Ibid., 2.243–247, 273–275.

himself but were already part of the traditions of the Roman Jewish community with which he came in contact. This emerges from an analysis of *Ag. Ap.* 2.145–278, where Josephus alters his way of arguing. In the earlier sections, he responded to specific charges made by different Greek writers, but in 2.145–278, he gives an overall exposition of the law and compares it with other law codes. He justifies this change by claiming that Apollonius Molon, unlike the writers treated up to then, did not group his accusations together but scattered them throughout his work. Because of this, Josephus thought it more appropriate to present a general exposition of the law and its superiority that would refute the various charges made by Apollonius. There is no reason, however, to think that Apollonius's charges were any more scattered than the writers Josephus explicitly refuted earlier. The justification is quite artificial. It really serves as a hook on which Josephus can now hang an overall exposition and justification of the Mosaic law. This exposition is only tangentially connected with Apollonius; Josephus mentions him only incidentally toward the end of the exposition (2.236, 254, 258, 270). The exposition is largely independent of any specific charges Apollonius may have made and was not composed for the specific purpose of refuting him. The overall structure of 2.145–278 was certainly Josephus's own, yet he returns to the same topics several times in the course of his exposition and comparison. This suggests that he probably used several already existing defenses of the Mosaic law that were available to him through the Roman Jewish community. He extensively edited them, but he did not create them out of whole cloth.

This means that the Roman Jewish community itself already had a self-understanding that strongly emphasized the superiority of the Mosaic law over other codes of law and the superiority of Jews' observance of their law over other peoples' nonobservance of their own laws. This superiority included the topics mentioned earlier: Jewish monotheism and antiquity, observance of the Sabbath rest, abstention from certain foods, density of community, and ethical superiority, especially in sexual matters. Roman Jews would have communicated this same sense of superiority to sympathetic Gentile inhabitants of Rome. Indeed, this claim to superiority was probably what some Gentile inhabitants of Rome found attractive, even though it clearly infuriated others.

After this somewhat detailed description of what some non-Jews found attractive in the Jewish way of life, one further issue needs attention. Among those who were sympathetic to the Jewish way of life, were there different levels of commitment to it? Were there different levels of association involvement with the Jewish community?[58] Were some more closely connected through their beliefs and practices to the Jewish community than others? From what we can know or plausibly surmise

---

[58] See Shaye J. D. Cohen, *The Beginnings of Jewishness: Boundaries, Varieties, Uncertainties* (Berkeley, Calif.: University of California Press, 1999), 140–74. Cohen lists seven ways in which a Gentile could show respect or affection for Judaism: (1) admiring some aspect of Judaism, (2) acknowledging the power of the God of the Jews, (3) benefiting the Jews or being conspicuously friendly to Jews, (4) practicing some or many of the rituals of the Jews, (5) venerating the God of the Jews and denying or ignoring all other gods, (6) joining the Jewish community with "conversion," e.g., in the case of Gentile wives and slaves, (7) converting to Judaism and "becoming a Jew."

about the Roman Jewish community, the evidence, although not plentiful, points to different levels of commitment and association. Some inhabitants of Rome who found the Jewish way of life attractive converted fully to it. Technically they became "proselytes" and were no longer "Gentiles."[59] For males, this would have involved circumcision. Both Juvenal and Tacitus took notice of this group of people.[60]

Among others, however, who adopted the various Jewish beliefs and practices mentioned above and associated regularly with the Roman Jewish community, the practice of the Jewish way of life was more limited in the sense that it did not entail circumcision and full "conversion." We have the names of several of them.[61] Suetonius was probably referring to such sympathizers when he related how the emperor Tiberius banished from Rome both Jews and "those who followed similar beliefs *[similia sectantes]*" in 19.[62] The most enlightening evidence, however, comes from Juvenal:

> Some, whose lot it was to have a Sabbath-fearing father,
> worship nothing but the clouds and the divinity of the heavens,
> and see no difference between human flesh and swine's flesh,
> from which their father abstained; then they take to circumcision.
> Having become accustomed to despise the laws of Rome,
> they learn and practice and reverence the Jewish law,
> all that Moses handed down in his secret tome. (*Sat.* 14.96–102 [Thackeray, LCL])[63]

Juvenal describes those whose fathers came to believe in the one God of the Jews, observed the Sabbath rest, and kept some of the dietary laws of the Jewish way of life. Their sons then took the final step and were circumcised. Although Juvenal takes a dim view of all this, his description of levels of belief and practice was probably accurate. Some Gentiles sympathetic to the Jewish way of life did not have themselves

---

[59] See Schürer, *History*, vol. 3, part 1, pp. 150–76. Five or six of the names found in the Jewish inscriptions of Rome are decribed as proselytes (*JIWE* 2:62 [*CIJ* 462], 2:218 [256], 2:224 [222], 2:392 [?] [202], 2:489 [21], 2:491 [68]). These inscriptions, however, probably all come from the third and fourth centuries.

[60] Tacitus, *Hist.* 5.5.2 (*GLAJJ* 2:281); Juvenal, *Sat.* 14.99 (*GLAJJ* 2:301).

[61] Quintus Caecilius Niger, a first-century B.C. Roman freedman who became quaestor (Plutarch, *Cic.* 7.6.5 [*GLAJJ* 1:263]); Flavius Clemens and his wife, Flavia Domatilla (late first century)(Dio Cassius, *Hist. rom.* 67.14.1–2 [*GLAJJ* 2:435]). Fulvia, the Roman aristocrat mentioned by Josephus in *Ant.* 18.81–85 in connection with the expulsion of the Jews from Rome in *Ant.* 19, may be another example. It is not clear, however, whether Josephus, in describing her as "practicing Jewish customs" (νομίμοις προσεληλυθυῖαν τοῖς Ἰουδαικοῖς), thought of her as an actual convert to Judaism (a proselyte) or as a sympathizer. Given her position in Roman society, one suspects the latter is more likely, no matter what Josephus actually thought. Another such sympathizer may have been Nero's wife, Poppaea (Josephus, *Ant.* 20.195). This, however, is less clear.

[62] Suetonius, *Tib.* 36 (*GLAJJ* 2:306).

[63] *Quidam sortiti metuentem sabbata patrem*
nil praeter nubes et caeli numen adorant,
nec distare putant humana carne suillam,
qua pater abstinuit, mox et praeputia ponunt.
Romanas autem soliti contemnere leges
Iudaicum ediscunt et servant ac metuunt ius,
tradidit arcano quodcumque volumine Moyses.

circumcised. In this way, they remained as Gentile sympathizers and associated with the Jewish community but were neither fully converted to the Jewish way of life nor fully part of the Jewish community. According to Juvenal, these Gentile sympathizers might associate with the Jewish community through the study of the Mosaic law. The most obvious way to do this was to attend synagogue services.[64]

Another helpful text comes again from Josephus, and it mirrors Juvenal's description in significant ways. In *Ag. Ap.* 2.209–210, Josephus describes Moses' legislation about the proper treatment of aliens (ἀλλοφύλους):

> It is also worthwhile considering how our legislator was concerned about the equitable treatment of aliens. For it will be clear that he took the best of all possible measures both so that we would not corrupt our customs and also so that we would not begrudge those who choose to share them. To all who desire to come and live under the same laws with us, he gives a gracious welcome, holding that this relationship is constituted not by birth alone but also by the choice of a way of life. On the other hand, he did not want casual visitors to be admitted to the intimacies of our daily life. (Thackeray, LCL)

One of Josephus's goals in this passage was to defend Jews against the charge that they were hostile to all those not of their own race.[65] Moses did indeed exclude casual visitors, the merely curious, from participation in Jews' daily life. But he did this lest their customs be corrupted and not out of any hatred for members of other races. The preservation of a people's customs was a justification readily understandable to inhabitants of the Greco-Roman world. After all, one of the complaints of Tacitus and Juvenal against the Jewish way of life was that Romans who became sympathetic to it also held the Roman way of life and its customs in contempt.[66] Yet Moses also decreed that Jews should graciously receive Gentiles who chose to share in their customs or to live under the same laws with them. This was not a matter of birth only but also of a choice of this way of life. Josephus described this group in fairly broad and indefinite terms. They must have been more than casual visitors, more than merely curious. But he did not claim that they must accept all Jewish customs and laws or that the males among them must be circumcised. Indeed Josephus never mentions circumcision in his exposition of the Mosaic law in 2.145–286.[67] This omission can hardly be accidental. Rather Josephus meant his description of non-Jews whom the Jewish community graciously accepted to be somewhat elastic and to include the different kinds of people mentioned by Juvenal, not only those who eventually became circumcised and

---

[64]There is a good deal of debate about whether words roughly translated as "God-fearer" (φοβούμενος, σεβόμενος, θεοσεβής) had a technical meaning, referring to Gentiles who were sympathetic to Judaism. The evidence for the first century comes from Josephus (*Ant.* 14.110, 195) and Acts (10:2, 22, 35; 13:16, 26, 43, 50; 16:14; 17:4, 17; 18:7), but it is unclear whether the terms are being used in a technical sense. The evidence for a technical use is stronger for the second and especially the third centuries. See Schürer, *History,* vol. 3, part 1, pp. 165–69; Feldman, *Jew and Gentile,* 342–69. Juvenal, in the quotation given above, is clearly not using the phrase "Sabbath-fearing father" *(metuentem sabbata patrem)* in any technical sense, since he uses the same verb *(metuunt)* several lines later (101) in a different way.

[65]See Josephus, *Ag. Ap.* 1.239, 304–311; 2.89–111, 121–124, for some examples.

[66]Tacitus, *Hist.* 5.5.1 (*GLAJJ* 2:281); Juvenal, *Sat.* 14.103–104 (*GLAJJ* 2:301).

[67]Josephus does mention the practice earlier (*Ag. Ap.* 1.169–171) and defends it against Apion (*Ag. Ap.* 2.137–142).

fully converted to the Jewish way of life but also those whose association with the Jewish community was much more than casual but stopped short of circumcision and full conversion. Again it is unlikely that Josephus was taking a view peculiar to himself in this description. Rather he was describing the views and practices of the broader Roman Jewish community.

The Jewish community almost certainly would not have considered as Jews those who, though regularly associating themselves with the community and following many of its beliefs and practices, did not finally become Jews through circumcision. But how did these individuals see themselves? Given the state of the evidence, it is virtually impossible to say. It is not unlikely, however, that such people would have clearly seen themselves on the Jewish side of the Jewish-Gentile divide. Although they were certainly not members of the Jewish community in the strict sense, they may well have seen themselves as part of it in a somewhat enlarged sense. The Jewish community itself may also have considered them the same way.[68]

It is impossible to determine the proportion between those who converted and became full members of the Jewish community and those whose commitment fell short of this. But one strongly suspects that the much larger of the two groups was made up of Gentiles whose association with the Jewish way of life stopped short of circumcision and full conversion. There are two reasons for this. First, adult circumcision in the ancient world was both painful and potentially dangerous. Second, and probably more important, was the social stigma attached to circumcision. Greek and Roman writers almost universally derided this practice.[69] Other aspects of the Jewish way of life sometimes found a sympathetic hearing, but virtually never circumcision.

To draw together all the strands of what we can know or plausibly surmise, the Roman Jewish community of the first century was fairly large, somewhere between twenty and fifty, but was not centrally organized. Rather the Jews of Rome were organized as local voluntary associations with no central authority. In addition, a number of Gentile inhabitants of Rome were sympathetic to Jewish beliefs and practices, especially monotheism, a superior ethic, observance of the Sabbath, and abstention from certain foods. They saw in the beliefs and practices of the Roman Jewish community a way of life superior to that of their fellow Romans. This superiority was also something emphasized by the Roman Jewish community itself. Some of these

---

[68] This description does not fit easily into Cohen's seven ways of showing respect for Judaism, listed in n. 58, above. It is more than either no. 4 (practicing some or many of the rituals of the Jews) or no. 5 (venerating the God of the Jews and denying or ignoring all other gods) but less than no. 7 (converting to Judaism and "becoming a Jew"). The problem with Cohen's otherwise very helpful categorization is that, until no. 7, it does not take into account the significance of regular association with a Jewish community. He also does not take adequately into account the kinds of things that Jewish authors claimed and Greco-Roman authors admitted were attractive about Judaism to non-Jews.

[69] Strabo, *Geogr.* 16.1.37 (*GLAJJ* 1:115); 16.4.9 (*GLAJJ* 1:118); 17.2.5 (*GLAJJ* 1:124); Horace, *Serm.* 1.9.69–70 (*GLAJJ* 1:129); Apion in Josephus, *Ag. Ap.* 2.137 (*GLAJJ* 1:176); Persius, *Sat.* 5.184 (*GLAJJ* 1:190); Petronius, *Sat.* 68.8 (*GLAJJ* 1:193); Martial, *Epigr.* 7.30.5 (*GLAJJ* 1:240); 7.35 (*GLAJJ* 1:241); 7.55.4–8 (*GLAJJ* 1:242); 7.82 (*GLAJJ* 1:243); 11.94 (*GLAJJ* 1:245); Tacitus, *Hist.* 5.5.2 (*GLAJJ* 2:281); Juvenal, *Sat.* 14.96–106 (*GLAJJ* 2:281); Suetonius, *Dom.* 12.2 (*GLAJJ* 2:301).

Gentiles, probably only a minority of them, eventually became circumcised and fully converted to the Jewish way of life. The majority, however, associated with the Roman Jewish community and accepted its beliefs and practices more selectively. Much of this evidence will be helpful as we now return to the history and character of the Christian communities of Rome.

THE CHRISTIAN COMMUNITY OF ROME

Suetonius's notice in *Claud.* 25.4 that the emperor Claudius "expelled from Rome Jews who were constantly making disturbances at the instigation of Chrestus" means that the earliest believers in Jesus in Rome were originally members of the Roman Jewish community.[70] The most obvious aspect of this belief in Jesus was that this he was the Messiah, the Christ. How or when believers first came to Rome is not clear. No reliable evidence exists in later Christian sources, however, that there was a single founder (e.g., the apostle Peter). Certainly Paul's letter to the Roman Christian community gives no indication that there was such a person. More likely belief in Jesus as the Christ first spread to the Jewish community in Rome through the frequent contacts between Jews in Rome and Jews in Jerusalem and Palestine. As seen above, contacts between the Roman Jewish community and Jews in Jerusalem and Palestine were frequent.

This view is strengthened by the probable dating for the earliest presence of believers in Jesus as the Christ within the Roman Jewish community. The expulsion by Claudius described by Suetonius took place in 49 or at least at the end of the 40s of the first century. Belief in Jesus as the Christ must have been around long enough in the Jewish community to have taken root and to have gained enough adherents to make the Roman authorities notice the disturbance they caused in the community. This pushes the origins of believers in Jesus in the community back at least to the late 30s or early 40s. Given the very limited presence of Christian communities outside Palestine at this time, belief in Jesus probably arrived in Rome through Jewish Christians coming from Jerusalem and Palestine or through Roman Jews visiting Palestine, especially Jerusalem, and coming in contact there with Jewish Christians.[71]

Apart from Paul's letter to the Roman Christians (to which we shall return shortly), the next evidence we have for Christians in Rome comes from the Roman historian Tacitus's description of their persecution under the emperor Nero (*Ann.* 15.44). In July of 64 a disastrous fire sweeping through the city of Rome destroyed

---

[70] On the Roman Christian community in general, see Rudolf Brändle and Ekkehard W. Stegemann, "The Formation of the First 'Christian Congregations' in Rome in the Context of the Jewish Congregations," in *Judaism and Christianity in First-Century Rome* (ed. Karl P. Donfried and Peter Richardson; Grand Rapids: Eerdmans, 1998), 117–27; James C. Walters, "Romans, Jews, and Christians: The Impact of the Romans on Jewish/Christian Relations in First-Century Rome," ibid., 175–95; William L. Lane, "Social Perspectives on Roman Christianity during the Formative Years from Nero to Nerva," ibid., 196–244.

[71] This view of the origins of Roman Christianity within the Roman Jewish community is indirectly confirmed by Ambrosiater in the late fourth century in the preface to his commentary on Romans (*In Epistulam ad Romanos*, part 1 of *Commentarius in epistulas paulinas* [ed. H. J. Vogels; CSEL 81.1; Vienna: Hoelder-Pichler-Temsky, 1961], 4–7).

or damaged ten of the city's fourteen districts. After the fire Nero contributed generously to rebuilding the burned-out districts of the city (15.43). But he also took 125 acres to build the Domus Aurea, a magnificent palace surrounded by elaborate gardens (15.42). None of Nero's generosity could prevent the public from suspecting that he had ordered the fire set in order to clear an area on which to build the Domus Aurea. Because of what it reveals about the Roman Christians in the mid-60s, Tacitus's account of Nero's attempt to find scapegoats for setting the fire bears quoting in full.

> Therefore, to suppress the rumor, Nero substituted as culprits, and punished with the utmost refinements of cruelty, those whom, loathed for their vices, the crowd called Christians. The founder of the same, Christ, was executed in the reign of Tiberius by the procurator Pontius Pilate. This pernicious superstition, checked for a moment, broke out once more, not only in Judaea, the home of the disease, but also in the city [Rome] itself, where all things horrible and shameful collect and come into vogue. First, then, the confessed members of the sect were arrested; next, on their disclosures, large numbers [*multitudo ingens*] were condemned, not so much for the crime of arson as for hatred of the human race [*odio humani generis*]. And derision accompanied their end: they were covered with wild beasts' skins and torn to death by dogs; or they were fastened on crosses, and, when daylight failed, were burned to serve as lamps by night. Nero had offered his Gardens for the spectacle, and gave an exhibition in his Circus, mixing with the crowd dressed as a charioteer, or standing in a chariot. Hence, in spite of a guilt which had earned the most exemplary punishment, there arose a sentiment of pity, due to the impression that they were being sacrificed not for the welfare of the state but to the ferocity of a single person. (15.44) (Jackson, LCL)

Two things are clear from Tacitus's account. First, by the mid-60s, when these events took place, there was a fairly large number of Christians in Rome. Tacitus may have exaggerated the number for dramatic effect. But even granted the exaggeration, the events described indicate that there were a substantial number of Christians in Rome. The apostles Peter and Paul were probably executed in Rome during this time.[72] Second, it is clear from Tacitus's narrative that by the mid-60s "Christians" were perceived by the emperor and the public alike as a separate group with no connection to the Jewish community of Rome. They even had their own name. There is not the slightest hint that Nero confused these Roman Christians with Roman Jews. And even though Tacitus was aware that their origins were in Judaea, he did not associate them with the Jewish way of life or the Roman Jewish community.[73]

The contrast between what Suetonius tells us about believers in Jesus as members of the Roman Jewish community toward the end of the 40s and what Tacitus tells us about Christians as a separate community in the mid-60 is startling. In a period of less than twenty years, members of the Roman Jewish community who believed in Jesus as the Christ had become "Christians" whom the Roman authorities

---

[72] From the end of the first century, *1 Clem.* 5–6 refers to the deaths of Peter and Paul as well as of a great multitude (πολὺ πλῆθον) of other Christians. *1 Clement*, however, does not explicitly mention Nero. For the explicit connection of the deaths of Peter and Paul to the persecution of Nero, see Eusebius, *Hist. eccl.* 5.25.5–7.

[73] Brown, *Antioch and Rome,* 99, highlights both of these facts.

perceived as quite separate from the Roman Jewish community. How and when did these changes take place? The easiest way is to begin with Tacitus and work back to Suetonius. From what Tacitus tells us, it is likely that the break between these Christians and the Roman Jewish community took place some years prior to Nero's persecution. It is difficult to imagine that either Nero or the Roman authorities would have been able to single out Christians so clearly had their break with the Roman Jewish community taken place immediately before the persecution. This is confirmed by Paul's letter to the Romans, probably written in 56–57, which gives no hint that there was an organizational connection between his Roman Christian audience and the Roman Jewish community.[74] Although this is an argument from silence, it is a significant silence, given the issues Paul deals with in the letter.[75] Had there been any institutional relationship between the Christian community and the much larger Roman Jewish community, Paul would have had to deal with it in some fashion. In addition, Paul's letter assumes that the organization of the Roman Christian community was not only freestanding and independent but also stable.[76] This form of organization, then, had already been in existence for some years. This brings us back to Suetonius's notice of the disturbances within the Roman Jewish community in 49. What were these disturbances about? Why were they disruptive enough to come to the attention of the emperor Claudius and even lead him to expel at least some Jews from Rome? The most plausible explanation is that the disturbances were over the expulsion of believers in Jesus as the Christ from the Roman Jewish community. The number of these believers had grown to such an extent that they could no longer be treated as a small group with odd opinions. Their presence was significant enough that something had to be done. What resulted were their expulsion and the ensuing disturbances. The notice in Suetonius, then, points to two expulsions. The first was the expulsion of believers in Jesus from the Roman Jewish synagogues. This resulted in disturbances in the Roman Jewish community and led to a second expulsion, this time the expulsion from Rome by Claudius of those involved in the disturbances. Included in this expulsion were Jewish Christians such as Prisca and Aquila, whom Paul met when he arrived at Corinth early in 51 (Acts 18:1–3). This scenario offers the most plausible explanation, first for the disturbances within the Jewish community in 49, then for the origins of the independence of the Roman Christian community from the Roman Jewish community reflected in Romans in 56–57, and finally for Tacitus's description of the persecution of the "Christians" by Nero in the mid-60s.

---

[74] Mark D. Nanos (*The Mystery of Romans: The Jewish Context of Paul's Letter* [Minneapolis: Fortress, 1996], 289–336) argues, on the basis of Rom 13:1–7, that Roman Christians were still part of the Roman Jewish community. But the reference to an authority's use of the sword (i.e., the power to execute) in 13:4 makes it impossible for 13:1–7 to be about Christian obedience to synagogue authority. Romans 13:1–7 is about obedience to Roman authority, not about submission to the authority of the Jewish community.

[75] These issues include the proper role of the Mosaic law, the place of Israel in God's plan, and the relationship between Jews and Gentiles. All these issues run throughout Romans.

[76] As we shall see shortly, the greetings in Rom 16:3–16 indicate that the Roman Christians were probably organized into house churches, based on the model of the organization of the Roman Jewish synagogues but independent of them.

Granted the basic accuracy of this scenario, four other important aspects of the Roman Christian community around the time of Paul's letter need to be clarified. The first is the makeup of the community. Were its members primarily Jewish Christians or Gentile Christians? From Paul's letter it is clear he thinks the majority of Roman Christians were of Gentile origin. In the elaborate greeting of the letter (Rom 1:1–7), Paul writes that through Jesus Christ "we have received grace and apostleship to bring about the obedience of faith among all the Gentiles [ἐν πᾶσιν τοῖς ἔθνεσιν] for the sake of his name, among whom are also you [ἐν οἷς ἐστε καὶ ὑμεῖς] who are called to belong to Jesus Christ" (1:5–6). A bit later, in the thanksgiving section of the letter (1:13), Paul claims that he often intended to come to Rome "in order that I might reap some harvest among you as I have among the other Gentiles [καθὼς καὶ ἐν τοῖς λοιποῖς ἔθνεσιν]." Finally, toward the end of the letter, Paul justifies the fact that he has written rather boldly to the Roman Christians because of the grace given to him by God "to be a minister [λειτουργόν] of Christ Jesus to the Gentiles [εἰς τὰ ἔθνη] in the priestly service [ἱερουργοῦντα] of the Gospel, so that the offering of the Gentiles [ἡ προσφορὰ τῶν ἐθνῶν] may be acceptable, sanctified by the Holy Spirit" (15:16). Paul was very much aware that the members of the Roman Christian community were primarily of Gentile origin.

This obviously does not mean that the Roman Christian community was made up only of Gentile Christians. Romans 16:3–16 contains a long list of Roman Christians to whom Paul sends greetings. An analysis of the names shows that a clear majority of the Roman Christians were probably of Gentile origin.[77] Of the twenty-six names mentioned in this list, about sixteen of them were probably of Gentile origin.[78] Five or six of the names, however, indicate Jewish origin, either because of the names themselves or because Paul indicates they are Jewish.[79] In addition, at least some of the members of the household of the Jewish couple Prisca and Aquila (16:3–5) were probably Jewish. If the Aristobulus mentioned in 16:10 was the grandson of Herod the Great and the brother of Agrippa I, the same would hold true of "those of the household of Aristobulus" (16:10). The presence of these Jewish Christians in the Roman community around 57 also indicates that Claudius's expulsion was no longer in effect or at least no longer being enforced. This is especially the case for Prisca and Aquila, who were now back in Rome (16:3–4) after being expelled in 49 (Acts 18:1–3). The Roman Christians, then, were primarily of Gentile origin, but there was also a significant minority of Jewish Christians.[80] Given the

---

[77] The most detailed analysis of the names in Rom 16:3–16 is found in Peter Lampe, *Die stadrömischen Christen in den ersten beiden Jahrhunderten: Untersuchungen zur Sozialgeschichte* (2d ed.; WUNT 18; Tübingen: Mohr, 1989), 124–53.

[78] Epaenetus, Ampliatus, Urbanus, Stachys, Tryphaena, Tryphosa, Persis, Rufus, Asyncritus, Phlegon, Hermes, Patrobas, Hermas, Philologus, Nereus, and Olympas.

[79] Prisca, Aquila, Andronicus and Junia (my fellow countrymen [τοὺς συγγενεῖς μου]), Herodion (my fellow countryman [τὸν συγγενῆ μου]), and possibly Mary.

[80] Scholars often point also to other passages in Romans to clarify the makeup of the Roman Christian community (e.g., 6:17–21; 9:3–5; 11:13, 17–18, 24, 28, 30–31). These passages will eventually prove helpful in understanding the viewpoints of this community, but because of their strongly rhetorical character, they are best not used to clarify the makeup of the community.

fact that the Christian community had been separate from the Jewish community for only seven or eight years, most of the Christians of Gentile origin almost certainly had already been sympathetic to the Jewish way of life and been associated with the Roman Jewish community before the separation in 49.

A more difficult question to answer is whether or how the expulsion from Rome in 49 affected the ratio of Gentile to Jewish believers in Jesus and whether this ratio was again altered once some of those who had been expelled returned to Rome after Claudius's death in 54. There is no clear answer to either question, but two things can be said with some assurance. First, the expulsion of believers in Jesus from the Roman Jewish community in 49 marked a fundamental shift in the community to which these believers in Jesus, both Jewish and Gentile, belonged. Before the expulsion, these believers belonged to, or were associated with, the Roman Jewish community. After the expulsion, the community to which they belonged became a separate community independent of the Roman Jewish community and ethnically predominantly Gentile. This is a significant shift. But one should not misinterpret its significance. As we shall see a bit later in this chapter, this separate Roman Christian community probably still maintained many of its fundamental convictions about, and commitment to, the Jewish way of life. In other words, its members still saw themselves as rooted in, and still part of, the Jewish way of life, even though the Roman Jewish community saw it quite differently. Second, even when Jewish Christians such as Prisca and Aquila returned to Rome after the death of Claudius in 54, Paul's letter to the Romans indicates that the community still remained largely Gentile. The return of Jewish Christians did not fundamentally alter the makeup of the Roman Christian community. In fact, as we shall see, the controversies among the Roman Christians reflected in Rom 14:1–15:6 did not divide along Jewish-versus-Gentile lines. After all, Prisca and Aquila, who would have been on Paul's side of the argument, were Jewish.

A second aspect of the Roman Christian community was the social status of its members. An analysis of the names in 16:3–16 again offers some guidance.[81] On the basis of their names, Prisca, Aquila, Urbanus, and Rufus were freeborn. Nereus, Hermes, Persis, Herodion, Tryphosa, Tryphaena, and Ampliatus were probably either slaves or freedmen or freedwomen. Julia, Junia, and Mary (if she was not Jewish) were freedwomen or descendants of freedwomen. For the other twelve on the list, there is no way to tell their social status on the basis of their names. The great majority of the Roman Christians, then, were probably from the lower social strata, slaves and freedmen and freedwomen. There were, however, some men and women of means among them. This was certainly true of Prisca and Aquila, at whose house one group of Christians met. It must also have been true for those at whose houses the two groups mentioned in 16:14–15 met.

A third aspect of the community was its mode of organization. The beginning and the end of Romans are again helpful. Both show that the Roman Christians were organized in ways similar to the decentralized structure of the Roman Jewish community from which they had been expelled. Like the Roman Jews, Roman Christians were organized as a number of voluntary associations. At the beginning

---

[81] See Lampe, *Die stadtrömischen Christen*, 135–53.

of the letter, Paul refers to the addressees as "all God's beloved in Rome, who are called to be saints" (1:7). This way of referring to the Roman Christians is unlike the way Paul described most of the other communities to which he wrote. With the exception of his letter to the Philippians, Paul referred to the Christian communities to which he was writing as a "church" or "assembly" (ἐκκλησία).[82] At each place the Christians seem to have formed a single community, that is, a single voluntary association. Paul did not refer to the Roman Christians as a "church" probably because he knew that they were not centrally organized as one community but as several independent but related voluntary associations. Paul uses the word "church" five times in Romans 16. In four of the instances (16:1, 4, 16, 23), he means the church in particular places other than Rome. The only time he uses the word to refer to the Roman Christians is in the mention of the "church" at the house of Prisca and Aquila (16:5), as one church among others in Rome.

The structure of Roman Christianity as a number of voluntary associations also emerges from an analysis of the elaborate list of greetings in 16:3–16. Paul's principle of organization for this list is not clear. But he seems to refer to at least five different house churches, that is, different groups of Christians who meet at the homes of individual Christians of some means: the church that meets at the house of Prisca and Aquila (16:5); those who belong to the household of Aristobulus (16:10); those who belong to the household of Narcissus (16:11); Asyncritus, Phlegon, Hermes, Patrobas, Hermas, and those with them (16:14); and Philologus, Julia, Nereus, his sister, Olympas, and those with them (16:15).[83] Given that thirteen of these names are connected to particular house churches, one wonders whether the other thirteen names might also have been members of yet other house churches. This would mean that Paul knew of up to fifteen house churches in Rome. The latter suggestion may be too speculative. But the list in 16:3–16 strongly supports the view that the Roman Christian community was not centrally organized. Rather it consisted of at least five, and probably more, independently organized house churches.[84] It is also clear from 3:3–16, however, that these different house churches were not sealed off from one another. Paul wrote his letter to the house churches as a whole and expected that the Roman Christians would pass his letter around and read it in these different house churches. In this way his greetings would be passed on to their members. This combination of the independent organization of the communities

---

[82] "To the church of the Thessalonians" (1 Thess 1:1); "to the churches of Galatia" (Gal 1:2); "to the church of God which is at Corinth" (1 Cor 1:2; 2 Cor 1:1); "to the saints in Christ who are at Philippi with the bishops and deacons" (Phil 1:1). The address in Gal 1:2 is "to the churches" because Paul was writing to several churches in a geographical area (Galatia) and not to a church in one city. The fact that Paul did not refer to the Christian community at Philippi as a church means that one must be cautious about making too much of the simple absence of the word in Rom 1:7. The significance of its absence there, however, becomes clear when one analyzes its use in Rom 16.

[83] The heads of at least the households of Aristobulus and Narcissus were not Christian. How meetings at these places would have taken place is not clear. In effect, the meetings may have been restricted to only those of each household.

[84] Lampe, *Die stadtrömischen Christen*, 301–02; William L. Lane, "Social Perspectives on Roman Christianity," 202–14.

and informal but very real relationships among them reflects that found in the Roman Jewish community.[85]

There was, however, probably one difference between the way the two different communities were organized. Because by this time the Roman Jewish community had been in Rome for at least 150 years and was much larger than the Roman Christian community, their meeting places were probably either existing buildings structurally modified to meet their needs or, less likely, buildings newly constructed for these purposes.[86] This was probably not the case with the Roman Christian community. Paul's way of greeting these communities suggests they met in private houses or apartments large enough to hold a number of people rather than in separate buildings or even spaces modified to serve their community needs.

A fourth and final aspect of the Roman Christian community was its beliefs and practices. Granted the ethnic makeup, social status, and community structure of the Roman Christians, how did they understand themselves? What can we plausibly say about their beliefs and practices at the time Paul wrote his letter to them? Were there any differences among Roman Christians about these beliefs and practices? In trying to answer these questions, we need to begin on a note of caution. The fact that the Roman Christian community was made up largely of Gentiles with a minority of Jews does not automatically tell us anything about their beliefs and practices. More specifically, it does not automatically mean that, as Gentiles, most of the community would have had no interest in the significance of the Mosaic law or in its observance.[87] There is ample evidence in earliest Christianity of diverse views about the relationship of Christian belief and practice to the Mosaic law and its observance.[88]

Given the different relationships between Jewish and Gentile Christians in earliest Christianity according to time and place, what can we know or plausibly surmise about the viewpoints, practices, and differences in the Roman Christian community? As seen above, the Roman Christians were expelled from the Roman Jewish community in 49. By the time Paul wrote his letter to them in 57, they had been independent

---

[85] This structure had changed, however, by the end of the first century. The openings of both *1 Clement,* from the end of the first century, and of Ignatius of Antioch's letter to the Roman Christians, from the beginning of the second century, refer to the Christians at Rome as a church (ἐκκλησία). The community had become more centralized but was still without a monoepiscopacy.

[86] For two somewhat different views on the issue of Jewish communal buildings in first-century Rome, see Richardson, "Augustan-Era Synagogues in Rome," 17–29, and White, "Synagogue and Society in Imperial Ostia,", 30–68.

[87] This view of Gentile Christianity was fairly common among an earlier generation of scholars, even in Rudolf Bultmann's classic *History of the Synoptic Tradition* (2d ed.; New York: Harper & Row, 1963).

[88] Raymond Brown (Brown and Meier, *Antioch and Rome,* 1–9) lists four different groups. Group 1 consisted of Jewish Christians and their Gentile converts who insisted on full observance of the Mosaic law, including circumcision. Group 2 consisted of Jewish Christians and their Gentile converts who did not insist on circumcision but did require converted Gentiles to keep some Jewish observances. Group 3 consisted of Jewish Christians and their Gentile converts who did not insist on circumcision and did not require observance of the Jewish food laws. Group 4 consisted of Jewish Christians and their Gentile converts who did not insist on circumcision or observance of the Jewish food laws and who saw no abiding significance in Jewish cult and feasts. The Roman Christians fell into groups 2 and 3.

of the Jewish community for a relatively short time, about seven or eight years. This means that most of the Gentile members of the community almost certainly came in contact with belief in Jesus as the Christ through their association with the Jewish community and its beliefs and practices. They were drawn primarily from among the Gentile sympathizers. Even after their expulsion from the Jewish community, the beliefs and practices of most Roman Christians, not only Jewish but also Gentile, probably still included not only the centrality of belief in Jesus as the Christ but also continued acceptance of central Jewish beliefs and practices in which their belief in Jesus was embedded. Most Jewish and Gentile Christians would have been committed to Jewish monotheism and to observance of the ethical precepts of the Mosaic law. Indeed, they would still have been convinced of the ethical superiority of the Mosaic law over the ethical practices of the Greco-Roman world. Some, a minority as we will see, also would have observed the Sabbath rest and the prohibition of certain foods. The Roman Christians also would have carried over a strong sense of community from the Jewish community to their now separate community. Even though institutionally separate from the Jewish community, they still saw themselves as committed to and as part of the Jewish way of life.

This view of the Roman Christian community finds support from the text of Romans itself. Three sections in Romans are particularly helpful.[89] First, it is clear from 14:1–15:6 that there was tension in the Roman Christian community over observance of the Sabbath and the dietary regulations of the Mosaic law. In this section of Romans, Paul deals with the tension between the "weak" (ὁ ἀσθενῶν) (14:1–2) and the "strong" (ὁ δυνατός) (15:1) over two issues.[90] The first concerns eating or abstaining from certain foods. The strong think that one can eat any kind of food; the weak, however, eat only vegetables (λάχανα, 14:1–2). The second concerns distinguishing some days from others (14:5–6). The strong do not distinguish one day from another, but the weak do. These two issues, then, concern the continued observance of the dietary rules and observance of the Sabbath and perhaps other festivals of the Mosaic law. Paul's own views clearly place him in the camp of the strong (14:14, 20): believers in Jesus are not obliged to observe either the dietary rules or the rules for the Sabbath of the Mosaic law. Yet in 14:1–15:6 Paul argues primarily on behalf of the weak. Among other things, he urges the strong not to despise the weak (14:3) and not to do injury to the weak for the sake of food and drink (14:15–17). Two points are especially important for our present purposes. First, this tension in the Roman Christian community is over two aspects of the Mosaic law that, as seen earlier, were attractive to Gentiles sympathetic to the Jewish way of life. Second and consistent with this, the tension is clearly not between Jewish and Gentile believers. Rather Paul describes the tension as one between the "strong" and the "weak." This means that there were Jewish and Gentile believers on both sides of the argument. Some Roman Christians, both Jewish and Gentile, thought that both

---

[89] For closer analyses of these sections, see ch. 14, below.

[90] The best analysis of this section is John M. G. Barclay, "'Do We Undermine the Law?': A Study of Romans 14.1–15.6," in *Paul and the Mosaic Law: The Third Durham-Tübingen Symposium on Earliest Christianity and Judaism* (ed. James D. G. Dunn; Grand Rapids: Eerdmans, 2001), 287–308.

sorts of regulations from the Mosaic law should still be observed; others, again both Jewish and Gentile, thought otherwise.

Second, despite their disagreements over these dietary and Sabbath rules, most Roman Christians seem to have been committed to observance of the ethical commandments of the Mosaic law. In Romans 7 Paul presents, among other things, a defense of the Mosaic law in which he tries to show that "the law is holy, and the commandment is holy and just and good" (7:12, 14, 16, 22). Paul casts much of this chapter in the first person singular (7:7–25). A great deal of debate surrounds the identity of the "I" in this section of the letter. There is good reason to think that the "I" is not autobiographical.[91] If it is not autobiographical, to whom does the "I" refer? The clue to the identity of the speaker is found in 7:7b–12, where the speaker describes his first encounter with the law and its results.[92]

> What then shall we say? That the law is sin? By no means! Yet if it had not been for the law, I should not have known sin. I should not have known what it is to "desire" if the law had not said, "You shall not desire." But sin, finding opportunity in the commandment, wrought in me every sort of desire. Apart from the law sin lies dead. I was once alive apart from the law, but when the commandment arrived, sin came alive and I died; the very commandment which promised life proved to be death to me. For sin, finding opportunity in the commandment, deceived me and by it killed me. So the law is holy, and the commandment is holy and just and good.

The speaker of these words has to be someone who at first did not know the law and so did not know sin. Then there came a time when the speaker both came to know the law and tried unsuccessfully to observe it. The result was that only through the law's commandment not to "desire" did the speaker come to know what desire was.[93] The speaker was once alive apart from the law, but when the law arrived, sin came alive and the speaker died. The transition from ignorance to knowledge and from non-observance to attempted observance does not fit with the speaker being Jewish. A Jew would have known the law from an early age. Rather, what Paul seems to be appealing to here, without explicitly saying so, is what he thinks was the experience of Gentiles sympathetic to the Jewish way of life who as adults came to observe the ethical commandments of the Mosaic law. They were born and grew up without the law, but as adults they took upon themselves its observance. Consistent with this, Paul's emphasis in 7:7b–25 is clearly on the ethical aspects of the law and not on dietary regulations or ritual purity. Paul, then, must have thought of the Roman Christian community as made up of Gentile Christians most of whom had come to feel obligated to observe the ethical commandments of the law.[94]

---

[91] The "you" in 8:2 indicates that Paul himself is not the speaker in 7:7–25. Other arguments against autobiographical interpretation of the "I" in 7:7–25 will be found in the detailed analysis of this passage in ch. 8, below.

[92] As we shall see in ch. 8, below, this is an example of prosopopoeia (speech-in-character).

[93] Paul is quoting the tenth commandment of the Decalogue. But he is clearly using it in the sense of "desire" (ἐπιθυμέω/ἐπιθυμία) rather than in the more restricted sense of "covet." Paul's emphasis is on the vice of desire so familiar to Greco-Roman moralists.

[94] The role that this plays in Paul's argument in this section of Romans will become clear in the analysis of Rom 7 in ch. 8, below.

Third, a passage from the very beginning of the letter further strengthens this view. Paul begins its first major section (1:18–3:20) with an indictment of Gentile religiosity (1:18–32). In it he first condemns Gentile failure to recognize God's invisible nature from the things that God made (1:19–21). This leads to idolatry because Gentiles have exchanged the glory of the immortal God for images of mortal human beings, birds, animals, and reptiles (1:22–23). This in turn leads to the practice of various sorts of vices, especially those of a sexual nature (1:26–27, 28–29). There is nothing peculiarly Christian about this critique. Rather this section of Romans is very much of a piece with other Hellenistic Jewish critiques of Gentile religion and the immorality to which such religion leads.[95] This critique also clearly resembles what we saw earlier in Josephus, *Ag. Ap.* 2.145–286. Integral to this critique and implicit in Paul's indictment is the superiority of Jewish belief and morality. Yet the comparatively small compass within which all this takes place shows that Paul is not really arguing a case. Rather he is stating what his Roman Christian audience would have taken to be obvious. His critique of Gentile religiosity and morality would certainly have appealed to Jewish Christians living in Rome. Yet only several verses earlier (1:5–6, 13) Paul has recognized that most Roman Christians were of Gentile origin. Why, then, would Paul begin the first major section of his letter to them with an indictment with which he thought they would have easily agreed? Such an indictment makes sense only if these Gentile Christians were already familiar with, and shared with Jewish Christians, the same Hellenistic Jewish view of Gentile religion and morality as well as a conviction about the superiority of Jewish belief and morality. This again supports the notion that most Roman Christians of Gentile origin, even after their expulsion from the Jewish community, continued to be convinced of the superiority of the Jewish way of life, especially its monotheism and ethical precepts and practices.

Finally, there is one crucial aspect of the Mosaic law about which the Roman Christian community did not seem to have disagreed. At no point in Romans does Paul deal with the issue of the circumcision of Gentile believers. Given Paul's views on this issue, especially in Galatians, this silence is significant. It must mean that entrance into the Roman Christian community by Gentile believers did not entail circumcision. Both Jewish and Gentile believers must have been in agreement on the issue; otherwise Paul certainly would have had to deal with it. This makes perfect sense, given the probability that most Gentile members of the community were drawn originally from sympathizers associated with the Jewish community rather than from full converts to the Jewish way of life. Part of the attractiveness for these Gentile believers would have been that, without the requirement of circumcision, they could be full members of the Christian community. Without circumcision this would have been impossible within the Jewish community. But this attractiveness, however, should not lead us to think that the other aspects of the Jewish way of life would have become less attractive to them. Those other aspects were what first attracted them to this way of life and continued to attract them as members of the Christian community. Paradoxically, apart from the Jewish community and without

---

[95] E.g., *Let. Arist.* 128–172; Wis 13:1–15:17; *Sib. Or.* 3:29–45, 184–187, 594–600, 764; Ps.-Phoc. 190–192, 213–214.

the requirement of circumcision, the ethnically Gentile majority among the Roman Christians could now, for the first time, understand themselves as full participants in a Jewish way of life. It was not something they would easily surrender or compromise.

This description covers the vast majority of Roman Christians. There was, however, within the Christian community one other group, whose members also saw themselves as participants in the Jewish way of life but whose configuration of it was quite different. This group, almost certainly fairly small, was made up of Prisca, Aquila, and other Christians whose views were essentially the same as Paul's. What these views were will become clearer in our next chapter. For the moment, let it suffice to say that, like Paul, they were convinced that Jewish and Gentile believers were now no longer obligated to observe even the ethical commandments of the Mosaic law as such. In addition to Prisca, Aquila, and the church at their house, this group probably included at least some of those Paul greeted in 16:3–16.[96] The most important, however, were Prisca and Aquila. They were prominent Christians who had been expelled from Rome in 49, and they were already at Corinth when Paul arrived there in 51 (Acts 18:2). There they came under Paul's influence and accepted his views about no longer being obligated to observe the Mosaic law. When they returned to Rome, they served as Paul's defenders. As we shall see in the next chapter, Prisca, Aquila, and these Roman Christians also served as the means by which Paul and the majority of Roman Christians came to know about each other's viewpoints.

CONCLUSIONS

What emerges from all these considerations is hardly a detailed portrait of either the Roman Jewish or Christian communities. At the same time, the evidence does allow us to sketch out important aspects of Roman Christian belief and practice in the middle of the first century. This is especially true of what must have been the complex relationship between the Christian community and Jewish beliefs and practices. A sense of this relationship will prove crucial for understanding the equally complex approach Paul takes to the Christian community in Romans.

It is clear from the evidence that the origins of the Roman Christian community lay within the much larger Roman Jewish community. In the late 30s or early 40s of the first century, Jewish believers in Jesus from Jerusalem or Palestine came to Rome. There they won over to belief in Jesus as the Christ some Roman Jews as well as some sympathetic Gentiles associated with the Jewish community. All of this took place within the Roman Jewish community. By the end of the 40s, however, serious conflict developed within the community over belief in Jesus. This led to the expulsion of both Jewish and Gentile believers in Jesus from the Jewish community. The number of these believers must have been large enough that the disturbances caused by their expulsion came to the attention of the Roman authorities. As a re-

---

[96] In addition to Prisca and Aquila, this included at least Epaenetus (the firstfruits of Paul's efforts in Asia), Andronicus and Junia (fellow Jews and prisoners with Paul), and Urbanus (a fellow worker of Paul's). It also may have included others on the list.

sult, the emperor Claudius in 49 expelled from Rome at least some of those involved in these disturbances.

By the time Paul wrote to the Roman Christians in 57, the Christian community had been separate from the Jewish community for seven or eight years. The Christians' organizational structure was similar to the decentralized structure of the Jewish community from which they had been expelled. They were organized as the separate house churches reflected in Paul's greetings in 16:3–16. Like the Jewish community, they would have been seen by the Roman authorities as voluntary associations, although not nearly as large and without the facilities available to the Jewish community.

From its beginning as a separate community in 49, the Roman Christian community was probably made up mostly of members who were ethnically Gentile. Even though by the time of Paul's letter many or most of those expelled from Rome had returned after Claudius's death in 54, this did not seem to have significantly altered the ratio of Gentile Christians to Jewish Christians. Even before 49, when they were still part of the Jewish community, belief in Jesus may already have been attractive especially to Gentiles associated with the Jewish community. In any case, the disagreements, reflected in 14:1–15:6, within the Christian community over observance of the Sabbath and dietary regulations did not break down along the lines of Jewish Christians versus Gentile Christians.

The continuity between the beliefs and practices of Roman Christians at the time of Romans and the Jewish way of life is striking. There are clear similarities between their beliefs and practices and what Gentiles found attractive in Jewish belief and practices as they were reflected in Roman writers such as Tacitus and Juvenal, on the one hand, and in a Jewish writer such as Josephus in *Ag. Ap.* 2:145–286, on the other. Obviously what distinguished Roman Christians from Roman Jews was the former's belief in Jesus as the Christ. But in other significant ways, Roman Christian belief and practice remained of a piece with Roman Jewish belief and practice. At first, this might seem counterintuitive, especially since the Christians had been expelled from the Jewish community and forced to form their own communities. Nevertheless, the evidence indicates that the Christians did not see themselves as members of a new religion. Even though now institutionally separate from the Jewish community and made up primarily of Gentile believers, they continued to see themselves as still connected with, and as part of, the Jewish way of life and its central beliefs and practices.

In this they did not differ from other Christians of the mid–first century, including Paul and the communities he founded. It is important, however, to get as clear a sense as possible of how they understood that continuity of belief and practice, because their understanding of it differed significantly from that of Paul and the small group of Roman believers such as Prisca and Aquila who agreed with Paul. This will also affect how we understand Paul's rhetorical strategy in Romans. The continuity was rooted first of all in Jewish monotheism, belief in one God and the rejection of all others. In addition, it included an emphasis on the superiority of the Mosaic law, specifically its ethical aspects, over what they saw as the degrading ethical practices of the Greco-Roman world. This was especially the case in areas of sexual morality. For a minority of the community, it also included continued observance of the Sabbath and perhaps other festivals as well as observance of some of the dietary laws; these aspects were a matter of controversy among the Roman Christians. There was, however, no demand that male Gentile believers undergo circumcision, and so no controversy over this.

Taken together, these beliefs and practices reflect a commitment to aspects of the Jewish way of life that both Roman writers and the Jewish writer Josephus emphasized as attractive to Gentiles who sympathized and associated with the Jewish community, but without the requirement of circumcision or, for most of the community, observance of the Sabbath and the festivals or the dietary and purity regulations. Without the latter, both Jewish and Gentile believers came to stand on the same footing. The result was that Gentile believers were no longer only sympathizers associated with the Jewish way of life but were now full participants.

The belief in Jesus as the Christ by both ethnically Jewish and Gentile believers was deeply embedded in what both regarded as the superiority of the Jewish way of life in its monotheism and in its ethical precepts. Conversely, they would have found it difficult, even impossible, to understand how anyone could be a believer in Jesus without also accepting the continued observance of the ethical commandments of the Mosaic law. Any challenge to the sanctity of this law or to observance of its ethical precepts would have appeared to them as perverse. As we shall see, they saw in Paul just such a challenge.

CHAPTER 2

Situating Romans:
Paul and the Roman Christians

*T*HIS CHAPTER TURNS TO PAUL'S SITUATION and his relationship to the Roman Christian community at the time he wrote to it. It first examines the immediate circumstances of his letter as he describes them in Rom 1:1–7, 8–15; 15:14–16:2. Next it examines a series of events in Paul's life that are crucial for understanding both his basic convictions and his situation at the time he wrote Romans. The events are his call and the crucial controversies in which he was involved leading up to Romans. These controversies concerned the status of Jewish and Gentile believers and the place of the Mosaic law. Finally it examines Paul's relationship to the Roman Christian community, especially how what they knew about him became a source of serious tension between themselves and Paul.

THE IMMEDIATE CIRCUMSTANCES OF ROMANS

Paul wrote his letter to the Roman Christians from the city of Corinth. In Rom 16:1–2 Paul writes a recommendation to them for Phoebe, a deaconess of the church in Cenchreae. Cenchreae was the eastern port for the city of Corinth. Phoebe was a prominent and fairly wealthy Christian; in 16:2 Paul refers to her as a "patroness" (προστάτις) of many in the community and of Paul himself. She was probably the one who brought Paul's letter to Rome. In addition, Paul mentions in 16:23 that a certain Gaius, who was Paul's host and host of the whole church, sent greetings to the Roman Christians. This Gaius is almost certainly the same Gaius whom Paul mentioned in 1 Cor 1:14 as one of the few Corinthian Christians whom he himself baptized. Another Christian whom Paul mentions in Rom 16:23 as sending greetings to Rome is Erastus, whom Paul describes as the "treasurer of the city" (ὁ οἰκονόμος τῆς πόλεως). He is probably to be identified with the Erastus of the first-century A.D. inscription from near the theater of ancient Corinth. The inscription reads, "Erastus, in return for his aedileship, laid (the pavement) at his own expense."[1] Like Gaius, he was a prominent Corinthian Christian.[2] Situating Paul's composition of Romans in Corinth is also consistent with Acts 20:1–6.[3] After leaving Ephesus, Paul traveled through Macedonia to Greece and stayed there three months; the most likely place for him to spend this time was Corinth. At the end of the three months, planning to return to Syria, he again went by way of Macedonia and was accompanied by a number of other Christians, among whom were Timothy and Sopater of Beroea.[4] Both are also mentioned in Rom 16:21 as sending greetings to the Roman Christian community. This would make perfect sense if Paul was writing Romans while he was in Corinth during this three-month period. This evidence, taken together, makes it virtually certain that Paul wrote Romans from Corinth.

There is more dispute, however, about the dating of the letter, which ranges over a four-year period, from early 55 to early 58, and depends on how one reconstructs the chronology of Paul's journeys preceding this stay in Corinth. For our purposes it makes little difference when Paul wrote Romans within that four-year period. My own preference, however, is for the winter of 56–57. This makes best sense of the chronology of Paul's journeys from the end of a previous stay in Corinth in the summer of 52, through his roughly three-year stay in Ephesus between the middle of 53 and the middle of 56 and his journey through Macedonia in the latter part of 56, to his arrival again in Corinth toward the end of 56.[5] On the basis of this chronology, Paul would have written his letter to the Roman Christians during his final three-month stay in Corinth during the winter of 56–57.

Toward the beginning of Romans (1:8–15) and again toward the end (15:14–33) Paul describes his current situation and his future plans. In 1:8–15 he writes of his long-standing desire to come to Rome, a desire that until now he has been prevented from fulfilling. In 15:14–33, immediately before the final greetings, Paul returns to write more specifically about his travel plans and about why, in spite of his desires, he has not come to Rome before this. He explains that he now plans to come to Rome on his way to Spain to preach the gospel there. He can now do this because he has completed preaching the gospel from Jerusalem as far around as Illyricum (15:19, 23), that is, throughout Asia Minor and Greece. Preaching the gospel to the Gentiles in these areas is what has prevented him from making his

---

[1] *Erastus pro aedilit[at]e s(ua) p(ecunia) stravit.* See John Harvey Kent, *The Inscriptions 1926–1950* (Corinth 8.3; Princeton, N.J.: American School of Classical Studies at Athens, 1966), 17–31, 99–100, pl. 21, no. 232. There is some dispute whether the Greek term Paul used (οἰκο-νόμος) translates the Latin *aedilis* or *quaestor.* As Fitzmyer (*Romans,* 750) points out, however, the term οἰκονόμος at least describes with reasonable accuracy the function of a Corinthian aedile.

[2] He is probably also the same Erastus mentioned in Acts 19:22 and 2 Tim 4:20.

[3] The extent to which one can use Acts for the biography or chronology of Paul's life is much disputed. It makes no sense, however, not to use Acts when it confirms evidence from Paul's letters. This is very different from using it to establish the framework for a chronology of Paul's life and then fitting the evidence of Paul's letters into that framework.

[4] The name is given as Sosipater in Rom 16:21 and as Sopater in Acts 20:4. It undoubtedly refers to the same person.

[5] Paul probably made a quick and unsuccessful journey to Corinth in the summer of 55 (2 Cor 13:14; 13:12; 2:1; 12:21). For a fuller discussion of the chronological issues, see Fitzmyer, *Romans,* 86–87; Robert Jewett, *A Chronology of Paul's Life* (Philadelphia: Fortress, 1979); Jerome Murphy-O'Connor, *Paul: A Critical Life* (Oxford: Clarendon, 1996), 1–31.

long desired trip to Rome (15:22). Before doing so, however, he first has to bring the collection he has taking up among the Christians of Macedonia and Achaia to the poor of the Jerusalem community (15:25–27, 30–32). Once he has successfully accomplished this, he will come to Rome to be refreshed by their company on his journey to Spain (15:24, 28, 32). He hopes, with their support, to move on to preach in Spain after only a short stay with them in Rome.

On the surface, all this seems quite straightforward. Yet just below the surface, these passages point to a situation that is more complicated, delicate, and tense. As one reads these passages closely, it becomes apparent how diplomatically Paul positions himself in relation to the Roman Christian community. In the address of the letter (1:1–7), Paul begins with a description of his call as an apostle. He already described himself as an apostle at the beginning of several other letters (Gal 1:1; 1 Cor 1:1; 2 Cor 1:1). But at the beginning of Romans, he does this much more elaborately, especially in describing his role as an apostle to the Gentiles. He has been "set apart for the gospel of God" (Rom 1:1). Through Jesus Christ he has "received grace and apostleship to bring about the obedience of faith for the sake of his name among all the Gentiles" (1:5). He explicitly includes the Roman Christians among these Gentiles (1:6). Since he did not found the Roman Christian community nor did he ever visit it, he needed to set out the basis on which he now writes to its members. Although he insists with them on his position as an apostle to the Gentiles, he is equally careful in the thanksgiving section of the letter (1:8–15) to be extremely respectful of the position of the community. He thanks God because the Roman Christians' "faith is proclaimed in all the world" (1:8). He offers an elaborate excuse about why he has been prevented from visiting them up until then, although he had long desired to do so (1:10–15). It is as if his very failure to visit them needed some sort of explanation. Perhaps the most revealing part of this thanksgiving, however, is in 1:11–12: "For I desire to see you, that I may impart to you some spiritual gift so that you may be strengthened, that is, that we may be mutually encouraged by each other's faith, both yours and mine." He begins by explaining that he desires to visit them so that he might impart something to them (1:11). But he immediately goes out of his way to clarify this by emphasizing the mutuality of the benefits of his visit to the Roman Christians (1:12). He will gain as much as they will. It is virtually impossible to convey in English how elaborate and even awkward the Greek of 1:12 is in emphasizing this mutuality.[6]

The same combination comes up again toward the end of the letter in 15:14–32. After the elaborate arguments of 1:16–15:13, Paul begins this section by expressing great confidence in the Roman Christians. They themselves are "full of goodness, filled with all knowledge and quite capable of correcting one another" (15:14). Only then does he go on in 15:15–21 to emphasize once again his own role as a minister (λειτουργόν) of Christ Jesus in relationship to the Gentiles and one who serves the gospel of God as a priest (ἱερουργοῦντα) so that the offering of the Gentiles may be acceptable to God. Even in doing this he admits in 15:15 that he

---

[6] The Greek reads, τοῦτο δέ ἐστιν συμπαρακληθῆναι ἐν ὑμῖν διὰ τῆς ἐν ἀλλήλοις πίστεως ὑμῶν τε καὶ ἐμοῦ. Paul tries to intertwine what both he and they will do for one another.

has written to them quite boldly in some respects (τολμηρότερον . . . ἀπὸ μέρους), but he has done this by way of reminder (ὡς ἐπαναμιμνῄσκων). He is not telling them something that they do not already know and understand. In addition, when he describes his travel plans to Rome in more detail in 15:22–32, he emphasizes what he will receive from them rather than the other way around. When he comes to Rome, he hopes to be sped on his way to Spain by them after he has enjoyed their company for a while (15:24). After his trip to Jerusalem with the collection, he hopes to come to them with joy and be refreshed together with them (15:32).

This rather elaborate rhetoric both at the beginning of the letter and immediately after the conclusion of his main arguments indicates how complex Paul realized his relationship was to this community. On the one hand, he insists on his role as an apostle to the Gentiles, among whom he includes the Roman Christians. On the other hand, he acknowledges that he does not have the same kind of authority over them that he has over communities he himself founded. His relationship with the Roman Christian community was much more a matter of equality, much more a matter of mutuality. He will receive as much from them as they will from him. If he expected them to be convinced of his various arguments, he had to acknowledge that reality openly and gracefully. It is striking how actively he sought to cultivate their benevolence. He had to win their benevolence and not simply assume it.

The complicated character of Paul's relationship to this community also emerges when we look more closely at 15:23–32, where Paul writes more specifically about his travel plans, first to Jerusalem and then to Rome. The question to keep in mind is why Paul includes at length, in the description of his travel plans to the Roman Christians, his trip to Jerusalem to bring the collection to the poor of the Jerusalem Christian community. Paul moves back and forth between writing about his trip to Rome and then to Spain (15:23–24, 28–29) and his trip to Jerusalem with the collection (15:25–27, 30–32). It is as if, for Paul, the two trips are connected to one another. What this connection was emerges when one looks more closely at how Paul wrote about his plans for his trip to Jerusalem with the collection.

First, however, something briefly needs to be said about the collection itself.[7] According to Paul, the collection for the "poor" (πτωχοί) of the Jewish Christian community of Jerusalem was part of the agreement reached at the meeting in Jerusalem between Paul and other representatives of the Christian community of Antioch, on the one hand, and the leaders of the Jerusalem Christian community such as Peter, James, and John, on the other (Gal 2:1–10).[8] One result of this meeting was Paul's promise to "remember the poor [of the Jerusalem Christian community], which very thing I was eager to do" (Gal 2:10). Subsequently Paul did just that. In 1 Cor 16:1–4 he instructed the Corinthian community about how it should take up

---

[7] For issues connected with the collection, see Keith F. Nickle, *The Collection: A Study in Paul's Strategy* (SBT 48; Naperville, Ill.: Allenson, 1966); Dieter Georgi, *Remembering the Poor: The History of Paul's Collection for Jerusalem* (Nashville: Abingdon, 1992); Hans Dieter Betz, *2 Corinthians 8 and 9: A Commentary on Two Administrative Letters of the Apostle Paul* (Hermeneia; Philadelphia: Fortress, 1985).

[8] The date of this meeting depends on what chronology of Paul's life one accepts. A date in the late 40s seems most likely, probably 48. We shall return to this meeting in more detail later in this chapter.

the collection. Like the churches of Galatia, the Corinthian Christians should set aside what they could on the first day of each week so that the collection did not have to be made when Paul himself arrived. Second Corinthians 8–9 contains fragments of two fund-raising letters Paul sent, one to the Corinthian Christians (2 Cor 8:1–24) and the other to the Christians of Achaia (9:1–15). In both letters he mentioned to them the churches of Macedonia as examples of generosity (8:1–5; 9:1–2). Their contributions were meant to be voluntary and not some sort of exaction (8:8; 9:5, 7). Yet he also urged them to be generous. He had already boasted of their generosity and would be humiliated if they failed in this (8:24; 9:1–5). Paul saw these contributions as a way of expressing the fellowship and unity (κοινωνία) between the communities he founded and the Christian community in Jerusalem (8:4; 9:13). He also offered several other reasons they should be generous. One was the example of Christ, who, though he was rich, became poor for their sake (8:9). Another included the concept, well known in the Greco-Roman world, of equality (ἰσότης) (8:13–14; 9:11–12).[9] Paul expresses this reason explicitly in 8:13–14: "I do not mean that others should be eased and you burdened, but that as a matter of equality [ἐχ ἰσότητος] your abundance at the present time should supply their want, so that their abundance may supply your want, that there may be equality [ἰσότης]." Their abundance should serve to relieve the needs of others and so establish a certain equality between the two. There is little doubt that from the start the collection had a symbolic aspect in addition to the obvious material support it provided for the poor of the Jerusalem community. It symbolized the obligation that the communities Paul founded had to the original community of believers of Jerusalem. Since the communities Paul founded were predominantly Gentile in origin, it also in effect symbolized the obligation these Gentile Christian communities had to the Jewish Christian community of Jerusalem. This was not, however, a justification Paul explicitly used in either 1 or 2 Corinthians.

When Paul returns to the subject of the collection in Rom 15:25–27, 30–32, there are two notable changes to the way he explains the collection. First, in 15:30–32, he explicitly expresses for the first time his fear that the Jewish Christians in Jerusalem might not accept the collection (15:31). Because of this he enlists the aid of the Roman Christians on his side. He appeals to them to "struggle along with" (συναγωνίσασθαί) him in prayers to God on his behalf that he might be delivered from the disobedient of Judea and that his service for Jerusalem may be acceptable to the saints (15:31).[10] His use of the verb "to struggle along with" expresses the seriousness of his fear.

---

[9] For the meaning of "equality" in this context, see Betz, *2 Corinthians 8 and 9*, 67–68; and Margaret E. Thrall, *A Critical and Exegetical Commentary on the Second Epistle to the Corinthians* (2 vols.; ICC; Edinburgh: T&T Clark, 1994–2000), 2.539–40.

[10] "The disobedient [τῶν ἀπειθούντων] in Judaea" and "the saints" (τοῖς ἁγίοις) were two different groups. The latter were the members of the Jewish Christian community of Jerusalem; the former were other Jews in Jerusalem. Fitzmyer (*Romans*, 726), however, may be right when he suggests that the "disobedient in Judaea" refers more specifically to Jewish acquaintances of Paul's who had not become believers in Jesus and who resented his becoming a Christian missionary.

Second, although in 15:25–27 Paul still preserves an "equality" of sorts, his justification for the collection becomes explicitly the repayment of a debt.

> At present, however, I am going to Jerusalem to bring aid to the saints. For Macedonia and Achaia have been pleased to make some common contribution [κοινωνίαν τινὰ ποιήσασθαι] for the poor among the saints at Jerusalem. They were pleased to do it, and indeed they are in their debt [ὀφειλέται], for if the Gentiles have come to share [ἐκοινώνησαν] in their spiritual benefits [τοῖς πνευματικοῖς], they are obligated [ὀφείλουσιν] to be of service to them in material benefits [τοῖς σαρκικοῖς].

More specifically, it is the repayment of a debt that the Gentile Christians of Macedonia and Achaia owe to the Jewish Christians of Jerusalem. Unlike the earlier justification for the collection, 15:25–27 is the first place where he puts the collection explicitly in the context of the relationship between Gentile and Jewish Christians and, more specifically, as a debt owed by the former to the latter. Although the collection had in fact always been a contribution made by Gentile Christians to Jewish Christians, Paul now emphasizes for the first time that the collection is a concrete expression of the recognition, on his part and on the part of the Gentile Christian communities he founded, of their debt to the Jewish Christians of Jerusalem. In addition, the fellowship or unity (κοινωνίαν [15:26]; ἐκοινώνησαν [15:27]) Paul and his communities seek to maintain is that between Gentile Christians and Jewish Christians.

Why did Paul make these changes? More specifically, what is the relation between Paul's fear that the collection would not be accepted in Jerusalem (15:30–32) and the new justification he gives for the collection (15:25–27)? There must be some relationship between the two. The most plausible explanation is that Paul meant his new interpretation of the collection—as the recognition of a debt owed by his Gentile Christian communities to the Jewish Christians of Jerusalem—to show why the latter should accept the collection. But why would they be so at odds with Paul that he feared they might not even accept what must have been a sizable financial contribution to the relief of their poorer members? The only plausible explanation is that the Jewish Christians of Jerusalem would have found the beliefs and practices of Paul and of the communities he founded so unacceptable that they would even refuse to accept financial help from them. In effect, they would refuse to maintain fellowship and unity with them. Given Paul's justification for the collection, these objections must have had something to do with how they understood Paul conceived of the relationship between Jewish believers and Gentile believers. What those objectionable beliefs and practices specifically were will emerge in the next section of this chapter.

There is, however, a more immediate question. Why does Paul rehearse in such detail for the *Roman* Christians both his fear for, and his new justification of, the collection? The most plausible explanation is that the Roman Christians had similar suspicions and objections about what they thought Paul's views were on the relationship of Jewish and Gentile Christians. How, then, is Paul able, at the end of the letter, to enlist their prayers that the Jewish Christians of Jerusalem would accept the collection? The answer can only be that he hoped that what he had written in the body of Romans (1:16–15:13) would have alleviated any fears or suspicions the Roman Christians had about him. With these fears and suspicions put to rest, they could now support by their prayers his trip to Jerusalem with the collection.[11] In addition, he could now come to Rome with joy, be refreshed by the company of the Roman Christians, and be sped on his way to Spain (15:23–24, 32).

All these passages (1:1–7, 8–15; 15:14–16:2) indicate how delicate and even tense the relationship between Paul and the Roman Christian community was at the time he wrote Romans. He could not count on their benevolence. He needed to allay their suspicions about him. But what were their suspicions? Why would they have found his views about the relationship between Jewish and Gentile Christians objectionable? For this we need to turn more broadly to an account of Paul's basic convictions and the controversies in which he was involved because of them before he wrote his letter to the Roman Christians.

PAUL'S CONVICTIONS AND THE CONTROVERSIES LEADING UP TO ROMANS

The controversies in which Paul was involved before writing Romans were deeply rooted in his own history and experience. Paul was a Hellenistic Jew, born in Tarsus in Cilicia, a prominent trading center in the southeastern corner of Asia Minor (Acts 9:11; 21:39; 22:3). The date of his birth is uncertain, but it probably was around A.D. 1–5. In Phil 3:5 Paul tell us that he was a Jew of the tribe of Benjamin and was circumcised on the eighth day. He also tells us that, although a Hellenistic Jew, he was a Pharisee by conviction.[12]

As Paul saw it, the two most prominent realities of his life before coming to believe in Jesus as the Christ were his observance of the law as a Pharisee and his persecution of those who did believe in Christ (Phil 3:5–6; Gal 1:13, 23; 1 Cor 15:9). He describes his observance of the Mosaic law as "blameless" (Phil 3:6). Even if we grant a certain amount of exaggeration on Paul's part, he certainly saw himself as a committed, observant Pharasaic Jew. Out of this commitment to Judaism, Paul came to persecute believers in Jesus. It is not altogether clear, however, what this persecution entailed.[13] The most likely explanation is that Paul urged subjecting

---

[11] Some have argued that one of Paul's purposes in writing Romans was to enlist the intervention of the Roman Christians on his behalf with the Jerusalem Christians, perhaps by sending a delegation or a letter to Jerusalem (see Fitzmyer, 75, 79). This is possible, but it is unclear whether Paul could have expected such a delegation or letter to have arrived in Jerusalem before or at the same time he did.

[12] On the Pharisees, see Schürer, *History*, 2:388–403; and Anthony J. Saldarini, *Pharisees, Scribes, and Sadducees in Palestinian Society: A Sociological Approach* (Wilmington, Del.: Michael Glazier, 1988).

[13] The accounts of his persecution of believers in Christ in Acts (8:3; 9:1; 26:9–12) have to be viewed skeptically. In Acts Paul is described first as persecuting Christians in Jerusalem. He arrests them and throws them into prison, and then, when they are faced with a sentence of death, he votes against them (26:10). In addition, he tries to persecute them even in Damascus (26:11). Armed with letters from the high priest to the synagogues in Damascus, he sets out for Damascus in order to bring any believers in Christ back to Jerusalem for punishment (9:1). There are, however, significant problems with this account. First, it seems that neither the Jewish high priest nor the Jewish Sanhedrin in Jerusalem had the authority to impose the death

Christians to the normal punishments of the synagogue, which included flogging and exclusion from the Jewish community. Such exclusion had significant social and economic consequences. It did not, however, involve either capital punishment or imprisonment.

One can only speculate on Paul's specific reasons for persecuting believers in Jesus. Some have suggested that the real motivation may have been early Christians' attitude toward observance of the Mosaic law, an observance about which Paul, as a Pharasaic Jew, had deep convictions. Paul and other Jews like him may have found the attitude of some early Christians toward the law intolerably lax. He may have felt that this attitude endangered the very foundations of the Jewish way of life. In this view, it was not early Christians' belief in Jesus as the Messiah but their attitude toward the Mosaic law that enraged Paul. Yet one suspects that a combination of both led Paul to persecute them. Early Christians undoubtedly appealed to Jesus and his words in order to justify their attitude toward observance or nonobservance of parts of the Mosaic law. Because their attitude toward the law was rooted in their belief in Jesus, Paul would have found both elements of Christian belief deeply troubling.

Paul's Call

On a journey to Damascus around A.D. 35, however, Paul experienced something that changed his life forever. It was a vision of the risen Jesus, whom God the Father had revealed to him: "But when he who had set me apart before I was born, and had called me through his grace, was pleased to reveal his Son to me, in order that I might preach him among the Gentiles, I did not confer with flesh and blood, nor did I go up to Jerusalem to those who were apostles before me, but I went away into Arabia; and again I returned to Damascus (Gal 1:15–17)." As Paul understood or came to understand this experience, it was not only a revelation of the risen Jesus; it was also a call to preach this risen Jesus to the Gentiles. Elsewhere Paul interpreted this experience as the last of the risen Jesus' appearances to his disciples and as the basis for his claim to be ranked as an apostle with the other apostles (1 Cor 9:1; 15:8–9). The language Paul used to describe this experience in Gal 1:15–17 was drawn from the calls of Israelite prophets, particularly Isaiah and Jeremiah. The language of God calling the prophet from his mother's womb and of God's speaking through him to the Gentiles is found in Isa 49:1, 5–6 and Jer 1:5.[14] Paul clearly understood this transforming experience as a prophetic call within the framework of

---

sentence on its own. Such a sentence could be imposed only with the approval of the Roman authorities. Second, it is very unlikely that either the high priest or the Sanhedrin had any authority beyond the borders of Palestine, i.e., in Damascus. See Helmut Koester, *History and Literature of Early Christianity* (vol. 2 of *Introduction to the New Testament;* New York: de Gruyter, 1982), 99–100.

[14] Isa 19:1, 5–6: "The Lord called me from the womb, from the body of my mother he named my name.... And now the Lord says, who formed me from the womb to be his servant, to bring Jacob back to him, and that Israel might be gathered to him, for I am honored in the eyes of the Lord, and my God has become my strength—he says: 'it is too light a thing that you should be my servant to raise up the tribes of Jacob and to restore the preserved of Israel; I will give you as a light to the nations [Gentiles], that my salvation may reach to the end of the

Judaism. He was not converting to another religion, Christianity. He clearly did not think of it as a desertion of Judaism or of Judaism's God. On the contrary, it was Judaism's God whom he experienced as calling him to preach the risen Jesus to the Gentiles. Paul's interpretation of his experience may seem eccentric in the light of the later parting of the ways between Judaism and Christianity. To understand how Paul interpreted this experience, however, it is crucial to realize that for him this experience was that of a Jew within the framework of Judaism's prophetic tradition.[15] This is especially important in light of another conclusion Paul drew from his vision of the risen Jesus and his call to preach to the Gentiles.

This additional conclusion was that the obligation to observe the Mosaic law as such had come to an end for both Jewish and Gentile believers. Paul came to see both his preaching to the Gentiles and the end of the obligation to observe the Mosaic law as central elements of his experience of the risen Jesus. What Paul meant by believers no longer being obliged to observe the Mosaic law and what was the reason for this obligation coming to an end are matters of much debate.[16] I cannot even pretend to set out the various positions on the issue.[17] The following position, however, is the most plausible and does most justice to the complexity of Paul's thought.

Paul's convictions about the status of the Mosaic law are best understood as rooted in his experience on the road to Damascus. He claimed to have experienced there a revelation from God of the risen Jesus and a call to preach the gospel of this risen Jesus to the Gentiles (Gal 1:15–17). The question, however, is why this experience also led him to the conviction that observance of the Mosaic law was no longer necessary for believers. The closest Paul comes to describing the experiential logic that led him to this conviction is in Phil 3:2–11. This passage bears a number of similarities to Gal 1:13–17. Both passages are explicitly autobiographical, and both occur in contexts that are concerned with the status of Gentile believers. In both passages Paul also strongly contrasts his life prior to his experience of the risen Jesus

---

earth.'" Jer 1:5: "Before I formed you in the womb I knew you, and before you were born I consecrated you; I appointed you a prophet to the nations [Gentiles]."

[15] The interpretation of Paul's experience as a call rather than a conversion is best set out by Stendahl, *Paul among Jews and Gentiles*, 7–23. Alan Segal (*Paul the Convert: The Apostolate and Apostasy of Saul the Pharisee* [New Haven: Yale University Press, 1990], 72–114), however, has argued that Paul's experience should be interpreted as a conversion rather than a call. I have argued elsewhere that Paul understood this experience as a call. The longer-term results (the eventual separation of Christianity from Judaism), however, make Paul's experience seem in retrospect like a conversion. See Thomas H. Tobin, *The Spirituality of Paul* (MBS 12; Wilmington, Del.: Michael Glazier, 1987), 43–59.

[16] For an excellent collection of essays on this much-debated issue, see James D. G. Dunn, ed., *Paul and the Mosaic Law: The Third Durham-Tübingen Symposium on Earliest Christianity and Judaism* (Grand Rapids: Eerdmans, 2001).

[17] For a very different position on these issues, see most recently Gager, *Reinventing Paul*. I agree with many of Gager's critiques of earlier views of Paul that read him against Judaism (pp. 21–42). I agree that Paul never saw himself as something other than a Jew, but I cannot agree with Gager's interpretations of either Galatians (77–99) or Romans (101–43). His arguments that Paul's views about no longer observing the Mosaic law apply only to Gentile believers are not at all convincing. In addition, Gager falls into the very traditional trap of trying to interpret Galatians and Romans as if they were of a piece. As will become clear in this study, they were not.

to his present life. Finally, in both passages, Paul emphasizes that his life prior to this experience was marked by observance of the law and by persecution of the church. His description, in Phil 3:7–11, of his life since his experience of the risen Lord differs significantly, however, from what he wrote in Gal 1:15–17. In Galatians Paul narrated the external events that immediately followed his experience.[18] In Phil 3:7–11, however, he describes the interior change he experienced and its consequences.

> But whatever gain I had, I counted as loss for the sake of Christ. Indeed I count every-thing as loss because of the surpassing worth of knowing Christ Jesus my Lord, for whose sake I have suffered the loss of all things, and count them as refuse, in order that I may gain Christ and be found in him, not having a righteousness of my own, based on the law, but that which is through faith in Christ, the righteousness from God based on faith; that I may know him and the power of his resurrection, and may share his suffer-ings, becoming conformed to his death, that if possible I may attain the resurrection from the dead.

The "gain" he refers to in Phil 3:7 is his own identity as a Jew, as a Pharisee, as an ob-server of the law and a persecutor of the church (3:5–6). All this he now considers as loss and as refuse because of the surpassing worth of knowing Christ. Paul is obvi-ously referring here to his experience on the road to Damascus and the profound change that it wrought in his life. To interpret this passage correctly, one must under-stand that Paul's evaluation of his own past life here is comparative and not absolute. Although he certainly regretted his persecution of the church, Paul was never ashamed of his previous observance of the law, which was not somehow wrong or misguided. Rather, compared with the righteousness based on faith in Christ, his past life of observance paled into insignificance. Compared to the experience on the Da-mascus road, all else was loss. Put another way, this experience crucially changed what Paul understood being a Jew meant. It did not make him something other than a Jew.

Paul's description of this experience and its consequences in this passage offers us an important insight into why he came to be so convinced that believers were no longer obliged to observe the Mosaic law. To require the continued observance of the law along with a life based on experience of the righteousness from God through faith would imply that both were on the same level, in the sense that both were still necessary. For Paul, this was impossible. It flew in the face of the experi-ence that had changed his life. This experiential logic, based as it was on the incom-parability of his vision of the risen Jesus, led him to reject the continued observance of the Mosaic law as something necessary for those who had faith in Christ.

This radical conviction also played into his view of his own calling to preach to the Gentiles, for it placed both Jews and Gentiles on the same footing. The obli-gation to observe the Mosaic law had ended for both Jewish and Gentile believers alike. Righteousness for both Jews and Gentiles was now rooted in faith in what God had accomplished in Christ and not in the continued observance of the Mosaic law. Paul's convictions about the present status of observance of the law for believers

---

[18] He did not go up to Jerusalem but traveled to Arabia (probably Nabatean territory) and then returned to Damascus (Gal 1:17).

was, at least as he saw it, rooted in the logic of his own experience and in its consequences for preaching the gospel to the Gentiles.

Paul's conviction that neither Jewish nor Gentile believers had to observe the
Mosaic law was quite radical in another way. It included not only the law's specifically Jewish dietary and purity regulations but also its broader ethical commandments. That Paul had much more in mind than simply the abolition of the law's
dietary and purity regulations becomes clear when one looks at the controversies in
which Paul was subsequently involved. The controversies reflected in Galatians and
Romans were not about observance of dietary and purity regulations. Rather, they
were about issues of ethics. It is difficult even to imagine how Paul would have become so intensely controversial had the issue been only the status of Jewish dietary
and purity regulations. This will become clearer when we look more closely at Paul's
controversy with the Galatian Christians later in this chapter.

There is, however, another, broader reason to maintain that Paul had more in
mind than simply the abolition of the law's specifically Jewish dietary and purity
regulations. This is important because it helps us to locate Paul within the larger
context of Hellenistic Jewish thought. Had Paul meant that only the dietary and purity regulations no longer needed to be observed, he could have used and reinterpreted a widely known and long-standing distinction made in Hellenistic Judaism
between the ethical commandments of the law, on the one hand, and all other regulations, on the other, especially the dietary and purity regulations of the law. The
purpose of this distinction for Hellenistic Jewish writers was to emphasize the superior ethical standards of the Mosaic law in comparison with the laws of other
peoples. While Jews were still to observe these other regulations of the law, their observance was not because of their inherent value. Rather, their observance was to
be maintained because they pointed to or symbolized some significant ethical
value. This pattern of legal interpretation first appeared in the middle of the second
century B.C. in the *Letter of Aristeas* (143–152, 162–166). In Jewish writers roughly
contemporary with Paul, the same distinction lay behind the overwhelming emphasis on the ethical aspects of the law in Philo of Alexandria,[19] Josephus,[20] and
Pseudo-Phocylides.[21]

Given how widespread this pattern of interpretation was in Hellenistic Judaism, it is difficult to imagine Paul being unaware of it. Indeed, there is good reason
to think that he was aware of it. In *Let. Arist.* 144, 162–166, in the Jewish high
priest Eleazar's speech, Eleazar argues that observance of the dietary and purity regulations of the Mosaic law is not for its own sake but for the sake of the ethical values that such observance symbolizes or to which it points. For example, the Mosaic
law forbids Jews to eat mice and weasels (Lev 11:29). Eleazar urges that Moses
surely did not enact this regulation out of any concern for mice or weasels (μυῶν
καὶ γαλῆς . . . περιεργίαν) but because he wanted to promote the perfecting of
character for the sake of righteousness (*Let. Arist.* 144). Later in the speech Eleazar

---

[19] See Philo's treatises *De decalogo* and *Spec.* 1–4.
[20] Josephus, *Ant.* 1.25; 3.259–260; *Ag. Ap.* 2.164–219.
[21] Ps.-Phoc. 3, 6, 8, 14, 15, 18, 22–30, 84–85, 99, 100–101, 109, 177–183, 184, 185, 186,
190–192, 198, 213–214, 220–222, 225–226.

explains that Moses forbade Jews to eat mice and weasels because they should avoid the vices that these creatures symbolize by their actions (162–166). In *Somn.* 1.93–94 Philo of Alexandria uses the same kind of argument. Paul does likewise in 1 Cor 9:8–11, where he claims that he has a right to be supported by the communities to which he preached:

> Do I say this on human authority? Does not even [καί] the law say the same? For it is written in the law of Moses, "You shall not muzzle an ox when it is treading out the grain [Deut 26:4]." Is it for oxen that God is concerned [μὴ τῶν βοῶν μέλει θεῷ]? Does he not speak entirely for our sake? It was written for our sake, because the plowman should plow in hope and the thresher thresh in hope of a share in the crop. If we have sown spiritual good among you, is it too much if we reap your material benefits?

Paul's argument in this passage shows he was aware of the Hellenistic Jewish framework of interpretation in which the nonethical regulations of the law have value only through their relationship to the ethical commandments of the law.

Still, apart from this isolated passage, Paul never appeals to this kind of argument. Although he was aware of it, it did not became part of the interpretative framework he used to clarify his understanding of the status of the Mosaic law. Had Paul intended to claim only that the dietary and purity regulations of the law no longer needed to be observed, all he had to do was appeal to this Hellenistic Jewish framework and reinterpret it. He could have distinguished, as Jewish writers did, the ethical commandments of the law from its dietary and purity regulations. He could then have claimed that because the gospel was now to be preached to the Gentiles, the peculiarly Jewish dietary and purity regulations no longer needed to be observed although the ethical commandments would still be in force. But Paul never did this. Although he was aware of the distinction between different parts of the Mosaic law, it was not part of his world of thought or operative in his basic arguments. For him, it was the whole law as such that no longer needed to be observed by believers, whether they were Jewish or Gentile.

Controversies and Consequences

Paul's convictions on these issues clearly made him a controversial figure in early Christianity. Two series of events, however, are particularly important for situating Romans. The first is the meeting in A.D. 48 in Jerusalem between the leaders of the Jewish Christian community there and a delegation from the Christian community of Antioch, with the subsequent confrontation at Antioch between Peter and Paul. The second is the controversy about 53–54 between Paul and the communities he founded in Galatia.

The first series of events was itself the result of a developing controversy. After his call in about 35, Paul's missionary work for the next three years centered around the city of Damascus and the area to the south and east of it (Gal 1:17).[22] Paul himself says that he did not go up to Jerusalem to meet with the community's leaders there until three years later, in 38 (1:18). At that time, he met with Peter and James

---

[22] Murphy-O'Connor, *Paul: A Critical Life*, 81–90.

(1:19–20). Paul does not tell us what took place during the meeting or what issues were discussed. He does, however, want to leave his Galatian audience with the impression that the meeting was cordial and uncontroversial. Paul, then, began his missionary activities in areas that were largely Gentile. This means that his first experiences of being a believer and a missionary took place in an environment quite different from the Jewish Christian environment of the Jerusalem church. Working in this largely Gentile environment probably clarified and strengthened Paul's own understanding of what was central to belief in Jesus and what was not, that is, continued observance of the Mosaic law.

For about the next ten years (38–48), Paul worked in the regions of Syria, Cilicia, Pamphylia, and Pisidia (Gal 1:21; Acts 13–14). During this time the base of his activities was Antioch in Syria (Acts 11:25–26; 13:1–3; 14:26–28).[23] Outside Jerusalem itself, Antioch was the main center of early Christianity at this time. The makeup of the Christian community at Antioch, however, differed significantly from that at Jerusalem. The Antiochene community included a number of Gentile converts and was perhaps made up primarily of such converts. Although this community shared with the Jerusalem community the same beliefs in Jesus, it probably did not share the Jerusalem community's same commitment to circumcision and continued observance of the Mosaic law. Over the ten-year period Paul used Antioch as his base, the tension between the believers at Antioch and those at Jerusalem over the question of continued observance of the Mosaic law built up. This tension may have been brought to a head when Jewish Christians from Jerusalem came to Antioch and claimed that all Christians, whether Jewish or Gentile, had to be circumcised and observe the Mosaic law in order to be true Christians (Acts 15:1). Paul and other Antiochene Christians objected to this position.

To clear up this difficulty, Paul, as part of a delegation of Christians from Antioch, went up to Jerusalem in 48 to meet with the leaders of the Jerusalem church. This meeting is described both in Gal 2:1–10 and in Acts 15:1–35. Even granted the polemical tone of Paul's account of the meeting, Gal 2:1–10 is probably the more reliable of the two accounts.[24] In his account, Paul claimed that the two sides came to an agreement. The "pillars" of the church in Jerusalem, James, Peter, and John, agreed that the gospel Paul and others were preaching to the Gentiles, a gospel without circumcision and observance of the Mosaic law, was legitimate. Paul and the rest of the delegation from Antioch likewise agreed that the gospel preached by the Jewish Christians of Jerusalem to their fellow Jews, a gospel that included

---

[23] The chronology of this part of Paul's life is much disputed. For different accounts, see Murphy-O'Connor, *Paul: A Critical Life*; Joseph A. Fitzmyer, *Paul and His Theology: A Brief Sketch* (2d ed.; Englewood Cliffs, N.J.: Prentice Hall, 1987) 12–14; *The Acts of the Apostles: A New Translation with Introduction and Commentary* (AB 31; New York: Doubleday, 1997), Rainer Riesner, *Paul's Early Period: Chronology, Mission Strategy, Theology* (Grand Rapids: Eerdmans, 1998). What is important for our purposes is that Paul's missionary activities led up to the meeting in Jerusalem.

[24] The account of the Jerusalem meeting in Acts 15:1–35 and its relationship to Gal 2:1–10 is complex and much in dispute. More recently see Fitzmyer, *The Acts of the Apostles*, 538–69. Whatever one thinks about the sources the author of Acts used, the final version of the meeting is the author's own and comes from the end of the first century.

both circumcision and observance of the Mosaic law, was also legitimate. Paul
described this compromise in Gal 2:6–9:

> And from those who were reputed to be something (what they were makes no difference
> to me: God shows no partiality)—those, I say, who were of repute added nothing to me;
> but on the contrary, when they saw that I had been entrusted with the gospel to the
> uncircumcised, just as Peter had been entrusted with the gospel to the circumcised (for
> the one who worked through Peter for the mission to the circumcised worked through
> me also for the Gentiles), and when they perceived the grace that was given to me, James
> and Cephas and John, who were reputed to be pillars, gave to me and Barnabas the right
> hand of fellowship, that we should go to the Gentiles and they to the circumcision.

In return for their acceptance, Paul and the other members of the delegation agreed to
remember the poor of the Jerusalem church. As is clear from 1 Cor 16:1–4 and 2 Corinthians 8–9, this meant a collection from among the Gentile Christian churches for
the poor of the Jerusalem church.

The agreement was obviously a compromise. And Paul's account of the meeting was clearly meant to serve the intensely polemical purposes in his letter to the
Galatians. He wanted to leave his Galatian audience with the impression that the
Jewish Christian leaders in Jerusalem had agreed with his preaching of the gospel to
the Gentiles without circumcision or observance of the Mosaic law. According to
Paul, they were willing to compromise and allow that circumcision and continued
observance of the Mosaic law were incumbent on Jewish believers but not on Gentiles believers. The real situation, however, was almost certainly more complex than
Paul allowed for in Gal 2:1–10. Compromises are usually more about what is left
unsaid than what is said. Because of this, it is difficult to gain clarity about the complex contours either of the controversy itself or of the resulting compromise. What
does seem clear, however, on the basis of what happened in Antioch after the meeting (2:11–14) is that the Jewish Christian leaders in Jerusalem were not of one mind
in their understanding or support of the compromise. Peter's commitment to the
compromise seems to have been stronger than that of James and his supporters.
Again, on the basis of what happened in Antioch after the meeting, one suspects
that the members of the Antiochene delegation were also not of one mind. Paul's
position that circumcision and observance of the Mosaic law were no longer required of any believer, Jewish or Gentile, was probably not shared by all the members of the delegation. Some members may well have thought that Gentile believers
would obviously continue to observe the ethical commandments of the law even
though they were not circumcised and did not observe its dietary or purity
regulations.

Whatever anyone's intentions were, the compromise was almost inherently
unstable. At a practical level, the compromise could work only if Gentile believers
and Jewish believers were never together in the same community. If they were together, whose position on observance of the Mosaic law would prevail? For example,
if they ate together, would they observe the dietary regulations of the Mosaic law or
not? At a deeper level, the logic of each position was irreconcilable with the other's.
At least Paul's position was that observance of the Mosaic law was no longer necessary for either Gentile believers or Jewish believers. In the same way, if the Mosaic

law was still in force, then its observance should be required of both Jewish and Gentile believers.

Indeed, the compromise began to unravel almost immediately. Paul's version of this unraveling is found in Gal 2:11–14. After the end of the conference, Paul and the delegation from Antioch returned home. Soon after, in the fall of 48, Peter came to Antioch. When he first arrived, Peter took part in the common meals of the largely Gentile community at Antioch. He seems not to have been concerned with issues of dietary regulations. Soon, however, supporters of James also came to Antioch from Jerusalem. At this point, Peter withdrew from eating the common meals with Gentile believers. This was due to pressure from James's supporters on the Jewish believers at Antioch to observe the Jewish dietary regulations at these common meals. Other Jewish believers, including even Barnabas, Paul's close friend and associate, followed Peter's example. Paul challenged Peter over what he considered Peter's hypocrisy. In 2:14, he angrily demanded how, Peter, though a Jew, could live like a Gentile and not like a Jew (ἐθνικῶς καὶ οὐχὶ Ἰουδαϊκῶς ζῆς) and then turn around and act in such a way that compelled Gentiles to live in a Jewish fashion (Ἰουδαΐζειν).[25] Paul's immediate point was that since Peter was willing to forego observance of the dietary regulations when he first came to Antioch, his later withdrawal from table fellowship because of pressure from James's supporters was hypocritical. But the way Paul formulated his rhetorical question to Peter was much wider than the response the immediate situation of table fellowship called for. Peter's conduct was for him a flash point for the wider issue of whether either Jewish or Gentile believers should be obliged to "live in a Jewish fashion," that is, should be obliged to observe the Mosaic law. Paul's implied answer to this question was that neither was obliged to observe the law.[26]

Paul does not tell us in 2:11–14 who won this confrontation. This probably means that Paul lost. The largely Gentile community at Antioch accommodated itself to the concerns of Peter and the other Jewish believers about observance of the Jewish dietary regulations. This may have meant that all of them were willing to observe these regulations in their common meals or that they would have provided food prepared in keeping with those regulations at least for the Jewish believers. In any case, Paul left Antioch for good the following spring (in 49).

Paul's confrontation with Peter at Antioch illustrates three important convictions of Paul and their consequences for his relationship with other Christian groups. First, it shows that Paul thought the regulations of the Mosaic law no longer needed to be observed either by Jewish or by Gentile believers. This is why he thought so much was at stake in his confrontation with Peter. Second, the fact that Paul seems to have lost the argument at Antioch suggests that the majority of believers at Antioch, including Gentile believers, took a different and less radical view

---

[25] See Cohen, *The Beginnings of Jewishness*, 175–97, esp. 182, for the various meanings of Ἰουδαΐζειν.

[26] For a fuller explanation of this position, see Hans Dieter Betz, *Galatians: A Commentary on Paul's Letter to the Churches in Galatia* (Hermeneia; Philadelphia: Fortress, 1979), 110–112. For a narrower interpretation, see James D. G. Dunn, *The Epistle to the Galatians* (BNTC 9; Peabody, Mass.: Hendrickson, 1993), 126–31. The broadness of Paul's formulation of the question suggests that Betz's interpretation is more to the point.

than Paul did about the status of the law. They were willing to accommodate themselves to the practices of Jewish believers in a way Paul was unwilling to do. They may also have taken a more positive position in general than Paul did about observance of the ethical commandments of the law. This set Paul at odds with the Antiochene Christian community. Finally, it indicates a fundamental disagreement between Paul and James and his supporters in Jerusalem. This disagreement would have further consequences for his relationship to the churches in Galatia several years later.

The second series of events took place about five years later. Paul's controversy with the Galatian Christian communities was again over the issues of circumcision and observance of the Mosaic law. Almost all we know of this controversy comes from Paul's intensely polemical letter to them. This letter differs from his other letters in that it was addressed to several communities in the same area, Galatia, rather than to one community in a specific city. Galatia was the name both of a territory in central Asia Minor and of a Roman province that included both the territory inhabited by the Galatians and the area south of it.[27] When Paul wrote to the Galatians, he was probably writing to inhabitants of the territory rather than of the larger Roman province. The Letter to the Galatians was probably written early in Paul's three-year stay at Ephesus, that is, about 53 or 54,[28] and probably after two previous visits to the Galatians (Gal 4:13; see Acts 16:6; 18:23).

The precise situation Paul is addressing in the letter is not altogether clear. This is due partially to its intensely polemical tone (polemical arguments are usually not fair representations of opponents' positions) and partially to the fact that both Paul and the Galatians already knew what we do not know but would like to know. The most plausible interpretation, however, is that Jewish Christian missionaries connected with either Jerusalem or perhaps Antioch came to the Galatian communities shortly after Paul's second visit to the area (Acts 18:23).[29] They clearly came from outside the Galatian communities, since Paul consistently distinguishes them (Gal 1:7, 9; 4:17; 5:10; 6:12–13) from the Galatian Christians themselves (1:11; 3:1–5, 15; 4:12, 28; 5:11, 13; 6:1, 18). These missionaries challenged Paul on two fronts. First, they claimed that Paul derived his authority from the leaders of the Jerusalem church. Insofar as Paul's gospel deviated from their gospel, it had no standing and should not be followed. Paul responds to this claim in 1:11–2:14. Second,

---

[27] For a description of Galatia, see Murphy-O'Connor, *Paul: A Critical Life*, 185–91. For a much fuller study, see Stephen Mitchell, *Anatolia: Land, Men, and Gods in Asia Minor* (2 vols.; Oxford: Clarendon, 1993).

[28] This is basically the position taken by Fitzmyer, "The Letter to the Galatians," *NJBC* 781; Murphy-O'Connor, *Paul: A Critical Life*, 184; Frank J. Matera, *Galatians* (SP 9; Collegeville, Minn.: Liturgical Press, 1992), 26. Both Dunn (*Galatians*, 19) and J. Louis Martyn (*Galatians: A New Translation with Introduction and Commentary* [AB 33a; New York: Doubleday, 1997]), 19–20) date Galatians to 50 and think that it was written somewhere in Greece. All except Matera think that it was written before 1–2 Corinthians and Romans. Matera thinks it was written after 1 Corinthians.

[29] Most scholars now think that Paul's opponents were Jewish Christian missionaries. Most also connect these missionaries with the Jerusalem church rather than with the church at Antioch. See Matera, *Galatians*, 1–11; Dunn, *Galatians*, 9–12; Betz, *Galatians*, 5–9; Martyn, *Galatians*,18. Murphy-O'Connor (*Paul: A Critical Life*, 193–94), however, opts for Antioch.

contrary to Paul, these missionaries preached that Gentile converts to Christianity must not only have faith in Christ but also be circumcised and observe the Mosaic law. Their interpretation of the gospel may have prominently featured three central figures: Abraham, Moses, and Jesus. Abraham turned from the worship of idols to serve the true God. God made a covenant with Abraham, and the sign of this covenant was circumcision. God also promised that Abraham would be the father of many nations. Moses was the one through whom God gave the law. And Jesus was the Messiah who confirmed both the promises made to Abraham and the law received through Moses.[30] All of this is reflected in Paul's arguments in 2:15–4:31. The appeal of their positions for the Galatian believers may have rested on the orderly way of life the Mosaic law offered to those who observed it. These Galatian believers had turned their backs on the various beliefs and practices of the religious world of which they had been a part. How were they to live in a properly religious and ethical fashion if there was, as Paul claimed, no law to guide them? Observance of the law offered them an articulated set of rules by which to lead their new way of life pleasing to God. Paul responds to these concerns in 5:1–6:10.

Although these Jewish Christian missionaries were always in the background, Paul addresses his letter to the Galatian believers themselves. Its most obvious characteristic is its intensely polemical tone. Paul even omits the thanksgiving with which he otherwise began his letters. Paul was deeply troubled by what was happening in Galatia. He felt that both his claim to authority and the central element of his own gospel—the preaching of Christ to the Gentiles without observance of the Mosaic law—were being challenged. The body of the letter is an example of deliberative rhetoric, in which Paul tries to persuade the Galatian believers to continue to have faith in Christ but without being circumcised or taking up observance of the Mosaic law.[31] The controversial nature of the arguments Paul makes in Galatians contributed significantly to the situation in which he found himself several years later as he began to dictate his letter to the Roman community. Because of this, it is important to have a fairly detailed sense of what these arguments were and why they would have proved so controversial.

The first part of the letter (Gal 1:11–2:14) is a very selective autobiographical narrative of Paul's own life. Its purpose is to establish his own authority as an apostle against the counterclaims of the Jewish Christian missionaries.[32] In doing so, Paul

---

[30] This interpretation is most fully argued by Martyn, *Galatians,* 302–6, and has been accepted by Murphy-O'Connor, *Paul: A Critical Life,* 196–99.

[31] My view of the rhetorical structure of Galatians is deeply indebted to Betz, *Galatians.* Galatians is better understood, however, as an example of deliberative rhetoric rather than of judicial rhetoric as Betz argues. Paul is primarily interested in the future, i.e., in what the Galatians should or should not do. This is the domain of deliberative rather than judicial rhetoric. George A. Kennedy, *New Testament Interpretation through Rhetorical Criticism* (Chapel Hill: University of North Carolina Press, 1984), 144–52, takes the same position.

[32] Rhetorically, this is the narrative-of-the-facts (*narratio,* διήγησις) section of the discourse. Deliberative rhetoric often did not have this section. External matters, however, that were relevant to the discussion were often introduced at this point, especially matters that established the authority of the speaker, since the authority of the speaker was central to deliberative rhetoric. See Quintilian, *Inst.* 3.8.10–12, and Kennedy, *New Testament Interpretation,* 145. This is obviously the case at this point in Galatians.

walks a very fine line. On the one hand, he insists that his gospel and his authority as an apostle were grounded in revelations from God and did not depend on authorization by any human authority (1:1). More specifically, he claims that both his call to preach Jesus among the Gentiles (1:16) and his later decision to go up to Jerusalem to meet with the leaders of the Jerusalem Christian community (2:1) were based on revelations (ἀποκαλύψαι/κατὰ ἀποκάλυψιν) from God. On the other hand, he also claims that the Jewish Christian leaders in Jerusalem supported his way of preaching the gospel to the Gentiles. This was true of his initial meeting in Jerusalem with Peter and James three years after his call (1:18–19). It was also true when Peter, James, and John all agreed to the compromise worked out at the Jerusalem meeting in 48 (2:1–10). He wanted their approval lest somehow he "should be running or had run in vain" (2:2). His attitude toward the Jewish Christian leaders in Jerusalem, however, is extraordinarily ambivalent. Even as he claims that Peter, James, and John supported his preaching of the gospel to the Gentiles at the meeting in Jerusalem, he consistently minimizes their authority (2:2, 6, 9). He describes them as "those who were reputed to be something (what they were makes no difference to me; God shows no partiality)" (2:6) and as those "who were reputed to be pillars" (Gal 2:9). Paul's ambivalence at the time he was writing Galatians reflected the uncomfortable reality that although the Jewish Christian leaders in Jerusalem had initially supported his preaching the gospel to the Gentiles, at least James and his supporters soon changed their minds and came to oppose it. Indeed, the Jewish Christians missionaries who came to Galatia and preached a "different gospel" (Gal 1:6) probably rightly claimed that they and not Paul had the authority of the Jewish Christian leaders in Jerusalem on their side.

In the second part of Galatians (2:15–4:31), Paul presents a series of arguments to dissuade the Galatian believers from being circumcised and observing the Mosaic law.[33] What is crucial for our purposes in situating Romans is the structure and character of the arguments Paul makes in Galatians. They are dialectical and marked by stark contrasts. The tone for this section is established by the basic proposition Paul sets out in 2:15–21:[34] righteousness is through faith in Christ and not by observance of the Mosaic law. Even Jewish believers like Paul have come to understand this. How much more should this be the case for Gentile believers such as the Galatians. If righteousness were through observance of the law, then Christ died

---

[33] It is not completely clear that the Galatians intended to observe the whole law (see Gal 4:10 and esp. 5:2). It is difficult to imagine, however, that the Jewish Christian missionaries preached anything other than observance of the whole law. Paul's arguments certainly presume this is the case. His remark in Gal 6:13 about those who are circumcised not observing the law (including the Jewish Christian missionaries) is about what they in fact do not do and not about what they should do.

[34] Rhetorically, Gal 2:15–21 is the proposition *(propositio)*. It concludes the narrative of the facts and sets out the basic position Paul will substantiate by the proofs that follow. The proposition is treated in Quintilian, *Inst.* 4.4.1–5.28. See Betz, *Galatians*, 113–14. Kennedy (*New Testament Interpretation*, 148–49) objects to calling 2:15–21 a proposition because it is argumentative. He prefers to call it an epicheireme. Galatians 2:15–21 is certainly argumentative. But Quintilian (*Inst.* 4.4.4) allows that a syllogism (which is argumentative) can be used as a proposition. Given its place in Galatians at the end of the narrative and the fact that it sets out Paul's basic position, 2:15–21 seems to function rhetorically as a proposition.

to no purpose. The logic of 2:15–21 is this: (a) righteousness comes either through faith in Christ or through observance of the law; (b) but righteousness comes through faith; (c) therefore it does not come through observance of the law. On the surface, 2:15–21 seems similar to Phil 3:7–11. There Paul claimed to count all as lost, even righteousness based on the law, in comparison with the surpassing worth of knowing Christ Jesus. But the similarity is only on the surface. However unequal the terms, Phil 3:7–11 was still a comparison. Galatians 2:15–21 is a stark contrast. Righteousness is through faith in Christ and so not through observance of the law. It is not, as the Jewish Christian missionaries tried to persuade the Galatians, both faith in Christ and observance of the law. The arguments of the Jewish Christian missionaries were both-and arguments; Paul's are either-or arguments.

The same structure of stark, either-or contrasts is also found in the six proofs that follow in Gal 3:1–4:31.[35] Paul's first proof (3:1–5) is an appeal to the Galatians' own experience. He asks how they first experienced the Spirit. Was it through observance of the law, or was it by hearing with faith? Since they only recently began to consider circumcision and observance of the law, the answer is obvious. Their original experience of the Spirit was through hearing with faith and not by observance of the law.

The second proof (3:6–14) is an elaborate interpretation of scriptural texts centered on the figure of Abraham.[36] In his interpretation of these scriptural passages, Paul links together Abraham's faith, righteousness, and a blessing for the Gentiles and contrasts them with observance of the law and the curse associated with it in Deut 27:26; 21:23. He then argues that Christ's death freed believers from the curse connected with the law and extended the blessing of Abraham to the Gentiles so that the promise of the Spirit might be received by faith.[37] The underlying contrast is between a blessing and a curse, and Paul astonishingly connects with the law and its observance the curse from which believers were delivered.[38]

In the third proof (Gal 3:15–18), Paul argues on the analogy of what he takes to be a commonplace law of inheritance. A will, once ratified, cannot be annulled or added to. So too the promise to Abraham and to his offspring was prior to the Mosaic law and so could not be annulled by the Mosaic law. In addition, the promise of inheritance was to Abraham's "offspring" (τῷ σπέρματι), in the singular, and not to his "offsprings," in the plural.[39] Paul interprets the "offspring" to whom the inheritance was promised as Christ. The implication at least is that the inheritance was

---

[35] These six proofs (*probationes*, πίστεις) form the central section of the letter. Proofs usually follow the narration and the proposition. On the necessity and centrality of this section, see Quintilian, *Inst.* 5.1.1.

[36] Gen 15:6; 12:3; Deut 27:26; Hab 2:4; Lev 18:5; Deut 21:23.

[37] This study will return several times to the difficult and highly artificial arguments of this passage.

[38] It may very well be that the curse in Deut 27:26 against those who do not observe the law may first have been used by the Jewish Christian missionaries who came to Galatia as an argument that the Galatian Christians should observe the law and that Paul then tried to turn this argument against them with less than complete success. This may also be reflected in Paul's rather acidic remark in Gal 5:2 that anyone who is circumcised is bound to observe the whole law.

[39] See Gen 12:7; 13:5; 17:7; 24:7.

not promised to the Jewish people, that is, to "offsprings" in the plural. He then concludes this proof with another stark contrast. The inheritance was based on the promise to Abraham and not on the law.

Paul's fourth proof (3:26–4:11) is an appeal to Christian baptismal language. Through baptism there is no longer "Jew or Greek, slave or free, male and female" (3:28). It is through baptism, and not through observance of the law, that believers receive their sonship and inheritance in Christ Jesus. Christ, who was born under the law, has delivered both Jews and Gentiles alike from slavery. They are no longer slaves but sons and heirs. For the Galatians to be circumcised and observe the law is in reality a return to their previous slavery to the weak and beggarly elemental principles of the universe, that is, to slavery to the gods they worshipped before their conversion.[40] Here again is a stark contrast. Sonship and inheritance came through baptism and all that it implied and not through the law or its observance, which is slavery to the elemental principles of the universe.

The fifth proof (4:12–20) is Paul's very personal appeal to the friendship between himself and the Galatians. He urges them not to destroy this friendship by being taken in by the Jewish Christian missionaries who are trying to persuade them to be circumcised and observe the Mosaic law. Here the contrast is between two friendships: a true friendship with Paul versus a false friendship with the Jewish Christian missionaries.

Paul's sixth and final proof (4:21–31) is an elaborate, difficult, and puzzling allegory based on a contrast between Abraham's two wives, Sarah and Hagar. Hagar was a slave woman, and her son, Ishmael, was born "according to the flesh." Sarah in contrast was a free woman, and her son, Isaac, was born "according to the promise" (4:21–23). Paul then interprets this contrast allegorically. He links Hagar with the covenant at Sinai and the present Jerusalem and its children, the Jewish people. By contrast, he links Sarah to a new covenant and the heavenly Jerusalem. Believers, Paul claims, are not children of the slave woman but of the free woman. They, and not the children of the slave woman, are to be the heirs. This is perhaps the starkest contrast of all. Paul allegorically places the Mosaic covenant, Jerusalem, and the Jewish people, astonishingly, with Hagar the slave woman and her son. In contrast, he places believers with Sarah the free woman and her son.[41]

---

[40] "The elemental principles of the universe" (τὰ στοιχεῖα τοῦ κόσμου) probably refers to the various deities they had previously worshipped. See Betz, *Galatians,* 205, and Dunn, *Galatians,* 223–26. For a different interpretation, see Matera, *Galatians,* 149–50. Note that Paul is not using a comparison. He is not saying that for the Galatians to observe to the law is *like* returning to slavery. It is actually returning to slavery to the elemental principles of the universe.

[41] Matera (*Galatians,* 167–79) and Martyn (*Galatians,* 447–66) argue that the allegory in 4:21–31 of Hagar and Sarah should be interpreted within the confines of Paul's intense polemic against the Jewish Christian missionaries who came to Galatia. Hagar, the present Jerusalem, and her children refer specifically to these Jewish Christian missionaries connected with Jerusalem and those who follow them. Hagar and her children do not refer to the broader category of the Jewish people at that time. Matera and Martyn are certainly right to claim that Paul's polemic was aimed at achieving a very specific result: to dissuade the Galatian believers from accepting the gospel of these Jewish Christian missionaries. The Galatians should not be circumcised or start to observe the Mosaic law. But the logic of Paul's argument in 4:21–31 is

The last section of the letter (5:1–6:10) is an exhortation.[42] Paul's introduction both sums up 2:15–4:31 and sets the tone for the exhortation that follows: "For freedom Christ has set us free; stand fast therefore, and do not submit again to a yoke of slavery" (5:1; see 5:7–12). The "yoke of slavery" he refers to in this context is clearly circumcision and observance of the Mosaic law, and he contrasts it with the freedom believers have because of Christ. Paul then argues that the basic principle of Christian life is "faith working through love" empowered by the Spirit (5:5–6). In addition, this freedom was not meant to lead to immorality. Rather, love means that they are to be become slaves of one another (5:13). On this basis he urges the Galatian believers in 5:19–23 to avoid a series of vices (the "works of the flesh") and to practice a series of virtues (the "fruits of the Spirit"). All this is made possible through the power and guidance of the Spirit (5:17–18, 22, 25). Finally, in 6:1–10 Paul offers admonitions about community cohesion and concludes with admonitions to do what is noble (τὸ καλόν) and good (τὸ ἀγαθόν).

The most striking aspect of this exhortation is its generality. Paul does not seem to be addressing specific ethical issues or problems in the Galatian communities. This very generality, however, gives us clues about why Paul wrote this exhortation and how he conceived of the ethical life of a believing community without observance of the Mosaic law. In the previous part of the letter, Paul tried to dissuade the Galatians from being circumcised and observing the Mosaic law. These arguments, however, must have raised an obvious question in the Galatians' minds: If we do not observe the Mosaic law, how then do we live ethically and in a way pleasing to God? If not by observing the Mosaic law, then how? If Paul's earlier arguments were to have any persuasive force, he needed to answer this question. Paul's exhortation in 5:1–6:10, then, was not something added on to the end of the letter but was an integral part of his overall argument. Without it his arguments in the earlier parts of the letter could not stand.

In describing how believers were now to live lives pleasing to God, Paul drew on an already existing pattern of interpretation in Hellenistic Judaism and significantly reinterpreted it. It was a commonplace among Hellenistic Jewish writers, such as the author of the *Letter of Aristeas,* Philo, and Josephus, that observance of the Mosaic law was meant to lead to the practice of virtue and the avoidance of vice. That was one of its primary purposes. Hellenistic Jewish writers redescribed observance of the law by using the categories of virtue and vice central to Greco-Roman ethical discourse. They claimed that observance of the law led to the practice of virtue and the avoidance of vice better than any Greco-Roman ethical philosophy or legal system did. The language of virtue and vice becomes an alternate way of understanding and expressing the value of observance of the law.[43] What Paul does in Gal 5:1–6:10 is to take this basic framework and reinterpret it in two ways. First,

---

in fact much broader than that. The allegory itself offers little reason to interpret it in the restrictive way suggested by Matera and Martyn. See Betz, *Galatians,* 238–52, and Dunn, *Galatians,* 242–59.

[42] The presence of this large exhortatory section also points to the deliberative, rather than judicial, character of the letter's rhetoric. See Kennedy, *New Testament Interpretation,* 145–46.

[43] For extended examples of this type of interpretation, see *Let. Aris.* 128–171; Philo, *De virtutibus* and *De decalogo,* and Josephus, *Ag. Ap.* 2.151–289.

rather than an alternate way of understanding and expressing the value of obser-vance of the law, the practice of virtue and the avoidance of vice becomes, in Paul's interpretation, an alternative to observing the law. Believers are exhorted directly to practice virtue and avoid vice without the mediation of observance of the law. Sec-ond, believers are guided and empowered by the Spirit to practice virtue and avoid vice. Paul's ethical alternative to observance of the law, then, is the Spirit-guided practice of virtue and the avoidance of vice. This leads to lives pleasing to God.

Paul seems to have prevailed in his arguments with the Galatians. At the end of 1 Corinthians, a letter he also wrote from Ephesus but about a year later (winter of 54–55), Paul instructed the Corinthian Christians about how the collection for the poor of the Jerusalem community was to be taken up (1 Cor 16:1–4). He asked them to do it in the same way as he had directed the churches of Galatia to do it (1 Cor 16:1). This shows that a year or so after he wrote to the Galatian churches, his relationship with them was once again on a firm footing. This would have been impossible had Paul's arguments not prevailed.[44]

But the victory came at a price. When one reads Paul's letter to the Galatians, one cannot but be struck by the starkness of its contrasts. On the one side is righ-teousness, the experience of the Spirit, sonship, inheritance, freedom, and those who have faith in Christ. On the other side is the law, its observance, slavery, and, appar-ently, the Jewish people. The two sides seem to be opposed to one another, almost inherently and in principle, to such an extent that it is difficult to imagine how the law or its observance could ever have been commanded by God. At least it is diffi-cult to see how Paul could ever have understood it in this way in Galatians.

What is one to make of all this? How are these stark contrasts to be inter-preted? The reason for asking these questions is not because Paul simply could not have meant what he wrote. Rather, the reason is that other parts of the letter seem to point in another direction. First, when Paul describes his life prior to his call, he proudly claims that he advanced in Judaism beyond many of his own age and is ex-tremely zealous for the traditions of his fathers (Gal 1:14). Even after his call, he is still proud of his earlier observance.[45] This pride implies a positive evaluation of the law that is at odds with his other arguments. Second, in a digression after his third argument, Paul explicitly raises the issue of the place of the law and whether it is op-posed to the promises (3:19–25). According to him, the law is not opposed to the promises. Rather, it was added because of transgressions. It was intended by God to be in effect until the coming of Christ and until what was promised in Christ was given to those who have faith. The law, then, though inferior to God's promises, was not opposed to them. Rather, it served as a kind of guardian (παιδαγωγός) until Christ came. Now that faith has come, however, believers were no longer under that guardianship. Both Paul's description of his observance of the law prior to his call and his analysis of the place of the law prior to Christ's coming share a common perspective. That perspective is a temporal one. In both cases the law was valid, but

---

[44] Paul's victory in this controversy also seems to be reflected in two later NT tests (2 Tim 4:10 and 1 Peter 1:1). See Dunn, *Galatians*, 19.

[45] Although Paul came to regret his persecution of the church, he never had similar re-grets about his observance of the law.

its validity was limited in terms of time. With Christ's coming and with Paul's call, the obligation to observe the law came to an end because something new had occurred that brought an end to the old. This temporal perspective on the role of the law is quite different from the almost inherent and in-principle opposition of Paul's other arguments against circumcision and observance of the law. The law and its observance had a valid function, but that function has now come to an end.

Third, Paul's references to the law in his exhortation in 5:1–6:10 are not of a piece. It is certainly true for Paul that Christ set believers free from the law and to return to its observance means to submit again to a yoke of slavery (5:1). Those who wish to be made righteous by observance of the law are severed from Christ (5:4). Believers who are now guided by the Spirit are no longer under the law (5:18). At the same time, however, Paul also claims in 5:14 that the whole law was fulfilled (πεπλήρωται) in one saying, "You shall love your neighbor as yourself," a quotation from Lev 19:18. Toward the end of the exhortation in Gal 6:2 Paul makes a somewhat similar claim that, by bearing each other's burdens, believers fulfill (ἀναπληρώσετε) the "law of Christ." Paul probably means by the "law of Christ" the Spirit-guided love of neighbor reflected in the practice of the virtues listed in 5:22–23 and not the Mosaic law. Yet he still uses the term "law" in both 5:14 and 6:2 to describe this way of living. In addition, the fulfillment of the law in 5:14 and the fulfillment of the "law of Christ" in 6:2 refer to the same kind of life guided by the love of one's neighbor.

How are we to interpret these verses? Is Paul somehow reintroducing observance of, at least, the ethical commandments of the law? Given the overall tone of his exhortation in 5:1–6:10, Paul clearly does not mean by "fulfilling" the law the same thing as "observance" of the law.[46] In addition, the verbs Paul uses for "fulfill" (πληρόω, ἀναπληρόω) were not used in the Septuagint to describe observance of the Mosaic law and its commandments. The verbs used in the Septuagint were ποιέω ("to do") or φυλάσσω ("to keep") and not πληρόω, ἀναπληρόω.[47] Because Paul uses both ποιέω in Gal 5:3 and φυλάσσω in 6:2 to refer to observance of the law, his choice of "fulfill" in 5:14 and 6:2 cannot be accidental. He clearly must mean by "fulfill" something other than "observe."[48] Rather, he is claiming that believers, by

---

[46] See Betz, *Galatians,* 274–76, 298–301; Dunn, *Galatians,* 288–92, 321–24; Matera, *Galatians,* 193, 214, 219; Martyn, *Galatians,* 486–91, 502–23, 547–49, 554–58 for a variety of interpretations of Gal 5:14; 6:2.

[47] The Greek verb ποιέω is used twenty-eight times and usually translates the Hebrew verb עשׂה ("to do"): Lev 19:37; 22:31; 26:15; Num 5:30; 15:22, 40; Deut 6:25; 15:5; 16:12; 17:19; 19:9; 27:10; 28:1, 15; 30:8, 10; Jos 22:3, 5; 1 Chr 22:12; 29:19; 2 Chr 14:3; Ezra 7:26; Neh 1:9; 9:34; 10:29; Tob 3:5; 1 Macc 13:48; Sus (Theodotion) 1:62. The Greek verb φυλάσσω ("to keep") is used seventy-four times and usually translates the Hebrew verb שׁמר ("to keep"): Gen 26:5; Exod 12:17; 13:10; Lev 19:19, 37; 22:31; Deut 4:2, 40; 5:29; 6:17; 7:9, 11; 8:2, 6, 11; 10:13; 11:8; 13:19; 15:5; 16:12; 17:19; 26:18; 27:1; 28:1, 15, 45; 30:10; Josh 22:3, 5; 1 Kgdms 13:13; 3 Kgdms 2:3, 43; 3:14; 8:58, 61; 9:6; 11:11, 38; 13:21; 17:13, 19; 18:6; 4 Kgdms 17:13; 23:3; 1 Chr 22:12; 28:7, 8; 2 Chr 34:31; Neh 1:5, 7, 9; 10:29; Ps (LXX) 104:45; 118:34, 45, 57, 60, 63, 134, 136, 168; Prov 4:5; 7:1, 2; 19:16; 29:18; Eccl 8:5; Jer 16:11; Ezek 18:21; Dan (Theodotion) 9:4; 1 Macc 2:52; 4 Macc 5:29; Sir 21:1; Wis 6:4.

[48] In Matt 5:17 Jesus claims not to have come to annul (καταλῦσαι) but to fulfill (πληρῶσαι) the law and the prophets. The interpretation of Matt 5:17–20 is much disputed. Because of the inclusion of the phrase "the prophets," the verb "fulfill" cannot be synonymous with "observe." It must mean to "fulfill" the Scriptures (i.e., the Law and the Prophets). For

being guided by the Spirit and loving one another through the practice of virtue, are equivalently carrying out what had been central to the Mosaic law. They are fulfilling the law, but they are not, as such, observing it.[49] This is, however, still a quite different and more positive understanding of the law than one finds either in the rest of the exhortation in 5:1–6:10 or in most of his earlier arguments. Although less clearly the case than in the previous two examples, Paul's references in 5:14; 6:2 to the Mosaic law and to the law of Christ also imply a temporal perspective. What was central to the fulfillment of the Mosaic law in the past is now fulfilled in the present through the "law of Christ," the Spirit-guided love of one's neighbor.

There are, then, two rather different perspectives on the Mosaic law in Galatians. One, clearly the dominant in Galatians, sees righteousness through faith in Christ as almost inherently opposed to righteousness through observance of the Mosaic law. Indeed, righteousness through observance of the law is impossible. This also has negative consequences for how one understands the place or, really, the lack of place for the Jewish people. The other perspective seems to be a more temporal one. There was a valid place or function for the law in the past, but all that has changed through the coming of Christ. These perspectives, at best, lie uneasily side by side. How can one reconcile this strange mixture, these mixed messages in Galatians? In one sense one cannot. The two perspectives are ultimately irreconcilable. Yet it is also clear that Paul wrote Galatians in the midst of bitter controversy. What was at stake for him was his status as an apostle to the Gentiles and his most deeply held convictions about righteousness by faith in Christ for both Jews and Gentiles without observance of the Mosaic law. These convictions were anything but theoretical for him. They were rooted in his own experiences, which had changed his whole life. To challenge them meant calling into question not only his perspective on the gospel but his very identity. That intensely polemical situation influenced the way Paul responded to what he regarded as a crisis in the Galatian Christian community. Paul used every argument he could muster to dissuade the Galatians from being circumcised and observing the Mosaic law. He marshaled his arguments so as to maximize the contrast between his own gospel and the gospel preached by the Jewish Christian missionaries who had come to Galatia, between a gospel that did not include observance of the Mosaic law and one that did. In doing this, however, his arguments had a logic that may well have gone beyond what he had either intended or foreseen. By attempting to quell one controversy, he had unintentionally created another, potentially more serious one.

PAUL AND THE ROMAN CHRISTIAN COMMUNITY AT THE TIME OF ROMANS

Paul wrote his letter to the Roman Christians in the winter of 56–57, during his last stay in the city of Corinth. He came there from Ephesus, where he had spent the previous three years, to strengthen a reconciliation between himself and the Co-

---

different interpretations of 5:17–20, see Ulrich Luz, *Matthew 1–7: A Continental Commentary* (Minneapolis: Fortress, 1992), 260–65.

[49] See also ch. 14, below, in the discussion of Rom 12:8–10.

rinthian Christians.[50] He seems to have prevailed in his conflicts with both the Corinthian and the Galatian communities. His relations, however, with the communities at both Jerusalem and Antioch were a different matter. As seen earlier in this chapter, his differences with both these communities were significant and persistent. While Paul seems to have maintained his authority in the communities he had founded, he risked being isolated because of his conflicts with the two most significant early Christian communities, those at Jerusalem and Antioch. It is within this context that Paul wrote to the Roman Christians.

But what did the Roman Christians and Paul know of each other's views, and how did they know them?[51] To answer these questions, one first has to keep in mind how Paul composed his letters. He did not go into some private study to write them. Nor did he write them without discussing their content with other Christian leaders involved in his missionary work. With the exception of Romans, Paul included other Christian leaders in the salutations of his letters.[52] Although the views expressed in the letters were certainly Paul's own, their contents were the result of discussions and probably arguments with at least some other prominent Christians. The letters have a public character to them. Their contents would have been known not only in the communities to which he wrote the letters but also in the communities where he wrote them.

The community where Paul wrote most of these letters was at Ephesus. He probably wrote Galatians, Philippians, 1 Corinthians, most of 2 Corinthians, and Philemon from there.[53] In the first century Ephesus was a major port on the western coast of Asia Minor and the principal city of the Roman province of Asia. Because of this there was a great deal of contact between Ephesus and Rome.[54] The Christian communities of Rome and Ephesus would have had frequent enough contact to be fairly well informed about each other. We need not depend, however, on this plausible but general observation alone. Romans 16:3–16 contains a long list of Christians in Rome to whom Paul sent greetings.[55] Although we can hardly be

---

[50] For two different accounts of the complicated relations between Paul and the Corinthian Christians, see Georgi, *The Opponents of Paul in Second Corinthians*, 1–25; and Thrall, *Second Epistle to the Corinthians*, 1.1–78; 2.926–65.

[51] Several of the essays in Karl P. Donfried, ed., *The Romans Debate* (rev. and expanded ed.; Peabody, Mass.: Hendrickson, 1991) helpfully set out the contours of this debate: Robert J. Karris, "Romans 14:1–15:6 and the Occasion of Romans," 65–84; Karl P. Donfried, "False Presuppositions in the Study of Romans," 102–24; Robert J. Karris, "The Occasion of Romans: A Response to Prof. Donfried," 125–27; Wilhelm Wuellner, "Paul's Rhetoric of Argumentation in Romans: An Alternative to the Donfried-Karris Debate over Romans," 128–46. Karris argues for the general character of the exhortations in Rom 12:1–15:6; Donfried, for the much more specific character; Wuellner, for a different approach altogether.

[52] "Paul, Silvanus, and Timothy" (1 Thess 1:1); "Paul ... and all the brethren who are with me" (Gal 1:1–2); "Paul and Timothy" (Phil 1:1); "Paul ... and our brother Sosthenes" (1 Cor 1:1); "Paul ... and Timothy our brother" (2 Cor 1:1); "Paul ... and Timothy our brother" (Phlm 1).

[53] The reasons for placing the composition of all these letters at Ephesus can be found in Murphy-O'Connor, *Paul: A Critical Life*, 166–84, 192–322.

[54] For contact between Rome and Asia Minor in general, see Noy, *Foreigners at Rome*, 227–34, 291–93.

[55] For detailed discussions of this list, see Lampe, *Die Stadrömischen Christen*, 124–53; Fitzmyer, *Romans*, 733–42; and Dunn, *Romans*, 884–907.

certain, it seems unlikely that Paul would be sending greetings to members of the Roman community whom he did not know at all. It is impossible to know when and where he met all these Christians. Five of the first six names on the list (Prisca and Aquila, Epaenetus, Andronicus and Junia), however, are plausibly connected not only with Rome but also earlier with Ephesus. The first two names were a Jewish Christian couple whom Paul met on his first visit to Corinth in 51. According to Acts 18:18–19, they then traveled with Paul from Corinth to Ephesus. They were still in Ephesus when Paul wrote 1 Corinthians in the winter of 54–55, since they sent their greetings to the Corinthian community (1 Cor 16:19). This means that they were in Ephesus for much of the time Paul was there. By the time he wrote Romans, however, they had obviously returned to Rome. The next name is Epaenetus. Paul described him in Rom 16:5 as the first convert in Asia for Christ. He was probably a Gentile. The most likely place for his conversion would have been Ephesus sometime earlier in Paul's three-year stay there. Finally, Andronicus and his wife, Junia, were Jewish Christians whom Paul described in Rom 16:7 as fellow prisoners (συναιχμαλώτους).[56] The most likely place for this imprisonment with Paul was at Ephesus (see Phil 1:7, 12, 14, 17; 2 Cor 1:8–10; 6:5; 11:23).[57] Given the length of his stay there, it would not be unlikely that Paul also met at Ephesus some of the other persons named in the list. Whether this was the case or not, it is clear that several of those to whom Paul sent greetings at Rome were in Ephesus during his stay there and thus during the period when he wrote his letters to the Galatians and Philippians and most of his correspondence with the Corinthians. They would have been aware of the conflicts in which Paul was involved with the communities in Galatia and Corinth. Given the rather public character of Paul's letter writing, they would also have been aware, in some detail, of Paul's responses in those conflicts.

In addition to the frequent contacts between the communities at Rome and Ephesus, there were also frequent contacts between the Christian communities of Rome and Corinth. In Rom 16:21–23, Paul listed the names of eight fellow Christians who were with him at Corinth while he was writing his letter to the Romans and who were also sending greetings to the Roman community. One was the scribe Tertius. Four others, Timothy, Lucius, Jason, and Sosipater, were Jewish Christians. The other three were probably Gentile Christians. We know nothing about one of them, Quartus, other than his name, but the other two must have been men of some means. Gaius, whom Paul also mentioned in 1 Cor 1:14, was wealthy enough to serve as the host (ξένος) for the whole Corinthian community. And Erastus is described as the "treasurer of the city" (ὁ οἰκονόμος τῆς πόλεως).[58] We have no way of knowing how many of the Roman Christians listed in Rom 16:3–16 these Corinthians knew, but they knew at least Prisca and Aquila, who had earlier lived in Corinth. They may have known others. In any case, these greetings indicate that there

---

[56] For evidence that Junia was a woman, see Lampe, *Die stadrömischen Christen,* 139–40, 147; Fitzmyer, *Romans,* 737–39; Dunn, *Romans,* 894–95.

[57] Evidence for Paul's imprisonment in Ephesus is found in Murphy-O'Connor, *Paul: A Critical Life,* 175–79.

[58] For further information on Gaius and Erastus, see pp. 47–48, above.

was also fairly frequent contact between the Christian communities of Rome and Corinth. Such would hardly be surprising, given that Corinth, like Ephesus, was a port city. This is important for our purposes because it offers evidence, even beyond what Prisca and Aquila would have provided, that the Roman Christians were also aware of the situation of the Corinthian community and of Paul's troubled relationship with it.

There is a good deal of evidence, then, that Paul and the Roman Christian community knew a good deal about each other. The Roman community would have had ample opportunity to learn in some detail about the controversies in which Paul had been involved with both the Galatian and the Corinthian communities and what his responses to these controversies were. For his part, Paul was probably also fairly well informed about the situation and viewpoints of the Roman community. More specifically, he would have been well aware of their attitudes toward him.

What were these attitudes? No doubt Paul and the Roman Christian community had some basic convictions in common. Yet there is also good reason to think that they differed on other significant issues and that these issues were a source of tension between Paul and the community. Various strands mentioned in this and the previous chapter bring out, from the perspective of the Roman Christians, some of the agreements but especially the primary sources of disagreement and tension between them and Paul.

Certainly both Paul and the Roman Christians saw themselves within the context of the Jewish way of life. Both were committed to Jewish monotheism, the belief in one God who was the God of Israel. Both accepted the Jewish scriptures as a central source of authority. Both were committed to the centrality of Jesus as the Messiah, or Christ, within the context of Jewish belief. And both saw their faith in Jesus as the Messiah as the fulfillment of their Jewish beliefs and expectations, not as a rejection of them. Although they did so for different reasons, both also agreed that circumcision was no longer necessary for full membership in the community. Because of this, both would have agreed that Gentile believers were now to have equal status with Jewish believers.

There were, however, significant differences between the viewpoints of the Roman Christians and what seemed to them to be Paul's views. These differences clustered first around their different interpretations of the basic value and continued observance of the Mosaic law. Apart from those associated with Paul, most Roman Christians, whether of Gentile or of Jewish origin, continued to observe the ethical commandments of the law. A minority or both Gentile and Jewish Christians at Rome also favored continued observance of the Sabbath and the dietary regulations of the law. Although the latter were a source of some controversy in the community, most members of the community agreed on the continued observance of the law's ethical commandments. Because of the ethical superiority of its commandments, the law was what distinguished them from their nonbelieving fellow citizens. The ethical superiority of the Mosaic law was what first attracted the Gentiles members of the community to Judaism in the first place. This attraction did not lessen when they came to believe in Jesus as the Christ. It was also, at least in their minds, what grounded their conviction that they were full and legitimate participants in the Jewish way of life, its history, its traditions, and its promises.

Given these convictions, most Roman Christians must have looked with alarm at some of the things they had learned Paul had written in his letter to the Galatians. Paul's views of the law in Galatians called into question much that was integral to their identity. They must have been scandalized by the sharp contrasts Paul continually drew in Galatians between the Mosaic law and its observance, on the one hand, and faith and righteousness, on the other. These contrasts were so stark that it would have been difficult for the Roman Christians even to imagine how Paul could ever have considered the Mosaic law to have been of divine origin or its observance to have been divinely commanded.

More concretely, Paul was claiming that no one was ever made righteous through observance of the law. He was thus calling into question not only the Roman Christians' present observance of the law but also the Jewish people's past observance of it, not simply the status of the law but also the status of the Jewish people, whether present or past. There seemed to be no present or past advantage to being members of the Jewish people. Paul's account of things even seemed to call into question the future of the Jewish people. The promises God made to Abraham and to his "seed" were not to the Jewish people but to Christ and, through Christ, to believers in him. The promises were not made to the Jewish people, and ultimately they even seemed to be excluded from the promises. To submit to the law meant being enslaved to the weak and beggarly elemental principles of the world. It was from just such an enslavement that Christ had delivered those under the law so they could become children and heirs of the promises rather than continue as slaves. Observance of the law allegorically meant they were not children of the free woman Sarah or of the heavenly Jerusalem but of the slave woman Hagar and the present Jerusalem. They could be neither sons nor heirs of God's promises to Abraham and so were excluded from the future, eschatological fulfillment of these promises. All of this must have deeply troubled most Roman Christians.

But they were probably also troubled by what they saw as the practical consequences of Paul's views about the law. For them, observance of the law provided a framework for conducting their lives in an orderly, ethical fashion pleasing to God. If the ethical commandments of the law were no longer to be observed, how were believers to lead their lives? What moral compass were they to use? How could proper order be maintained in the community? Paul's answer in Galatians was that believers were to be guided by the Spirit rather than controlled by the flesh. Empowered by the Spirit, they would be able to practice virtue and avoid vice and so lead lives pleasing to God.

The Roman Christians must have feared that all this was too vague and quite unsatisfactory, compared with observance of the law. In addition, they saw the problems of the Corinthian Christians as ample evidence that their fears were well founded. Given the frequent contact between Christians in Rome and in Corinth, the Roman Christians must have been aware of the situation, which is reflected in 1 Corinthians.[59] One member of the community had committed incest with his fa-

---

[59] For surveys of the issues connected with 1 Corinthians, see Wolfgang Schrage, *Der erste Brief an die Korinther* (4 vols.; EKKNT; Zurich: Benziger, 1991-2001), 1:1–94; and Raymond F. Collins, *First Corinthians* (SP 7; Collegeville, Minn.: Liturgical Press, 1999), 1–31.

ther's wife (1 Cor 5:1–13). Other members advocated sexual asceticism even in marriage (7:1–40). Some were taking other members before Corinthian civil courts instead of solving their differences within the community (6:1–11). There were disputes about the propriety of eating meat that had first been offered to idols in the temples in Corinth (1 Cor 8–10). There were issues about proper conduct at community meals at which the Eucharist was celebrated: the veiling of women (11:1–16), differentiation between rich and poor at community meals and the Eucharist (11:17–34), and the disruption of community gatherings by speaking in tongues (1 Cor 12–14). There were also divisions and quarrels in the community over the issue of whose baptism was superior and over who was therefore initiated into a superior form of divine wisdom (1 Cor 1–4). Finally, they seemed to have been convinced that they were somehow already "raised" from the dead (1 Cor 15).

The Roman Christians probably saw the number and variety of these problems as the predictable results of abandoning observance of the Mosaic law, and as the results of the kind of emphasis Paul gave to the notions both of freedom and of guidance by the Spirit in Galatians 5–6. Certainly Paul's emphases on freedom and the Spirit, however misunderstood by the Corinthian Christians, seem to have played important roles in the issues he was dealing with in 1 Corinthians. Notions of freedom seem to lie behind the Corinthians' seemingly tolerant attitude toward the man who had committed incest (1 Cor 5:1–13)[60] and the cavalier attitude of some community members about the appropriateness of eating meat previously offered in pagan temples (8:1, 4; 9:1, 19).[61] Similarly, emphasis on the possession of the Spirit seems to lie behind not only some Corinthians' disruptive emphasis on speaking in tongues (1 Cor 12–14)[62] but also their claims to possess a special divine wisdom based on their baptism (1 Cor 1–4).[63] Finally, some Corinthians were also apparently convinced that, through their reception of the Spirit in their baptism into the risen body of Christ (12:12–13), they were already "raised" from the dead (1 Cor 15) and possessed special divine wisdom.[64]

---

[60] In 1 Cor 5:2, 6, Paul accuses the Corinthian Christians of even being proud of their tolerant attitude to the man who had committed incest. In the same context, Paul seems to be replying in 1 Cor 6:12–14 to a claim by the Corinthian Christians that "everything is permitted" for them. See Collins, *First Corinthians*, 243–44; and Schrage, *Der erste Brief an die Korinther*, 2:8–20.

[61] In 1 Cor 8:1, 4, Paul seems to be quoting a Corinthian slogan that because they have knowledge (γνῶσις) that idols have no existence, eating food offered to idols is a matter of indifference. Similarly in 1 Cor 9:1, 19, Paul seems to be countering the Corinthians' claim to be "free" (ἐλεύθερος) with an emphasis on subordinating individual freedom to the common good.

[62] The word "spirit" (πνεῦμα) appears fourteen times in 1 Cor 12–14.

[63] Πνεῦμα appears eleven times in 1 Cor 2–4. One of Paul's goals in 1 Cor 1–4 is obviously to correct the Corinthians' claim to have acquired a special wisdom through their reception of the Spirit at baptism. He sets the cross of Christ and its "wisdom" over against the Corinthians' claim to wisdom. See Collins, *First Corinthians*, 86–203; and Schrage, *Der erste Brief an die Korinther*, 1:108–367.

[64] It is difficult to avoid the conclusion that the Corinthian Christians seemed to have assimilated their understanding of baptism and its results to initiation into a mystery cult. The parallels with the initiation of Lucius at Cenchreae into the mysteries of Isis in Apuleius, *Metam.* 11.1–26, are too strong to dismiss. Their assimilation of the unknown (baptism) to the known (initiation into a mystery cult) is quite understandable.

No doubt Paul was as opposed to what was happening in Corinth as the Roman Christians would have been. He wrote 1 Corinthians to correct their mis-understandings of both freedom and the role of the Spirit, urging them to end their divisions and to correct their ethical lapses. He consistently tried to show in 1 Corinthians that the guidance of the Spirit was meant to lead to unity in the community and to placing the common good of the community over the exercise of one's individual "rights."[65] Finally, he argued for the reality of a bodily resurrection but that this bodily resurrection was still in the future. The Roman Christians, however, probably saw the cause of these divisions and lapses in a quite different light. It is what was to be expected when one abandoned observance of the Mosaic law and so no longer had the law as a compass to provide direction and order for living lives pleasing to God. For the Roman Christians, Paul's abandonment of the obligation of believers to observe the ethical commandments of the law in favor of the practice of virtue through the guidance of the Spirit was itself a primary cause of the ethical confusion and disarray in Corinth.

RETROSPECTIVE

Paul's relationship with the Roman Christians, then, was complex, made more difficult by the fact that they knew each other only through third parties. Hints of this complexity began to emerge with the elaborately respectful way in which Paul approached the Roman Christian community and with his emphasis on how they could mutually benefit each other. It also emerged in Paul's explicit concern that his collection for the poor of the Jerusalem community would not be accepted. This concern was not simply a matter of charity; it was also about maintaining or perhaps even reestablishing the bond of unity, which the collection symbolized, between his largely Gentile Christian communities and the Jewish Christian community of Jerusalem.

Paul and the Roman Christians certainly had a great deal in common. Both believed in Jewish monotheism, in Jesus as the Messiah, or Christ, as the fulfillment of their Jewish hopes and expectations, in the authority of the Jewish scriptures, and in the equality of Jewish and Gentile members of the community. Neither believed that circumcision was now required to become full members of the community. The beliefs and practices they held in common were what made an exchange between them possible.

But there were also significant differences, embedded in their distinct histories and centered around issues of how properly to understand and appropriate their common Jewish heritage. The Roman Christians saw their beliefs and practices in continuity with the Jewish way of life, to which they had originally been attracted even before they came to believe in Jesus as the Messiah. For them, the Mosaic law

---

[65] The centrality of the theme of unity has been demonstrated especially by Margaret M. Mitchell, *Paul and the Rhetoric of Reconciliation: An Exegetical Investigation of the Language and Composition of 1 Corinthians* (Louisville: Westminster John Knox, 1991).

was superior to every other ethical or legal code, and observance of its ethical commandments provided a sure guide to living an orderly, ethical life acceptable to God.

Paul's convictions were also rooted in a history. His, however, was both more personal and more controversial. Rooted in his experience of the risen Lord, Paul was convinced of his call to preach the gospel to the Gentiles based on faith in Jesus as the Christ but without either circumcision or observance of the Mosaic law. Both Jewish and Gentile believers were to live their lives in love of neighbor guided by the Spirit and in the practice of virtue. These convictions embroiled him in controversies with the churches of Jerusalem, Antioch, and eventually with the Galatian community he himself had founded. The intensity of his controversy with the Galatians led Paul to so sharpen the contrasts between righteousness through faith and observance of the law that it became difficult to see how the law or its observance could ever have been commanded by God. These same stark contrasts seemed even to exclude the Jewish people from ultimately receiving the inheritance promised to them by God in the Scriptures.

The contrasts Paul drew must have seemed incomprehensible to most Roman Christians. His rejection of the value of observance of the Mosaic law must have seemed scandalous to them. His arguments in Galatians called into question not only the value of their observance of the law but also the value of observance of the law by the Jewish people as a whole in the course of their history. His arguments even seemed to call into question the future of the Jewish people, to which they were convinced they belonged. Finally, as the example of the Corinthian Christians showed, his views about how to live ethically led predictably to confusion and disarray.

As Paul began to dictate his letter to the Roman Christians during his stay in Corinth during the winter of 56–57, how was he going to deal with this situation? He not only risked losing their support for his mission to Spain; he also risked alienating himself and his communities from the important community in Rome in addition to the communities in Jerusalem and Antioch. Paul obviously needed and wanted to persuade the Roman Christians of the correctness of the gospel he preached. To do this, he needed to persuade them that his gospel was indeed based on convictions they held in common and that it flowed from these same common convictions.

But he also needed to do this with integrity and without compromising his own basic convictions. But what were these basic convictions, which he needed to maintain and defend with integrity? For example, did they in fact include all the arguments in his letter to the Galatians? These arguments are not all of a piece. Side by side with stark, in-principle contrasts between righteousness through faith and observance of the law lie views about the place of the law and its observance that are less sharp and more temporally oriented. In reality there are two frameworks present in Galatians. One is the dominant dialectical framework, which strongly contrasts righteousness through faith with observance of the law. The other is a much less obvious temporal framework, which sees the law and its observance as ordained by God for a specific purpose during a limited period of time. With the coming of Christ, that period of time had now come to an end.

As Paul began to dictate Romans, it was not as simple as trying to convince the Roman Christians of the correctness of the views for which he had become so controversial. His own views were also changing. No doubt this was partly due to how these views were understood or, as he thought, misunderstood by the Roman Christians. But to a significant degree, it was also due to the ways Paul himself was coming to rethink and revise significantly many of the earlier, polemical views he so forcefully argued in Galatians. As we shall see, Paul is not simply defending his previous convictions in a less controversial manner. He is sorting out what these basic convictions really are, discarding some, revising others, and recasting all of them within a different framework.

CHAPTER 3

The Structure, Genre, and Purposes of Romans

*T*HIS CHAPTER, WHICH TURNS DIRECTLY to the Letter to the Romans itself, deals with three basic issues in its interpretation. The first is the structure of the letter; the second, its genre; and the third, the purpose or, more correctly, the purposes of the letter. Two aspects of the letter have not received adequate attention. The first aspect is the importance of the literary cues the letter provides; they are crucial for understanding how Paul structured the letter. These literary cues need to be distinguished from more explicitly theological ways of understanding the letter's structure. The second aspect is what Paul thought the issues were in the letter. These issues need to be distinguished from the broader theological "themes" of the letter. Interpreters of Romans have often, and rightly, pointed to themes such as righteousness or salvation as central. But how and why did these themes become issues between Paul and the Roman Christian community? In order to understand what Paul was about in Romans, one also has to understand what was at stake for Paul in his arguments about these themes. Put another way, one has to understand why Paul used these themes and what he was trying to persuade the Roman Christians of by using them.

THE OVERALL LITERARY STRUCTURE OF ROMANS

When one turns to the literary structure of Romans, the easiest places to start are at the beginning (1:1–15) and the end of the letter (15:14–16:24).[1] Virtually everyone agrees that 1:1–15 and 15:14–16:24 form the letter framework of Romans. Paul begins with an address and greeting to the Roman Christian community (1:1–7). This is followed by a thanksgiving (1:8–10). Both these elements, although

---

[1] I take the original letter to be 1:1–16:24; 16:25–27 is a later non-Pauline addition. For a defense of this position, see Harry Y. Gamble, Jr., *The Textual History of the Letter to the Romans: A Study in Textual and Literary Criticism* (SD 42; Grand Rapids: Eerdmans, 1977).

expanded somewhat, were standard ways in which Paul began his letters.[2] Then, in 1:11–15, Paul explains to the Roman Christians his long-standing desire to come to Rome. As the previous chapter of this study showed, Paul in these verses carefully tries to establish with the Roman Christian community a relationship that was marked by mutuality. He expresses the hope that his visit to the Christian community in Rome will be one through which both he and the Roman Christians are mutually encouraged by each other's faith. Since Paul had not founded the community and so had no authority over it, he first needed to gain an attentive and benevolent hearing from the community. The emphasis on mutual encouragement was an attempt to gain just such a hearing.

At the end of the letter, in 15:14–16:24, Paul returns to the letter framework. He first takes up again the reasons why he has not previously traveled to Rome and why he now wants to come to Rome on his way to Spain (15:14–21). He has completed his work of preaching Christ to the Gentiles of the eastern Mediterranean and now wants to travel by way of Rome to Spain to preach the Gospel there. He then goes on to explain his travel plans more specifically. He must first go to Jerusalem with the collection for the poor among the Jerusalem Christians. After this he will travel to Rome to spend some time with the Roman Christian community and then be sped by the community on his way to preach the gospel in Spain (15:22–33). As seen in the previous chapter of this study, one purpose for Paul's explanation may well have been to enlist their prayerful support that the Jerusalem Christians would accept the collection he was bringing to them. In Romans 16, Paul concludes the letter with a recommendation for Phoebe, who was bringing the letter to Rome; an elaborate list of greetings to various Roman Christians and the house churches to which they belong; and a concluding benediction. Although much more elaborate than usual, Romans 16 basically follows the pattern Paul customarily used to conclude his letters.[3]

There is also a consensus on two aspects of the structure of the body of the letter (1:16–15:13). First, nearly everyone agrees that Paul intended the arguments of 1:16–15:13 to be taken as a whole. This is because the beginning and the end of the body of the letter are marked by an inclusion. In 1:16–17 Paul states the basic proposition or thesis of 1:16–15:13 by claiming that the gospel is the power of God to everyone who has faith, to the Jew first and also to the Greek (i.e., Gentiles). In 15:7–13 he restates this proposition about the centrality of Christ for both Jews and Gentiles and concludes the arguments he has made in the letter. Second, nearly everyone also agrees that 12:1–15:7 forms a distinct exhortatory section of the letter. This section is similar to exhortatory sections found in several of Paul's other letters (1 Thess 4:1–2; 5:12–22; Gal 5:1–6:10; Phil 1:17–2:18).[4]

---

[2]John L. White, "Saint Paul and the Apostolic Letter Tradition," *CBQ* 45(1983): 437–39. For ancient letter writing in general and its relationship to NT letters, see John L. White, *Light from Ancient Letters* (FF; Philadelphia: Fortress, 1986); Stanley K. Stowers, *Letter Writing in Greco-Roman Antiquity* (LEC 5; Philadelphia: Westminster, 1986).

[3]White, "Saint Paul," 439–42.

[4]I accept the view that both 1 Thessalonians and Philippians are made up of several letters. First Thessalonians is made up of two letter fragments (Letter A: 2:12–4:2; Letter B: 1:1–2:12; 4:3–5:28); 4:1–2 and 5:12–22 are exhortations that come toward the end of each of the fragments. See Murphy-O'Connor, *Paul: A Critical Life*, 106–10; Earl J. Richard, *First and*

There are, however, significant variations in how interpreters understand the structure of what comes between 1:16–17 and 15:7–13. Three recent commentaries on Romans illustrate these variations. In the first, Joseph A. Fitzmyer divides 1:16–15:13 into four major parts:[5]

1. Through the gospel the uprightness of God is revealed as justifying people of faith (1:16–4:25).

2. The love of God further assures salvation to those justified by faith (5:1–8:39).

3. This justification and salvation through faith do not contradict God's promises to Israel (9:1–11:36).

4. The demands of upright life in Christ (12:1–15:13).[6]

The second commentary is by Ulrich Wilckens. Although Wilckens agrees with Fitzmyer that there are four major sections to the body of the letter, he divides the sections somewhat differently:[7]

1. Justification of the godless on the basis of faith in Jesus Christ (1:18–5:21).

2. The reality of justification in Christian life (6:1–8:39).

3. The paradoxical reality of election (9:1–11:36).

4. Exhortation (12:1–15:13).[8]

What basically distinguishes Wilckens's division from Fitzmyer's is their placement of Romans 5. For Fitzmyer, Romans 5 goes with what follows (Rom 6–8); for Wilckens, it goes with what precedes (1:18–4:25).

The third example is from James D. G. Dunn's commentary. Unlike either Fitzmyer or Wilckens, Dunn divides the body of Romans into five major parts:[9]

1. The wrath of God on man's unrighteousness (1:18–3:20).

2. God's saving righteousness to faith (3:21–5:21).

3. The outworking of the gospel in relation to the individual (6:1–8:39).

4. The righteousness of God—from God's faithfulness: The outworking of the gospel in relation to Israel (9:1–11:36).

5. The outworking of the gospel for the redefined people of God in everyday terms (12:1–15:13).

Second Thessalonians (SP 11; Collegeville, Minn.: Liturgical Press, 1995), 11–19. Philippians is made up of three letter fragments (Letter A: 1:1–2; 4:10–20; Letter B: 1:3–3:1; 4:4–9, 21–23; Letter C: 3:2–4:3); 1:17–2:18 is the exhortatory section that comes toward the end of Letter B. See Murphy-O'Connor, *Paul: A Critical Life*, 216–20.

[5] Fitzmyer, *Romans*, 96–101.

[6] The commentaries of Byrne (*Romans*, 26–28), Cranfield (*Romans*, 1.27–29), and Moo (*Romans*, 32–35) agree with this division.

[7] Wilckens, *Römer*, 1:ix–x; 2:vii–viii; 3:vii.

[8] Morris (*Romans*, 33–34) also divides the body of Romans in this way.

[9] Dunn, *Romans*, vii–xi.

Dunn also groups together 1:18–3:20 and 3:21–5:21 under the broader rubric of "the righteousness of God—to man's faith," and 6:1–8:39 and 9:1–11:36 under the broader rubric of "the outworking of this gospel in relation to the individual and to the election of grace." Dunn agrees with Wilckens in placing Romans 5 with what precedes. But unlike Fitzmyer or Wilckens, Dunn understands 1:18–3:20 and 3:21–5:21 as distinct sections.[10]

There are two basic differences in these various divisions. The first difference is between Dunn, who distinguishes 1:18–3:20 from what follows, and the other interpreters who do not. This difference, however, is less significant than it appears. Both Fitzmyer and Wilckens also distinguish 1:18–3:20 from what follows. Neither, however, thinks of the division as representing a major break in the development of Paul's thought. The second and more important difference is the placement of Romans 5. For both Wilckens and Dunn, Romans 5 goes with what precedes. For Wilckens, this is because it is still part of Paul's larger argument in 1:18–5:21 about the justification of the godless on the basis of faith in Jesus Christ. In a similar way, for Dunn, Romans 5 draws the conclusions about the new perspective of faith in relation to the individual and to humanity at large that Paul has developed in 1:18–4:25. For Fitzmyer, however, Romans 5 goes with 6:1–8:39 because it moves from the theme of justifying human beings by faith, the theme of 1:16–4:25, to the theme of the love of God as assuring salvation to those justified by faith, the theme of Romans 5–8.

Despite these differences, however, the three interpreters seem to share an underlying presupposition, that Paul structured his letter to the Roman Christian community primarily on the basis of theological themes. This is clearest in Fitzmyer.[11] He describes 1:16–11:36 as the "doctrinal section" of the letter. Within the first two major sections of the letter (1:16–4:25; 5:1–8:39), he also sees the structure in thematic terms. In 1:16–4:25, the theme is first announced (1:16–17), then explained negatively (1:18–3:20), then explained positively (3:21–31), and finally illustrated in the law by the example of Abraham (4:1–25). Similarly in 5:1–8:39, the theme is first announced (5:1–11), then explained (5:1–8:13), and finally developed (8:14–39). Although not as explicitly, the same broadly thematic structuring of Romans is shared by Wilckens and Dunn. All three interpreters see 1:16–11:36 as the development of three basic theological themes: (1) God's wrath and righteousness in relation to faith; (2) Christian living as the outgrowth of God's justification of men and women of faith; and (3) the relationship of all this to God's perduring promises to Israel. Each interpreter may place one or another passage under a different theme. For example, Wilckens and Dunn place Romans 5 under the first theme whereas Fitzmyer places it under the second. All three, however, view the structure of most of the letter under these three general theological themes.[12]

Although these themes no doubt are present in Romans and are important, there are three significant problems with understanding the structure of Romans primarily on the basis of these themes. The first problem is that this way of under-

---

[10] In distinguishing 1:18–3:20 from what follows, Schreiner (*Romans*, 23–27) agrees with Dunn.

[11] See Fitzmyer, *Romans*, 96–102.

[12] The same is true of the other commentators mentioned.

standing clearly reflects the concerns of later theological controversies, that is, some of the central theological controversies rooted in the Reformation and concerning especially the interpretation of Paul. It is not that Fitzmyer, Wilckens, and Dunn are apologists for their respective religious communities' viewpoints. They clearly are not; on the contrary, all three are ecumenically minded and make significant use of the work of scholars of other denominations and of no denomination. Nevertheless, their views of the structure of Romans reflect in important ways later theological controversies about the proper interpretation especially of Paul's notions of justification, faith, and salvation. This does not necessarily mean that their interpretations of the letter's structure are wrong. But it does make one suspect that the varnish of long-standing theological controversies may have obscured the original grain of Paul's letter to the Roman Christian community.

A second problem with structuring Romans along thematic lines is that it tends to inhibit attempts to locate Paul's arguments in Romans consistently within the particular contexts of the Roman Christian community, of Paul's own situation, and of the relationship between the two. It is not that recent interpreters of Romans are unaware of the importance of the various contexts of Romans or that they consider them unimportant. Nevertheless, these contexts do not consistently impinge on their interpretations of the letter. The reason appears to be that when one structures Romans thematically, the theological themes maintain a life of their own. Because these themes have been so central and controversial over the centuries, consistently contextualizing Paul's arguments is difficult. Structuring Romans on the basis of theological themes emphasizes the different subjects treated in Romans, for example, righteousness, faith, or salvation. But it does not take seriously enough the ways in which these different themes become central issues with which Paul has do deal in his relationship with the Roman Christian community.

This leads to the third and most important problem with understanding the structure of Romans. Seeing its structure primarily in thematic terms inhibits attempts to deal adequately with the literary structure of the letter. Like any writer, Paul lived and wrote in a particular time and place and was influenced by the literary conventions of his culture. This does not necessarily mean that he had the wide and deep education of upper-class Greeks and Romans such as Plutarch or Cicero. Nor does it mean that he slavishly followed the literary conventions of his world. But in the end one cannot plausibly maintain that Paul was not affected, or was affected only superficially, by these conventions.[13] After all, Paul was born and raised in Tarsus in Cilicia, a Greek-speaking city. His first language was Greek, and he received a Greek rhetorical education and perhaps some Greek philosophical education at

---

[13] There is considerable controversy about Paul's awareness and use of ancient rhetoric. For a positive assessment, see most recently Margaret M. Mitchell, *The Heavenly Trumpet: John Chrysostom and the Art of Pauline Interpretation* (Louisville: Westminster John Knox, 2002). A much more negative assessment is argued by Stanley E. Porter, "Paul of Tarsus and His Letters," in *Handbook of Classical Rhetoric in the Hellenistic Period (330 BC–AD 400)* (ed. Stanley E. Porter; Leiden: Brill, 1997), 533–85. Mitchell's view is much more persuasive for two reasons. First, John Chrysostom, no mean rhetorician himself, found it quite easy to place Paul's arguments within the context of Greco-Roman rhetoric. Second, the result of Porter's arguments is to leave Paul in a kind of rhetorical limbo, which in the end makes very little sense of Paul's rhetoric.

Tarsus.[14] Thus the least one must do is analyze thoroughly what literary conventions Paul made use of and how he used them. More specifically, are there literary rather than theological cues in Romans that reveal how Paul structured his arguments in the letter?

The following pages will argue three points. First, there are literary cues in Romans that would have guided his Roman Christian audience in understanding the structure of Paul's arguments. Second, the body of Romans (1:16–11:36) is best understood as a diatribe. Third, once one understands the structure of Romans on the basis of these literary cues as a diatribe, one can also understand more clearly the issues that Paul is addressing and not simply the subjects he is discussing. In this way, one can better understand the specific context within which Paul is writing the letter. All of this contributes to an interpretation of Romans that gets below the varnish of centuries of theological controversy to the grain of the letter itself.

LITERARY CUES IN ROMANS

Literary cues in Romans provide guidance for understanding its structure. As mentioned earlier, when one reads the main body of Romans (1:16–11:36), one cannot but be struck by the differences in style between different sections of the text. On the one hand, some sections read like expositions or explanations of a topic. Their tone is calm and not explicitly argumentative. Romans 1:18–32, 3:21–26, 5:1–21, and 8:1–30 are of this sort. On the other hand, other sections of Romans are quite argumentative or polemical in style. Romans 2:1–3:20, 3:27–4:25, 6:1–7:25, and 8:31–11:36 are of this sort; these sections are marked by various literary devices that create a much livelier, more engaged, and argumentative tone.[15] These literary devices include rhetorical questions,[16] apostrophes (addresses to imaginary interlocutors),[17] dialogues with imaginary interlocutors,[18] refutations of objections and false conclusions,[19] speeches-in-character,[20] comparisons of various sorts,[21] and

---

[14] Murphy-O'Connor, *Paul: A Critical Life*, 32–51, esp. 46–51, makes the case for Paul receiving a good Greek education in Tarsus. Most recently, Troels Engberg-Pedersen (*Paul and the Stoics* [Louisville: Westminster John Knox, 2000]) argues that Paul was influenced by the Stoics. One needs to take with a grain of salt Paul's claim in Acts 22:3 that he grew up in Jerusalem. The claim represents Luke's later interest in linking Paul as closely as possible to Jerusalem.

[15] For explanations of many of these terms, see R. Dean Anderson, Jr., *Glossary of Greek Rhetorical Terms Connected to Methods of Argumentation, Figures, and Tropes from Anaximenes to Quintilian* (Louvain: Peeters, 2000); and Heinrich Lausberg, *Handbook of Literary Rhetoric: A Foundation for Literary Study* (ed. David E. Orton and R. Dean Anderson; trans. Matthew T. Bliss, Annemiek Jansen, and David E. Orton; Leiden: Brill, 1998).

[16] Rom 2:3, 4, 21, 22, 23, 26; 3:1, 3, 5, 6, 7, 8, 9, 27, 29, 31; 4:1, 3, 9, 10; 6:1, 2, 3, 15, 16, 21; 7:1, 7, 13, 24; 8:31, 32, 33, 34, 35; 9:14, 19, 20, 21, 24, 30, 32; 10:7, 8, 14, 15, 16, 18, 19; 11:1, 2, 4, 7, 11, 15, 34, 35.

[17] Rom 2:1–11, 17–29; 9:20–29; 11:11–24.

[18] Rom 3:1–10; 3:27–4:2.

[19] Rom 3:1–9, 27–31; 4:1–2; 6:1–3, 15–16; 7:7, 13–14; 9:14–15, 19–20; 11:1, 19.

[20] Rom 7:7–25; 10:6–8.

[21] Rom 2:6–10, 12–16; 6:4–11, 15–23; 7:1–6; 8:5–17; 9:30–33; 11:17–24.

examples.[22] The style of these passages is also enlivened by the frequent use of phrases such as "What then?" (τί οὖν;) in 3:9; 6:15; 11:7; "What then shall we say?" (τί οὖν ἐροῦμεν;) in 3:5; 4:1; 6:1; 7:7; 8:31; 9:14, 30; "Certainly not!" (μὴ γένοιτο) in 3:4, 6, 31; 6:2, 15; 7:7, 13; 9:14, 30; and "O man!" (ὦ ἄνθρωπε) in 2:1, 3; 9:20. Paul's use of these literary devices and phrases in the argumentative sections creates a very different tone from that found in the expository sections, from which they are almost completely missing.

All this may seem like an interesting rhetorical or literary observation, but there are important reasons to think that it is much more than that. These expository and argumentative passages are distinct from one another in two other important ways. First, with the exception of 1:18–32, the expository sections have in common that they draw on and develop traditional cultic language and imagery about Christ's death as a sacrifice. This is most clearly the case in 3:24–26, where Paul quotes fragments of a traditional creedal formula that confesses Christ as one "whom God put forth as an expiation . . . by means of his blood" (3:25). Although less obvious, traditional cultic language about the death of Christ lies behind 5:8–9, where Paul describes believers as being made righteous by "the blood of Christ," who "died on our behalf." This same is also true of 8:3, where Paul likewise uses traditional cultic language and imagery to describe "God sending his own Son in the likeness of sinful flesh and as a sin-offering." The language is traditional in all three cases.[23] This cultic language about the death of Christ is, then, something Paul and his Roman Christian audience have in common. It is also clear that 1:18–32 is a fairly traditional and uncontroversial piece of Hellenistic Jewish critique of pagan religion. Paul, then, also shared the viewpoints expressed in 1:18–32 with his Roman Christian audience, much as he shared the cultic language and imagery of the other expository sections with them. All four expository sections, then, have in common that they are rooted in, or appeal to, traditional viewpoints shared by Paul and his Roman Christian audience.

In addition, odd as it may seem, none of these expository sections ever quotes from the Jewish scriptures. The argumentative sections of the letter, however, are marked, for the most part, by Paul's extensive use of the Scriptures. This is clearly the case for 2:1–3:20, where Paul employs them to argue for the equal sinfulness of Jews and Gentiles, and for 3:27–4:25, where he appeals extensively to them for his interpretation of Abraham's faith. It is also true of 8:31–11:36, where Paul draws extensively on the Scriptures to defend God's faithfulness to the promises made to Israel. Even in 6:1–7:25, where Paul uses only one scriptural quotation ("you shall not covet/desire") in 7:7 from Exod 20:17//Deut 5:18, this quotation is the basis for his whole argument in 7:8–25.

These expository and argumentative sections, however, are not only distinct from one another; they are also interrelated to one another in four fairly complex ways. First, each of the livelier, more argumentative sections takes off from some aspect of the preceding expository section. In 2:1, Paul begins by drawing a conclusion

---

[22] Rom 4:1–25; 9:6–9, 10–15, 16–18.

[23] The justification for this will be found later in the detailed interpretations of the particular passages.

from 1:18–32, "Therefore [διό] you have no excuse, whoever you are when you judge another." In 6:1, he begins with, "What shall we say then [οὖν]?" referring back to what he wrote in 5:1–21. Finally, in 8:31, Paul begins with, "What then [οὖν] shall we say to this?" referring back to 8:1–30. Each of the argumentative sections turns to issues raised by the expository sections of the letter. In terms of ancient rhetoric, the expository sections roughly correspond to the positive argumentation of a speech; the more polemical sections correspond to the part of the speech devoted to the refutation of objections.[24]

Second, in 3:21–26, 5:1–21, and 8:1–30 (the second, third, and fourth expository sections), Paul consistently moves beyond the previous argumentative section to a new stage in his argument. In 3:21, Paul begins with, "But now [Νυνὶ δέ] the righteousness of God has been manifested apart from the law." Paul is contrasting the past situation described in 1:18–3:20 with the present situation of the manifestation of God's righteousness in 3:21–26. In 5:1, Paul begins with, "Therefore [οὖν], being made righteous by faith, let us have peace with God through our Lord Jesus Christ." In Romans 5 Paul moves from the issue of 3:21–4:25, righteousness for Jews and Gentiles alike through faith apart from the law, to the issue of the incompatibility of this righteousness with sin. The latter issue dominates all of Romans 5–7. Finally, in 8:1, Paul claims, "There is therefore now [ἄρα νῦν] no condemnation for those who are in Christ Jesus." This stands in contrast to the terrible situation of the man whose speech-in-character is found in 7:7–25. Paul then introduces the Spirit, contrasts it with the flesh, and describes its role in making believers sons of God and heirs. He moves his whole argument in the direction of a universalizing eschatology, which is explicitly the subject of 8:18–30 and 8:31–11:36.

Third, Paul clearly intends the larger arguments of 1:18–3:20, 3:21–4:25, 5:1–7:25, and 8:1–11:36 to be taken as an articulated whole and not as four discrete arguments. His larger arguments are linear in the sense of being sequential and interlocking. This is clear, first of all, from the literary cues in 3:21; 5:1, 8:1 just mentioned. More broadly, however, Paul intends his larger arguments in 1:18–11:36 to be sequential and interlocking in that each successive stage is a development of, and a response to, the previous stage. His argument in 3:21–4:25 is that the righteousness of God is *now* made manifest apart from the law for both Jews and Greeks equally. This new manifestation of God's righteousness upholds, as the example of Abraham shows, the Jewish scriptures. Paul intends this argument as both a development from, and a response to, his previous claim in 1:18–3:20 about the equal sinfulness of both Jews and Greeks. Likewise, his arguments in 5:1–7:25 are that this new righteousness through faith apart from the law is incompatible with continued sinfulness. This section concerns the issue of how believers can live lives pleasing to God apart from the observance of the law. This issue was implicit in Paul's earlier claim in 3:21–4:25 that righteousness is now no longer connected with

---

[24] Both of these parts of a speech fall under the general rubric of "proofs." The terms used to describe them vary. Cicero, *Inv.* 1.19, distinguishes between *confirmatio* and *reprehensio;* the author of *Rhet. Her.* 1.4, between *confirmatio* and *confutatio;* and Quintilian, *Inst.* 3.9.1, between *probatio* and *refutatio.* Aristotle, *Rhet.* 3.13.4–5, with wonderful impatience, simply includes refutation (ἔλεγχος) as part of the section of speeches devoted to proofs.

observance of the law. Finally, Paul's struggles in 8:1–11:36 over the interlocking eschatological fate of Jews and Gentiles are attempts to come to terms with an issue implicit in 1:18–7:25 as whole. If God intends this righteousness for Jews and Gentiles equally, what does one make of the present reality that most Jews have not accepted it? More important, in the light of God's promises to Israel, what does this present rejection by most of Israel mean for the future eschatological fate of Israel? Have God's promises to Israel failed? Paul means all of the arguments of 1:16–11:36, then, to form one articulated and interlocking argument that responds to these issues.

Finally, Paul's arguments are also linear in the sense that he places them in a temporal sequence. Romans 1:18–3:20 deals with the previous equally sinful situation of both Jews and Gentiles. Romans 3:21–4:25 deals with the new situation of righteousness through faith made possible by the death of Christ. This new righteousness is apart from the law and intended for Jews and Gentiles alike. Romans 5:1–7:25 deals with the ethical consequences for both Jews and Gentiles that follow on this new righteousness. Finally, 8:1–11:36 deals with the future eschatological fate of Jews and Gentiles. The framework of Paul's arguments in Romans, then, is intentionally and essentially temporal or historical in character. It is crucial to understand from the beginning how different this framework in Romans is from the dominant framework of his arguments in Galatians. As seen in the previous chapter, the dominant framework of most of Paul's arguments in Galatians was dialectical, a series of stark, almost in-principle contrasts that allow for no resolution. Even though Paul deals with many of the same themes in both letters, the interpretive framework he uses in each of them is very different. In Romans he uses the temporal or historical framework that he had previously used in Phil 3:2–11 to interpret his initial experience of the risen Jesus and its consequences.[25] This temporal or historical framework was even present at several points in Galatians (1:14; 3:19–25; 5:1; 6:2).[26] But in Galatians, this temporal or historical framework was overwhelmed by the dominance of stark, almost in-principle contrasts. In Romans, however, it becomes the dominant framework. The importance of this different interpretive framework and how it fundamentally changes the character of Paul's arguments will become clearer from a more detailed look at Paul's arguments, contrasting them with Paul's more dialectical arguments in his earlier letter to the Galatians.

If one takes all of these cues seriously, then the overall structure of much of the letter looks significantly different from the proposals mentioned earlier in this chapter:

1:16–17 (proposition)

1. 1:18–3:20

    a. 1:18–32 (expository)
    b. 2:1–3:20 (argumentative)

---

[25] See pp. 55–56, above.
[26] See pp. 168–70, above.

2. 3:21–4:25

    a. 3:21–26 (expository)

    b. 3:27–4:25 (argumentative)

3. 5:1–7:25

    a. 5:1–21 (expository)

    b. 6:1–7:25 (argumentative)

4. 8:1–11:36

    a. 8:1–30 (expository)

    b. 8:31–11:36 (argumentative)

5. 12:1–15:7 (exhortatory)

    15:8–13 (conclusion)

Each expository or explanatory section develops a position based on traditional views Paul believes he and his Roman Christian audience have in common. These expositions of shared beliefs then serve as the basis for the much more argumentative sections that follow the expository ones. In these argumentative sections, Paul seems to be defending his positions on various issues, for the most part on the basis of interpretations of the Jewish scriptures. In addition, the structure of Paul's arguments is linear or sequential in terms of logical development but especially in terms of a temporal or historical framework. Each successive section is either a development of, or a response to, the previous section. Finally, it is crucial to realize, on the basis of this literary analysis, that each argumentative section of the letter is significantly longer than the preceding expository section. About three-quarters of 1:18–11:36 is argumentative, and only one-quarter is expository. This especially highlights the importance of understanding what Paul wrote in Romans not primarily in terms of themes or subject matter but in terms of issues between himself and the Roman Christian audience he was addressing.

The Diatribe and the Genre of Romans 1:16–11:36

Before turning to these issues, however, a further literary question about Romans is in order. When Paul was writing Romans, what sort of document did he think he was writing? When the Roman Christian community heard his letter read to them, what kind of document did they think they were hearing? Put another way, to what rhetorical or literary genre did they think the body of Romans belonged? The answer is important for the interpretation of Romans because it establishes the interpretive framework within which Paul wrote the letter and within which his Roman Christian audience would have heard it.

The issue of genre is very complex, both today and in the ancient Greco-Roman world. This study, which deals specifically with the argument of Paul's letter to the Romans, cannot hope to deal adequately with this complexity. But something needs to be said about genre in the context of the Greco-Roman world and what the genre is to which the body of Romans belongs. The position here is that both Paul and the Roman Christians would have understood the body of Romans (1:16–11:36) as a diatribe.

Literary and rhetorical genres in the Greco-Roman world concerned especially conventions and expectations.[27] When ancient readers or hearers read or heard something, they expected writers or orators to do different things in order to accomplish different purposes. How the authors composed something obviously depended on what they wanted to accomplish. Conversely, readers and hearers understood the purposes of a work by recognizing how it was composed. This meant that authors and audiences shared sets of conventions. These conventions, of necessity, were not individual or private but common and public. Ancient readers had certain expectations about what historians did and other expectations about what philosophers did. Ancient audiences expected one kind of oratory in the courtroom and another in the public assembly. These shared expectations and conventions are what is meant here by "genre."

In the Greco-Roman world, the conventions of some genres received considerable explicit attention. This was especially the case for rhetoric intended for public occasions. For example, we have a number of works intended to describe and, to a certain extent, prescribe how judicial rhetoric should be used in the courtroom and how deliberative rhetoric should be used in the public assembly. These treatises were quite explicit about the structure of such works, the kinds of arguments to be used, even their style and diction.[28] To a lesser extent, the same was also true for the conventions of letter writing.[29] The conventions of other genres, however, such as history and biography, philosophical treatises, moral exhortations of various sorts, and novels were given much less explicit attention. In the case of histories and biographies, writers often signaled what they thought they were doing through the preface to their work or by remarks in the body of the work itself.[30]

The conventions were of various types, but they are not susceptible to a systematic presentation. In prose works, some conventions concerned the subject of the work, its size, whether it was written or originally oral, its function, occasion, context, and purpose. Other conventions concerned the structure of the work. For example, is the work a narrative, a collection, a dialogue, an argument, or a series of arguments? Still other conventions concerned the various kinds of literary units in a

---

[27] In this discussion of genres, I am much indebted to two works. The first is Alastair Fowler, *Kinds of Literature: An Introduction to the Theory of Genres and Modes* (Cambridge: Harvard University Press, 1982); and Richard A. Burridge, *What Are the Gospels? A Comparison with Graeco-Roman Biography* (SNTSMS 70; Cambridge: Cambridge University Press, 1992), esp. 26–54.

[28] E.g., Aristotle, *Rhetorica;* Cicero, *De oratore, De inventione rhetorica,* and *Orator ad M. Brutum; Rhetorica ad Herennium;* Quintillian, *Institutio oratoria.*

[29] For examples, see Abraham J. Malherbe, *Ancient Epistolary Theorists* (SBLSBS 19; Atlanta: Scholars Press, 1988).

[30] For histories see, e.g., Herodotus, *Hist.* 1.1; Thucydides, *Hist.* 1.1–2; Polybius, *Hist.* 1.1.1–1.2.8; Diodorus Siculus, *Bibl. hist.* 1.1.1–14.7; Sallust, *Bell. Cat.* 1.1–4.5; Livy, praef.; Josephus, *J.W.* 1.1–30; *Ant.* 1.1–26. For biographies, see, e.g., Nepos, *Pel.* 1.1; Plutarch, *Alex.* 1.1–3; Tacitus, *Agr.* 1.

work (e.g., speeches, anecdotes, maxims, catalogues, examples, syllogisms, enthymemes); style (e.g., high, popular, comic) and the topics treated in the work; or the relationship of the writer to his or her audience (e.g., is the author trying to persuade, reprove, edify, entertain, encourage, or instruct?). A genre was the fairly stable clustering of different conventions such that they formed a commonly recognized pattern. These patterns then informed the ways in which authors composed, and readers and hearers understood, these compositions.

In trying to understand how genres functioned in the ancient Greek and Roman worlds, we also need to keep in mind five other points. First, ancient readers and audiences were able to recognize particular genres even when these genres were not the subject of explicit treatments. They were recognized by means of the different sets of literary or rhetorical conventions used in them. This was certainly the case, for example, for ancient novels or romances. We have no specific explanations from the ancient world about how they should be composed. Nevertheless, they fall into recognizable patterns.[31]

Second, concerning ancient genres, reference has been made here to sets of conventions and sets of expectations rather than to definitions. Definitions are often not very helpful in understanding genres and sometimes are even misleading. They tend to be prescriptive rather than descriptive of what an ancient literary or rhetorical genre was and how it was recognized and functioned. In addition, definitions often have to be so general that they prove virtually useless in understanding the conventions and expectations of ancient works of literature or rhetoric. For example, to define "history" as "a longer prose narrative of significant events" contributes little to our understanding of how the conventions and expectations of ancient histories differ from those of modern histories.

Third, the same conventions were often shared by different genres. The boundaries between them were often porous and overlapping. For example, ancient biographies often shared conventions with histories, encomia, moral philosophy, and several other genres.[32] What made a genre recognizable was not so much features unique to it but the clustering and concentration of certain conventions that individually it shared with other genres. Genres were flexible.

Fourth, genres developed and changed over time. One often cannot understand a work's genre simply by appealing to the conventions of a previous age. The clustering and concentration of conventions shift.

Finally, it is important to take one's cues about ancient genres from actual examples rather than from ancient literary or rhetorical handbooks. Consulting such handbooks is certainly useful, but they tend to present what someone thought a genre should be rather than what it actually was in all of its variety. For example, Cicero, in good lawyerly fashion, often violated in his speeches the rules he laid down in his own treatises on rhetoric.

---

[31] See B. P. Reardon, *The Form of Greek Romance* (Princeton, N.J.: Princeton University Press, 1991); and *Collected Ancient Greek Novels* (Berkeley, Calif.: University of California Press, 1989), 1–16; Tomas Hägg, *The Novel in Antiquity* (Berkeley, Calif.: University of California Press, 1983), 81–124.

[32] Burridge, *What Are the Gospels?* 66.

With this in mind, we can turn to the issue of the diatribe itself. In modern English, the word "diatribe" usually refers to bitter or abusive speech or writing. This usage needs to be distinguished from the way the word was used in the Greco-Roman world. In Greek, the word διατριβή ("diatribe") itself had a range of meanings. It could mean "pastime" or "amusement," or, in a negative sense, "waste of time." It could also refer to study or even a school of philosophy.[33] The range of meanings that interests us, however, is "classroom instruction" or "school discourse," usually of an ethical-religious nature.[34] The classroom or school in question was the philosophical school rather than a primary or secondary school.

The most important study on the diatribe in recent years is that of Stanley K. Stowers.[35] Stowers reviews the history, from the late nineteenth century on, of scholarship about the diatribe. He then analyzes various ancient texts that have been described as diatribes and draws several very helpful conclusions. First, "diatribe" was not a technical term for a genre in antiquity. It is, however, an appropriate and useful term for certain works that originated in the philosophical schools or imitated the style of the school discourse.[36] Against Bultmann, Stowers convincingly shows that the diatribe should not be located in popular Cynic-Stoic preaching before crowds. Second, the diatribe needs to be distinguished from technical instructions in logic, physics, philosophy, and so forth. Diatribes were discourses or instructions of a more popular sort in which there was a strong dialogical or Socratic component. They were not, however, dialogues. The purpose of diatribes was not simply to impart knowledge but to transform students, to point out error and cure it.[37] Stowers's reassessment of texts usually classified as diatribes has shown that they all employed a similar dialogical style in varying degrees and also that they grew out of the context of the philosophical school rather than out of popular Cynic-Stoic preaching.[38]

The discourses of Teles (fl. ca. 235 B.C.), Musonius Rufus (ca. 30–100), Musonius's pupil Epictetus (ca. 55–135), and some of the discourses of Dio of Prusa (ca. 45–112) and Plutarch of Chaeronea (before 50 to after 120) have usually been classed as diatribes. In addition, certain works of Philo of Alexandria (ca. 10 B.C. to after A.D. 40), Seneca the Younger (ca. 2 B.C.–A.D. 65), and Maximus of Tyre (second century A.D.) have been said to contain the style of the diatribe.[39] From among

---

[33] See LSJ, s.v. διατριβή.

[34] The definition of Hermogenes is often cited in this regard: "A diatribe is the extension of a short thought of an ethical nature so that the moral character of the speaker might become fixed in the mind of the hearer" (διατριβή ἐστι βραχέος διανοήματος ἠθικοῦ ἔκτασις, ἵνα ἐμμείνῃ τὸ ἦθος τοῦ λέγοντος ἐν τῇ γνώμῃ τοῦ ἀκούοντος). This is, however, misleading. Hermogenes is actually referring to a rhetorical figure and not to a kind of ethical discourse or instruction.

[35] Stanley K. Stowers, *The Diatribe and Paul's Letter to the Romans* (SBLDS 57; Chico, Calif.: Scholars Press, 1981). Two other recent works also need to be mentioned, although neither is as helpful as Stowers's: George L. Kustas, *Diatribe in Ancient Rhetorical Theory* (Berkeley, Calif.: Center for Hermeneutical Studies, 1976); Thomas Schmeller, *Paulus und die "Diatribe": Eine Vergleichende Stilinterpretation* (NTAbh NF 19; Münster: Aschendorff, 1987).

[36] Stowers, *Diatribe,* 77.

[37] Ibid., 76.

[38] Ibid.

[39] Ibid. 49.

these authors, the most helpful for our purposes is Epictetus. There are two reasons for this. First, unlike either Teles or Maximus of Tyre, Epictetus wrote only a generation or two after Paul. Second and more important, the discourses of Epictetus have preserved the lively oral character and style of the diatribe much better than the works of Musonius, Plutarch, Seneca, or Philo. The diatribes of Musonius and Plutarch and the diatribe style in Seneca and Philo of Alexandria have all, to a greater or lesser extent, undergone a process of *letteraturizzazione*, that is, the movement of the rhetoric of the diatribe in the direction of more literary composition.[40]

We owe the preservation of Epictetus's discourses to his pupil Arrian. In his letter to Lucius Gellius at the beginning of his collections of the discourses, Arrian claimed that he tried as best as he could to write down word for word what he heard from Epictetus (*Ep.* 2). There is some reason to think that the process was more complicated than that. In his recent commentary on the first book of Epictetus's discourses *(Diatribae [Dissertationes])*, Robert F. Dobbin has argued that the discourses as we now have them are too polished to be simply impromptu. He suspects that Epictetus himself was responsible for the discourses as we now have them but that he also tried to "preserve the dramatic context from which they probably developed."[41] That is certainly possible. It is also possible that Arrian himself was responsible for some editorial additions, such as placing some of the discourses in a particular situation. In any case, there is little doubt that the discourses as we now have them still maintain the lively character and style of their original oral presentation in a school setting.

As Arrian indicates in his letter, Epictetus delivered his discourses as instructions to hearers in a school context. Their purpose was to "incite the minds of his hearers to the best things." Their effect, according to Arrian, was such that "when Epictetus himself spoke them, the hearer could not help but feel exactly what Epictetus wanted him to feel." His audience would have consisted mostly of men who came to hear his discourses of their own free will. They would have been attracted to him by his reputation for teaching others how to live "in accord with nature."[42] The contents of these discourses were, for the most part, of an ethical-religious nature. Those who heard them were not schoolboys whose parents had sent them to him for primary or secondary education; they were not a captive audience. Since the relationship between Epictetus and his audience was voluntary and not compulsory, his ability to hold an audience depended on the persuasive power of the discourses themselves and not on any external coercion.

There is considerable variety in Epictetus's discourses.[43] Their size varies widely. The shortest (*Diatr.* 2.25), which is an apothegm rather than a discourse, is

---

[40] Ibid. 65.

[41] Robert F. Dobbin in Epictetus, *Discourses, Book I* (trans. Robert F. Dobbin; Oxford: Clarendon, 1998), xxii.

[42] The phrase "according to nature" (κατὰ φύσιν) appears fifty-two times in Epictetus's discourses.

[43] We are still in need of a thorough study of the rhetorical structure of Epictetus's discourses. The purpose here is more limited. It is to show how aspects of the rhetorical structure and techniques in Epictetus's discourses throw light on the rhetorical structure and techniques of Romans.

only 65 words long. The longest (4.1) is more than 5,800 words. About 44 of the discourses range between 150 and 700 words. Another 35 range between 800 and 1,300. Twelve range between 1,300 and 1,700. Finally, the three longest discourses (3.22, 24; 4.1) are about 3,350, 3,800, and 5,850 words respectively. In addition, several discourses (1.11, 13; 2.24; 3.1, 4, 5, 7, 9; 4.6, 7) should be classified as dialogues rather than diatribes. With the exception of 4.6, 7, these dialogues are introduced with a brief description of the occasion.

Most of the discourses, however, also have a good deal in common. The common elements establish the conventions and expectations that make the diatribe recognizable. These common elements are especially apparent in the rhetorical techniques Epictetus uses. Above all else, they establish and maintain the lively, dialogical style of the diatribes.[44] They include, first of all, rhetorical questions, with which Epictetus's diatribes are filled. In addition, they include apostrophes (addresses to imaginary interlocutors),[45] dialogues with imaginary interlocutors,[46] objections and false conclusions,[47] speeches-in-character,[48] comparisons,[49] and examples.[50] Several phrases occur frequently that also contribute to the lively, dialogical flavor: "O man!" (ἄνθρωπε); "What then . . . ?" (τί οὖν); and "Not at all!" (μὴ γένοιτο).[51] Epictetus also frequently uses quotations, mostly from Homer, as authorities to support arguments he is making.[52]

Through these rhetorical devices Epictetus often created lively exchanges between himself and imaginary interlocutors or addressees. In these exchanges, he was, first, trying to point out some failing or misunderstanding on the part of these interlocutors or addressees. Second, he was also trying to persuade them about how to live their lives properly, in accord with nature. In neither case, however, was he directly addressing his actual hearers. Rather, he was addressing them only indirectly. This indirection played an important role in the way in which these diatribes functioned. Because Epictetus was not directly accusing his audience of the faults and failings he was talking about, the audience could identify themselves with him in both what he was censuring and what he was advocating. They could then take to heart what he was saying without feeling that they were being directly attacked. Of

---

[44] For a survey of the devices used by authors of diatribes, see Heinrich Weber, *De Senecae philosophi dicendi genere Bioneo* (Marburg: F. Soemmering, 1895), 6–33.

[45] E.g., Epictetus, *Diatr.* 1.2.33; 1.4.14–17; 1.6.23–28, 37–38, 40–43; 2.8.9–14; 2.14.18–22; 2.22.83–85; 3.24.75–77, 78–83.

[46] E.g., Epictetus, *Diatr.* 1.2.2–3, 9–11, 36–29, 30–31; 1.6.3–7; 1.7.6–9; 2.22.7–12, 19–22; 2.14.14–17; 3.22.26–44; 3.24.22–30, 45–55.

[47] E.g., Epictetus, *Diatr.* 1.2.34–35; 1.6.30–32.

[48] E.g., Epictetus, *Diatr.* 1.4.28–29; 1.9.12–16; 1.26.5–7, 10, 20–22, 26–49; 3.24.68–70, 97–102.

[49] E.g., Epictetus, *Diatr.* 1.4.20–21, 30–32; 1.6.12–22, 23–24; 1.16.4–5; 2.8.15–23; 2.11.2–4; 2.14.4–6, 23–25; 3.22.3–8, 14–18; 3.24.31–37, 91.

[50] E.g., Epictetus, *Diatr.* 1.2.2, 8–11, 12–18, 19–24, 25, 32; 1.4.13; 1.6.32–36; 1.9.22–26; 1.26.11–12; 2.22.57–58, 78–80, 90–92.

[51] "O man!" occurs sixty-two times; "What then?" occurs eighty times; "Not at all!" occurs thirty-two times.

[52] Epictetus, *Diatr.* 1.12.3; 1.24.16; 1.28.7; 2.1.13; 2.8.26; 2.12.16; 2.18.32; 2.19.12; 2.22.11, 14; 2.24.23; 3.1.38–39; 3.10.2–3; 3.11.4; 3.22.30, 72, 92, 108; 3.24.13; 4.1.20, 131; 4.4.34; 4.8.32; 4.10.35.

course, this was a rhetorical fiction. But it was a useful, even necessary, one. His hearers were not schoolboys who could simply be lectured at or berated. This fiction enabled Epictetus to address the faults and failings of his hearers without directly attacking and alienating them. It also enabled his hearers to identify themselves with Epictetus and to feel superior to those whose faults and failings Epictetus was censuring, even though these faults and failings were actually their own.

Finally, we need to look beyond the rhetorical devices, which give diatribes their recognizable character, to their larger structure. As mentioned, the diatribes of Epictetus contain considerable variety. Most of them begin with a statement of the proposition, the position he is going to argue. After this, however, there is much fluidity to their structure. The extent to which he uses the rhetorical devices mentioned above varies. Sometimes a diatribe is made up almost entirely of these devices. Sometimes, however, Epictetus's discourses also include expository passages, which usually function to clarify and support the other arguments he is making. They serve as a less controversial explanation or foundation for the other arguments. Examples of diatribes making use of such expository passages are *Diatr.* 1.2; 1.4; 1.6; 1.12; 1.27; 2.1; 2.10; 2.11; 3.24.[53] For our purposes, these diatribes are the most helpful in understanding the genre of Rom 1:16–11:36.

Since these expository passages all tended to serve a similar function, perhaps the best way to get a sense of how they functioned is to use an example. The subject of *Diatr.* 1.6 is providence (πρόνοια).[54] The proposition Epictetus wants to argue is that it is easy to praise providence on two conditions. First, one needs a comprehensive view of the things that happen to each person; and second, one needs a sense of gratitude (1.6.1–2). In the rest of the discourse, he argues for each of these points in turn. In 1.6.3–22, Epictetus argues that the order and design of the universe point to an intelligent designer who has providentially created this order and design. In 1.6.23–43, he argues that the order and design of the universe call for gratitude rather than complaining. In most of his arguments, Epictetus uses rhetorical devices such as example (1.6.3–9, 30–31, 32–36), comparison (1.6.23–27), apostrophe (1.6.37–39, 41–43), dialogue with an imaginary interlocutor (1.6.3–9), and numerous rhetorical questions (e.g., 1.6.23–26).

At several points in this discourse, however, Epictetus uses exposition to explain more clearly the point he is making. In 1.6.7 he explains the basic comparison between human-made objects and natural objects. This comparison then serves as the basis for his argument from design for the existence of God as maker. In 1.6.10, he explains how the human intellect not only has the forms of sensible objects impressed on it but also is able to manipulate these forms in various ways. Such a wonderful capacity points beyond mere chance to the existence of a designer who made the human intellect.[55] In 1.6.13–22, Epictetus explains the providentially designed relationship between human beings and the animal world. Because they are made

---

[53] The expository sections in these discourses are the following: Epictetus, *Diatr.* 1.2.1, 5–7; 1.4.1–4, 18–21; 1.6.1–3, 13–22, 40; 1.12.1–4, 7, 17; 1.27.1–4, 7; 2.1.2–3, 6–7, 10–14, 29, 40; 2.10.1–3, 5–6; 2.11.1–2, 13, 23–25; 3.14.1–3, 9–12, 22–24, 84–87.

[54] For a more thorough commentary on this discourse, see Dobbin in Epictetus, *Discourses*, 101–13.

[55] For Stoics such as Epictetus, this designer is God or nature. See ibid., 101–3.

for human use, animals need to make use of sensible impressions in order to drink, eat, copulate, and whatever else satisfies them. But they do not need to understand their use. Human beings, however, are designed by God to be both spectators and interpreters of his works. Because of this, God made them not only with the faculty to make use of sensible impressions but also with the faculty to understand them. Both of these explanations deal with God's providential order and design of the universe. The final expository section deals with the issue of complaint versus gratitude. In 1.6.40, Epictetus explains how God has not only given human beings the faculties to endure all that happens; he has also given them these faculties in such a way as to enable them to control them completely. There can thus be no grounds for moaning or complaining against God, but only gratitude toward him who is the benefactor of the human race in all things. Although these expository sections made up only about 25 percent of the discourse, they play an important role in clarifying and supporting the other arguments Epictetus is making in the rest of the discourse. In themselves, they are meant to be fairly uncontroversial and serve as the foundation or basis for Epictetus's more controversial applications of them to the ways in which human beings should conduct their lives.

There are obvious similarities between the conventions of the diatribe and the body of Paul's letter to the Romans. As mentioned, the most obvious is Paul's frequent use of many of the same rhetorical devices found in the diatribe.[56] The polemical sections of Romans are all marked by the lively, argumentative, dialogical style of the diatribe. Although Paul made use of some of these devices in his other letters, their use in Romans is much more varied and frequent than in his other letters. But the similarities also go beyond the use of rhetorical devices in several significant ways. First, although Rom 1:16–11:36 is certainly longer than almost all of Epictetus's discourses, it is shorter than *Diatr.* 4.1, the longest of the discourses. About 5,000 words in length, Rom 1:16–11:36 stands between *Diatr.* 3.24 (ca. 3,800 words) and *Diatr.* 4.1 (ca. 5,800 words); it is within the range of what would be thought of as a diatribe. Second, Paul employs a number of quotations from the Jewish scriptures both as a basis of, and as a support for, his arguments in Rom 1:16–11:36. This is similar to, although not identical with, the citations of authority, especially of Homer, used by Epictetus in his discourses. Third, like several of Epictetus's diatribes, Rom 1:16–11:36 alternates between expository passages and much more argumentative passages. Like the diatribes of Epictetus, these calmer, more expository passages are also much shorter than the longer and more argumentative ones. In Romans they make up roughly a quarter of the text; the same is true for the expository passages in Epictetus, *Diatr.* 1.6; 2.1.[57] The expository sections in both Epictetus and Rom 1:16–11:36 also serve similar functions, as the bases and the supports of the more argumentative sections.

Taken together, the similarities between Rom 1:16–11:36 and some of Epictetus's discourses indicate that Paul's Roman audience probably would have understood this section of Romans as a diatribe and that Paul himself was intentionally using the conventions of the diatribe as he wrote this section of the letter. The

---

[56] See above, p. 93, for examples of these devices in Romans.

[57] The relative size of the expository sections in the other discourses is smaller.

contention that 1:16–11:36 should be understood as a Greco-Roman diatribe goes beyond what other interpreters of Romans have advocated. This is even true of Stowers, who has made the strongest case for diatribal elements in Romans. Even he is reluctant about claiming that 1:16–11:36 as a whole should be seen as a diatribe.[58]

There are several reasons for this reluctance, and these reasons point, at least initially, to what seem to be obvious differences between Romans and the diatribe. In reality, however, they point to how Paul recognized the conventions of the diatribe and used them for his own purposes. First, it is true that the overall literary genre of Romans is a letter and not a diatribe. But the bodies of ancient letters were their most variable part and often contained a variety of genres. This is the case in some of Paul's other letters. For example, the bodies of Galatians and 1 Corinthians are best taken as examples of deliberative rhetoric.[59] In addition, we have several collections of pseudonymous Cynic "letters" attributed to earlier Greek sages such as Anacharsis, Crates, Diogenes, and Heraclitus.[60] Many of them actually originated during the first century B.C. or the first two centuries A.D.[61] Several of these letters are really diatribes placed in a letter framework.[62] The framing genre of a letter therefore does not necessarily indicate the genre or genres found in the body of the letter itself. In the case of Romans, the obvious fact that the framework of Romans is that of a letter does not make what is found in Rom 1:16–11:36 any less a diatribe.

A second reason for the reluctance to think of 1:16–11:36 as a diatribe is the presence of the expository passages contained in it (1:18–32; 3:21–26; 5:1–21; 8:1–30). In the past, the presence of these passages seemed to preclude Romans from being understood as a diatribe. The comparison of Romans with some of Epictetus's discourses, however, shows that this is not really the case. Some of Epictetus's diatribes contain expository passages, and these passages usually serve as explanations or foundations for the longer, more argumentative passages. The presence of these expository passages, then, is well within the conventions of a diatribe. This initial reluctance, however, does highlight how Paul uses these expository passages in his arguments in Romans: they play a more important and structural role in Romans than they do in Epictetus's discourses. In Romans they mark major stages in Paul's arguments in a way they do not in Epictetus. But the structural role played by these passages does not mean that Rom 1:16–11:36 is less of a diatribe. Rather, it means that Paul has used the conventions of the diatribe for his own purposes. This is something most writers and orators do when they employ literary or rhetorical conventions. Paul's use of these conventions for his own purposes is itself a recognition of their existence.

---

[58] Stowers, *Diatribe,* 178–84.

[59] Betz (*Galatians,* 14–26) argues that Galatians is an example of apologetic rhetoric. Kennedy (*New Testament Interpretation,* 144–52) has argued convincingly, however, that Galatians is better taken as an example of deliberative rhetoric. Mitchell (*Paul and the Rhetoric of Reconciliation)* has shown that 1 Corinthians should also be understood as an example of deliberative rhetoric.

[60] These epistles are conveniently collected in Abraham J. Malherbe, *The Cynic Epistles: A Study Edition* (SBLSBS 12; Missoula, Mont.: Scholars Press, 1977).

[61] The issues of dating are discussed ibid., 6–34.

[62] E.g., see Heraclitus, *Ep.* 4, 7, 9 (Malherbe, *Cynic Epistles,* 190–93, 200–7, 210–15).

A third reason for this reluctance is that Paul's extensive use and interpretation of the Jewish scriptures make 1:16–11:36 look very different from Epictetus's discourses. This is true enough as far as it goes. But one needs to be clearer about what the difference actually is and what it means for understanding the rhetorical genre of 1:16–11:36. The difference between Paul and Epictetus at this point is in the use of arguments from authority. Both Epictetus in his discourses and Paul in this section of Romans frequently cite authorities to support their arguments. In the case of Epictetus, this is especially Homer and, to some extent, Euripides; in the case of Paul, it is the Jewish scriptures. The difference is that citations and interpretations of the Jewish scriptures play a much more significant role for Paul than do the citations of Homer and Euripides in Epictetus's diatribes. The reason is that the Jewish scriptures had a greater authority and significance for Paul and early Christians than Homer and Euripides ever did for ancient Greeks and Romans. This difference, however, should not blind us to the similarity between Paul and Epictetus. The appeal to authority, whether to Homer and Euripides or to the Jewish scriptures, served an important function in both writers. Paul certainly made more extensive use of the Jewish scriptures than Epictetus did of Homer or Euripides. In this sense, Paul again turned the conventions of the diatribe to his own purposes. It is equally important to realize, however, that he was still making use of the same rhetorical convention and that his use of it would have been recognizable to his Roman audience.

A fourth reason for the reluctance to think of 1:16–11:36 as a diatribe concerns the level of generality of the diatribe in comparison with Romans. For the most part, diatribes, including those of Epictetus, are not addressed to a particular audience or to a particular situation. Their advocacy of virtues and rebuke of vices are usually at a more general level and appropriate to a school context. Romans, on the other hand, seems much more specific in the way Paul addresses the issues of a particular community, in this case the Roman Christian community. This view, however, is misleading on two counts. On the one hand, although most diatribes are of a quite general nature, it is not true for all of them. Some of Epictetus's discourses begin with a brief description of the occasion on which he delivered it or of the person to whom he directed it.[63] In addition, several of the discourses are directed to individuals in particular situations.[64] Diatribes, then, are not always as general as might be supposed. On the other hand, Paul's letter to the Roman community is significantly more general than his letters to other communities. In his other letters, Paul was dealing mostly with quite specific problems or issues in the communities to which he wrote. He was dealing with *their* issues or problems. As seen above in the previous chapter, Galatians and 1 Corinthians are good examples of this. In Rom 1:16–11:36, however, Paul is not dealing with issues and problems of the Roman

---

[63] Epictetus, *Diatr.* 1.11, 13, 14, 15; 2.4, 24; 3.1, 4, 5, 7, 9, 22; 4.6.

[64] Epictetus, *Diatr.* 1.15, was a response to a man who asked Epictetus how he could persuade his brother to stop being angry with him; *Diatr.* 2.4 was directed to a man who had been caught in adultery; *Diatr.* 3.1, to a young student of rhetoric whose hair was elaborately dressed; *Diatr.* 3.4, to the procurator of Epirus who took the side of a comic actor in a somewhat undignified manner; and *Diatr.* 3.9, to a rhetorician who was going to Rome for a lawsuit.

Christians themselves but with issues and problems they have with him and his understanding of the gospel. His response is his attempt to persuade them of the correctness of his gospel as it touched on a whole range of issues that they found troubling. Romans, then, is noticeably more general in that it is an explanation and defense of his understanding of the gospel.[65] In this sense, Romans is roughly comparable, in a Christian context, to Epictetus's explanation and defense of his philosophical positions.

The final reason for the reluctance is of a broader sort. When one reads Rom 1:16–11:36 and Epictetus's discourses, they simply look very different. They seem to inhabit different worlds, one the world of Greek philosophy and religiosity and the other the world of Judaism and its early Christian reinterpretation. Most educated inhabitants of the Greco-Roman world probably would have found the specific content of much of 1:16–11:36 quite incomprehensible. They would not have known what to make of much of it. Once again this is true enough as far as it goes. But what is it about this central section of Romans that they would have found incomprehensible? It would not have been the broad subject matter. Much of this section of Romans was recognizably concerned with ethical-religious matters, about how human beings should live their lives. Nor would it have been the rhetorical devices Paul used. These too would have been familiar to them. Rather, what they would have found incomprehensible is the specifically Jewish/Christian contents of Romans. In other words, they probably would have recognized 1:16–11:36 as a diatribe, but a very odd-sounding one. The situation obviously would have been different, however, for Paul's Roman Christian audience. They would have recognized both the conventions of the diatribe and how Paul was using these conventions for his own specific purposes.

This central section of Romans, then, is best understood as an example of a diatribe. And Paul's use of the various conventions of a diatribe would have been recognizable to his Roman Christian audience. Paul certainly used these conventions for his own purposes. But his use of these conventions was still well within the range of what his Roman Christian audience would have recognized as a diatribe.

THE PURPOSES OF ROMANS

Why, then, did Paul write his letter to the Roman Christian community? What did he hope to convince the Roman Christians of, and how did he go about doing this? Detailed answers to these questions will become clear only in the course of the arguments in the following chapters. Given the complexity of Romans, however, there is always a danger of losing sight of the forest because of the number of trees. This section therefore draws together the arguments made up until now and lays out in a preliminary way how Paul set out to deal with the complex of issues between himself and the Roman Christian community. This broader view will serve as a helpful guide to the more detailed arguments of the following chapters.

---

[65] This has been recognized by Kennedy, *New Testament Interpretation,* 155–56.

On the surface, Paul's purposes in writing Romans seem fairly simple and straightforward. They are found in the letter framework of Romans (1:1–15; 15:14–16:24). He hopes to visit them in the near future, to be encouraged by their faith as they by his, and to be supported by them on his trip to preach the gospel in Spain. First, however, he plans to travel to Jerusalem with the collection for the poor of Jerusalem. He requests that, in this matter, they pray on his behalf that the collection will be acceptable to the Jewish Christian community in Jerusalem.

As already seen, both of these purposes pointed to more complicated issues between Paul and the Jewish Christian community in Jerusalem but also, more important, between him and the Roman Christian community. The exploration of both of these situations and the histories that lay behind them provided a more specific sense of what the complexities were and an explanation for why Paul wrote such a complex and difficult letter introducing himself to the Roman Christians. If Paul expected to be received cordially by the Roman Christians and to be supported by them on his journey to Spain, he first had to persuade them of the truth of his gospel and to dispel the deep misgivings they were bound to have about him and his gospel. More broadly, Paul needed to do this if he and his communities were not to be isolated from the growing Christian community at the center of the Roman Empire.

Perhaps the best way to get a preliminary sense of how Paul dealt with the issues at the heart of the Roman Christians' misgivings about him and his gospel is to look again briefly at the four major stages in his argument (1:18–3:20; 3:21–4:25; 5:1–7:25; 8:1–11:36). The emphasis here is not on the subject of each stage but on the issues Paul seems to be dealing with. In each stage, Paul begins by appealing to beliefs or convictions he and the Roman Christians have in common. He then develops these beliefs or convictions in such a way as to support some central aspect of his gospel. Finally, he tries to show how the controversial aspects of his gospel should be acceptable to them and should not raise misgivings for them either about him or about his gospel. For the most part, he supports the apparently controversial aspects of his gospel by appealing to the Jewish scriptures to show how the gospel he preaches is in continuity with them and with Jewish tradition.

In 1:18–3:20, Paul argues for the equal sinfulness of Jews and Gentiles. He begins with the claim that the wrath of God is being revealed against *all* ungodliness and wickedness. Since God's invisible nature can be perceived from creation, human beings are without excuse for not recognizing God (1:18–20). Paul then moves on to a conventional Hellenistic Jewish critique of Gentile religion and morality (1:21–32). Both his initial claim and his subsequent critique would have found ready acceptance with the Roman Christians. Only in 2:1–3:20 does Paul then argue more controversially that Jews as a group are as sinful as Gentiles as a group. Although for different reasons, they are both under the power of sin. Gentiles are sinful because of their foolish religious beliefs and depraved moral practices. Jews are sinful because in fact they have not observed the law. God's wrath against "all ungodliness and wickedness" includes Jews and Gentiles equally.

Paul seems well aware of how offensive this claim would be to the Roman Christians. How could someone such as Paul place Jews on the same level as Gentiles? If it is true, what good is either being a Jew or circumcision? For the Roman

Christians, the very value of the whole Jewish tradition would have been at issue. Because of this, Paul argues his case on the basis of a scriptural principle, God's impartiality (2:1–11), and on the basis of the Jewish scriptures (3:10–18). More important, he goes out of his way to reaffirm the value of both circumcision and being a Jew (2:25–3:8). Circumcision is of value if one obeys the law. And Jews have been privileged because they have been entrusted with God's scriptures. Paul obviously hoped that these traditional Jewish arguments would appeal to the Roman Christians and convince them that his views about the equal sinfulness of Jews and Gentiles was indeed rooted in Jewish tradition itself. In comparison with Galatians, Paul also fundamentally and intentionally alters how he now frames the issue. He refers to Ps 143:2 ("For no one will be made righteous before him") both in Rom 3:20 and earlier in Gal 2:16. In Gal 2:16, Paul's point in using Ps 143:2 was that it was impossible for anyone, whether Jew or Gentile, to be made righteous through observance of the law. His use of it at the end of Rom 2:1–3:20, however, serves a quite different purpose. No one is made righteous by God through observance of the law because Jews as a group are as sinful as Gentiles as a group; in the course of their history, Scripture shows that they in fact have not observed the law (3:10–18).

In 3:21–4:25, Paul moves to the next stage of his argument. He begins in 3:21 by claiming that "now the righteousness of God has been manifested apart from the law, although the law and the prophets bear witness to it." In 3:22–26, Paul draws on a traditional creedal formula that he has in common with the Roman Christians. He then comments on it to show that this righteousness, which comes through the death of Christ, is received through faith and is for both Jews and Gentiles without distinction. In 3:27–4:25, he then argues that although this righteousness is both apart from the law and intended for Jews and Gentiles alike, this still does not annul the law. Rather, it upholds the law. In support of this, he uses the example of Abraham. He argues, primarily on the basis of texts from Genesis, that Abraham was made righteous by his faith in God and not by his observance of the law.[66] In addition, through the promises made to him because of his faith, Abraham is the father of both Jews and Gentiles.

The issues at stake in 3:21–4:25 again become clear when set against the backdrop of Paul's earlier arguments in Galatians. In Galatians, Paul starkly contrasted righteousness through faith with observance of the law. The contrast seemed to be a matter of principle. But in Rom 3:21–26, Paul does not contrast righteousness through faith with the law. Rather, righteousness takes place "apart from the law." In addition, the contrast Paul does draw is not one in principle but a temporal one. The righteousness of God is *now* being manifested apart from the law.[67] Second, Paul clearly uses the figure of Abraham very differently than he did in Galatians. In Gal 3:6–14, the promises to Abraham seemed to be intended for the Gentiles but not really for the Jews. These promises seemed to bypass the Jewish people and come directly to Christ (Gal 3:15–18). In Rom 4:1–25, however, Paul emphasizes the role of Abraham as the father of both Jews and Gentiles. Paul's very

---

[66] See Gen 12:3; 15:5–6; 17:5, 10–11; 18:18.

[67] This temporal notion is clearly important for Paul. He returns to it in Rom 3:26 when he refers to the demonstration of God's righteousness "in the present time" (ἐν τῷ νῦν καιρῷ).

different view of Abraham is shown most starkly in his radically different use of the phrase "and to your seed" (καὶ τῷ σμέρματί σου) from Gen 12:7. In Gal 3:16, Paul interpreted "seed" as a singular noun referring specifically to Christ and not to the Jewish people. In Rom 4:13–17, however, he specifically interprets "seed" as a collective noun that includes both Jews and Gentiles. It is difficult to imagine a starker reversal of interpretation.

In Rom 5:1–7:25, Paul is primarily concerned with issues of how believers are to live their lives once they have been made righteous by faith. In 5:1–21, he explains how righteousness through faith, apart from the law and its observance, is still incompatible with sin. He does this first by appealing to the conviction, shared by him and the Roman Christians, that Christ's death was meant to reconcile sinners to God (5:6–11). He then uses a comparison and contrast between Adam and Christ to show how sin is incompatible with the grace in which believers, Jews and Gentiles alike, now stand (5:12–21). In 6:1–7:25, Paul moves once again to defend and significantly revise some of his earlier controversial views on ethics. The first part (6:1–23) is based on a reinterpretation of baptism and its consequences. In baptism, by dying with Christ, believers also die to sin in order to live to God in Christ Jesus (6:1–14). Thus freed from sin, they are now slaves to God through righteousness (6:15– 23). In the second part (7:1–25), Paul defends the holiness of the law itself and contrasts it with the weakness of human beings. As we shall see, he appeals especially to the difficulties the Gentile Roman Christians experienced in their attempt to observe the ethical commandments of the law (7:7–25).

In Romans 5–7, Paul is clearly struggling with two issues that trouble his relationship with the Roman Christians. The first is their deep misgivings about his view of ethics, expressed in Gal 5:1–6:10, as freedom from the law and as the practice of virtue guided by the Spirit. For the Roman Christians, these views are largely responsible for many of the problems experienced by the Corinthian Christians. In Romans 6, Paul significantly revises his rhetoric about ethics. He emphasizes not freedom from the law but freedom from sin. In addition, he emphasizes for the first time that baptism is a dying with Christ to sin. The second issue is the Roman Christians' deep misgivings about Paul's earlier denigration of the value of the law. Romans 7 is the point at which Paul deals in detail with this vexing issue. It is the first time in any of his letters that he writes of the holiness of the law. On both these issues, Paul seems very aware that these problems were, to a great extent, of his own making and were largely caused by his own intemperate rhetoric in Galatians.

The final stage of Paul's argument (Rom 8:1–11:36) is by far his longest and most complicated. It is concerned primarily with issues of eschatology. The first part (8:1–30) is an explanation of the role of the Spirit in believers' lives. By walking according to the Spirit rather than according to the flesh, believers become sons of God and heirs destined for glory (8:1–17). The Spirit also serves as the basis for an inclusive, universalizing eschatology (8:18–30). The second and much more argumentative part (8:31–11:36) is an anguished series of arguments about the ultimate incorporation of the Jewish people in the mysterious plan of God. Paul develops these reflections in three stages. First, he reflects on God's original choice of Israel and God's extension of it to the Gentiles (9:6–29). He then deals with the present situation of Israel's unbelief in relation to Gentiles' belief (9:30–10:21). Finally, he deals with the mystery of God's future plan, in which there will be final salvation for Israel and the Gentiles alike (11:1–36).

This section is clearly the climax of Paul's argument. It also reflects the personal anguish that this issue came to cause Paul. On the one hand, he would not and could not give up on his basic conviction that in Christ salvation was offered equally to Gentiles as well as to Jews. On the other hand, he realized that even though most of his fellow Jews had not come to have faith in Christ, God's promises to Israel still could not fail. He also came to understand that some of his own rhetoric in Galatians seemed to cast doubts on the trustworthiness of these promises. Above all, it is in Romans 8–11 that Paul struggles with the truth of the Roman Christians' accusation that, in his intense polemic in Galatians, he seemed to exclude Jews from the inheritance promised to them by God in the Scriptures.

Even this preliminary overview of the central section of Romans reveals how complex Paul's relationship to the Roman Christians was and so how complex his purposes were in writing Romans. This overview also reveals some of the central issues that lay just below the surface of the letter's "themes." These issues can be grouped into three distinct but related clusters. The first cluster concerns the status and the value of the Mosaic law and its observance. Paul's views that believers are no longer obliged to obey the Mosaic law seem to devalue even its observance in the past. The observance of the Mosaic law seems never to have been of value. The second cluster concerns how believers are to live their lives in an ethical fashion. What are the consequences of no longer being obliged to observe the law? Can the consequences be anything but disastrous? The third cluster concerns the status of the Jewish people, Israel, and their relationship to the Gentiles. Do not Paul's views place Jews and Gentiles on the same level? Do they not lead to a devaluation of the Jewish people, its history, and even God's promises to Israel? Do they not consistently seem even to exclude the Jewish people from these promises?

Paul's responses to these issues are equally complex. He does not respond simply by expanding on his earlier arguments in Galatians. In the light of objections from the Roman Christians to his earlier controversial views, Paul radically revised and even reversed some of the central arguments he made in Galatians. At the same time, however, there is also continuity in his basic convictions. He is still convinced, and tries to convince the Roman Christians, that in Christ righteousness is through faith apart from observance of the Mosaic law and is meant equally for both Jews and Gentiles. These convictions were so rooted in his own experience that he would not and could not change them. His confrontation with the Roman Christians over these issues, however, forced him to rethink and sort out what his basic convictions really were and, perhaps as important, what they were not. This confrontation also forced him to reconsider whether, in the intensely polemical atmosphere of his controversy with the Galatians, he had in fact lost sight of some of his other basic convictions. More specifically, had he lost sight of the importance of the Jewish people and of God's promises to them?

This confrontation also led Paul not only to reconsider the controversial views that were specifically at issue between himself and the Roman Christians; it also forced him to reconsider the framework within which he formulated these views. The interpretive framework of Romans differs radically from the framework of

Galatians. Whereas Galatians is dominated by stark contrasts that seem to allow of no resolution, Paul's interpretive framework in Romans is temporal and historical. The four major stages of his argument in Rom 1:16–11:36 are arranged in a temporal sequence. Paul begins with the equally sinful situation of Jews and Gentiles prior to the manifestation of God's righteousness and mercy in Christ (1:18–3:20), then deals with that manifestation itself (3:21–4:25) and its consequences (5:1–7:25), and concludes with the salvation of Jews and Gentiles together (8:1–11:36). In addition, Paul also sets his struggle to understand the situation of his fellow Jews in Romans 9–11 within a temporal framework: past (9:6–29), present (9:30–10:21), and future (11:1–36).

Finally, this overview suggests why Paul's use and adaptation of the genre of the diatribe would have proved so attractive. The bias of the diatribe genre was toward broader issues rather than toward particular problems. In Romans Paul tries to deal with, is indeed forced to deal with, a much broader range of issues than he does in any of his other letters. In effect, he defends and tries to persuade the Roman Christians of the correctness of his understanding of central aspects of the gospel. In addition, the diatribe has a certain indirectness to it that also would have appealed to Paul. Given his standing or lack of it with the Roman Christians, it would have been difficult for him directly to confront their misgivings about him and his views. But the diatribe allowed Paul to place them rhetorically on his side from the beginning. All the rhetorical devices of the diatribe would have enabled him to respond to their issues and misunderstandings of him without ever having to confront them directly.

CHAPTER 4

Jews, Gentiles, and the Impartiality of God

AUL BEGINS HIS ARGUMENT IN ROM 1:16–17, as the authors of most diatribes do, by setting out the basic proposition he wants to argue in the body
of the letter:[1] "For I am not ashamed of the gospel; for it is the power of
God for salvation to every one who has faith [παντὶ τῷ πιστεύοντι], to the Jew
first and also to the Greek. For in it the righteousness of God is revealed through
faith for faith [ἐκ πίστεως εἰς πίστιν]; as it is written, 'He who is righteous
through faith [ἐκ πίστεως] shall live' [Hab 2:4]." This seemingly straightforward
statement gives us important clues about Paul's overall approach in the letter both to
the issues in the minds of the Roman Christians and to his own rethinking of some
of his earlier controversial positions. All these ideas (righteousness, salvation, faith,
Jew and Greek) will play central roles in Paul's arguments in Romans. But they also
played central roles in Galatians and, as we saw earlier, in very controversial ways.
But here, at the beginning of Romans, Paul intentionally formulates this proposition
in a positive and quite uncontroversial way so that it could be easily understood and
accepted by the Roman Christians. Given what we know of the controversies in
which Paul has been involved, the way Paul states this proposition is extremely significant. In Rom 1:16–17, Paul certainly emphasizes the centrality of faith, but he
does not contrast it with observance of the law. This is very different from his statement of the proposition in Gal 2:15–21. There Paul starkly contrasted faith in
Christ with observance of the law. Righteousness is through faith in Christ and not
by observance of the law (Gal 2:15–16). Indeed, no one is made righteous through
observance of the law (Gal 2:16). In Gal 2:21, Paul even claimed that if righteousness were through the law, then Christ died in vain. These stark contrasts are entirely missing in Rom 1:16–17.

In addition, Paul emphasizes in Rom 1:16–17 not only that the gospel is the
power of God for salvation to everyone who believes, both Jew and Greek, but also
that a priority is accorded to the Jew. This is something Paul has never done before.

---

[1] Most of Epictetus's diatribes begin with a statement of the proposition.

It too is at odds with what we saw of Paul's arguments in Galatians in 3:6–14, 3:26–4:11, and 4:21–31, where he seemed even to have excluded the Jews from God's promises. What this priority consists in will become clear only in the course of Paul's arguments in the body of the letter. Perhaps emblematic of this difference is Paul's use of Hab 2:4 in Rom 1:17 to emphasize the centrality of faith. Paul also used Hab 2:4 in Gal 3:11. But there he starkly contrasted the faith mentioned in Hab 2:4 with the law. He even connected those who observe the law with the curse mentioned in Deut 27:26 (Gal 3:10, 12). But in Rom 1:17, Paul has completely dropped this contrast. From the very beginning of Romans, then, Paul signals that he is intentionally taking a very different approach than he did in Galatians and specifically with regard to the elements of his gospel that would have been most objectionable to the Roman Christians.

Paul begins the first major stage of his argument (Rom 1:18–3:20) with the subproposition in 1:18–20:[2] "For the wrath of God is revealed from heaven against all ungodliness and wickedness of human beings who by their wickedness suppress the truth. For what can be known about God is plain to them, because God has shown it to them. Ever since the creation of the world his invisible nature, namely, his eternal power and deity, has been clearly perceived in the things that have been made. So they are without excuse." Toward the end of the section, he makes the claim more specific: "For we have already charged that all, both Jews and Greeks, are under the power of sin" (3:9). He follows this with a list of quotations from the Jewish scriptures (3:10–18) that he claims refer to the sinfulness of Jews because "whatever the law says it speaks to those who are under the law" (3:19). The result is that the whole world (and by this he means both Jews and Gentiles as groups) are equally held accountable to God (3:19).

In one sense, the point of Paul's argument is clear. He is arguing for the equality in sinfulness of Jews and Gentiles as groups. But what more specifically is at issue in the argument? Why does Paul make this argument to the Roman Christians at the very beginning of his letter to them? As argued in chapters 1 and 2 above, the Jewish historian Josephus offers us some clues in his defense of Judaism in *Against Apion*. In *Ag. Ap.* 2.145–286, Josephus makes four claims that are helpful for understanding what is at issue in Rom 1:18–3:20 between Paul and the Roman Christians. First, Josephus asserts the superiority of Jewish monotheism: the belief in one God who is the Creator and Ruler of all, whose work can plainly be seen from what exists (*Ag. Ap.* 2.190–192, 164–167). Second, he contrasts this with Greek polytheism and especially with the immorality of the Greek gods and goddesses (2.232–249). Third, he asserts the superiority of various aspects of the Mosaic law, its concept of God and its morality, especially its sexual morality (2.190–219). Finally, and for our purposes most important, Josephus repeatedly emphasizes that, unlike the Greeks and other peoples, the Jews observe and put their laws into practice (2.168–174, 220–225, 271–278).

---

[2] Paul begins 1:18–3:20, 3:21–4:25, and 5:1–7:25 with a statement of what he is arguing in the respective section. For the sake of convenience, these statements are here called subpropositions.

Josephus's views about the superiority of the Jewish way of life were probably not simply his own but also represented the views of the Roman Jewish community. Since most of the members of the Roman Christian community had previously been either members of, or Gentile sympathizers associated with, the Roman Jewish community, many of these views were then carried over into the Roman Christian community as a whole and were affirmed even by members of the community who were ethnically Gentile. What would their reaction have been to a prominent Christian who claimed that in reality both Jews and Gentiles were equally sinful, that in effect Josephus's fourth claim was not true? They almost certainly would have been astounded and scandalized by such a view. In addition, they would have thought that he was also implicitly challenging the superiority of the Mosaic law itself, that is, Josephus's third claim. After all, if the superiority of the Mosaic law does not lead to the practice of that law, in what does its superiority really consist? At the very least, it is no more effective than the legal systems of the Greeks and other peoples. As we shall see, this suspicion probably lies behind Paul's reply to the objection in Rom 3:1–3.

It is these issues that Paul addresses in 1:18–3:20. He deals with them first because the reality of the equal sinfulness of Jews and Gentiles inevitably conditions any further arguments he will make in the letter about the salvific role of Christ, the righteousness of believers before God, the ethical consequences of this righteousness, and the future fate of both Jews and Gentiles as groups. Paul also deals with them first because he now takes a more temporal or historically oriented approach in Romans. This is quite different from his approach in Galatians, which, as pointed out in chapter 2 above,[3] was marked by stark contrasts. In Rom 1:18–3:20, Paul deals with what has been the case, then he turns in 3:21 ("But now . . . ") to what now is changed through the manifestation of God's righteousness in Christ.

These issues of the equal sinfulness of Jews and Gentiles also account for the specific ways in which Paul argues his case. He tries to ground his controversial conclusions about equal sinfulness by appeals to the Jewish scriptures and to traditional Jewish viewpoints that were current in contemporary, especially Hellenistic, Judaism. He rhetorically juxtaposes these appeals in an attempt to persuade his Roman Christian audience that his apparently scandalous conclusions about the equal status of Jews and Gentiles as groups are in reality grounded in the Jewish scriptures and in other traditional Jewish concepts. Even the juxtaposition itself is grounded in the Jewish scriptures, specifically in the traditional Jewish concept of God's impartiality.[4] Paul hopes to show the Roman Christian community that his challenge to the kind of claim Josephus made about Jewish observance of the law did not invalidate Josephus's third claim about the superiority of the law. Paul claims that he is in fact upholding the validity of the law. This is because the knowledge of the equal sinfulness of both Jews and Gentiles comes through the law (3:20). In effect, Paul is appealing to their own self-understanding and using that self-understanding as the basis for showing the similar status of Jews and Gentiles in regard to sinfulness.

---

[3] See above, pp. 64–66.

[4] For the importance of this concept in understanding this section of Romans, see Jouette M. Bassler, *Divine Impartiality: Paul and a Theological Axiom* (SBLDS 59; Chico, Calif.: Scholars Press, 1982).

Paul's attempt to root his seemingly scandalous views about the equality of Jews and Gentiles is also reflected in the kinds of arguments he uses and in the way he structures the sequence of his arguments. In the first place, two of the most important arguments he uses are (1) the argument from authority and (2) the argument from previous judgments in similar cases. Both of these arguments were familiar ones in Greco-Roman rhetoric, and both play into the traditional character of the arguments Paul is making.

Although the argument from authority was not one of the more common, it nevertheless was one of the arguments used in Greco-Roman rhetoric.[5] Quintilian described such arguments in the following way:

> Authority also may be drawn from external sources to support a case. Those who follow the Greeks, who call them κρίσεις, style such arguments *judgments* or *adjudications*, thereby referring not to matters on which judicial sentence has been pronounced (for such decisions fall into the category of precedents), but to whatever may be regarded as expressing the opinion of nations, peoples, philosophers, distinguished citizens, or illustrious poets. Even common sayings and popular beliefs may not be without use. For they are testimonies, which are all the more impressive because they were not given to suit special cases, but were the utterances and actions of minds free of antipathy or partiality, done simply because they seemed the most honorable or honest things to say or do. (Quintilian, *Inst.* 5.11.36–37 [Butler, LCL])

Quintilian also included in this type of argument the "authority of the gods" *(deorum auctoritas)* *(Inst.* 5.11.42).[6] The author of the *Rhetorica ad Herennium* (2.48) also included ancestors, sages, and laws in this category. At each stage of his argument, Paul will appeal to the authority either of the Jewish scriptures (i.e., *dei auctoritas* and the Jewish "laws") or of traditional Jewish outlooks (i.e., ancestors and sages). Although Paul uses the argument from authority to a greater extent than Greek or Roman orators did, the argument nevertheless would have had a familiar ring to the ears of his Roman audience.

The argument from previous judgments on similar cases was also a standard topic in Greco-Roman rhetoric. It was described this way in *Rhet. Her.* 2.13.19:

> It is a previous judgment *[iudicatum]* when on the same question a sentence has been passed or a decree interposed. These are often contradictory, according as one judge, praetor, consul, or tribune of the plebs has determined differently from another; and it often happens that on the same matter one has decreed or decided differently from another. . . . Therefore, because different past judgments can be offered for a like case, we shall, when this comes to pass, compare the judges, the circumstances, and the number of decisions. (Caplan, LCL)

---

[5] Arguments from authority were used far more extensively in Jewish and Christian rhetoric than in Greco-Roman rhetoric. See George A. Kennedy, *Classical Rhetoric and Its Christian and Secular Tradition from Ancient to Modern Times* (Chapel Hill: University of North Carolina Press, 1980), 121–29.

[6] Whereas *Rhet. Her.* 2.30.48 and Cicero (*Inv.* 1.53.101) place the argument from authority at the conclusion of a speech as a form of *amplificatio,* Quintilian places it among the regular proofs used in argumentation (*Inst.* 5.11.36–44). As Quintilian points out (*Inst.* 5.11.43), Cicero himself made use of such arguments in several of his orations (*Cat.* 3.9.21; *Lig.* 6.19).

One appeals to a previous judgment as a precedent for the judgment that one wants in the present case. The argument is based on the similarity between the previous case and the present one.[7] Paul will make use of this argument at the crucial point where he moves from a consideration of wickedness in general to an explicit consideration of Jewish transgression of the law.

Second, these issues also affect the way in which Paul structures the sequence of his arguments. He begins with the subproposition of this section of the letter in Rom 1:18–20, that "the wrath of God is revealed from heaven against all ungodliness and wickedness of human beings who by their wickedness suppress the truth" and that "what can be known about God is plain to them, because God has shown it to them." In 1:21–32, he describes this idolatry and wickedness and its consequences. Although Paul clearly derived the thought of this passage from Hellenistic Jewish critiques of *Gentile* religiosity and morality, he never explicitly mentions Gentiles. This section is meant to be quite conventional and uncontroversial for his audience. On this basis, Paul then moves through a series of steps leading to the conclusion that, on the basis of the Jewish scriptures and traditional Jewish viewpoints, both Jews and Gentiles as groups are equally sinful:

1. Apostrophe to someone who condemns immorality but who also acts immorally. This leads to the conclusion of the impartiality of God's judgment (2:1–11).

2. Comparison of the impartial judgment of those under the law with those not under the law (2:12–16).

3. Parallel apostrophe to a Jew who boasts of knowledge of the law and yet who does what is condemned by the law. Circumcision is of benefit only if one obeys the law (2:17–29).

4. Objections from, and replies to, a Christian "skeptic" about the value of being a Jew and about God's faithfulness in the face of human unfaithfulness (3:1–18).

5. Conclusion: The whole world (i.e., both Jews and Gentiles as groups) are accountable to God (3:19–20).

Romans 1:18–32: The Subproposition and the Exposition

The first stage of Paul's argument (1:18–32) begins with the subproposition that the wrath of God is revealed against *all* human ungodliness and wickedness. Because what can be known about God has been made manifest by God, human beings are without excuse for not recognizing God's eternal power and deity, which can be clearly perceived in creation (1:18–20). This is followed in 1:21–32 with a more extended description divided into three parts. In each part Paul describes first human beings' failure to recognize God (1:21–23, 25, 28a) and then the conse-

---

[7] For other explanations and examples of this kind of argument, see Aristotle, *Rhet.* 2.23.12, and Quintilian, *Inst.* 5.2.1–5.

quences of this failure (1:24, 26–27, 28b–32).[8] This failure leads to the degrading beliefs and practices of the Gentiles: exchanging the glory of the immortal God for images of mortal human beings, birds, animals, and even reptiles (1:21–23) and also exchanging the truth about God for a lie, serving the creature instead of the Creator (1:25), and not acknowledging God (1:28a). Paul describes with ever greater specificity the ethical consequences of the failure to recognize and worship God. In 1:24, God hands human beings over to the desires of their hearts and to the dishonoring of their bodies among themselves. In 1:26–27, god hands them over to dishonorable passions. Here Paul specifically describes homosexual practices among both women and men.[9] Finally, in 1:28b–32, he gives a whole catalogue of specific vices.

In presenting this description, Paul quite clearly used standard Hellenistic Jewish apologetic motifs against *Gentile* religiosity and conduct, and his Roman Christian audience naturally would have understood it in this way, at least at first. Examples of such apologetic are found in Wisdom 13–15 and in *Sib. Or.* 3:8–45 (also 3:184–187, 594–600, 764); frgs. 1–3. Both of these texts were directed against Gentile refusal to recognize and worship the one, true God who can be recognized from creation.[10] Both also claimed that this failure to recognize God leads to idolatry and a myriad of other vices.[11] This same critique is also found in Josephus, *Ag. Ap.* 2.145–286. God is the Creator and Ruler of all, whose work can be plainly seen from what exists (1.190–192). Failure to recognize this leads to all kinds of vices condemned by the law (2.199–203, 206–208). Elsewhere in *Against Apion,* Josephus specifically ridicules and condemns the worship, especially prevalent among the Egyptians, of various sorts of animals (1.225, 239, 244, 249, 254; 2.66, 81, 86, 128–129, 139). In addition, all these texts, like Paul, highlight Jewish condemnation of homosexual practices, a condemnation that Hellenistic Jews thought set them apart from the Greco-Roman world.[12] Paul's description of human godlessness and wickedness clearly reflects this specifically Jewish perspective on Gentile religiosity and conduct. Because his description basically followed the pattern of traditional Hellenistic Jewish apologetic against Gentile religion and morality, his Roman Christian audience would have easily understood it and agreed with it. In this sense, Rom 1:18–32 is not so much an argument as an exposition of viewpoints he and the

---

[8] This division basically follows that suggested by Byrne, *Romans,* 64–72.

[9] For an interpretation of 1:26–27 and its relationship to wider attitudes in the Greco-Roman world, see esp. Bernadette J. Brooten, *Love between Women: Early Christian Responses to Female Homoeroticism* (Chicago: University of Chicago Press, 1996).

[10] Wis 13:1–9; *Sib. Or.* 3:15–23; frgs. 1:3–17, 32–35; 3:3–14.

[11] Idolatry: Wis 13:10–14:11; *Sib. Or.* 3:29–35; frgs. 1:18–21; 3:21–33. Other vices: Wis 14:12–31; *Sib. Or.* 3:36–45; frgs. 1:19, 23–25; 3:19. For other examples of this kind of apologetic, see *Let. Aris.* 132–141, 152; Ps.-Phoc. 109–192, 213–214; Philo, *Leg.* 3.36; *Abr.* 135–136; *Spec.* 3.37–42; *Contempl.* 59–62.

[12] See Wis 14:26; *Sib. Or.* 3:184–187, 594–600, 764; *Let. Aris.* 152; Philo, *Abr.* 135–137; *Spec.* 3.37–42; Ps. Phoc. 3, 190–192, 213–214; Josephus. *Ag. Ap.* 2.273–275. Attitudes toward homosexuality in the Greco-Roman world were much more complex than one would gather from either Paul or these Hellenistic Jewish authors. See the article and bibliography in *OCD* 720–23. Condemnation of homosexual practices, however, became a widespread marker among Hellenistic Jews, who claimed that such condemnation showed the ethical superiority of Judaism.

Roman Christians shared. On the surface at least, there was nothing controversial about it. Paul could not be accused of being soft on Gentiles.

There are, however, two elements in this otherwise conventional Jewish apologetic that set the stage for Paul's later arguments about the equally sinful status of Jews and Gentiles. First, in all of 1:18–32, Paul never uses the word "Gentiles." His audience may have at first assumed that he was in fact referring to Gentiles, but he never uses the word. Second, Paul begins his description with the claim that the wrath of God is revealed against all (πᾶσαν) human ungodliness and wickedness (1:18). Emphasis on *all* human ungodliness and wickedness was not characteristic of this kind of Jewish apologetic, but it did serve Paul's purposes very well. If the wrath of God is indeed revealed against all human ungodliness and wickedness, then, by implication, Jewish misconduct must also be included. Paul makes this implication explicit, however, only gradually in the course of 2:1–3:20. At this point, however, Paul only insinuates this into his Roman audience's minds.[13] In effect, Paul rhetorically has laid a foundation that both he and his Roman Christian audience would agree on, even though this foundation may not turn out to be exactly what his Roman Christian audience thought it was.

ROMANS 2:1–3:20: DEFENSE AND PROOFS

After the description and condemnation of apparently Gentile idolatry and immorality, Paul's rhetoric suddenly becomes sharper and more argumentative in 2:1–3:20. It is at this point that he moves to a defense of his convictions about the equal sinfulness of Jews and Gentiles. These are the convictions that the Roman Christians would have found controversial and even scandalous. But Paul approaches the issue only gradually and indirectly. He builds on the viewpoints of 1:18–32 that he shares with them, and he does not directly attack their views of him on these issues. This indirection is also commonly found in diatribes.

Romans 2:1–11: Apostrophe to Someone Who Acts Hypocritically

This section, rhetorically in the form of an apostrophe, is addressed to a fictitious person ("whoever [πᾶς] you are who judges") who hypocritically condemns those who commit the acts described in 1:18–32 but who also commits the same acts.[14] As in 1:18, he again uses the word πᾶς ("all," "every"), insinuating, but not stating explicitly, that both Jews and Gentiles are included. Paul rhetorically asks whether such a person thinks that he will escape the judgment of God or whether he is ignorant of the fact that God's kindness, forbearance, and patience are meant to lead to repentance. Such a person is storing up wrath for the day when God's just judgment will be revealed. On that day, God will render to everyone according to his works, to the Jew first and also the Greek, for God shows no partiality. It is only at

---

[13] For the use of insinuation in Greco-Roman rhetoric, see Quintilian, *Inst.* 4.1.42–48.

[14] Apostrophe is a "turning away" from the actual audience to address absent persons as if present or things as if listening. See Quintilian, *Inst.* 4.1.63–70. Although writers like Quintilian thought that it should be used sparingly, it was a common figure in diatribes. See Anderson, *Glossary of Greek Rhetorical Terms*, 25.

the end of this section, however, that Paul first mentions explicitly that he includes Jews as well as Gentiles.

Once again a good deal of Paul's argument is conventional. The imagery of God judging on the "day of wrath" in 2:5–10 is certainly widespread in Judaism and early Christianity.[15] In 2:2, Paul appeals to the notion that the judgment of God is truthful against those who do such things. Such a viewpoint was a commonplace in Jewish thought.[16] Romans 2:6 ("For He will render to each according to his works") is a combined quotation from Ps 62:12 and Prov 24:12. Finally and most important, Rom 2:11, which explicitly states the principle of God's impartiality, is also a concept that is rooted in Jewish scripture and tradition. This principle is central to Paul's argument. Its classical formulation is found in Deut 10:17: "For the Lord your God is God of gods and Lord of lords, the great, the mighty, and the terrible God, who is not partial and takes no bribe." But it is also found elsewhere in the Jewish scriptures, in Jewish apocalyptic literature, and in other Jewish literature, including Philo of Alexandria.[17] It refers specifically to the way in which God judges, which of course is also the context of Rom 2:5–11. Paul then uses and reinterprets this widely accepted principle rooted in the Jewish scriptures as the fulcrum for his argument about the equal sinfulness of Jews and Gentiles.

For all of its conventionality, however, two elements in this passage are at first puzzling. First, why does Paul keep anonymous this fictitious addressee who condemns idolatry and morality and yet does the same things? Second, why is it that, at this point, Paul first introduces the notion that God will punish everyone (πᾶσαν ψυχήν) who has done evil, *the Jew first and also the Greek,* and will reward everyone (παντί) who has done good, *the Jew first and also the Greek* (2:9–10)?

These two apparently puzzling elements, however, help us to understand how Paul uses traditional Jewish viewpoints for his own purposes. First, what is important for Paul in his fictitious addressee is the discrepancy between the addressee's claim to have a higher morality and the reality of the addressee's practice. Paul obviously expects his Roman Christian audience to react with indignation and to condemn this discrepancy, this hypocrisy. Indignation, that is, grief over someone else's *undeserved* good fortune, was one of the emotions that an orator often wanted to arouse in his audience.[18] This condemnation will serve as a precedent when Paul

---

[15] The biblical roots of the "day of wrath" can be seen in Isa 2:12; 13:6; 24:21; Jer 46:10; Ezek 7:7; 30:3; Joel 2:1–2; Amos 5:18; Zeph 1:7, 15, 18; 2:2–3. The imagery is much expanded in Jewish apocalypticism (*1 En.* 45:2–6; *Pss. Sol.* 15:12–13; *4 Ezra* 6:17–24; 7:102). Paul uses this imagery elsewhere in his letters (1 Cor 1:8; 5:5; 2 Cor 1:14; Phil 1:6, 10; 2:16; 1 Thess 5:2). Paul and his Roman Christian audience undoubtedly had this imagery in common.

[16] See Isa 13:6–16; 34:8; Dan 7:9–11; Joel 2:1–3; Zeph 1:4–2:3; 3:8; Mal 4:1; *Jub.* 5:10–16; *1 En.* 90:20–27.

[17] 2 Chr 19:7; Ps 82:1–4; Sir 35:12–13; *Jub.* 5:16; 21:4; 30:16; 33:18; *2 Bar.* 13:8; 44:4; *1 En.* 63:8; *L.A.B.* 20:4; Philo, *Spec.* 1.307; 4.177; *Decal.* 41; *Mos.* 2.238. See Bassler, *Divine Impartiality,* 7–44, 77–119, who has also shown the centrality of this theological axiom in Paul's argument. One needs to be aware, of course, that numerous biblical texts emphasize God's favor toward Israel.

[18] Aristotle, *Rhet.* 2.9.1–16; *Rhet. Her.* 4.15.22; 39.51; Cicero, *Inv.* 1.53.100. *Rhet. Her.* 4.15.22 connects the arousal of indignation with the use of apostrophe, which is quite similar to what we have in Rom 2:1–6.

moves on in 2:17–29 to use the same kind of apostrophe to condemn the same kind of discrepancy in a fictitious Jewish addressee who claims to know the law but does not observe it. The condemnation in 2:1–11 gives Paul, as we shall see, the rhetorical foundation he needs to speak explicitly in 2:17–29 about Jewish conduct in the same way that he has been speaking about the conduct of this anonymous addressee.

Second, Paul makes much the same kind of move when he claims in 2:9–10 that God will punish and reward each according to his deeds, *the Jew first and also the Greek*. Based on the testimony of Scripture (Ps 62:12; Prov 24:12) that God rewards each according to his deeds and upon the familiar Jewish theological principle that God really is impartial (Rom 2:11), Paul claims that divine reward and punishment must apply both to Jews and to Gentiles. At this point Paul turns the principle of God's impartiality in a somewhat different direction. It is here that Paul explicitly mentions Jews and Gentiles in the argument. Paul will now apply these scriptural texts and the principle of God's impartiality to the parallel situations of Jews and Gentiles. This will set him apart from the normal, traditional uses of this principle as primarily a support for the hope and ultimate vindication of those unjustly treated within Israel.[19]

This section is crucial for understanding the development of Paul's argument. Rhetorically, Paul's use of apostrophe gives the section sharpness and immediacy. But it is equally important to understand how the apostrophe functions in the argument. At this point Paul introduces the two types of Greco-Roman rhetorical argument or topic mentioned earlier (the appeal to authority and the appeal to previous judgments in similar cases) to show that God judges both Gentiles and Jews by the same standards. The appeal to authority is straightforward. He quotes Ps 62:12 and Prov 24:12 in Rom 2:6, that God rewards each according to his deeds, and then in Rom 2:11 restates the same claim by an appeal to the principle of God's impartiality. This appeal to scriptural authority also serves as Paul's justification for using the argument from previous judgments in similar matters. The argument, however, is also a bit more subtle. In 2:9–11, Paul claims that these rewards and punishments are for the Jew first and also for the Greek. Rhetorically in the form of a suppressed enthymeme, Paul is claiming that if you agree that God judges impartially (and you must) and if you agree (as you have) with God's condemnation of idolatry and immorality (1:18–32) as well as hypocrisy (2:1–5), then you must also agree that God condemns similar kinds of acts when done by Jews.[20] In other words, God's previous judgment on idolatry and immorality must apply equally to Jews and Gentiles. At the end of this section, in 2:9–11, Paul makes explicit what he has only insinuated up until now, that what he has written in 1:18–20 applies to both Jews and Gentiles. Although his audience would have assumed that 1:18–2:8 was meant to apply to Gentile religiosity and morality, he now makes it clear that it applies to Gentiles and Jews alike.

---

[19] See the texts mentioned above in nn. 16 and 17, and Bassler, *Divine Impartiality*, 7–44, 121–70.

[20] In ancient rhetoric, proofs were often rooted in syllogisms, but they were often not expressed in syllogistic form. See Aristotle, *Rhet.* 1.2.13; 2.22.1–3; Cicero, *Inv.* 1.41.77; Quintilian, *Inst.* 5.14.24–26.

Both Paul's appeal to the authority of Scripture and his argument based on previous judgments in similar cases have enabled him to use traditional Jewish viewpoints and traditionally oriented Greco-Roman rhetorical topics to draw apparently untraditional conclusions. For Paul, of course, the rhetorical effect was meant to be quite the reverse, that is, that his apparently untraditional conclusions were in reality rooted in the Jewish scriptures and traditional Jewish viewpoints.

Romans 2:12–29: God's Impartiality and Its Consequences

The next stage of Paul's argument is found in 2:12–29, in which Paul explicitly discusses the situation of Jews specifically in relation to their observance of the Mosaic law. The word "law" (νόμος) appears nineteen times in this section.[21] In 2:12–16, he first introduces the notion of the law and its relationship to the conduct of both Gentiles and Jews. In 2:17–29, he again uses another apostrophe, this time, however, to a fictitious *Jewish* addressee. The apostrophe first concerns the discrepancy between Jewish claims about knowing the law and actual observance of the law (2:17–24). In 2:25–29, Paul then turns to the question of circumcision. He draws out the implications of the principles established in 1:18–32; 2:1–11, specifically applying them to the situation of Jews and their relationship to the Mosaic law. Because of this, passages in 2:12–29 are often parallel to 1:18–2:11.

Although these parallels are crucial for Paul's argument, it is equally important to note the lack of parallelism in two significant ways. First, there is no overall parallel in Paul's discussion of the situation of his fellow Jews with 1:21–32, his general indictment of Gentile religion and morality. Because Jewish religion and culture are rooted in the Mosaic law, they are not susceptible to the kind of indictment to which non-Jewish religion and morality are. There is no parallel between the two at this level. The parallelisms Paul draws are at the level of actual Gentile and Jewish *conduct*, not at the level of religion or morality as such. This points to the second lack of parallelism. As we shall see, Paul will argue that it is possible for some Gentiles to do by nature (φύσει) what the law requires (2:14–15). But they do this by *rejecting* their own Gentile culture and religiosity, something accomplished by only a few Gentiles. On the other hand, Jews become transgressors by *failing* to observe the law that is the basis of their culture and religion (2:17–29). In this way Paul upholds the validity and significance of the central reality of Jewish religion and ethics, the Mosaic law, while clearly condemning Gentile religion and ethics. This twofold lack of parallelism helps greatly to explain why Paul's critique of his fellow Jews is far more limited than was his critique in 1:18–2:11. It brings out once again the consciously traditional character of Paul's assumptions and arguments as well as the rhetorical importance of 2:1–11 in establishing the specific parallelism that Paul needs for his argument.

Romans 2:12–16: The Impartiality of God

Romans 2:12–16 serves as a transitional passage from an argument that apparently deals primarily with Gentiles (1:18–2:11) to an argument that deals primarily

---

[21] Rom 2:12 (bis), 13 (bis), 14 (bis), 15, 17, 18, 20, 23 (bis), 25 (bis), 26, 27 (bis).

with Jews (2:17–29). When Paul claims in 2:6–11 that God shows no partiality in rewarding and punishing both Jews and Gentiles on the same basis, this basis is whether each has done either good or evil (2:9–10). This is another way of stating the criterion of God's impartial judgment. In 2:12–16, Paul restates and interprets this general principle in more specifically Jewish terms, that is, in relationship to the Mosaic law. This more specific principle is stated in 2:12–13: "For those who have sinned without the law [ἀνόμως] will also perish without the law [ἀνόμως], and those who have sinned under the law [ἐν νόμῳ] will be judged through the law [διὰ νόμου].For it is not the hearers of the law who are righteous before God, but the doers of the law who will be made righteous."[22] Paul claims that, on the basis of God's impartiality, Jews who have sinned under the law will be punished just as Gentiles are punished who have sinned without the law.[23] In this, Paul reflects a fairly traditional Jewish viewpoint, that the law was the criterion for God's judgment on the conduct of human beings.[24] Conversely, Gentiles who do not have the law but who do by nature (φύσει) the things the law calls for have the reality of the law written in their hearts, and on the day of judgment their thoughts will accuse them or even excuse them (2:14–16).[25] Paul has reformulated the principle enunciated in 2:6–11 specifically in relation to the observance of the Mosaic law.

At first, 2:12–16 seems confusing and at odds with what Paul has written earlier in the letter. First, how can those "without the law," that is, Gentiles (2:12, 14), do by nature what the law requires and even have the reality of the law written in their hearts? Is he using the word "law" in two very different senses, one in the sense of the Mosaic law and the other in the sense of some sort of "natural law"? Second, given Paul's condemnation of Gentile religion and morality in 1:18–32, how can he now write of Gentiles who by nature do what the law requires and whose thoughts may even excuse them on the day of judgment (2:14, 16)?

The apparent inconsistencies in this passage reflect Paul's use of a view common in Hellenistic Jewish thought. When Paul uses the word "law" (νόμος) in this section, he ultimately does mean the Mosaic law. But he understands the Mosaic law in a way similar to that found in some strands of Hellenistic Judaism. The law was explicitly revealed to Moses on Mount Sinai. But for Hellenistic Jews such as Philo of Alexandria, this same law was also reflected in the structures of the universe and was embedded in nature (φύσις) itself. For Philo, the world is in harmony with the Mosaic law, and the law with the world. Human beings who observe the law

---

[22] The Greek adverb ἀνόμως normally means "lawlessly." Paul obviously does not mean this here; he means "without the law." He seems to be playing with the meaning of the word, taking it to mean "law-lessly." Paul has a similar wordplay on ἄνομος in 1 Cor 9:21.

[23] The γάρ at the beginning of 2:12 clearly indicates that 2:12–16 was meant to explain 2:6–11. Bassler, *Divine Impartiality*, 199, points out the parallels between 2:6–11 and 2:12–16.

[24] *Jub.* 5:12–19; *2 Bar.* 48:45–47; *L.A.B.* 11:1–3.

[25] There is some dispute about whether the Greek word φύσει ("by nature") goes with what precedes ("who do not have the law by nature") or with what follows ("who do by nature"). It probably goes with what follows. Had Paul intended the word to go with what precedes, he would have place it within the preceding participial phrase. See Fitzmyer, *Romans*, 310; Dunn, *Romans*, 98–99; Byrne, *Romans*, 92–93; Wilckens, *Römer*, 1.133–34. For a different view, see Cranfield, *Romans*, 1.156–57.

regulate their actions in accord with the purpose and will of nature (φύσις).[26] Philo often uses the term "law or laws of nature."[27] For him, these laws find their highest and clearest expression in the Mosaic law.[28] The two "laws" are ultimately identical. Because of this, Philo can speak of human beings who either before the explicit revelation of the Mosaic law or apart from the explicit commandments of the Mosaic law are nevertheless "living law"(νόμος ἔμψυχος) by observing the "unwritten laws" (νόμοι ἄγραφοι).[29] Similarly, Paul also speaks of Gentiles who do not have the law as it was explicitly revealed on Mount Sinai but who nevertheless do by nature (φύσει) what the law requires and so become a law for themselves (2:12, 14–15).

Yet Paul, like many other Jews (including, to some extent, Philo), thought that such observance of the law by nature was not common among Gentiles.[30] This emerges when he points out that on the day of judgment their thoughts will condemn or even excuse them (2:15). Gentiles being excused by their consciences, while possible, is still exceptional because it means that they have rejected their own religious beliefs and practices. Paul's point in 2:14–16 is that, on the basis of God's impartiality, both Jews and Gentiles are judged by the same criterion of the observance of the law. He is not arguing that Gentiles commonly do by nature what the law requires but only that such observance by nature is nevertheless possible and that it does sometimes happen.

The question still persists, however, about why Paul finds it necessary to emphasize at least the possibility that Gentiles could observe by nature the requirements of the law. The answer lies in the nature of the argument Paul is making. His overall argument is that Jews and Gentiles, in terms of their conduct, are in parallel situations. If this is so, then Gentiles whose conduct reflects the observance of the law by nature must be in the same situation as Jews who observe the law as it was explicitly revealed on Sinai.

Romans 2:17–29: Apostrophe to a Jew Who Acts Hypocritically

This parallelism becomes clearer when Paul again uses an apostrophe in 2:17–29. This time, however, the fictitious addressee is a Jew rather than a Gentile. Paul castigates the Jew who, while claiming to know the law and to be able to instruct others in it, does not himself observe the commandments of the law. Such a person dishonors God. In addition, although circumcision is useful if one practices the law, it is useless for someone who is a transgressor of the law. Conversely, someone who is uncircumcised but who observes the requirements of the law is

---

[26] Philo, *Opif.* 3; *Ebr.* 141–142; *Mos.* 2.48.

[27] Philo, *Opif.* 171; *Post.* 185; *Agr.* 31, 66; *Abr.* 249; *Ios.* 29; *Mos.* 2.81, 245; *Spec.* 3.32, 189; *Praem.* 108; *Prob.* 30, 37; *Contempl.* 59; *Aet.* 59. See Helmut Koester, "ΝΟΜΟΣ ΦΥΣΕΩΣ: The Concept of Natural Law in Greek Thought," in *Religions in Antiquity: Essays in Memory of Erwin Ramsdell Goodenough* (ed. Jacob Neusner; NumenSup 14; Leiden: Brill, 1968), 521–41.

[28] Philo, *Leg.* 3.167–168; *Ebr.* 37–38; *Mos.* 2.14; *Somn.* 2.174–175, 223; *Spec.* 1.202, 306; 2.13.

[29] Philo, *Abr.* 5, 275–276; *Mos.* 1.162; 2.4; *Decal.* 1; *Spec.* 4.149–150; *Virt.* 194.

[30] See Philo, *Sobr.* 25; *Mos.* 2.13; *Decal.* 2–9. For a detailed analysis, see Alan Mendelson, *Philo's Jewish Identity* (BJS 161; Atlanta: Scholars Press, 1988), 77–138.

considered circumcised by God and will even judge those who, though circumcised, are transgressors of the law. The argument of this section leads to the conclusion of 2:28–29: "For he is not a Jew who is one externally [ἐν τῷ φανερῷ], nor is circumcision something external in the flesh [ἐν τῷ φανερῷ ἐν σαρκί]. He is a Jew who is one inwardly [ἐν κρυπτῷ] and circumcision is a matter of the heart [καρδίας], spiritual not literal [ἐν πνεύματι οὐ γράμματι]. His praise is not from human beings but from God." In order to understand the argument of 2:17–29, one must first understand how Paul uses the Jewish scriptures and traditional Jewish viewpoints and, second, how he turns them to his own purposes. This second element entails understanding how the apostrophe Paul uses in 2:17–29 parallels 2:1–11, 12–16.

First, the most obvious use of the Jewish scriptures in this part of his argument is found in 2:23–24: "You who boast in the law, through your transgression of the law you dishonor God. For 'the name of God is blasphemed among the Gentiles because of you' [Isa 52:5], as it is written." Paul uses a quotation from scripture (Isa 52:5 [LXX]) to support his claim that those who pride themselves on having the law but who also transgress this same law dishonor God.[31] Paul's point is that, on the basis of the Jewish scriptures, Jewish transgressions of the law have in fact contributed to God's name being dishonored.

In emphasizing the value of circumcision of the heart rather than of the flesh (2:25–29), Paul also appeals to another element of Jewish thought. Some Hellenistic Jews saw circumcision as primarily of symbolic importance. Philo reflects this attitude. Circumcision symbolically represented the cutting out of sensual pleasures and the other passions; it was a circumcision of the heart (Philo, Q.E. 2.2).[32] Although Paul did not share Philo's Platonic views about the structure of human beings, he

---

[31] Romans 2:24 is not an exact quotation. The wording is close to Isa 52:5 ("Thus says the Lord, 'On account of you my name is continually blasphemed among the Gentiles.'"), but Paul's point in using the quotation seems closer to Ezek 36:20 ("And they went to the Gentiles, among whom they went, and they profaned my holy name, in that it was said of them, 'These are the people of the Lord, and yet they went out of his land.'"). Only the text of Ezek 36:20 emphasizes that the Jews were forced to leave their own land because of their transgressions of the law and that this departure caused God's name to be dishonored among the Gentiles.

[32] (Exod 22:21) "Why does (Scripture) in admonishing 'Thou shalt not oppress a sojourner,' add, 'For you were sojourners in the land of the Egyptians'?"

"(Scripture) first makes it clearly apparent and demonstrable that in reality the sojourner is one who circumcises not his uncircumcision but his desires and sensual pleasures and the other passions of the soul. For in Egypt the Hebrew nation was not circumcised but being mistreated with all (kinds of) mistreatment by the inhabitants in their hatred of strangers, it lived with them in self-restraint and endurance, not by necessity but rather of its own free choice, because it took refuge in God the Savior . . . But strangers are also those who by themselves have run to the truth, not in the same way as those who made their sojourn by Egypt. For these are newcomers to the land, while those are (newcomers) to laws and customs" (Philo, Q.E. 2.2 [Marcus, LCL]).

See also Philo, Migr. 92; Spec. 1.305. For discussion of this question, see Mendelson, Philo's Jewish Identity, 54–58; Peder Borgen, "Debates on Circumcision" and "Debates on Circumcision in Paul and Philo," in Philo, John, and Paul: New Perspectives on Judaism and Early Christianity (BJS 131; Atlanta: Scholars Press, 1987), 61–71, 233–54; and Richard D. Hecht, "The Exegetical Contexts of Philo's Interpretation of Circumcision," in Nourished with Peace: Studies in Hellenistic Judaism in Memory of Samuel Sandmel (ed. Frederick E. Greenspahn, Earle Hilgert, and Burton L. Mack; Homage Series 9; Chico, Calif.: Scholars Press, 1984), 51–79.

did share the view that what was important was the "circumcision of the heart." Philo certainly would have rejected the conclusions Paul drew about the ultimate status of the law and of circumcision.[33] Yet Paul's view of the value of circumcision, that it is a matter of the heart rather than of the flesh, still reflects a view of circumcision similar to Philo's.

Paul may well have meant this argument to appeal especially to the Gentile Christian majority in the Roman Christian community without, however, alienating its Jewish Christian minority. As pointed out earlier, circumcision seems not to have been an issue in the Roman Christian community.[34] Had it been an issue, Paul would have felt compelled to deal explicitly with it in the letter. As it was, however, the majority of male believers of Gentile origin, although originally sympathetically associated with the Roman Jewish community, were not circumcised and were not being called on to be circumcised in order to be members of the Christian community. Similarly, male Jewish Christian members of the community would have already been circumcised. Paul's argument about the true value of circumcision would have appealed to each group, although in somewhat different ways. On the one hand, it would have appealed to the Jewish Christian minority because Paul affirmed that circumcision would be of value (ὠφελεῖ) if one obeyed the law (Rom 2:25). On the other hand, although he affirmed its value, he did not affirm its necessity. This would have appealed to the Gentile Christian majority, since Paul claimed that for someone who was uncircumcised but obeyed the commandments of the law, his uncircumcision could be accounted as equivalent to circumcision (2:26). In this way, his interpretation of circumcision, rooted as it was in traditional Jewish viewpoints, could affirm the equal status of both Jewish and Gentile members of the Roman Christian community.

Second, how Paul turns these traditional viewpoints to his own purposes emerges in the way he uses the apostrophe in 2:17–29.[35] Paul's apostrophe to a fictitious Jewish addressee in 2:17–29 is meant to parallel 2:1–11, the apostrophe to a fictitious Gentile addressee. In 2:1–11, Paul expects his readers to condemn the hypocrisy of the Gentile addressee, who, while condemning Gentile idolatry and immorality, engaged in the same kind of conduct. In 2:17–24, Paul offers an equivalent apostrophe to a fictitious Jewish addressee who, while claiming to know the law and to be able to instruct others in the law (2:17–19), nevertheless dishonors God by not observing the requirements of the law. If God is impartial as Paul claims in 2:6–11, then the equivalent conduct of Jews must be equally condemned.[36] The same point is made in 2:25–29, this time using circumcision as an example. In a way similar to 2:12–16, Paul claims that circumcision is of value only if one practices the law. But if one is a transgressor of the law, then circumcision is of no value. Conversely if someone who is uncircumcised observes the requirements of the law, this observance

---

[33] Though interpreting the law allegorically, Philo thought that the law also had to be observed literally (*Migr.* 89–94).

[34] See above, pp. 43–44.

[35] See Stowers, *Diatribe*, 97–98.

[36] Notice that in 2:21–22 Paul does not accuse Jews of the same conduct as Gentiles (i.e., idolatry and homosexual practices) but of equivalent conduct condemned by the law (i.e., stealing, adultery, and perhaps sacrilege). On the meaning of ἱεροσυλέω, see Dunn, *Romans*, 114–15, 138.

will be counted by God as circumcision. Both 2:25–29 and 2:12–16 compare Jews and Gentiles and claim that observance of the "law" (whether by Jews or by Gentiles) is what is important.

The parallelism of the two apostrophes (2:1–11, 17–29) is meant to flesh out rhetorically the consequences of the theological principle that God judges impartially (2:6, 11). On the basis of this impartiality, both Gentiles and Jews, in terms of their conduct (although not in terms of their respective religious traditions), are similarly liable to God's judgment. If Gentiles' knowledge of what is right means that they have no excuse (ἀναπολόγητος, 2:1) for doing wrong, then similarly Jews' knowledge of the law is not a privilege that can be appealed to in transgressing the law (2:21–24).[37] This rhetorical parallelism, based on the conservatively oriented argument from previous judgments on similar cases, puts flesh on the bones of the theological principle of divine impartiality.

What Paul has done in 2:12–29 is to argue that the conduct of Jews must be judged on the same basis as the conduct of Gentiles. He demonstrates this, however, through the use of quotations from the Jewish scriptures as well as through the use of other traditional Jewish viewpoints. Where Paul moves beyond those viewpoints is in juxtaposing them in a conservatively oriented argument from previous judgments on similar cases. This juxtaposition itself is rooted in what Paul claims is a scripturally grounded, traditional Jewish argument, that is, the impartiality of God. In reality, Paul has argued for untraditional conclusions on what he hopes his audience would regard as traditional assumptions and viewpoints.

Romans 3:1–20: Objections and Replies

Once Paul has made his argument, on what he considers traditional grounds, that Jews and Gentiles are in similar situations, he then deals with objections that might be raised against his position. From a rhetorical point of view, 3:1–20 is a refutation *(reprehensio* or *confutatio)* of these objections.[38] All the objections are to arguments in 2:12–29, that is, to the controversial aspects of Paul's arguments. As seen above in chapter 3, the use of objections and replies was a common rhetorical device in the diatribe.[39] For the most part, this section is made up of a series of objections from, and replies to, a fictitious interlocutor, again a rhetorical figure common in diatribes.[40] Paul does not specify the identity of this fictitious interlocutor. At first, he might seem to be the same as the fictitious Jewish addressee in 2:17–29. This, how-

---

[37] Notice that Paul is not attacking the law but transgressions of the law and claims to privilege when one is even transgressing the law.

[38] See Quintilian, *Inst.* 5.13, for a discussion of refutation.

[39] For rhetorical analyses of this section, see Stanley K. Stowers, *Diatribe,* 119–120, 133–137, 148–154; "Paul's Dialogue with a Fellow Jew in Romans 3:1–9," *CBQ* 46 (1984): 707–22; *A Reading of Romans: Justice, Jews, and Gentiles* (New Haven: Yale University Press, 1994), 163–75; and A. J. Malherbe, "*Mē genoito* in the Diatribe and Paul," in *Paul and the Popular Philosophers* (Minneapolis: Fortress, 1989), 25–33.

[40] The technical name for this figure is *subiectio.* See *Rhet. Her.* 4.33; Quintilian, *Inst.* 5.11.3, 5; 9.2.14–15; and Lausberg, *Handbook of Literary Rhetoric,* §§ 771–75. It has been traced back to the Cynic Teles (third century B.C.). See Theodore C. Burgess, *Epideictic Literature* (Chicago: University of Chicago Press, 1902), 237.

ever, is unlikely. The Jewish addressee in 2:17–29 was a hypocrite who claimed to know the law but did not keep its commandments. The interlocutor in 3:1–8, however, is someone quite different. He is someone concerned over the negative implications of Paul's views about the equal sinfulness of Jews and Gentiles for the value of the whole Jewish tradition. In reality, Paul's fictitious interlocutor in 3:1–8 is the Roman Christian who is suspicious of, or hostile to, what he sees as the implications of Paul's controversial arguments.[41] But it is important in this context to recall again the indirection of these objections and replies. This indirection was common to the rhetorical devices used in the diatribe. Although Paul is addressing what he thinks are objections from his Roman Christian audience, he does not reply directly to them but to a fictitious interlocutor. He therefore does not explicitly identify him. Rhetorically, this allows Paul to avoid any direct confrontation with the Roman Christians and allows them to identify more easily with his responses, since they are not being directly attacked. The common element that runs through these objections is that Paul's views about the similar situations of both Jews and Gentiles compromise God, either God's faithfulness to the Jews or God's righteousness in judging transgressors. Once again Paul's answers to the objections are rooted in the Jewish scriptures and traditional Jewish viewpoints.

The first objection (3:1–2) asks what value there is in being a Jew or in circumcision if Jews and Gentiles are in the same situation. Paul answers that there is great value in both, especially because the Jews have been entrusted with the oracles of God, that is, with the Jewish scriptures. This in itself would be advantage enough, even if there were no other advantage to circumcision and being a Jew. Since this answer appealed to the value of the Jewish scriptures, none of Paul's Roman Christian audience would have objected to Paul's reply to this fictitious interlocutor.

The second objection (3:3–4) is that if some Jews have been unfaithful, this does not nullify God's faithfulness. Paul readily agrees that it certainly does not and again appeals to Scripture, first by alluding to Ps 115:2 (LXX) and then by quoting Ps 50:6 (LXX): "That you may be justified in your words and prevail if you are taken to court [κρίνεσθαί σε]."[42] The context of Psalm 50 (LXX) is one in which the sinner admits his or her sinfulness and the justice of God's judgment. By his appeal to this psalm, Paul points out that God is shown to be just even in judging the sinner and that the unfaithfulness of some does not negate the truthfulness of God's judgment.[43]

---

[41] In seeing Paul's imaginary interlocutor in this section as a Roman Christian suspicious of the consequences of Paul's arguments, I disagree with Stowers, "Paul's Dialogue," 715. The problem with Stowers's interpretation of the interlocutor as a fellow Jew is that Paul's concern at this point is not the Jewish reaction to his positions but the suspicious or even hostile reaction of the Roman Christians. It is their objections with which he must come to terms.

[42] The Greek infinitive κρίνεσθαι could be either middle or passive voice. In this context, it is better taken as the middle voice with an active meaning. This is because the word "prevail" (νικᾶν) is being used in the technical sense of winning a lawsuit. See Byrne, *Romans*, 113; and William Sanday and Arthur C. Headlam, *A Critical and Exegetical Commentary on the Epistle to the Romans* (5th ed.; ICC; Edinburgh: T&T Clark, 1902), 72.

[43] Stowers ("Paul's Dialogue," 716–17) places Rom 3:3 in Paul's mouth and 3:4 in the interlocutor's mouth. Throughout Romans 1–3, however, Paul appeals to Scripture, and so the scriptural references in 3:4 (Ps 115:2 [LXX]; 50:6 [LXX]) are more naturally placed in his mouth. Romans 3:3, then, has the words of the interlocutor.

The third objection (Rom 3:5–6) concerns God's justice in judging. If even human wickedness demonstrates the righteousness of God, the God who inflicts wrath is not unjust, is he? Paul again agrees that God is certainly not unjust. His reason is that if God were unjust in inflicting wrath, then God could not judge the world at all. Such a patently absurd conclusion, so contrary to the Jewish scriptures, was obviously out of the question not only for Paul but also for his fictitious inter-locutor and for his Roman Christian audience as well.[44]

Paul's answers to the first three objections are very short. His answers to the second and third objections even agree with the fictitious interlocutor's positions. Rhetorically, this has the indirect effect of leading Paul's Roman Christian audience to see him as someone who agrees with them, as someone who maintains the same traditional Jewish positions as they do about the value of the Jewish scriptures and about God's faithfulness and judgment. He also intends these first three replies to render his Roman Christian audience benevolent as he moves on to the fourth and fifth objections, probably the real objections made against his positions.

The fourth objection (3:7–8) takes up the alleged ethical consequences of Paul's position. The interlocutor asks why, if by his lie God's truthfulness abounds to God's glory, he is still judged a sinner. Why not indeed do evil in order that God may draw good from it?[45] In this objection Paul explicitly mentions that there are some who blasphemously claim that this is indeed his position (3:8). Paul very care-fully does not identify these "some" with his Roman audience. They remain dis-creetly anonymous. Paul summarily condemns them for claiming that this was his position. It is difficult to imagine that someone could charge that Paul explicitly claimed that Christians should do evil in order that good might come of it. The charge was probably more indirect. If righteousness now takes place apart from ob-servance of the Mosaic law, then what role could ethical conduct play in the life of believers? Could not even sinning work to the greater glory of God? The rumor or suspicion about Paul's position may have claimed that, although not explicitly, in ef-fect Paul was saying, "Let us do evil that good might come of it." At this point in the letter, Paul dismisses this charge out of hand: "Their condemnation is well de-served." But as we shall see, Paul took this charge more seriously than his sharp, quick reply here would indicate. He will return to the charge and deal with it much more fully in Romans 5–7.

But even here he takes up the charge in a somewhat modified form in the fifth and final objection (3:9–19): "What then? Are we making excuses [προεχόμεθα]?[46]

---

[44] Stowers (ibid., 715, 717) places 3:5 in Paul's mouth and 3:6 in the interlocutor's mouth. Since Paul, however, is defending himself and answering objections, it is more natural to place the answers in Paul's mouth (3:6) and the objection in his interlocutor's. The end of 3:6 (κατὰ ἄνθρωπον λέγω) is Paul's editorial comment lest even the mention of the possibility of God being unjust be taken amiss.

[45] This objection is actually in the first person singular. In the diatribe, however, objec-tions and false conclusions are stated in a number of different ways with no appreciable differ-ence in meaning (Stowers, Diatribe, 128–29). The point of the objection is obviously not restricted to Paul alone. Paul may have used the first person singular because "some say" (3:8) that this was Paul's position.

[46] The meaning of προεχόμεθα is disputed. Various translations have been suggested: "What then do we plead in our defense?" (Dunn, Romans, 145–48); "Do we [Jews] have an ad-

Not at all!"[47] Here the rhetoric changes, and Paul raises the objection as a rhetorical question in the first person. This objection is not that Paul is encouraging sin that good might come from it but that he is nevertheless offering excuses for human sinfulness. Once again, he denies this by pointing out that he has previously charged that both Jews and Gentiles are all (πάντας) under sin (3:9). The reference to the previous charge is to the whole argument that Paul has made in 1:18–2:29, that both Gentiles and Jews are sinful. Here he finally states clearly and explicitly what he has only insinuated at crucial points earlier in his argument (1:18; 2:1, 6–10), that the wrath of God is revealed on all (πᾶσαν) human ungodliness and wickedness. This "all" is now seen to include not only Gentiles but also Jews. He is making excuses for no group, neither for Jews nor for Gentiles.

He then substantiates this claim in 3:10–18 by a catena of scriptural quotations (Eccl 7:20[?]; Ps 14:1–3//53:2–4; Ps 5:10; Ps 10:7; Isa 59:7–8; Ps 36:2). In order to make the point of this appeal to Scripture as clear as possible, he also appeals to what he takes to be a principle of scriptural interpretation familiar to his readers: "We know that whatever the law says it speaks to those under the law" (Rom 3:19). The scriptural quotations describing human sinfulness must therefore also apply to Jews. He then adds that the purpose of this is that "every [πᾶν] mouth may be stopped, and the whole [πᾶς] world may be held accountable to God" (3:19). It is important to emphasize that Paul's argument here is not about all individuals but about all groups, that is, about Jews and Gentiles. Since both occurrences of πᾶς in 3:19 take up the use of πᾶς in 3:9 (as well as the πᾶς of 1:18; 2:1, 6–10), the point of the πᾶς is that both Jews and Gentiles as groups are similarly liable to God's judgment.[48]

---

vantage?" (Cranfield, *Romans,* 1.187–90); "Do we have an advantage?" (Wilckens, *Römer,* 1:172); "Are we any better?" (Morris, *Romans,* 162–65); "Have we any advantage?" (E. Käsemann, *Commentary on Romans* [ed. and trans. G. W. Bromiley; Grand Rapids: Eerdmans, 1980], 85); "Are we Jews at a disadvantage?" (Stowers, "Paul's Dialogue," 719–20). The most natural interpretation of προεχόμεθα is to take it in its customary middle sense ("to hold something before oneself for protection" [BDAG 869]). Since the "we" of προεχόμεθα must be the same as the "we" of προητιασάμεθα (3:9b), i.e., Paul, the translation would be, "Are we protecting ourselves?" or "Are we making excuses?" This translation is closest to Dunn; but I do not find Dunn's alternate punctuation or his omission of οὐ πάντως convincing.

[47] Both the meaning and the presence of οὐ πάντως are matters of some dispute. While one would expect οὐ πάντως to mean "not entirely," in the context of 3:1–9 it must mean "not at all." This meaning is attested in Epictetus, *Diatr.* 4.8.2. Dunn (*Romans,* 145), following Nils A. Dahl ("Romans 3:9: Text and Meaning," in *Paul and Paulinism: Essays in Honour of C. K. Barrett* [ed. M. D. Hooker and S. G. Wilson; London: SPCK, 1982], 184–204) omits the phrase altogether. The preponderance of the MS evidence is in favor of retaining the phrase. The phrase is absent from MSS whose ancestry can be traced to the edition of Romans that lacked Romans 15–16. The fact that Romans probably originally contained Romans 15–16 counts against the omission of οὐ πάντως as original. The phrase could have been omitted for either of two reasons: (1) if the scribe took the phrase to mean "not entirely," he could have omitted it because it would have had no meaning in its context, or (2) if the scribe took προεχόμεθα with Τί οὖν, he would have omitted οὐ πάντως because it would have made no sense in the context.

[48] Given the way in which Paul interprets the significance of the catena of scriptural quotations in 3:10–18 by 3:9,19, these quotations (even the allusion to Eccl 7:20 in Rom 3:10) are best understood as referring to all groups (i.e., Jews and Gentiles) rather than to all individuals.

This leads to his concluding statement in 3:20: "For 'no one shall be made righteous before him' [Ps 143:1–2] by works of the law, for through the law comes knowledge of sin." He uses Ps 143:1–2 as his final statement that neither group, Gentile or Jewish, is made righteous through observance of the law. Why is this the case? Because neither group has in fact observed the law. It is crucial to emphasize how much his use of Ps 143:1–2 here differs from his use of it in Gal 2:16. In Gal 2:16, Paul interprets Ps 143:1–2 as a *principle* meant to deny that righteousness was ever possible through the observance of the law.[49] Given his argument in Rom 1:18–3:19, however, Paul's point in using this quotation from Ps 143:1–2 in Rom 3:20 is not that observation of the law could not result in righteousness or even that the law was impossible to observe but that as a *matter of fact* neither Jews nor Gentiles as groups have observed the law. This quite different interpretation of Ps 143:1–2 is once again in keeping with Paul's consistent attempt in this section of Romans to explain his position to his Roman readers in terms that had roots in traditional Jewish viewpoints.

In addition, and crucial for the way he has argued up until now, Paul ends by claiming that the knowledge of that sinfulness comes through the law itself (Rom 3:20). Given his appeal to the Jewish scriptures (i.e., the law) throughout his argument, the emphasis of this final phrase is not that the law brings *only* knowledge of sin. Rather, it is the law itself and the knowledge of human sinfulness (both Gentile and Jewish) that it provides that have supported Paul's arguments. In 3:20 one can see clearly and in summary fashion both the position Paul has argued—the equal sinfulness of Jews and Gentiles—and the grounds on which Paul claims that he has argued it, the law itself.

CONCLUSIONS

For the Roman Christian community, Paul's convictions about the equal sinfulness of Jews and Gentiles as groups must have seemed incompatible with their convictions about the ethical superiority of the Mosaic law and its observance. In the light of this, Paul crafted his rhetoric very carefully in order to persuade his audience that his apparently controversial positions about the equal sinfulness of both Jews and Gentiles were really rooted in, and supported by, the Jewish scriptures and Jewish tradition, both of which he and the Roman Christian community shared. Paul did this by consistently appealing to the Jewish scriptures and to traditional Jewish viewpoints about Gentiles and about God's impartiality. Paul argued that his viewpoints were in continuity with them and not in conflict with them. He also used various arguments and devices of Greco-Roman rhetoric associated with the diatribe that were familiar to his Roman readers and had a conservatively oriented bias. In this way, he hoped to allay their suspicions and hostility. He was really a sheep in wolf's clothing.

In reflecting more broadly on 1:18–3:20, it is also important to be aware of the perspective Paul takes in his arguments. He certainly appeals to the Jewish scriptures

---

[49] Betz, *Galatians*, 116–19; Martyn, *Galatians*, 252–53.

and to traditional Jewish viewpoints to support his arguments for the equal sinfulness of Jews and Gentiles as groups. But it is even more important to realize the extent to which Paul sees these arguments as temporally or historically oriented. That Paul sees his arguments in this way becomes very clear at the beginning of the next stage of his argument (3:21–26): "Now [Νυνί] the righteousness of God has been manifested apart from the law . . . to prove at the present time [ἐν τῷ νῦν καιρῷ] his righteousness." It is also clear from the arguments he makes in 1:18–3:20 itself. He is arguing that in fact Jews and Gentiles have in the course of time been equally sinful even though in different ways. Paul thus sees what he argues for in 1:18–3:20 as an analysis of what has been the case in the past but now, through the manifestation of God's righteousness in Christ, has been irrevocably changed. This temporally or historically oriented perspective is very different from that of his letter to the Galatians, which was dominated by stark and virtually unresolvable contrasts. This very different perspective, which surfaces in the first stage of Paul's argument, will continue to play a crucial role in how he continues, in the rest of Romans, to reshape radically the stark and seemingly unresolvable contrasts of Galatians.

CHAPTER 5

The Paradox of Righteousness, Abraham, and Upholding the Law

I N ROM 3:21–4:25 WE COME FACE TO FACE again with the complexity of
Paul's relationship to both his own past (especially his interpretation of the significance of Abraham as reflected in his letter to the Galatians) and the Roman
Christian community (especially how this interpretation provoked grave misgivings
among the Roman Christians). The complexities of both these relationships affect
the way Paul argues in 3:21–4:25. He significantly revises some of his own previously held views. The section reflects his struggle to rethink the assumptions and
implications of his own basic convictions about righteousness through faith and the
equality of Jews and Gentiles before God. As will be seen, he does this partially by
continuing to place these convictions in a temporally oriented framework rather
than in the dialectical framework that dominated Galatians and also by showing
how this different framework and the implications he draws from it are rooted in
views that he and his Roman Christian audience share.

At first reading, Paul's arguments in this section of Romans, although complicated, seem fairly straightforward. He argues for three interrelated positions, all of
which he states in the subproposition in 3:21–22c:

1. The righteousness of God has *now* been manifested *apart from* the Mosaic
   law.

2. This righteousness of God is witnessed to by the Jewish scriptures (i.e., the
   Law and the Prophets).

3. This righteousness is *through faith* in Jesus Christ for *all* who have faith
   (i.e., both Jews and Gentiles).

Paul is obviously taking up again the central elements of his "gospel" that he first
stated in the proposition of his argument in 1:16–17. Paul claimed there that in his
gospel the righteousness of God is being revealed on the basis of faith. This revelation
of God's righteousness is the power of God for the salvation of everyone who has
faith, the Jew first and also the Gentile. All these elements recur in 3:21–22c. But Paul

also emphasizes two additional elements in this subproposition. First, the manifestation of God's righteousness *now* takes place *apart from* observance of the law. Second, this righteousness is witnessed to in the Jewish scriptures. Both these elements will play important roles in his argument in 3:21–4:25.

Most of this section is taken up with an interpretation of the example of Abraham (4:1–25). Paul explicitly meant the example of Abraham to substantiate his second position, that the Jewish scriptures witness to the righteousness of God (Rom 3:31). But he also meant it to support the first and third positions. In support of the first position, Paul argues that righteousness was reckoned by God to Abraham through his faith and apart from his observance of the law (4:1–8). Also in support of the first position is the fact that the promise given to Abraham and to his "seed" was given on the basis of faith and was not mediated through the Mosaic law (4:13–17a). In support of the third position, Paul argues that the blessing through faith to Abraham and to his "seed" was given to Abraham before his circumcision so that he would be the father of both the circumcised and the uncircumcised (4:11–12, 16–17). Finally, the example of Abraham and his faith was meant not only for Abraham himself but also "for us," that is, for all who have faith in the God who raised Jesus from the dead (4:23–25). Abraham is not only an example from the past but also a paradigm for the present.

These arguments, although not simple, seem at first to be straightforward. They are, however, much less straightforward than they appear. This does not mean that Paul is being devious. Rather, the issues underlying this section of Romans as well as Paul's responses to them are deeply influenced by his complex relationships with both his Roman Christian audience and his own past, specifically with what he wrote in Galatians. But before we look at these issues, something needs to be said about the structure of the passage and its unity.

The structure of 3:21–4:25 is fairly clear and is similar to the structure found in 1:18–3:20:

A. Subproposition: The righteousness of God is now revealed through faith in Jesus Christ apart from observance of the law for all who believe; the Law and the Prophets witness to this (3:21–22c).

B. Exposition of this position through the use of a traditional creedal formula about redemption through Jesus' death as an expiation (3:22d–26).

C. Defense of the controversial position that righteousness for both Jews and Gentiles through faith apart from observance of the law upholds the law rather than nullifies it (3:27–4:25).

    1. Rhetorical questions and replies claiming that righteousness through faith apart from observance of the law for Jews and Gentiles alike upholds and does not nullify the law (3:27–31).

    2. Argument by means of the example or paradigm of Abraham (4:1–25).

        a. Abraham was reckoned righteous by his faith apart from his observance (4:1–8).

> b. Abraham's righteousness was prior to his circumcision so that he could be the father of both the circumcised and the uncircumcised, both Jews and Gentiles (4:9–12).
>
> c. The promise comes through faith and not through the law to all Abraham's "seed," not only to Jews but also to Gentiles; but if it comes through the law, then God's promise is rendered void (4:13–17a).
>
> d. An emotionally heightened description of how Abraham had faith in God's promise even if it concerned God's giving life to the dead (4:17b–22).

D. Conclusion applying the example or paradigm of Abraham's faith to those who have faith in the God who raised Jesus from the dead (4:23–25).

As in 1:18–20, Paul begins 3:21–22c with a statement of the subproposition that he will be arguing. As in 1:21–32, the expository section in 3:22d–26 draws on material that both Paul and the Roman Christian community have in common, in this case a traditional creedal formula. Finally, as in 2:1–3:20, Paul makes use in 3:27–4:25 of the rhetorical questions, replies, and comparisons commonly found in diatribes. He also makes extensive use of an example, that of Abraham's faith. This too is a rhetorical device common in diatribes. Finally, as in 2:1–3:20, he makes extensive use of the Jewish scriptures and for much the same purpose, to show how they support his position (4:1–25).

The unity of the passage is also fairly clear. Both the beginning of this section ("But now . . ." [3:21]) and the beginning of the next section of the letter ("Therefore, since we are made righteous by faith . . ." [5:1]) indicate that what falls between must be seen as a unit. There are also a number of parallels between the two major parts of the section (3:21–26 and 3:27–4:25):

Righteousness apart from the law	3:21	3: 28; 4:6
Righteousness through faith	3:22	3:27; 4:5, 11
To all who believe	3:22	3:29; 4:11–12, 16
By grace	3:23	4:4, 16
Use of traditional creedal formula	3:24–26	4:25
Not make void the law	3:21	3:31; 4:14

These extensive parallels make clear that Paul is dealing with the same issues throughout the section.

What specifically are the issues that Paul is dealing with in this passage? Here we need to keep clearly in mind two characteristics of his earlier letter to the Galatians. The first and more general characteristic was mentioned above in chapter 3: the consistently dialectical structure of Paul's arguments in Galatians. When Paul wrote his letter to the Galatians, his purpose was to persuade them not to be deceived into being circumcised and practicing the Mosaic law in order to be considered full believers in Christ. Because of its polemical intensity, Paul's arguments in

Gal 3:1–4:31 consistently contrast faith in Christ with observance of the Mosaic law. This contrast is to the great detriment of the latter. His arguments are of the either-or sort, in which one alternative is accepted and the other rejected.

The second and more specific characteristic of Galatians is his treatment of the patriarch Abraham in three of his arguments (3:6–14; 15–18; 4:21–31). Although his treatment of Abraham there bears some similarity to his use of Abraham in Rom 4:1–25, it is astonishing how different the interpretations of Abraham in Galatians and in Romans are. Because the example of Abraham in Rom 4:1–25 plays such a dominant role in 3:21–4:25, these crucial differences must be taken account of and explained if one is to understand at all what Paul is about in 3:21–4:25.

The patriarch Abraham first appears in Gal 3:6–14. Beginning with Gen 15:6, he is the basis of a scriptural proof that in Christ righteousness would come to the Gentiles through faith and not through observance of the Mosaic law. Although the argument is complex, Paul clearly states his point in Gal 3:14: "so that in Christ Jesus the blessing of Abraham might come to the Gentiles [τὰ ἔθνη], so that we might receive the promise [ἐπαγγελίαν] of the Spirit through faith [διὰ τῆς πίστεως]." His argument in 3:6–14 connects the Gentiles who have faith in Christ with the precedent of the patriarch Abraham, who also had faith and so was reckoned as righteous (Gen 15:6) and in whom God promised that all the Gentiles would be blessed (Gen 18:18; 12:3).

But in Gal 3:10–13 Paul also sharply contrasts Abraham and Gentile believers with those who are rooted in the observance of the law (ὅσοι ἐξ ἔργων νόμου). Quoting Deut 27:26 ("Cursed be everyone who does not abide by all things written in the book of the law, and do them"), Paul claims that all who observe the law are under a curse. Further, it is clear that no one is made righteous before God by observing the law. To establish this, Paul quotes Hab 2:4 ("The one who is righteous shall live by faith") and contrasts it with Lev 18:5 ("Whoever does the works of the law will live by them"). The point of the contrast is that Lev 18:5, in referring to those who do the works of the law, does not speak of them either as having "faith" or as "righteous."[1] Finally, Paul claims that Christ, through his crucifixion on a cross, has delivered believers from the curse mentioned in Deut 27:26 by himself becoming accursed. To establish this point, he quotes Deut 21:23 ("Cursed is everyone who hangs on a tree"). The connection of the curse mentioned in Deut 27:26 with the one in Deut 21:23 is made, at least in Paul's mind, on the basis of the hermeneutical principle known from later rabbinic literature as *gᵉzērāh šāwāh*, an analogy made on the basis of the occurrence of the same words in two different scriptural passages.[2] In this case, the word that appears in both passages is "cursed"

---

[1] See Betz, *Galatians*, 146–48.

[2] The hermeneutical principle of "equal ordinance" is the second of Hillel's seven rules *(middôt)(t. Sanh.* 7.11). See Herman L. Strack and Günter Stemberger, *Introduction to the Talmud and Midrash* (Edinburgh: T&T Clark, 1991), 20–21. The situation, however, is more complicated than it seems at first. In quoting Deut 27:26 and Deut 21:23, Paul uses the identical word for "cursed" in both places (ἐπικατάρατος). In the MSS, however, ἐπικατάρατος is found only in Deut 27:26; Deut 21:23 has κεκαταραμένος. The words for "cursed" are also different in the MT (*'ārûr* in Deut 27:26; *qillat* in Deut 21:23). Paul may have been quoting from memory, or he may have changed κεκαταραμένος to ἐπικατάρατος to make his point.

(ἐπικατάρατος). Christ, by being crucified took on himself the "curse" of Deut 21:23 and so overcame for believers the "curse" of Deut 27:26.[3] The overcoming of the curse took place presumably through God's raising Jesus from the dead.

In the situation reflected in Galatians, Paul's purpose in using this argument is to show, on the basis of the Jewish scriptures, that Gentile believers such as the Galatians, through their faith in Christ, are free of any obligation to observe the Mosaic law. Yet Paul's argument raises as many questions as it tried to answer. The basic contrast in the argument is between Abraham and Gentiles who by their faith are the true "sons of Abraham," on the one hand (Gal 3:6–9, 14), and those who observe the Mosaic law, on the other (3:10–12). On the basis of this contrast, one could logically conclude that Paul viewed Abraham as connected with the Gentiles but as standing over against those who observed the Mosaic law, that is, the Jewish people. In this way, Abraham is the father of the Gentiles who have faith, but he no longer appears, at least in any religious sense, to be the father of the Jews. This impression could only have been strengthened by Paul's claim that those who observe the law are under a curse (3:10–13).

In Gal 3:15–18 Paul moves on to another argument, which, however unintentionally, raises the same problems as 3:6–14. Galatians 3:15–18 is about the relationship between the promise made by God to Abraham and his "seed" and the Mosaic law.[4] The overall argument is based on what Paul claims is a familiar legal practice.[5] Once someone's will has been ratified, no one can annul it or add to it. So too the promise made by God to Abraham and to his "seed" cannot be annulled or changed by the Mosaic law, which was given 430 years later. Otherwise the promise made by God to Abraham and to his "seed" would be nullified (καταργῆσαι) because the inheritance would be mediated by the law rather than by the promise (3:17–18).

As part of the argument, Paul also specifies more precisely in 3:16 to whom he thinks the word "seed" refers: "Now the promises were made to Abraham and to his 'seed' [σπέρματι, Gen 12:3; 13:15; 17:17; 22:18; 24:7]; it does not say 'and to his seeds' [καὶ τοῖς σπέρμασιν], as of many; but it says, 'and to your seed' [καί τῷ σπέρματί σου], who is Christ." The purpose of interpreting the references to Abraham's "seed" in Genesis as a singular noun rather than as a collective noun is first, to connect Christ directly with Abraham and the promises made to him by God and, second, to show that the promises were not mediated through the law. The second

---

[3] For the association of Deut 21:23 with crucifixion, see 4QpNah, fragments 3–4, col. 1, lines 7–8, and 11QTᵃ 66:11–13. See Joseph A. Fitzmyer, "Crucifixion in Ancient Palestine, Qumran Literature, and the New Testament," in *To Advance the Gospel* (New York: Crossroad, 1981), 125–46.

[4] From its context in Galatians, the promise made to Abraham included all of the blessings Paul mentions, esp. that in Gal 3:14, i.e., the Gentiles' reception of the promise of the Spirit through faith. See Betz, *Galatians*, 156.

[5] What this common legal practice was, however, is not clear. In Greek and Roman law a testament could be changed at any time. Paul may be referring to a specifically Jewish institution (the *mattenat bari'*) that could not be changed. The question is how widespread this institution was. See Betz, *Galatians*, 155–56; Reuven Yaron, *Gifts in Contemplation of Death in Jewish and Roman Law* (Oxford: Clarendon, 1960), 19–21, 49–51; Walter Selb, "Διαθήκη im Neuen Testament: Randbemerkungen eines Juristen zu einem Theologenstreit," *JJS* 25 (1974): 183–96.

purpose is probably the more important in Paul's mind in Galatians. Because the Mosaic law played no role in the promises or their transmission to Abraham's "seed"—that is, Christ—the inheritance (3:18) that believers receive does not come through the law. The implied conclusion is that the Galatians should have no interest in being circumcised and observing the Mosaic law.

Whatever Paul's intended purpose, the argument, specifically his interpretation of the term "seed," raises the same kind of problem as did 3:6–14. If the term "seed" is a singular noun and refers only to Christ, then it seems that it cannot refer to the Jewish people, its most obvious and certainly its traditional Jewish referent in Genesis.[6] Not only does Abraham seem to be the father of the Gentile believers rather than of the Jews; the promise given by God to his "seed" also seems to bypass the Jews by referring directly to Christ.

Abraham appears for the last time in the allegory of Sarah and Hagar (4:21–31). This passage is Paul's final argument against the Galatian believers who want to put themselves under obligation to observe the Mosaic law (4:21). The allegory is quite difficult for us today to understand, especially in its details, and may well have been as difficult for the Galatians.[7] From the conclusion Paul drew in 4:31 ("we are children, not of the slave woman but of the free woman"), however, the purpose of the allegorical interpretation is to affirm the status of the Gentile believers of Galatia and to argue against any demand that they be circumcised and observe the Mosaic law. Yet his allegorical interpretation of the relationship between Sarah and Hagar presents a very odd picture. The Jews (Sinai, the present Jerusalem) are associated with Hagar and with slavery whereas the Gentile believers (the Jerusalem above) are associated with Sarah and Isaac and with freedom. The allegorical interpretation reverses the "ancestry" of Jews and Gentile believers. In addition, because Ishmael, the son of the slave woman, persecuted Isaac, the son of the free woman, Scripture says (Gen 21:10) that the slave woman and her son should be driven out (Gal 4:29–30).[8] The point of this interpretation no doubt is to show that the Galatian believers should reject anyone who claims that they not only have to have faith in Christ but also have to observe the Mosaic law. Nevertheless, whatever Paul's actual intention is, it again plausibly leads to the conclusion that the Jews are not the true children of Abraham and that, in reality, they are hostile to those who are Abraham's true children, that is, to the Gentile believers. This suspicion would hardly have been allayed by Paul's description of the Galatians' wish to observe the Mosaic law as submitting again "to a yoke of slavery" (5:1) or as being in bondage to weak and beggarly elemental principles of the universe, to "beings that by nature are not gods" (4:8–10).

As one reads Paul's arguments in Galatians and particularly his appeals to Abraham in 3:6–14, 15–18; 4:21–31, one can argue that his intention was to defend

---

[6] Sir 44:21; *Jub.* 12:24; 13:4, 19–21; 14:5, 7, 13, 18; 15:9–10, 19; 16:17–19, 26, 28; 18:15–16; 19:21–25; 21:22, 25; *3 Macc* 6:3; 1QapGen 21:10, 12; *Pss. Sol.* 9:9; 18:3; *4 Ezra* 3:15; *L.A.B.* 18:5; 23:5; Philo, *Leg.* 3.203; *Her.* 8, 86, 313–314; *T. Ab.* 2:6; 8:7 [recension A]; *Apoc. Ab.* 20:5; *T. Mos.* 3:9.

[7] For a discussion of this difficult passage, see esp. Betz, *Galatians*, 238–52.

[8] On the notion of Ishmael "persecuting" Isaac, see Josephus, *Ant.* 1.215; *t. Soṭah* 6.6; *Gen. Rab.* 53.11; *Tg. Ps.-J.* Gen 22:1. For a discussion, see Betz, *Galatians*, 250–51.

the enfranchisement of Gentile Christians as Gentiles and not to advocate the dis-inheritance of the Jews. Certainly Paul's excursus in 3:19–25, on the role of the Mo-saic law, as well as his own sense of himself as a believing Jew point in this direction.[9] But it is difficult to deny that Paul's use of the example of Abraham in Galatians left him open to the accusation that he had enfranchised Gentile believers at the price, in effect, of disinheriting the Jews. In addition, the way Paul used the Jewish scriptures to make these arguments must have seemed perverse to most Roman Christians. He seemed to annul the obvious intent of the very scriptures he was interpreting. None of this would have endeared Paul either to his fellow Jews or, more to the point, to most Roman Christians, who saw their own beliefs in close continuity with both the Jewish scriptures and the Jewish people. All this will sig-nificantly affect, as we shall see, the way Paul argues in Rom 3:21–4:25.

ROMANS 3:21–26: THE SUBPROPOSITION AND THE EXPOSITION

With these issues in mind, we can now turn to Rom 3:21–26. Although the passage is quite brief, it is difficult to think of another passage in Paul's letters that has generated more controversy. At this point in the letter, however, Paul was actu-ally trying to be anything but controversial. The structure of the passage is fairly simple. In 3:21–22c Paul states the subproposition that will serve as the basis for his further arguments in 3:27–4:25 (see above, at the beginning of this chapter, how the subproposition consists of three parts). As is clear from the rest of the passage, the righteousness of God Paul is referring to is the righteousness that is manifested through the death of Christ and its consequences. In 3:22d–26, he then offers two reasons in support of this subproposition. First, there is no distinction between Jews and Gentiles, for all sinned and fall short of the glory of God (3:22d–23). Second, Paul appeals to, and comments on, a traditional creedal formula he has in common with the Roman Christians (3:24–26). He hoped that the Roman Christians would have found both these reasons uncontroversial by this point in his argument.

Each part of the subproposition, however, needs some explanation. Paul claims in the first part that the righteousness of God has *now* been manifested *apart* from the law. The Greek word "now" (νυνί) has both a temporal and a logical sense. Both senses are operative here, but the emphasis is on its temporal meaning. This is clear from 3:26, where Paul describes the death of Christ as a demonstration of God's righteousness "in the present time" (ἐν τῷ νῦν καιρῷ). The perspective in his argu-ments is once again temporal. He emphasizes this by placing νυνί as the first word in the sentence. God's manifestation of righteousness in the present time in the death of Christ certainly differs from how God manifested his righteousness in the past, but it is not necessarily in opposition to it.

What is distinctive about the present manifestation of God's righteousness is that it takes place "apart from the law" (χωρὶς νόμου). The context in which the phrase occurs makes clear that Paul means "apart from observance of the law." Im-mediately preceding this passage, in 3:20, he claimed that no one is made righteous

---

[9] See above, pp. 68–69.

on the basis of works of the law (ἐξ ἔργων νόμου). Immediately following the passage, in 3:28, Paul will claim that a person is made righteous "apart from works of the law" (χωρὶς ἔργων νόμου). And in 4:6 he will write about the person whom God considers righteous "apart from works" (χωρὶς ἔργων). This manifestation of God's righteousness now takes place apart from observance of the Mosaic law. Because he places the phrase second in the sentence and out of its natural word order, Paul obviously intends to emphasize it. This emphasis is even clearer when one realizes that he has never used the phrase "apart from [observance] of the law" before but now uses it three times in 3:21–4:25.[10] But what is the point he is actually emphasizing? This becomes clearer when one remembers once again the very different way Paul wrote about the law and its observance in Galatians. As seen above in chapter 2, Paul starkly and consistently contrasted throughout his arguments in Galatians a righteousness based on faith with one based on observance of the law. But in Rom 3:21 Paul pointedly does not describe the present manifestation of God's righteousness in opposition to observance of the law but as "apart from [observance of] the law." This change is clearly intentional and quite significant. Especially in conjunction with his use of "now," it represents a significant shift in the way Paul views the law and its observance. From this new perspective, the law and its observance played a legitimate and divinely ordained role in the past. As Paul stated at the end of the preceding section (3:20), the recognition of sin came through the law. It is difficult to overestimate the importance of this new and different perspective. This temporally oriented perspective allows Paul to maintain his basic conviction that in Christ righteousness is now through faith apart from observance of the law and at the same time not denigrate the divinely ordained role of the law in the past.

In the second part of the subproposition, Paul emphasizes that the Law and the Prophets witness to the present manifestation of God's righteousness apart from observance of the Mosaic law. As he did in 1:18–3:20, Paul wants to claim that his position is in continuity with, and is supported by, the Jewish scriptures. He does not, however, immediately explain how this is the case. Rather, he returns to it in 3:27, where he claims that his position does not annul the law but upholds it. In support of this, he then offers a much revised interpretation of the example of Abraham in 4:1–25.

In the third part of the subproposition (3:22a–c), Paul clarifies the meaning of this present manifestation of the righteousness of God through the use of an appositional phrase. This righteouness takes place through faith in Jesus Christ (διὰ πίστεως Ἰησοῦ Χριστοῦ) and is meant for all who have faith (εἰς πάντας τοὺς πιστεύοντας), for both Jews and Gentiles. Neither element in itself would have been controversial for the Roman Christians. They, like Paul, had faith in Jesus Christ, and like Paul, they were convinced that this faith was meant for all who believed, for both Jews and Gentiles. What would have been controversial, however, is the context within which Paul places these two elements. He links them with his conviction that God's righteousness is now manifested apart from observance of the Mosaic law rather than in conjunction with its observance. In addition, as Paul explains the significance of the subproposition in 3:22d–26, it will become clear that

---

[10] He will also use the phrase "apart from the law" again in 7:7, 8.

he means not simply "for both Jews and Gentiles now" but, more specifically, "for both Jews and Gentiles now" on the same basis, that is, on the basis of faith apart from observance of the Mosaic law.

In recent years, there has been considerable discussion about whether the phrase Ἰησοῦ Χριστοῦ in Rom 3:22, following πίστις in the same verse, should be construed as a subjective genitive ("the faith[fulness] of Jesus Christ") or as an objective genitive ("faith in Jesus Christ"). The same question also arises in the interpretation of the same or similar genitive constructions a bit later in 3:26 and in five other passages in Paul (Gal 2:16 [bis]; 2:20; 3:22; Phil 3:9).[11] The issue is not, as such, grammatical, since the Greek word πίστις can be followed by either a subjective or an objective genitive. Although the subjective genitive is more common, we also have examples of the objective genitive in both the New Testament and elsewhere.[12]

This study cannot go into all the complexities of the issue. But before its examination of what Paul appeals to in support of his subproposition in Rom 3:22d–26, here are the principal reasons I take the genitives in all these passages as objective rather than subjective. The first is a fairly broad and yet crucial reason. It sets the context within which the individual passages in question need to be interpreted. If Ἰησοῦ Χριστοῦ or its equivalent in these passages were a subjective genitive, one could reasonably expect that "Jesus Christ" or its equivalent would also appear as the subject of the verb πιστεύω ("to believe," "to have faith") at some point in Paul's letters. Such, however, is not the case. The verb πιστεύω appears forty-two times in Paul's letters. Not once is "Jesus Christ" or its equivalent the subject of this verb. Given the number of times Paul uses the verb in his letters and its importance for his thought, this absence must be more than accidental. In addition, the adjective πιστός ("faithful," "trustworthy") appears nine times in Paul's letters. Four times it refers to God (1 Thess 5:24; 1 Cor 1:9; 10:13; 2 Cor 1:18), once to Abraham (Gal 3:9), once to Paul alone (1 Cor 7:25), once to Paul and Apollos (1 Cor 4:2), once to Timothy (1 Cor 4:17), and once to a believer versus an unbeliever (2 Cor 6:15). Not once, however, is Jesus referred to as πιστός. Again, it is highly unlikely that this absence is accidental. The absence of examples of Jesus as the subject of the verb πιστεύω or as a noun modified by πιστός indicates that when Jesus appears after the noun πίστις, "Jesus Christ" or its equivalent is probably not the subject but the object of πίστις. It means "faith in Jesus Christ" and not the "faith[fulness] of Jesus Christ." This broader context needs to be kept in mind, since it has too often been overlooked.[13]

Second, when one turns, with this in mind, to the interpretation of the specific passages in Paul mentioned above, the more plausible interpretation of the phrase πίστις Ἰησοῦ Χριστοῦ or its equivalent is as an objective genitive. This is clearest in the two occurrences in Gal 2:15–16: "We ourselves, who are Jews by birth and not

---

[11] The recent discussion of this issue began with Richard B. Hays, *The Faith of Jesus Christ* (SBLDS 56; Chico, Calif.: Scholars Press, 1983). For a good collection of important articles reflecting the different positions, see David M. Hay and E. Elizabeth Johnson, eds., *Romans* (vol. 4 of *Pauline Theology;* SBLSymS 4; Atlanta: Scholars Press, 1997).

[12] Mark 11:22; Acts 3:16; Phil 1:27; Col 2:12; 2 Thess 2:13; Jas 2:1; Rev 14:12; Josephus, *Ant.* 19.16; *Diogn.* 11.6.

[13] The exception is Fitzmyer, *Romans*, 345.

sinners from among the Gentiles, yet who know that a person is not made righteous by works of the law [ἐξ ἔργων νόμου] but through faith in Jesus Christ [διὰ πίστεως Ἰησοῦ Χριστοῦ], even we have believed in Christ Jesus [καὶ ἡμεῖς εἰς Χριστὸν Ἰησοῦν ἐπιστεύσαμεν], so that we might be made righteous by faith in Christ [ἐκ πίστεως Χριστοῦ] and not by works of the law [ἐξ ἔργων νόμου]." The clause "even we have believed in Christ Jesus" takes up the language of the preceding clause, "who know that a person is not made righteous by works of the law but through faith in Jesus Christ." Paul's point in the whole sentence makes sense only if the phrase διὰ πίστεως Ἰησοῦ Χριστοῦ is taken to mean "faith in Jesus Christ." Just as εἰς Χριστὸν Ἰησοῦν is the object of ἐπιστεύσαμεν, so too Ἰησοῦ Χριστοῦ must be an objective genitive dependent on διὰ πίστεως.[14] This also means that the phrase ἐκ πίστεως Χριστοῦ ("by faith in Christ") in the following verse must also be an objective genitive. A bit later in the same argument (Gal 2:20), Paul also claims that he no longer lives but Christ lives in him and that the life he now lives in the flesh he lives "by faith in the son of God" (ἐν πίστει . . . τῇ τοῦ υἱοῦ τοῦ θεοῦ), who loved him and gave himself for him. Because the argument Paul began in 2:15 runs through 2:21, the phrase ἐν πίστει . . . τῇ τοῦ υἱοῦ τοῦ θεοῦ must also be an objective genitive because of its obvious similarity to the equivalent phrases in 2:15–16.

An argument often made against taking the phrase "Jesus Christ" (or its equivalent), when it follows πίστις, as an objective rather than as a subjective genitive is based on apparent redundancy. This is especially the case with Gal 3:22, Phil 3:9, and the first occurrence (Rom 3:22) in our present passage (Rom 3:21–26). In the end, however, this argument is in each case unconvincing. In all three cases, what appears at first to be redundant is actually Paul's attempt at emphasis. In Gal 3:22, Paul claims that Scripture has confined all things to sin "so that the promise based on faith in Jesus Christ [πίστεως Ἰησοῦ Χριστοῦ] might be given to those who have faith [τοῖς πιστεύουσιν]." Paul used exactly the same phrase earlier in Gal 2:16. There the genitive Ἰησοῦ Χριστοῦ was clearly an objective genitive. It makes most sense to interpret it the same way here. The apparent redundancy is due to Paul's insistence throughout Gal 3:6–29 that the promise made to Abraham was meant to be given to those who have faith in Jesus Christ and not to those who observe the law.[15] The same also seems to be the case in Phil 3:9. Paul expresses his hope to be found in Christ, not having a righteousness of his own based on the law (τὴν ἐκ νόμου) but a righteousness through faith in Christ (τὴν διὰ πίστεως Χριστοῦ), the righteousness of God that depends on faith (ἐπὶ τῇ πίστει). Once again Paul is emphasizing that there are two kinds of righteousness, one based on the law and the other based on faith in Christ. It is this second kind of righteousness, dependent on faith, that is, in his own experience, the righteousness of God.[16] Again it is a matter of emphasis, not of redundancy.

---

[14] Betz, *Galatians*, 117–18; Dunn, *Galatians*, 138–39. I find the arguments of both Matera (*Galatians*, 98–102) and Martyn, *Galatians*, 270–71, that "Jesus Christ" is a subjective genitive strained. The clause "even we have believed in Christ Jesus" is clearly not redundant. It is an emphatic conclusion based on the entire preceding clause.

[15] Betz, *Galatians*, 175–77; Dunn, *Galatians*, 195–96.

[16] Gordon Fee, *Paul's Letter to the Philippians* (NICNT; Grand Rapids: Eerdmans, 1995), 321–26. Fee also points out the parallelisms between the two parts of Phil 3:9:

Finally, the objective genitive is also clearly the case in Rom 3:22. When Paul writes that the righteousness of God is now manifest "through faith in Jesus Christ [διὰ πίστεως Ἰησοῦ Χριστοῦ] for all who have faith [εἰς πάντας τοὺς πιστεύοντας]," he is not being at all redundant. Rather, by using the phrase "for all who have faith," he is emphasizing that righteousness through faith in Jesus Christ is for all who have faith, that is, for Jews and Gentiles alike. There is no distinction because all sinned and all fall short of the glory of God (3:22d–23). This also means that the somewhat cryptic Greek phrase "the one who is of faith in Jesus" [τὸν ἐκ πίστεως Ἰησοῦ] in the final clause in 3:26 ("that he [God] might be righteous and make righteous the one who is of faith in Jesus") should also be taken as an objective genitive.

We can now turn to Rom 3:22d–26, where Paul offers two reasons in support of the subproposition in 3:21–22c. In 3:22d–23, he first sums up and appeals to what he has already established in 1:18–3:20: there is no distinction between Jews and Gentiles because all, both Jews and Gentiles, sinned and so fall short or are in need of God's glory. Given its brevity, Paul obviously takes this point as something already established by his arguments in 1:18–3:20. In its present context, it serves as the basis for a further development in his argument. If both Jews and Gentiles are similarly situated in terms of sin, then the present manifestation of God's righteousness through faith in Jesus Christ should also affect both Jews and Gentiles in a similar fashion. The equality of Jews and Gentiles in relation to sin sets the stage for the similar equality of Jews and Gentiles in relation to God's present manifestion of his righteousness now in Jesus Christ and through faith in him. This first appeal to 1:18–3:20 also illustrates how Paul's major arguments in Romans build on and are dependent on one another. His arguments in 3:21–4:25 build on the arguments he has just made in 1:18–3:20. The order of Paul's arguments in Romans is crucial for establishing their persuasiveness. As we shall see later, the same is true for Romans 5–7 and 8–11.

Based on this first appeal, Paul then makes a second appeal (3:24–26) to 1:18–3:20. He uses a traditional creedal formula that he shares with the Roman Christians and that he also amplifies and comments on in order to clarify its relevance for its present context. Both the extent and the meaning of this formula must have been familiar to his Roman Christian audience. The same, however, cannot be said of Paul's modern readers. Its extent, its original meaning, and how Paul made use of it are all matters of dispute. This study's interest is primarily in the third issue: how did Paul make use of this formula, and to what purpose did he put it in the context of 3:21–4:25? The other two issues, however, also need to be taken into account, since they affect what use one thinks Paul put the material to in the larger context of 3:21–4:25.

The first issue is the extent of the traditional creedal formula. A rather literal translation of 3:23–26 is as follows:

---

(1) (a) not having my own righteousness (b) that comes from the law (c) but that which is through faith in Christ; and (2) (a) the righteousness (b) that comes from God (c) and is based on faith. The apparent redundancy is intentional for the sake of emphasis.

For all sinned and lack the glory of God,

> *being made righteous* [δικαιούμενοι] *as a gift* [δωρεάν] by his grace [τῇ αὐτοῦ χάριτι],
>
> *through the redemption* [ἀπολυτρώσεως] *which is in Christ Jesus,*
>
> *whom God put forward* [προέθετο] *as an expiation* [ἱλαστήριον],[17]
>
> through faith [διὰ πίστεως], *by his blood* [ἐν τῷ αὐτοῦ αἵματι]
>
> *for a demonstration* [ἔνδειξιν] *of his righteousness*
>
> *for the remission* [πάρεσιν][18] *of the sins* [ἁμαρτημάτων] *formerly committed* [προγεγονότων]
>
> *in [the time of] God's patience* [ἐν τῇ ἀνοχῇ του θεοῦ]

for the "demonstration [τὴν ἔνδειξιν] of his righteousness"[19] in the present time [ἐν τῷ νῦν καιρῷ],

so that he may be righteous and make righteous the one who has faith in Jesus [τὸν ἐκ πίστεως Ἰησοῦ].

The sections in italics are taken to be parts of the traditional creedal formula. Most interpreters agree that, with the exception of "through faith," 3:25–26a is part of it. The reason is the unusual clustering, in these verses, of words that Paul rarely uses or uses nowhere else. Three words occur nowhere else in Paul: ἱλαστήριον ("expiation"), πάρεσις ("remission"), and προγίνομαι ("to happen" or "to be done before"). In addition, the Greek verb προτίθημι occurs elsewhere in Paul only in 1:13, where it almost certainly has a different meaning ("to intend," "to propose," rather than "to put forward").[20] In addition, two other words are used only once elsewhere in Paul: ἁμάρτημα (1 Cor 6:18) and ἀνοχή (Rom 2:4). Paul, then, is clearly quoting from a traditional creedal formulation in Rom 3:25–26a. Faith is a central concept for Paul,

---

[17] "Expiation" or "means of expiation" are probably the best translations for ἱλαστήριον. Paul's Roman Christian audience probably would have heard echoes of the description of the "mercy seat" (ἱλαστήριον ἐπίθεμα) above the ark in Exod 25:17–22 and the description of the ritual on the Day of Atonement in Leviticus 16. But such echoes should not lead us to translate ἱλαστήριον as "mercy seat" or try to force the interpretation of Jesus' death in this passage into the straightjacket of the ritual of the Day of Atonement. The language is metaphorical. It uses cultic language and imagery to interpret a noncultic event. For a very sensible explanation of these issues, see Byrne, *Romans,* 126–27, 132–33. For an interpretation that takes ἱλαστήριον as "mercy seat," see Wilckens, *Römer,* 1:190–92.

[18] The meaning "remission," "forgiveness," "dismissal" for πάρεσις is found in Phalaris, *Ep.* 81.1; Dionysius of Halicarnassus, *Ant. rom.* 7.37.2; *SIG* 742, 33; 39; *OGIS* 669, 50. The most enlightening use of πάρεσις is in the letter of Phalaris. Phalaris quite easily characterizes the "remission of debts" (πάρεσις τῶν χρημάτων) discussed in the letter as both a χάρις ("benefit," "gift") and a δωρεά ("gift"). In addition, he uses the verb παρίημι in the sense of "remit." This suggests that πάρεσις in Rom 3:25 should be translated as "remission" rather than as "passing over." See also BDAG 776.

[19] The presence of the article (τήν) indicates that Paul is quoting the phrase from the traditional creedal material.

[20] See BDAG 889.

and the phrase "through faith" is clearly an insertion by Paul because it breaks up the pre-Pauline phrase "an expiation by his blood."

Although it is much more disputed, it also seems that Rom 3:24, with the exception of "by his grace," is also part of the traditional formula Paul is quoting.[21] The first reason for suggesting this is again a matter of vocabulary. The Greek adverb δωρεάν ("as a gift") appears only twice elsewhere in Paul, and in neither case does it have the same meaning.[22] In addition, the Greek noun ἀπολύτρωσις ("redemption") also occurs only twice elsewhere in Paul. Later, in 8:23, it has an eschatological meaning rather than the meaning here. The other occurrence is in 1 Cor 1:30, in a list that itself seems to be made up of traditional terms.[23]

A second and more convincing reason for taking 3:24 as part of the preexisting formula Paul is quoting is the redundancy in its opening phrase ("being made righteous as a gift by his grace"). Paul often uses the word "grace" (χάρις), and it is important for him. But in this context, the phrase "by his grace" (τῇ αὐτοῦ χάριτι) seems redundant, since it carries basically the same meaning as the immediately preceding "as a gift" (δωρεάν). This awkwardness is best explained by taking the phase "by his grace" as Paul's own clarification or gloss of the preceding word, δωρεάν. If this is the case, then the preceding phrase "being made righteous as a gift" probably belongs to the pre-Pauline creedal formula.

Finally, the opening phrase of 3:24, "being made righteous as a gift," is grammatically awkward. The participle δικαιούμενοι ("being made righteous") grammatically governs all of 3:24–26 and itself depends on πάντες ("all") at the beginning of 3:23.[24] Thus the participle in effect carries on the thought of the two finite verbs "have sinned" and "lack" in 3:23. Given this, one would have expected a series of coordinated clauses in which the last was an adversative clause: "All have sinned and lack the glory of God but are now made righteous as a gift." It is true that Paul uses participial clauses elsewhere to carry on the thought of finite verbs (2 Cor 5:12; 7:5; 10:14–15). But in 2 Cor 10:14–16, the participial clauses that follow the finite verbs are circumstantial rather than adversative in meaning. In 2 Cor 5:12; 7:5, the participial clauses do have an adversative meaning. But in both cases, Paul indicates this by his use of "but" (ἀλλά) before the participial clauses. Given all this, it makes much more sense to explain the awkwardness in Rom 3:24 as caused by the fact that, with the exception of the phrase "by his grace," the participial clause in 3:24 was also part of the traditional formula Paul was quoting. All these reasons taken together indicate that the traditional formula Paul was using probably included all of 3:24–26a, with the exception of "as a gift" in 3:24 and "through faith" in 3:25.

The second issue concerns the original meaning of the traditional creedal formula. Even more than the question of the extent of the traditional formula, its interpretation is a matter of dispute. Again, because the interest here is primarily in Paul's use of this traditional material, a thorough discussion of the disputes about its

---

[21] For a fuller explanation for the inclusion of Rom 3:24 in the traditional creedal formula Paul draws on, see Fitzmyer, *Romans*, 342–43, 347–50.

[22] In 2 Cor 11:7, it means "without cost," and in Gal 2:21, it means "for nothing, in vain."

[23] The other terms are "righteousness" and "holiness."

[24] For the range of possibilities, see Cranfield, *Romans*, 1.205.

meaning would go too far afield.[25] The most plausible interpretation of its meaning is presented here. The purpose of this traditional creedal formula is fairly clear: to interpret the meaning and significance of the death of Jesus. In this sense, it is similar to numerous other texts from earliest Christianity that also interpreted Jesus' death.[26] The thought of 3:24–26a is that human beings are made righteous before God by the redemption that takes place in Christ Jesus. This redemption includes the remission of sins that were previously been committed during the period of God's patience or forbearance. This redemption in Christ Jesus is brought about at God's initiative and is a demonstration of God's righteousness. At God's own initiative, God put Jesus forward as an expiation by means of his blood. This expiation is the source of righteousness for human beings and of the remission of their sins and is the demonstration of God's own righteousness.

The background and sources of this creedal formula are complex. The notion of God's righteousness as expressed in the Jewish scriptures provides the overall framework for the formula. A central attribute of God in the Jewish scriptures was righteousness.[27] This righteousness often carried with it a forensic notion of God's acts of judging justly.[28] Especially in the postexilic period, this righteousness also took on the additional quality of mercy or graciousness.[29] It is this notion of God's righteousness as merciful and gracious that is central to 3:24–26a. God's demonstration of God's own righteousness leads to the remission of sins by means of the death of Jesus.

The notion of the death of a human being as a means of expiation to a deity, however, has its roots outside Judaism in the Greco-Roman world. Greek and Roman literature is filled with examples of human beings who were willing to die nobly for the sake of some cause, whether for the city, for friends, for the law, or for truth.[30] For the most part, these noble deaths were not interpreted explicitly through the use of cultic imagery or language. There are also famous examples, in Greek and Roman literature, of human sacrifices whose purpose was to placate a deity for the good of the community.[31] These were themselves cultic acts. But there was also a phenomenon in which the noble deaths especially of those who gave their lives for the sake of the community came to be described and interpreted using cultic imagery and language. The use of this language and imagery was usually not exact. There

---

[25] For a bibliography, see Fitzmyer, *Romans*, 354–58.

[26] Two recent studies on the various interpretations of Jesus' death in early Christianity are John T. Carroll and Joel B. Green, *The Death of Jesus in Early Christianity* (Peabody, Mass.: Hendrickson, 1995); and Morna D. Hooker, *Not Ashamed of the Gospel: New Testament Interpretations of the Death of Jesus* (Grand Rapids: Eerdmans, 1995).

[27] See Ps 35:28; 36:7; 51:16; 103:17; 112:9; Prov 16:10; Isa 46:13; 59:16. For a fuller treatment of the concept of God's righteousness, see Fitzmyer, *Romans*, 105–7; and Wilckens, *Römer*, 1:212–20.

[28] See Isa 3:13; Jer 12:1; Hos 4:1–2; 12:3; Mic 6:12; Ps 9:9; 96:13; 98:2.

[29] See Isa 51:5, 6, 8; 56:1; 61:10; Ps 40:9–10.

[30] For the city: Homer, *Il.* 15.495–498; Thucydides, *Hist.* 2.43.1–2; Horace, *Carm.* 3.2.13. For friends: Plato, *Symp.* 179b. For the laws: Demosthenes, *2 Aristog.* 23. For philosophy: Plato, *Apol.* 32a; D.L. 5.7–8. For a fuller treatment, see Martin Hengel, *The Atonement: The Origins of the Doctrine in the New Testament* (Philadelphia: Fortress, 1981), 6–18.

[31] Plutarch provides a list in *Pel.* 20–21. It was also a favorite theme of Euripides (see *Phoen.* 911–1018, 1090–1092; *Hec.* 342–378, 432–437). See also Seneca, *Tro.* 193–202.

was often an awareness of the metaphorical nature of the language and that the cultic language and imagery were being used to interpret a noncultic reality. This was obviously made easier by the broadly religious context within which dying for the sake of the community was already seen.[32] For example, the Roman historian Livy (8.9.10) described how in 340 B.C. the Roman general Decius plunged to his death in the thick of the Latin enemy "as though *[sicut]* sent from heaven as an expiatory offering *[piaculum]* of all the anger of the gods, and to turn aside destruction from his people and bring it on their adversaries."[33] Plutarch, *Pel.* 20–21, could even list together both human sacrifices and soldiers dying for their country. In the middle of references to human sacrifices, he listed the Spartan king Leonidas, who died in the battle of Thermopylae and "who, in obedience to the oracle, sacrificed himself, as it were [τρόπον τινά], for the sake of [ὑπέρ] Greece."[34]

This same phenomenon, in which cultic language and imagery were used to describe and interpret the significance of someone's noble death for the sake of the community, also found its way into Hellenistic Judaism. Although it is debatable, this may have been the case for the stories of the deaths of the Jewish mother and her seven sons in 2 Maccabees 7 and of the Jewish elder Razis in 2 Macc 14:37–46. The way their deaths are described in 2 Maccabees seems to imply that they died as some sort of vicarious atonement for the Jewish people.[35] It is certainly the case, however, that cultic imagery and language were used to interpret the noble deaths of the Jewish martyrs in 4 Maccabees. In 4 Macc 6:27–29, the Jewish leader Eleazer, as he is dying in torment, lifts his eyes and addresses God: "You know, O God, that though I might have saved myself, I am dying in burning torments on behalf of [διά] the law. Be merciful to your people and be satisfied by our punishment for their sake [ὑπέρ αὐτῶν]. Make my blood their purification [καθάρσιον], and take my life as an exchange [ἀντίψυχον] for theirs." Eleazer dies a noble death on behalf of the law and the Jewish people. At the same time, however, his death is interpreted by means of the cultic language and imagery of purification through his blood. The same is even clearer in the final interpretation of all of the martyrs' deaths in 4 Macc 17:20–22:

> These, then, who have been consecrated [ἁγιασθέντες] on behalf of [διά] God, are honored, not only with this honor, but also by the fact that because of them our enemies did not rule over our nation, the tyrant was punished, and the homeland purified [καθαρισθῆναι]—they having become, as it were, a ransom [ἀντίψυχον] for the sin of our nation. And through the blood [διά τοῦ αἵματος] of those devout ones and their expiating death [τοῦ ἱλαστηρίου θανάτου],[36] divine Providence preserved Israel that previously had been afflicted.

---

[32] Hengel (*Atonement*, 10) makes this point.

[33] Livy (*Urbe cond.* 10.28.12–13 [Foster, LCL]) describes a similar act by Decius's son also as an expiatory offering *(piaculum)*.

[34] Λεωνίδαν τε τῷ χρησμῷ τρόπον τινὰ προθυσάμενον ἑαυτὸν ὑπὲρ τῆς Ἑλλάδος (Plutarch, *Pel.* 21.4 [Perrin]). The oracle Plutarch refers to is found in Herodotus, *Hist.* 7.220.

[35] The case for this interpretation has been made most recently by Jan Willem van Henten, *The Maccabean Martyrs as Saviors of the Jewish People: A Study of 2 and 4 Maccabees* (JSJSup 57; New York: Brill, 1997), 140–56.

[36] This the reading of MSS A and B. This reading, which takes ἱλαστηρίου as an adjective modifying the noun θανάτου, is preferable to the reading of MS ℵ, which reads τοῦ ἱλαστηρίου τοῦ θανάτου and takes ἱλαστηρίου as a noun.

Once again, all of the martyrs died a noble death for the sake of God. But their deaths are also extensively interpreted by means of cultic language and imagery. They are consecrated; through their deaths the homeland is purified; through their blood and their expiating deaths, God preserves Israel.

The traditional creedal formula Paul uses in Rom 3:24–26a clearly reflects the same kind of development. In this case, Jesus's death is interpreted as an expiation by the shedding of his blood. This results in the remission of sins and so reestablishes a proper relationship with God. There are crucial differences, however, between the interpretation of Jesus' death in 3:24–26a and the previous texts. First, in 3:24–26a, it is God who takes the initiative, who puts Jesus forward as an expiation, and who demonstrates in Jesus' death God's merciful righteousness. Early Christians obviously took over the kind of interpretation found in 4 Maccabees and used it to interpret the death of Jesus. But they placed it within the framework of the larger Jewish notion of the righteousness of God mentioned above. This is quite different from the other texts in which human beings take the initiative and the person's death is accepted by the deity as reestablishing the proper relationship. Second, the expiation has a universal significance. Unlike what was found in the previous texts, the expiation described in 3:24–26a is not confined to a particular set of circumstances, nor are the effects confined to a particular group of people. It is at God's initiative and for the benefit of all human beings.

It is also important to realize that Paul at two other crucial junctures in Romans uses similar traditional creedal language in which Jesus' death is interpreted through the use of cultic language and imagery.[37] In 8:3, Paul uses a fragment of traditional creedal material about how God, by sending his own Son as a sin-offering (περὶ ἁμαρτίας), condemned sin.[38] Paul also uses traditional creedal language in 5:6–11. But here the situation is more complicated. Paul seems to be using three different creedal fragments, two of which he has used before.[39] The first is found in 5:8: "Christ died for our sake [ὑπὲρ ἡμῶν]." The second is in 5:10, where Paul affirms that "we have been reconciled [κατηλλάγημεν] to God through the death [διὰ τοῦ θανάτου] of his son." Paul had already used language similar to both of these fragments together in 2 Cor 5:14–15, 18–19. The language was obviously important for how Paul understood Jesus' significance. It is important to keep in mind in this context that neither of these traditional creedal fragments as such involved the use of cultic imagery or language.[40] In Rom 5:9, between these two formulas

---

[37] The term "creedal language" is used here rather than "creedal formula" because, in comparison with Rom 3:24–26a, they are too fragmentary to be called formulas.

[38] For a fuller explanation, see below, pp. 282–84.

[39] For a fuller explanation, see below, pp. 163–65.

[40] One needs to be very careful about too quickly connecting various christological formulas with the temple cult. For discussions of this complex issue, see Klaus Wengst, *Christologische Formeln und Lieder des Urchristentums* (Gütersloh: Mohn, 1972); Sam K. Williams, *Jesus' Death as Saving Event: The Background and Origin of a Concept* (HDR 2; Missoula, Mont.: Scholars Press, 1972); Cilliers Breytenbach, *Versöhnung: Eine Studie zur paulinischen Soterologie* (WMANT 60; Neukirchen-Vluyn: Neukirchener Verlag, 1989); "Versöhnung, Stellvertretung, und Sühne: Semantische und traditionsgeschichtliche Bemerkungen am Beispiel der paulinischen Briefe," *NTS* 39 (1993), 59–79; David Seeley, *The Noble Death: Graeco-Roman Martyrology and Paul's Concept of Salvation* (JSNTSup 28; Sheffield, England: Sheffield Academic Press, 1990).

and linking them together, Paul paraphrases part of the traditional creedal formula from 3:24–26a: "made righteous now by his blood."[41] This formula, as seen earlier, does involve cultic imagery and language. In 5:9, Paul intentionally introduces traditional creedal language taken from the formula in 3:24–26a, which uses cultic imagery and language, into the context of two other traditional creedal fragments which he used before but which did not involve the use of cultic imagery and language. In this way he draws these two other fragments into an explicitly cultic context.

Thus, in three of the expository sections of Romans (3:21–26; 5:1–21; 8:1–30), Paul roots his explanations in traditional creedal material that involves, in some way, cultic language and imagery. Why does Paul do this at these points in the argument? The most plausible explanation is that interpretations of Christ's death through cultic language and imagery were especially important to the Roman Christian community. By placing them in each of the expository sections and then commenting and expanding on them for his own purposes, Paul tries to show how his seemingly controversial views about righteousness through faith, apart from observance of the law, for both Jews and Gentiles are in fact rooted in traditional interpretations of Jesus that are especially important for them. This is especially the case for creedal language that interprets Jesus' death in cultic terms. Romans 3:24–26a is the first and most prominent example of Paul's use of this traditional creedal material. But with its explicit use of cultic language and imagery, it is also the traditional creedal material most unlike Paul's other ways of interpreting Jesus' death. It was probably more important to the Roman Christian community, at least initially, than it was to Paul. All of this supports the suspicion that cultic interpretations of Jesus' death may well have been of particular importance to the Roman Christians. In using this material at this crucial point in Romans, Paul is trying to show the compatibility of his own positions with viewpoints that were especially important for them.[42]

The third and, for our purposes, the most important issue is how Paul uses this material in its present context. His basic approach is to use this traditional creedal formula, which he shares with the Roman Christians, for explaining how this shared foundation supports his central convictions about faith and its relation to observance of the law and about the relationship between Jews and Gentiles. He goes about this in several ways. First, however grammatically awkward it is, Paul connects the long participial clause of the traditional creedal formula in 3:24–26a to "all" (πάντες) of the preceding finite clause. He thus creates a parallelism. Just as all sinned and lack the glory of God, so now all are made righteous as a gift by his grace. His justification for this is that there is no distinction between Jews and Gentiles in this regard.

Second, he inserts two clarifying phrases within the traditional creedal formula itself. The first insertion is "by his grace" (τῇ αὐτοῦ χάριτι) in 3:24, which he uses to clarify the phrase "as a gift" (δωρεάν). The point of this clarification is to

---

[41] For a fuller explanation, see below, pp. 163–65.

[42] An indirect confirmation of this is that the later letter to the Hebrews, which is filled with cultic language and imagery used to interpret the death of Jesus, was probably addressed to the Roman Christians (Heb 13:24). See Harold W. Attridge, *The Epistle to the Hebrews* (Hermeneia; Philadelphia: Fortress, 1989), 9–10.

connect the word χάρις, which Paul uses often and is a central idea for him, to the closely related word δωρεά, which is part of the traditional creedal formula.[43] Apart from the greeting in 1:5, 7, this is the first time Paul uses the word "grace" in Romans. To understand why Paul does this, one has to understand how he has used the word in his earlier letters and how it plays a central role for him later in Romans itself. In both Galatians (1:15; 2:9) and 1 Corinthians (15:10), Paul uses "grace" as a way to describe both his own call and to legitimate his own identity as an apostle. It is a word central to his own experience. But it was also an important concept in his controversies with the Galatian Christians. This is especially the case in his stark contrast between righteousness through observance of the law and righteousness through grace. In Gal 1:6, Paul is astonished that the Galatians have so quickly turned from the God, who called them by grace to another gospel. In 2:21, he claims that he does not nullify the grace of God. For if righteousness were through the law, then Christ died for nothing. Finally, in 5:4, he claims that those who would be made righteous through observance of the law have cut themselves off from Christ. They have fallen away from grace. In all three cases, grace is an integral part of the stark contrasts Paul drew between his gospel of righteousness through grace and faith and righteousness through observance of the law. But in Rom 3:24 Paul intentionally realigns the meaning of "grace." "Grace" is another way of describing something he and the Roman Christians actually have in common rather than something that drives them apart. In addition, it characterizes a righteousness that Paul has just described as something that "now" has been manifested (3:21). Grace is no longer, as it was in Galatians, part of a stark, in-principle contrast to observance of the law. It becomes part of the very different temporal framework that dominates Romans. Righteousness by grace is now apart from observance of the law. It is different from righteousness through observance of the law, and it now takes the place of observance of the law. But it is not as such opposed to the law, and it does not empty the law of its divinely sanctioned authority in the past, as it seemed to do in Galatians. Once Paul has realigned the meaning of the word "grace," he will then use it at a number of crucial points in his arguments in the rest of Romans.[44]

The second insertion Paul makes in the traditional creedal formula is "through faith" (διὰ πίστεως) in 3:25.[45] The insertion is awkward, coming as it does between "as an expiation" and "by his blood," which obviously went together in the traditional material. Given its awkwardness, why does Paul place it where he does? The reason is that he wants to characterize the way in which this expiation is received or appropriated by human beings. It is an expiation experienced through faith. The purpose of this insertion differs, however, from that of the previous one. Here Paul's purpose is not to reinterpret a previously controversial concept but to emphasize the importance of faith. This is something that he and the Roman Christians have in common but was not specifically contained in the traditional creedal formula. Paul did not expect that this addition would have been controversial for the Roman Christians.

---

[43] The word χάρις appears sixty-five times in Paul's letters.
[44] Rom 4:4, 16; 5:2, 15, 17, 20, 21; 6:1, 14, 15, 17; 7:25; 11:5, 6.
[45] The MSS are fairly divided between διὰ πίστεως and διὰ τῆς πίστεως.

The third and final way Paul interprets the traditional creedal formula for his purposes is to add two comments of his own in 3:26b–c immediately after it. Both comments emphasize aspects of what he has just written. In the first comment, Paul repeats the phrase "demonstration of his righteousness," from the traditional formula, and adds to it "in the present time" (ἐν τῷ νῦν καιρῷ). This harks back to the very beginning of the passage ("But now apart from the law . . ."). It emphasizes again the temporal perspective on which Paul is now insisting. This again is quite different from the earlier in-principle contrasts of Galatians. The warrant in Paul's mind for the additional comment, "in the present time," was probably the phrase "because of the passing over of the sins formerly committed [τῶν προγεγονότων ἁμαρτημάτων]." He takes this to mean that the way in which God deals with sins "in the present time" differs from the way he dealt with them in the past. In the second comment, Paul adds that all of this now happens "so that he [God] may be righteous and make righteous the one who has faith in Jesus [τὸν ἐκ πίστεως Ἰησοῦ]." This comment is not so much for emphasis as for clarity. He wants to make sure his Roman Christian audience does not miss the point of his awkward insertion of the phrase "through faith" in 3:25. He tries to clarify the connection of "through faith" to God's putting Jesus forward as an expiation by his blood. In the present manifestation of his righteousness, God's purpose in doing this is that God might be righteous and make righteous the one who has faith in Jesus.

In 3:21–26, then, Paul moves to a new stage in his argument. He begins in 3:21–22c by stating the three-part subproposition: (1) the righteousness of God is now manifested apart from observance of the law; (2) the Jewish scriptures witness to this; and (3) this righteousness is through faith for Jews and Gentiles on the same basis. He then goes on to offer two reasons in support of this subproposition. The first (3:22d–23) is really an appeal to what he argued in 1:18–3:20, that Jews and Gentiles are similarly placed in relation to sinfulness. The second (3:24–26) is an appeal to a traditional creedal formula he has in common with the Roman Christians and on which he comments. Paul does all of this in as irenic and uncontroversial a way as possible. He tries to root the controversial aspects of his argument in beliefs he and the Roman Christians have in common. Righteousness is now through faith and apart from the law, and this righteousness is for both Jews and Gentiles on the same basis. The point of all this becomes clear when we realize that Paul is doing all of this against the background of what he wrote earlier in Galatians. Instead of the stark contrast and opposition between faith and observance of the law so central to Galatians, Paul turns the difference between the two into a temporal one. It is now that righteousness of God is manifested through faith and apart from the law. Paul does not surrender his central conviction about faith and its present relation to observance of the law, but he does put it into a temporal framework that no longer denigrates the law or its earlier observance.

Romans 3:21–26 parallels 1:18–32 in appealing to what Paul and the Roman Christians have in common; 3:21–26 does it, however, in a different way. Romans 1:18–32 appealed to Hellenistic Jewish viewpoints about Gentile religiosity that Paul and the Roman Christians had in common. Romans 3:21–26, however, appeals explicitly to traditional Christian material that they share. This establishes a precedent. As shall be seen, Paul will make similar appeals to traditional Christian material in both 5:6–10 and 8:3. Both of these texts are parts of passages (5:1–20; 8:1–30) that play roles in the next two stages of Paul's arguments similar to that played by 3:21–26.

ROMANS 3:27–4:25: ARGUMENT BASED ON THE EXAMPLE OF ABRAHAM

At 3:27, Paul's tone suddenly changes. He becomes much more argumentative. The argumentative tone continues through 4:25. This section is similar in tone to 2:1–3:10. Like 2:1–3:20, it is also marked by extensive use of the Jewish scriptures (3:30; 4:1–25). Romans 3:27–4:25 falls into two parts of unequal length. Romans 3:27–31 is made up of four rhetorical questions and replies. This is followed in 4:1–25 by an extended example based on the interpretation of passages from the Jewish scriptures about the life of the patriarch Abraham. As already seen, this section too needs to be interpreted against the background of the Roman Christian audience's deep misgivings about how Paul interpreted the significance of Abraham in his letter to the Galatians. It also needs to be understood as Paul's attempt to revise significantly some of his earlier views while still maintaining his basic convictions about righteousness through faith for Jews and Gentiles alike apart from observance of the law. Whereas Paul attempted in 3:21–26 to embed these controversial convictions in traditions he shared with his Roman Christian audience, in 3:27–4:25 he attempts to deal more explicitly with their strong misgivings about these controversial views. This explicitness, however, should not be confused with directness. In 3:27–4:25, Paul is not directly attacking views held by the Roman Christians. As in 2:1–3:20, he continues to maintain the fiction of indirectness common in diatribes. He continues to hope that the Roman Christians will be persuaded by his arguments without feeling that their positions are being directly attacked.

Romans 3:27–31: Rhetorical Questions and Replies

Romans 3:27–31 is composed of four rhetorical questions and replies.[46] Paul's first question (3:27a) is about what has become of boasting. His reply is that it has been excluded. His second question (3:27b–28) is about what the principle (νόμος) is by which it has been excluded.[47] Is it a principle about works, that is, about observance of the law? His reply is, "No." It is, rather, based on a principle about faith. This principle is that "a human being is now made righteous by faith apart from works of the law." His third question (3:29–30) is about whether God is the God of the Jews only. Is God not also God of the Gentiles? Paul's answer is that God is of course God also of the Gentiles. Because God is one (and here Paul refers to Deut 6:4), God will make the circumcised righteous on the basis of faith (ἐκ πίστεως)

---

[46] These verses are better taken as rhetorical questions and replies rather than objections and responses to an imaginary interlocutor. Both 3:28 (a reply) and 3:31 (a question) are in the first person plural. In terms of the rhetoric of the passage, this indicates that Paul himself is both asking the questions and making the replies.

[47] Paul uses the word νόμος with a variety of meanings. One of those meanings is that of "principle." He also uses it in this sense in 7:21, 23. See Fitzmyer, *Romans*, 131–32.

and also the uncircumcised righteous through faith (διὰ τῆς πίστεως).[48] The final question (Rom 3:31) moves in a somewhat different direction. Do we annul the law by this faith? His answer is, "By no means." We actually confirm the law.

These rhetorical questions and replies touch on the three aspects of 3:21–26 that would have remained controversial. All are meant to set the stage for the much longer example of Abraham in 4:1–25. The first two questions and replies (3:27–28) go together and deal with the issue of righteousness by faith apart from observance of the law. They take up Paul's claim in 3:21–22 that the righteousness of God has now been manifested apart from observance of the law. Paul's exclusion of boasting should not be misunderstood. It is not some general condemnation of boasting. Paul often uses the word positively.[49] As is clear from 4:2, he means something more specific here, boasting about the observance of the law. In addition, the reason for excluding such boasting is also very specific. It is that human beings are now made righteous by God through faith.

The third question and reply (3:29–30) is a bit more complicated and takes up Paul's claim in 3:22 that this righteousness of God is meant for all who have faith. Essentially it is a reductio ad absurdum argument. If righteousness necessarily involves observance of the law, the conclusion must be that God is God only of the Jews. But this conclusion is absurd, since God is one (Deut 6:4) and so must be the God of Jews and Gentiles alike. If this is the case, then God will make both Jews and Gentiles righteous by faith apart from observance of the Mosaic law.

The final question and reply (Rom 3:31) is meant to deal with the issue of whether Paul's conviction about righteousness through faith apart from observance of the law annuls the law. He claims that it does no such thing. Rather, it confirms the law. This harks back to 3:21b, where Paul claimed that the Law and the Prophets witnessed to all this.[50] This last rhetorical question and reply leads immediately into the example of Abraham, which Paul uses to show how his viewpoint on righteousness through faith apart from observance in fact confirms what is written in the law.

To understand what Paul is about in 3:27–31, we have to keep in mind that he is using these rhetorical questions and replies to provide the framework for how his audience should understand the example of Abraham in 4:1–25. In 3:27–31, Paul obviously intends to maintain his basic convictions that God's righteousness is now manifested through faith apart from observance of the law. Equally, what lies behind this insistence is his conviction about the equal status of Jewish and Gentile believers. At the same time, however, Paul significantly rethinks the meaning of these two central convictions. This rethinking becomes visible when the framework he establishes in 3:27–31 is read against the background of his Roman Christian audience's misgivings about how he interpreted the significance of Abraham in Galatians. There Abraham's faith was set over against observance of the law. In addition, Paul seemed to take Abraham as the father of the Gentiles only and almost to exclude

---

[48] The use of ἐκ and διά is an elegant variation rather than an attempt to distinguish between how Jews and Gentiles are made righteous.

[49] See 1 Thess 2:19; Gal 6:4; Phil 1:26; 2:16; 3:3; 1 Cor 1:31; 9:15; 15:31; 2 Cor 1:12, 14; 5:12; 7:4, 13; 8:24; 9:2, 3; 11:10.

[50] It also means that Paul uses the word "law" (νόμος) in 3:31 in the wider sense of the Jewish scriptures as a whole.

the Jews. For the Roman Christians, such an interpretation of Abraham's significance also seemed a perversion of the clear intent of the Jewish scriptures. It seemed, in that sense, to "annul" the scriptures. The framework Paul establishes in 3:27–31 points them in a very different direction. First, God's righteousness is now manifested "apart from the law." But it is not set over against the law, nor is it a condemnation of past observance of the law. In addition, Paul clearly takes up what he wrote in 1:16, that his gospel is the power of God for everyone who has faith, the Jew first and then the Greek. In 3:30, Paul also mentions first the circumcised whom God will make righteous on the basis of faith and then the uncircumcised whom God will make righteous through the same faith. As in 1:16, Jews are specifically included. Finally, this view supports rather than annuls the law, as can be seen from the very revised interpretation of the example of Abraham that Paul presents in 4:1–25.

Romans 4:1–25: The Example of Abraham's Faith apart from Observance of the Law

Romans 4:1–25 is a fairly lengthy argument from the Jewish scriptures, based on interpretations of texts about Abraham from Genesis and from other traditional Jewish material. Romans 4:1–25 takes up the language of 3:21–31 and serves, from a rhetorical viewpoint, as an extended scriptural example and proof for the truth of these verses. The central text Paul uses is again, as in Gal 3:6–14, Gen 15:6: "Abraham believed God and it was reckoned to him as righteousness." Yet Paul's interpretation of this and related scriptural texts differs significantly and, I think, intentionally from those found in Galatians. More specifically, Paul's purpose in Rom 4:1–25 is to show, through the example of Abraham, how righteousness through faith apart from observance of the Mosaic law is both rooted in the Jewish scriptures and includes Jews and Gentiles alike. Romans 4:1–25 falls into five sections:

A. 4:1–8: Abraham's faith was reckoned to him as righteousness.

B. 4:9–12: Abraham's righteousness was prior to his circumcision so that he could be the father not only of the circumcised but also of the uncircumcised.

C. 4:13–17a: The promise comes through faith and not through the law to all Abraham's "seed," not only to Jews but also to Gentiles.

D. 4:17b–22: Abraham had faith in God's promise even if it concerned God's giving life to the dead.

E. 4:23–25: Abraham's example is applied to those who have faith in the God who raised Jesus from the dead.[51]

---

[51] This division of Romans 4 is based partly on literary cues and partly on considerations of content. Romans 4:1–8 and 9–12 each begin with a question (4:1,9), which is then answered in the following verses (4:2–8,10–12). Romans 4:13–17a deals with the promise to Abraham's "seed" and how it is mediated. Although 4:17b–22 is loosely connected to 4:17a grammatically, the former's concern is not the promise or its mediation but a dramatic retelling of part of the

Romans 4:1–8: Abraham's Faith Reckoned to Him as Righteousness

Paul begins rhetorically with a question: "What then are we to say Abraham our forefather according to the flesh found?"[52] The answer he gives in 4:2–3 is that Abraham found righteousness through faith in God. This righteousness, however, was not through observance of the law.[53] The scriptural proof Paul offers is Gen 15:6: "Abraham believed in God and it was reckoned to him as righteousness."[54] Because of this, Abraham has nothing to boast of before God.[55] Paul then goes on in Rom 4:4–5 to explain his point by appealing to the example of a laborer and his wages: "To someone who works the reward is not reckoned as a favor but as a debt; but to someone who does not work but rather believes in the one who makes righteous the ungodly, his faith is reckoned to him as righteousness." Finally Paul offers as an additional scriptural proof in 4:6 the "beatitudes" of Ps 32:1–2:

Abraham story in order to bring out the depth of Abraham's faith and its similarity to the faith of believers in Jesus. After 4:22 quotes Gen 15:6 again as the conclusion to Paul's interpretation of this verse, Rom 4:23–25 explicitly applies the interpretation to the typologically similar situation of believers in Christ.

[52] There are two issues connected with 4:1. The first concerns εὑρηκέναι. Some MSS (ℵ*, A, C*, 81, 365, 1506, and the Coptic versions) place it after ἐροῦμεν; others, after ἡμῶν (33, 1881, *Byz al*); and in a few it is not found at all (B, 6, 1739). The most likely solution is that originally εὑρηκέναι stood after ἐροῦμεν. Were it not originally in the text, it is difficult to explain why any copyist would have added it. In addition, εὑρηκέναι after ἐροῦμεν makes better sense and has stronger external support. The word εὑρηκέναι may have dropped out because of homoeoarchy with ἐροῦμεν. See Bruce M. Metzger, *A Textual Commentary on the Greek New Testament* (2d ed.; New York: United Bible Societies, 1994), 450. The second issue concerns the punctuation and translation of 4:1. Richard B. Hays has argued that 4:1 should be punctuated and translated as follows: "What shall we say? Have we found Abraham to be our forefather according to the flesh?" ("Have We Found Abraham to Be Our Forefather according to the Flesh?" *NovT* 16 [1985]: 76–98). Though seductive, this punctuation and translation awkwardly leave the infinitive εὑρηκέναι without an expressed accusative subject. This is not the case with the other instances cited by Hays of τί ἐροῦμεν in 3:5; 6:1; 7:7; 8:31; 9:14, 30. Other problems with Hays's position are found in Dunn, *Romans*, 199.

[53] It was not uncommon in Jewish literature of this period to see Abraham already as an observer of the "law" (Sir 44:20; *2 Bar.* 57:1–2; Philo, *Abr.* 276). Abraham's observance of the law is a recurring theme in *Jub.* 11:14–23:7.

[54] A number of Jewish texts highlight Abraham's faith or trust in God (e.g., Sir 44:20; 1 Macc 2:52; 2 Macc 1:2; *L.A.B.* 23:5). This is esp. the case with Philo (*Leg.* 3.228; *Deus* 4; *Migr.* 43–44, 132; *Her.* 14, 90–93, 96–99; *Mut.* 181–187, 201–2; *Praem.* 49; *QG* 3.2, 58; 4.17). In Sir 44:19 and 1 Macc 2:52, Abraham's faith seems to be connected with the story of the sacrifice of Isaac in Gen 22. More commonly, as in Paul, this interpretation of Abraham is connected with Gen 15:6 (1 Macc 2:52; *L.A.B.* 23:5; Philo, *Leg.* 3.228; *Migr.* 43–44; *Her.* 90–93, 96–99; *Mut.* 181–187; *QG* 3.2) or with the story of the God's promise of a child to Abraham and Sarah in Genesis 18 (Philo, *Migr.* 132; *QG* 3.56, 58; 4.17). Unlike Paul, however, none of these texts takes as significant the fact that Abraham's faith and righteousness in Gen 15:6 were prior to his circumcision and consequently "apart from the law."

[55] Romans 4:2 is a suppressed enthymeme. The full form of the enthymeme would have been this: if Abraham was made righteous by works, he would have something to boast of before God; but Abraham was made righteous by faith and not by works; therefore Abraham does not have anything to boast of before God. Rhetorical proofs or enthymemes were often rooted in syllogisms but were often not expressed in syllogistic form. See Aristotle, *Rhet.* 1.2.13; 2.22.1–3; Cicero, *Inv.* 1.41.77; Quintilian, *Inst.* 5.14.24–26.

> Blessed are those whose lawless deeds have been forgiven,
> and whose sins have been covered;
> Blessed is the man whose sin the Lord will not at all reckon.

Paul interprets this passage to mean that David, the traditional author of the psalm, is speaking of the blessedness of the one to whom God reckons righteousness without works (of the law). Here Paul takes up the language of Rom 3:21, 28. His justification for this interpretation was probably that David did not mention "works of the law" as a reason for God's forgiveness.

Several elements in this section need to be emphasized. First, Paul makes much the same point in using the example of Abraham and in quoting Gen 15:6 in Rom 4:3 as he did in Gal 3:6, that is, that Abraham was made righteous by God because of his faith and not because of his observance of the law. But in Rom 4:1–8, Paul entirely changes that to which he contrasts righteousness through faith. In Gal 3:7–12, Paul immediately associates Abraham's faith with the Gentiles and contrasts it and the Gentiles with those who are "of works of the law" (ὅσοι ἐξ ἔργων νόμου) and under a curse (ὑπὸ κατάραν, Gal 3:10), that is, with the Jewish people. In Rom 4:1–8, however, Paul avoids this contrast altogether. Rather, he contrasts Abraham's righteousness through faith with the more general, colorless example taken from the commercial sphere, of the worker whose reward is reckoned to him as a debt and not as a favor (4:4). The contrast is no longer between Abraham (and the Gentiles) and those who are "of works of the law" (the Jewish people).

Second, in 4:1 Paul refers to Abraham as "our forefather according to the flesh" (τὸν προπάτορα ἡμῶν κατὰ σάρκα). Although referring to Abraham as "forefather" was not a common way for Jews during this period to refer to Abraham, it was not unkown. Josephus refers to him in *J. W.* 5.380 as "Abraham our forefather" (προπάτωρ ἡμέτερος) with no apparent sense that the term was unusual. The use of the full term, "our forefather according to the flesh," at the very beginning of Paul's argument in Rom 4:1–25 emphasizes the connection of Abraham to the Jewish people ("according to the flesh") and of Paul and other believers ("our") to both Abraham and the Jewish people.[56] One does not want to make too much of what may have been a traditional, if not common, way of referring to Abraham. Yet referring to Abraham in this way at the very beginning of the argument does set the tone for the rest of 4:1–25. It sets a different and much less controversial tone than is found in Gal 3:7–10, where Abraham's fatherhood is associated explicitly only with the Gentiles.

Finally, Paul's use of Ps 32:1–2 in Rom 4:6–8 functions as more than simply an additional scriptural proof of the same thing found in Gen 15:6. Since David is the speaker in the psalm, what is said in the psalm must refer to Jews; that is, the forgiveness of sins to which the psalm refers and that takes place apart from works of the law must already be part of Jewish experience.[57] This also breaks down the contrast, which dominated Gal 3:6–14, of Gentiles made righteous by faith versus

---

[56] The phrase κατὰ σάρκα in Rom 4:1 does not have a negative connotation. The same is true of its use in 1:3; 9:5. For another view, see Dunn, *Romans*, 199.

[57] While one should not make too much of it, it may also have been important for Paul that Ps 32:11 spoke of the righteous (δίκαιοι) boasting or exulting (καυχᾶσθε) in the Lord. Both of these themes are obviously important in Romans.

Jews under the curse of the law. As we shall see shortly, it also sets the stage for the next step in Paul's argument (Rom 4:9–12).

As one looks at Rom 4:1–8, both in its appeal to Scripture and in its treatment of the relationship of Abraham to the Jewish people, one begins to see that Paul's initial interpretation of Abraham moves in a quite different and much less problematic direction than the one he took in Gal 3:6–14. This shift of direction will continue throughout the rest of the chapter.

Romans 4:9–12: Abraham's Righteousness prior to His Circumcision

The next question Paul asks is whether the "blessing" mentioned by David in Ps 32:1 is meant for the circumcised (ἐπὶ τὴν περιτομήν), that is, the Jewish people, or also (ἢ καί) for the uncircumcised (ἐπὶ τὴν ἀκροβυστίαν), that is, the Gentiles (Rom 4:9). To answer this question, he asks another question: how was righteousness reckoned to Abraham; that is, did it take place when he was circumcised or when he was uncircumcised (4:10)? Paul's answer is that it took place while Abraham was still uncircumcised. Abraham's faith was reckoned to him as righteousness in Gen 15:6, but the command about circumcision was not given until Gen 17:10–11. In Paul's interpretation, the sign (σημεῖον) of circumcision was a seal (σφραγίς) of Abraham's righteousness by faith while he was still uncircumcised, but not its cause (Rom 4:11). According to Paul, the reason for this sequence was so that Abraham could be the father both of those who believe in a state of uncircumcision and of those who are circumcised (4:11–12).

To understand Paul's argument in this section, one needs first to pay careful attention to how Paul poses the question. The question is not whether righteousness through faith was meant for the circumcised or for the uncircumcised, that is, for the Jews or for the Gentiles, but whether this righteousness through faith was meant for the circumcised or also (ἢ καί) for the uncircumcised (4:9). The very framing of the question assumes that Abraham's righteousness through faith had significance for the Jewish people. The question, as Paul poses it here, is rather whether the Gentiles are also included, whether Abraham's righteousness through faith has significance also for them. The importance of posing the question in this way is further highlighted by the fact that he formulates the question based on the "beatitude" (τὸν μακαρισμόν [Rom 4:6]; ὁ μακαρισμὸς οὖν οὗτος [Rom 4:9]) spoken by David in Ps 32:1 and not on Gen 15:6. Rhetorically, then, Paul poses the question from a Jewish perspective, that is, from the perspective of someone for whom it is obvious that David's blessing (and Abraham's righteousness) is significant for the Jewish people.

Second, Paul maintains the same perspective in the way he answers the question. The reason Abraham's righteousness through faith took place before his circumcision was so that (εἰς τὸ εἶναι) Abraham would be the father of all who believed while uncircumcised as well as father of those who were circumcised. In Rom 4:11–12, Paul explains Abraham's significance for Jews and for Gentiles in a rhetorically balanced way:

> a. so that he is father of all those who believe while uncircumcised (δι' ἀκροβυστίας), that righteousness might be reckoned also (καί) to them,

> b. and father of the circumcised (περιτομῆς),

b'. for those who are not only (οὐκ . . . μόνον) of the circumcision (ἐκ περιτομῆς)

a'. but also (ἀλλὰ καί) for those who walk in the footsteps of the faith while still uncircumcised (ἐν ἀκροβυστίᾳ) of our father Abraham.[58]

The passage is arranged in a chiastic pattern: *a//a'* is about the Gentiles, and *b//b'* is about the Jewish people. Within this pattern there is also a parallelism: *a* and *b* refer first to Abraham as father of the uncircumcised and then as father of the circumcised; *b'* and *a'* refer to Abraham as significant not only (οὐκ . . . μόνον) for the circumcised but also (ἀλλὰ καί) for the uncircumcised. Because the two extremes of the chiasmus are more developed, emphasis falls on them, that is, on Abraham's significance as father for the Gentiles. Yet it is equally important to notice the way in which his fatherhood for the Gentiles is described. Abraham's significance for righteousness is framed in such a way as to include not only the Jewish people but also (και, ἀλλὰ καί) the Gentiles. The description of Abraham's significance is from a Jewish perspective that now includes, that also takes in, the Gentiles.

Third, this perspective is strengthened by the way Paul uses the word "father" (πατήρ) in this section. In 4:11–12 he describes Abraham as "father of all who believe while uncircumcised . . . and father of the circumcised." Then, at the end of Rom 4:12, he calls him "our father Abraham." This is a typically Jewish way to characterize Abraham.[59] Juxtaposing it to references to Abraham as father of both Jews and Gentiles would impress on Paul's Roman Christian audience that Abraham, the father of the Jews, is now seen as also father of the Gentiles.

Without ever explicitly adverting to it, Paul takes a perspective in 4:9–12 quite different from the one he took in Galatians. As pointed out above, in Gal 3:6–14, Paul wrote explicitly only about Abraham's relationship to the Gentiles. One could even argue that he excluded, albeit unintentionally, the Jewish people from having Abraham as their father in any religious sense. By contrast, in Rom 4:9–12, Paul has so reformulated both the question and its answer that Abraham is obviously the father of the Jewish people ("our father"); but he is also the father of the Gentiles. The perspective in 4:9–12 is no longer one of contrast or potential exclusion but one that, though clearly aiming to include the Gentiles on an equal footing, is nevertheless rooted in a perspective that begins with the assumption that Abraham is the father of the Jewish people. This interpretation of Abraham is obviously much more in continuity with traditional Jewish interpretations of Abraham than was Gal 3:6–9.[60] But it is also in continuity with Paul's statement of the whole letter's

---

[58] The use of the definite article τοῖς in both 4:12b and 4:12c indicates that he is writing about two separate groups (i.e., the Jews and the Gentiles) and not simply about one group (i.e., Jews). Grammatically, 4:12bc stands in a chiastic parallelism with 4:11b–12a depending on 4:11 rather than as a phrase depending on 4:12a. See James Swetnam, "The Curious Crux at Romans 4,12," *Bib* 61 (1980): 110–15.

[59] See, e.g., *2 Bar.* 78:4; *4 Bar.* 4:10; *Pss. Sol.* 9:9–10; *L.A.B.* 23:4; 32:1; Josephus, *Ant.* 11.169; 14.255.

[60] "Abraham was the great father of a multitude of nations. . . . Therefore he [God] assured him with an oath that the nations would be blessed through his seed" (Sir 44:19, 21, referring to Gen 17:4–6); "and all the nations of the earth will bless themselves by you" (*Jub.*

proposition in Rom 1:16–17, that the gospel is the power of God for everyone who has faith, for the Jew first and also the the Greek.

Romans 4:13–17a: The Promise through Faith to All Abraham's "Seed"

In the previous section the emphasis was on Abraham as the "father" of both Jewish and Gentile believers. In 4:13–17a Paul turns his attention more specifically to Abraham's "seed" and how the promise made to Abraham is mediated to this seed. His claim is that the promise made to Abraham and to his seed is through righteousness by faith and not through the Mosaic law (4:13). If the heirs of Abraham are such on the basis of the law, then faith is rendered invalid and God's promise nullified (4:14). Since this cannot be so, the promise must be mediated through faith. The promise is through faith so that it might be made firm to all of Abraham's seed, both to those of the law and to those who share Abraham's faith, that is, to both Jews and Gentiles (4:15–16). As proof of this, Paul quotes Gen 17:5: "I have made you the father of many nations."

Given that Paul interpreted "seed" (σπέρμα) in Gal 3:15–18 as referring only to Christ, his very different interpretation of the same word in Rom 4:13–17a is striking. Here he takes it as a collective rather than as a singular noun.[61] But more important, he connects it with an interpretation of Gen 17:5: "I have made you the father of many nations [πολλῶν ἐθνῶν]." One must remember that the word ἔθνη means both "nations" and "Gentiles." If God established Abraham as the father of many nations/Gentiles, Abraham's seed must include not only Jews but also Gentiles. Whereas his interpretation of "seed" in Gal 3:15–18 as referring only to Christ apparently excluded the Jews from being the seed of Abraham in connection to the promise, his interpretation in Rom 4:13–17a includes both them and the Gentiles.

12:23); "and you [Abraham] will be the father of many nations" (*Jub.* 15:6); Abraham's descendants, "from whom [were to come] peoples and kings" (Philo, *QG* 3.54, interpreting Gen 17:6); "the multitude of peoples, which are made many through you [Abraham]" (*L.A.B.* 23:7); God revealed to Abraham "how great nations and kings would spring from him [Isaac]. . . . Abraham then inquiring concerning Ishmael also, whether he was to live, God made known to him that he would live to an advanced age and become the father of great nations" (Josephus, *Ant.* 1.191–193, interpreting Gen 17:1–8, 11–22); God "foretold that their race would swell into a multitude of nations, with increasing wealth, nations whose founders would be had in everlasting remembrance" (*Ant.* 1.235, interpreting Gen 22:15–18). Jewish views of Abraham's relationship to non-Jewish peoples, however, are complex. Several texts emphasize Abraham as a culture bringer, esp. as a teacher of astrology to the Egyptians and Phoenicians (Artapanus, frg. 1 [Eusebius, *Praep. ev.* 9.18.1]; Eupolemus [Eusebius, *Praep. ev.* 9.17.3–4, 8]; *Jub.* 11:18–24; Josephus, *Ant.* 1.167–168). Many texts claim that Abraham is the ancestor of *particular* Gentile peoples: Moab and Ammon (Josephus, *Ant.* 1.205–206 [Gen 19:30]; Assyria and Africa (Cleodemus Malchus and Josephus, *Ant.* 1.238–241; 2.257 [Gen 25:1–6, the descendants of Abraham by Keturah]; Arabia and Nabataea (Josephus, *Ant.* 1.220–221 [Gen 25:12–15]; *Jub.* 20:11–13); the Spartans (1 Macc 12:6, 21; 2 Macc 5:9; Josephus, *Ant.* 12.226; 14.255). Paul, however, shows no interest in Abraham either as a culture bringer or as the ancestor of any particular Gentile people or group of peoples. His interest is in the more general notion that Abraham was the father of many nations and that these nations would prosper or be blessed because of him.

[61] In Romans, Paul always takes σπέρμα as a collective noun (1:3; 4:13, 16, 18; 9:7–8, 29; 11:1).

The way Paul writes about the inclusion of the Gentiles, however, reflects the same "not only . . . but also" pattern he used in 4:12. The mediation of the promise is through faith so that the promise may be made firm not only (οὐ . . . μόνον) to those of the law but also (ἀλλὰ καί) to those who are adherents of Abraham's faith (4:16). The perspective is again one in which the Jews are obviously included but in which the Gentiles are now also included.

This same perspective is reflected in Paul's reference in 4:16 to Abraham as the "father of us all" (πατὴρ πάντων ἡμῶν), that is, the father of both Jews and Gentiles. In 4:1, he began by referring to Abraham as "our forefather according to the flesh"; in 4:11–12, he referred to Abraham as "father of all who believe while still uncircumcised . . . and father of the circumcised." This movement in the way Paul writes of Abraham as "father" subtly reflects the stages in Paul's argument in this chapter and the way in which he wants his Roman Christian audience to understand the significance of Abraham. Abraham is not only the forefather of the Jews (4:1), which he certainly is; on the basis of the Jewish scriptures themselves, he is the father also of the Gentiles (4:11–12), indeed the "father of us all" (4:16). Once again Paul's argument is rooted in continuity rather than in the kind of contrast that dominated Galatians, and it again reflects the proposition in 1:16–17.

Romans 4:17b–22: Abraham's Firm Faith in God's Promise

At this point Paul selectively retells a small portion of the story of Abraham's faith in God's promise in the face of his own and his wife Sarah's old age (Gen 17:15–21).[62] He does so in such a way as both to emphasize the depth of Abraham's faith and also to show the similarity of his faith to that of believers in Christ. Abraham believed that God would keep his promise to make Abraham the father of many nations/Gentiles, even though both he and his wife Sarah were well beyond childbearing age. He also believed that the God who could give life to the dead could also give life to their "dead" bodies.

In retelling the story, Paul brings together important themes from the previous sections of Romans 4. Yet the passage does more than simply retell the story of Abraham or summarize previous themes. Paul retells the story in such a way as to heighten its pathos. The opening sentence sets the tone for the whole passage. Abraham believed in a God "who gives life to the dead and calls things which have no existence into existence" (4:17).[63] Abraham's own body and that of his wife Sarah are as good as dead (4:19). Nevertheless, Abraham believes "against hope in hope" (4:18); he does not weaken in faith even when he realizes that his own body and that of his wife are as good as dead (4:19); he does not doubt in disbelief the promise of God but is strengthened by faith (4:20–21). In vivid contrast to Abraham's

---

[62] The selective and dramatic retelling of biblical stories was quite common in Jewish literature of this period. For examples of such retelling of stories about Abraham, see *Jub.* 11:14–23.7; 1QapGen 18–22; *L.A.B.* 6:1–8:14; *Testament of Abraham*; Philo, *De Abrahamo*; Josephus, *Ant.* 1.151–256; and *Apocalypse of Abraham*.

[63] The exact sense of the phrase καὶ καλοῦντος τὰ μὴ ὄντα ὡς ὄντα in 4:17b is problematic. Simply taking the phrase ὡς ὄντα to mean "as if they existed" makes no sense in this context. It is better to take the phrase as an elliptical consecutive clause ("so that they exist"). For phrases with similar meaning, see *2 Bar.* 21:4; 48:8.

and Sarah's seemingly hopeless situation stands the promise of God, the God who gives life to the dead (4:17) and who is able to accomplish what was promised (4:21). All of this heightens Paul's Roman Christian audience's sense of the depth of Abraham's faith as well as sense of the power of the God who keeps the promise made to Abraham.

The dramatic heightening of the story serves two purposes. First, it is retold is such a way that Abraham serves as a model for faith. But the purpose of this faith is so that he might become the "father of many nations" (4:18). In the context of 4:1–25, this clearly means "father" of both Jews and Gentiles. Abraham is meant to be a model of faith for both Jewish and Gentile believers. This view of Abraham's significance is again quite different from that found in Gal 3:6–14, in which Abraham's significance was explicitly for the Gentiles, effectively if not intentionally bypassing the Jews. In Rom 4:17b–22, Abraham is a model for both. Second, because the story is retold in a way that emphasizes the power of God to give life to the "dead," Abraham's faith is similar to believers' faith in the God who raised Jesus from the dead. It is to this aspect that Paul turns in the concluding section of this chapter.

Romans 4:23–25: Application to the Present of the Example of Abraham's Faith

In the concluding section of the argument, Paul claims that Gen 15:6, where Abraham's faith "was reckoned to him as righteousness," was written not only for the sake of Abraham "but also for us, to whom it is to be reckoned, who believe in him who raised Jesus our Lord from the dead" (Rom 4:23–24). The way Paul retold the story of Abraham in 4:17b–22 makes the claim itself much easier to accept. Central elements in the story of Abraham are now taken up in 4:23–25 when Paul writes of the faith of those who believe that God raised Jesus from the dead. The type of appeal Paul makes in 4:23–25 is one that he has used elsewhere (1 Cor 9:9–10; 10:11), where the Jewish scriptures are interpreted to refer not only to events of the past but also to the present situation of believers. The Scriptures have a meaning "for our sake" (δι' ἡμᾶς, 1 Cor 9:10) or "for our instruction" (πρὸς νουθεσίαν ἡμῶν, 1 Cor 10:11). He will also use it again in Rom 15:3. This kind of appeal was traditional in both early Christianity and contemporary Judaism. Its traditional character is also present in the closing words of this section (Rom 4:24–25): "for those who believe in him who raised Jesus our Lord from the dead, who was handed over for our transgressions and raised for our righteousness." Referring to God as the one who raised Jesus from the dead is quite common in the New Testament.[64] Paul is using traditional language when he refers to Jesus being "handed over for our transgression and raised for our righteousness."[65] These verses also echo the equally traditional language of 3:24–26a. In this way, all of 4:1–25 is linked back to 3:21–26, for which it serves as a scriptural example and proof. Paul's final summary of the meaning of Abraham and his relevance for believers, then, is cast in a form meant to be taken as quite traditional and, as far as possible, uncontroversial for his Roman Christian audience.

---

[64] Rom 8:11; 10:9; 1 Cor 6:14; 15:15; 2 Cor 4:14; Acts 3:15; 4:10; 1 Pet 1:21. See Cranfield, *Romans,* 1.251.

[65] The formula seems to have been based on Isa 52:13–53:12.

CONCLUSIONS

One gets a much more three-dimensional perspective on Paul's concerns in Rom 3:21–4:25 when read against the background of Galatians. The Abraham who emerges in Rom 4:1–25 is certainly very different from the one in Galatians. He is the father of both Jews and Gentile believers. His "seed" once again is interpreted as a collective noun referring to both Jews and Gentile believers rather than as a singular noun that, by referring to Christ alone, excludes Jews as the "seed of Abraham." Paul's interpretation of Abraham in 4:1–25 is one in which a Jewish perspective on Abraham is broadened to include Gentile believers, unlike the interpretation found in Galatians, in which Abraham is virtually excluded, however unintentionally, as the father of the Jewish people in connection with the promise. The either-or arguments of Galatians are replaced by the both-and arguments of Rom 4:1–25.

More broadly, Rom 3:21–4:25 reflects the significant ways in which Paul has rethought and revised his understanding of some of his basic convictions about the manifestation of God's righteousness in Christ. The most fundamental change, although not the most obvious, is one of perspective. The stark contrasts and oppositions of Galatians have given way to a temporally oriented, historical perspective in which the righteousness of God is now made manifest apart from observance of the law for Jews and Gentiles alike. This change of perspective also allows Paul to revise some of his other views. The Mosaic law no longer needs to be placed in stark opposition to faith or grace. What takes place now in Christ is apart from the law, but this is no longer seen as an in-principle opposition to observance of the law even in the past. The law does not need to be denigrated, nor does its divinely sanctioned observance in the past need to be challenged. Nor does Abraham need to be seen as father of the Gentiles only. He is once again the father of many nations, of both Jews and Gentiles.

In doing all this, Paul is also careful to appeal to early Christian creedal traditions as well as to interpretations of the Jewish scriptures. He shared both these authorities with his Roman Christian audience. He carefully roots the arguments in favor of his controversial positions in authoritative sources that both he and the Roman Christians accept. In 3:21–4:25 Paul tries to bring out the common ground and the continuity of his positions about righteousness, for Jews and Gentiles alike apart from observance of the law, with the convictions and beliefs he shares with the Roman Christians.

The extent to which these efforts were successful with the Roman Christians is, of course, another question. One has to wonder, though, whether at least some Roman Christians still would have found his views unacceptable. However reformulated his arguments may have been, Paul still refused to compromise his basic convictions about the present manifestation of God's righteousness in Christ for Jews and Gentiles alike through faith apart from observance of the law. No matter how strongly or cogently Paul emphasized the continuity of his convictions with the creedal traditions and the Jewish scriptures he shared with them, at least some Roman Christians probably still would have objected to his insistence that righteousness no longer involved observance of the law and that Jews and Gentiles were similarly situated.

All of this is speculation. But what is much less speculative is that the Roman Christians saw in the observance of the ethical commandments of the Mosaic law a higher ethic and a way of life superior to that of their Gentile neighbors. They saw Paul's insistence on righteousness apart from observance of the law in Galatians as an invitation to ethical confusion and disarray. For them, this confusion and disarray were not simply theoretical possibilities. The Roman Christians saw them in practice in the problems experienced by the Christian community in Corinth. It is to this that Paul turns in Romans 5–7.

CHAPTER 6

The Incompatibility of This Grace and Sin

*F*OR JEWS LIVING IN THE GRECO-ROMAN WORLD as well as for the Roman Christian community, the Mosaic law served not only as a guide for ethical actions and a way of being obedient to God's will but also as the basis for their claim to moral superiority over their Greco-Roman neighbors. When Paul gained a reputation for preaching a gospel apart from observance of the Mosaic law, many Roman Christians were understandably concerned about what the basis of Christian ethical behavior could now be. If not the ethical commandments of the Mosaic law, then what? Paul already adverted to this issue in Rom 3:8 when he condemned those who had slandered him by claiming that, without the Mosaic law, his position led to moral confusion and disarray. In 3:1–8 this slander was part of a larger concern on the part of most Roman Christians that Paul's views not only risked doing away with ethical norms but also put in doubt the value of the Mosaic law as the basis for their moral superiority over their Greco-Roman neighbors (3:1). Christian ethical behavior and the ethical content of the Mosaic law were inextricably intertwined for them. They could not conceive of one without the other.

Some of Paul's previous attempts to state positively the new basis of Christian ethical behavior compounded their misgivings about him. In his exhortation in Gal 5:1–6:10, Paul tried to provide the Galatian Christians with an alternative ethical perspective to observance of the Mosaic law. One must realize how integral this section is to Paul's overall argument in Galatians. If the Galatian Christians were to be persuaded that they should not allow themselves to be circumcised or oblige themselves to observe the Mosaic law, he had to show them how they could live ethically as Christians on some other basis.[1] Three central principles dominated this alternative perspective. The first was freedom (ἐλευθερία): "For freedom Christ has set us

---

[1] Given the general character of the exhortation in this passage, even in Gal 6:1–10, Paul does not seem concerned with "antinomianism" or with specific moral lapses on the Galatian Christians' part. His concern was, rather, to show them how they could lead ethical lives without the observance of the law. For recent surveys of opinions on the place of this section of Galatians, see John M. G. Barclay, *Obeying the Truth: A Study of Paul's Ethics in Galatians*

free. Stand firm, therefore, and do not submit again to a yoke of slavery" (Gal 5:1).
In this passage, the "yoke of slavery" is the Mosaic law and its observance. Paul
contrasted the freedom of believers in Christ with the slavery of observance of the
Mosaic law. This same viewpoint was basically restated in 5:13. The second principle was guidance by the Spirit. This Spirit is a divine power by which believers
have the capacity to act ethically, to walk (περιπατεῖτε) by the Spirit (5:16), to let
themselves be led (ἄγεσθε) by the Spirit (5:17), to live (ζῶμεν) and be guided
(στοιχῶμεν) by the Spirit (5:25).[2] The final principle was love (ἀγάπη): "For in
Christ Jesus neither circumcision nor uncircumcision count for anything; the only
thing that counts is faith working through love [πίστις δι' ἀγάπης ἐνεργουμένη]"
(5:6); "Through love become slaves [δουλεύετε] to one another" (5:13). Love was
also listed first in Paul's catalogue of virtues in 5:22.

Paul undoubtedly saw in all this a way of living no less demanding than the
observance of the Mosaic law. In 5:14, he wrote that the whole law is summed up in
the single commandment, quoting Lev 19:18, to love one's neighbor as one's self
(Gal 5:14). Indeed, through love the Galatian Christians were to become slaves of
one another (5:13). He also warned them not to use their freedom from the yoke
of the law as an opportunity (ἀφορμήν) for the flesh (5:13) and then went on to
offer catalogues of vices and virtues (5:19–23) that are in fact consonant with the
Mosaic law.[3]

Yet for Roman Christians who saw the Mosaic law as a divinely sanctioned,
superior ethical code, Paul's emphasis on freedom, guidance by the Spirit, and love
as the new bases for living a Christian life must have seemed hopelessly vague and
inadequate in comparison with the specificity of the law. How could Paul's emphasis
on righteousness through faith apart from observance of the law result in anything
but a kind of moral anarchy, the very anarchy that the law enabled them to overcome? In the eyes of the Roman Christians, this was not just a theoretical question.
They could point to the situation of ethical disarray in the Christian community of
Corinth reflected in 1 Corinthians. Without the observance of the Mosaic law,
this largely Gentile community at Corinth came to be troubled by divisions over
a variety of ethical issues. The situation of the community there served as a negative
confirmation, for the largely Gentile Christian community at Rome, of its conviction that all believers should remain bound by the ethical commandments of the
Mosaic law.

Finally, Paul's characterization of the law as a yoke of slavery (Gal 5:1), of
those who observe the law as being under a curse (3:10), and of those Gentile believers who want to observe the law as turning back to the slavery to the weak and

---

(Studies of the New Testament and Its World; Edinburgh: T&T Clark, 1988), 9–23; Matera,
Galatians, 194–96; and Martyn, *Galatians*, 467–558.

[2] The term πνεῦμα occurs ten times in this section of Galatians (5:5, 16, 17 [bis], 18, 22,
25 [bis]; 6:1, 8). In all but one of them (6:1), it is best understood as referring to a divine power.

[3] Hellenistic Jews had for some time understood the law as a code of conduct meant to
instill the practice of virtue and the avoidance of vice (e.g., *Let. Arist.* 130–171, 187–300;
Josephus, *Ag. Ap.* 2.145–296; Philo, *De decalogo* and *Spec.* 1–4). Paul, however, used the practice
of virtue and the avoidance of vice as alternatives to the observance of the law. This also set
Paul apart from the position of most Roman Christians.

beggarly elemental principles that they had previously served (4:9) must especially have struck most Roman Christians as scandalous. Paul's rhetoric seemed to impugn the goodness of the God-given law itself.

It is to this web of issues, accusations, and suspicions that Paul turns in Romans 5–7. That Paul was aware of these issues and the problems they created for Roman Christians will become clearer in the course of our analysis of his arguments in Romans 5–7. In these chapters Paul significantly rethinks and revises how he understands the relationship between Christian living and righteousness through faith apart from observance of the law. He intends this to allay their suspicions that his views would lead, however unintentionally, to moral confusion and disarray, especially in the case of Gentile believers. He also deals at greater length with what he sees as the place of the law. If Christian living and the ethical commandments of the law are inextricably intertwined in the minds of most Roman Christians, then Paul must also deal explicitly with the role of the law. How can the law be anything but good? And if it is good, why are believers in Christ now to live their lives "apart from the law"?

The rhetorical structure of Romans 5–7 is similar to both 1:18–3:20 and 3:21–4:25. This similarity and the fact that these chapters follow, as did the first two parts, recognizable Greco-Roman rhetorical conventions, especially those associated with the diatribe, point to their unity.[4] Paul presents his positive exposition in 5:1–21 whereas in 6:1–7:25 his tone is much more argumentative. Once again he uses rhetorical questions, apostrophe, speech-in-character, and personification to answer objections to, or misunderstandings of, his views. More specifically, Romans 5 consists of (1) a statement of the subproposition, in 5:1–5, which stresses the ethical seriousness and earnestness of Paul's view of "this grace in which we stand" (5:2), and (2) his development of the subproposition, in which he tries to show the incompatibility of "this grace" with sin (5:6–21). Once again Paul develops these arguments on the basis of traditional Christian viewpoints he shares with his Roman Christian audience. On the basis of these shared viewpoints, he tries to show how his convictions about righteousness through faith apart from observance of the law, that is, "this grace in which we stand," are incompatible with sin for Gentile as well as for Jewish believers. Romans 6–7, the argumentative part of the passage, is structured around a series of rhetorical questions: 6:1–14, 15–23; 7:1–6, 7–12, 13–25. The first two concern the relationship of grace to sin and to the law respectively; the last three deal with Paul' defense of the goodness of the law and its relationship to sin. All of these are intended to answer Roman Christians' misgivings about, or objections to, what they take to be his positions in Galatians and 1 Corinthians.

---

[4]The structure of Romans 5–7, specifically whether Romans 5 belongs with Romans 1–4 or with Romans 6–7 (8), is much disputed. For a list of the various positions and their proponents, see Fitzmyer, *Romans*, 96–98. Fitzmyer correctly places Romans 5 with what follows. In addition to those listed by Fitzmyer, Morris (*Romans*, 172, 217–18, 243–44) and P. Stuhlmacher (*Paul's Letter to the Romans: A Commentary* [Louisville: Westminster John Knox, 1994], 57, 78–79, 88–89) place Romans 5 with the preceding chapters. Their arguments ignore the relationship of Paul's argumentation to the conventions of Greco-Roman rhetoric. When one takes these conventions into consideration, Romans 5 clearly belongs with Romans 6–7.

The unity of these three chapters is not only one of overall rhetorical structure but also of content and vocabulary. Certain words either occur frequently in these three chapters or are clustered in them:[5]

grace (χάρις): 11/24 (Romans 5, 6, 7)
gift (χάρισμα): 3/6 (Romans 5, 6)
free gift (δωρεά): 2/2 (Romans 5)
free gift (δώρημα): 1/1 (Romans 5)

sin (ἁμαρτία): 37/48 (Romans 5, 6, 7)
to sin (ἁμαρτάνω): 4/7 (Romans 5, 6)
sinner (ἁμαρτωλός): 3/4 (Romans 5, 7)
transgression (παράβασις): 1/3 (Romans 5)
trespass (παράπτωμα): 5/9 (Romans 5)

death (θάνατος): 18/22 (Romans 5, 6, 7)

law (νόμος): 28/74 (Romans 5, 6, 7)

These words do not simply cluster in Romans 5–7; they also establish a series of contrasts that run through Romans 5–7. Paul consistently contrasts the first group of words with the second group. In addition, he gives considerable emphasis to arguing about how both death (θάνατος) and law (νόμος) are related to these two groups. This clustering provides clear evidence of the unity of his argument in Romans 5–7. The contrasts indicate what is at stake: the relationship of sin, death, grace, and Christian living, how the first two stand in opposition to the last two, and how the law is related to both groups. Why Paul spends so much time dealing with these relationships and what his rhetorical strategy is will become clearer in the more detailed analysis of Romans 5 in this chapter and of Romans 6–7 in our chapters 7 and 8.

ROMANS 5:1–5: THE SUBPROPOSITION

Romans 5 begins with the subproposition for this part of letter (5:1–5). The subproposition consists of two main clauses, both in the first-person-plural subjunctive: (1) "let us have peace with God" (5:1) and (2) "let us boast in the hope of God's glory" (5:2).[6] The second of these clauses is then expanded in 5:3–5, again with a verb in the first-person-plural subjunctive. The use both of the first-person plural

---

[5] The first number indicates the number of times the word appears in Romans 5–7; the second number, the times the word occurs in all of Romans.

[6] There is debate over the correct reading in 5:1: ἔχομεν in the indicative or ἔχωμεν in the subjunctive. This also affects whether one takes καυχώμεθα in 5:2, 3 as an indicative or as a subjunctive. Most modern commentators take the two verbs as indicative. The subjunctive, however, is much better attested textually and was so understood by patristic writers (Fitzmyer, *Romans* 395). Given the strongly ethical bent of Romans 5–7, the subjunctive for both words seems more appropriate. For another view, see Metzger, *Textual Commentary*, 452. The committee's argument in favor of the indicative is odd in the sense that they concede that Tertius, Paul's amanuensis, may well have written the subjunctive. If this were the case, then Paul could have corrected the mistake when he read over the letter in preparation for making the final copy that would have been sent to the Roman Christian community.

and of the subjunctive sets these verses apart from what follows (5:6–21). In addition, 5:6 begins with the particle "for" (γάρ), which indicates that what follows in 5:6–21 is meant to offer arguments or explanations for why what is found in 5:1–5 is the case. Romans 5:1–5 is cast in the form of a short ethical exhortation. Paul's purpose is to emphasize from the start that his viewpoint about being made righteous by grace is not devoid of ethical consequences but, rather, is fraught with them. By using the first-person-plural subjunctive rather than the second-person-plural imperative, Paul also rhetorically unites himself with his audience. They are both of one mind in realizing the serious ethical consequences of Christian believing.

In 5:1–2, Paul begins by connecting this passage with 3:21–4:25. He does this by taking up two central concepts found in 3:21–26: being made righteous by faith (5:1) and grace (5:2). Believers, who have been made righteous by faith, should now have peace with God through Jesus Christ and access to "this grace in which we stand." It is crucial to note how Paul describes this situation. By describing it as "*this grace* in which we stand," he means something specific. What this something appears is at the beginning of 5:1, "Made righteous, therefore, by faith." Given what Paul has just argued in 3:21–4:25 through the example of Abraham, this righteousness through faith occurs apart from observance of the Mosaic law (3:21, 28; 4:1–8, 13, 16) and applies to Jews and Gentiles alike (3:22–26; 28–31; 4:11–12, 16). It is the seriousness of the ethical consequences of "this grace" that Paul wants to emphasize in Romans 5. That this is one of Paul's primary concerns in Romans 5 is also indicated by the fact that he returns to "this grace" in 5:20–21 to claim that where sin increased, grace abounded all the more, with the result that, just as sin reigned in death, so too grace now reigns through righteousness for eternal life.

These verses also bring together again in an ethical context terms that appeared together earlier in Gal 5:2–5: grace, righteousness, faith, hope, and love. The concepts that appear at the beginning (faith in Rom 5:1) and at the end (love in Rom 5:5) formed Paul's basic ethical principle in Gal 5:5: faith working through love. The connection between love and the Holy Spirit in Rom 5:5 as central to Christian living was also emphasized in Galatians 5. Although love in Rom 5:5 is explicitly God's love and the love mentioned in Gal 5:5 refers to the love Christians are to have for one another, the power of the Spirit joins the two together.[7] One has in Rom 5:1–5 a concatenation of terms that cannot but bring to mind Galatians 5. But this view of Christian living, especially opposed as it explicitly was in Galatians 5 to observance of the law, was also what must have provoked suspicion among most Roman Christians. Such a view of ethics must have seemed to them too vague and lacking in ethical seriousness. In Rom 5:1–5, Paul begins to address this issue.

Paul does this by connecting righteousness through faith and "this grace in which we stand" with boasting in the practice of three virtues: patience, character, and hope. In doing this, Paul draws on ethical material he used in earlier letters. This is most obvious in his use of the virtue of hope, which he connects with faith (Rom 5:1) and love (5:5), a triad that previously appeared in 1 Thess 1:3; 5:8; 1 Cor 13:13. It is also true of the two virtues of patience (ὑπομονή) and character

---

[7] The role of the Spirit in Rom 5:5, by *insinuatio,* also points ahead to Romans 8. In Romans 8, however, Paul will also significantly revise the way he describes the role of the Spirit.

(δοκιμή); both have appeared in his earlier letters (patience in 1 Thess 1:3; 2 Cor 1:6; 6:4; 12:12; character in 2 Cor 2:9; 8:2; 9:13; 13:3; Phil 2:22).

Quite significantly, Paul places the exercise of these virtues in the context of afflictions (θλίψεσιν, Rom 5:3) and uses the rhetorical figure of κλῖμαξ or *gradatio*[8] to bring out their relationship: Afflictions produce patience; patience produces character; character produces hope. In emphasizing the reality and value of afflictions, Paul again draws on his earlier letters (1 Thess 1:6; 3:3, 7; but esp. 2 Cor 1:4, 8; 2:4; 4:17; 6:4–10; 7:4; 8:2, 13). Though not using the word "afflictions," Paul also connected both grace and boasting with similar realities in 2 Cor 12:7–10 in speaking about his own experience:

> Therefore, to keep me from being too elated by the abundance of revelations, a thorn was given me in the flesh, a messenger of Satan, to harass me, to keep me from being too elated. Three times I besought the Lord about this, that it should leave me; but he said to me, "My grace is sufficient for you, for my power is made perfect in weakness." I will all the more gladly boast of my weaknesses, that the power of Christ may rest upon me. For the sake of Christ, then, I am content with weaknesses, insults, hardships, persecutions, and calamities, for whenever I am weak, then I am strong.

By drawing on his earlier letters and his own experience, Paul in Rom 5:1–5 is placing in an obviously serious ethical context both his views about righteousness through faith as a grace and Christian living as God's love empowering believers through the Spirit. He emphasizes the reality and significance of afflictions and encourages the practice of the virtues of patience, character, and hope. This grace and righteousness through faith are not cheap or easy; they are fraught with afflictions. Such an emphasis would have provided the Roman believers an ethos different, at least in emphasis, from that found in Galatians 5 and more in keeping with their own views. The creation of such an ethos, that is, the sense of Paul as an ethically serious person, would have been crucial in persuading his Roman audience to take seriously the arguments he is about to make in the rest of Romans 5 and his defense in Romans 6–7. This emphasis on the value and importance of afflictions, not insignificantly, also paralleled their own experience, especially since some of them had suffered expulsion from Rome only six or seven years earlier. The fact that Romans 5 begins with a short ethical exhortation and that this exhortation contains the point that Paul wants to develop in the rest of the chapter is not at all accidental. The issue at stake is the ethical seriousness of Paul's gospel.

ROMANS 5:6–21: THE EXPOSITION—CHRIST'S DEATH IS INCOMPATIBLE WITH SIN

Once Paul has stated his conviction that righteousness through faith and "this grace in which we stand" have significant ethical consequences, he goes on in 5:6–21 to show they are also incompatible with sin. As in 3:23–26, he tries to do this on the

---

[8]This rhetorical figure involves a progression in the form *a . . . b; b . . . c; c . . . d . . .* See Demetrius, *Eloc.* 270; Quintilian, *Inst.* 9.3.54.

basis of traditional Christian beliefs that he has in common with his Roman Christian audience. The interpretation of this section of Romans, especially 5:12–21, is difficult and has been the subject of almost endless contention. The debates swirl around issues such as the universal character of human sinfulness, "original sin" and its nature and propagation, the relationship between sin and death, and between the sinful human condition and individual sinfulness and sinning.[9]

All these questions are important, and all are occasioned by what Paul wrote. They do not serve, however, as good starting points for understanding what Paul is concerned about in this passage. Paul's concerns are of a different sort. In the attempt to understand 5:6–21, perhaps the best place to begin is at the end, at the point to which Paul intends his argument in these verses to move. This comes in 5:21:

> so that, just as sin reigned in death,
> so too grace might reign through righteousness to eternal life
> through Jesus Christ our Lord.

Paul's conclusion contrasts sin and death, on the one hand, with grace and righteousness, on the other. Set within the context of Romans 5, this conclusion emphasizes again the utter incompatibility of "this grace," mentioned in 5:2, with sin and death. Keeping this conclusion in mind obviously does not solve all the issues occasioned by Paul's language and thought in Romans 5. But it does serve as a guide to what is at stake for Paul as he presents his arguments to the Roman Christians.

Four additional points need to be made before examining 5:6–21 in detail. The first concerns the rhetorical strategy of this section—specifically, the dominant form of argumentation. For much of 5:6–21, Paul employs a rhetorical device familiar to Greek and Roman audiences, that of comparison. Ancient rhetoric recognized three kinds of arguments from comparison: from the greater to the lesser *(a maiore ad minus);* from the lesser to the greater *(a minore ad maius);* and between equals *(paria ex paribus).*[10] In 5:6–21, Paul uses all three: from the greater to the lesser in 5:9–10, from the lesser to the greater in 5:15–17, and between equals in 6:18–21.[11]

Second, throughout 5:6–21, Paul establishes an extensive series of contrasts between two sets of terms. What is obvious in all these contrasts is the incompatibility of human sinfulness with what has been accomplished by God in Christ.

---

[9] For discussions of some of these issues, see Cranfield, *Romans,* 1.269–95; Fitzmyer, *Romans,* 406–23; Wilckens, *Römer,* 1:305–37. There is no doubt that these debates are deeply colored by the controversies between Protestants and Catholics since the sixteenth century. But the origins of the debate certainly go back to the time of Augustine and the Pelagian controversies in the early fifth century. These debates were also influenced by the theological controversies of Western medieval Christianity. It is worthwhile noting that these controversies are not nearly as important in Eastern Christian history and theology.

[10] Aristotle, *Rhet.* 2.23.4–5 1397b 12–27 (ἐκ τοῦ μᾶλλον καὶ ἧττον); *Top.* 2.10 114b 25–115a 24; Cicero, *Top.* 23, 68–71; Quintilian, *Inst.* 5.10.86–93.

[11] One finds a similar form of argumentation in rabbinic literature: "the light and the heavy" *(qal wa-ḥomer).* Given that Paul uses all three forms of the topic of comparison from Greco-Roman rhetoric, one suspects that he is drawing on this Greco-Roman rhetorical topic rather than on the similar rabbinic technique. For a description of the Rabbinic technique, see Strack and Stemberger, *Introduction to the Talmud and Midrash,* 21.

These contrasts also serve as important guides to what Paul is about in this passage. The contrasts are the following:[12]

weak (ἀσθενῶν, 5:6)	Christ (Χριστός, 5:6, 8)
godless (ἀσεβῶν, 5:6)	love (ἀγάπην, 5:8)
sinners (ἁμαρτωλῶν, 5:8)	God (θεός, 5:8)
enemies (ἐχθροί, 5:10)	reconciliation (καταλλάγω, καταλαγήν, 5:10–11)
through one man (Adam) (δι' ἑνὸς ἀνθρώπου, 5:12)	one man (Christ) (ἑνὸς ἀνθρώπου, 5:15)
sin (ἡ ἁμαρτία, 5:12, 13, 20, 21)	grace (ἡ χάρις, 5:15, 17, 20, 21)
death (ὁ θάνατος, 5:12, 14, 17, 21)	(eternal) life (ἡ ζωή [αἰώνιος], 5:17, 18, 21)
sinners (οἱ ἁμαρτωλοί, 5:19)	righteous (οἱ δίκαιοι, 5:19)
disobedience (τῆς παρακοῆς, 5:19)	obedience (τῆς ὑποκοῆς, 5:19)
trespass (τὸ παράπτωμα, 5:15, 16, 17, 18, 20)	gift (τὸ χάρισμα, 5:15, 16)
	grace (ἡ χάρις, 5:15, 17, 20, 21)
	the free gift (of righteousness) (ἡ δωρεά [τῆς δικαιοσύνης], 5:15, 17)
condemnation (τὸ κατάκριμα, 5:16, 18)	righteousness (ἡ δικαίωσιν, 5:18)
	righteous deed (τὸ δικαίωμα, 5:16, 18)
judgment (τὸ κρίμα, 5:16)	gift (τὸ χάρισμα, 5:15, 16)
through one man sinning (δι' ἑνὸς ἁμαρτήσαντος, 5:16)	the free gift (τὸ δώρημα, 5:16)

Third, Paul makes use of viewpoints and language he already used in his other letters, especially in 1 and 2 Corinthians, as well as earlier in Romans. Some of this, as we will see, appears to be traditional material that Paul has taken up and made use of here. This again shows that Paul is appealing in Rom 5:6–21 to viewpoints he probably had in common with the Roman Christians.

Fourth, Paul's arguments in 5:6–21 are part of the larger argument of Romans as a whole. One needs to be aware of how his arguments here take up and develop the arguments and language he used earlier in the letter. As we will see, this helps us to understand the meaning of some of the language Paul uses in Romans 5,

---

[12] The translation of some of these words as Paul uses them in 5:6–21 is difficult. The reason is that Paul especially uses Greek nouns ending in -μα because of their sound and for the sake of contrast rather than for their precise meaning.

especially his emphasis on "all" and its relationship to the "many," terms prominent in 5:12–21.[13]

The argument of 5:6–21 moves through a series of steps. Paul first uses traditional cultic imagery to describe the significance of Christ's death (5:6–8) and then its significance for believers (5:9–11). He then uses this explanation as the basis for a comparison between Adam and Christ (5:12–21). The comparison is first set up in an elliptical fashion (5:12–14), then an explicit contrast is drawn between the effects of Adam's trespass and the effects of what God accomplished in Christ (5:15–17). Finally, a comparison is drawn between those affected by Adam's trespass and those affected by Christ's act of righteousness (5:18–21). Paul's purpose in using these comparisons is, first, to show how his gospel of righteousness through faith apart from observance of the Mosaic law; that is, "this grace in which we stand," is incompatible with sin. He argues that this is so on the basis of traditional Christian beliefs he and his Roman audience share in common. Second, especially through the comparison between Adam and Christ, these shared beliefs also show that this incompatibility between this grace and sin is the case for all believers, Jewish and Gentile alike.

Romans 5:6–11: The Significance of Christ's Death

Paul develops his interpretation of the significance of Christ's death for believers in 5:6–11 primarily by appealing to three creedal traditions he and the Roman Christians have in common. In 5:6–8 he, first describes how God showed his love through Christ's dying for us (ὑπὲρ ἡμῶν ἀπέθανεν) while we were yet sinners (ἁμαρτωλῶν ὄντων). The passage echoes, in a shortened form, the fuller, explicitly traditional creedal formula in 1 Cor 15:3 ("Christ died for our sins"). Given his reference to Christ's death while "we were yet sinners" in Rom 5:8, Paul clearly has this fuller form in view. Paul also makes use of this traditional creedal formula elsewhere in his letters.[14] The most relevant parallel for our purposes, however, is 2 Cor 5:14–15, where Paul uses a variation on the same traditional creedal formula to describe Christ as dying for all (ὑπὲρ πάντων ἀπέθανεν).[15] We shall return to this parallel shortly. As in Rom 3:24–26a, Paul is again drawing in Rom 6:6–8 on language and images that he and the Roman Christians have in common. At the same time, he gives his own emphasis to it. He emphasizes the extraordinary character of God's love for us through Christ's death in that it occurred while we were yet weak (5:6), ungodly (5:6), and sinners (5:8). By insistently setting God's love and action in Christ over against human sin and weakness, he establishes the implied contrast and the consequent incompatibility between God and sin that he explicitly develops in the rest of the chapter.

On the basis of what he establishes in 5:6–8, Paul goes on in 5:9–11 to claim that believers will be saved from the future wrath by Christ's life (i.e., his resurrection). The emphasis shifts from what God has done in Christ's death to the

---

13 "All" (πάντες) in 5:12 (bis), 18 (bis); "the many (οἱ πολλοί)" in 5:15 (bis), 16, 19 (bis).

14 1 Thess 5:10; Gal 2:21; 1 Cor 1:13; 8:11; 2 Cor 5:14–15; Rom 14:15. It is also found in 1 Pet 3:18.

15 For the traditional elements in these verses, see Victor Paul Furnish, *II Corinthians* (AB 32A; Garden City, N.Y.: Doubleday, 1984), 310; and Thrall, *Second Corinthians*, 1.409.

consequences, for believers, of his resurrection. The type of argument Paul uses in these verses, part of the topic of comparison, is from the greater to the lesser *(a maiore ad minus)*. The form of the argument is this: if *a* (the greater) is the case, how much more so is *b* (the lesser) the case. If, while we were enemies, we were reconciled to God through the death of God's Son (the greater, the more difficult, the more unexpected [5:6–8]), how much more so will we, now reconciled, be saved from wrath by his life (the lesser, the less difficult).[16] In using this argument in 5:10–11, Paul emphasizes the reality of reconciliation: "For if while we were ene- mies, we were reconciled [κατηλλάγημεν] to God through [διά] the death of his Son, how much more, now that we are reconciled [καταλλαγέντες], shall we be saved by his life. Not only so, but we even boast in God through [διά] our Lord Jesus Christ, through whom [δι' οὗ] we have now received reconciliation [τὴν καταλλαγήν]." Paul views Christ's death as that event through (διά) which God has reconciled sinners to himself. They are no longer enemies, and so by implication, they are now at peace with God. This language clearly expands on the notion of being at peace with God from 5:1.

In using the metaphor of reconciliation, Paul also is taking up another creedal tradition he previously used in 2 Cor 5:18–21:

> All this is from God, who through Christ reconciled [καταλλάξαντος] us to himself, and gave us the ministry of reconciliation [καταλλαγῆς]; as it is said [ὡς ὅτι], in Christ God was reconciling [ἦν . . . καταλλάσσων] the world to himself, not counting their trespasses against them, and entrusting to us the message of reconciliation [καταλλαγῆς]. So we are ambassadors for Christ, God making his appeal though us. We beseech you on behalf of Christ, be reconciled [καταλλάγητε] to God. For our sake he made him to be sin who knew no sin, so that in him we might become the righteous- ness of God.

This passage follows almost immediately on 2 Cor 5:14–15, where Paul appeals to the creedal tradition mentioned above about Christ dying for all. Although disputed, there is good reason to think that the language about reconciliation in this passage is also traditional.[17] The strongest case can be made for 2 Cor 5:19a, "in Christ God was reconciling the world to himself," since the ὡς ὅτι is best translated "as it is said." In addition, the use of the paraphrastic imperfect (ἦν . . . καταλλάσσων) is rare in Paul.[18] Given that the language of reconciliation was already traditional in 5:19a, its use in Rom 5:10–11 indicates that Paul is again using material he shares with his Roman Christian audience. At the same time, his use of the notion that all this took place "while we were enemies" (Rom 5:10) connects these verses with the weak, the

---

[16] Although Byrne (*Romans*, 168, 171) associates this argument with the *qal wa-homer* technique of rabbinic literature rather than with the Greco-Roman topic of comparison, he correctly notes that the argument is a comparison from the greater to the lesser.

[17] Since there is little evidence for the use of the idea of reconciliation in a religious sense either in Greek literature or in Hellenistic Judaism, the traditional character of the language is within early Christianity itself. See Byrne, *Romans*, 172; and esp. Breytenbach, *Versöhnung*, 40–104, 107–20, 143–72.

[18] Furnish, *II Corinthians*, 317–18, 334. For other views, see Ralph P. Martin, *2 Corinthi- ans* (WBC 40; Waco, Tex.: Word, 1986), 138–59; and Thrall, *Second Corinthians*, 1:445–49.

ungodly, and the sinners of 5:6–8, and once again emphasizes the incompatibility between what God accomplished in Christ and sinfulness. This contrast then serves as the basis for Paul's extended comparison of Christ with Adam in 5:12–21.

In addition to the creedal traditions Paul uses in 5:6–8 and 5:10–11, he also uses a third creedal tradition in 5:9 to connect the two. On the basis of what he established in 5:6–8, Paul goes on in 5:9 to draw the conclusion ("therefore" [οὖν] in 5:9) that if believers have been "made righteous by his blood" (δικαιωθέντες νῦν ἐν τῷ αἵματι αὐτοῦ), how much more will they be saved from future wrath by Christ's life (i.e., his resurrection). Paul is obviously paraphrasing here a section of the traditional creedal formula he used in 3:24–25. In using this third creedal tradition to connect the other two, Paul gives the whole passage a somewhat different complexion. Neither the creedal tradition in 5:6–8, about Christ dying for us, nor that in 5:10–11, about the reconciliation with God that believers have received through the death of Christ, involved the use of cultic language or imagery.[19] By paraphrasing a crucial section from 3:24–26 and placing it between these two creedal traditions, Paul brings them into a context in which Jesus' death is again interpreted in cultic terms. As suggested above in the last chapter, this was probably due to the importance, for the Roman Christians, of the interpretation of Jesus' death in cultic terms.[20]

The purpose and character of the arguments Paul uses in 5:6–11 deserve highlighting. Much of the argumentation in the rest of Romans 5 will be of the same sort. He anchors the argument of this section in traditional material he shares with his Roman Christian audience. On this basis, he then tries to show how the agreement extends to the incompatibility between what God has accomplished in Christ and human sinfulness. It is also crucial to understand what Paul does not appeal to in this argumentation. He does not appeal to the ethical commandments of the Mosaic law. He does not appeal to the law as the way to demonstrate the incompatibility of God and sin. All that Paul describes God doing through Christ takes place "apart from the law." Paul tries to show the incompatibility between God and sin through the use of traditional beliefs he shares with the Roman Christians but without any appeal to the law. In this sense, the argument in 5:6–11 is similar to that in 3:21–26. It even includes an explicit paraphrasing of 3:24–25. What has changed is the emphasis. In 3:21–26, Paul was concerned with the reality of being made righteous through faith apart from the law. In 5:6–11, he shifts the emphasis to the ethical consequences of this reality. His purpose is obviously not to persuade the Roman Christians that such an incompatibility exists. They needed no persuading in the matter. Rather, his purpose is to persuade them that he too, in the face of their suspicions, is fully convinced of the same incompatibility. At the same time, he tries to show that this shared conviction about the incompatibility between what God has accomplished in Christ and sin is based on something other than the the ethical commandments of the law. In 5:12–21, he will continue to build on this common conviction. The basic type of argument, however, will remain the same.

---

[19] This has been convincingly argued by Breytenbach, "Versöhnung, Stellvertretung, und Sühne."

[20] See above, pp. 139–40.

Romans 5:12–21: Comparison and Contrast of Christ and Adam

Paul now turns to an extended comparison between Adam and Christ. The interpretation of this section of the letter, as mentioned above, has been extremely controversial over the ages, especially with regard to the nature and extent of "original sin." None of the questions raised by this section of the letter is unimportant for Christian belief. Still, some of them are not the questions Paul had in mind when he wrote this part of the letter. Given the history of its interpretation, it is no easy task to get at what Paul did have in mind, that is, what Paul thought this section contributed to the argument of Romans 5–7.

Perhaps the most helpful way to start is to look at the beginning and the end of the section. Paul begins the section with the phrase διὰ τοῦτο, "because of this" or "therefore." He sees this section, in some fashion, as a development of 5:1–11, that is, of his insistence on the incompatibility between what God has accomplished in Christ and human sin.[21]

Something similar emerges when we turn to the parallel structure in the conclusion of the passage in 5:21:

so that,

> just as sin [ἡ ἁμαρτία] ruled in death [ἐν τῷ θανάτῳ],
>
> so too grace [ἡ χάρις] might rule through righteousness [διὰ δικαιοσύνης]
>
> > for eternal life [εἰς ζωὴν αἰώνιον] through Jesus Christ our Lord.

In order to sum up the point of the comparison between Adam and Christ, Paul contrasts the rule of sin in death, connected with Adam, to the rule of grace through righteousness for eternal life, connected with Jesus Christ. The contrasts are between sin and death, on the one hand, and grace and eternal life, on the other. In the fuller second half of the parallelism, Paul also adds "through righteousness" and "through Jesus Christ our Lord." This vocabulary leads us immediately back to 5:1–2, where Paul began this section of the letter:

> Made righteous [δικαιωθέντες] through faith let us have peace with God through our Lord Jesus Christ [διὰ τοῦ κυρίου ἡμῶν Ἰησοῦ Χριστοῦ], through whom we have gained access by faith to this grace [εἰς τὴν χάριν ταύτην] in which we stand.

In 5:21, Paul takes up again the vocabulary of 5:1–2, so central to Paul's own convictions, and thus links the beginning and the end of the argument. But in 5:21, he also contrasts this vocabulary with sin and death. The purpose of the comparison between Adam and Christ in 5:12–21 is to bring out especially the contrast and incompatibility between "this grace in which we stand" and righteousness through faith, on the one hand, and sin and death, on the other. Paul was not so much interested in analyzing the origins or propagation of human sinfulness as he was in showing by means of contrasts the incompatibility of grace and righteousness with sin and death. He insists

---

[21] Paul uses the phrase elsewhere in his letters in similar ways. See 1 Thess 2:13; 3:5, 7; 1 Cor 4:17; 11:10, 30; 2 Cor 4:1; 7:13; 13:10; Phlm 15; Rom 1:16; 4:16; 13:6; 15:9.

on this not because his Roman Christian audience would have considered grace and sin compatible but because they suspected *he* did. In addition, as we shall see below in the next two chapters, Paul's argument in Romans 5 will also serve as the basis for the defense of his own positions in Romans 6–7, a defense in the face of precisely these suspicions on the part of the Roman Christian community.

There is, however, another purpose for the comparison between Adam and Christ: it enables Paul to include all humanity. For Paul, this again means both Jews and Gentiles, the two fundamental groups into which humanity is divided. More specifically, the comparison between Adam and Christ provides Paul with a way to show how the incompatibility of grace and righteousness with sin and death includes both Jews and Gentiles. In addition, it does this in such a way as to bypass again the ethical commandments of the Mosaic law. Because of Christ, one does not now need the law to establish this incompatibility.

Adam's Sin and Its Consequences in Judaism and Earliest Christianity

In order to locate Paul's argument in 5:12–21, it is first necessary to understand in some detail two contexts out of which Paul's comparison between Adam and Christ comes. The first is the variety of ways in which Genesis 1–3, but especially Genesis 3, was understood in early Judaism.[22] This is especially important for understanding Rom 5:12–14, where Paul writes that death entered the world through Adam's sin and that both sin and death spread to other human beings. The second is the way in which Adam and Christ had already been compared in earliest Christianity. This comparison is already found in 1 Cor 15:21–22, 45–49. The comparison in 1 Cor 15:21–22 is especially important for understanding Rom 5:15–21, since the basic comparison between Adam and Christ in these verses shows that it was already traditional in earliest Christianity. As we shall see, Paul takes over this comparison and develops it for his own particular purposes.[23]

Concerning interpretation of Adam's sin in Jewish writings roughly contemporary with Paul and from a century or two earlier, the figure of Adam appears in several different contexts and is used for several different purposes in these writings. It is important to keep this in mind lest one think there was a unified "Adam myth" lying behind what one finds in Paul; rather, there was a variety of interpretations of Adam in early Judaism, and this variety was conditioned by the purposes and viewpoints of the different authors.[24]

---

[22] This has been studied by John R. Levison, *Portraits of Adam in Early Judaism: From Sirach to 2 Baruch* (JSPSup 1; Sheffield, England: JSOT Press, 1988).

[23] Earlier studies on these two interrelated topics include the following: Charles K. Barrett, *From First Adam to Last: A Study in Pauline Theology* (New York: Charles Scribner's Sons, 1962); Egon Brandenburger, *Adam und Christus: exegetisch-religionsgeschichtliche Untersuchung zu Röm. 5, 12–21 (1. Kor. 15)* (WMANT 7; Neukirchen-Vluyn: Neukirchener Verlag, 1962); Robin Scroggs, *The Last Adam: A Study in Pauline Anthropology* (Philadelphia: Fortress, 1966). See also William D. Davies, *Paul and Rabbinic Judaism: Some Rabbinic Elements in Pauline Theology* (4th ed.; Philadelphia: Fortress, 1980), 36–57; Jacob Jervell, *Imago Dei: Gen 1, 26f. im Spätjudentum, in der Gnosis, und in den paulinischen Briefen* (FRLANT 58; Göttingen: Vandenhoeck & Ruprecht, 1960), 26–50.

[24] Levison, *Portraits*, 1–28, has rightly emphasized both of these points. He also rightly criticizes earlier works in this area for their lack of recognition of this variety.

For our purposes, these interpretations can be grouped under three different headings. Under the first heading, language connected with, or alluding to, Genesis 1–3 about Adam is used to explain the general human condition, especially its mortality; but the emphasis is on the human condition rather than on Adam. Examples of this are found especially in Sirach and Wisdom of Solomon.[25] The most elaborate passage of this type is Sir 17:1–4:

> The Lord from the earth created man,
>> and makes him return to earth again.
> Limited days of life he gives them,
>> with power over all things else on earth.
> He endows them with a strength that befits them;
>> in God's own image he made them.
> He puts the fear of him in all flesh,
>> and allows them power over beasts and birds.[26]

In this passage Sirach draws on the language of Gen 1:26–28; 3:19; his interest, however, is not in Adam but in how the language of Genesis can be used to describe the general human situation.

Under the second heading, the figures and accounts of Genesis 1–3 are used as exemplary of the human condition. Here the writer's attention is focused on the interpretation of Genesis 1–3. Yet the purpose is to show how the Genesis text illustrates (rather than explains) the general human condition, especially in its moral and religious aspects. Examples of this use of Genesis are found in the Jewish historian Josephus and in the Jewish exegete Philo of Alexandria.

Josephus's interpretation of Genesis 1–3 is found in *Ant.* 1.32–72. They are of a piece with his overall goals in the *Antiquities*. Josephus adapts the conventions of rhetorical historiography found in the *Antiquitates romanae* of Dionysius of Halicarnassus. Both Dionysius and Josephus retell history in order to teach contemporary, especially ethical, lessons. In the case of Josephus, it was to show that those who conform to the will of God prosper whereas those who do not suffer disaster.[27] Josephus interprets Adam and Eve's disobedience within this overarching ethical and religious scheme. After the creation of Adam and Eve, God placed them in the garden, commanding them at the same time to abstain from the tree of wisdom, "forewarning them that, if they touched it, it would lead to their destruction" (Josephus, *Ant.* 1.40). Through the jealousy of the serpent, however, they brought disaster upon themselves by disobeying God's command. When God entered the garden, they withdrew and were afraid to answer God's question to them, conscious

---

[25] Sir 14:17; 15:14; 17:1–24, 30–32; 18:7–14; 24:28; 33:7–13; 40:1, 11; Wis 2:23–24; 7:1–6; 9:1–3; 15:11.

[26] Translation from Patrick W. Skehan and Alexander A. Di Lella, *The Wisdom of Ben Sira* (AB 39; New York: Doubleday, 1987), 276 (slightly revised).

[27] Josephus, *Ant.* 1.14, 20. See Harold W. Attridge, *The Interpretation of Biblical History in the "Antiquitates judaicae" of Flavius Josephus* (HDR 7; Missoula, Mont.: Scholars Press, 1976), 56, 67–68, 92–98.

of having transgressed God's command. In keeping with the conventions of rhetorical history, Josephus provides God with a speech appropriate to the occasion:

> I had decreed for you to live a life of happiness, unmolested by any ill, with no care to fret your souls; all things that contribute to enjoyment and pleasure were, through my providence, to spring up for you spontaneously, without toil or distress of yours; blessed with these gifts, old age would not soon have overtaken you and your life would have been long. But now you have flouted this purpose of mine by disobeying my commands; for it is through no virtue that you keep silence but through an evil conscience. (*Ant.* 1.46 [Thackeray, LCL])

Josephus then goes on to describe the appropriate punishments for Adam, Eve, and the serpent. These are basically the punishments described in Gen 3:14–19. As is clear from God's speech, Josephus does not use the Genesis story to provide an explanation for the origin of death; he assumes that they would have died in any case. Rather, he uses the story as the first of many illustrations of how those who obey God's commands will live long and prosperous lives free of care whereas those who do not will suffer disaster. The extent to which Josephus's interpretation is illustrative rather than explanatory becomes even more apparent in his treatment of Seth and his descendants to the seventh generation (*Ant.* 1.68–69, 72):

> He [Seth], after being brought up and attaining to years of discretion, cultivated virtue, excelled in it himself, and left descendants who imitated his ways. These, being all of virtuous character, inhabited the same country without dissension and in prosperity, meeting with no untoward incident to the day of their death. . . .

> For seven generations they continued to believe in God as Lord of the Universe and in everything to take virtue for their guide; then, in course of time, they abandoned the customs of their fathers for a life of depravity. They no longer rendered to God his due honors, nor took account of justice towards human beings, but displayed by their actions a zeal for vice twofold greater than they had formerly shown for virtue, and thereby drew upon themselves the enmity of God. (Thackeray, LCL)

The prosperity experienced by Seth and the first seven generations of his descendants is also in stark contrast to the disasters that befell Cain and his descendants for their indulgence in various sorts of vice (*Ant.* 1.60–66). For Josephus, the early narratives of Genesis function primarily as illustrations for the larger framework of interpretation enunciated in *Ant.* 1.14, 20: through God's providence, the good prosper and the evil are punished.

The interpretations of the same narratives by Philo, though considerably more complex and philosophical, fall into a similar pattern in the sense that they are interpreted as exemplary narratives. Philo's interpretations of Genesis 1–3 are concentrated in three places in his works: *Opif.* 65–88, 134–170a; *Leg.* 2–3; and *QG* 1.4–57. These interpretations are not all of a piece and were the result of a complex history extending back several generations before Philo.[28]

---

[28] For a detailed analysis of this history, see Thomas H. Tobin, *The Creation of Man: Philo and the History of Interpretation* (CBQMS 14; Washington, D.C.: Catholic Biblical Association of America, 1983).

Perhaps the most helpful way to get at Philo's interpretations of Genesis 3 is to look briefly at *Opif.* 151–170a.[29] In this section, there are two distinct but inter-related interpretations of Genesis 3. Philo was responsible for only the second of them. The first, a generalizing and moralizing interpretation of Genesis 3, is found in *Opif.* 151–152, 156, 167–170a. It is summarized in *Opif.* 156:

> It is said that in olden time the venomous earthborn crawling thing could send forth a human voice and that one day it approached the wife of the first man and upbraided her for her irresoluteness and excessive scrupulosity in delaying and hesitating to pluck a fruit most beautiful to behold and most luscious to taste, and most useful into the bargain, since by its means she would have power to recognize things good and evil. It is said that she, without looking into the suggestion, prompted by a mind devoid of steadfastness and firm foundation, gave her consent and ate of the fruit, and gave some of it to her husband; this instantly brought them out of a state of simplicity and innocence into one of wickedness: whereat the Father in anger appointed for them the punishments that were fitting. For their conduct well merited wrath, inasmuch as they had passed by the tree of life immortal [τὸ ζωῆς ἀθανάτου φυτόν], the consummation of virtue, from which they could have gathered a long and happy life [μακραίωνα καὶ εὐδαίμονα βίον]. Yet they chose that fleeting and mortal [ἐφήμερον καὶ θνητὸν] life which is not a life but a period of time full of misery. (Colson and Whitaker, LCL)

Like Josephus, Philo interprets the story in an exemplary, moralizing way. The story is about choosing vice over virtue. But the emphasis is different, due to the more philosophical interests both of Philo and of the interpretative tradition of Alexandrian Judaism to which he belonged. Although by eating of the fruit the first man and woman lost the possibility for a long and happy life, the emphasis in Philo is on their disastrous choice of a fleeting and mortal life rather of an immortal one. For this reason, Philo emphasizes the importance of Gen 2:17; 3:22 in a way Josephus did not. Earlier in this interpretation (*Opif.* 152), Philo connected the roots of this choice with love (ἔρως), desire (πόθος), and ultimately bodily pleasure (ἡδονή):

> And this desire begat likewise bodily pleasure, that pleasure which is the beginning of wrongs and violation of law, the pleasure for the sake of which they bring on themselves a mortal and unhappy life [τὸν θνητὸν καὶ κακοδαίμονα βίον] in place of that of an immortal and happy one [ἀντ' ἀθανάτου καὶ εὐδαίμονος]. (Colson and Whitaker, LCL)

Philo again correlates happiness and unhappiness with immortality and mortality. Yet it is clear that the interpretation is not meant to explain the origins of death. Rather, it is meant to be exemplary of the choice placed before human beings.

The second kind of interpretation of Genesis 3 in Philo is found in *Opif.* 154–155, 157–166. Philo refers to this kind of interpretation as symbolic (συμβολικῶς [*Opif.* 154]) or allegorical (ἐπ' ἀλληγορίαν [*Opif.* 157]). It is Philo's own interpretation. In it the figures of Adam, Eve, and the serpent are interpreted as aspects of each individual human being. The figures of the Genesis narrative are

---

[29] The other main interpretations of Genesis 3 are found in Philo, *Leg.* 2.71–108; 3.1–253 and *QG* 1.31–57.

internalized.[30] In this allegorical interpretation, the man is a symbol of mind (νοῦς); the woman, of sense perception (αἴσθησις); and the serpent, of pleasure (ἡδονή):

> Pleasure does not venture to bring her wiles and deceptions to bear on the man, but on the woman, and by her means on him. This is a telling and well-made point: for in us mind corresponds to man, the senses to woman; and pleasure encounters and holds parley with the senses first, and through them cheats with her quackeries the sovereign mind itself. . . . Reason is forthwith ensnared and becomes a subject instead of a ruler, a slave instead of a master, an alien instead of a citizen, and a mortal instead of an immortal [θνητὸς ἀντ᾽ ἀθανάτου]. (*Opif.* 165 [Colson and Whitaker, LCL])

In this allegorical type of interpretation, the figures of the narrative are no longer part of the external world. Rather, they have become aspects of each individual human being. There is, however, considerable continuity between this kind of interpretation and the previous one. Both are concerned with bodily pleasure as the origin of vice; both are concerned with the contrasting choices of immortality and mortality; and both take the narrative of Genesis 3 as exemplary of the human condition and of the choices to be made as part of it.

Under the third and final heading, the narratives of Genesis 1–3 are taken as explanatory rather than only as exemplary of the present condition of human beings. These interpretations are the most relevant for understanding Rom 5:12–21. Sometimes these explanatory interpretations are part of a larger framework of an interpretation of biblical history. For example, *Sib. Or.* 1:22–86 is part of a larger interpretation of world history that divides history into ten generations (*Sib. Or.* 1–2).[31] In the interpretation of Genesis 3, the role of Eve is emphasized. She betrayed Adam because it was she who persuaded him to sin (*Sib. Or.* 1:40–45). Because of their deed, they received evil rather than good and were expelled from the "place of immortals" (*Sib. Or.* 1:50–54). Similarly *Jub.* 2:13–4:6 and 4:29–30 are part of a larger interpretation of world history, this time from creation through Moses. The purpose of *Jubilees* is to expound and defend its own particular interpretation of the law, especially of the Jewish calender.[32] For example, in *Jub.* 3:8–14 and 3:26–31, laws concerning purification after childbirth and laws against nudity respectively are connected with interpretations of Genesis 1–3. The story of the disobedience of the first man and woman in Genesis 3 is retold in a straightforward fashion, except that Adam's repentance is emphasized by his sacrifice to God on the day they were expelled from the garden (*Jub.* 3:27).

In other texts the interpretations of Genesis 1–3, and again especially of Genesis 3, are meant to be explanatory in themselves; that is, the actions narrated in the beginning of Genesis are understood as having direct consequences for the present state of human beings. These interpretations are found in four texts,

---

[30] See Tobin, *Creation*, 135–76.

[31] The origins of the *Sibylline Oracles* are disparate. The most plausible location for *Sib. Or.* 1–2 is the first century A.D. in Phrygia. See John J. Collins, "Sibylline Oracles," *OTP* 1:330–34.

[32] *Jubilees* was probably composed in Hebrew in the first half of the second century B.C. in Palestine. Fragments of *Jubilees* have been found in several of the caves at Qumran. See O. S. Wintermute, "Jubilees," *OTP* 2:35–50.

all of which probably originated in Palestine in the first or early second century
A.D.: *Apocalypse of Moses/Life of Adam and Eve; 4 Ezra; 2 Baruch (Syriac Apocalypse);*
and *Liber antiquitatum biblicarum* (Pseudo-Philo). These interpretations, though
containing significant variations, are nevertheless similar in pattern: (1) Adam's
(or, in one case, Eve's) transgression brings about their death (2) and death for
all their descendants; (3) nevertheless, human beings are still responsible for their
own actions.

Perhaps the best place to begin is with three texts from *4 Ezra*, a Palestinian-
Jewish apocalypse written toward the end of the first century A.D. in the wake of the
destruction of the temple in 70:[33]

> And thou didst lay upon him [Adam] one commandment; but he transgressed it, and
> immediately thou didst appoint death for him and for his descendants. From him
> there sprang nations and tribes, peoples and clans, without number. And every nation
> walked after its own will and did ungodly things before thee and scorned thee, and
> thou didst not hinder them. But again, in its time thou didst bring the flood upon the
> earth and the inhabitants of the world and destroy them. And the same fate befell
> them: as death came upon Adam, so the flood upon them. (*4 Ezra* 3:7–10)

> For the first Adam, burdened with an evil heart *[cor malignum]*, transgressed and was
> overcome, as were also all who were descended from him. Thus the disease became
> permanent; the Torah was in the people's heart along with the evil root *[malignitate
> radicis]*, but what was good departed, and the evil remained. So the times passed and
> the years were completed, and you raised up for yourself a servant, named David. And
> thou didst command him to build a city for thy name, and in it to offer thee oblations
> from what is thine. This was done for many years; but the inhabitants of the city trans-
> gressed, everyone doing as Adam and all his descendants had done, for they also had
> the evil heart *[cor malignum]*. So thou didst deliver the city into the hands of thy ene-
> mies. (3:21–27)

> O Adam, what have you done? For though it was you who sinned, the misfortune was
> not yours alone, but ours also who are your descendants. For what good is it to us, if an
> immortal age has been promised to us, but we have done deeds that bring death? Or
> that an everlasting hope has been predicted to us, but we have erred wickedly? Or that
> safe and healthful treasuries have been reserved for us, but we have erred wickedly?
> (7:118–21)

Adam's transgression is connected with an evil heart *(cor malignum)*, and as a result of
his transgression, death becomes the fate of his descendants. At the same time, although Adam's transgression has consequences for later generations, this does not
lessen their responsibility for their own transgressions. Adam's transgression is connected with the reality that he and all his descendants are burdened with an evil heart
(cor malignum) or an evil root *(malignitate radicis, 3:21–22, 26)*. Yet the presence of
this evil heart or root does not do away with human responsibility. The two lie side by
side, though perhaps uneasily so.

---

[33] For the date and place of origin, see Michael Edward Stone, *Fourth Ezra* (Hermeneia;
Minneapolis: Fortress, 1990), 9–11. The translations are from Stone.

The same basic pattern is found in *2 Baruch*, again a Palestinian Jewish apocalypse, probably from the early second century A.D.:[34]

> For with your counsel, you reign over all creation which your right hand has created, and you have established the whole fountain of light with yourself, and you have prepared under your throne the treasures of wisdom. And those who do not love your law are justly perishing. And the torment of judgment will fall upon those who have not subjected themselves to your power. For, although Adam sinned first and has brought death upon all who were not in his own time, yet each of them who has been born from him has prepared for himself the coming torment. And further, each of them has chosen for himself the coming glory. For truly, the one who believes will receive reward. But now, turn yourselves to destruction, you unrighteous ones who are living now, for you will be visited suddenly, since you have once rejected the understanding of the Most High. For his works have not taught you, nor has the artful work of his creation which has existed always persuaded you. Adam is, therefore not the cause, except only for himself, but each of us has become his own Adam. (*2 Bar.* 54:13–19)

In spite of their obvious similarities, there is a significant difference of interpretation between *4 Ezra* and *2 Baruch*. The latter insists on emphasizing the reality of human beings' responsibility for their actions. In addition, this passage from *2 Baruch* omits any mention of an evil heart or root. Both this insistence on human responsibility and the omission of any mention of the evil heart or root seems to be in reaction to what is found in *4 Ezra*.

The third text, *Apocalypse of Moses/Life of Adam and Eve*, is preserved in two distinct recensions, one in Greek *(Apocalypse of Moses)* and the other in Latin *(Life of Adam and Eve)*.[35] Despite the title, neither is an apocalypse. Their provenance is disputed. M. D. Johnson argues that the earliest version was written in Hebrew in Palestine toward the end of the first century A.D.[36] M. Whittaker, however, thinks that the earliest version was in Greek, composed perhaps by a Jew in Alexandria also toward the end of the first century A.D.[37] Although certainty on this matter is impossible, Johnson's arguments seem more plausible.[38]

In any case, the same basic pattern again emerges, with the exception that emphasis is placed on the role of Eve. The consequences of the transgression of Adam

---

[34] For the date and place of *2 Baruch*, see A. Frederik J. Klijn, "2 (Syriac Apocalpyse of) Baruch," *OTP* 1:616–17. The relationship between *4 Ezra* and *2 Baruch* is unclear. Given the material common to both of them, there must be some literary relationship, although its nature is disputed. The most probable explanation may be that both drew extensively on the same traditions. If one did depend literarily on the other, *2 Baruch* probably depended on *4 Ezra*, rather than the other way around. See Bruce M. Metzger, "The Fourth Book of Ezra," *OTP* 1:522; Klijn, "2 (Syriac Apocalpyse of) Baruch," 1:619–20; Stone, *Fourth Ezra*, 39–40, 60.

[35] The text of *Apocalypse of Moses/Life of Adam and Eve* was quite fluid. This has been studied most recently by John R. Levison, *Texts in Transition: The Greek "Life of Adam and Eve"* (SBLEJL 16; Atlanta: Society of Biblical Literature, 2000).

[36] M. D. Johnson, "Life of Adam and Eve," *OTP* 2:251–52.

[37] M. Whittaker, "The Life of Adam and Eve," *AOT* 141–43.

[38] Johnson's position depends on the thorough analysis by J. L. Sharpe, *Prolegomena to the Establishment of the Critical Text of the Greek Apocalypse of Moses* (Ph.D. diss., Duke University, 1969; Ann Arbor, Mich.: University Microfilms, 1969). Whittaker seems unfamiliar with this work.

and Eve were, first of all, seventy plagues (*Apoc. Mos.* 8:2; *L.A.E.* 34:2), which, according to *L.A.E.* 34:3, extend to all subsequent generations. More important, because of the transgression of Adam and Eve, death is a punishment not only for them but also for later generations: "Adam said to Eve, 'Why have you wrought destruction among us and brought upon us great wrath, which is death gaining rule over all our race [παντὸς τοῦ γένους ἡμῶν]?'" (*Apoc. Mos.* 14:2)[39] This punishment, however, does not do away with the responsibility of human beings for their own actions. For example, Adam still exhorts his children: "Now, then, my children, I have shown you the way in which we were deceived. But you watch yourselves so that you do not forsake the good" (*Apoc. Mos.* 30:1).[40] The assumption is that Adam's descendants are still responsible for their actions. Even the presence of the "evil heart" (ἡ καρδία ἡ πονηρά, *Apoc. Mos.* 13:5) in human beings, which will be removed at the resurrection, does not do away with this responsibility.[41]

Finally, the same combination is also found in *Liber antiquitatum biblicarum* (Pseudo-Philo). Pseudo-Philo's work is not an apocalypse but rather a retelling of biblical history from Adam through the death of Saul. It comes from Palestine, was originally composed in Hebrew, and is most likely from the first half of the first century A.D.[42] The passage about the consequences of Adam's transgression comes from a section in which God speaks to Moses in the tent of meeting:

> Then he [God] gave him [Moses] the command regarding the year of the lifetime of Noah, and he said to him, "These are the years that I ordained after the weeks in which I visited the city of men, at which time I showed them the place of creation and the serpent." And he said, "This is the place concerning which I taught the first man, saying, 'If you do not transgress what I have commanded you, all things will be subject to you.' But that man transgressed my ways and was persuaded by his wife; and she was deceived by the serpent. And then death was ordained for the generations of men." And the Lord continued to show him the ways of paradise and said to him, "These are the ways that men have lost by not walking in them, because they have sinned against me." And the Lord commanded him regarding the salvation of the souls of the people and said, "If they will walk in my ways, I will not abandon them but will have mercy on them always and bless their seed; and the earth will quickly yield its fruit, and there will be rains for their advantage, and it will not be barren. But I know for sure that they will make their

---

[39] The parallel in *L.A.E.* 44:4 is, "Our parents who were from the beginning have brought upon us all evils." See also *Apoc. Mos.* 32, where Eve confesses that "all sin in creation has come about through me."

[40] See also *Apoc. Mos.* 19:3; 28:4.

[41] This is the only mention of the evil heart in the *Apocalypse of Moses*. In addition, its mention appears in a section found in only a minority of the Greek manuscripts. See Johnson, "Life of Adam and Eve," 2:275.

[42] There is a debate about the dating of Pseudo-Philo, specifically whether it was composed before or after the destruction of the second temple in A.D. 70. Those proposing a date prior to A.D. 70 include Daniel J. Harrington, "Pseudo-Philo," *OTP* 2:299–300; and Pierre-Maurice Bogaert, in Pseudo-Philo, *Les Antiquités bibliques* (ed. Daniel J. Harrington et al.; 2 vols.; SC 229, 230; Paris: Cerf, 1976), 2:66–74. Those proposing a date after A.D. 70 include L. Cohn, "An Apocryphal Work Ascribed to Philo of Alexandria" (*JQR* 10 [1898]: 277–332); and most recently Howard Jacobson, *A Commentary on Pseudo-Philo's "Liber antiquitatum biblicarum"* (2 vols.; AGJU 31; Leiden: Brill, 1996), 199–210. The earlier dating seems to be more likely. The translation is from Harrington.

ways corrupt and I will abandon them, and they will forget the covenants that I have established with their fathers; but nevertheless I will not forget them forever. For they will know in the last days that on account of their own sins their seed has been abandoned, because I am faithful in my ways." (*L.A.B.* 13.8–10)

The result of Adam's (and Eve's) transgression is death for later generations. At the same time, there is again no lessening of human responsibility. Indeed, because of the lack of any mention of the evil heart or evil root, the question does not even arise.

The particular articulation of this pattern in Pseudo-Philo is important for two reasons. First, it is characteristic of Pseudo-Philo that he cannot be placed within any of the sectarian groups known to us from first-century A.D. Judaism. "Pseudo-Philo seems rather to reflect the milieu of the Palestinian synagogues at the turn of the common era."[43] This lack of peculiarity suggests that his viewpoint, which combines the belief in the baleful consequences of Adam and Eve's transgression for later generations with the conviction that later generations are responsible for their own transgressions, was not restricted to narrowly apocalyptic circles.[44] Although it was hardly the only viewpoint, it represented one that had fairly wide currency in Judaism in the first century A.D.

Second, Pseudo-Philo lacks any mention of an evil heart or an evil root in conjunction with the transgression of Adam and its consequences. This suggests that the connection of these two motifs is secondary and was made after the composition of Pseudo-Philo, that is, toward the very end of the first century A.D. This connection probably occurred in conjunction with the anguished reflections, found in *4 Ezra* and *2 Baruch*, in the wake of the destruction of the temple This view is strengthened by the fact that the phrase "evil heart" or similar phrases occur in Qumran literature but are not connected with the transgression of Adam and its consequences for later generations.[45]

There is, then, within Judaism during this period a variety of ways in which the narrative in Genesis 3 is used. As we shall see, Paul's interpretation of Adam's sin and its consequences in Rom 5:12–14 most closely resembles those found in texts such as *4 Ezra, 2 Baruch, Apocalypse of Moses/Life of Adam and Eve,* and Pseudo-Philo. More specifically, the closest resemblance is to Pseudo-Philo.

In addition to taking into account the variety of views of Adam in Jewish literature of the period, it is also necessary to be aware that Paul had already explicitly used the contrast between Adam and Christ earlier in his letters, 1 Cor 15:21–22; 45–49.[46] Of these two texts, the second (15:45–49) is much more difficult to understand. It almost certainly depends on some sort of speculation on the part of the Corinthian Christians about their connection, perhaps through baptism, with the

---

[43] Harrington, "Pseudo-Philo," 2:300. See also Frederick J. Murphy, *Pseudo-Philo: Rewriting the Bible* (New York: Oxford University Press, 1993), 6–7; and Bogaert in Pseudo-Philo, *Les Antiquités bibliques,* 2:28–39.

[44] This view is supported by the presence of this pattern also in *Apocalypse of Moses/Life of Adam and Eve.*

[45] See, e.g., 1QS 1:6 and CD 2:16.

[46] It is also possible that there is an implicit contrast between Adam and Christ in the hymn in Phil 2:6–11. The Jewish background of this hymn, however, is much disputed. The most likely background is found in Philo, esp. *Conf.* 40–41, 62–63, 146–147.

"heavenly man" created in Gen 1:27 as opposed to the "earthly man" created in Gen 2:7. Similar speculation figures prominently in Philo's treatises.[47] Neither this speculation nor Paul's response to it in 1 Cor 15:42–49 plays any role in Romans.

The situation, however, is quite different with 1 Cor 15:21–22. These verses give us important clues to what Paul is about in contrasting Adam with Christ in Romans 5:12–21. In structure, the passage is made up of four short balanced clauses. The first two clauses *(ab)* are parallel to the second two *(a'b')*, and within each pair the clauses stand in contrast to one another:

> a. Through a man came death,
> b. through a man also comes resurrection of the dead;
> a'. for as in Adam all die,
> b'. so also in Christ all will be made alive.

The view of Adam's significance in this contrast is very much like the view found in *4 Ezra, 2 Baruch, Apocalypse of Moses/Life of Adam and Eve,* and Pseudo-Philo. Through Adam, death entered the world and was passed on to following generations. The viewpoint found in these Jewish texts forms the background out of which the contrast in 1 Cor 15:21–22 was constructed. It is also important to note that although Adam's transgression is obviously presumed in 1 Cor 15:21–22, it is not mentioned. Rather, the emphasis of the contrast between Adam and Christ is between death and resurrection of the dead and between "all die" and "all will be made alive."

The structure of short, balanced parallel clauses is similar to the creedal statement in 1 Cor 15:3–5. Thus there is reason to think that 1 Cor 15:21–22, like 15:3–5, reflects a traditional early Christian creedal statement that Paul employs in dealing with the Corinthian Christians.[48] The context in which these verses occur points in the same direction. The argument Paul makes in 15:20–28 concerns the order (τάγμα) in which the resurrection of the dead takes place: "Each in his own order [τάγματι]: Christ the first fruits [ἀπαρχή], and then at his coming those who belong to Christ" (15:23). This verse specifies and explains what is said in 15:20, that Christ has in fact been raised from the dead and is the "firstfruits" of those who have fallen asleep. First Corinthians 15:23, by taking up the word "firstfruits" mentioned in 15:20, is meant to explain the significance of the firstfruits in terms of an "order" or sequence in the resurrection of the dead. Yet these words do not occur in 15:21–22. What is central in 15:21–22, the contrast between what happened in Adam and what happens in Christ, plays no role in Paul's argument in 15:20, 23–28. Order or sequence is what is central to his argument in 15:20–28, not the contrast

---

[47] E.g., see Philo, *Opif.* 69–88, 129–130, 134–147; Tobin, *Creation,* 102–34; Gregory E. Sterling, "'Wisdom among the Perfect': Creation Traditions in Alexandrian Judaism and Corinthian Christianity," *NovT* 37 (1995): 355–84.

[48] The traditional character of 1 Cor 15:21–22 is affirmed by Hans Conzelmann, *1 Corinthians: A Commentary on the First Epistle to the Corinthians* (Hermeneia; Philadelphia: Fortress, 1975), 268; Hans-Josef Klauck, *1. Korintherbrief* (NEchtB 7; Würzburg: Echter, 1984), 113; and Wolfgang Schrage, *Der erste Brief an die Korinther,* 4:162. Conzelmann's connection of these verses with a primal-man mythology is misplaced. Collins (*First Corinthians,* 548) wrongly interprets 1 Cor 15:21–22 in the light of Rom 5:12–21 and so misses the traditional character of these verses.

between Adam and Christ. Rather, Paul seems to have taken a traditional early Christian creedal statement that contrasted Adam and Christ and used it to substantiate his argument that there is an order to the resurrection. He does this by implication, based on the fact that the verb ζωοποιηθήσονται ("will be made alive") is in the future tense. Christ has been raised, but Christians *will* be made alive. Paul's argument in 15:20–28, however, is persuasive only if he can presume that what is found in 15:21–22 is a statement of belief that both he and the Corinthian Christians already hold in common, that is, a common creedal statement.

What emerges from this admittedly lengthy analysis is the capacity to locate Paul's interpretations, in Rom 5:12–21, of Adam's sin and its consequences for human beings, as well as his comparison between Adam and Christ, within the broader contexts of both contemporary Judaism and earliest Christianity. Both of these contexts enable us to get a more specific sense of what Paul is actually concerned about in these verses. With these contexts in mind, we can now turn to a more detailed analysis first of Rom 5:12–14 and then of Rom 5:15–21.

Romans 5:12–14: Adam's Sin

In 5:12–14, Paul introduces the figure of Adam. His interest in Adam is Adam's sin and its consequence (death) and how both sin and death subsequently came to *all* human beings. In addition, he tries to clarify the status of sin and death for human beings living after Adam but before the introduction of the Mosaic law. There are several difficult grammatical problems in 5:12–14. These problems, however, do not seem to be insurmountable. The most likely way to construe the passage is fairly straightforward:

> Therefore, just as [ὥσπερ] sin entered the world through one human being,
>> and through sin death,
> even so [καὶ οὕτως] did death spread to all human beings,
>> with the result that [ἐφ' ᾧ] all sinned.
> For until the law sin was in the world,
>> though sin is not "accounted" without the existence of the law;
> but death reigned from Adam until Moses,
>>> even over those who did not sin in a way similar
>>>> to the transgression [τῆς παραβάσεως] of Adam,
>>>>> who is a type of the one to come.

The first problem is the meaning of the Greek phrase καὶ οὕτως in 5:12, translated here as "even so." Because 5:12 is part of a passage (5:12–21) dominated by a comparison between Adam and Christ, most interpreters take the word ὥσπερ ("just as") in 5:12 as the beginning of a comparison between Adam and Christ that is not completed by a "so too" (οὕτως καί) clause.[49] The καὶ οὕτως in 5:12 is then translated "and so," with the following clause taken as dependent on, rather than as coordinated

---

[49] See, e.g., Fitzmyer, *Romans*, 413; Byrne, *Romans*, 183; Cranfield, *Romans*, 1:272–73; Dunn, *Romans*, 273; Wilckens, *Römer*, 1:314–15.

with, the preceding ὥσπερ clause. Romans 5:12 is thus treated as an anacoluthon, and 5:13–14 is the digression that occasions the anacoluthon. This rather complicated solution, however, seems unnecessary if one takes the phrase καὶ οὕτως as "even so," an acceptable meaning of the Greek.[50] The following clause, then, is coordinated with the previous ὥσπερ clause, and the anacoluthon disappears. This way of construing the passage also makes more sense because the comparison and contrast between Adam and Christ begins only in 5:15.

The second problem, the meaning of the phrase ἐφ' ᾧ, is more complicated, if for no other reason than that its interpretation has important theological implications for the understanding of original sin. Numerous interpretations of the phrase have been offered.[51] Most recently Joseph A. Fitzmyer has cogently argued that the most likely meaning of the phrase is consecutive, "with the result that, so that"; it is equivalent to the consecutive conjunction ὥστε and an infinitive.[52] Fitzmyer cites a number of classical texts in support of this interpretation.[53]

The third problem is broader in nature. How should one understand Paul's language, in these verses, about sin and death entering the world and about death spreading to all human beings? At first it may seem that Paul is writing about sin and death as two personified malevolent forces that exercise power over human beings; they are real forces that Paul has personified.[54] In this interpretation, Paul is thought to conceive of sin and death as cosmic forces of some sort. But on closer examination, Paul's language is much less theologically loaded. What does he mean by claiming that sin and death entered the world or that death spread to all human beings? From what he goes on to write in 5:15–21, he means that, because of Adam's sin, Adam died and all his descendants were also condemned to die. For the sake of vividness, he is using one form of the rhetorical figure of personification, the personification of concepts.[55] One must avoid turning Paul's metaphorical language,

---

[50] See Herbert Weir Smyth, *Greek Grammar* (rev. ed.; Cambridge: Harvard University Press, 1956), no. 2882b. For a similar view, see J. T. Kirby, "The Syntax of Romans 5:12: A Rhetorical Approach," *NTS* 33 (1987): 283–86; Scroggs, *The Last Adam*, 79; C. K. Barrett, *The Epistle to the Romans* (New York: Harper & Row, 1957), 109–10.

[51] Fitzmyer, *Romans* 413–16, lists eleven possibilities. The first eight take ἐφ' ᾧ as introducing a genuine relative clause: (1) "in whom," i.e., Adam; (2) "because of whom," i.e., Adam; (3) "because of the one by whom," i.e., Adam; (4) "to the extend that"; (5) "on the grounds of which"; (6) "toward which"; (7) "on the basis of what (law)"; (8) "on the basis of which" or "under which circumstances." The other three take the phase as equivalent to a conjunction: (9) "since, because, inasmuch as"; (10) "in view of the fact that, on condition that"; (11) "with the result that, so that."

[52] Joseph A. Fitzmyer, "The Consecutive Meaning of ἐφ' ᾧ in Romans 5.12," *NTS* 39 (1993): 321–39; *Romans*, 416–17. For a different evaluation of the arguments, see Byrne, *Romans*, 183.

[53] E.g., Plutarch, *Cim.* 8.6.4; *Arat.* 44.4.1; *Curios.* 552E.4–6; Athenaeus, *Deipn.* 2.49d; Dio Cassius, *Hist. rom.* 59.19.1–2; 59.20.3; 61.33.8; 63.28.5; 67.4.6; 73.18.1; Diogenes Laertius, 7.173.1–5.

[54] This seems to be the view of Fitzmyer, *Romans*, 411–12.

[55] See Lausberg, *Literary Rhetoric*, §829, for this type of *fictio personae*. Lausberg points out that this type of personification is often used with the personification of concepts that are set in a "family relationship" of some sort. This is the case in Rom 5:12–14, where sin brings about death. In the NT a similar use of the figure is found in Jas 1:15. For classical examples, see Quintilian, *Inst.* 9.3.89; Rutilius Lupus, *Fig. sent.* 2.6; Aeschylus, *Sept.* 224; Sophocles, *Phil.* 1360; Xenophon, *Oec.* 5.17.

used for the sake of vividness, about sin and death into some broader theological claim about sin and death as cosmic forces of some sort.[56] This also needs to be kept in mind in the interpretation of the rest of Romans 5–7.

Although this may solve several important issues, other crucial issues of interpretation still remain. In dealing with them, it is important to see them in light of the arguments Paul is making in Romans. This may seem obvious, but given the role played by these verses in later theological controversies, this focus on their place in Paul's arguments is easily overlooked.

Two observations are apropos. The first is that 5:12–21 begins with "therefore" (διὰ τοῦτο). This means that Paul views what follows as flowing from what he has written in 5:6–11. The major point of 5:6–11 was to show the incompatibility between what God accomplished in Christ and sinfulness. One would therefore expect what Paul writes in 5:12–21 to develop this contrast. Paul thus may be less interested in stating precisely, much less in developing a theory about, the significance and consequences of Adam's transgression for later generations than in contrasting Adam's transgression and its consequences with what God accomplished in Christ and its consequences.

This first observation is supported by a second, which concerns the way Paul uses Jewish interpretations of Adam's transgression. Paul's interpretation in 5:12 clearly falls into the third type of interpretation mentioned above, in which Adam's transgression had consequences for later generations, specifically the punishment of death.[57] At the same time, Paul also clearly affirms continuing human responsibility for sin. In all four works in which this interpretation occurred (*4 Ezra, 2 Baruch, Apocalypse of Moses/Life of Adam and Eve,* and Pseudo-Philo), both death as a consequence of Adam's transgression for later generations and continuing human responsibility for sin lie side by side. In addition, the elements of the interpretation Paul employs in 5:12 seem closest to Pseudo-Philo, the earliest of the four texts and the only text likely to be contemporary with Paul. Neither Paul nor *L.A.B.* 13:8–10 connects Adam's transgression or its consequences with an evil heart or an evil root, which play a role in the other three texts. Both Paul and Pseudo-Philo reflect an interpretation prior to the connection of the evil heart or evil root to Adam's transgression and its consequences, a connection found in the other three texts. Given that Paul describes Adam's transgression and its consequences in only one sentence (Rom 5:12), it is highly unlikely he is trying to offer here a new interpretation of Adam's transgression and its consequences. Rather, he is offering his Roman audience an interpretation they are already aware of, that is, the fairly commonplace Jewish interpretation witnessed to by Pseudo-Philo. In this way, Paul is not concerned to offer any precise interpretation of the relationship between the consequences of Adam's sin and continuing human responsibility; rather, he seems simply to be drawing his audience's attention to this common Jewish viewpoint.

---

[56] See Byrne, *Romans,* 175–76; Cranfield, *Romans,* 1:274; Dunn, *Romans,* 272–73; and Wilckens, *Römer,* 1:315–16, all of whom take basically the same position.

[57] Obviously this does not exclude Paul using language from texts of one of the other types. In 5:12, Paul's image of sin and death "entering the world" is very close to Wis 2:24. But the purpose to which he puts the language is different.

Paul's purpose in using this viewpoint lies elsewhere. What this purpose is emerges when one examines more closely two other interrelated elements in 5:12–14. The first is his use of the word "all" (πάντες) twice in 5:12. The second is the purpose of 5:13–14 as an interpretation of the relationship of the Mosaic law to sin and death.

First, when Paul claims in 5:12 that "death spread to *all* human beings, with the result that *all* sinned," he at first seems to be saying no more than what is found in *4 Ezra* 3:21; *2 Bar.* 48:42; 54:15; *Apoc. Mos.* 14:2; and *L.A.B.* 13:8, that Adam's transgression brought death on all his descendants.[58] He seems also to be saying no more than what was found in the traditional creedal statement of 1 Cor 15:22 mentioned above: "For as all die in Adam, so all will be made alive in Christ." Yet when this passage is viewed in the context of his arguments earlier in Romans, Paul is interpreting the meaning of "all" as something more specific, that is, as both Jews and Gentiles. For Paul, the gospel is the power of God for everyone (παντί) who believes, to the Jew first and also to the Greek (1:16); there will be anguish for everyone (πᾶσαν) who does evil, the Jew first and also the Greek, and glory for everyone (παντί) who does good, the Jew first and also the Greek (Rom 2:9–10); and all (πάντας), both Jews and Greeks, are under the power of sin (Rom 3:9). The use of "all" to mean "both Jews and Gentiles" is also found in Paul's interpretation of the Abraham story in 4:11, 16, the section immediately preceding Romans 5. Finally and most important, Paul used the exact phrase "all sinned" (πάντες ἥμαρτον) (5:12) previously in 3:23: "For all sinned [πάντες γὰρ ἥμαρτον] and fall short of the glory of God." In the context of 3:21–26, he clearly meant "both Jews and Gentiles." Given this pattern, the same is true of 5:12. All have sinned, that is, both Jews and Gentiles, and all die, that is, both Jews and Gentiles.

This leads to the consideration of the second element, the function of 5:13–14. The interpretation of "all" in 5:12 is both strengthened by, and helps explain the purpose of, 5:13–14. The latter text, which is about the place of the law, at first seems like a digression. Why does Paul think it necessary to emphasize at this point that sin and death were still in the world in the period between Adam and Moses, the period before the existence of the law? When one realizes that "all" in 5:12 means "both Jews and Gentiles," the reason for the presence of 5:13–14 becomes clearer. If "all" in 5:12 means Jews and Gentiles, then one might ask about the situation of those who, living between Adam and Moses, did not disobey God's explicit command as Adam had (Gen 2:16–17; 3:1–6, 17) but for whom the Mosaic law did not yet exist. This question would refer particularly to "Gentiles" between Adam and Moses, since the patriarchs in Genesis 12–50 were guided by God either through explicit commands or their equivalent.[59] In this way, the patriarchs were similar to Adam. But what of the others? Without the Mosaic law or analogously

---

[58] *4 Ezra* 3:21: "For the first Adam, burdened with an evil heart, transgressed and was overcome, as were also all who were descended from him"; *2 Bar.* 48:42: "And I answered and said: O Adam, what did you do to all who were born after you?"; *2 Bar.* 54:15: "For, although Adam sinned first and has brought death upon all who were not in his own time"; *Apoc. Mos.* 14:2: "death is gaining rule over all our race"; *L.A.B.* 13:8: "And then death was ordained for the generations of men."

[59] E.g., see also *Jub.* 12–46.

explicit commands by God, these "Gentiles" would have come perilously close to having no morality at all. The underlying assumption of Paul's Roman Christian audience would have been that ethical standards depend on the existence of the Mosaic law. Without the Mosaic law there would be no way to distinguish between virtue and vice, good and evil. This is what some Roman Christians suspected was the consequence of Paul's conviction about righteousness apart from the law.

Paul forestalls this objection by arguing in Rom 5:13–14 that although sin is not "accounted" (ἐλλογεῖται) before the existence of the law, both sin and death were still in the world from Adam to Moses and affected even those (i.e., Gentiles) who had not sinned in a way similar to the transgression of Adam. In offering this explanation, Paul draws on an image common in Jewish literature, that human actions, both good and evil, are recorded in heavenly ledgers that would be opened at the time of God's final judgment.[60] But he revises the image so as to distinguish between sins being committed and sins being both committed and "accounted" in the heavenly ledgers. This distinction was not originally part of the image in Jewish literature. One purpose of the distinction is to corroborate Paul's view in Romans that the purpose of the Mosaic law was the recognition of what is sinful (3:20) and so to increase the trespass (5:20).[61] A second purpose is to insinuate that the ethical character of human actions, either good or evil, does not depend exclusively on the existence of the Mosaic law as such and so the ethical character is possible apart from the law (as Paul argued in 1:18–32 and esp. in 2:12–16). As part of Romans 5–7, this distinction also indirectly buttresses Paul's overall argument that righteousness through faith apart from observance of the Mosaic law does not result in the moral confusion and disarray to which most Roman Christians suspected his ethical views led.

In 5:12–14, two interlocking concerns emerge: (1) Paul's continuing concern about the relationship between Jews and Gentiles and (2) his continuing desire to articulate the relationship of "this grace" (5:2), that is, righteousness through faith apart from the law, to the question of ethical actions. These concerns set the stage for what he writes in the rest of Romans 5. They also explain why the figure of Adam and his comparison with Christ would be so attractive to Paul in his arguments in Romans 5–7. Even more than Abraham, Adam is a figure prior to the Mosaic law and prior to the distinction between Jews and Gentiles. Because he stands at the ultimate origin of both Jews and Gentiles, he serves as an apt foil to Christ, who for Paul unites both Jews and Gentiles.

Finally, Paul's ethical interests are signaled by the way in which he introduces the explicit comparison between Adam and Christ (5:15–21) in the last clause in 5:14: "Adam, who is the type of the one to come" (Ἀδάμ, ὅς ἐστιν τύπος τοῦ μέλλοντος). The word τύπος appears four other times in Paul's letters (Rom 6:17; 1 Cor 10:6; Phil 3:17; 1 Thess 1:7).[62] In all five cases, although the precise meaning of the word varies, the context in which Paul uses it is always an ethical one. The use

---

[60] Ps 106:31; Dan 7:10; 1 Macc 2:52; *2 Bar.* 24:1; *T. Benj.* 11:4; *Jub.* 30:17; *1 En.* 104:7.

[61] Paul will expand on this understanding of the role of the Mosaic law in Romans 7.

[62] It is important to distinguish Paul's use of τύπος and τυπικῶς as "example" from the "typology" of later Christian interpretation of the OT. Paul's use is in continuity with other Greek literature of the period. See LSJ 1835. BDAG 1020 distinguishes too sharply the use in Rom 5:14 from the more usual uses of the word in Greek.

of the word closest to that in Rom 5:14 is 1 Cor 10:6: "Now these things occurred as examples [τύποι] for us, so that we might not desire evil as they did." "These things" to which Paul refers were events of the exodus and the wilderness. More specifically, he is referring to the Israelites' idolatry and subsequent punishment narrated in Numbers 21, 25, in which twenty-three thousand fell in a single day. "These things happened to them to serve as an example [τυπικῶς], and they were written down to instruct us, on whom the ends of the ages have come" (1 Cor 10:11). These events, then, serve as negative ethical examples for believers of Paul's own day. The strongly ethical character of the way in which Paul uses the word also gives us another clue to his strongly ethical concern in his extended comparison of Adam and Christ in the following verses.

Romans 5:15–21: Comparison and Contrast with Christ
    In Rom 5:15–21 Paul moves to an explicit comparison between Adam and Christ. Again he makes use of the topic of comparison familiar from Greco-Roman rhetoric. Whereas in 5:9–10 he used the comparison from the greater to the lesser, in 5:15–21 he makes use of the other two kinds of comparison, that from the lesser to the greater (*a minore ad maius,* 5:15–17) and that between equals (*paria ex paribus,* 5:18–21).
    As mentioned above, Paul already used the comparison between Adam and Christ in 1 Cor 15:21–22. He clearly has this comparison in mind when he writes Rom 5:15–21. In both passages the fate of all is affected by the actions of individual human beings (Adam and Christ); because of Adam all die, and because of Christ all will be made alive (ζωοποιηθήσονται [1 Cor 15:21]) or will reign in life (ἐν ζωῇ βασιλεύσουσιν [Rom 5:17]), or grace will reign for eternal life (ἡ χάρις βασιλεύσῃ . . . εἰς ζωὴν αἰώνιον [Rom 5:21]). In addition, the verbs used in both texts are either in the future tense (1 Cor 15:21; Rom 5:17) or future oriented (Rom 5:21).
    First Corinthians 15:21–22 was a traditional Christian creedal statement that Paul used in his argument with the Corinthian Christians about the reality of the bodily resurrection. When he uses the comparison between Adam and Christ in Rom 5:15–21, he is beginning with a creedal statement he and the Roman Christians have in common. But he also expands on it by emphasizing its ethical implications, an interpretation in keeping with what he has already done in Rom 5:1–14. In 1 Cor 15:21–22, the contrast between Adam and Christ concerned death and resurrection, dying in Adam and ultimately being made alive in Christ. Since the contrast was rooted in the viewpoints about the consequences of Adam's trespass found in the Jewish texts mentioned above, the reality of Adam's sin was certainly implicit in 1 Cor 15:21–22. It was, nevertheless, not explicitly part of the contrast. Paul, however, makes Adam's trespass explicit and central to the contrast between Adam and Christ in Rom 5:15–21. This expansion of the place of sin in the contrast becomes clear when one looks at the vocabulary of these verses. Death and dying remain important; "death" (θάνατος) appears five times (5:12 [bis], 14, 17, 21), and "die" (ἀποθνήσκω) once (5:15). But there is also a shift in the contrast; "sin" (ἡ ἁμαρτία) appears five times (5:12 [bis], 13, 20, 21), "to sin"(ἁμαρτάνω) three times (5:12, 14, 16), and "sinner" once (5:19). Other words of the same sort also appear in these verses: "trespass" (παράπτωμα, 5:12 [bis], 16, 17, 18, 20), "disobedience" (παρακοή,

5:19), and "condemnation" (κατάκριμα, 5:16, 18). The character of the contrast between Adam and Christ has shifted to emphasize the issue of sin.

A parallel shift takes place on the other side of the contrast. In 1 Cor 15:21–22, the emphasis was on resurrection (15:21) and future life (15:22). Although future life is still important in Rom 5:15–21, other elements become the real point of this side of the contrast. Once again this becomes clear when one looks at the vocabulary of 5:15–21. These verses are filled with words connected with grace and righteousness, the central concepts of Paul's own viewpoint: "grace" (χάρις) in 5:12 (bis), 17, 20, 21; "gift" (χάρισμα) in 5:15, 16; "free gift" in 5:15, 17 (δωρεά) and in 5:16 (δώρημα); "righteousness" in 5:17, 21 (δικαιοσύνη), in 5:16, 18 (δικαίωμα), and in 5:18 (δικαίωσις); and "righteous" (δίκαιος) in 5:19.

When one steps back from the words themselves, it becomes clear that Paul has taken the traditional creedal statement of 1 Cor 15:21–22, which he shares with his Roman Christian audience, and has drawn out implications that are very much in keeping with what he has already done in Rom 5:1–14. What emerges is, once again, the incompatibility of sin with what God has accomplished in Christ. But by developing this contrast through the use of the vocabulary of grace and righteousness or their synonyms, he makes two points crucial for the defense of his position before the Roman Christians. First, his own central convictions about grace and righteousness are really implications drawn from what he and the Roman Christians share in common. Second, these implications, no less than the common creedal statement they are based on, are incompatible with sin. Once again, as in 5:1–14, these arguments are meant to allay whatever suspicions the Roman Christians have about Paul's viewpoints about righteousness apart from the law leading to ethical disarray.

Romans 5:15–17 is an argument from the lesser to the greater *(a minore ad maius)*, a series of contrasts between the effects of Adam's trespass and the effects of God's free gift through Christ. These contrasts bring out the disproportion between the effects of the trespass and the effects of the free gift. On the one hand, because of the one man's trespass, the many have died, have been condemned, and death has come to reign over them. On the other hand, how much more so has the free gift led to righteousness and the expectation of eternal life for the many. The effectiveness of this argument *a minore ad maius* depends partly on Paul's previous argument in 5:6–11 about the lavishness of Christ's dying not on behalf of the just or the good but on behalf of those who were still sinners and enemies of God. Given this lavishness, the effects of God's free gift must greatly exceed the effects of Adam's trespass.

The argument's effectiveness also depends on the effect of the rhetoric. This effect is accomplished in three ways. First, there is the commonplace contrast between the one and the many, how what happens to the many through one man, Adam, is more than overcome for the many through one man, Christ. Second, the phrase "the grace and the gift" (ἡ χάρις καὶ ἡ δωρεά), which occurs twice (5:15, 17), appears elsewhere in Greek and Hellenistic Jewish literature and was probably a commonplace phrase, which now Paul takes up.[63] Third, these verses are filled with words ending in -μα: παράπτωμα, κρίμα, κατάκριμα, on one side of the contrast,

---

[63] Demosthenes, *Mid.* 172; Polybius, *Hist.* 1.31.6; Diodorus Siculus, *Bibl. hist.* 3.73.6; Philo, *Her.* 26; Josephus, *Ant.* 5.54.

and χάρισμα (bis), δώρημα, and δικαίωμα, on the other side. Paul is using these words less for their precise meaning than for the rhetorical effect they have in emphasizing the contrast and especially the disproportion between the effects of the sin and the effects of the free gift.

Given this emphasis, it is crucial to understand the intended effect of the contrast and disproportion. On the one side, there is a whole series of words connected with trespass, sin, judgment, condemnation, and death. On the other side, however, there is a whole series of words connected with grace and righteousness, two words central to Paul's basic and controversial convictions: χάρις (5:12 [bis]), χάρισμα (5:15–16), δικαιοσύνη (5:17), δικαίωμα (5:16). These words are interlaced with other, less controversial yet basically synonymous, words meaning "free gift" (ἡ δωρεά [5:15, 17] and τὸ δώρημα [5:16]). The effect of the contrast and disproportion between the two sides emphasizes the incompatibility between such things as trespass and sin and Paul's controversial convictions about grace and righteousness. In addition, by also using less controversial yet synonymous words, he offers his Roman audience a less terminologically charged way of understanding his view.[64] That Paul has these effects in mind becomes clear when, in the final, climactic contrast in these verses, he writes of "the grace and free gift of righteousness" (τῆς χάριτος καὶ τῆς δωρεᾶς τῆς δικαιοσύνης), thus both bringing together two of his most controversial terms and offering a less controversial yet synonymous formulation of his point.

Romans 5:18–21 is the second part of the comparison between Adam and Christ. Unlike 5:15–17, these verses are a comparison not from the lesser to the greater but between equals *(paria ex paribus)*, the third type of the topic of comparison. This is indicated by the "just as . . . so too" (ὡς/ὥσπερ . . . οὕτως καί) structure of 5:18, 19, 21. Paul intends these verses as an inference drawn from what was said in 5:15–17. This is indicated by his use of the inferential phrase "therefore" (ἄρα οὖν) at the beginning of 5:18.[65] The inferential sense of these verses is also strengthened by Paul's use of words taken up from 5:15–17 (παράπτωμα, κατάκριμα, δικαίωμα, δικαίωσις). Given that the structure of the comparison is meant to emphasize similarity or equality, the emphasis in these verses inevitably falls on the phrases "all human beings" and "the many," since these are the terms that are the same in each comparison:

Therefore, just as through one trespass condemnation came

> to all human beings [εἰς πάντας ἀνθρώπους],

so too through one righteous act righteousness and life came

> to all human beings [εἰς πάντας ἀνθρώπους].

---

[64] Neither ἡ δωρεά nor τὸ δώρημα are important words for Paul. Apart from these verses, τὸ δώρημα is not used at all by Paul, and ἡ δωρεά is used only in 2 Cor 9:5. This also indicates that, in Romans 5, Paul uses these two words to offer his audience a less controversial, alternative way of understanding what he is driving at.

[65] Paul also uses this inferential phrase in 1 Thess 5:6; Gal 6:10; Rom 7:3, 25; 8:12; 9:16, 18; 14:12, 19.

> For just as through the disobedience of one human being
>
> > the many [οἱ πολλοί] were made sinners [ἁμαρτωλοί],
>
> so too through the obedience of one human being
>
> > the many [οἱ πολλοί] will be made righteous [δίκαιοι].
>
> But the law slipped in so that the trespass might increase,
>
> but where sin increased, grace has abounded all the more,
>
> > so that, just as sin reigned in death,
> >
> > > so too grace [ἡ χάρις] might reign through righteousness [διὰ δικαιοσύνης]
> >
> > for eternal life through Jesus Christ our Lord. (5:18–21)

The comparison concerns the similarity of the extent of those affected respectively by Adam's trespass and Christ's act of righteousness. In both cases, the acts affect "all human beings" or "the many." Given the character of the comparison, the emphasis falls on these two phrases. In the comparison from the lesser to the greater in 5:15–17, Paul used the phrase "the many" rather than "all human beings" in contrast to "the one." But at the beginning of 5:18, he reverts to the phrase "all human beings," which he previously used in 5:12 to indicate the extent of the spread of death and sin. Given the overall argument of Romans up to that point (5:12) and the immediate context of 5:12–14, the phrase refers to "Jews and Gentiles." By taking up this phrase again in 5:18, Paul reminds his audience of this meaning. Since the phrase is used in parallel with "the many" in 5:19, Paul also indicates to his audience that he means the two phrases to be synonymous; that is, both refer to "Jews and Gentiles."[66]

This interpretation is strengthened by 5:20. Paul again takes up the question of the place of the Mosaic law, just as he had in 5:13. Paul's comment in 5:20, that the law slipped in that trespass might increase, is occasioned by the immediately preceding clause, "so through the obedience of one human being the many will be made upright [δίκαιοι]." The implication of the comment is that since the many will be made upright through the obedience of Christ, they are not made upright through observance of the Mosaic law. Rather, the place of the law was to increase the trespass, a role similar to that mentioned in 3:20. The conclusion implied in this comment is that if the many will not be made righteous through the law, then the distinction between Jews and Gentiles is no longer relevant. Rather, righteousness comes to "all human beings," to "the many," that is, Jews and Gentiles alike, through the obedience of Christ apart from the law.

The conclusion to the whole argument of Romans 5 comes in 5:21, where Paul once again sets sin, which reigns in death, over against the grace that reigns

---

[66] Given that Paul uses the words οἱ πολλοί and πάντες synonymously in this passage basically to mean "both Jews and Gentiles," it is pointless to press the interpretation of the two words further. Although questions about the absolute universality of human sinfulness and the possibility of righteousness and salvation in Christ are both valid and important theological questions, they go beyond what Paul is concerned with in this passage. His concern here, as earlier in Romans, is with "both Jews and Gentiles" as groups.

through righteousness for the eternal life that comes through Christ. In this conclusion Paul draws from the various terms he has used in this chapter those central to the argument he is making, sin and death in contrast to grace through righteousness and eternal life. Once again, as he did at the conclusion of the earlier comparison in 5:15–17, he uses both the words "grace" (χάρις) and "righteousness" (δικαιοσύνης), two of his concepts most controversial for the Roman Christians, and contrasts them with sin and death. The grammar of this verse highlights more precisely the emphasis Paul intends. The subjects of the two clauses are "sin," on the one hand, and "grace," on the other. By placing them in contrast to one another, he once more emphasizes their incompatibility. The addition of the phrase "through righteousness" also points to the incompatibility of righteousness with sin and death. Given Paul's view of righteousness in the letter up until now, it can only be a righteousness apart from the law; and this righteousness is to be contrasted with sin, which reigns in death.

CONCLUSIONS

Paul's use of the word "grace" in 5:21 takes us back to "this grace in which we stand" in 5:2. But what has happened between 5:2 and 5:21 is Paul's claim and supporting arguments that "this grace" is incompatible with sin. When one steps back from the details of the arguments, one notices the extent to which his arguments are rooted in traditional Christian beliefs, that is, in language and viewpoints Paul has in common with his Roman Christian audience. These include imagery and language about the significance of Christ's death and resurrection in 5:6–11, the significance of Adam's trespass in 5:12–14, and the basic comparison itself between Adam and Christ in 5:15–21.

By using this material, Paul highlights the common ground he shares with his Roman Christian audience. He uses this common ground not for its own sake but as the basis for showing them first of all how "this grace in which we stand" (5:2) is incompatible with sin (5:21). Given the place in Romans where this phrase occurs and its immediate context in 5:1–11, including its references back to 3:21–26 and 3:27–4:25, "this grace" is shorthand for righteousness through faith apart from observance of the law. Paul's argument is that "this grace" and everything of which it is emblematic flow from traditional Christian beliefs he and his Roman Christian audience share, and this grace is incompatible with sin.

Second, especially by using the traditional Christian comparison between Adam and Christ, Paul also shows that this incompatibility between grace and sin encompasses both Jews and Gentiles, that is, "all human beings" (5:12, 18). This grace, which again is apart from observance of the law, is incompatible with sin for Jews and Gentiles alike. This is highlighted by his comments in 5:13, 20 about the role of the Mosaic law. The Mosaic law enables sin to be "accounted," but it does not create the sole basis for morality (5:13). Rather, because of the law, the trespass increases (5:20). The full implications of these comments, as well as of similar comments in 3:20; 4:15, will become apparent especially in Romans 7.

In all of this, there is a certain obliqueness or indirection. In making these arguments, does Paul think that the Roman Christians do not believe that what happens because of Christ is incompatible with sin? Obviously not. Rather, the arguments in Romans 5 serve as the basis for the refutations in Romans 6–7. As we shall see in detail below, in the analysis of Romans 6–7, the arguments of Romans 5, by establishing how Paul's convictions about grace and all it stands for are incompatible with continuing in sin for both Jews and Gentiles, serve as the basis for his refutation of charges made against him that "this grace" of his leads to moral anarchy.

A note of caution is apropos. If Paul's purpose is as described here, one needs to beware of drawing conclusions from Romans 5 that are based on concerns peripheral for Paul. Two of these are the intertwined concepts of original sin and the universality of human sinfulness. Although Paul assumed, as did at least some other Jews and early Christians, that the origins of sin and death go back to Adam, he also assumed, as they did, that human beings were responsible for their own actions. He took both for granted. His purpose, however, in Romans 5 was not to explain how these two viewpoints are related or reconcilable. The same is true of the question of the universality of human sinfulness. In Romans 2, Paul placed responsibility for sin on the shoulders of Jews and Gentiles alike and allowed for the possibility even of some Gentiles not sinning (2:14–16). Human sinfulness is general; that is, it encompasses both Jews and Gentiles. In Romans 5, human sinfulness, given how Paul connects the origins of sin with Adam, appears at first glance to not simply be general but universal, that is, without any exception whatsoever. Can these two viewpoints be reconciled? This is certainly an important question for Christian theology, but it was not Paul's question or concern in Romans. Paul's concern for the fate of "all human beings" remained a concern for the fate of both "Jews and Gentiles," "all" in the sense that both groups are equally included. To ask Paul for a resolution of these tensions between the general and the universal, however important such a resolution is theologically, is to ask for more than Paul intended to give and for something he was not concerned about in Romans.

CHAPTER 7

Baptism and Ethics

AUL'S PURPOSE IN WRITING ROMANS 5 was to convince his Roman Christian audience that "this grace in which we stand" was incompatible with sin. He did this by developing traditional themes whose viewpoints he and his Roman Christian audience had in common. The issue was not that the Roman Christians thought that "this grace" was somehow compatible with sin; rather, it was that they suspected that Paul did. "This grace" that Paul emphasized in 5:2 was the grace he had been explaining and defending in Romans 1–4. "This grace" was emblematic of his deepest convictions about the nature of the gospel. Righteousness is now through faith in Christ Jesus, but apart from observance of the Mosaic law and intended equally for both Jews and Gentiles. Paul wanted to show his Roman Christian audience that this grace was also incompatible with sin and that this incompatibility was based on their shared beliefs about Christ. In the course of Romans 5, Paul also commented on the functions of the Mosaic law, that without the law sin was not "accounted" (5:13) and that the law's coming "increased" the trespass (5:20). Given the nature of the gospel as he understood it, Paul tried to explain all this within the widest possible context by using an already traditional contrast between Adam and Christ. He did this because this contrast encompassed both Jews and Gentiles. But he also developed the contrast specifically by emphasizing its ethical implications, by the contrast between the effects of Adam's sin and the effects of what God accomplished in Christ's death and resurrection, between those affected by Adam's sin and those affected by Christ's death and resurrection. The latter contrast was also meant to include both Jews and Gentiles alike.

On the basis of what he hopes are now shared convictions, Paul turns in Romans 6–7 to deal more specifically and directly with the Roman Christians' suspicions of, and objections to, his convictions about the nature of his gospel, that is, about "this grace in which we stand." This is apparent from the very opening question in 6:1: "What, then, shall we say? Should we continue in sin so that *grace* may abound?" In Romans 6–7, he deals especially with the relationship of this grace to both sin (Romans 6) and the Mosaic law (Romans 7). In doing this, he continues to use the contrasts between sin and death, on the one hand, and grace and life, on the other, that were so central to Romans 5.[1] The continued use of these contrasts emphasizes the continuity of Paul's arguments in Romans 5–7. In reading Romans 6–7, it is also crucial to keep in mind that Paul makes no distinction between Jewish and Gentile believers. He clearly intends that his arguments about the ethical dispositions believers should have must apply equally to both groups in the community.

Before examining Romans 6–7 in detail, however, we need to recall what the issues were and how they were related in the minds of his Roman Christian audience. This is crucial lest we think that Paul's arguments about sin in Romans 6 and about the law in Romans 7 are completely parallel, that is, that just as Romans 6 is about freedom from sin, so too Romans 7 is about freedom from the law. As we shall see, this would be to misconstrue what Paul is actually arguing.

One of the basic suspicions most Roman Christians must have had about Paul was connected with his conviction that righteousness through faith was apart from the observance of the Mosaic law for both Jews and Gentiles. Although the majority of the Roman Christian community were ethnically Gentile, they nevertheless understood their beliefs in Christ as of a piece with continued observance of the ethical commandments of the law. For them, Paul's insistence that righteousness is now by faith as a gift apart from the observance of the law raised two distinct but interrelated questions. First, without continued observance of the ethical commandments of the law, on what ethical basis do believers live their lives in obedience to God? The Roman Christians were aware that in Gal 5:1–6:10 Paul emphasized the guidance of the Spirit and that "walking by the Spirit" (Gal 5:16) and being "guided by the Spirit" (5:18) led to becoming slaves of one another (5:13), the practice of various virtues (5:22–23), and the avoidance of an array of vices (5:19–21). Living and walking by the Spirit also led believers to "crucify the flesh with its passions and desires" (5:24–25). Paul was not an antinomian in any ordinary sense. Yet he also insisted that this meant "freedom" from the law and that believers should not submit again to the "yoke of slavery," by which he clearly meant the Mosaic law (5:1). Although he warned the Galatian believers against using their freedom as an opportunity for the flesh (5:13), he still insisted on their freedom from the yoke of the law.

For most Roman Christians, with their continued observance of the ethical commandments of the law, this combination of freedom from the law and guidance by the Spirit as the basis for living out one's life as a believer must have seemed vague and naive at best. This skepticism and these suspicions were not simply theoretical. Rather, on the basis of what they knew from Priscilla and Aquila, they saw what seemed to them to be the ethical disarray of the Corinthian believers as the consequence of Paul's insistence on freedom from the law and guidance by the Spirit.[2] In addition, as we shall see shortly, the situation in Corinth was also partially

---

[1] "Sin" (ἁμαρτία): Rom 6:1, 2, 6 (bis), 7, 10, 11, 12, 13, 14, 16, 17, 20, 22, 23; 7:5, 7 (bis), 8, 9, 11, 13 (ter), 14, 17, 20, 23, 25; "to sin" (ἁμαρτάνω): 6:15; "sinner, sinful" (ἁμαρτωλός): 7:13; "death" (θάνατος): 6:3, 4, 5, 9, 16, 21, 23; 7:5, 10, 13 (bis), 24; "life" (ζωή): 6:4, 22, 23; 7:10; "grace" (χάρις): 6:1, 14, 15, 17; 7:25.

[2] Such issues included factionalism (1 Cor 1:18–4:21), incest (5:1–13), possible involvement with prostitutes (6:12–20), inappropriate sexual asceticism (7:1–40), indifference about the effects on the community of eating foods once offered to idols (8:1–11:1), and various sorts of disorder and disunity in the community's worship (11:2–14:40). It is not clear whether the

due to the Corinthian Christians' understanding—or misunderstanding—of baptism and its consequences. Whatever Paul's intentions were, the practical results in Corinth, as far as the Roman Christians were concerned, were disastrous.

Paul's insistence on freedom from the law also raised a second, distinct but clearly related issue. Why was Paul so insistent about believers being free from observance of the law? What does this say about the character of the law itself? Was there something wrong with it that it should no longer be observed, that it should no longer contain the criteria for living in obedience to God? This second issue was no doubt compounded by what Paul had previously written about the law, especially in Galatians. As we have seen, in Galatians Paul described the law as a "yoke of slavery," submission to which was equivalent to submitting again to the "weak and beggarly elemental principles" of the universe (Gal 4:9). The law was something from which, in the fullness of time, Christ had delivered believers (4:5). Certainly Paul could also write about how the law had a role ordained by God (3:19–25), that in God's plan the law's function was to imprison and guard people until faith came (3:23). But taken together, it would be difficult to think that Paul's views of the law left much room for describing the law as "good." In any case, Paul had never described it this way. Not to see the law explicitly as something good, especially because it had been given by God, must have also been very troubling to most Roman Christians.

These two issues and Paul's attempts to deal with them in the light of the skepticism and suspicion of the Roman Christian community are the subject of Romans 6–7. As he did in the parallel passages in Rom 2:1–3:20 and 3:27–4:25, Paul once again uses rhetoric familiar from the diatribe. He structures Romans 6–7 again around a series of rhetorical questions (6:1, 14; 7:1, 7, 13). In these chapters, he will also use other techniques associated with the diatribe. In Romans 6, he is primarily concerned with the issue of the relationship between grace and sin; in Romans 7, with the issue of the goodness of the law.

There is, however, a significant difference between Paul's arguments in 2:1–3:20 and 3:27–4:25 and his arguments now in Romans 6–7. Unlike the two earlier passages, Paul's arguments in Romans 6–7 are not primarily scriptural. With the exception of 7:7, where he quotes the tenth commandment (Exod 20:17; Deut 5:18), he does not quote the Jewish scriptures. This is all the more surprising since Rom 8:31–11:36, the fourth and final rhetorically parallel passage, is once again filled with scriptural quotations. But when one considers the issues Paul deals with in Romans 6–7, it becomes much less surprising. All the issues addressed in these other passages are directly related to the Jewish scriptures and their interpretation. Both 3:27–4:25 and, as we shall see later, 8:31–11:36 concern whether Paul's views uphold the Scriptures (3:27) or whether his views impugn the trustworthiness of the Scriptures (9:6). The issues in Romans 6–7 are somewhat different. In Romans 6, the issue is whether Paul's views about how believers are to lead their lives "apart from the law" result in ethical disarray. Because this way of living is "apart from the law," arguments based on quotations from the ethical commandments of the Jewish scrip-

---

issue of involvement with prostitutes was a real one or a rhetorical topos that Paul employed. See Collins, *First Corinthians*, 240; Schrage, *Der erste Brief an die Korinther*, 2:8–38.

tures would be counterproductive. His arguments must be placed on a different basis. In Romans 7, the issue is Paul's view about the "goodness" of the law. It is his defense of the goodness of the law. At first one might think Paul would call on a myriad of quotations to support the law's goodness. But the issue at stake for Paul in Romans 7 is both more personal and more complex. First, it is more personal because the issue is not so much the goodness of the law itself as how Paul himself evaluates the law. Second, the issue is more complex, in that establishing the goodness of the law simply by quoting the Jewish scriptures would harm rather than help Paul's case, since such quotations would also argue for the law's continued observance. Rather, what Paul wants to do is affirm the goodness of the law while at the same time offering an explanation for why observance of the law is now no longer the basis for believers living their lives in obedience to God. In this way, Paul's arguments for both these positions would be ill served by quotations from the Jewish scriptures.

The rhetorical structure of Romans 6–7 is determined by a series of five questions. They are meant to take up the objections Roman Christians have to his convictions about how believers are to live their lives in obedience to God:

> What shall we say then? Should we persist in sin so that grace may abound? Certainly not! (6:1)

> What then? Should we continue in sin since we are not under the law but under grace? Certainly not! (6:15)

> Or are you ignorant, brothers,—I speak to people who know the law—that the law has authority over a person as long as he lives? (7:1)

> What shall we say then? That the law is sin? Certainly not! (7:7)

> Did what is good [i.e., the law], then, prove to be death for me? Certainly not! (7:13)

The first two questions concern the relationship of grace to sin, but the second also introduces the question of the law. The other three questions are concerned directly with the place of the law. The last two questions deal specifically with the relationship of the law to sin and to death. Although these five questions are not completely parallel to one another, they nevertheless provide the rhetorical framework for Paul's arguments.[3] Once again it is important to keep in mind the rhetorical perspective of these questions, which give Romans 6–7 its polemical character. The polemic is carried on once again by way of indirection. It is not that the Roman Christians hold the views Paul is arguing against. Rather, in one way or another, they suspect him of holding these views. Paul is trying to show that he too rejects such views.

The unity of the argument of Romans 6 is indicated in three ways. First, the question at the beginning of each section explicitly concerns the relationship of grace to the issue of continuing in sin (6:1, 15). Second, the second question (6:15) explicitly takes up the conclusion of the first section, that "you are not under the law

---

[3] The rhetorical question in 7:13 is not entirely parallel to the other four questions because it is spoken by the fictive speaker of 7:7b–25. The other four questions are in Paul's own voice.

but under grace," and turns it into the subject of the following section (6:15–23). Finally, both 6:1–14 and 6:15–23 end with references to sin and to grace (χάριν, 6:14) or the closely related term "gracious gift" (χάρισμα, 6:23).

ROMANS 6:1–14: THE REINTERPRETATION OF BAPTISM

Paul's argument in 6:1–14 moves through four steps. He begins in 6:1–2 with the question whether believers should persist in sin that "grace may abound," and answers with an emphatic denial. He also asks another rhetorical question, which in effect states the basic position he develops in the passage, that it is inconceivable that those who have died to sin should still continue to live in it (6:2). In 6:3–4, he appeals to an interpretation of baptism, which he partially shares with his Roman Christian audience, that believers have been baptized into Christ Jesus so that just as Christ was raised from the dead, so too they might walk in newness of life. What is new in these verses is Paul's insistence that in baptism believers have been baptized specifically into Christ's death. In 6:5–11 he then draws out the ethical implications of this new interpretation, arguing that they are also dead to sin and alive to God through being baptized into the death of Christ. Finally, he ends the passage in 6:12–14 with a short exhortation based on these ethical implications, urging his audience not to let sin reign over them. Concerning the development of the passage itself, Paul's argumentation is fairly complicated. The intended force of his arguments, however, can be understood only in the broader context of his interpretation of baptism in his other letters, especially in the context of 1 Corinthians and the ethical issues he was dealing with there.

Romans 6:1–2: Rhetorical Questions about Continuing in Sin

In 6:1–2 Paul begins with the rhetorical question about whether believers should persist in sin so that grace may abound. His answer is an emphatic denial. The question is, in one sense, occasioned by what Paul wrote in 5:1–21 with its emphasis on "this grace in which we stand" (5:2) abounding even more than sin did (5:20–21). Yet throughout Romans 5, Paul has already consistently contrasted sin with grace to show their incompatibility. Thus, by the end of Romans 5, Paul could emphasize that grace reigns "through righteousness" for eternal life (5:21), a righteousness incompatible with sin. For Paul, Romans 5 already provides the basis for just such a rejection.

The primary reason for Paul raising the issue again in 6:1–2 must lie elsewhere. It lies specifically in 3:8, where, in an almost parenthetical aside, Paul denounced those who maliciously claim that he says that believers should do evil so that good may come. As pointed out above in chapter 4, the accusation against Paul may not have been quite that boldfaced.[4] But the issue that provoked the accusation or something similar to it was Paul's insistence that righteousness is by grace apart from observance of the law, and the ethical implications seemingly entailed by this

---

[4] See above, p. 120.

insistence. If grace is not connected with observance of the law, then why not do whatever one wants, however wrong it may otherwise be? In 6:1–2, Paul now returns to deal with the issue. He provides his basic answer to this accusation in 6:2, again in the form of a question the answer to which is obvious: "How can we who have died to sin still live in it?" The implied answer is that it is impossible. The logic of the implied answer is simple enough: One cannot "live" in the very thing (i.e., sin) to which one has "died." Paul then uses this same logic in his arguments in the rest of 6:1–14. In arguing this way, Paul is building on the contrasts he already developed in Romans 5.

Romans 6:3–4: Baptism into the Death of Christ

But what Paul needs to show is how believers have indeed "died" to sin. He does this first in 6:3–4 by appealing to an interpretation of baptism that he partially shares with his Roman Christian audience. He asks if they are "unaware" (ἢ ἀγνοεῖτε) that those who were baptized into Christ Jesus were baptized "into his death." Therefore (οὖν), he concludes, they were "buried with" Christ through their baptism into his death so that just as Christ was raised from the dead, they too might walk in newness of life. Paul uses the phrase ἢ ἀγνοεῖτε ("Or are you unaware") both here and in 7:1. In both cases, he is suggesting that something the Roman Christians already know has a deeper meaning.[5] In 6:3, Paul shares with his Roman Christian audience the interpretation of baptism as a baptism "into Christ Jesus." What he now wants to show is that baptism into Christ Jesus is more specifically a baptism "into his death" (εἰς τὸν θάνατον αὐτοῦ).[6] In this, Paul's interpretation of baptism seems to draw on the traditional creedal formula found in 1 Cor 15:3–5, which Paul also would have had in common with the Roman Christian community:

Christ died [ἀπέθανεν] for our sins according to the scriptures,
and he was buried [ἐτάφη],
and he was raised [ἐγήγερται] on the third day according to the scriptures,
and he appeared to Cephas and then the twelve.

That Paul has this traditional formula in mind is clear from Rom 6:4, where he concludes that believers were therefore (οὖν) "buried with him" (συνετάφημεν αὐτῷ) and then goes on to mention Christ being raised (ἠγέρθη). The presence of all three elements (death, burial, and resurrection), especially that of the much less common element of burial, shows that Paul is drawing on this traditional, shared formula in his interpretation of baptism. Although this interpretation of baptism into Christ Jesus as a baptism "into his death" was itself unfamiliar to the Roman Christians, Paul presents it to them as the consequence of a christological confession they have in common.

---

[5] Byrne, *Romans*, 195.

[6] Other than this passage from Paul, we have no evidence of an interpretation of baptism as a baptism "into Christ's death" either earlier than, or contemporary with, Paul. See Wilckens, *Römer*, 2:50.

There is, however, an aspect of this interpretation that is unexpected. For this very reason, it is helpful in understanding the purpose to which Paul is putting his arguments in 6:1–14. Paul writes that believers are buried with Christ through baptism into his death "in order that, just as Christ was raised from the dead by the glory of the father, so we too might walk [περιπατήσωμεν] in newness of life" (6:4). Given that Paul has just connected believers' baptism with Christ's death and burial, one would expect a similar connection to be made between Christ's resurrection and believers' resurrection. But this is not the case. Rather, the parallel with Christ being raised is that believers should "walk in newness of life." "Walk" is a common biblical idiom for conduct or behavior; Paul himself has often used it this way.[7] The purpose of baptism into Christ's death and burial is, at least partially, that believers may conduct themselves in a new and different way. It is this new way of living that Paul places in parallel with Christ's resurrection. Paul thereby emphasizes the ethical consequences of baptism, how believers are to live in a new and different way.[8] In the rest of 6:1–14, Paul will continue both to emphasize the ethical implications of baptism and to refrain from connecting Christ's resurrection directly with what happens to believers in baptism.

Romans 6:5–11: Dying to Sin and Living to God in Christ Jesus

Paul then draws out the ethical implications of baptism more fully in 6:5–11, in two complex parallel sentences (6:5–7, 8–11), both of which are primarily concerned with believers "dying" to sin.

> a. For if we have been conformed [σύμφυτοι] to the likeness [τῷ ὁμοιώματι] of his death,[9]
>
>   then certainly we shall also be [ἐσόμεθα] [conformed to the likeness] of his resurrection,[10]
>
>   b. knowing [γινώσκοντες] that our old self has been crucified with him,
>
>   in order that the body of sin might be done away with

---

[7] 1 Thess 2:12; 4:1, 12; Gal 5:16; 1 Cor 3:3; 7:17; 2 Cor 4:2; 5:7; 10:2; 12:18; Phil 3:17; Rom 8:4; 13:13; 14:15.

[8] The image of newly baptized believers "walking in newness of life" may have already been connected with an interpretation of baptism. By placing it in parallel with Christ's resurrection, however, Paul gives it added emphasis.

[9] The precise meanings of the words σύμφυτοι and τῷ ὁμοιώματι are difficult to determine. In addition, it is not clear whether τῷ ὁμοιώματι should be taken with σύμφυτοι or as an instrumental dative. The translation given here basically follows the interpretation of Byrne, *Romans*, 196. Romans 6:6 suggests that "likeness" (ὁμοίωμα) in 6:5 should be taken to mean that believers' old selves have been crucified with Christ, so that the body of sin has been done away with and they no longer should be enslaved to sin. Although this is to take place through baptism, the word "likeness" does not refer to baptism directly but to the reality that should be the result of baptism. For a different view and other interpretations, see Fitzmyer, *Romans*, 435.

[10] The parallel structure of Rom 6:5ab clearly calls for "conformed to the likeness (σύφυτοι τῷ ὁμοιώματι)" to be understood in the second part of the verse.

so that we would no longer be enslaved to sin.

    c. For the one who has died has been freed from sin.

a'. If we have died with Christ,

    we believe that we will also live [συζήσομεν] with him,

        b'. knowing [εἰδότες] that Christ once raised from the dead no longer dies;

        death no longer has power over him.

          c'. For the death he died, he died to sin once and for all.

        But the life he lives he lives for God.

Thus you too should consider yourselves dead to sin but alive to God in Christ Jesus.

Paul begins each section with a conditional sentence (*a/a'*; 6:5, 8). This is followed in each section by clauses beginning with participles meaning "know" (γινώσκοντες, εἰδότες) (*b/b'*; 6:6, 9). Finally, each section ends with a statement about how dying with Christ also inherently entails death to sin (*c/c'*; 6:7, 10–11). Granted this parallelism, the two sections are not simply reversible. There is a development from one to the other. Although both these sections draw on an interpretation of baptism he and the Roman Christians hold in common, Paul also introduces certain nuances that help us to understand what he is really trying to persuade the Roman Christians of.

Paul begins 6:5–7 with a conditional sentence that continues the interpretation of baptism found in 6:3–4. If believers have been conformed to the likeness of Christ's death, then certainly they will also eventually be conformed to the likeness of his resurrection. The protasis refers to what has already been taking place (the perfect tense); the apodosis, however, refers to the future (ἐσόμεθα). Once again Paul does not place the effects of baptism directly in parallel with Christ's resurrection. Conformity to the likeness of Christ's resurrection is still in the future. Paul spells out for believers' present way of living the implications of this connection between the present reality of being conformed to the likeness of Christ' death and the ultimate outcome of also becoming conformed to the likeness of his resurrection. Believers know that in baptism their old self (lit. "our old man" [ὁ παλαιὸς ἡμῶν ἄνθρωπος]) has been crucified with Christ and that the purpose of this is that the "body of sin" (τὸ σῶμα τῆς ἁμαρτίας) may be done away with so that they may no longer be enslaved to sin.[11] Once again Paul emphasizes the ethical consequences of baptism, that the "crucifixion" of the old—that is, sinful—self with Christ entails a new way of living. This new way of living is no longer bound in slavery to sin. He then concludes this first section by stating very briefly why this is so: "For [γάρ] the one who has died has been freed from sin" (6:7). Although elliptical, the point of the verse is not a general one, that anyone who has died is freed from sin. Rather, it is

---

[11] The phrases "our old self" (literally "our old man") and the "body of sin" need to be understood in conjunction with one another. The point of the second phrase is not that the body itself is sinful. Rather Paul is referring to the body in so far as it is controlled by sin. Paul is referring to the same reality as the first phrase. See Byrne, *Romans*, 196–97; Fitzmyer, *Romans*, 436.

more specific. One who has "died" in baptism with Christ, that is, one whose old self has been crucified with Christ and who is no longer enslaved to sin, has indeed been freed from sin. This more specific interpretation of the verse is clear from the beginning of the following verse ("If we have died with Christ . . ."), in which this "dying" is explicitly dying "with Christ."

The second section (6:8–11) begins with another conditional sentence, the protasis of which takes up the conclusion of the previous verse. If believers have died with Christ, they also believe they will eventually live with him. Once again the connection between the protasis and the apodosis is based on the interpretation of baptism found in 6:3–4. Once again the apodosis about living with Christ is also in the future tense (συζήσομεν). As he did in the previous section, he then expands on this in 6:9 by using another participial clause. Believers know that Christ, once raised from the dead, no longer dies; death no longer has any power over him. In the parallel passage in the previous section (6:6), the emphasis was on the old self being crucified with Christ. In this section, the emphasis is on the consequences, for believers, of Christ being raised; that is, that death no longer has any power over him. In 6:10–11, he again concludes by emphasizing the ethical implications of this for believers, here through a parallel formulation, first about Christ, then about believers. The death Christ died he died to sin, and the life he lives he now lives to God; so too believers should consider themselves dead to sin but living to God in Christ Jesus. Once again the parallel between Christ having been raised and believers' present situation is put in ethical terms. They should consider themselves dead to sin but alive to God "in Christ Jesus" (ἐν Χριστῷ Ἰησοῦ). Although believers are now to account themselves alive in the realm of Christ Jesus, Paul very carefully does not refer to believers as now actually raised as Christ is. Such resurrection of believers is still outstanding, still in the future.

Romans 6:12–14: Let Not Sin Reign in You but Offer Yourselves to God

On this basis, Paul then concludes this stage of his argument with a short ethical exhortation in 6:12–14. He urges his audience not to let sin reign in their mortal bodies nor to obey the mortal body's desires. They should not offer (παριστάνετε) themselves as weapons or instruments (ὅπλα) of wickedness to sin. Rather, they should offer (παραστήσατε) themselves to God as though (ὡσεί) being alive from the dead and their members as weapons or instruments (ὅπλα) of righteousness to God.[12] Paul's wider use of the noun ὅπλον would suggest the meaning "weapons."[13] Paul's metaphor, then, would be a military one, of soldiers offering their weapons in the service of their commander. But the immediate context of 6:16–19, where the imagery of slavery plays such an important role, suggests the broader meaning "instruments," in which slaves offer themselves in the service of their master. In fact,

---

[12] Although not explicit, the language of "offering" (παρίστημι) Paul uses in 6:12–14 may also have cultic overtones. This is especially the case because it is an offering to God. When Paul again uses the verb in 12:1–2 at the beginning of his exhortation, it explicitly has a cultic meaning.

[13] Rom 13:12; 2 Cor 6:7; 10:1.

Paul may be playing on both meanings of the word.[14] He then concludes this section by claiming that just as death has no power over Christ, so sin will have no power (οὐ κυριεύσει) over them, for they are living not under the law (ὑπὸ νόμον) but under grace (ὑπὸ χάριν).

Once again Paul emphasizes the ethical implications of baptism and that baptism involves a rejection of sin. But once again he puts it in such a way as to avoid a direct parallel between Christ's resurrection and believers' present situation. In presenting themselves to God, believers do so "as though alive from the dead" (ὡσεὶ ἐκ νεκρῶν ζῶντας). The compound Greek particle ὡσεί can mean nothing more than the simpler ὡς ("as"), but often it has the stronger meaning of "as if" or "as though."[15] Paul's use of it in 6:13 reflects the stronger meaning. This becomes clear when one compares the phrase "as though living from the dead" in 6:13 with the parallel formulation in 6:11 ("living for God in Christ Jesus"), where the particle ὡσεί is lacking. Paul can use the phrase in 6:11 without qualification because, by standing in parallel to the preceding phrase "dead to sin," its emphasis is clearly ethical. But he is unwilling to do so with the phrase "living from the dead" in 6:3. In the present, believers can act only "as though" alive from the dead. Paul's point is not that, in the present, believers' acting "as if" alive from the dead is a pretense. Rather, their present living from the dead can be so only in a qualified sense; their actual resurrection is still something outstanding. This same reticence even affects the way Paul writes about the relationship between believers and sin in 6:14. He puts it in the future tense: "Sin will have no power [οὐ κυριεύσει] over you." Although Paul's whole thrust in 6:1–14 is to show how, as a consequence of baptism, believers should no longer be enslaved to sin, he is reluctant simply to claim that at present sin has no power at all over believers. That too is something in the future.

Paul concludes this section in 6:14 by returning to the notion of grace with which he began in 6:1: "For you are not under the law but under grace." This final sentence serves two purposes. First, it reminds his audience of the issue with which the passage began, whether believers should remain in sin that grace may abound. The intervening arguments about the ethical implications of baptism showed that this is impossible. Being "under grace" is fundamentally antithetical to persisting in sin. Second, the contrast between being "under the law" and being "under grace" also leads into the next section (6:15–23).

THE BROADER CONTEXT OF PAUL'S ARGUMENTS IN ROMANS 6:1–14

Paul's arguments in 6:1–14 raise several questions that force us to place his arguments in a broader context. To begin with, what did Paul think he was persuading the Roman Christian community of? At first the answer seems obvious. He was trying to persuade them of the ethical consequences of baptism. By being baptized into Christ's death, believers should no longer allow sin to have power over them.

---

[14] See Byrne, *Romans,* 198; Fitzmyer, *Romans,* 446–47; Cranfield, *Romans,* 1:318.
[15] For this stronger meaning, see Byrne, *Romans,* 198; BDAG 1106.

But did the Roman Christians think there were no ethical responsibilities connected with their baptism and so need to be shown that there were? This seems unlikely. Rather, Paul is trying to persuade them that he himself believes that there are ethical consequences of baptism, ethical consequences that they suspected he did not take seriously.

But why did they suspect that Paul saw no ethical implications specifically in baptism? Perhaps the best way to get at the answer to this question is to recall several important aspects of Paul's arguments in 6:1–14. First, the rhetorical question with which Paul begins this section is whether believers should continue in sin so that grace may abound (6:1). This question takes up an accusation made against him and to which he refers in 3:8. That accusation is that he, in effect, is saying that we should do evil that good may come of it. When Paul returns to deal with this accusation in 6:1–14, he does so by immediately appealing to an interpretation of baptism. This suggests that there is some connection between this accusation and Paul's interpretation of baptism. Second, Paul's interpretation of baptism as a baptism into Christ's death marks the first appearance of this interpretation in early Christian literature. It does not appear in any of Paul's earlier letters or in any other early Christian text prior to Paul or contemporary with him.[16] Paul himself is reinterpreting baptism as a baptism into Christ's death, and this reinterpretation emphasizes the ethical implications of baptism. Third, when Paul refers in 6:1–14 to the resurrection of Christians in parallel with Christ's resurrection, he consistently does so in the future tense (6:5, 8). The resurrection of Christians is still in the future. When he places believers' present situation in parallel with Christ's resurrection, the emphasis is on conduct (6:4, 11). The same care is reflected in his qualified characterization of believers' present situation "as though living from the dead" (6:13). In 6:14, he even goes so far as to write that "sin will not reign [οὐ κυριεύσει] over you," again a future tense. Given the care with which Paul wrote all this, he must have done it quite intentionally.

For an understanding of the connections between all these elements and their presence together in 6:1–14, it is necessary to see how Paul interpreted baptism in his earlier letters and what problems or issues these interpretations may have occasioned, if not caused. We shall look primarily at passages where Paul explicitly mentions baptism or where he uses images that he has explicitly linked to baptism elsewhere in his letters prior to Romans. This is important so as not to overlook Paul's reinterpretations of baptism in his letters or bring them together in an uncritical synthesis.[17]

Galatians 3:26–28

Paul explicitly interpreted the meaning of baptism in two earlier letters, Galatians and 1 Corinthians. His first interpretation of baptism is found in Gal 3:26–28. It comes at the beginning of an argument from Christian tradition (3:26–4:11). The point of his argument as a whole is to persuade the Galatian Christians that in

---

[16] Wilckens, *Römer*, 2:50, makes this point.
[17] See esp. Betz, *Galatians*, 187–89, for the importance of this.

Christ believers have become both sons and heirs and so are no longer slaves subject to the Mosaic law. He begins his argument in 3:26–28 by appealing to what may have been a pre-Pauline baptismal tradition:[18]

> For all of you are sons of God in Christ Jesus [ἐν Χριστῷ Ἰησοῦ] through faith [διὰ τῆς πίστεως]. For as many of you as were baptized into Christ [εἰς Χριστόν] have put on [ἐνεδύσασθε] Christ. There is neither Jew nor Greek; there is neither slave nor free; there is no "male and female." For you are all one [εἷς] in Christ Jesus [ἐν Χριστῷ Ἰησοῦ].

Although brief, this passage is both complex and, at crucial points, difficult to interpret. The beginning and the end of the passage claim that believers are "in Christ Jesus" (3:26, 28). They become such both "through faith" (3:26) and by being baptized "into Christ" (3:27). In addition, this baptism into Christ also means they have "put on Christ" and have become "one" in Christ. There is considerable dispute about the meaning and especially the background of virtually all these expressions. This study cannot settle these questions here, nor is it its purpose.[19] But several aspects of this passage are crucial for understanding what Paul eventually argues in Rom 6:1–14. This is clearly indicated by the fact that in both Gal 3:27 and Rom 6:3 believers are baptized "into Christ" (εἰς Χριστόν). In addition, Gal 3:27 and Rom 6:3 are syntactically parallel. Both begin with a relative clause about being baptized into Christ, followed by a main clause that explains the meaning of this baptism into Christ. The contents of the two main clauses, however, are strikingly different. In Gal 3:27, believers "put on Christ"; in Rom 6:3, they are "baptized into his death." This is a significant difference.

The meaning of being baptized "into Christ" is by no means completely clear. Its meaning should probably be distinguished from that of being baptized "into the name" (εἰς τὸ ὄνομα) of Christ, which was another baptismal formula used in early Christianity (Acts 8:16; 19:5; see 1 Cor 1:13; Matt 28:19). The latter expression was derived from Greco-Roman legal and commercial language about the transfer of a possession from one person to another. By baptism "into the name" of Christ, the one baptized becomes the possession of, or under the protection or power of, Christ, into whose name one is baptized.[20] The interpretation of the expression "into Christ," is more difficult, and its meaning probably shifted depending on different contexts. In Gal 3:27–28, Paul clarifies its meaning by claiming that "as many of you as were baptized into Christ have put on Christ [Χριστὸν ἐνεδύσασθε]," with the

---

[18] The strongest reason for thinking that Gal 3:27–28 is a pre-Pauline tradition connected with baptism is that 3:26, 29 contains the two terms central to Paul's argument in 3:26–4:11 ("sons" and "heirs"). Neither term is found in 3:27–28. Rather, the beginning of 3:29 seems meant to link 3:27–28 to its present context. For a fuller treatment of this section, see Betz, *Galatians*, 181–85. For the purposes of this study, whether 3:37–28 is traditional or not, however, is not crucial. In either case Paul has made this interpretation his own.

[19] The relationship between any ritual and its interpretation is complex. A ritual can and almost always does have several interpretations. These interpretations may or may not take up different aspects of the ritual itself. One therefore has to be aware that apparent distances of interpretations from the seemingly obvious elements of the ritual itself do not necessarily point to interpretations that are secondary or peripheral.

[20] BDAG 713; *"onoma," TDNT* 5:245.

result that "all of you are one [εἶς] in Christ Jesus [ἐν Χριστῷ Ἰησοῦ]." It is clear that underlying the meaning of "putting on" Christ is the image of putting on or taking off garments. This verb was already used in the LXX in a similarly metaphorical sense: being clothed with salvation (2 Chr 6:41; Isa 61:10); being clothed with righteousness (Job 29:14; Ps 131:9 [LXX]; Isa 59:17); being clothed with shame (Ps 34:26 [LXX]); iniquity being taken away (Zech 3:3–5). Paul uses the word in a similar way in 1 Thess 5:8 and Rom 13:12.[21] All these expressions concern being clothed metaphorically with something. In Gal 3:27, however, believers are clothed with someone; that is, they are clothed with Christ. This is a significant difference. In addition, with the possible exception of 2 Chr 6:41, these biblical passages are not connected with a specific ritual or its interpretation.[22] Rather, the imagery of Gal 3:27 seems closer to that of Greco-Roman mystery initiations in which putting on garments symbolized some sort of unification with the deity in whose garments the initiate was clothed. The best examples are found in Plutarch, *Is. Os.* 3 (352B), and Apuleius, *Met.* 11.24, in which initiates of Isis are clothed with special garments that symbolize their unity with the goddess.[23] Although one needs to be cautious about making too much of these similarities, especially about using them to explain the origins of Christian baptism, they are helpful in understanding the reasons for Paul's reinterpretation of baptism in Rom 6:1–14.[24]

Equally important for understanding the changes in Paul's interpretation of baptism in Romans is the answer to another question about the meaning of "putting on Christ." What Christ is it that the baptized put on? The answer in Galatians is fairly clear. It is the risen Christ. The interpretation of baptism in Gal 3:27–28 is that, in this rite, believers put on the risen Christ and are united with him to such an extent that they are now all "one in Christ Jesus" (Gal 3:28). Because of this, all other distinctions between human beings are relativized, even those between Jew and Greek, slave and free, and male and female.

First Corinthians

With this interpretation of baptism and the cluster of images associated with it in mind, we can now turn to 1 Corinthians, the other letter in which Paul explic-

---

[21] Both these passages take up the imagery of Isa 59:17.

[22] In 2 Chr 6:41, Solomon prays that God will clothe his priests with salvation. No doubt this is connected with the priests' garments, but there is no reference to a ritual by which the priests are clothed with the garments. See also Philo, *Fug.* 110.

[23] Both are concerned with the cult of the Egyptian goddess Isis. See also Ephippus in Athenaeus, *Deipn.* 12.53, about Alexander the Great clothing himself with the garments of different gods and goddesses (Ammon, Artemis, Hermes, and Heracles). This kind of imagery is also found in later gnostic texts. See Betz, *Galatians,* 188.

[24] E.g., at the time of Paul, did the baptismal ritual already include the newly baptized being clothed in new garments? Although Gal 3:27 suggests that this was already the case, the evidence is simply too meager to draw anything approaching a strong conclusion. For the extraordinarily complex question of the origins of Christian baptism, see Hans Dieter Betz, "Transferring a Ritual: Paul's Interpretation of Baptism in Romans 6," in *Paul in His Hellenistic Context* (ed. Troels Engberg-Pedersen; Minneapolis: Fortress, 1995), 84–118. Although my understanding of some of Paul's changing interpretations of baptism differs from Betz, his analysis of the complexity of the issues is most helpful.

itly writes about baptism and its significance. He writes about baptism at four different points in 1 Corinthians (1:10–17; 10:1–2; 12:12–13; 15:29), three of which are important for our purposes.[25] The passage most similar to Gal 3:26–29 is 1 Cor 12:12–13: "For just as the body is one and has many members, and all the members of the body, though many, are one, so it is with Christ. For by one Spirit [ἐν ἑνὶ πνεύματι] we were all baptized [ἐβαπτίσθημεν] into one body [εἰς ἓν σῶμα]—Jews or Greeks, slaves or free—and all were made to drink of one Spirit [ἓν πνεῦμα]." These verses are part of a section of 1 Corinthians (11:2–14:40) where Paul deals with the manifestations of the Corinthian community's factionalism when they come together in worship. More specifically, in 12:1–14:40, Paul writes about the issues of unity and the possession of various "spiritual gifts" (πνευματικά, χαρίσματα) by different members of the community. In 12:12–31 he compares the community's unity in diversity to the unity of the members of the human body. First Corinthians 12:12–13 is the beginning of the comparison.

These verses about the significance of baptism bear several important similarities to Gal 3:27–28. Most obvious is Paul's use again of the phrases "Jews or Greeks" and "slaves or free" from Gal 3:28.[26] Less obvious but equally important is the notion that in baptism believers are baptized "into Christ." In 1 Cor 12:13, Paul writes that "all of you were baptized into one body [εἰς ἓν σῶμα]." It is clear from the end of 1 Cor 12:12 that this is an alternative formulation of "into Christ" found in Gal 3:27. The importance of this formula of being baptized "into Christ" for Paul is also highlighted by his use of it in 1 Cor 10:1–2, where he writes of the analogous example of "our fathers" being "baptized into Moses [εἰς Μωϋσῆν]" in the cloud and in the sea during the exodus from Egypt.

First Corinthians 12:12–13 also contains several other important elements that are not found in Gal 3:27–28 but were probably also part of the same interpretation of the ritual of baptism. In baptism, believers are baptized "into one body" "by one Spirit." In this case the "one body" must be the risen body of Christ into which believers are baptized.[27] In addition, this is accomplished in baptism by the power of the "one Spirit." In order for the argument to be effective, Paul must be appealing to something both he and the Corinthian believers already have in common. Given the presence of the notion of all believers being "one in Christ Jesus" in Gal 3:28, the notion of being united into one body (the risen body of Christ) must also have been part of the same traditional baptismal language found in Gal 3:27–28. This also makes more specific the image, in Gal 3:27, of being clothed with Christ. It means putting on the risen body of Christ. The same is true for the belief that this takes

---

[25] The fourth passage (1 Cor 15:29) mentions some Corinthian Christians' practice of being baptized on behalf of the dead (ὑπὲρ τῶν νεκρῶν). Because of the obscurity of this custom, it can contribute little to our understanding of the development of Paul's interpretations of baptism.

[26] Paul probably does not include the polarity "male and female" from Gal 3:28 because of the previous controversy about women wearing veils in 1 Cor 11:2–16.

[27] This is clear from the end of 1 Cor 12:12 ("so it is with Christ"). The body referred to in 1 Cor 12:13 must be Christ's resurrected body. See Schrage, *Der erste Brief an die Korinther,* 2:211–18; and Collins, *First Corinthians,* 462, although he does not emphasize enough this aspect of the comparison.

place by the power of the Spirit. In 3:2, Paul challenged the Galatian believers with the question of how they received the Spirit: was it by observance of the law, or was it through hearing with faith? It was, of course, by the latter. More specifically, however, when did this reception of the Spirit take place? Was there a ritual by which this took place? The obvious answer is, "At baptism." This is also consistent with his ethical appeals to the Galatians in 5:1–26 to walk by the Spirit (5:16), to be led by the Spirit (6:18), and to live by the Spirit (6:25) rather than to observe the Mosaic law. In 1 Cor 12:12–31, Paul then uses this traditional baptismal language already familiar to the Corinthian community to argue against the factionalism so prevalent among them.

What emerges from an examination of these passages in Galatians and 1 Corinthians is a fairly coherent interpretation of baptism. Through baptism, believers are united by the one Spirit into the risen body of Christ, so that even distinctions between Jews and Greeks, slaves and free, male and female are relativized. This interpretation is both traditional and something Paul has accepted, made his own, and used for his own purposes.

At the same time, however, this interpretation was at least partially the occasion, if not the cause, of the factionalism and some of the other difficulties Paul was forced to address in 1 Corinthians. In 1 Cor 1:10–17, Paul describes the situation in Corinth as one full of factions (σχίσματα) and quarrels (ἔριδες). On the basis of his description, these factions and quarrels are connected with baptism, specifically with the person by whom someone was baptized (1:13–17). Paul lists four different factions. Some claim to be of Paul, others of Apollos, others of Cephas (Peter), and still others of Christ (1:12). Although he mentions four factions, the two real factions seem to be those of Paul and Apollos.[28] After listing them, Paul immediately turns in 1:13–17 to the question of baptism and whom he baptized.

> Is Christ divided? Was Paul crucified for you? Or were you baptized into the name of Paul [εἰς τὸ ὄνομα Παύλου]? I am thankful that I baptized none of you except Crispus and Gaius; lest any one should say that you were baptized into my name [εἰς τὸ ἐμὸν ὄνομα]. (I did baptize also the household of Stephanas. Beyond that, I do not know whether I baptized any one else.) For Christ did not send me to baptize but to preach the gospel, and not with eloquent wisdom, lest the cross of Christ be emptied of its power.

The factions' break down on the basis of the person by whom one was baptized. By claiming that he baptized very few of the Corinthian believers and had not been sent to baptize but to preach the gospel, Paul is not minimizing the importance of baptism itself but discounting the importance of who the baptizer was and how "wise" he was. In addition, these factions seemed to have been generated from within the Corinthian community itself and did not represent disagreements between Paul and Apollos themselves. In 16:12, Paul tells the Corinthians that he had urged Apollos, who was

---

[28] Scholars have unsuccessfully tried to provide plausible identifications for the factions of Cephas and Christ. In 3:22, Paul lists three factions (Paul, Apollos, and Peter); in 3:1–9, Paul lists only two factions (Paul and Apollos). The most plausible explanation is that there were really only two factions, those of Paul and Apollos. The other factions mentioned in 1:12 and in 3:22 were probably for rhetorical effect. See Schrage, *Der erste Brief an die Korinther,* 2:142–48; Collins, *First Corinthians,* 80–81.

then with him at Ephesus, to go to Corinth and that Apollos had declined. Had the factions at Corinth represented real disagreements between Apollos and himself, Paul would hardly have urged Apollos to return to Corinth.[29]

This fact also helps to put into proper perspective Paul's language about baptism in this passage as a baptism "into the name of Christ." As we saw both in Gal 3:26–28 and in 1 Cor 12:12–13 (see also 1 Cor 10:1–4), Paul's basic interpretation of baptism is that one is baptized "into Christ" (εἰς Χριστόν) rather than "into the name [εἰς τὸ ὄνομα] of Christ" The latter interpretation at first seems to be the interpretation of baptism in 1 Cor 1:13, 15. Does this suggest that the roots of the factionalism in the Corinthian community lie in different interpretations of baptism, one by Paul ("into Christ") and the other by Apollos ("into the name of Christ")? In that case, Apollos's interpretation of baptism would be that the baptized becomes the possession of, or under the protection or power of, Christ, into whose name one is baptized.[30] If there is no significant disagreement between Paul and Apollos, why, then, does Paul use this alternate expression—"into the name of . . ."—in connection with baptism at this point? It is certainly possible that the expression represents the Corinthian community's own interpretation of baptism, an interpretation that differs from both Paul's and Apollos's. This seems unlikely, however, since neither Paul nor Apollos would have provided them with such an interpretation.[31] A more likely explanation is that Paul uses this expression because it serves his immediate purpose in 1:10–17 to describe the foolish factionalism of the Corinthian community. All the Corinthian Christians were baptized "into Christ," the formula Paul presumes to be the case in 12:12–13. It is impossible to imagine that any of the Corinthian believers would have described their baptism as a baptism "into Paul" or "into Apollos." They were baptized "into Christ." But Paul uses the alternate expression about being baptized "into the name of . . . " as a pointed way of bringing out the foolishness of their factionalism. In baptism, they did not come into the possession of, or under the power of, either Paul or Apollos. The factionalism of the Corinthian community is connected, then, with their interpretation of baptism. But the factionalism is not in terms of whether they understood their baptism as a baptism "into Christ" or "into the name" of Christ. All were baptized "into Christ."

Their factionalism is connected, rather, with how they interpret different aspects of this baptism "into Christ," that is, with how they understand or misunderstand *Paul's* understanding of baptism as a baptism "into Christ" by which they were united to the risen body of Christ by means of the Spirit. If this is the case, then many of the apparently disparate issues treated by Paul in 1 Corinthians fall into a

---

[29] Paul's rhetoric in 3:1–9 also indicates that both he and Apollos are opposed to the factionalism at Corinth.

[30] See above, p. 199.

[31] Acts 18:24–28 tells the story of Apollos, already a believer in Jesus, who came to Ephesus and spoke in the synagogue about Jesus. He knew, however, only of the baptism of John. Paul's fellow missionaries, Priscilla and Aquila, then expounded to him the way of God more accurately. This presumably included a better understanding of baptism. It is very difficult to sort out what is going on in this story or how historically reliable it is. In any case, Apollos's understanding of baptism had already been corrected by Priscilla and Aquila by the time he arrived in Corinth (Acts 19:1). By that time it would have been the same as Paul's.

fairly coherent pattern. By being baptized into Christ and being united with the risen body of Christ, the Corinthian believers came to see themselves as already in some fashion "raised," so they no longer look forward to some future resurrection of their bodies (the issue of 1 Corinthians 15). Such a baptism also gave them a new "wisdom" (one of the other issues of 1 Corinthians 1–4) and empowered them with manifestations of the Spirit they received at baptism (the issue of 1 Corinthians 12–14). At the ethical level, this new state of being also placed them beyond the boundaries of conventional morality (the issues of 1 Corinthians 5, 7, 8–10). This was especially the case since, as Paul insisted, they were no longer bound by the strictures of the Mosaic law but were to be led by the Spirit they received at baptism.[32] Within this interpretation of baptism, the specific cause of their factionalism concerns who baptized them. Was it Paul or was it Apollos, and why is this important? Given Paul's concern with the correct understanding of "wisdom" in 1 Corinthians 1–4, the importance of whom someone was baptized by seems to lie in the issue of who led those whom he baptized to a greater "wisdom." The different factions in the Corinthian community seem to have developed a particular allegiance to whoever had instructed them in preparation for baptism and to have claimed that this person communicated to them a greater "wisdom."

Paul is clearly opposed to the Corinthians' interpretation of baptism and the ethical implications they draw from it. First Corinthians reflects his attempt to correct these misinterpretations. One can see, however, how such views could have been plausibly derived from understanding baptism "into Christ" as a baptism into the risen body of Christ by means of the Spirit. Such interpretations would have gained even greater plausibility when seen in the context of the widespread practice of initiations into mystery cults. This study cannot go in detail about the complex issues of the character of such cults or their connection with Christian interpretations of baptism. The presence of such cults in the cultural and religious environment of Corinth, however, would have offered ready analogies for the Corinthian community's attempt to understand the significance of their baptism. After all, both were initiation rituals; both united their respective initiates with a deity; both promised immortality and wisdom of an extraordinary sort.[33] In addition, at least in some cases, there was even a special bond established between the initiated and the one who prepared the person for initiation.[34]

---

[32] One must assume that the kind of ethical stance Paul took in Gal 5:1–6:10 was what he also first preached to the Corinthian believers.

[33] The relationship between the Corinthian Christians' views of baptism and initiations into mystery cults is complex and much debated. On the one hand, it is clear that initiations into mystery cults do not explain the origins of Christian baptism. See Günter Wagner, *Pauline Baptism and the Pagan Mysteries: The Problem of the Pauline Doctrine of Baptism in Romans VI.1–11* (Edinburgh: Oliver & Boyd, 1967), for a thorough critique of older notions. On the other hand, one can make little sense of what Paul wrote in 1 Corinthians if one fails to recognize that the Corinthian Christians seem to have come to understand their own baptism on the analogy with mystery initiations. For a good guide to these mystery cults, see Walter Burkert, *Ancient Mystery Cults* (Carl Newell Jackson Lectures; Cambridge: Harvard University Press, 1987).

[34] See esp. Apuleius, *Met.* 11.13–15, 21–23, 25.

For the purpose of understanding Paul's arguments in Rom 6:1–14, several aspects of both the situation in Corinth and Paul's response to it are especially relevant. The Corinthian community's ethical confusion and disarray were partially rooted in their interpretation of baptism as being united to the risen body of Christ by means of the Spirit. Paul himself gave them this interpretation. In addition, Paul's insistence that ethical behavior should be guided by the Spirit rather than by observance of the Mosaic law meant that the Corinthian community had no ethical code of behavior in a conventional sense, which would have provided them with clear ethical norms. Paul obviously disagreed with how they interpreted their baptism. But their interpretations, however misguided, were rooted partly in interpretations of baptism that Paul had preached to them.

Several of Paul's responses to the situation at Corinth are also relevant for understanding Rom 6:1–14, specifically his arguments about the resurrection of believers in 1 Corinthians 15. Paul's arguments in 1 Corinthians 15 are not about belief in the resurrection of Christ. Both he and the Corinthian Christians believe in Christ's resurrection. Rather, Paul's arguments are meant to correct their beliefs about their own resurrection. They seem to have believed that they were already in some fashion "raised." They probably also believed that this new status came about through their baptism in the Spirit into the risen body of Christ. What precisely they meant by this new status is difficult to determine. Given that they seemed to have understood baptism on the analogy of an initiation into a mystery cult, they probably understood their new status of being "raised" as an immortality of the soul rather than as some form of a present resurrection of the body.[35] In 1 Corinthians 15, Paul tries to persuade them, first, of the future resurrection of their bodies (1 Cor 15:1–34) and second, of the difference between such a resurrection and any notion of a crudely physical, bodily resuscitation (15:35–49).

For the purpose of understanding Rom 6:1–14, the most relevant section is 1 Cor 15:1–28. First, in 1 Cor 15:1–11, Paul roots his arguments for a future bodily resurrection of believers in a traditional creedal formula he has in common with the Corinthians (15:3–5).[36] This creedal formula was most likely used in connection

---

[35] Both Greeks and Romans would have found the notion of a resurrection of the body very odd. They would have understood it as a resuscitation of the body, a concept that would have had no appeal for them. Paul's arguments in 1 Cor 15:35–49 seem to have been aimed at explaining how this was not the case, how the future resurrection of their bodies entailed a radical transformation and not a resuscation. See Dale B. Martin, *The Corinthian Body* (New Haven: Yale University Press, 1995), 108–17. In addition, the issue in 1 Corinthians 15 is not about some sort of "realized" eschatology in which the Corinthian Christians believed that their bodies had already been raised. The issue instead is concerned with a different frame of reference, that of the immortality of the soul rather than the resurrection (whether present or future) of the body.

[36] The traditional formula is contained in 15:3–5. Paul probably added 15:6–7 himself. The formula, on the basis of an analysis of content and vocabulary, was probably Palestinian in origin, although it may have been modified in the Hellenistic church. See Schrage, *Der erste Brief an die Korinther*, 3:19–26; Collins, *First Corinthians*, 528–37; and John S. Kloppenborg, "An Analysis of the Pre-Pauline Formula in 1 Cor 15:3b–5 in Light of Some Recent Literature," *CBQ* 40 (1978): 351–67, for a fuller explanation.

with the ritual of baptism.[37] The formula lists in order that Christ (1) died for our sins according to the Scriptures, (2) was buried, (3) was raised on the third day according to the Scriptures, (4) and was seen by Cephas (Peter) and the Twelve. This creedal formula about Christ's death and resurrection, which Paul emphasizes as something shared by himself and the Corinthians (15:11), then serves as a foundation for the arguments that follow. Second, in 15:12–19, Paul then insists on the inextricable connection between Christ's bodily resurrection and that of believers. The one makes no sense without the other. The function of this section in his argument is to establish a symmetry between these two realities. In doing this, Paul is implicitly criticizing the Corinthians' belief that they are already "raised" by being united to the risen body of Christ. This is because such a "resurrection," whatever else it is, is not from the dead as Christ's was (15:12, 13, 15, 16). Third, in 15:20–28, Paul then emphasizes that there is an order to the resurrection: first Christ as the "first fruits of those who have fallen asleep" and then, "at his coming" (ἐν τῇ παρουσίᾳ αὐτοῦ), those who belong to Christ (15:23). He emphasizes that the resurrection of believers is an event that is still outstanding, still in the future. It will take place only at Christ's coming in power and will immediately precede all things being subjected to Christ (15:24–27). By arguing as he does, Paul in effect juxtaposes the traditional creedal formula in 15:3–5 over against the Corinthians' quite different interpretation of the effects of baptism. More specifically, because the context for the use of this creedal formula was itself the ritual of baptism, he uses this element of the baptismal ritual as a way to understand the significance of the ritual as a whole. He thus interprets baptism, understood as being united to the risen body of Christ, in such a way that this baptism does not preclude the bodily resurrection of believers as an event still in the future but indeed demands it.

With all this in mind, we can now return to Rom 6:1–14 and see more clearly how the issues of 1 Corinthians affected Paul's reinterpretation of baptism in this passage. Most obvious is the close connection on which Paul insists between baptism and its ethical implications. As the result of baptism, believers should die to sin; they should walk in newness of life; they should no longer be slaves to sin; sin should not longer have power over them. Baptism should not be understood as allowing for the kind of ethical confusion and disarray found in the Corinthian community. Equally obvious is the care with which Paul, in connecting baptism with Christ, places the actual resurrection of believers in the future. Although he is still able to describe believers as "putting on the Lord Jesus Christ" in Rom 13:14, he does so only within the strongly ethical context of 13:11–14, which in turn must be seen in light of 6:1–14. In this way, Paul distinguishes between believers' being united through baptism to the risen body of Christ and their own bodily resurrection, an event that is still in the future.

Less obvious but no less important is the way Paul reinterprets the significance of baptism itself. He does this in ways that go beyond even what he wrote in 1 Corinthians. In 1 Cor 15:3–5, he used the traditional creedal formula as a counterweight to the Corinthians' view that, by being united to the risen body of Christ

---

[37] See Collins, *First Corinthians*, 531; and Schrage, *Der erste Brief an die Korinther,* 4.18–19.

in baptism, they were in fact already "raised" in the sense that they had already become immortal. But in 1 Cor 15:3–5, he did not use the creedal formula to reinterpret the meaning of the baptismal ritual itself. In Rom 6:1–14, however, Paul reinterprets the meaning of the ritual, on the basis of the traditional creedal formula of 1 Cor 15:3–5, as dying with Christ (1 Cor 15:3; Rom 6:3), being buried with Christ (1 Cor 15:4a; Rom 6:4a), so that just as Christ was raised from the dead, believers might walk in newness of life (1 Cor 15:4b; Rom 6:4bc). This reinterpretation was certainly made easier because Paul already understood the life of believers after baptism, especially in their sufferings, as an assimilation to the death of Christ, so that they would also ultimately be assimilated to the resurrection of Christ.[38] But he never before used this pattern of assimilation to interpret the baptismal ritual itself. That Paul is using this pattern to reinterpret baptism in Rom 6:1–14 becomes clear when one notices one of the striking features of this pattern in Paul's earlier letters: the prominence given to expressions with the preposition "with" (σύν) (1 Thess 4:14, 17; 5:10; 2 Cor 4:14) and to words compounded with this preposition (2 Cor 7:3; Gal 2:19; Phil 3:10–11, 21). This same pattern now figures prominently in Rom 6:1–14, where Paul frequently uses words compounded with this preposition (Rom 6:4, 5, 6, 8). Indeed Paul previously used two verbs, "to be crucified with" (συσταυρόομαι) in 6:6 and "to live with" (συζάω) in 6:8, to describe this pattern of assimilation, the former in Gal 2:19 and the latter in 2 Cor 7:3. This indicates that Paul is now intentionally using this broader pattern of believers' assimilation to the death and resurrection of Christ to reinterpret the meaning of baptism itself.

When one sees Rom 6:1–14 against this complex background, what concerns Paul in the passage becomes much clearer. The Roman Christian community's suspicions about Paul were not simply matters of theology in some general sense. Rather, they were rooted in a knowledge of the excesses that had taken place in Corinth. To the Roman Christians, these excesses were rooted in the combination of (1) an interpretation of baptism as a ritual through which believers were not only united to the risen body of Christ but were already actually "raised" in the sense of becoming immortal and (2) an ethics that depended on the guidance of the Spirit but was devoid of the framework provided by observance of the Mosaic law. As 1 Corinthians shows, Paul was certainly as appalled as they were by the Corinthians' conduct and sought to correct it. Yet it is not difficult to imagine that the Roman Christians would have perceived the situation at Corinth as the result, however unintended, of some of Paul's views about Christian belief and practice. In part, Paul came to agree with them. He came to see that the meaning of baptism needed to be understood in a rather different way. It could still be understood as "putting on Christ," as it is in Rom 13:11–14, but what "putting on Christ" means needed to be understood in a different framework. In 6:1–14 he articulates this new framework on the basis not only of Christ's resurrection but especially on the basis of his suffering and death. This reinterpretation enables Paul to emphasize the ethical implications of baptism. To be baptized into Christ's death means for believers a death to sin. Building on Romans 5, Paul insists that one cannot be baptized into Christ's death without also

---

[38] Examples of this pattern in one form or another are found in 1 Thess 4:13–18; 5:10; Gal 2:19–20; Phil 3:4–11, 20–21; 2 Cor 4:7–14; 6:1–10; 7:3; 13:3–4.

dying to sin. But this reinterpretation also offers Paul a way to insist that the bodily resurrection of believers is still something in the future. The consequence is that believers are not beyond everyday earthly existence and so are not beyond the ethical requirements that are a part of such an existence. But this interpretation allows Paul to insist on this without involving observance of the Mosaic law as a necessary means to this end. The implication of Paul's argument is that dying to sin is already an integral part of, and a necessary consequence of, baptism. All of this is still "apart from the law," and so one need not invoke observance of the law to establish or maintain the incompatibility of sin and grace. Baptism is a ritual that Jewish and Gentile believers alike undergo. It is this common ritual and its consequences, and not observance of the law, that serve as the basis for ethical behavior for both Jewish and Gentile believers.

ROMANS 6:15–23: FREED FROM SIN BUT SLAVES TO RIGHTEOUSNESS

In 6:15, Paul asks another rhetorical question: "What then? Shall we continue to sin, since we are not under the law but under grace?" He replies, "Certainly not." The question obviously takes up the conclusion in 6:14, that sin will not reign over believers, "for [γάρ] you are not under the law but under grace." Paul thinks it appropriate or even necessary to deal with this question in conjunction with his reinterpretation of baptism. This provides further evidence that the issue he is dealing with is the conjunction, in the Roman Christians' minds, between his previous interpretations of baptism and his conviction that righteousness is now by grace and not by observance of the Mosaic law. It also reminds us again that he is still dealing with the issue of the ethical implications of "this grace in which we stand" in 5:2.

Romans 6:16–19: Slaves Either to Sin or to Righteousness

The rest of the passage develops in two steps. First, in 6:16–19, Paul states a principle and then explains the significance of the principle in the present context. The principle is that when you offer yourselves as slaves in obedience, you are slaves to whom or what you obey. In stating this principle, he immediately specifies it for the present context: You are slaves "either of sin which leads to death, or of obedience which leads to righteousness" (6:16).[39] By introducing this principle and its specification as a rhetorical question ("Do you not know that . . . ?"), Paul obviously assumes that the Roman Christians would readily agree with both the principle and its specification. He expects their immediate agreement. Paul's answer in 6:16 to the question in 6:15, whether believers should continue to sin because they are not under the law but under grace, does not immediately take up most of the language of that verse; it takes up only the matter of sin. Rather, in his explanation, he shifts the issue to whom or what one is a slave to and whom or what one is obedient to.

---

[39] The grammar of this verse is clumsy, but its meaning is fairly clear. See Cranfield, *Romans*, 1:322–23.

The purpose of this shift will become apparent only a little later. What is important at this point is the way Paul chooses to deal with the issue. The issue is to whom or what one is an obedient slave.

In 6:17–18, Paul then describes how believers changed from being slaves of sin to become, once freed (ἐλευθερωθέντες) from sin, enslaved to righteousness (ἐδουλώθητε τῇ δικαιοσύνῃ). Then, resuming the metaphor of "offering oneself" from 6:13, 16, he presents a contrast in 6:19 between their past and what their present should be. Just as in the past they offered their members as slaves "in uncleanness and lawlessness leading to lawlessness" (τῇ ἀκαθαρσίᾳ καὶ τῇ ἀνομίᾳ εἰς τὴν ἀνομίαν), so too in the present they should offer their members as slaves "in righteousness leading to holiness" (τῇ δικαιοσύνῃ εἰς ἁγιασμόν). Although he does describe believers as being freed from sin (6:18), the emphasis of the language is again predominantly on obedience and slavery. Paul himself seems to realize how weighted this language is in the direction of obedience and slavery. At the beginning of 6:19, he almost apologizes for speaking in such "human terms" (ἀνθρώπινον) to the Roman believers. But he defends himself by claiming that he puts it this way because of their human weakness. Above all he does not want his notion of freedom to be misunderstood as license.[40] Paul also emphasizes that their past was characterized by "lawlessness leading to lawlessness," and contrasts this with their present situation, which is marked by "righteousness leading to holiness" (6:19). Given his insistence that believers are now not under the law but under grace (6:14–15), this contrast is particularly striking and will prove helpful for placing 6:15–23 in its larger context. Paul's description of the change they have undergone is similar to his description, in 1 Thess 1:9, of the Thessalonian believers "turning to God from idols to serve the living and true God." Since the Roman Christian community was made up of mostly Gentile believers, they would have found this description quite apt.

Romans 6:20–23: The Consequences

In the second half of the passage, Rom 6:20–23, Paul uses the same framework but concentrates on the consequences or results of these two different situations, slavery to sin or slavery to God. Again the perspective is temporal. While they were slaves of sin and free with regard to righteousness, they gained no fruit (καρπόν) from the things of which they are now ashamed and that lead to death.[41] But now that they are freed from sin and enslaved to God, they possess fruit (καρπόν) that leads to holiness and ultimately to eternal life. The reason is that the wages of sin is death whereas the gift of God (τὸ χάρισμα τοῦ θεοῦ) is eternal life in Christ Jesus. In this final contrast, Paul again insists on the incompatibility of sin and death, on the one hand, and God's gift and eternal life, on the other. This is something Paul has emphasized again and again both in Romans 5 and in Romans

---

[40] See Fitzmyer, *Romans*, 450.

[41] There is a question about whether the relative clause "those things of which you are ashamed" (ἐφ᾽ οἷς νῦν ἐπαισχύνεσθε) should be taken with the preceding or with the following clause. Since the following clause provides the reason for being ashamed ("For their end is death."), the relative clause goes better with the preceding clause ("What fruit did you have from those things of which you are ashamed?").

6. At the same time, it is again crucial to be aware that, in the immediate context of 6:15–23, this "gift" is such that believers are no longer "under the law." This also means Paul intends the argument of 6:15–23 to be taken with the larger context beginning with Romans 5.

THE BROADER CONTEXT OF PAUL'S ARGUMENTS IN ROMANS 6:15–23

With this sense of the structure and language of 6:15–23, we need to ask more specifically what Paul hopes to convince the Roman Christians of. Is he trying to convince them that they should no longer be slaves of sin and should become slaves to God and to righteousness? Are they in any real danger of "offering their members to uncleanness and lawlessness"? The answer is clearly no. Just as in 6:1–14, Paul's purpose in 6:15–23 is of a less direct sort. He is trying to convince them that his gospel about righteousness free from the observance of the law does not lead to some sort of moral disarray.

Perhaps the best way to get at the issue is to return to an earlier comment about the very beginning of the passage. Paul's rhetorical question in 6:15 is whether believers should continue to sin because "you are not under the law but under grace." In 6:14, not being under the law but under grace is clearly Paul's own position. The supposed issue in 6:15–23 is whether this means that believers should continue to sin, since they are no longer under the law but under grace. Paul obviously thinks not and tries to show how this is not the case. But in what follows, he does not mention the law or even grace (χάρις) until the very end of the passage, where he uses the closely related term "gift" (χάρισμα). What, then, is the connection between the question in 6:15 and the argument in 6:16–23? Paul certainly thought that his audience would have readily made the connection. But how?

The answer begins to emerge when one realizes that Paul's claim that believers are no longer under the law is not new. He already explicitly made just such a claim in Gal 5:18. When one looks at the context surrounding Gal 5:18, one begins to understand more specifically what Paul is now trying to do in Rom 6:15–23. Galatians 5:18 was part of Paul's moral exhortation to the Galatian believers in Gal 5:1–6:10. The passage was not simply a moral exhortation added on to an already completed series of arguments in 3:1–4:31. Because he tried to dissuade the Galatian believers from being circumcised and observing the Mosaic law in 3:1–4:31, he also had to present them with an alternate way of living ethically. This was his goal in 5:1–6:10, and it was integral to his argument in Galatians.

This passage has important similarities to Rom 6:15–23, including the use of language contrasting freedom and slavery. In Gal 5:1, Paul both sums up his previous arguments and sets the stage for the exhortation to follow: "For freedom [τῇ ἐλευθερίᾳ] Christ has set you free. Stand firm therefore, and do not submit again to a yoke of slavery [ζυγῷ δουλείας]." In this context, the "yoke of slavery" is clearly the obligation to observe the Mosaic law. Paul returns to this theme in Gal 5:13 when he again insists that the Galatian believers "were called to freedom." But he is equally insistent that this freedom should not be used as an excuse for immorality (5:13). The purpose of 5:1–6:10 is to show how this is possible. Believers are to "become slaves of one another in love" (διὰ τῆς ἀγάπης δουλεύετε ἀλλήλοις, 5:14). In doing this, they fulfill the "law of Christ" (τὸν νόμον τοῦ Χριστοῦ, 6:2) and the "whole [Mosaic] law" (πᾶς νόμος), which is summed up in one saying, quoting Lev 19:18: "You shall love your neighbor as yourself" (Gal 5:14). By "fulfilling the law," however, Paul clearly does not mean observance of the Mosaic law, since this would contradict all his previous arguments. Rather, he means that, by this alternative way of living, that is, by becoming slaves of one another, believers in effect fulfill the purpose of the law.[42] All this becomes possible through the power of the Spirit. Believers are to conduct themselves by the power of the Spirit and give no place to the "flesh" (5:16); they are to be led by the Spirit (5:18) and live by the Spirit (5:25). To specify this even more, Paul provides a list of vices that, as "works of the flesh," are to be avoided (5:19–21) and a list of virtues that, as the "fruit of the Spirit," are to be practiced (5:22–23). Against the latter "there is no law" (5:23).

In order to understand Rom 6:15–23, one needs to understand the ethical framework Paul established in Gal 5:1–6:10 and what he contrasted it to. Believers have been set free from the law and are now to be lead by the Spirit and thereby become slaves of one another and practice virtues appropriate to this status. He contrasts this freedom with the Mosaic law and its observance as a yoke of slavery. Paul certainly understands this ethic of becoming slaves of one another as no less stringent than observing the Mosaic law, and he warns against using this newly experienced freedom as an excuse for the flesh (Gal 5:13). Nevertheless, there is still a fundamental contrast Paul insists on between the law as a yoke of slavery from which believers have been freed and the freedom of the life of the Spirit by which they are now empowered. This contrast is very much of a piece with his arguments elsewhere in Galatians. For example, in his version, in 2:1–10, of the meeting in Jerusalem about A.D. 48, Paul describes some of his opponents as "false brethren secretly brought in, who slipped in to spy out our freedom [τὴν ἐλευθερίαν ἡμῶν] which we have in Christ Jesus, that they might enslave [καταδουλώσουσιν] us" (2:4). Although the specific identity of these "false brethren" is not clear, they were certainly Jewish Christians who were convinced that Gentile Christians should also be circumcised and observe the Mosaic law. The enslavement Paul is alluding to means placing Gentile Christians under the obligation of observing the law.

Much the same viewpoint about the Mosaic law is found in two more extended passages, Gal 4:1–11 and 4:21–31, seen earlier in this study in conjunction with Paul's interpretation of the promises to Abraham in Romans 4.[43] Here several other aspects of the passages need highlighting. In Gal 4:1–11, Paul presents a complex comparison about the status of believers on the basis of the different statuses of sons and heirs, on the one hand, and slaves, on the other. Paul characterizes those who are "under the law" (ὑπὸ νόμον) as "enslaved" (δεδουλωμένοι) to

---

[42] For the complex issues in the interpretation of Gal 5:14; 6:2, see Betz, *Galatians*, 274–76, 298–301; Matera, *Galatians*, 192–98, 218–21; Dunn, *Galatians*, 288–92, 321–24; Martyn, *Galatians*, 486–91, 502–18, 547–49. It is crucial to keep in mind that Paul intended Gal 5:1–6:10 as an alternative to the observance of the law and not as an alternative way of describing observance. See above, pp. 67–68.

[43] See above, pp. 145–51.

the elemental principles of the universe (4:3). In the fullness of time, God sent his Son to buy back or deliver those "under the law" so that they could become sons and heirs and receive the Spirit (4:4–6). Paul pleads with the Gentile believers of Galatia not to become slaves (ἐδουλεύσατε) again to forces that are by nature not divine or to return and become slaves (δουλεύειν) again to these weak and beggarly forces (4:8–9). He clearly means by this Gentile Galatian believers' being circumcised and observing the Mosaic law. In the intensely polemical atmosphere of Galatians, Paul seems to elide being "under the law" with being enslaved to the same elemental principles of the universe the Gentile Galatians served before their conversion. As seen above in the analysis of Romans 4, Paul came to see how inappropriate this elision actually was. But it is important to notice the way Paul characterizes being "under the law" as a kind of slavery. Much the same picture emerges when one looks at the elaborate allegory of Sarah and Hagar in 4:21–31. Here too Paul connects being "under the law" (see 4:21), this time allegorically (4:24), with Hagar and her children being enslaved (δουλεύει) (4:25). In contrast, he allegorically connects believers with Sarah, the free woman (ἐλευθέρα) (4:22, 23, 26, 30, 31). At the conclusion of the allegory, Paul urges the Galatians to stand firm in the freedom for which Christ has set them free and not to submit again to a yoke of slavery, the observance of the law (5:1).

What emerges from these considerations is a fairly consistent configuration emphasizing that believers' lives should be characterized by freedom from the law and guidance of the Spirit. In contrast, circumcision and observance of the law are connected with the kind of slavery from which believers have been delivered and to which they should not again submit. It is certainly true that Paul insists that this freedom and guidance by the Spirit entail becoming slaves of one another and not providing an opportunity for the flesh. It is also true that Paul insists that this means practicing virtues that are the fruit of the Spirit's guidance and avoiding vices that are the works of the flesh. Still, Paul's overall framework emphasizes freedom guided by the Spirit and consistently contrasts this with the observance of the law as a kind of slavery.

It is this twofold emphasis that partly, although unintentionally, occasioned some of the problems reflected in 1 Corinthians. These problems led Paul to rethink and reformulate the way he thought about the notion of freedom guided by the Spirit. This rethinking is reflected especially in 1 Corinthians 8–10 and 12–14. In 1 Corinthians 8–10, Paul deals with divisions in the Corinthian community over eating meat previously offered to idols. Some within the community, probably those of higher social and economic status, claimed that because of their knowledge that there was only one God and other gods did not exist, eating meat previously offered to such nonexistent deities was not a problem. Others less prosperous and less knowledgeable, seeing them dining in a temple precinct, were scandalized by such conduct, and their consciences were harmed. Paul finds the conduct of these upper-class believers unacceptable. He readily concedes they are right that there is only one God. But he objects to their eating in temple precincts because not all the members of the community are so firmly grounded in such knowledge. At some level of principle, they indeed have the right (ἐχουσία) to do it, but it is unacceptable to exercise this right if it would harm other, admittedly weaker, members of the community.

Paul argues that, in doing this, these believers sin against the consciences of the weaker members of the community, members for whom Christ died. In this way they sin against Christ himself (1 Cor 8:10–12).

In 1 Corinthians 9, Paul then offers his own conduct as exemplary. As an apostle and as one who has seen the risen Christ, he has the right (ἐχουσία) to be supported in his ministry by the communities he founded. But he stoutly refuses such support even though he has every right to it. He does this for the sake of the gospel, in the hope of gaining more people to Christ. Underlying Paul's arguments in this controversy is his conviction that, in the Christian community, a person's individual "right" must cede to the well-being of the whole community. The word he uses for "right" in 1 Corinthians 8–9 is ἐχουσία, which means both "right" and "freedom."[44] He uses it so frequently because it is the word the Corinthians themselves probably used to justify their conduct. In using his own conduct as an example in 1 Corinthians 9, he also uses the word ἐλεύθερος ("free") at two crucial points, and this indicates that he is using it as synonymous with ἐχουσία. In 9:1 he begins his argument with a rhetorical question, "Am I not free [ἐλεύθερος]?" The implied answer is "yes." But he chooses not to exercise this freedom; as he writes in 9:19, "For being free [ἐλεύθερος] of all I made myself a slave [ἐδούλωσα] to all, that I might win the more." In one way he is claiming no more than he did in Gal 5:13 when he warned the Galatian believers not to use their freedom as an opportunity for the flesh but to be slaves to one another in love. But a change has taken place. Although the individual believer's freedom remains a value for Paul, he now places it in the larger context of the community's well-being. In this way, he is also forced to reconsider the framework of his thought because of this controversy. He emphasizes less the value of freedom and insists more on the value of the spiritual well-being of the community, of becoming slaves of one another.

A similar rethinking takes place in 1 Corinthians 12–14, where the issue is the role of the "spiritual gifts" (πνευματικά), especially that of speaking in tongues. Throughout these three chapters, Paul emphasizes again and again that the various gifts of the Spirit are all meant for the building up of the community and their relative value must be judged on this basis. Believers are certainly to be guided by the Spirit, but this guidance is intended primarily for the common good of the community as a body. Indeed, through baptism all were baptized through the one Spirit into the one body of Christ (12:12–13). Once again Paul's thought on this issue is in some ways in continuity with what he wrote in Galatians 5 about believers being guided by the Spirit. But the framework and the emphasis have changed. The guidance of the Spirit has become a much more communally oriented reality, into which the individual believer's guidance by the Spirit must be fitted and to which it must be subordinated.

When one steps back from the details of these controversies about eating meat offered to idols and speaking in tongues, one cannot but be struck by the fact that underlying both are two elements Paul himself emphasized in his exhortation to the Galatians: freedom and guidance by the Spirit. While it is true enough that the Corinthians significantly misunderstood Paul on both issues, nevertheless these

---

[44] The word appears in 1 Cor 8:9; 9:4, 5, 6, 12, 18. See BDAG 352–53.

misunderstandings have some foundation in Paul's own preaching. Paul himself seems to have understood this. In his interpretations of both freedom and guidance by the Spirit in 1 Corinthians, he shifts the emphasis of his language in a much more community-oriented direction. The values of freedom and guidance by the Spirit are still present; they no longer form, however, the framework itself but are subordinated to a different, larger framework, the good of the community as a whole.

These controversies and the shifts occasioned by them also help us to understand more clearly what Paul is concerned about in Rom 6:15–23. This is especially the case once one realizes how the Roman Christian community probably interpreted what happened in Corinth. For them, the anarchic situation in Corinth was what should be expected once observance of the ethical commandments of the Mosaic law were abandoned, once being believers "under grace" also meant that they were not "under the law." Yet Paul's own deepest convictions would not allow believers to become subject to the law. In 1 Corinthians it does not even seem to have occurred to Paul to appeal to commandments of the Mosaic law to correct the abuses at Corinth.[45] But as we saw above, it did lead him to reorient the ways he thought about both freedom and guidance by the Spirit so that they would no longer be open to the kinds of interpretation and application as was found in Corinth. He came to insist much more on the community-oriented aspects of both.

In Rom 6:15–23 he carries this reorientation even further. Though still maintaining that believers are indeed under grace and not under the law, he seems to have taken much more seriously the values that observance of the ethical commandments of the law represent for the Roman community and the issues his viewpoints would have raised for them. Perhaps the best place to begin to understand Paul's rethinking of these issues is to note his emphasis on obedience at the beginning of the passage, in 6:16–17. The principle he states in 6:16 is that when believers offer themselves as slaves leading to obedience (εἰς ὑπακοήν), they become slaves to what or whom they obey (ὑπακούετε), whether slaves of sin leading to death or slaves of obedience (ὑπακοῆς) leading to righteousness. When he describes in 6:17 the change that has taken place in believers, he again describes it in terms of obedience: "Thanks be to God, that, though you were once slaves of sin, you have become obedient [ὑπηκούσατε] from the heart."[46] These two verses are almost overloaded with references to obedience, and they clearly establish the context for the rest of the passage. In addition, Paul clearly thinks of obedience in positive terms. Obedience is what leads to righteousness (6:16); the change that believers have undergone is a change to obedience from the heart (6:17).

At first glance, this emphasis might seem unexceptional. Yet Paul very rarely used language about obedience in his other letters. The adjective (ὑπήκοος) appears

---

[45] For a quite different approach, see Peter J. Tomson, *Paul and the Jewish Law: Halakha in the Letters of the Apostle to the Gentiles* (CRINT 3.1; Minneapolis: Fortress, 1990), 187–220. In the end, I do not find that analyzing Paul's arguments in 1 Corinthians 8–10 primarily in halakhic terms very helpful.

[46] The two clauses are actually coordinated clauses, but the first must be translated by a subordinate clause. For an explanation of this, see Fitzmyer, *Romans*, 449; and Max Zerwick, *Biblical Greek: Illustrated by Examples* (trans. Joseph Smith; SPIB 114; Rome: Pontifical Biblical Institute, 1963), 152–53.

only in Phil 2:8 as part of a hymn Paul is quoting. In Phil 2:12, he uses the verb for the only time apart from Romans. It refers to the Philippian believers' previous conduct, as part of an exhortation to them to continue to work out their salvation in fear and trembling. Obedience becomes important only in Romans. Paul describes his own apostolate in Rom 1:5 as intended to lead "to the obedience [εἰς ὑποκοήν] of faith among all the Gentiles." He repeats virtually the same phrase in 15:18, again as part of a description of his own ministry.[47] Paul also twice uses language about obedience earlier in Romans 5–7. In 5:19, he contrasts Adam's disobedience (παρα-κοῆς), by which the many were made sinners, with Christ's obedience (ὑπακοῆς), by which the many are made righteous. He also uses this language as part of his exhortation earlier in Romans 6, that sin should not be allowed to rule over believers' mortal bodies, so that they would obey (ὑπακούειν) its desires (6:12). The new emphasis on the importance of obedience elsewhere in Romans is very much of a piece with what he calls for in 6:16–17, with its emphasis on the contrast between sin and obedience. Paul's goal is to work toward the obedience of the Gentiles. This obedience is the result of Christ's own act of obedience. More proximately, by their baptism, believers are no longer to obey desires rooted in their mortal bodies. The accent in Romans now falls in a very different place than it did in Galatians with its emphasis on freedom. This is especially the case for Rom 6:16–17 with its multiple references to obedience. But in 6:16–17, Paul also moves beyond even what he wrote in 1 Corinthians, by using the language of obedience as the framework for his characterization of the way believers are to live.

Paul's purpose in reformulating the ethical framework for the way believers ought to live was influenced, then, by both his own experience with the community at Corinth and the Roman community's concerns about his views and what they thought were the results of such views in Corinth. But Paul's revision of his thinking was also influenced by the Roman community's concerns in a more specific way. One of their concerns was the confusion and disarray that resulted when the ethical commandments of the Mosaic law were no longer normative. In trying to meet their concerns, Paul explains how living "under grace" rather than "under the law" really upholds rather than destroys central values underlying the law itself. This purpose is reflected in the vocabulary he uses in Rom 6:15–23, vocabulary that reflects what the Jewish scriptures demand both be observed and be shunned. This is true, first of all, of his emphasis on obedience. Whereas the noun "obedience" (ὑπακοή) appears only once in the LXX, the verb "to obey" (ὑπακούω) appears about seventy times.[48] It appears in statements about the importance of Israel's obeying God and God's commandments (Lev 26:14, 18, 21, 27; Deut 26:14, 17, 30:2; Sir 4:15; 24:22). It is also used in descriptions of the consequences both of obedience (Gen 22:18; 26:5) and especially of disobedience to God and God's commandments (Judg 2:17, 20; Isa 65:12; 66:4; Jer 13:10, 13, 25; 16:12; Dan 3:29). The same is also true of other vocabulary in Rom 6:15–23. Both the noun "slave" or "servant" (δοῦλος) and the verb

---

[47] Paul also uses the noun in 16:19 to refer to the Roman believers themselves.

[48] The noun appears in 2 Kgs 22:36. The adjective ὑπήκοος appears five times in the LXX (Deut 20:11; Josh 17:13; Prov 4:3; 13:1; 21:28), but none of them are relevant to our concerns.

"to be a slave" (δουλεύω) are often used in the Jewish scriptures in connection with slavery or service to God.[49] The same is true of the contrast Paul draws in Rom 6:19 between the believers' previous life as marked by uncleanness (ἀκαθαρσία) and their present life as one that should lead to holiness (ἁγιασμόν), a contrast that also draws on scriptural language (2 Sam 11:4; 2 Chr 29:5, 16; 1 Esdr 1:47; *Pss. Sol.* 8:22). Last but perhaps most important of all is Paul's stark contrast of believers' present lives, marked by righteousness and holiness, with their previous lives, which he emphasizes were dominated by "lawlessness leading to lawlessness" (τῇ ἀνομίᾳ εἰς τὴν ἀνομίαν) (Rom 6:19). Although believers are now "under grace" rather than "under the law," it was their previous lives that were in fact "lawless" and not their present lives. In contrasting their previous lives as lawless, Paul uses the word "lawlessness" (ἀνομία), the most common word in the LXX to describe anything that was ethically wrong.[50]

What emerges from this analysis of Rom 6:15–23, against the backgrounds of both the situations in Galatia and in Corinth and the reactions to these events both by the Roman community and by Paul himself, is a much more nuanced view of Paul's purposes in this passage and the rhetorical strategy he uses to accomplish them. Paul is trying to convince the Roman community that his convictions about believers being under grace and not under the law do not led to ethical anarchy. To do this, Paul inverts the ethical framework of Galatians 5, where freedom guided by the Spirit formed the framework within which slavery to one another was fitted, to a framework in Rom 6:15–23 where obedience and slavery to God and to righteousness form the framework and freedom becomes primarily freedom from sin. The language of Rom 6:15–23 is a language of orderliness whereas Galatians 5 is much more a language of freedom. As seen in 1 Corinthians 8–10 and 12–14, this emphasis on orderliness did not emerge first in Romans. Paul's arguments in these passages in 1 Corinthians already emphasized the importance of social harmony and cohesion in ways that go beyond Galatians. Paul's change of perspective, then, is not simply the result of the necessity of responding to the Roman community's suspicions. Paul himself saw the need for this kind of rethinking as a result of his own experience with the Corinthian community. But the Roman community's suspicions did lead Paul to rethink even further the ethical implications of being under grace and not under the law. This is because the Roman community saw the anarchic situation in Corinth specifically as the expected result of not demanding that believers observe the ethical commandments of the Mosaic law. In the light of this criticism, Paul emphasizes in Rom 6:15–23 not only orderliness but also that living "under grace" entails the practice of central virtues called for by the law and the shunning of vices prohibited by it. None of this means, however, that Paul has surrendered his basic conviction that believers are no longer under the law but under grace. But it

---

[49] The noun is connected with the Lord (κύριος) in Josh 24:30; Judg 2:8; 1 Sam 20:8; 23:11; 2 Sam 7:5, 8, 20; 2 Kgs 10:23; 1 Chr 17:7; Ps (LXX) 85:4; 118:65; 122:2; 133:1; 134:1; Dan 3:85; Jon 1:9. The verb is used in the same way in Judg 2:7; 10:16; 1 Sam 7:4; 12:20, 23; 2 Chr 30:8; 33:16; 34:33; Ps (LXX) 2:11; 21:31; 99:2; 101:23; Sir 2:1.

[50] The word ἀνομία occurs more than 220 times in the LXX and is used to translate over twenty different Hebrew words. Philo also frequently uses the word, but it appears in Josephus only 3 times.

does mean that he becomes more explicit and specific about what the notion found in Gal 5:14, about the whole law being fulfilled in the command to love one another, entails.

CONCLUSIONS

In Romans 6, Paul is primarily concerned with the ethical dispositions that believers should have. He emphasizes how these dispositions are completely incompatible with sin or with any notion of freedom as a license to do whatever one wants. Paul is not trying to convince the Roman Christians of this. They are already convinced. Rather, he is trying to convince them that he is of the same opinion. He is trying to do this in the face of their suspicions that his insistence that believers are no longer obliged to observe the commandments of the Mosaic law and his emphasis on the role of the Spirit in ethics lead to ethical disarray.

Perhaps the best way to understand Paul's response to these suspicions is to note what Paul leaves out of Romans 6. The importance of omissions is admittedly difficult to gauge. Still, given what Paul has previously emphasized in Galatians and 1 Corinthians, two omissions at this point in his argument seem significant. One concerns the role of the Spirit; the other, the role of the law. Regarding the first, it is impossible to miss, especially in the wake of 1 Corinthians 12–14 and Galatians 5, that Paul does not appeal in Romans 6 to the role of the Spirit as an integral part of how believers are to live their lives. He will turn to the role of the Spirit later in the letter, in Rom 8:1–30. But as we shall see below in chapter 10, he will shift his understanding of the function of guidance by the Spirit significantly away from the way he understood it either in Galatians 5 or in 1 Corinthians 12–14. Yet its omission at this point is in itself significant. The reason for the omission is not difficult to find. Given his emphasis on obedience and slavery to God and to righteousness rather than slavery to sin, as well as his contrast between holiness and righteousness, on the one hand, over against uncleanness and lawlessness, on the other, references to living by the guidance of the Spirit would have been out of place or even counterproductive. Given the issues raised in the minds of Roman believers about the anarchic role played by the Spirit and the "gifts of the Spirit" among Corinthian believers, Paul's introduction of a role for the Spirit at this point would have subverted his emphasis on the orderliness of Christian living in Romans 6. The omission of any role for the Spirit at this point is not because the Spirit is no longer important for Paul. Quite the contrary, it remains important for him. Yet he has significantly rethought its role. As we shall see when he turns to the Spirit in 8:1–30, Paul will shift his understanding of the Spirit's role in a direction that is at once more orderly and more oriented toward the grounding of eschatological hopes rather than as an important guide for ethical living in the present.

The other omission concerns the law. Here the issue is a bit more complex and less clear. On the one hand, although Paul begins 6:15–23 with the question whether we should continue to sin because we are not under the law but under grace, he makes no further mention of the law in the rest of the passage. On the other hand, he does take up the issue of the place of the law immediately following this passage in 7:1–25. In this way Paul clearly sees the two issues of Christian living and the law as closely related. But in 6:15–23, Paul first tries to show how an orderly Christian life can be understood apart from observance of the law. His omission of any further reference to the law in 6:15–23, however, has a further significance. In comparison with Galatians, it also means that he no longer contrasts the framework for Christian living he describes in Romans 6 with the observance of the law. More specifically, he does not describe the law as a "yoke of slavery" or the observance of the law as being enslaved again to "the weak and beggarly principles" of the universe as he did in Gal 5:1 and 4:9. The reason for this omission is twofold. First, if Christian living is now understood as obedience to God and even as "slavery" to God, then to contrast the law as a "yoke of slavery" with how believers now live no longer makes any sense. Second and more important, Paul seems to have realized that his characterization of the law in the heat of his argument with the Galatians was, in significant ways, wrong. The Roman Christian community's deep misgivings about him brought this home to him. Paul has not changed his mind about the fact that believers in Christ are no longer under the law but under grace. But the reasons he gives for this are not the same. The issue of the law is not its very "goodness," as it seemed to be at points in Galatians, but the effects the realities of sin and death had on it. It is to this issue that Paul turns in Romans 7.

CHAPTER 8

The Goodness of the Law and Human Limitations

*I*N ROMANS 7, PAUL IS CONCERNED with the character, function, and limitations of the Mosaic law. The subject follows naturally enough on 6:15–23. If we are "not under the law but under grace," what does that say about the law? What is it about the law that believers should now no longer be under it? Paul's understanding of the character of the law, both its goodness and its limitations, in Romans 7 differs in significant ways from what he wrote in Galatians. There Paul said that those under the law are under a curse from which Christ redeemed them (Gal 3:10, 13) and that to begin to observe the law would be to turn back to slavery to the weak and beggarly elemental principles of the universe (Gal 4:9). Given these views, one would expect Paul to return to, and expand on, this kind of critique of the law in Romans to justify why believers are no longer under it but under grace.

But Paul does something very different. One goal of Romans 7 is actually to defend the goodness of the law and the holiness of its commandments (7:12, 14, 16, 22). Yet Paul's attempt to defend the goodness of the law in Romans 7 does not come without any preparation for it. At four points earlier in Romans, Paul made brief, almost cryptic remarks about the role of the law. Through the law comes knowledge of sin (3:20); the law brings about wrath (4:15); until the law, sin was in the world, but sin was not "accounted" when there was no law (5:13); the law entered in so that the trespass might increase (5:20). All these remarks occur, as we saw earlier, almost in passing. Paul made no effort to expand on them or explain them in any detail. All of them, however, more or less cluster around the notion that the function of the law is primarily to provide the knowledge of what is sinful and in that way make explicit the sinfulness of already sinful actions. There is no reason to think that Paul, in making these remarks about the function of the law, intended to impugn its goodness. Rather, by insinuation, they point to the function of the law Paul emphasizes in Romans 7, where he will insist that this function shows the law's goodness. By making these earlier remarks, Paul was also preparing his Roman Christian audience, even before Romans 7, to understand that his view of the law is significantly different from what he wrote in Galatians.

The overall structure of Romans 7 is fairly simple. Paul begins in 7:1–6 by addressing those who "know the law," and he offers an example from Jewish marriage law and applies it to believers who are no longer under the Mosaic law. The rest of the chapter (7:7–25) is primarily a speech in the first person singular, which has as its starting point a quotation from the Decalogue (Exod 20:17; Deut 5:18): "You shall not desire . . ." In it the speaker both defends the goodness of the Mosaic law and laments his inability to observe its admittedly holy commandments. The speech is structured around two rhetorical questions and denials: "What shall we say? Is the law sin? Certainly not!" (Rom 7:7); "Did that which is good, then, become death for me? Certainly not!" (7:13).

ROMANS 7:1–6: FREEDOM FROM THE LAW COMPARED TO MARRIAGE LAW

Paul begins by rhetorically asking his Roman Christian audience whether they who know the law are unaware of the principle that the law has power over a person only as long as the person is alive. He takes this as a principle that should be obvious to all who know the Mosaic law (7:1).[1] He then gives an illustration. A woman is bound to her husband by marriage law only as long as her husband is alive. Once her husband dies, she is freed from the marriage law that bound her to her husband (7:1–3).[2] So too believers have been freed from the Mosaic law through the death and resurrection of Christ in order to serve in the newness of the Spirit rather than in the oldness of the letter (7:4–6).

Although the structure of 7:1–6 is fairly simple, its simplicity is deceptive; the passage is more complex than it appears at first. The causes of this complexity are two. One is the odd relationship between the example from Jewish marriage law in 7:2–3 and Paul's claim about the effects of the death and resurrection of Christ on believers and their relationship to the Mosaic law in 7:4–6. The other is Paul's complex interpretation of Christ's death and resurrection and their consequences for believers in 7:4–6 itself.

First, in the example take from Jewish marriage in 7:2–3, the wife is bound to her husband as long as the husband is alive. Should she leave her husband for another man while her husband is still alive, she would be considered an adulteress. Once her husband has died, however, she is freed from the law binding her to her husband. The emphasis is on the change in the woman's legal status due to her husband's death. But in the principle that Paul enunciates in 7:1 and that the example is presumably meant to illustrate, the emphasis is elsewhere: "The law has power [κυρεύει] over a person as long as the person is alive." The principle in 7:1 in fact applies to the situation of the husband who dies, whereas the example in 7:2–3 is about the situation of the wife who is still alive. In addition, it is the principle rather

---

[1] In rabbinic literature, the principle is found in *m. Qidd.* 1:1; *b. Šabb.* 30a; *b. Nid.* 61b.

[2] For illustrations of various elements of this marriage law in Scripture, see Exod 20:17; Num 30:10–15; Deut 24:1. For use of the word ὕπανδρος to express the married state of a woman, see Prov (LXX) 6:24, 29; Sir 9:9.

than the example that Paul develops in 7:4–6. Believers have been put to death (ἐθανατώθητε) to the law through the body of Christ (7:4); believers are removed from the power of the law by dying (ἀποθανόντες) to that by which they were held bound (7:6). In relationship to the example in 7:2–3, believers are in the position of the husband and not of the wife. Although a good deal of ink has been spilled trying to reconcile the two, these efforts have not been successful.[3]

The uneasy relationship between the example in 7:2–3 and the rest of the passage (7:1, 4–6) helps us to understand what Paul is driving at in Romans 7. In enunciating the legal principle in 7:1 and applying it to the situation of believers in 7:4–6, Paul's interest clearly lies in showing how believers are freed from the law through the death and resurrection of Christ. One can almost move from 7:1 to 7:4–6 without sensing the loss of 7:2–3.

What role, then, does the example from Jewish marriage law play in 7:1–6? Its role is twofold. First, since he is appealing, perhaps with a bit of irony, to the Roman Christians as "those who know the law," this example serves as an illustration from within the law itself of how a law can cease to have force when a death occurs. In spite of all the dissimilarities between 7:1, 4–6 and the example in 7:2–3, the point of similarity is this: death can bring about the cessation of the binding force of a law.

Second and more important, one needs to see Paul's use of the example from Jewish marriage law against the background of the rather different way he wrote earlier about the cessation of the binding force of the Mosaic law on believers. In Gal 3:10–14, Paul described those who observe the law as being under a curse (ὑπὸ κατάραν), a curse from which (ἐκ τῆς κατάρας) Christ redeemed (ἐξηγόρασεν) believers. Paul interpreted the change of status for believers from being under the law to not being under the law as a change from being under a curse to not being under a curse. A similar viewpoint seems to lie behind what Paul wrote in Gal 4:4–5. When the fullness of time came, God sent his son, born under the law (ὑπὸ νόμον), in order to redeem (ἐξαγοράσῃ) those under the law (τοὺς ὑπὸ νόμον). In the context of 4:1–11, being under the law is similar to being a slave (4:1, 3, 7–8), and redemption is like being released from slavery into the status of adopted sonship (4:5, 7). What is common to these ways of describing believers' change of status is that they imply a negative evaluation of the law itself. To be redeemed from the law is to be redeemed from a curse or from slavery. Given their views of the law, most Roman Christians must have found these ways of characterizing the law as scandalous. Against this background, the example from Jewish marriage law furnished Paul with an illustration of how the cessation of the binding force of a law did not imply anything negative about the law itself. Paul did not criticize the law about marriage. The law itself is good. But it also ceases to bind the wife once her husband has died. This is very much in keeping with what follows in Rom 7:7–25. This example from Jewish marriage law affords Paul a way to illustrate for his Roman Christian audience, on the basis of the law itself, how the cessation of the binding force of the Mosaic law for believers through the death and resurrection of Christ does not impugn

---

[3] Part of the problem is that Paul uses 7:2–3 as an example rather than as part of a comparison. But by taking up some of the language of 7:2–3 and using it in 7:4, Paul himself creates some of the difficulty. See Wilckens, *Römer*, 2:64; Cranfield, *Romans*, 1:335.

the goodness of the law itself. It furnishes Paul with an image to begin his discussion of the place of the law—an image very different from the images of being redeemed from a curse or from slavery in Galatians.

The second issue concerns the rather complex arguments found in Rom 7:4–6. In 7:4, Paul again addresses the Roman Christians and claims that they too were put to death (ἐθανατώθητε) with regard to the law through the body of Christ (διὰ τοῦ σώματος τοῦ Χριστοῦ) in order to belong to Christ, who was raised from the dead so that they might bear fruit to God. Then, in 7:5–6, he contrasts their past situation "in the flesh" (ἐν τῇ σαρκί), in which sinful passions (τὰ παθήματα τῶν ἁμαρτιῶν) connected with the law (τὰ διὰ τοῦ νομοῦ) were at work and that bore fruit for death, with their present situation, in which they have been released (κατηργήθημεν) from the law (ἀπὸ τοῦ νομοῦ) by dying to that by which they were bound (ἀποθανόντες ἐν ᾧ κατειχόμεθα). As a result, they are now to serve (δουλεύειν ἡμᾶς) in the newness of the Spirit rather than the oldness of the letter.[4]

One can begin to understand this rather complex passage only by realizing the extent to which Paul draws on and develops the vocabulary and viewpoints of Romans 6. Much of the vocabulary he uses in 7:4–6 he already used in Romans 6.[5] In 7:4–6, Paul draws out the consequences of the legal principle, that the law has power over a person only as long as the person is alive (7:1), in the light of the arguments he developed in Romans 6. In 7:4, he claims believers "were put to death" (ἐθανατώθητε) in relation to the law (τῷ νόμῳ) through the body of Christ. When one asks about the odd use of the passive "put to death," that is, how believers are "put to death," and about the meaning of the phrase "through the body of Christ," the answer is not hard to find. Paul is referring to baptism and its consequences. Although the phrase "through the body of Christ" may be a way of referring to Christ's death, the more likely interpretation connects the phrase with the conviction that through baptism believers are united to the body of Christ. Paul used this imagery in 1 Cor 12:12–13, and he will use it again later in Rom 12:4–5. The same is true for the odd use of the passive, "put to death." It immediately calls to mind Rom 6:3, where Paul used a passive verb to claim that in baptism believers have been baptized (ἐβαπτίσθημεν) into Christ's death. In 7:4, Paul builds on his interpretation of baptism found in 6:3–4, that in baptism believers were baptized into Christ's death; they were buried with him through baptism into his death. In 6:5–14, Paul then explained that one result of this death with Christ through baptism is the separation of believers from sin so that sin should no longer reign in their mortal bodies, so that they would no longer obey its desires (ταῖς ἐπιθυμίαις αὐτοῦ). Rather, they should present themselves to God as if risen from the dead and present their members to God not as instruments of wickedness but as instruments of righteousness. In 7:4, Paul now claims that another result is that, because of this same baptism and its consequences, believers have also been put to death in relation

---

[4] In 7:5–6, Paul moves from the second person plural of 7:4 to the first person plural and so associates himself with his Roman Christian audience.

[5] E.g., "risen from the dead" (6:4, 8; 7:4); "newness" (6:4, 8; 7:4); "old," "oldness" (6:6; 7:6); "death" (6:3, 4, 5, 8, 9; 7:5); "die" (6:2, 7, 8, 10); "serve" (6:6; 7:6); "members" (6:13; 7:5); "sin" (6:1, 2, 5, 7, 10; 7:5).

to the law. What is the logic behind this further claim? Were Paul's argument put into syllogistic form, it would run something like this: the law has power over a person (only) as long as the person is alive; but in baptism believers have been "put to death" through the body of Christ; therefore, as a result of baptism, the law no longer has power over them.[6] The major premise is an uncontroversial legal principle (to which Paul had appended the equally uncontroversial example of Jewish marriage law), and the minor premise is a restatement of Paul's interpretation of baptism in 6:3–4. The conclusion is that, as a result of baptism, the law no longer has any power over believers.

In 7:5–6, Paul expands on this argument by contrasting the Roman Christians' situation prior to belief in Christ with their present situation. He once again uses vocabulary and viewpoints found in Romans 6 but draws consequences from these for a change in believers' relationship to the law.

> For when [ὅτε] we were in the flesh [ἐν τῇ σαρκί], the sinful passions [τὰ παθήματα τῶν ἁμαρτιῶν] provoked through the law [τὰ διὰ νόμου] were at work in our members [ἐν τοῖς μέλεσιν ἡμῶν] so that we bore fruit for death. But now [νυνὶ δέ] we have been released from the law [κατηργήθημεν ἀπὸ τοῦ νόμου] by dying [ἀποθανόντες] to that by which we were bound [ἐν ᾧ κατειχόμεθα] so that we might serve in the newness of the Spirit [ἐν καινότητι πνεύματος] and not in the oldness of the letter [παλαιότητι γράμματος].

The temporal character of the contrast is emphasized by the "then" and "now" contrast at the beginning of each verse. In order to understand the contrast properly, one must keep in mind that Paul is trying to explain more clearly how in baptism believers have been put to death "in relation to the law" (7:4). In the past, before baptism, their sinful passions, those provoked through the law, were at work in them so that they bore fruit for death (7:5). Paul seems to be using the phrase "sinful passions" (τὰ παθήματα τῶν ἁμαρτιῶν) here with the same meaning as the mortal body's "desires" (ταῖς ἐπιθυμίαις) in 6:12.[7] Their past was one dominated by the vices condemned in Greco-Roman ethical discourses. Paul also connects these sinful passions in some way with the law. What specifically that way is, what the specific meaning of διὰ νόμου is in this context, will become clear only in 7:7–25. What is important at this point for his argument is simply that Paul makes the connection between the two.

In 7:6, Paul then contrasts all this with believers' present situation. They are now released from the law (ἀπὸ τοῦ νόμου) by dying to that by which (ἐν ᾧ) they were held. As a result, they now serve (δουλεύειν) God in the newness of the Spirit rather than in the oldness of the law. In describing the result, Paul once again uses the verb "to serve," "to be a slave" to describe this new situation, a verb he also used in 6:6 to emphasize that believers' present ethical behavior should not be at all disorderly or chaotic.[8] But his emphasis in 7:6 is on what this change means for believers' relationship to the law: "But now we have been released from the law by dying to that by which we were bound."

---

[6] One must again remember that in rhetorical arguments the form of the syllogism is often suppressed lest the speech end up being logical but so uninteresting as to be unpersuasive.

[7] He has already used them synonymously in Gal 5:24.

[8] See also δοῦλος in 6:16, 17, 19, 20.

The point Paul is arguing in this verse is not immediately clear. Part of the lack of clarity concerns interpretation of the clause "dying to that by which we were bound"—more specifically, the antecedent of the relative "that by which" (ἐν ᾧ).[9] Most interpreters take the relative pronoun as grammatically masculine and think the antecedent is "the law." They appeal, quite understandably, to the preceding phrase ("we have been released from the law") and to the opening clause in 7:4 ("we have been put to death in relation to the law [τῷ νόμῳ]").[10]

But there is good reason to think otherwise. First, if one takes the antecedent of the relative pronoun as "the law," then the first two clauses about being released from the law and dying to the law seem redundant. They are two different ways of saying the same thing. But Paul seems to be saying more. The second clause is an explanation why the first clause is so. Second, it also seems clear that Paul means what he writes in 7:6 to be parallel to 7:5 and to stand in contrast to it. But if the relative "that by which" in 7:6 refers to "the law," then the phrase "the sinful passions" in 7:5 has no parallel in 7:6. If the relative "that by which" is neuter, however, rather than masculine, then it refers collectively to the "sinful passions" in the preceding verse.[11] Correlative to this, the aorist participle ἀποθανόντες ("dying") is easily understood as a circumstantial participle indicating cause.[12] This interpretation makes better sense of the immediate argument Paul is making because it provides an explanation for believers' release from the law. Paul's argument, then, in 7:5–6 is that in baptism believers have been released from the law by dying to *the sinful passions* by which they were once held. This interpretation better maintains the parallelism between 7:5 and 7:6. More important, it makes better sense of his immediate argument in that it offers an explanation for believers' being released from the law. If believers die in baptism to the sinful passions by which they were once held, then the law through which these sinful passions were once provoked no longer has a function and so is something from which believers have been released. The point Paul wants to make is that believers' release from the law is the result of having died to the sinful passions by which they were once held.

This interpretation also makes much better sense within the immediately preceding context of Romans 6. In this regard, the parallel between "dying [ἀποθανόντες] to that by which we were held" in 7:6 and "you have been put to death [ἐθανατώθητε] to the law" in 7:4 is somewhat misleading in that, although related, the two verbs are different.[13] The same verb that appears in 7:6 (the second aorist of ἀποθνῄσκω), however, also occurs in 6:2, 7, 10, and, in all three cases, the dying that takes place is to sin (ἁμαρτία). In addition, Paul went on in 6:15–23 to describe the result of this dying to sin as becoming slaves to righteousness or slaves to God. This is the same result Paul describes at the end of 7:6. Believers now serve (δουλεύειν) God in the newness of the Spirit and not in the oldness of the letter. The broader

---

[9] Everyone agrees the phrase is an ellipsis for τούτῳ ἐν ᾧ. This is quite common in Greek. The question is what the τούτῳ refers to.

[10] Byrne, *Romans*, 215; Cranfield, *Romans*, 1:338–39; Dunn, *Romans*, 365–66; Wilckens, *Römer*, 2:69–70.

[11] Fitzmyer (*Romans*, 459) mentions this as a possibility.

[12] See Smythe, *Greek Grammar*, §2064.

[13] Θανατόω in 7:4 but ἀποθνῄσκω in 7:6.

context, then, also argues for taking the antecedent of the relative ἐν ᾧ in 7:6 as "the sinful passions" in 7:5 rather than "the law."

When one steps back from the details of this analysis, the overall contours of Paul's arguments in 7:1–6 become clearer. Paul takes both his reinterpretation of baptism as a baptism into the death of Christ and his strongly ethical emphasis on the consequences of baptism and combines them with the commonly accepted legal principle about the cessation of the binding force of the law at death. All this then serves as the basis for his explanation of how in baptism believers, by dying with Christ to sinful passions, have also been released from the law. At the same time, he prefaces his explanation with the example taken from Jewish marriage law. This example leads his audience to understand the explanation as one that, though maintaining that believers are released from the binding force of the law, does not impugn the value of the law itself.

There are, however, two phrases in 7:1–6 whose ambivalence also serves to introduce Paul's fuller explanation of both the goodness of the law and its limitations. The first phrase is found at the end of 7:6. Believers now serve God "in the newness of the Spirit and not in the oldness of the letter."[14] Obviously, in Paul's mind, the first is superior to the second. But there is still an ambivalence to the contrast. Although the first is superior, does it mean that the second is not simply inferior but also wrong? The second and even more ambivalent phrase is found in 7:5: "the sinful passions provoked through the law [τὰ διὰ νόμου]." What is the point of characterizing the sinful passions as τὰ διὰ νόμου? The Greek preposition διά ("through") with the genitive indicates that the sinful passions are somehow provoked through the law or that they work through the law or by means of the law. If this is so, what does this say about the law? The obviously intentional ambivalence on Paul's part about the oldness of the letter and especially about the relationship of the law to the sinful passions serves as the occasion for Paul explicitly to face up to how he understands the character of the law in 7:7–25.

ROMANS 7:7–25: SPEECH-IN-CHARACTER ABOUT THE GOODNESS OF THE LAW AND HUMAN LIMITATIONS

Over the centuries Rom 7:7–25 has generated diverse and conflicting interpretations. At the center is the issue of the identity of the speaker here. Paul has cast most of the passage in the first person singular, and the question is who the "I" is. Is it Paul himself, or is it someone else?[15] The simplest answer is that it is Paul himself. But when one looks more closely at the passage, this apparent simplicity quickly dissolves. Does the "I" refer to Paul's own present experience as a believer? Or does it

---

[14] As in 5:5, Paul mentions the Spirit but makes nothing more of it. He does not deal with the role of the Spirit until Romans 8. The significance of this will become clearer in the analysis of Romans 8 below in ch. 10 (pp. 273–98).

[15] Surveys of the various opinions listed below are found in Cranfield, *Romans*, 1:342–47; Fitzmyer, *Romans*, 463–65; and Jan Lambrecht, *The Wretched "I" and Its Liberation: Paul in Romans 7 and 8* (Louvain Theological and Pastoral Monographs 14; Louvain: Peeters, 1992), 59–91.

refer to his past experience, that is, his experience prior to his call or conversion? Or does it refer to his past experience but viewed from the perspective of his present experience of faith? If the passage is not autobiographical, however, to whom does the "I" refer? Here again there have been a variety of suggestions, many of which see the "I" as a typical figure of some sort. Is the "I" the typical Jew's experience of the law, whether as seen by himself or as seen from Paul's point of view? Or does the "I" represent the experience of the believer? If so, is it the believer's past experience or the believer's present experience? If it is the believer's present experience, does it represent the experience of all believers, or does it represent the experience of believers who are still immature and struggling? More broadly still, does it represent the experience of human beings in general; that is, is it one of our earliest and classical examples of what Krister Stendahl has called the "introspective conscience of the West"?[16] In a quite different vein, is Paul speaking in this passage in the name of Adam? Or is he using the "I" as a way of rehearsing the experience of human beings through different stages in the course of history from Adam through life under the Mosaic law?

Given this kaleidoscope of interpretations, one is tempted to give up in despair of ever understanding Paul's purposes in writing this passage. Yet the passage itself and the larger argument of which it is a part offer important clues to its interpretation. One clue is a matter of detail whereas the others are of a broader sort. It is best to begin with the detail. This is found in 8:2. Although 8:1–4 marks a new stage in his argument, Paul begins by referring back to 7:24–25, the anguished first-person-singular cry to be delivered from the sinful body by one who serves the law of God with his mind and with his flesh serves the law of sin. In 8:1–2, Paul gives a response to this cry: "There is therefore now no condemnation for those who are in Christ Jesus. For the law of the Spirit of life in Christ Jesus has set you [σε] free from the law of sin and of death." The "you" in 8:2 is obviously a reference to the anguished speaker of 7:24–25.[17] This means that the speaker in 7:24–25, and therefore in 7:7–25 as a whole, is someone other than Paul, since Paul refers to the speaker in 8:2 as "you." Thus Paul does not intend 7:7–25 to be autobiographical but is giving a speech-in-character.[18] Who that speaker is will become clear only later (see below). That the speaker of 7:7–25 is someone other than Paul is also supported by Paul's own description of his previous observance of the law in Gal 1:13–14 and Phil 3:5–6. In neither passage does he express the kind of anguish over the inability to observe the Mosaic law found in Rom 7:7–25. Rather, Paul seemed proud of his own earlier observance.

---

[16] Stendahl, *Paul among Jews and Gentiles*, 78–96.

[17] There are variant readings for the σε of 8:2: σε (‫א‬ B F G 1506* 1739* a b sy^p Tertullian Ambrosiaster); με (A D 1739^c 1881 Byz lat sy^h sa Clement); ἡμᾶς (Ψ bo Methodius). The third reading is clearly a secondary modification introduced to make the passage apply to all Christians. Of the first two readings, the first is almost certain. It is the more difficult reading, since με would have brought 8:2 into line with the first person singular in 7:7–25. The first reading also has the weight of the combination of Alexandrian and Western witnesses on its side. See Metzger, *Textual Commentary*, 456.

[18] Stowers, *Rereading of Romans*, 281–82, especially has rightly insisted on this, but other recent commentators on Romans also make this point.

If Paul is not speaking autobiographically in 7:7–25, he is not speaking in propria persona. Rather, he is taking on a different persona. This technique (προσω-ποποιία or ἠθοποιία in Greek and *fictio personae* or *conformatio* in Latin) was a well-known rhetorical figure in the ancient world.[19] Essentially it is "speech-in-character," in which the writer or speaker produces a speech in which he takes on the character of someone else.[20] Perhaps the clearest definition comes from Theon's *Progymnasmata:* "Speech-in-character is the introduction of a character who speaks words clearly appropriate to himself and to the matters being presented."[21] This character may be a real historical person or someone fictional.[22] The character need not be an individual, whether real or fictional, but may be typical of a certain kind of person, such as a husband or a general.[23] The character may not even be "personal" at all but may be gods or the dead or cities or whole peoples, even virtues and vices.[24] Its use was meant to add vividness and color and to appeal to the emotions of the audience, often the emotion of pity.[25] It is perhaps for this reason that speeches-in-character were fairly common in diatribes.[26] Writers on the subject frequently emphasized the importance of composing the speech in a way that was appropriate to the character being imitated.[27] From the prominence given to it in the handbooks of rhetorical exercises *(progymnasmata)* of Theon and Hermogenes, it must have been part of the standard fare of an ancient rhetorical education and so almost certainly part of Paul's own Greek education.[28] In most cases, the character's identity was explicitly mentioned at the beginning of the speech-in-character. But as Quintilian (*Inst.* 9.2.36–37) points out, this was not always necessary. The speech-in-character could begin (as it does in Rom 7:7) without identifying the speaker. In such a case, the speech-in-character is combined with another figure, that of the ellipse *(detractio)*, which here consists in the omission of any explicit indication of who the speaker is.

---

[19] For descriptions of this figure, see Theon, *Prog.* 2.115.11–118.5; Hermogenes, *Prog.* 9.1–43; Demetrius, *Eloc.* 265–266; *Rhet. Her.* 4.66; Cicero, *Inv.* 1.99–100; *Part. or.* 55, 57; *De or.* 3.205; *Or. Brut.* 85, 138; *Top.* 45; Quintilian, *Inst.* 1.8.3; 3.8.49–54; 4.1.28, 69; 6.1.3, 25–27; 9.2.29–39; 11.1.39–41.

[20] The translation of the word as "speech-in-character" is from James M. Butts, "The *Progymnasmata* of Theon: A New Text with Translation and Commentary" (Ph.D. Diss., Claremont Graduate School, 1987). The best treatment of speech-in-character in relation to Paul is by Stanley K. Stowers, "Romans 7.7–25 as a Speech-in-Character (προσωποποιία)," in *Paul in His Hellenistic Context* (ed. Troels Engberg-Pedersen; Minneapolis: Fortress, 1995), 180–202.

[21] Theon, *Prog.* 2.118.12–14.

[22] Quintilian, *Inst.* 4.1.28, 69.

[23] Theon, *Prog.* 2.115.14–19; Hermogenes, *Prog.* 9.13–17.

[24] Hermogenes, *Prog.* 9.4–6; *Rhet. Her.* 4.66; Cicero, *Inv.* 1.99–100; Quintilian, *Inst.* 9.2.31.

[25] Demetrius, *Eloc.* 265–266; Theon, *Prog.* 2.117.6–32; Hermogenes, *Prog.* 9.28–35; Quintilian, *Inst.* 4.1.28; 6.1.25–27; 9.2.29–30.

[26] E.g., see Epictetus, *Diatr.* 1.4.28–29; 1.9.12–15; 1.26.5–7; 3.24.68–70.

[27] Theon, *Prog.* 2.115.11–2.117.6; Hermogenes, *Prog.* 9.42–43; Quintilian, *Inst.* 3.8.49–51; 11.1.39–40.

[28] See Abraham J. Malherbe, *Social Aspects of Early Christianity* (2d ed.; Philadelphia: Fortress, 1983), 29–59; Martin Hengel, *The Pre-Christian Paul* (Philadelphia: Trinity, 1991), 34–37; Murphy-O'Connor, *Paul: A Critical Life,* 46–51.

The Identity of the Speaker in Romans 7:7–25 and
Greco-Roman Philosophy

Since Paul omitted any indication of who the speaker was in Rom 7:7–25, he must have thought the speaker's identity would be clear enough to his Roman audience. Given the variety of opinions listed above, the same is plainly not the case for the rest of us. To understand the identity of the speaker, we have to take the more roundabout way of first trying to understand the content and, to some extent, the apparent purpose or function of the speech before grasping the identity of the speaker. In addition, we need to be aware of how the speaker, whoever he is, seems to speak about himself. Fortunately, there are several clues in the speech itself and in its context that point in a particular direction.

First, 7:7–25, like 7:1–6, is in various ways concerned with the character and function of the Mosaic law. The word νόμος ("law") appears sixteen times in the chapter. Paul is concerned to show the relationship of the law to sin and to death, two central realities also in Romans 5–6, and to defend the goodness of the Mosaic law. The first concern lies behind the overall structure of 7:7–25. Romans 7:7–12 is meant to answer the rhetorical question in 7:7: "What shall we say? Is the law sin? Certainly not!" Romans 7:13–25 is meant to answer a second rhetorical question in 7:13: "Therefore, did what is good [i.e., the law] become death for me? Certainly not!" In the course of answering these questions, the speaker strongly defends the goodness of the law: "So the law [ὁ νόμος] is holy, and the commandment [ἡ ἐντολή] is holy and just and good" (7:12); "For we know that the law is spiritual" (7:14); "If I do that which I do not wish, I agree with the law that it is holy" (7:16); "I take delight in the law in my inner self" (7:22).

Second, while defending the goodness of the law and strongly denying that it is sin or that it leads to death, the speaker also points more specifically to the function of the law and especially to the limitations involved in this function. In 7:7, the speaker claims that he did not know sin except through the law and, in 7:12, that the purpose of the law was so that (ἵνα) sin might become manifest and so that (ἵνα) sin might become utterly sinful through the commandment of the law. The function and purpose of the law are to provide those who encounter it with clear knowledge of what is sinful. But there is also a further consequence of this knowledge that the law provides. Without the law commanding that "you shall not desire" (οὐκ ἐπιθυμήσεις, Exod 20:17; Deut 5:18), the speaker claims he would not have known what desire (τὴν ἐπιθυμίαν) is (Rom 7:7). Further, sin, by using the commandment against desire as an opportunity (ἀφορμήν), produced all manner of desire in him. As a result, the commandment prohibiting desire, which was meant to lead to life, led to death instead (7:10). In 7:14–23, the speaker goes on to describe this terrifying situation in more detail, that he, though agreeing with the law that desire is wrong, nevertheless is incapable of resisting it, that he does not do what he knows is good but instead does the evil he does not want to do. In this sense, the law is limited: it provides the knowledge of what is sinful, but it does not provide the power or capacity to avoid doing what is sinful. Indeed, sin uses this knowledge of what is sinful as a way of provoking the speaker to act sinfully even though he does not "want" to. From the experience of the speaker, the function and purpose of the law are to provide knowledge of sin, and so the law is good and holy. But sin also perversely uses such knowledge to provoke all kinds of sinful desires in the speaker, desires that the speaker finds himself unable to resist.

The third clue is found in the way Paul uses the quotation "you shall not desire" (Exod 20:17; Deut 5:18) from the Decalogue in Rom 7:7. This quotation serves as the starting point for the whole of the speech-in-character that follows (7:7–25). Paul does not, however, quote the whole tenth commandment but only its first two words, οὐκ ἐπιθυμήσεις ("you shall not desire"). He does not list the objects that it is forbidden to desire: "your neighbor's house . . . your neighbor's wife, or his male servant or his female servant, or his ox, or his ass, or anything that is your neighbor's." In one way, this is perfectly understandable. Paul expected his audience to be familiar with the Decalogue and so with the objects that it was forbidden to desire; there was no need to quote the whole passage. Although this is true enough, his primary reason for presenting this truncated quotation lies elsewhere: he is not interested here in the objects forbidden to desire but in desire (ἐπιθυμία) itself. This is clear from 7:7–8: "For I should not have known [οὐκ ᾔδειν] desire [ἐπιθυμίαν] if the law did not say, 'You shall not desire.' But sin, finding opportunity [ἀφορμήν] through the commandment, worked in me all sorts of desire [πᾶσαν ἐπιθυμίαν]." Whereas the tenth commandment, in the context of the Decalogue, is concerned with the social disruption caused by coveting, or desiring, what belongs to other members of the community, Paul is interested in desire itself, desire as an individual vice. By taking the tenth commandment to forbid the vice of desire, he has moved it from its original context within the Decalogue and placed it within a different kind of context, that of popular Greco-Roman moral philosophy.

Desire (ἐπιθυμία) was one of the principal vices in Greco-Roman moral philosophy. Different philosophical schools understood the nature of desire differently and consequently understood the remedies for it differently. Whereas Aristotle and the Peripatetics thought that the virtuous person moderated his or her appetites, including desire, the Epicureans, the Stoics, and the Middle Platonists, for the most part, urged their extirpation.[29] Paul's anthropology does not fall exclusively into any one of these schools but is more ad hoc.[30] That said, his overall evaluation of desire, as distinct from any elaborate theory, is much closer to that of the Stoics than to those of Aristotle or the Epicureans.[31] Like the Stoics, when Paul uses the noun "desire" or the verb "to desire" (ἐπιθυμέω), he almost always uses it negatively, indicating vices.[32] The same is true for words referring to the passions in general.[33] This

---

[29] For an analysis of these different approaches, see A. A. Long, *Hellenistic Philosophy* (2nd ed.; London: Duckworth, 1986) 56–59, 179–209; A. A. Long and D. N. Sedley, *The Hellenistic Philosophers* (2 vols.; Cambridge: Cambridge University Press, 1987), 1:102–25, 410–23; 2:104–29, 404–18; Nussbaum, *Therapy of Desire*.

[30] See David E. Aune, "Human Nature and Ethics in Hellenistic Philosophical Traditions and Paul: Some Issues and Problems," in *Paul in His Hellenistic Context* (ed. Troels Engberg-Pedersen; Minneapolis: Fortress, 1995), 291–312.

[31] This has been emphasized most recently by Engberg-Pedersen, *Paul and the Stoics*.

[32] The noun ἐπιθυμία: 1 Thess 4:5; Gal 5:16, 24; Rom 1:24; 6:12; 13:14; the verb ἐπιθυμέω: Gal 5:17; 1 Cor 10:6; Rom 13:9. The noun is used in a positive sense only in 1 Thess 2:17 and Phil 1:23.

[33] The nouns πάθος (1 Thess 4:5; Rom 1:26) and πάθημα (Gal 5:24; Phil 3:10).

is unlike Aristotle, for whom the passions, when moderated and controlled by reason, have a proper place in the life of a virtuous person. Paul is clearly not an Epicurean, in that pleasure (ἡδονή), however interpreted, is obviously not a goal for him. Indeed, he never uses the word in any of his letters.

There were two common ways of describing the experience of desire in Greco-Roman philosophy and especially in the Stoics. Both are reflected in the way Paul describes desire. The first description is in terms of internal disorder or conflict between aspects of the human person. This is found in Rom 7:7–25, where mind or the inner self is set against the flesh or the law at work in one's members. It is also found in Gal 5:17 in the stark antithesis between the Spirit and the flesh. This view of desire as a source of internal chaos or struggle is common in Greco-Roman moral philosophy. For example, the Stoics thought that desire, an irrational craving for some apparent good, like all the passions, was an appetite disobedient to reason.[34] The second description is that desire has a seemingly overpowering character to it.[35] Again this characteristic is found in Rom 7:7–25, where, because of desire, the speaker is unable to do what he knows is right and wants to do. This too is a common way to characterize desire in Greco-Roman philosophical texts. Stoics routinely wrote about the overpowering (βιαστικόν) character of the passions, including desire, and how people are carried away by them and unable to be obedient to reason.[36] Paul has taken over and used these popular philosophical motifs about the passions, particularly desire, in 7:7–25 as a way of interpreting the tenth commandment.

Paul, however, was hardly the only Jew to do this. Other Hellenistic Jews also used these popular philosophical motifs to interpret this commandment. What Paul wants to argue in Romans 7 needs to be seen in this context. One finds two examples in 4 Maccabees and Philo. Fourth Maccabees was probably written a generation after Paul, perhaps in Antioch, by a Diaspora Jew who had a good Greek rhetorical education. The work exhibits a kind of eclectic Stoicism popular at the time. The author's thesis in 4 Macc 1:12–13 is that reason (λογισμός) is able to be sovereign over the passions (τὰ πάθη). He argues this thesis through a series of examples. The most important example is the story of the martyrdoms of Eleazer, the seven brothers, and their mother, first found in 2 Maccabees. Two of the earlier examples he gives, however, are more helpful for our purposes, those of the patriarch Joseph and King David. Joseph was able to overcome desires (ἐπιθυμίαι) for the enjoyment of beauty, that is, the desire for intercourse with Potiphar's wife, through

[34] Stobaeus, *Ecl.* 2.90.7 (*SVF* 3:384). A similar sense of internal disorder or struggle between two aspects of the person is found in Aristotle, *Eth. nic.* 3.10–12; and, for the Epicureans, in Diogenes Laertius 10.127–28.

[35] The word "seemingly" is used here on purpose, since all the schools of Hellenistic philosophy thought that desire and the rest of the passions could be controlled or extirpated through philosophy.

[36] Stobaeus, *Ecl.* 2.89.4–90.6 (*SVF* 3:389); see also Epictetus, *Diatr.* 2.16.47; 2.18.8–9; and Galen, *Plac. Hip. et Plat.* 4.2.10–18 (*SVF* 3:462). For an analogous view in Aristotle, see *Eth. nic.* 3.5 –21; and for the Epicureans, see D.L. 10.149. The references to Galen are according to the numbering system found in Galen, *On the Doctrines of Hippocrates and Plato* (ed. and trans. Phillip De Lacy; 3 vols.; Corpus medicorum graecorum 5.4.1.2 (Berlin: Akademie, 1980–1984). The translations are also from De Lacy's edition.

reason (λογισμός) (4 Macc 2:1–6).[37] David, thirsty after a day of campaigning against the Philistines, was able through reason (λογισμός) to overcome his irrational desire (ἀλόγιστος ἐπιθυμία) for water (3:6–18).[38] When he gives the example of Joseph, the author in 2:4–6 explicitly quotes the tenth commandment:

> Not only is reason proved to rule over the frenzied urge of sexual desire, but also over every desire [πάσης ἐπιθυμίας]. Thus the law says, "You shall not desire [οὐκ ἐπιθυμήσεις] your neighbor's wife or anything that is your neighbor's." In fact, since the law has told us not to desire, I could prove to you all the more that reason is able to control desires.

The author of 4 Maccabees interprets the tenth commandment in much the same way that Paul does in Rom 7:14–25, as forbidding the vice of desire. Earlier, in 4 Macc 1:15–17, the author explains the role the law plays in overcoming the passions:

> Now reason [λογισμός] is the mind [νοῦς] that with right reasoning [ὀρθοῦ λογοῦ] prefers the life of wisdom. Wisdom [σοφία], next, is the knowledge of divine and human matters and the causes of these. This, in turn, is education in the law [ἡ τοῦ νόμου παιδεία], by which we learn divine matters reverently and human affairs to our advantage.

The law is that by which a person learns what wisdom is, and wisdom is the attribute of the mind by which reason can function properly. The role of the law, then, is educational. Through it a person learns what is right and what is wrong. This is again a role quite similar to the one Paul attributes to the law in Rom 7:7–25. Three other similarities between 4 Maccabees and Rom 7:7–25 are also important to highlight. First, the author of 4 Maccabees describes David's extreme thirst as an "irrational desire" (ἀλόγιστος ἐπιθυμία), which "tormented and inflamed him, undid and consumed him" (4 Macc 3:11). Desire is a passion that virtually overwhelms the person. Second, the relationship of reason to desire and the passions is one of conflict in which reason must conquer desire and all the other passions (3:17; 6:33; 7:4; 13:2, 7). Finally, the author of 4 Maccabees, like Paul, locates the capacity to act in accord with right reason in the mind (νοῦς) of human beings. It is the temperate mind (ὁ σώφρων νοῦς) that overcomes the passions (1:35; 2:16, 18; 3:17).[39] Although the author of 4 Maccabees is much more explicitly philosophical, both he and Paul nevertheless are working with many of the same categories and inhabit similar worlds of thought.

When Philo discusses the tenth commandment in *Decal.* 142–153, 173–174 and in *Spec.* 4.79–131, he also takes it in the broad sense of forbidding the familiar vice of desire. Philo's treatment of desire is much more extended and more philosophically sophisticated than that found either in Paul or in 4 Maccabees.[40] For

---

[37] See Gen 39:7–12.

[38] See 2 Sam 23:13–17; 1 Chr 11:15–19.

[39] For a sense of the complexity of the use of the word νοῦς in Greek philosophy, see Francis E. Peters, *Greek Philosophical Terms: A Historical Lexicon* (New York: New York University Press, 1967), 132–39.

[40] Philo's anthropology or psychology is primarily Platonic, but he is also heavily influenced by Stoicism, especially in his ethics.

Philo, desire stands at the opposite extreme from reason (λόγος) or mind (νοῦς) (*Spec.* 4.92–94, 123). Because he is also aware that there are four primary passions in Stoicism (desire, pleasure, fear, and pain), he tries to explain why Moses singles out desire in the tenth commandment rather than any of the other three. Of all the passions, desire is the hardest to deal with (*Decal.* 142); it is the font of all evils and the originating passion (*Spec.* 4.84–85). Philo characterizes desire in basically the same way Paul and 4 Maccabees do, as a passion that overwhelms a person (*Decal.* 146, 149; *Spec.* 4.79–82, 92–94). The role of the law is obviously to forbid desire. But the law also forbids things that can foment desire. It is under this commandment, for example, that Philo places the various food regulations of the law, which he emphasizes are also symbolic ways of forbidding various aspects of desire (*Spec.* 4.100–125). Though it is by far the most philosophically sophisticated, Philo's basic treatment of desire is of a piece with both Paul and 4 Maccabees. Romans 7:7–25, then, reflects broader discussions within Hellenistic Judaism about the function of the law in relation to theories about the nature of the passions, particularly desire, in Greco-Roman philosophy. As will be seen shortly, however, Paul turns these Hellenistic Jewish discussions, which he has in common with Philo and 4 Maccabees, in a quite different direction.

A fourth and very important clue to the identity of the speaker is provided by allusions in Rom 7:15–16, 18–21 that resemble several lines from Euripides' *Medea*.[41]

> For I do not know [οὐ γινώσκω] what I bring about. For I do not do [οὐ ... πράσσω] what I want to [ὃ θέλω], but I do [ποιῶ] what I hate [ὃ μισῶ]. Yet if I do [ποιῶ] what I do not want [ὃ οὐ θέλω], I agree with the law that it is right. (Rom 7:15–16)

> I can want [τὸ θέλειν] what is right [τὸ καλόν], but I cannot bring it about [τὸ κατεργάζεσθαι]. For I do not do [οὐ ... ποιῶ] the good [ἀγαθόν] I want [ὃ θέλω], but the evil [κακόν] I do not want [ὃ οὐ θέλω] I do [πράσσω]. But if I do what I do not want, it is no longer I who brings it about [οὐκέτι ἐγὼ κατεργάζομαι] but sin which dwells within me [ἡ οἰκοῦσα ἐν ἐμοὶ ἁμαρτία]. So I find this principle [τὸν νόμον] at work, that when I want to do what is right [τῷ θέλοντι ἐμοὶ ποιεῖν τὸ καλόν], what is evil is ready at hand (Rom 7:18–21)[42]

These verses are the anguished expression of the conflict between what the speaker wants to do (τὸ θέλειν) and what he actually does (πράσσω, ποιῶ), between wanting to do what is right (τὸ ἀγαθόν, τὸ καλόν) and actually doing what is evil (τὸ κακόν). The roots of this lie in the conflict between the mind (ὁ νοῦς, 7:23, 25), on the one hand, and desire (ἡ ἐπιθυμία, 7:7–8) and the other passions (τὰ παθήματα, 7:5), on the other.

The lines in Euripides' *Medea* to which they are related come in the fifth scene of the play, at the end of a speech Medea has made about her two sons just after they

---

[41] This insight has been most clearly developed by Stowers in *Rereading of Romans*, 260–64, 269–72; and "Romans 7.7–25," 198–202. Although I disagree with Stowers at several points in what follows, I am clearly dependent on his basic insights.

[42] Although it is difficult, I have tried to maintain the play on words in translating this passage. The Greek is very concise.

have left the stage. She expresses her anguish over the overwhelming anger that is compelling her to murder them as part of her vengeance against Jason, her unfaithful husband:

> . . . Yet I am conquered by evils.
> And I understand the deeds I am about to do are evil,
> But anger is greater than my resolves,
> Anger, the cause for mortals of the greatest evils. (*Med.* 1077b–1080 [Way, LCL])[43]

These lines express an anguish similar to that found in Rom 7:14–25, the conflict between knowing what is right and doing what is evil, between rational resolve and overwhelming passion. The language in the two passages, however, is different. Paul is neither quoting nor paraphrasing these lines from Euripides. Rather, he is using what had become a commonplace in Greco-Roman ethical debates about how to understand the conflict between wanting to do what is right and yet not actually being able to do it, even doing what one knows to be wrong.

As early as the third century B.C., the Stoic philosopher Chrysippus (280–207) used these lines from Euripides as a parade example of this conflict.[44] This debate concerned several distinct issues. One was whether the conflict between willing and doing was entirely within the mind or ruling faculty (τὸ ἡγεμονικόν) of a human being. Most Stoics, including Chrysippus, thought that it was. Others, such as Galen, used this example from Euripides as evidence that the conflict was between the reasoning faculty (τὸ λογιστικόν) of a human being and other faculties, such as the appetitive (τὸ ἐπιθυμητικόν) and the passionate (τὸ θυμικόν).[45] Related to this was the issue of whether a person could know what was right and yet not do it, that is, whether not acting ethically was due to ignorance or to being overwhelmed by passions even though one knew what was right.[46]

The details of these debates need not detain us. What is important for understanding Paul is the language that was used. One apparently common framework for the debate was the relationship between knowing what is right, willing what is right, and doing what is right. This is found in several texts from the Stoic philosopher Epictetus that illustrate the contrast between willing and doing:

> I want something [θέλω] and it does not happen; and what creature is more wretched than I? I do not want something [οὐ θέλω], and it does happen; and what creature is more wretched than I? Medea, for example, because she could not endure this, came to the point of killing her children. In this respect at least hers was the act of a great spirit. For she had the proper conception of what it means for anyone's wishes [ἃ θέλει] not to come true. . . . For she did not know [οὐ ᾔδει] where the power lies to do [τὸ ποιεῖν] what we wish [ἃ θέλομεν]. (Epictetus, *Diatr.* 2.17.18–19, 21 [Oldfather, LCL])

---

43 . . . ἀλλὰ νικῶμαι κακοῖς.
    καὶ μανθάνω μὲν οἷα δρᾶν μέλλω κακά,
    θυμὸς δὲ κρείσσων τῶν ἐμῶν βουλευμάτων,
    ὅσπερ μεγίστων αἴτιος κακῶν βροτοῖς.
44 Galen, *Plac. Hip. et Plat.* 3.3.13; 4.6.20.
45 Galen, *Plat. Hip. et Plat.* 3.4.23–27.
46 Epictetus, *Diatr.* 1.28.5–9; 2.26.1–7.

Every error involves a contradiction. For since he who is in error does not want [οὐ θέλει] to err, but to be right, it is clear he is not doing what he wants [ὃ μὲν θέλει οὐ ποιεῖ].... He, then, who can show to each one the contradiction which causes him to err, and can clearly bring home to him how he is not doing what he wants [ὃ θέλει οὐ ποιεῖ], and is doing what he does not want [ὃ μὴ θέλει ποιεῖ] is strong in argument, and at the same time effective both in encouragement and refutation. (*Diatr.* 2.26.1, 4 [Oldfather, LCL])[47]

In these two passages, Epictetus, in agreement with Chrysippus, takes the common Stoic position that the conflict between wanting what is right and doing what is right is due to a mistaken judgment. If one can be shown how one's judgment is mistaken, the problem can be corrected. Another way he puts the issue is that Medea had been deceived (ἐξηπάτηται), but if she could have been shown how she had been deceived, she would not have murdered her sons.[48]

Epictetus is also aware that others claim that the issue is not a matter of knowledge but the conflict between knowing and willing, on the one hand, and being overwhelmed by passion and so being unable to do what one knows to be right and what one want to do, on the other hand. He is also aware that they use the lines from Euripides' *Medea* to support their position.[49] The physician Galen represents this other position very clearly, and he appeals to these lines from Euripides' *Medea*. After quoting them, Galen writes:

If Euripides was to give evidence in support of the teaching of Chrysippus [also the position of Epictetus], he should not have said that she understands [μανθάνειν] but the very opposite, that she is ignorant and does not understand what evils she is going to do. But to say that she knows [γινώσκειν] this and yet is overcome by anger—what is that but the act of a person who introduces two sources for Medea's appetitions, one by which we know [γιγνώσκομεν] things and have knowledge of them, which is the rational power, and another irrational (power) whose function it is to be angry? (Galen, *Plac. Hip. et Plat.* 4.6.20–21)

For Galen, the problem is not a matter of knowledge but the conflict between the rational and the irrational faculties of a human being.[50] Human beings know what is right, but they do not do what is right because they are overwhelmed by their passions. In Latin literature this same conflict finds its classic statement in the lines from Ovid's *Metamorphoses*, again spoken by Medea:

But some strange power *(nova vis)* draws me against my will *(invitam)*,
   and desire *(cupido)* persuades me one way,
and my mind *(mens)* another. I see *(video)* the better and approve,
but I follow the worse (Ovid, *Metam.* 7.19–21 [Miller, LCL]).[51]

---

[47] See also Epictetus, *Diatr.* 4.1.147.

[48] Epictetus, *Diatr.* 1.28.8.

[49] Epictetus, *Diatr.* 1.28.5–9.

[50] Galen, *Plac. Hip. et Plat.* 3.3.13–18; 3.4.23–27; 4.2.27. Galen uses the example of Medea in all three texts.

[51] *Sed trahit invitam nova vis, aliudque cupido,*
   mens aliud suadet: video meliora proboque,
   deteriora sequor.

Once again the problem is not knowledge. Medea knows what is right. Rather, it is this strange power, this desire that overwhelms her mind and forces her against her will *(invitam)* to do what she knows to be wrong.[52] This same sense of conflict that leads Medea to act against her own will *(invita)* is also found in Seneca, *Med.* 952, 991.

When one compares these passages with Rom 7:15–16, 18–21, it is not clear where Paul stands in these debates. Most of what is in these verses is quite un-Stoic. The problem is not one of knowledge. The speaker knows the law and what it requires, and knows that it is good. In addition, the conflict is not within the mind or the rational faculty of the speaker but between the speaker's mind and flesh, between knowing what is right and yet being overwhelmed by desire. But Paul can also have the speaker claim in 7:15 that "I do not know [οὐ γινώσκω] what I bring about" or in 7:11 that "sin . . . deceived me." These certainly would fit well into the standard Stoic view that the issue is really one of knowledge or of mistaken judgment.

Paul, however, is probably not taking a stand in these philosophical debates. Rather, what he seems to aware of and makes use of is the skein of thought and language used in these debates: the conflict between knowing, willing, and doing; the conflict between a rational faculty and an appetitive faculty; the experience of being deceived; and the seemingly overwhelming character of the passions. He would have learned this language as part of his Greek rhetorical education. Such an education would have included practice in the use of speech-in-character. And certainly such speeches often entailed taking on the character of famous figures from literature, including Medea.[53] This in itself is very helpful in understanding what Paul is driving at in 7:7–25. Since he is drawing on literary and philosophical commonplaces often connected with the figure of Medea (both in Greek and in Latin literature), he probably expects that his Roman Christian audience will recognize them and readily understand not only the literary allusions but also the kinds of internal conflicts to which he is appealing.

When one steps back from the mosaic of these four clues, a pattern emerges that points to both Paul's rhetorical context and his rhetorical strategy in Romans 7. This pattern also helps us to identity the speaker in 7:7–25. The rhetorical context of the passage is Hellenistic Jewish discussions of the function of the law, specifically the function of the tenth commandment. From the parallel discussions in both 4 Maccabees and Philo of Alexandria, we see that these discussions were deeply influenced by Greco-Roman philosophical debates, whether popular or learned, about how to lead a virtuous life and avoid vice. The function of the tenth commandment in the law was to prohibit the vice of desire. In prohibiting this vice, the tenth commandment, along with the rest of the law, also served an educational function in that it served as a guide to how one could lead a virtuous life. The function of the law was reinterpreted in the categories of Greco-Roman ethics. The understanding of the law by the speaker in 7:7–25 is, in important respects, similar to this. The law provides the knowledge that desire is sinful, and without the law the speaker would

---

[52] These words of Medea refer not to the murder of her children but to her initial contact with Jason, which eventually led to her murdering her own brother.

[53] See Theon, *Prog.* 2.94.17; 96.11; 123.22; Hermogenes, *Prog.* 2.19–22.

not have known this (7:7). The law is therefore holy, and its commandments are holy and just and good (7:12, 12, 14, 16). In affirming the goodness of the law, specifically the goodness of this function of the law, the speaker is in agreement with this Hellenistic Jewish understanding of the law and its value.

But Paul also has the speaker say much more than this. And this turns the speech in a very different direction and reveals Paul's strategy in using the speech. Although the speaker affirms the goodness of the law, he also anguishes over the tragic reality that he cannot observe the law. He knows what is right and intends to do what is right, but he is unable to do it because of the overwhelming character of desire, this power that resides in his members, in his flesh. In constructing this speech, Paul has made use of a common view in Greco-Roman ethical discussions of the often overwhelming character of desire and the other passions. More specifically, he has used the language of the ethical debates associated with the tragic figure of Medea to illustrate how knowledge of what is right and wrong, the knowledge furnished by the law, is not enough. The result is that the speaker can both affirm the goodness of the law and, at the same time, illustrate its limitations.

When one asks further who would have understood this kind of speech, the obvious answer would be Hellenistic Jews familiar with both this kind of defense of the goodness of the law and popular Greco-Roman discussions about the overwhelming nature of the passions and the tragic conflict between knowing and wanting what is right and yet doing what is wrong. But this is obviously not Paul's audience. Paul's audience is the Roman *Christian* community. Yet, as we have seen, the Roman Christian community was probably made up of a majority of ethnically Gentile Christians who, as believers in Jesus and without being circumcised, nevertheless observed the ethical commandments of the Mosaic law. Most of them were drawn from Gentiles who were originally sympathetic to, and associated with, the Roman Jewish community. These Roman Christians were also suspicious of, and even scandalized by, what they thought Paul's views of the law were. Paul's rhetorical strategy in Romans 7 is to illustrate how the Mosaic law can be both good and, at the same time, inadequate for living a virtuous life. This inadequacy is not due to what the law commands or forbids but to the overwhelming character of desire experienced by someone who wants to observe it. Paul tries to do all of this by using viewpoints and discussions that already would have been intelligible to them.

It is important to notice how Paul does this. He uses an illustration, the rhetorical device of speech-in-character. But why did he think this would have been effective? After all, most ancient rhetoricians thought of speech-in-character as important because of its vividness, not because of its value as an argument in itself.[54] This leads us to the fifth and final clue to the identity of the speaker in 7:7–25 and the function of the passage in Paul's larger argument. In 7:7–12, the speaker describes a change in his status and the consequences of this change. He claims that he would not have known sin except through the law, that he would not have known desire except that the law forbade it (7:7). There was a time (ποτέ) when he lived (ἔζων) without the law (χωρὶς νόμου). But when he came to know the commandment against desire, sin came to life (ἀνέζησεν), but he died (ἐγὼ δὲ ἀπέθανον)

---

[54] Quintilian, *Inst.* 9.2.29–30.

(7:9–10).[55] There was a time earlier in the speaker's life when he neither knew nor observed the law against desire. When he came to know and accept the law in its prohibition of desire, the law (which is good) and the commandment (which is intended to be life-giving) against desire had the paradoxical effect of bringing him death, since he could not observe the commandment because of the overwhelming character of desire.

Of whom is this a description? Whose experience is this meant to illustrate? The most natural answer is the Gentile majority of the Roman Christian community. There was a time when they did not know or observe the law. There was also a time when they did come to observe it, when they came to be associated with the Roman Jewish community. The way the speaker talks about this change fits this identification better than it fits any of the other possibilities mentioned earlier in this chapter. There is no mention of either circumcision or a full conversion to Judaism. Nor is there any indication the speaker is describing a coming-of-age, a point at which he becomes subject to the observance of the commandments. He is not describing a typical Jew or a typical Christian or Adam or the history of Israel. Rather, the speaker describes the situation of someone who, at one time, had not known the law but who had come to know it and accept its ethical commandments, symbolized here by the commandment forbidding desire. The speaker is describing what Paul thinks or imagines is the experience of the typical Gentile Roman Christian. The speaker is describing the situation of someone in whom Paul thinks the Gentile Roman Christians will see themselves and their own experience of trying to observe the ethical commandments of the law. In addition, the speaker does this by using language and categories about the function of the law from Hellenistic Judaism and about the nature of desire from Greco-Roman moral philsophy. Both would have been familiar to the Roman Christians and would have had a kind of antecedent plausibility for them.

This also explains why Paul uses speech-in-character and yet does not explicitly identify the speaker. He uses this figure of speech-in-character without any explicit identification of the speaker because it allows him to avoid directly accusing Gentile Roman Christians of not being able to observe successfully the ethical commandments of the law. It allows him to appeal to their experience, or what he suspects is their experience, in ways familiar to them, without ever having to argue directly over the issue of their observance or nonobservance of the ethical commandments of the law. It allows him to maintain the same rhetorical indirection he has already used a number of times in the letter.

---

[55] The meaning of ἀναζάω in 7:9 is "come to life" rather than "come to life again." See BDAG 62. The reason for this is the context. In 7:7–12, the speaker divides his life into *two* stages, one before he knew sin and the commandment not to desire and the other after he came to know sin through the law forbidding desire. For the translation of the word ἀναζάω as "come alive *again*" to make any sense, one would have to assume that the speaker also experienced another stage at which sin had been alive but then had somehow died, only to come to life again when the speaker came to know the law. This makes no sense in the context of 7:7–12. Most commentators also take it in the sense of "come to life." See Fitzmyer, *Romans*, 467; Dunn, *Romans*, 383; Byrne, *Romans*, 222; Sanday and Headlam, *Romans*, 180; Cranfield, *Romans*, 1:353; Wilckens, *Römer*, 2:282; Morris, *Romans*, 282.

Finally, it is also important to keep in mind the perspective from which Paul composed this speech-in-character: the perspective of the common faith in Christ he and the Roman Christians share. At first this may seem too obvious even to mention. In trying to redescribe indirectly through the speaker in 7:7–25 their experience of trying to observe the Mosaic law and the difficulties he assumes this entailed, Paul is not supposing that this is also identical to their present experience, that is, after they came to have faith in Christ. There is an asymmetry between the situation the speaker describes and the present situation of Roman Christian believers in Christ. This is important to remember lest one forget that 7:7–25 is meant to illustrate, albeit indirectly, something rather specific. Paul uses the speech-in-character to illustrate something he hopes the Roman Christians will see reflected in their own experience so that, through seeing this reflection, they come to understand how the law can be both good yet limited and something by which believers in Christ are no longer bound. The importance of this will become clear in the next section.

A Detailed Analysis of the Speech-in-Character of Romans 7:7–25

Once we understand Paul's rhetorical context and basic strategy in 7:7–25 as well as the identity of the speaker, we can turn to a more detailed analysis of the argument of the passage. The passage falls into three sections of somewhat unequal length (7:7–12, 13–23, 24–25). The first two sections each begin with a rhetorical question followed by the emphatic reply "Certainly not" (μὴ γένοιτο). This is identical to the way Paul began 6:1–14; 15–23. The final section begins with the anguished cry "Wretch that I am!" and is followed by the question "Who will deliver me from the body of this death?" In addition to the rhetorical questions, there is a temporal progression. In 7:7–12, the verbs are in the aorist tense; in 7:13–23, they are in the present tense; and in 7:24–25 the question is in the future tense. This concern with temporal sequence partially reflects the way in which speeches-in-character were supposed to be constructed. In *Prog.* 9.37–41, Hermogenes recommended that the speaker begin with the present, then move to the past, and finally to the future. The speaker in Rom 7:7–25 reverses the first two. He moves from past to present. Nevertheless, he does cover all three time periods. In addition, the way the speaker characterizes the three periods of time reflects the recommendations found in Hermogenes. The speaker should describe first the present difficulties, then contrast them with a happy past, and finally turn to the dire consequences for the future. The speaker in 7:7–25, although not in quite the same order, contrasts his present difficulties with his happy past and then goes on to describe the dire consequences for the future. The first two questions, about whether the law is sin and whether the law has become death, also reflect Paul's continuing concern about sin and death, a concern that runs throughout Romans 5–7. Nearly the whole passage, with the possible exception of 7:25a, is in the first person singular and is a speech-in-character. The character in question, as already seen, is meant to be typical of most of his Roman Christian audience. It is someone with whom Paul hopes they can identify in their experience of having come to observe the ethical commandments of the law.

Paul begins 7:7–12 in his own voice, with two brief rhetorical questions and an emphatic reply: "What then shall we say? Is the law sin? Certainly not!" Paul intends that what follows should, at least in part, substantiate this emphatic denial that the law is sin. Rhetorically, the question about whether the law is sin is occasioned by Paul's assertion in 7:5 that the sinful passions that were provoked through the law (τὰ διὰ τοῦ νόμου) were at work in our members. What does the phrase "through the law" mean? Does it mean that the law is sin? Paul's repeated use of the phrases "through the law" (διὰ νόμου) (7:7) and "through the commandment" (διὰ τῆς ἐντολῆς) (7:8, 11 [2]) in 7:7b–12 makes clear that he means for what follows to show how this is certainly not the case. It is also at this point that Paul begins the speech-in-character by moving from the first person plural to the first person singular.

In the first part of the speech-in-character (7:7b–12), the speaker describes his encounter with the law and its consequences. Although the law is certainly not sin, the speaker claims in 7:7b that he would not have known sin except through the law or, more specifically, would not have known desire unless the law forbade desire in the tenth commandment. The function of the law is to provide the knowledge of sin, the knowledge of what is right and wrong. This is in keeping with 4 Maccabees and Philo and was a common Hellenistic Jewish viewpoint on the function of the law. It is also in keeping with Paul's earlier description of the law in 3:20 as providing knowledge of sin. In 7:8–11, the speaker then describes the consequences of this knowledge. Both at the beginning (7:8a) and at the end of the section (7:12), he states the consequences in basically the same way. Sin, by grasping the opportunity, through the commandment (διὰ τῆς ἐντολῆς) prohibiting desire, either brought about every kind of desire in him or deceived him and through the commandment (δι' αὐτῆς) led to death.[56] Between these two verses the speaker uses language of life and death to describe the paradoxical consequences of his encounter with the law: "For without the law sin is dead. I once was living without the law. But when the commandment came, sin sprang to life, but I died. And the commandment, which was meant to lead to life, turned out for me to lead to death" (7:8–10). The speaker then draws a conclusion (ὥστε) from this: "So the law is holy, and the commandment is holy and just and good" (7:12). Why is this so? The law is not sin but provides knowledge of sin, and this knowledge is good. Rather, it is sin that grasps the opportunity to bring about all kinds of desire through the commandment prohibiting desire.

In the attempt to interpret these verses, there is an almost irresistible temptation to overinterpret them. This is especially due to the metaphorical language Paul has the speaker use. It is the language of life and death. This temptation needs to be resisted. If one begins, however, with the most plausible identification of the speaker as a Gentile who has come to observe the ethical commandments of the law, as someone who Paul thinks is typical of most members of the Roman Christian community, then this temptation becomes easier to resist. In coming to observe these

---

[56] The phrase διὰ τῆς ἐντολῆς in 7:8, 11 seems to go with the main verb in each sentence rather than with the participle. This becomes clear when one notices that the parallel phrase δι' αὐτῆς at the end of 7:11 must go with the finite verb ἀπέκτεινεν.

ethical commandments, the speaker experiences them as both appealing and difficult, and for the same reason. They represent for the speaker the expression of a higher morality. That the Mosaic law represented such a higher morality was a constant in Hellenistic Jewish literature. For a Gentile to decide to observe the ethical commandments of the law meant that the Gentile became convinced of the higher morality of the Mosaic law. It meant the law was holy and its commandments holy and just and good. At the same time, however, Paul has the speaker describe as extremely difficult this experience of trying to practice such a higher morality as is found in the law. In order to convey the seriousness of this experience of coming to observe the Mosaic law, Paul has the speaker use the paradoxical language of life and death to describe how difficult this is. Without the law sin seemed dead, and I was once living without the law. But when the commandment came, sin came alive, but I died. The commandment that was intended to lead to life has paradoxically led instead to death.

One reason Paul uses this language is to convey the depths of the speaker's dilemma. But another, equally important reason is that it continues the connection he made throughout Romans 5–6 between sin and death. In 7:7–12, however, he adds the paradoxical role of the law. The law, which in itself is good since it provides the knowledge of sin, paradoxically leads to death because sin is able to use the commandment that, by prohibiting desire, increases its wrongfulness. Perhaps the best way to understand what Paul is driving at in these verses comes through recognizing how metaphorical the speaker's language is. This is most obviously the case with the images of dying and death. Put at its simplest, the speaker is still alive even though he refers to himself as having died and to sin as having deceived and killed him. Since he is not describing some eschatological punishment in these verses, the speaker is using this language metaphorically to describe his own experience of coming to observe the law. Likewise, sin is hypostatized as an active force that can grasp the opportunity to use the commandment, to bring about all kinds of desire and finally to deceive and bring about death. Recognizing the extent of the metaphorical language also helps us to understand the speaker's otherwise odd description of his life prior to the law in 7:8: "For without the law sin is 'dead.'" Obviously he is using the term "dead" metaphorically. But in what way is he is using it metaphorically? Given what Paul wrote in 1:18–32 about the presence of sin without the law and in 5:12–14 about the reality of sin between Adam and Moses, Paul can hardly have the speaker mean in 7:8 that without the law there is no sin. But when one realizes the extent of the speaker's use of metaphorical language of life and death in these verses, the point of 7:8 in its present context becomes clearer. The metaphorical timbre of 7:8 finds its resonance at the beginning of the next section of the speech-in-character (7:13). Through the commandment, sin can appear as it really is, as exceedingly sinful. Without the law or the commandment, sin is still sin, but it cannot appear as exceedingly sinful without the law or the commandment. In this comparative sense, sin is "dead" without the law. But in describing the paradoxical experience of coming to observe the law, the speaker nevertheless affirms the goodness of the law and of the commandment prohibiting desire.

But the speaker has not finished. After describing the paradoxical experience of coming to observe the law, he goes on in 7:13–23 to describe in more detail what this experience is like, what this metaphorical dying is like. The speaker, in doing this, once again affirms the goodness of the law. Romans 7:13–23 develops in several stages. First, 7:13 opens with another rhetorical question, this time about whether what was good, that is, the law, becomes death for the speaker. The speaker immediately answers, "Certainly not." He then expands on this answer by explaining that it is sin, by working through what is good, that is, the commandment, that brings about death in order that sin might appear as exceedingly sinful. In 7:14–16, the speaker goes on to contrast the law, which is spiritual (πνευματικός), with himself, who is fleshly (σάρκινος) and sold under sin. He expands on this in 7:15–16 by using the contrast between willing and doing that we saw was similar to contrasts in Greco-Roman ethical discussions revolving around the lines from Euripides' *Medea*. He once again affirms that he agrees with the law that the law is right. In 7:17–20, he describes the same situation under a somewhat different rubric, that it is now no longer "I" who do this but sin dwelling in me (ἡ οἰκοῦσα ἐν ἐμοὶ ἁμαρτία). In 7:18–20, the speaker again uses the contrast between willing and doing and ends with an *inclusio* in 7:20 by asserting that it is no longer I who do this but sin dwelling in me. Finally, in 7:21–23, by contrasting two "laws" (νόμοι) at work in him, he concludes by explaining what all this has to do with the law. He finds it to be the rule (τὸν νόμον) that when he wants to do what is right, what is wrong lies ready at hand for him. While he rejoices in the law of God (τῷ νόμῳ τοῦ θεοῦ) in his inner self, he also finds another "law active in his members" (ἕτερον νόμον ἐν τοῖς μέλεσίν μου), the "law of sin" (τῷ νόμῳ τῆς ἁμαρτίας), which fights against the "law of his mind" (τῷ νόμῳ τοῦ νοός μού). It is important to remember that, in doing this, the speaker once again affirms the goodness of the law. The law itself is something in which he rejoices.

To understand what Paul is doing in this passage, one has to remember that the whole passage is still in the first person singular. In this way he is maintaining the persona he adopted in 7:7–12, that is, someone who once did not observe the ethical commandments of the law but now does them or tries to do so. The maintenance of this persona means that even 7:13, the rhetorical question and answer with which the passage begins, should be attributed to the fictive speaker and not to Paul himself.[57] Although Paul's other uses of these rhetorical questions and answers at the beginning of sections in Romans 6–7 are obviously in Paul's own voice (6:1, 15; 7:1, 7a), they are also all in the first person plural. The fact that the rhetorical question in 7:13 uses the first person singular (ἐμοί) indicates that Paul is maintaining the persona he adopted in 7:7b. Where 7:13–23 differs from 7:7–12, however, is that in 7:13–23 the speaker is describing his situation after coming to observe the Mosaic law. Paul's purpose in doing this is to appeal indirectly to what he thinks his Roman Christian audience's own experience is. Through the speaker in 7:13–23, he

---

[57] This also means that the beginning of 7:14 should be read as, "for I know" (οἶδα μὲν γάρ) rather than as, "for we know" (οἴδαμεν γάρ). Although the MS evidence for the first reading is weak (i.e., 33 and a few other MSS and church fathers), the context strongly suggests that it is the better reading. Romans 7:14a is meant to contrast with 7:14b, which is in the first person singular. In addition, it is parallel to the beginning of 7:18a (οἶδα γάρ). Conversely, to read οἴδαμεν γάρ in 7:14a makes the verse virtually impossible to interpret plausibly. See Wilckens, *Römer*, 2:85.

is redescribing their situation in such a way as to show both the goodness of the law and the dilemma of their own experience.

More specifically, he does this by juxtaposing language about the law, sin, death, and the flesh with language drawn from the popular Greco-Roman ethical discussions occasioned by Euripides' *Medea*. In Rom 7:14, the speaker contrasts the law, which he knows to be spiritual, with himself, who is fleshly, sold under sin; and in 7:16b, he claims to agree with the law that it is right.[58] Between these two affirmations of the value of the law, the speaker describes his own situation as one in which he does not do what he wants but does do what he hates (7:15–16a). Similarly, in 7:17, he claims that it is no longer he who acts but sin, which dwells in him, that is, in his flesh. Then in 7:18–20, he again describes his own situation as one in which he wants to do what is right and good but is unable to do it and in the end does what is evil. From 7:12, what is right and what is good clearly mean what the law commands. In order to make specific and vivid what it means to be fleshly or what it means for the speaker to have sin dwell in him, Paul has the speaker use commonplace language from Greco-Roman ethical discussions about the conflict between wanting and doing. For the most part, however, the two languages remain distinct. The sections contrasting willing and doing do not mention sin, flesh, or the law. Conversely, the sections about sin, flesh, and the law do not mention the contrast between willing and doing. These two languages come from different worlds of discourse. By having the speaker use the commonplace philosophical language contrasting willing and doing and through the recognition that goes with it, Paul is indirectly providing his mostly Gentile Roman Christian audience with a way to understand what he takes to be their experience of trying to observe the ethical commandments of the law. The juxtaposition provides Paul with a way to both affirm the goodness of the law and display to his audience the law's limitations in a way that would be readily understandable to them.

To understand this more clearly, we need to return to 7:21–23, where the speaker most explicitly describes the place of the law in this experience. In these verses the two different languages come most together:

> I find this to be the rule [τὸν νόμον]: when I want to do what is right, what is evil lies ready to hand for me. For I rejoice at the law of God [τῷ νόμῳ τοῦ θεοῦ] according to my inner self, but I see another law [ἕτερον νόμον] in my members, fighting against the law recognized by my mind [τῷ νόμῳ τοῦ νοός μου] and making me captive to the law of sin [ἐν τῷ νόμῳ τῆς ἁμαρτίας] which is in my members.

The interpretation of these verses is the subject of considerable debate. It centers on whether or to what extent the Greek word νόμος has the same meaning in these

---

[58] The contrast between "spiritual" (πνευματικός) and "fleshly" (σάρκινος) is also found in 1 Cor 3:1. In 1 Cor 9:11 and Rom 15:27, Paul contrasts "spiritual" with "material" (σαρκικός); in 1 Cor 15:44–45 he contrasts it with "psychic" (ψυκικός). By "psychic" in 1 Cor 15:44–45, he seems to mean something like "physical." Given the variability of Paul's anthropological terms, the specific meaning of these contrasts cannot be pressed. But it is important that only in Rom 7:14 does Paul ever refer to the law as "spiritual." This is consistent with the more positive way in which Paul understands the law in Romans, in contrast especially to Galatians.

verses and in 7:25b and whether or how it refers specifically to the Mosaic law in some or all of the verses.[59] As one tries to sort out the meaning or meanings of the word in these verses, it is important to keep in mind how highly rhetorical 7:7–25 as a whole is. The passage is full of metaphorical language and plays on words.[60] It would be odd if, after using these rhetorical devices so liberally, Paul would have the speaker suddenly use the word νόμος univocally. Rather, one should expect the speaker to continue the rhetorical display he has used up to this point. This indeed is the case.

First, in 7:21, the speaker seems to use the word νόμον in the sense of "general rule." He finds this to be the rule, that when he wants to do what is right, what is evil lies ready to hand. That the word νόμος can be used in Greek literature in this more general sense is clear.[61] Two texts from Epictetus are especially close to Paul's use of the word νόμον in this verse:

> This is the rule governing hypotheses [νόμος ὑποθετικός]: we must accept what the hypothesis demands. (Epictetus, *Diatr.* 1.26.1 [Oldfather, LCL])[62]

> This is a law of nature [νόμος φυσικός]: the superior has the better of the inferior, in respect to which he is superior. (*Diatr.* 3.17.6 [Oldfather, LCL])[63]

In both cases, Epictetus notes the existence of a general law or rule and then follows this immediately with a statement of its content. The same is true in Rom 7:21. The speaker notes that he has found it to be a rule and follows this with a statement of its content, that when he wants to do what is right, what is evil is ready to hand.

Second, with this in mind, we can now turn to the series of contrasts in 7:22–23, 25b in which the word νόμος is used:

the law of God	another law
according to my inner self (7:22)	in my members (7:23)
the law of my mind (7:23)	the law of sin in my members (7:23)
with my mind I serve the law of God (7:25b)	with my flesh I serve the law of sin (7:25b)

The first contrast in 7:22–23 is between the "law of God according to my inner self" and "another law in my members." The phrase "the law of God" also appears in 7:25b, "with my mind I serve the law of God." This indicates that the phrases "with my mind" in 7:25b and "according to my inner self" in 7:22 are equivalent. This in turn

---

[59] See Byrne, *Romans*, 231–33; Cranfield, *Romans*, 1:361–65; Dunn, *Romans*, 392–96; Fitzmyer, *Romans*, 375–76; Wilckens, *Römer*, 2:89–94.

[60] E.g., metaphorical use of language of life and death; hypostasis of sin and commandment; contrasts between wanting and doing; piling up words with similar meanings ("holy," "just," "good"; "what is good," "what is right").

[61] Instances of this meaning have been collected by Heikki Räisänen, *Paul and the Law* (Philadelphia: Fortress, 1986), 50–51. Such examples include Josephus, *J.W.* 1.11; 2.90; 5.20; 6.239, 346, 353; *Ant.* 1.230, 315; 15.157; Polybius, *Hist.* 2.18.10; Appian, *Hist. rom.* 1.2; Philo, *Somn.* 1.102; *Spec.* 2.197; 4.96. H. Kleinknecht's view in "nomos," *TDNT* 4:1022–29 that νόμος is not used this way is simply wrong. See also BDAG 677.

[62] Νόμος ὑποθετικός ἐστι καὶ οὗτος τὸ ἀκόλουθον τῇ ὑποθέσει παραδέχεσθαι.

[63] Νόμος οὗτος φυσικὸς τὸν κρείττονα τοῦ χείρονος πλέον ἔχειν, ἐν ᾧ κρείττων ἐστίν.

indicates that the phrase translated literally as "the law of my mind" in 7:23 is also equivalent and must mean something like "the law recognized by my mind." Given the context of 7:7–25, this law must be the Mosaic law. The other side of the contrasts begins with "but I see another law in my members" (7:23). Given that the speaker refers to this law as "another law," it would be odd if by this he were also referring to the Mosaic law, even if under a different aspect. Rather, this law must really be seen as "another" law that is at work in the speaker's members. The other two phrases that are part of this side of the contrast, "the law of sin, which is in my members" (7:23), and "the law of sin," which the speaker serves in his flesh (7:25b), clearly indicate that the other "law" in 7:23 is the "law of sin." The question then becomes this: what does the speaker mean by the "law of sin"? Given what he says about sin elsewhere in the passage, that it dwells in him, in his flesh, and that it is sin rather than he who acts (7:17, 20), it is difficult to think he means anything other than sin itself. The reason for using the phrase "law of sin" is simple enough. It serves as an obvious contrast to the "law of God." The genitive "of sin" (τῆς ἁμαρτίας) is a genitive of apposition. Not surprisingly, he is using the word νόμος in two somewhat different senses. The first is a specific reference to the Mosaic law as the "law of God." The second is more general, a kind of pattern, rule, or principle that is active in the speaker's members. It is oxymoronic to characterize sin as a "law" when sin is almost by definition opposed to law, but it fits very well into the speaker's pathos-laden rhetoric at this point in the speech-in-character.

Once one realizes this, it becomes clearer what Paul is driving at in these verses. He has the speaker play with the various meanings of the word νόμος in order to bring his audience, toward the end of the passage, back to its central subject, the way the speaker experiences the law. By playing on the various meanings of the word, he brings out in a rhetorically striking way the Mosaic law as something in which the speaker rejoices in his mind, in his inner self, but also as something that is limited because there is another rule or principle at work in his flesh, in his members, the "law of sin."

Finally, in Rom 7:24–25 the speaker turns to the future. He laments how wretched he is (ταλαίπωρος ἐγὼ ἄνθρωπος), and asks who will deliver him from this body of death (7:24).[64] He also summarizes his present situation as one in which he himself serves the law of God with his mind but the law of sin with his flesh (7:25b). Between these two is the exclamation "Thanks be to God through Jesus Christ our Lord!" (7:25a). The speaker, in describing himself as wretched, uses a characterization common in Greco-Roman literature to describe someone in this kind of situation.[65] It is quite common in Greek tragedies, whose characters were also often the subject of speeches-in-character. The most difficult part of this concluding section to interpret is the exclamation in 7:25a. It seems out of place in the context of 7:7–25 and especially in the concluding lament of 7:24–25. One could easily imagine some pious

---

[64] The phrase "this body of death" could also be translated, "the body of this death." The Greek τοῦ σώματος τοῦ θανάτου τούτου could be translated either way. The difference between the two is negligible.

[65] See Sophocles, *Ant.* 1211; *Aj.* 981; *Phil.* 744; *Oed. col.* 753, 847, 1338, 1401; Euripides, *Hipp.* 875; *Andr.* 1200; *Phoen.* 1335, 1346, 1599; *Iph. aul.* 536; Epictetus, *Diatr.* 1.3.3–6; 1.12.28; 2.17.18; 3.13.4; Ovid, *Metam.* 7.18.

scribe adding it to break the seemingly unrelieved despair of the previous verses. But the textual evidence is against this.[66] The pious scribe in this case was Paul himself, but the reason for his insertion of the explanation is not clear. Perhaps the best way to account for it is to recall that Paul is writing to Roman Christians. They may well be observing the ethical commandments of the Mosaic law. But they are, like him, also believers in Christ; they, like him, have faith; they, like him, have been baptized into the death of Christ and so have died to sin. It is from the perspective of their common belief in Christ that Paul writes to the Roman Christian community in the first place. In this sense, the story does not have an unhappy ending. More specifically, the present plight of the speaker, in whose attempt to observe the Mosaic law Paul hopes the Roman Christian community will indirectly see its own practice reflected, is not final. In spite of the speaker's failed attempts to observe the law, God has accomplished something new and different through Christ. Paul's insertion of the exclamation points to this something that God has accomplished through Christ. Although it would be too much to say that this completely removes the awkwardness of the exclamation, it makes sense within the context of the speaker indirectly reflecting Paul's attempt to appeal to the Roman Christians' own experience of coming to observe the ethical commandments of the Mosaic law.

CONCLUSIONS

At the end of Romans 7, what does Paul expect or hope his Roman Christian audience to be persuaded of? Most obviously he hopes they are persuaded of his affirmation of the goodness and holiness of the Mosaic law. It is not that they are in any doubt of this. Rather, they doubt that Paul is persuaded of its goodness and holiness. The point of his repeated assertions about the goodness and holiness of the law is to show that he also strongly affirms these qualities. Through the law one comes to know clearly what is right and what is wrong, and through the law what is sinful is manifested as utterly sinful. Both these functions reflect the law's goodness and holiness. They are also consistent with what Paul hinted at earlier in the letter about the functions of the law (3:20; 4:15; 5:13, 20). In this way, Paul tries to show how his own view of the law is in some fundamental ways consistent with their own.

But he also wants to claim more than this. He continues to argue for one of his fundamental convictions, that believers are no longer bound by the Mosaic law. But in Romans 7, he tries to show how this conviction does not impugn the goodness or holiness of the law. This argument begins to emerge from the very start of the chapter, with the example of the woman who is freed from the law by her husband's death (7:1–3). Such a release implies nothing negative about the law either before or after her husband's death. This example establishes the framework within which Paul then describes how believers are no longer bound by the law (7:4–6). Here he draws on his interpretation of baptism in 6:1–14. In baptism believers have

---

[66] There are several minor variations in the text of 7:25a that try to reduce its jarring character, but there is no text-critical reason to consider it a gloss. See Metzger, *Textual Commentary*, 455.

been put to death in relation to the law through being baptized into the body of Christ. They have been released from the law through dying in baptism to all the sinful passions by which they had been bound. Such a release, however, is not a license to do what they want. Instead it enables them to bear fruit to God and to serve God or be slaves of God in the newness of the Spirit rather than the oldness of the letter. Here he is drawing on what he argued in 6:15–23, that believers are freed from sin in order to becomes slaves of righteousness, slaves of God. This release from the law, then, results from "dying" in baptism to sinful passions, by which they had seen bound, so as to serve God.

Finally, he argues this position through an indirect appeal to their own presumed experience of observing the ethical commandments of the law. The speaker in 7:7–25, in describing his own experience of how he came to accept the goodness and binding force of the law and the internal conflicts that prevented him from observing it, is meant by Paul to reflect, without ever explicitly saying so, the experience of the largely Gentile Christian community of Rome in their efforts to observe the law. To what extent this was actually the case is impossible to say. By using both Hellenistic Jewish explanations of the value of the law and popular Greco-Roman philosophical views about the overpowering effects of desire, however, he hopes they will see in the speaker's anguish something of their own experience. This experience was one in which they could affirm both the goodness of the law but also its limitations due to the power of desire and the other sinful passions. In this way Paul can affirm with them the law's goodness and holiness and at the same time, by indirectly appealing to their own experience, show how, because of sin, the law did not provide them with the capacity to die to sin. Rather, they received such a capacity by dying to sin through their baptism into the body of Christ. Paul also hopes to show how his own convictions are in continuity with two of their basic convictions, the goodness and holiness of the law, on the one hand, and the necessity for believers in Christ to live ethical lives, on the other. He tries to show further that the second of these convictions was brought about not through observance of the law but through being baptized into the body of Christ in such a way as to serve God in the newness of the Spirit rather than in the oldness of the letter. Whether the Roman Christians would have found this further argument convincing is impossible to say. But Paul hoped they would be persuaded that his convictions about righteousness apart from the law were still in keeping with basic convictions they held about the goodness of the law and the necessity of living ethical lives. He hoped further that they would come to understand that these two convictions became reality not through observance of the law but by dying to sin through baptism into the body of Christ and its consequences, serving God in the newness of the Spirit.

One can see in this way how intricately interwoven Paul's arguments in Romans 7 are with the larger arguments of Romans 5–7 as a whole. The underlying concerns of Romans 5–7 are with the intricate relationship between ethics and the Mosaic law.[67] From the point of view of the Roman Christian community, Paul's

---

[67] The question of Paul's understanding of the Mosaic law and its relationship to Christian believers is complicated and controversial. For a range of opinions on this issue, see Dunn, *Paul and the Mosaic Law*.

conviction that righteousness was a gift of God received through faith by Jews and Gentiles alike apart from observance of the Mosaic law raised two distinct but clearly interrelated concerns. First, if righteousness comes through faith apart from the observance of the law, how are believers to lead ethical lives? How are they to know what is right and what is wrong? If believers are freed from the yoke of the law and should now be guided by the Spirit, as Paul claimed in Galatians 5, in the end does this not lead to the kind of ethical disarray reflected in the issues Paul tried to deal with in 1 Corinthians? Second, if righteousness is apart from observance of the law, what does this say about the law itself? Can there be something inherently wrong with the law, which both Paul and his Roman Christian audience believe was God-given, such that its observance is no longer intimately bound up with righteousness in God's sight?

As was the case earlier in Romans, both these concerns are again part of the broader issue of the relationship between Jews and Gentiles, between Jewish believers and Gentile believers. In Romans 5–7, however, the issue takes a different turn. If Gentile believers come from the kind of world described in 1:18–32, do they not need the law at least as much as, if not more than, Jewish believers? For Gentile believers, does not righteousness through faith apart from observance of the law lead to exactly the kind of ethical disarray reflected in the Gentile Christian community in Corinth? The latter issue would have been particularly sensitive for Roman believers, most of whom were of Gentile origin but who also observed the ethical commandments of the law. For these Gentile believers, observance of the law justifiably provided them with an ethical code that set them apart from and above their nonbelieving neighbors. It is to this web of issues (or, from Paul's perspective, misunderstandings) that he turns in Romans 5–7.

As he did in 3:21–4:25, Paul begins by explaining how his own views are rooted in traditional Christian beliefs that he shared with his Roman Christian audience. In Romans 5, Paul tries to show how "this grace in which we stand," that is, God's free gift of righteousness through faith and apart from the law, is antithetical to sin. He does this first by once again expanding on traditional language about Christ's death on behalf of the godless, through which God has reconciled sinners to himself (5:1–12). He then develops this through an elaborate comparison between Adam and Christ and between the results of Adam's sin and the results of Christ's death. The basic comparison between Adam and Christ is also traditional and is meant to contrast how in Adam all human beings died but in Christ all will be made alive. Paul expands on and emphasizes the ethical consequences of the comparison. He sets the free gift of God in Christ's death and resurrection and its consequences over against Adam's transgression and the sin and death that are its consequences. In comparing Adam and Christ, Paul also emphasizes how both the consequences of Adam's transgression and those of Christ's death and resurrection affected "all" or "the many." Following on his previous arguments in 1:18–4:25, Paul means by "all" and "the many" both Jews and Gentiles. All this took place essentially apart from the law, for the law's role, when it came into existence, was to "increase the trespass." The force of Paul's explanation is first to show how "this grace in which we stand" is absolutely antithetical to sin and not at all indifferent to sin or a way of making allowances for sin. Second, by expanding on the traditional contrast between Adam and Christ, Paul can emphasize that this antithesis between grace and sin involves all human beings, both Jews and Gentiles. The fact that all this took place apart from the law did not in any way lessen the antithesis between this grace, with the life it brought, and sin, with its consequence death. All this Paul develops on the basis of convictions he believes he shares with his Roman Christian audience. This grace, then, which comes through faith apart from the law, is in continuity with, and rooted in, shared convictions. It is not something extreme or at odds with these shared beliefs.

On the basis of these explanations, Paul then turns in Romans 6–7 more specifically to the problems troubling his Roman Christian audience about his views. In Romans 6, Paul deals with two distinct but interrelated issues in the minds of his Roman Christian audience. First, lying behind Rom 6:1–14 was their perception of the ethical disarray in the Gentile Christian community in Corinth. They saw this anarchy as the result of Paul's interpretation of baptism as a baptism into the risen body of Christ. At least some of the Corinthian believers saw themselves as already raised and so beyond the range of normal ethical norms. For the Roman community, this situation was only made worse by Paul's claim that believers were no longer bound by observance of the Mosaic law. Paul's own response is to reinterpret baptism in such a way as to emphasize that believers were baptized into the death of Christ. And just as Christ had died to sin, so too believers, by being baptized into his death, also died to sin. He reinterprets baptism in such a way as to emphasize its ethical implications. Second, lying behind 6:15–23 was the Roman Christian perception that Paul's emphasis in Galatians 5 on freedom from the law and guidance by the Spirit and on being under grace and not under the law also contributed to what happened in Corinth. Once again Paul reinterprets the position that he took earlier in Galatians 5. The central metaphors Paul uses change from freedom to slavery and obedience. What believers were "freed from" is not the law but sin. What they were "freed for" is righteousness. Just as they had been slaves of sin, which resulted in death, so now they have become slaves of God, which leads to eternal life. In all this, however, Paul does not relinquish his basic conviction that righteousness is now still apart from observance of the law. He tries to show that not being under the law but under grace does not lead to ethical confusion or disarray. Rather, it brings believers to lead deeply ethical lives.

Paul's arguments in Romans 5–7 are clearly a blend of continuity and change, of restatement and revision. His interpretations of baptism in Romans 6 and some of his earlier ethical metaphors represent significant revisions of what he wrote earlier, especially in 1 Corinthians and Galatians. These reinterpretations are not simply attempts to rephrase his earlier positions in more palatable terms for the benefit of his Roman Christian audience. They represent real revisions of his earlier views in the light of the problems he himself had to deal with in Corinth. These revisions reflect his own realization that some of his earlier views contributed to these problems. Likewise his interpretations of the character and function of the Mosaic law in Romans 7 represent a significant shift. This shift, however, differs from those found in Romans 6. In Romans 7, Paul certainly writes more positively about the Mosaic law than he did in any of his earlier letters. Yet the primary function Paul attributes to the law in Romans 7, that of distinguishing what is right from what is wrong and so exhibiting sin as utterly sinful, is one he also attributed to it in Gal 3:19–25. Rather, in Romans 7 and in Romans as a whole, Paul drops any kind of language that could be interpreted as impugning the goodness of the law itself. Gone are any references to those under the law being under a curse (Gal 3:10) or to those who seek to observe the law as turning back to the weak and beggarly elemental principles of the universe (Gal 4:9). Paul realized that this characterization of the law was not only rhetorically excessive and understandably offensive to his Roman Christian audience but also at odds with his own basic convictions as a Jew.[68]

At the same time, there is a good deal of continuity in Paul's arguments in Romans 5–7. This continuity is of two quite different sorts. First, throughout his arguments in Romans 5–7, Paul does not budge from his earlier conviction that believers are no longer required to observe the Mosaic law. His arguments are meant to show the Roman Christians how and why this should be so. Righteousness through faith in Christ for both Jews and Gentiles and apart from observance of the law is "this grace in which we stand." Paul has not changed his fundamental conviction on this issue. In this way, he is in continuity with what he wrote earlier in Galatians. There is also, however, a second and different kind of continuity Paul tries to establish. In Romans 5–7, he tries to show how his views about ethics and the law are in continuity with some of the fundamental beliefs about Christ that he holds in common with the Roman Christian community. He is at pains to establish that their problems with his views about ethics and the law are unfounded. And the reason they are unfounded is that his apparently offensive views are really the consequences or implications of what he and they have in common.

Two final comments need to be made about Romans 5–7. Both situate the arguments of Romans 5–7 within a broader framework. First, as one reads Paul's letters, one has a sense that Paul is seldom in doubt about what is right and wrong. Rather, the real ethical issue for Paul is not about what is right or wrong but how or by what capacity one is able to do what is right and avoid what is wrong. This is true of Romans 7, but it is also true of Galatians 5 and Paul's other letters.[69] For Paul, both the knowledge of what is right and what is wrong and the capacity to do what is right and avoid what is wrong are connected in various ways with believers' incorporation into the body of Christ and with the guidance of the Spirit. His ethical exhortations, quite strikingly, do not explicitly appeal to the ethical commandments of the Mosaic law. Yet given Paul's own identity as a Jew, it is clear that his sense of what was right and wrong was often based on his knowledge of the law. This is the case even though Paul claims that such knowledge now comes to believers from elsewhere. There is an unacknowledged tension in his thought between his insistence that the Mosaic law is no longer binding on believers and the reality that many of his views on ethical questions are in keeping with that same law. Put rather scholastically, the Mosaic law is in principle no longer the formal norm of Christian ethics, but in fact the law remains in significant ways the material norm.

---

[68] The extent to which these basic convictions were still with Paul will become clearer in Romans 9–11.

[69] 1 Thess 5:12–24; Phil 4:4–9, 10–14; 1 Corinthians 12–14.

The second comment, although related to the first, moves in a different direction. Paul's view of ethics and his view of the law are rooted in his own transforming experience of call or conversion. As he briefly described it in Gal 1:13–17, God's revelation of his Son to Paul was so that he would preach the gospel to the Gentiles. Paul also became convinced that one could not do this and at the same time maintain continued observance of the Mosaic law, the institution that was the basis for the distinction between Jews and Gentiles. That other Christians were not of the same opinion is clear from the Gospel of Matthew.[70] But it certainly was the conclusion that Paul reached. In addition, in Phil 3:2–11, where he warns against those who would preach circumcision and continued observance of the law, Paul insists, on the basis of his own experience of knowing Christ, that all else is in comparison rubbish. He includes the Mosaic law in this. Again put rather scholastically, if the surpassing worth of knowing Christ is sufficient, then the law is no longer necessary. On the other hand, if observance of the law is still necessary, then the surpassing worth of knowing Christ is not sufficient. Although Paul did not express himself in these terms, they bring out the point that Paul's view that the law was no longer binding on believers was deeply rooted in his own experience. Both these elements, his commitment to preach the gospel to the Gentiles and his experience of the surpassing worth of knowing Christ, help us to understand why Paul continued to insist, with all the revisions his thought underwent on these issues, that believers were no longer bound by the Mosaic law.

---

[70] The author of the Gospel of Matthew clearly took it for granted that believers would continue to observe the Mosaic law (Matt 5:17–20).

CHAPTER 9

The Unity of Romans 8-11

*T*HE PLACE OF ROMANS 8–11 IN THE STRUCTURE of Romans and its function in Paul's overall argument are much disputed. The following four chapters will explain in detail how Romans 8–11 belongs together both thematically and rhetorically. This chapter takes up three broader issues concerning the place and function of Romans 8–11. First, a discussion of how recent commentators have understood these chapters will highlight several outstanding issues in the interpretation of Romans 8–11. (Putting these four chapters of Romans together is at odds with the approach of recent commentators.) Second, general arguments based on subject matter and overall rhetorical structure will present reasons these four chapters belong together. The more detailed analyses in the following chapters will provide more extensive proof. Finally, Romans 8–11 needs to be set within two other broader ancient contexts. One is that of Jewish eschatological expectations, specifically those of Hellenistic Judaism. Whatever else one thinks of Romans 8–11, Jewish eschatology certainly provides the conceptual and imaginative framework within which Paul develops his arguments. The other context, distinct from, but closely related to, the first, is Paul's own eschatology as it is found in his earlier letters. As already seen, Paul's arguments in Romans often involve rethinking and revising the arguments found in his earlier letters. The same is true of Romans 8–11. For the purposes here, the most important passages are found in 1 Thessalonians 4, 1 Corinthians 15, and Galatians 3–4. These passages provide both the framework for Paul's arguments in Romans 8–11 and the issues with which he feels compelled to deal.

RECENT INTERPRETATIONS OF ROMANS 8–11

Recent discussion has centered mostly on the place and function of Romans 9–11 in the letter. Commentators, especially early in the twentieth century, often thought of Romans 9–11 as a kind of excursus or appendix, an almost self-contained unit whose excision would not have broken the thought between the end of Romans 8 and the beginning of Romans 12. C. H. Dodd expressed this view most sharply:

"Chaps. IX–XI form a compact and continuous whole, which can be read quite satisfactorily without reference to the rest of the epistle . . . the epistle could be read without any gap, if these chapters were omitted."[1] Most recent commentators, however, see Romans 9–11 as an integral part of the letter, if not its actual climax.[2]

Joseph A. Fitzmyer sees Romans 9–11 as the climax of 1:16–11:36, the doctrinal section of the letter. For Fitzmyer, this climax is not primarily polemical but, rather, apologetic in nature. Paul is seeking to understand how the Jewish people fit into the new plan of God. He engages in this apologetic because he must face up to the obvious objection that his fellow Jews have resisted his teaching about the salvation of both Jews and Gentiles.[3] In other words, "divine freedom and grace are now manifested toward both Jew and Gentile, but Paul tries to cope with the fact that despite its privileges and his efforts to evangelize his own people, Israel has not reacted as Paul thinks it should have."[4]

James D. G. Dunn also points to the climactic character of these chapters. In a sense, Romans 1–8 create the problem for which Romans 9–11 is the solution. The problem is how to square Israel's nonacceptance of Christ with God's call and promise to Abraham. For Dunn, this is the problem to which the whole preceding exposition (1:18–8:39) is leading. Dunn also points out the various ways in which Romans 9–11 take up themes and viewpoints found earlier in the letter.[5]

C. E. B. Cranfield begins by admitting that "one stubborn problem is that of the relation of these three chapters [Romans 9–11] to the rest of Romans."[6] But he does point out that many features in Romans 1–8 cannot be understood fully until they are seen in the light of Romans 9–11. Cranfield offers several examples from the very beginning of the letter. In 1:16–17, Paul describes the gospel as the power of God for salvation and as the revelation of God's righteousness. But this gospel cannot be understood apart from its definition in 1:1–4 as God's gospel concerning his Son, who was "born of David's seed according to the flesh." It cannot be understood therefore except in relation to Israel. Further, in 1:1–4, this gospel was promised beforehand through God's prophets in the Jewish scriptures. But there is no making sense of the Jewish scriptures without taking Israel into account. The questions dealt with in Romans 9–11, then, are crucial for a full understandings of Romans 1–8.[7]

Ulrich Wilckens sees Romans 9–11 as parallel to Romans 6–8. For him, Romans 6–11 is concerned with the two principal objections raised against Paul's gospel by his imaginary Jewish dialogue partner. In Romans 6–8, Paul shows how

---

[1] C. H. Dodd, *The Epistle of Paul to the Romans* (rev. ed.; MNTC 6; London: Collins, 1959), 148–49. Although less sharply expressed, similar views are found in Sanday and Headlam, *Romans*, 225; Francis W. Beare, *St. Paul and His Letters* (Nashville: Abingdon, 1962), 103; Rudolf Bultmann, *Theology of the New Testament* (2 vols.; New York: Scribner, 1951–1955), 2:132.

[2] Krister Stendahl (*Paul among Jews and Gentiles*, 28, 85) sees Romans 9–11 as the climax of the letter.

[3] Fitzmyer, *Romans*, 539–43.

[4] Ibid., 543.

[5] Dunn, *Romans*, 518–21.

[6] Cranfield, *Romans*, 2:445.

[7] Ibid., 2:445–47.

Christian righteousness is real righteousness. He does this in the face of the objection that if all are sinners, Jews and Gentiles alike, there can be no real righteousness because there is no real distinction between righteousness and unrighteousness.[8] In Romans 9–11, Paul turns to the second objection and tries to show how the righteousness he preaches is the same covenant righteousness by which God chose Israel. This is so even though Israel as the chosen people now opposes the church as the new covenant community. In these chapters Paul wants to, and indeed must, answer the second objection of his Jewish partner, that his gospel's universal preaching of salvation for Jews and Gentiles alike has been purchased at the price of God's breaking his promise of Israel's election. If this is so, how can any promise of God be anything but an empty word, devoid of reality?[9]

Finally, Brendan Byrne points out that chapters 9–11 of Romans "form an integral and necessary element of Paul's total project in Romans."[10] In Byrne's view, Romans 9–11 is crucial because the credibility of Paul's gospel rests on the satisfactory solution of a paradox that for Paul is both theological and personal. This paradox is the gospel's "success" with the Gentiles versus its apparent failure with the Jews. "The gospel presented by Paul so 'inclusively' with respect to the Gentiles has proved to be overwhelmingly 'exclusive' with respect to Israel. Has God 'included' the Gentiles at the terrible cost of 'excluding' the People to whom the promises were originally entrusted?"[11] Just as Romans 1–8 argues for the inclusion of the Gentiles, so Romans 9–11 argues for the inclusion of Israel.[12]

By contrast, the place of Romans 8 in the structure of the letter has been much less controversial. All the commentators mentioned above place Romans 8 as the concluding section either of Romans 5–8 or of Romans 6–8.[13] Whether they place the beginning of this major section at the beginning or Romans 5 or at the beginning of Romans 6, all of them see Romans 8 as part of a section that deals primarily with how the righteousness described earlier in the letter is worked out in the present lives of Christians. Romans 8 deals especially with one aspect of this, the indwelling role of the Spirit.[14] Often parts of Romans 8, especially 8:31–39, are seen as the climax of either Romans 5–8,[15] or Romans 6–8,[16] or even 1:16–8:30 altogether.[17]

The reevaluation of the place of Romans 9–11 in the letter as a whole has certainly made a significant contribution to the interpretation of Romans. It is difficult

---

[8] Wilckens, *Römer*, 2:2–5.
[9] Ibid., 2:181–83.
[10] Byrne, *Romans*, 282.
[11] Ibid.
[12] Ibid., 283.
[13] Romans 5–8 as a unit: Cranfield, *Romans*, 1:28–29, 252–54, 370–71; Fitzmyer, *Romans*, 96–98, 393–94, 479–80, 497; Byrne, *Romans*, 26, 162–64. Romans 6–8 as a unit: Wilckens, *Römer*, 1:17–19; 2:3–5, 118–21, 145–51 170–72; Dunn, *Romans*, 301–3, 412–13. In addition, both Morris (*Romans*, 19, 33–34, 243–44, 299) and Stuhlmacher (*Romans*, 15, 88–89) also place Romans 8 with Romans 6–8.
[14] See the references in the preceding footnote for more specific descriptions.
[15] Fitzmyer, *Romans*, 529; Byrne, *Romans*, 274–75, Wilckens, *Römer*, 2:177–80.
[16] Dunn, *Romans*, 497.
[17] Cranfield, *Romans*, 1:434–35; Dunn, *Romans*, 499.

to imagine that such a long and elaborate passage as Romans 9–11 could ever have been anything but central to Paul's concerns. This reevaluation has also brought to the fore various ways in which Romans 9–11 is linked to other sections of the letter. Yet for all this, significant problems about the place of Romans 9–11 and its relationship to other sections of the letter, particularly Romans 8, still remain.

First, although one can now see more clearly how themes, motifs, and vocabulary in Romans 9–11 fit into the rest of the letter, Romans 9–11 still remains *structurally* isolated. Although the issues dealt with in Romans 9–11 are now seen as central, one could still move from Romans 8 to Romans 12 without disturbing the structure of the letter.[18] Second, although Romans 8 and especially 8:18–39 contain material taken up again in Romans 9–11, this fails to affect the way in which the structure of these four chapters is understood.[19] Third, commentators have noted how the tone of the letter changes significantly in 8:1. Yet this too has not affected their interpretation of the place of Romans 8 in the letter or of its relationship to Romans 9–11.[20] Fourth, commentators have also noted the extent to which 8:1–17 takes up material found in Galatians 4.[21] Yet they have not taken seriously how significantly Paul has revised this material and how this revision contributes to understanding the relationship of Romans 8 to Romans 9–11. Finally, little attention has been paid to the rhetorical structure of these chapters and their relation to Greco-Roman rhetorical conventions. Once again, the point is certainly not that Paul slavishly followed these conventions. Very few good Greco-Roman rhetoricians ever did. Nevertheless, the question of what the relationship of these chapters is to these conventions is never really asked, let alone seriously pursued. This again gives interpretations of this part of Romans an almost entirely theological coloring and ignores the rhetorical aspects of the arguments. Given these problems, a reexamination of Romans 8–11 is called for. This reexamination must take more seriously both their thematic and rhetorical character as well as their relationship to Paul's other letters, especially in Galatians and 1 Corinthians.

THE THEMATIC AND RHETORICAL STRUCTURE OF ROMANS 8–11

When one tries to understand the relationship between Romans 8 and Romans 9–11, it is crucial, first of all, to take seriously the unity of subject matter in these chapters. All four chapters are concerned primarily with eschatology. This is clearly the case with Romans 9–11, which deals with the ultimate fate of Israel and

---

[18] See Cranfield, *Romans*, 2:447, where Romans 9–11 is described as an "insertion," even though not an undesirable one.

[19] See, e.g., Cranfield, *Romans*, 2:446–47; Dunn, *Romans*, 467.

[20] E.g., Byrne, *Romans*, 234–35; Fitzmyer, *Romans*, 481.

[21] For Galatians 4, see Wilckens, *Römer*, 2:138–39, who both draws on and reworks Peter von der Osten-Sacken, *Römer 8 als Beispiel paulinischer Soterologie* (FRLANT 112; Göttingen: Vandenhoeck & Ruprecht, 1975), 128–139. See also Fitzmyer, *Romans*, 498; Dunn, *Romans*, 447. For Galatians 5, see Henning Paulsen, *Überlieferung und Auslegung in Römer 8* (WMANT 43; Neukirchen-Vluyn: Neukirchener Verlag, 1974), 67.

its relationship to the fate of the Gentiles and the world as a whole. It is likewise clear for 8:18–39, which deals with the eager expectation of creation and of humankind for the revelation of the sons of God (8:18–23), the role of the Spirit in this expectation (8:26–27), and how all things ultimately work to the good for those who love God (8:28–30).[22] Though at first less obvious, the same is true for 8:1–17. The explanation of the role of the Spirit and its contrast with the flesh in 8:1–8 is primarily meant to prepare for the eschatologically oriented claims that "if the Spirit of him who raised Jesus from the dead dwells in you, he who raised Christ from the dead will give life to your mortal bodies also" (8:11) and that "if by the Spirit you put to death the deeds of the body, you will live" (8:13). Finally, Paul's use of the terms "sons of God" (υἱοὶ θεοῦ), "adoption" (υἱοθεσίας), "children of God" (τέκνα θεοῦ), "heirs" (κληρονόμοι), and "joint heirs" (συγκληρονόμοι) in 8:14–17 all have an eschatological orientation. Romans 8:17 makes this abundantly clear: "and if children, then heirs, heirs of God and joint heirs with Christ—if, in fact, we suffer with him so that we may also be glorified with him." These four chapters of Romans, then, are united by the same subject matter: eschatology.[23]

Their unity is also clear from their rhetorical structure. The most obvious rhetorical division is between 8:1–30, on the one hand, and 8:31–11:36, on the other. Romans 8:1–30 is calm in tone and explanatory in character. It is marked by a positive exposition that lays the foundation for an inclusive eschatology. Romans 8:31–11:36, by contrast, is argumentative and controversial in tone and filled with the rhetorical devices so common in diatribes.[24] These divisions parallel the divisions of the earlier parts of the letter:

| Exposition: | 1:18–32 | 3:21–26 | 5:1–21 | 8:1–30 |
| Controversy/refutation: | 2:1–3:20 | 3:27–4:25 | 6:1–7:25 | 8:31–11:36 |

Romans 8–11 also shares other elements in common with the earlier divisions of the letter. First, 8:1–30, like 3:21–26 and 5:1–21, begins by taking up the issue of the previous section. The primary thrust, however, of each passage is to move the argument to a new stage.[25] Second, in presenting and developing his view of eschatology, Paul uses material in 8:1–30 he has in common with his Roman Christian audience. For example, in 8:3–4, he again uses cultic language and imagery to explain what God has done in Christ in much the same way he did earlier in 3:24–26 and 5:6–9. He also uses it for a similar purpose, to establish common ground, which he then develops for his own purposes, with his Roman Christian audience. Paul also had much of the eschatological imagery in 8:18–30 in common with his

---

[22] The connections between 8:18–39 and Romans 9–11 have been noted especially by Dunn (*Romans*, 467). Dunn does not, however, draw any conclusions from this about the structural relationship between these passages.

[23] How Paul articulates this unity of subject matter will become more apparent in the detailed analyses of the following three chapters of this study.

[24] E.g., the use of μὴ γένοιτο (9:14; 11:1, 11); the use of τὶ οὖν (8:31; 9:14, 10; 11:7); numerous rhetorical questions (8:30–35; 9:14, 19–22, 30; 10:8, 14–18, 19; 11:1–2, 7, 11; and apostrophe (9:19–20; 11:13–24).

[25] This movement is marked by "now" (νυνί) in 3:21, "therefore" (οὖν) in 5:1, and "therefore now" (ἄρα νῦν) in 8:1.

audience. This is similar to his use of imagery about Adam and Christ in 5:12–21. Third, 8:1–30, again like 1:18–31; 3:21–26; 5:1–21, contains no quotations of Scripture. By contrast, the arguments of 8:31–11:36, like 2:1–3:20; 3:27–4:25; 6:1–7:25, depend for their force on quotations from Scripture and arguments about their proper interpretation.[26] Finally, in Romans 8–11, especially Romans 8, Paul takes up and significantly reinterprets language and viewpoints found in Galatians in much the same way he did in Rom 3:27–4:21 and Romans 6–7. In Romans 8–11, these include the contrast between "Spirit" and "flesh" and the meaning of such terms as "sons," "children of God," "adoptive sonship," and "heirs." The extent and significance of these common elements will become clearer through the detailed analysis of the following chapters in this study. Yet even from these general similarities, there are thematic and rhetorical reasons to think of Romans 8–11 as a unit parallel to 1:18–3:20; 3:21–4:25; 5:1–7:25.

THE ESCHATOLOGICAL CONTEXTS OF ROMANS 8–11

It is also crucial to explore two other areas that place what Paul does in Romans 8–11 in a wider and more nuanced context. First, one of his primary concerns in Romans 8–11 clearly is the eschatological fate of Israel. The eschatological imagery Paul uses to struggle with this issue here is rooted in the eschatological language and imagery of Second Temple Judaism. The place of Israel in this imagery thus calls for investigation. Specifically, since Paul is a Hellenistic Jew and is writing to a Christian community that emerged from the already existing Hellenistic Jewish community in Rome, it is important here to explore how Israel was viewed in the eschatologies of Hellenistic Judaism, especially since the place of Israel as a whole in Hellenistic Jewish eschatology is often underestimated. Second, Paul used eschatological imagery in his earlier letters. It is therefore appropriate to examine how he used this imagery and how his use of it may even have created some of the problems he now tries to deal with in Romans 8–11. As we shall see, this applies especially to the language of Galatians 3–4. A more specific sense of both these contexts will also provide a plausible explanation for how Paul struggles with the ultimate fate of Israel in this letter to the Roman Christian community and how this struggle is also the subject of Romans 8 and not only of Romans 9–11.

Israel in Hellenistic Jewish Eschatology

The eschatological expectations of Jews during the Hellenistic and Roman periods were complex, almost certainly more complex than the available evidence allows us to see. This complexity cannot be studied here in detail.[27] What is important for understanding Romans 8–11, however, is the role played by Israel as a

---

[26] This is less true of Romans 6–7, where there is only one scriptural quotation (Exod 20:17/Deut 5:18 in Rom 7:7). But even here the quotation serves as the basis for the whole argument of Rom 7:7–25.

[27] E.g., see John J. Collins, *The Scepter and the Star: The Messiahs of the Dead Sea Scrolls and Other Ancient Literature* (ABRL; New York: Doubleday, 1995), who shows how complex

corporate entity in the eschatological expectations of Hellenistic Jews. Given that the Roman Christian community grew out of the Roman Jewish community, the probable persistence of the role of Israel in their expectations provide us with an important window on some of the Roman Christians' concerns to which Paul thought it necessary to respond in Romans 8–11.

There is little dispute about the importance Israel or the "true" Israel, the righteous of Israel, and its vindication play in the eschatological expectations of the Jewish literature composed in Palestine during this period. This literature is of a wide variety, both apocalyptic and nonapocalyptic. Some of the literature is clearly sectarian, and some shows no clear sign of particular sectarian viewpoints. This does not mean that the role Israel plays in these expectations is uniform. Quite the contrary, there is considerable variation. The importance of Israel's role is, however, a constant in this literature.[28]

When one turns to the eschatological expectations of Jewish literature from the Hellenistic Diaspora, the role played by Israel in these expectations is more complex and disputed. Both the complexity and the disputes arise from the extent to which the eschatological expectations in these documents become either so individualized or so universalized that Israel as a corporate entity no longer plays a significant role. Individualization in this context refers to the notion that God's judgment is viewed as a judgment of individuals rather than of Israel as a corporate entity.[29] Universalization refers to the lessening or even absence of the observance of the Mosaic law as a criterion for God's judgment. God renders judgment, rather, on the basis of the practice of virtues and vices that are not specifically Jewish.[30] In both cases, the role of Israel, that is, Jews as a corporate entity, fades toward insignificance.

Although both of these phenomena occurred, the eschatological expectations of Diaspora Judaism remained inextricably bound up with the fate of corporate Israel. For all of the variations in these expectations, Israel almost never entirely lost its privileged position. This can best be illustrated by briefly examining the place of Israel in eschatological expectations of Jewish literature that can plausibly be placed in the Hellenistic Diaspora of this period.

The continuing place of Israel in Hellenistic Jewish eschatological expectations emerges very clearly in some texts. Both Israel and the Gentiles have important roles

---

the messianic expectations of this period were. See also George W. E. Nickelsburg, "Eschatology (Early Jewish)," *ABD* 2:579–94.

[28] For the important place of Israel in these expectations as well as their variety see, e.g., Dan 7:19–27; 8:23–25; 12:1–3; *1 En.* 1:1–9; 5:1–10; 45–57; 91–104; *L.A.B.* 11:1–5; 19:12–13; 23:13; *Pss. Sol.* 7:1–10; 8:23–24; 17:21–46; 18:1–9; *4 Ezra* 6:1–28; 7:28–61; 9:26–10:59; 12:31–39; 13:21–56; *2 Bar.* 13:8–12; 19:1–8; 30:1–2; 51:3–6; 72:1–73:7; 77:1–10; 78:7; 83:1–85:13; 1QS 4:16–25; 1QM 12:2–8; 4Q 285.

[29] Ulrich Fischer, *Eschatologie und Jenseitserwartung im hellenistischen Diasporajudentum* (BZNW 44; Berlin: de Gruyter, 1978). Because of the narrow band of literature Fischer analyzes, he underestimates the continued importance played by Israel in the eschatological expectations of Hellenistic Judaism.

[30] John J. Collins, "The Genre Apocalypse in Hellenistic Judaism," in *Apocalypticism in the Mediterranean World and the Near East* (ed. David Hellholm; 2d ed.; Tübingen: Mohr [Siebeck], 1989), 531–48.

to play in the eschatological expectations of the *Testaments of the Twelve Patriarchs.*[31] In *T. Jud.* 22:1–3, after being ruled by foreigners, Israel will find salvation through the coming of the God of righteousness and will enjoy tranquility and peace along with the Gentiles. In *T. Jud.* 25:5, "the deer of Jacob shall run with gladness; the eagles of Jacob shall fly with joy." In *T. Sim.* 7:2, the Lord "will raise up from Levi someone as high priest and from Judah someone as king. He will save all the gentiles and the tribe of Israel." A similar image is found in *T. Benj.* 9:2: "The twelve tribes shall be gathered there and all the nations, until such time as the Most High shall send forth his salvation through the ministration of the unique prophet."

The importance of Israel also emerges in books 3 and 5 of the *Sibylline Oracles,* Jewish "oracular" texts from Egypt, ranging from the middle of the second century B.C. through the early second century A.D.[32] In *Sib. Or.* 3:702–709, from the middle of the second century B.C., the future place of Israel is described this way:

> But the sons of the great God will all live
> peacefully around the Temple, rejoicing in these things
> which the Creator, just judge and sole ruler, will give.
> For he alone will shield them, standing by them magnificently
> as if he had a wall of blazing fire round about.
> They will be free from war in town and country.
> No hand of evil war, but rather the Immortal himself
> and the hand of the Holy One will be fighting for them.[33]

A similar expectation about the importance of the place of the Jews as a corporate entity is found in *Sib. Or.* 5:248–255 from the end of the first century A.D.:

> then on that day it will come to pass that
> the divine and heavenly race of the blessed Jews,
> who live around the city of God in the middle of the earth,
> are raised up even to the dark clouds,
> having built a great wall round about, as far as Joppa.
> No longer will trumpet whistle the sound of war,
> and no longer will they perish at raging hostile hands,
> but they will set up trophies won from the wicked, forever.

---

[31] Much about the *Testaments of the Twelve Patriarchs* is disputed, particularly whether it is a Jewish composition with Christian interpolations or a Christian document that uses traditional Jewish material. This affects the dating of the document and its place of origin. The stronger case has been made for its Jewish origins by H. C. Kee, "Testaments of the Twelve Patriarchs," *OTP* 1:775–80. For Kee, it is a Jewish composition written in Greek by a Hellenized Jew in the second century B.C. in Syria rather than in Egypt or Palestine. For the case for Christian authorship, see Marinus de Jonge, *The Testaments of the Twelve Patriarchs: A Study of Their Text, Composition, and Origin* (Assen: Van Gorcum 1953). More recently de Jonge ("The Testaments of the Twelve Patriarchs," *AOT* 508–12) has offered a slightly revised position. See also Harm W. Hollander and Marinus de Jonge, *The Testaments of the Twelve Patriarchs: A Commentary* (SVTP 8; Leiden: Brill, 1985).

[32] The most helpful recent studies are John J. Collins, *The Sibylline Oracles of Egyptian Judaism* (SBLDS 13; Missoula, Mont.: Scholars Press, 1974); "The Development of the Sibylline Tradition," *ANRW* 20.1:421–59; Valentin Nikiprowetzky, *La troisième Sibylle* (Paris: Mouton, 1970). See also Schürer, *History,* vol. 3, part 1, pp. 618–54.

[33] The translations are from John J. Collins, "Sibylline Oracles," *OTP* 1:317–472.

The eschatological expectations of both Sibylline books concern God's establishment of an ideal earthly kingdom for Jews who will live in peace around the exalted Jerusalem temple.[34] Conversely, it also concerns the destruction of lawless Gentiles who, in one way or another, oppose God and God's people (*Sib. Or.* 3:660–701; 5:179–237).

These eschatological expectations also affected Philo, even as he was probably reacting against the more political aspects of *Sib. Or.* 3 and 5.[35] In *De praemiis et poenis*, after lengthy descriptions of the curses against lawbreakers and transgressors (*Praem.* 127–162), Philo turns to a description, based on Deut 30:1–7, of the reversal that will take place when the Jewish nation repents of its lawlessness and is converted as a body to virtue. In this scenario, conversion to virtue (πρὸς ἀρετὴν μεταβολῆς) will lead Jews' masters to set them free, being ashamed to rule over those better than themselves (*Praem.* 164). Once freed, those scattered all over Greece and the barbarian world will with one impulse return from exile to their homeland, led by a divine vision (*Praem.* 165). Once they arrive, they will experience great prosperity such that the prosperity of their ancestors will seem a tiny fragment, all of this flowing from the gracious bounty of God (*Praem.* 168). Conversely, God will turn the curses against their enemies who rejoiced at the nation's misfortunes and did not understand that these misfortunes were meant for the nation's correction and not for its perdition (*Praem.* 169–170). They will realize that they have mistreated not some obscure and unworthy nation but one of high lineage whose sparks of noble birth needed only to be fanned into a flame (*Praem.* 171). The fact that such corporate expectations appear even in Philo is a tribute to their persistence and pervasiveness.

Three documents often cited as illustrating the phenomena of individualization and universalization are *2 Enoch, Testament of Abraham,* and *3 Baruch (Greek Apocalypse).* Yet only *3 Baruch,* written in Greek in Egypt perhaps about the beginning of the second century A.D., is without expectations for Israel as a corporate entity.[36] Although its provenance is disputed, *2 Enoch* was probably a Jewish composition written in Greek sometime during the first century A.D. in Egypt.[37] It contains purported revelations to the biblical Enoch, including a tour of the seven heavens and other instructions. Some of these revelations are concerned with God's judgment. Although it shows an emphasis is on God's judgment of the individual, rewarding the good and punishing the evil, there are also frequent references to a final, more general judgment leading to both reward and punishment.[38] It is true

---

[34] In both *Sib. Or.* 3 and 5, this is usually accomplished through an intermediate figure. See *Sib. Or.* 3:49, 191–195, 286–294, 652–656; 5:108, 155, 256, 414.

[35] See Thomas H. Tobin, "Philo and the Sibyl: Interpreting Philo's Eschatology," *SPhA* 9 (1997): 84–103.

[36] It is disputed whether *3 Baruch* is a Jewish document that has undergone Christian reworking or a Christian document that has incorporated Jewish traditions. The former seems more likely, but what is important for our purposes is the presence of Jewish traditions. See H. E. Gaylord, Jr., "3 (Greek Apocalypse of) Baruch," *OTP* 1:653–60; and Fischer, *Eschatologie,* 71–84.

[37] Collins, "Genre Apocalypse," 533–34. For other views, see F. I. Andersen, "2 (Slavonic Apocalypse of) Enoch," *OTP* 1:91–100; and A. Pennington, "2 Enoch," *AOT* 321–28.

[38] *2 En.* 11:37 (36:3); 13:44 (39:3); 13:48 (46:3); 13:59 (50:4); 13:71 (52:15); 17:4–6 (65:6–11). The references are to the short recension; the numbers in parathenses are to Andersen's renumbering in "2 (Slavonic Apocalypse of) Enoch," 102–213.

that there is little emphasis on distinctively Jewish customs as the basis for the judgment and more on virtues such as feeding the hungry and clothing the naked.[39] Yet the situation is more complicated than it first appears. *Second Enoch* is filled with denunciations of idolatry and exhortations to fear the Lord.[40] Imagining Jews reading *2 Enoch* in Roman Egypt, one can hardly avoid the conclusion that these denunciations and exhortations were meant to keep Jews faithful to their own religious tradition and apart from the polytheistic world of their Egyptian, Greek, and Roman neighbors.[41] In this way, *2 Enoch* is both more corporate and less universal than it first appears. Without ever using the word, the author of *2 Enoch* still maintains a privileged place for "Israel" as a corporate entity set over against the larger Gentile world.[42] The third text, the *Testament of Abraham*, is also a Jewish composition written in Greek sometime about the end of the first century A.D. in Egypt.[43] Although it is primarily concerned with the fate of the individual, *T. Ab.* 13:5–6 (recension A) looks to a final general judgment of both the righteous and the wicked. This is to take place in three stages, in the second of which human beings will be judged by the twelve tribes of Israel.[44] A privileged place for Israel over against the Gentile world persists even in a document where the emphasis is elsewhere.

Josephus is in many ways allergic to things eschatological, given his position in Rome after the disastrous Jewish War of 66–70.[45] But in spite of himself, he attests to the persistence of eschatological expectations for the future of Israel as a corporate entity and for its triumph over Gentile nations. In addition, he probably also reflects to some extent the expectations of the Roman Jewish community. Two passages are of particular importance here. The first is *J.W.* 6.312–314:

> But what more than all else incited them [the Jews of Palestine] to the war was an ambiguous oracle [χρησμὸς ἀμφίβολος], likewise found in their sacred writings [ἐν τοῖς ἱεροῖς εὑρημένος γράμμασιν], to the effect that at that time someone from their country [ἀπὸ τῆς χώρας αὐτῶν τις] would rule the world [ἄρχει τῆς οἰκουμένης]. This they understood to mean someone of their own race [οἰκεῖον], and many of their wise men went astray in their intepretation of it. The oracle, however, in reality signified the sovereignty of Vespasian, who was proclaimed Emperor on Jewish soil. (Thackeray, LCL)

This passage is part of a larger section (*J.W.* 6.288–315) that describes various portents leading up to the Jewish War. It is very similar to a passage found in Tacitus,

---

[39] Collins, "Genre Apocalypse," 535.

[40] *2 En.* 2:2 (2:2); 5:10 (9:1); 5:17–18 (10:6); 10:22 (33:8); 10:31 (34:10); 13:28 (42:6–7); 13:35 (42:14); 13:51 (47:3); 17:2 (66:2); 22:2 (70:1).

[41] Collins ("Genre Apocalypse," 535) underestimates the importance of these denunciations of idolatry for maintaining a corporate Jewish identity.

[42] The same can be said for the function of the denunciation of idolatry in Wisdom of Solomon 13–15.

[43] E. P. Sanders, "Testament of Abraham," *OTP* 1:871–80.

[44] Although the reference to Israel appears only in recension A, this recension probably better represents the original contents and order of the composition than recension B; see ibid., 1:872, and the literature cited there. The same image lies behind Wis 3:8, where the righteous "will govern nations [ἔθνη] and rule over peoples [λαῶν]."

[45] Fischer, *Eschatologie*, 144–83.

Hist. 5.13.1–2. These similarities show that Josephus was probably relying in this passage on a Roman source he had in common with Tacitus.[46] Josephus, however, is not quoting the Roman source verbatim. In his paraphrase, he clearly connects the oracle with the "messianic" texts of Num (LXX) 24:7, 17: "There shall come forth a man from his seed, and he will rule over many nations . . . a star will rise from Jacob and a man will arise from Israel, and he will break the rulers of Moab and plunder all the sons of Sheth."[47] It is significant that Josephus is using the LXX version here, not the Hebrew, which at crucial points is quite different. Both his use of the Roman source and his revision of it on the basis of the LXX text of Num 24:7, 17 indicate that he has done this on the basis of Jewish eschatological interpretations of these LXX passages available to him after his arrival in Rome in 71. Although he rejects these interpretations, he nevertheless attests to their existence in the Roman Jewish community.

The second passage is found in Josephus, *Ant.* 10.210, as part of Josephus's interpretation of the book of Daniel.

> And Daniel also revealed to the king the meaning of the stone, but I have not thought it proper to relate this, since I am expected to write of what is past and done and not what is to be [οὐ τὰ μέλλοντα]; if, however, there is anyone who has so keen a desire for exact information that he will not stop short of inquiring more closely but wishes to learn about the hidden things that are to come [περὶ τῶν ἀδήλων τί γενήσεται], let him take the trouble to read the Book of Daniel, which he will find among the sacred writings. (Marcus, LCL)

The passage to which Josephus is referring but that he is very reticent to quote is Dan 2:44–45. It describes God setting up a kingdom that will last forever and will crush all other kingdoms. In the context of Daniel, this kingdom is obviously Israel. Given his situation, it is understandable why Josephus is unwilling to quote it. What is surprising is that he still understands the passage as something that will come to pass in the future. However reluctantly, Josephus attests to eschatological expectations about the Jewish people that are yet to be fulfilled. It is difficult to imagine that Josephus would have even alluded to these views had they been held by only a small minority of Jews. These expectations were probably those of the Roman Jewish community as much as, or even more than, they were Josephus's own. That such views persisted in the Roman Jewish community even after the Jewish War points to their almost certain presence prior to the war, that is, during the period when Paul wrote his letter to the Roman Christian community.

When one steps back from the particular eschatological expectations of Hellenistic Judaism found in these texts, the persistence of the presence of Israel, that is, Jews as a corporate entity, in these expectations is striking. Certainly the specific role played by Israel, and whether it is central or more peripheral, varies a good deal. But some privileged place for Israel is almost never absent from these expectations. In

---

[46] Ibid., 158–67.

[47] Num 24:7 (LXX): ἐξελεύσεται ἄνθρωπος ἐκ τοῦ σπέρματος αὐτοῦ, καὶ κυριεύσει ἐθνῶν πολλῶν; Num 24:17 (LXX): ἀνατελεῖ ἄστρον ἐξ Ιακωβ, καὶ ἀναστήσεται ἄνθρωπος ἐξ Ισραηλ, καὶ θραύσει τοὺς ἀρχηγοὺς Μωαβ καὶ προνομεύσει πάντας υἱοὺς Σηθ. Num 24:7 (LXX) also plays an important role in *Sib. Or.* 5 and, to a lesser extent, in Philo, *Praem.* 95.

addition, it is almost always a place that includes some sort of triumph over Israel's enemies or over the unjust in general. The continued presence of Israel and of its vindication in these eschatological expectations in Hellenistic Jewish literature in general and in Josephus in particular also helps us understand the context in which Paul wrote Romans 8–11. The Roman Christian community arose out of the Roman Jewish community, and the former's viewpoints on a number of issues, as already seen, were more of a piece with those of the Roman Jewish community than were Paul's views, or at least what they took to be his views. Another of these viewpoints was probably eschatology. For the Roman Christians, as much as for the Roman Jewish community, eschatological expectations included an important place for corporate Israel and its vindication. But in order to understand more specifically what they would have found suspicious or even offensive in Paul's views in this matter, it is necessary to look more specifically at aspects of Paul's eschatology found in his earlier letters.

Israel and the Eschatology of Paul's Earlier Letters

Earliest Christianity took over and adapted significant elements of Jewish eschatological language and imagery. How this occurred and what the relationship of this development was to the historical Jesus are very complicated and disputed issues.[48] These disputes, however, lie beyond the scope of this study. What is important for understanding Romans 8–11 is the nature of the basic eschatological framework of earliest Christianity that Paul took over and how he reinterpreted it in the course of his letters.[49] Some of these reinterpretations also contributed to the problems Paul felt compelled to address in Romans 8–11. The issues concern the place of Israel or, more specifically, the perceived lack of such a place in Paul's interpretations of early Christian eschatological expectations. Who are included in the "we" of such expectations? As these expectations move in a universalizing direction, what place, if any, does Israel have in them? Put differently, how does one deal with the tension between a universalizing eschatology and the fact that the roots of this eschatology are deeply embedded in Jewish expectations about the future of Israel as a corporate entity? Given the origins of early Christian eschatological expectations in Judaism, these questions are virtually unavoidable. But they were also made sharper by some of Paul's reinterpretations of the eschatological framework of earliest Christianity.

Perhaps the best place to begin to understand this framework and Paul's reinterpretations of it is 1 Thessalonians.[50] Toward the beginning of 1 Thessalonians, Paul describes how the Thessalonian Christians turned from idols to serve the living

---

[48] See John S. Kloppenborg, "The Sayings Gospel Q and the Quest of the Historical Jesus," *HTR* 89 (1996), 307–44.

[49] See David E. Aune, "Eschatology (Early Christian)," *ABD* 2:602–3.

[50] The integrity of 1 Thessalonians is open to question. See most recently Richard, *First and Second Thessalonians*, 11–19; and Murphy-O'Connor, *Paul: A Critical Life*, 104–14. Both argue that 1 Thessalonians was originally two letters (an earlier letter consisting of 1 Thess 2:13–4:2, and a slightly later letter consisting of 1 Thess 1:1–2:12; 4:3–5:28). All the passages referred to here come from the later letter.

and true God and "to wait for his Son from heaven, whom he raised from the dead, Jesus who rescues us from the wrath [ὀργῆς] that is coming" (1 Thess 1:10).[51] Elsewhere in 1 Thessalonians, Paul further describes this event as "the coming [παρουσία] of our Lord Jesus with all his saints" (3:13; see also 2:19; 4:15; 5:23) and associates it with a judgment scene (2:19). This coming is also called the "day of the Lord" (5:2, 4). The most circumstantial description of these events is found in 4:16–17:

> For the Lord himself, with a cry of command, with the archangel's call and with the sound of God's trumpet, will descend from heaven, and the dead in Christ [οἱ νεκροὶ ἐν Χριστῷ] will rise first. Then we who are alive, who are left, will be caught up in the clouds together with them to meet the Lord in the air; and so we will be with the Lord forever.

The coming of the Lord is the occasion and the cause of the resurrection of the dead in Christ. Given the reference to "we who are alive, who are left" (4:17), this coming of the Lord is expected to take place in the near future. Paul connects all this with the consequences of Christ's own death and resurrection (1:10; 4:14–15; 5:9–10). Because of Christ's death and resurrection, God has destined believers not for wrath (ὀργήν) but for salvation (σωτηρίας). The period between the present and Christ's future coming is also to be marked by afflictions (3:3–4; see also 1:6; 3:7), but believers will be strengthened in their afflictions by the power of the Spirit (1:5–6).

With the exception of the description of the fate of those who are alive at Christ's coming in 4:17, this scenario probably represents fairly widespread eschatological expectations in earliest Christianity and is not peculiarly Pauline.[52] These expectations about a future deliverer are rooted in Jewish eschatological imagery.[53] There are, however, two significant changes, both obvious but more complex than they at first appear. First, the figure in Jewish eschatological literature who is to come in judgment is identified with Jesus. Second, the group that at his coming is to be delivered from God's wrath and saved is identified with "the dead in Christ" and "we who are alive" at his coming (4:16–17). This means all believers in Christ. Put negatively, the group to be preserved from wrath and saved is not identified with Israel or the righteous of Israel. Judging by what one finds in 1 Thessalonians, the purpose of the change was not the exclusion of Israel.[54] Israel and its fate are simply

---

[51] In 1 Thess 1:9–10, Paul was probably using and editing the ideas of fellow Jewish Christian missionaries. See Richard, *First and Second Thessalonians,* 53–58.

[52] With the exception of 4:17, Paul mentions these expectations as if they represent a common viewpoint shared by him with his Thessalonian audience. See Richard, *First and Second Thessalonians,* 241–45.

[53] See, e.g., Dan 7:13–14; 12:1–2; *1 En.* 45:1–46:8; 48:2–10; 51:1–5; 61:8–13; 62:7–16; 69:26–29; 71:15–17; *Pss. Sol.* 17:26, 32; *4 Ezra* 6:11–28; 12:31–34; *2 Bar.* 30:1–3. See A. Frederik J. Klijn, "1 Thessalonians 4.13–18 and Its Background in Apocalyptic Literature," in *Paul and Paulinism: Essays in Honour of C. K. Barrett* (ed. M. D. Hooker and S. G. Wilson; London: SPCK, 1982), 67–73.

[54] First Thessalonians 2:14–16 is best taken as a later interpolation. See Richard, *First and Second Thessalonians,* 17–19; Birger Pearson, "1 Thessalonians 2:13–16: A Deutero-Pauline Interpolation," *HTR* 64 (1971), 79–91. For a different position, see James M. Scott, "Paul's Use of Deuteronomic Tradition," *JBL* 112 (1993): 651–57.

not mentioned. First Thessalonians reflects a stage in earliest Christianity before the recognition that the place of Israel or the lack of it was an issue. At this stage, the earliest Christians probably saw themselves quite naturally as part of Israel in some way. By applying this imagery to themselves, they were quite unself-consciously doing so as part of Israel. This second change and the issues it eventually provoked will prove especially important for understanding Romans 8–11.

Paul maintained substantially this same framework throughout his letters.[55] This is not to say that he left the framework untouched or that he made no contributions of his own. He often made his contributions, however, by rethinking the stages within this framework. The two most significant examples of this apart from Romans 8–11 are in 1 Thess 4:13–18 and in 1 Corinthians 15.

In 1 Thess 4:13–18, Paul deals with concerns raised by the Thessalonian Christians about whether believers who have already died will be at a disadvantage at Jesus' coming (4:13–15). He replies that, at the Lord's coming, those who have died in Christ will be raised first and only then will those who are still alive be caught up into the clouds to meet the Lord (4:16–17).[56] Those who have died will thus not be at a disadvantage. The framework remains basically the same, but the stages of the events are clarified so as to meet the concerns of the Thessalonian Christians.[57]

The situation reflected in 1 Corinthians 15 is rather different. Although it is not entirely clear, the Corinthian Christians seem to have believed that through baptism they were already substantially "raised" and so did not look forward to some future resurrection of the dead. They saw their new status of being "raised" as an immortality of the soul rather than as some form of a present resurrection of the body. They may have seen death as no more than sloughing off the body, something that did not really affect who they had already become through baptism.[58] In 1 Corinthians 15, Paul tries to persuade them through a complex series of arguments that things are quite otherwise. He starts from a conviction they both hold in common, the resurrection of Christ (1 Cor 15:1–11). He then argues that the resurrection of Christ cannot be separated from their own resurrection. If they will not be raised, then Christ was not raised, and vice versa (15:12–19). He goes one step further to argue in 15:20–28 that there is an order (τάγματι), that is, stages, to these events. First Christ, the firstfruits (ἀπαρχή) of those who have fallen asleep, has been raised, and then, at his coming (παρουσία), those who belong to Christ. Only then will the end come when Christ hands over the kingdom to God the Father after he

---

[55] 1 Thess 2:19; 3:13; 5:1–11, 23; Gal 1:4; Phil 1:6, 10; 2:15–16; 3:10–11, 20–21; 1 Cor 1:7–8; 3:13; 4:5; 6:2; 7:25–35; 11:26; 2 Cor 1:9–10, 14; 2:15–16; 4:3–4, 14; 5:10.

[56] For an analysis of background of the images that Paul uses especially in 4:17, see Richard, *First and Second Thessalonians*, 245–48.

[57] Although the precise nature of the Thessalonians' concerns is not clear, one has to keep in mind that for non-Jewish converts to belief in Jesus, as was the case with the Thessalonian Christians (1:9), these scenarios, especially about a bodily resurrection, must have been quite unfamiliar and so open to all sorts of misunderstandings. See Martin, *Corinthian Body*, 108–23.

[58] For the importance of baptism for understanding the Corinthian Christians' viewpoint, see Klauck, *1. Korintherbrief*, 22–23.

has destroyed every ruler and authority and power. The last of these is death. Death will be finally destroyed only at the end, not in the present through baptism, as some Corinthian Christians believe. Once again the framework remains basically the same. The resurrection of believers from the dead is again connected with Christ's coming in power. But what happens within the framework, that there is an "order" to the resurrection of the dead, is articulated in such a way as to persuade the Corinthian believers to abandon their erroneous views about their present "raised" state.

In 1 Corinthians 15, another development emerges that will also prove significant to our understanding of the central issues of Romans 8–11. In 1 Cor 15:20–28, the traditional eschatological framework is partially maintained, especially in 15:23. Christ was the first to be raised, and at his coming in power, all those who belong to Christ will be raised. The resurrection again seems limited to those who believe in Christ, a comparatively small group. Yet the language that surrounds this verse moves in a different, much broader direction. In 15:21–22, Paul sets Christ over against Adam. Through Adam death entered the world and death became universal, that is, "all die" (πάντες ἀποθνῄσκουσιν), but in Christ "all will be made alive" (πάντες ζῳοποιηθήσονται). The language moves in the direction of claiming that in Christ the resurrection of the dead is something meant for all human beings. Just as in Adam death became a universal reality of human life, so in Christ the overcoming of death has now become something for all human beings.

The note of universality is resumed in 15:24–26. Christ will deliver the kingdom to God the Father after destroying every rule and authority and power, and the last of these is death. In this context, "rule," "authority," and "power" are not human rulers or authorities but demonic cosmic rulers and authorities, symbolized most clearly by death, all of which oppress human beings (see Gal 4:8–11; 1 Cor 2:6–9).[59] It is significant that nowhere in this list of enemies does Paul mention other human beings or groups of human beings. The real enemies of Christ are not human enemies but these demonic cosmic powers. This differs from the viewpoint of Dan 12:1–3, where those who are not part of the group of the "wise" are to rise to everlasting contempt (Dan 12:2). It also differs from the viewpoints found in *Sib. Or.* 3 and 5,[60] in the passages from Philo's *De praemiis et poenis*,[61] and in the two passages from Josephus mentioned above.[62] In this respect, this passage differs from most Jewish and early Christian eschatological scenarios, even some found elsewhere in Paul.[63] These two developments, the tendency toward universalization and the lack of any mention of hostile human groups, are closely related in the sense that the universalization of eschatological expectations tends to preclude scenarios that set one group to be rewarded against the mass of those to be punished.[64]

---

[59] Conzelmann, *1 Corinthians*, 271–72; Collins, *First Corinthians*, 552–54.

[60] *Sib. Or.* 3:660–701; 5:179–237.

[61] Philo, *Praem.* 79, 91–97, 169–70.

[62] Josephus, *J.W.* 6.312–314; *Ant.* 10.210.

[63] E.g., 1 Thess 1:9–10; 5:1–11; Gal 1:4; 5:21; 6:2, 9–10; Phil 1:28; 2:15; 2 Cor 2:15; 4:3–4; 5:10.

[64] The word "tendency" is intentionally used here because eschatological scenarios are expressions of hope and not literal descriptions of future events. First Corinthians 15:20–28 itself is an example of how such scenarios can contain two inconsistent elements in this regard.

A similar tension between particularity and universality is also found in 1 Cor 15:42–49, where Paul writes more directly about the resurrection of the dead. Here he describes the contrast between the earthly body and the resurrected body. Paul once again introduces the comparison between Christ and Adam and between those who are of Christ and those who are of Adam. On the one hand, this comparison introduces a division within humanity, between those who are of Christ and therefore "of heaven" (ἐπουράνιοι) and those who are of Adam and therefore "of dust" (ἐχοϊκοί) (15:47–49). On the other hand, there is also a more universal element within the comparison. If all of humanity is of Adam, of dust, all of humanity can also through Christ come to be of heaven. The comparison of Christ with Adam almost inevitably leads to a more universalistic and inclusive eschatology, especially when seen in conjunction with 15:20–28.[65]

Finally, this tension again surfaces in Paul's highly rhetorical conclusion to the passage (15:50–57):

> What I am saying, brethren, is this: flesh and blood cannot inherit [κληρονομῆσαι] the kingdom of God, nor does the perishable inherit [κληρονομεῖ] the imperishable. Behold! I tell you a mystery. We shall not all fall asleep, but we shall all be changed, in a moment, in the twinkling of an eye, at the last trumpet. For the trumpet will sound, and the dead will be raised imperishable, and we shall be changed. For this perishable nature must put on the imperishable, and this mortal nature must put on immortality. When the perishable puts on the imperishable, and the mortal puts on immortality, then shall come to pass the saying that is written: "Death is swallowed up in victory" [Isa 25:8]. "O death, where is your victory? O death, where is your sting?" [Hos 13:14]. The sting of death is sin, and the power of sin is the law. But thanks be to God, who gives us the victory through our Lord Jesus Christ.

The scenario's images remain in some respects traditional, especially in 15:51–52, 57 where the "we" and the "us" refer to members of the Christian community. But other aspects of the imagery again move in a more universalistic direction. In 15:52, it is the dead generally who will be raised imperishable, not some limited group.[66] In addition, the Christian community is again not set over against other groups of human beings. The real enemy is death, the power that, along with sin, oppresses *all* human beings. As in 15:20–28, Paul's imagery points to a hope that no human being need be excluded from being delivered from the power of death.

There is a tension, then, in Paul's thought in 1 Corinthians 15 between a vision of the consummation of the world limited to a relatively small group of believers and one much more universal and inclusive in scope. The reason for the more universalistic side of the tension is not difficult to find. It is rooted in Paul's conviction about the inclusion of the Gentiles. Their inclusion allows for, even demands, the reinterpretation of traditional Jewish and early Christian expectations about the consummation of the world in just such a direction. Yet there is a tension between the two, and this tension remains.

---

[65] Paul himself clearly makes this connection, since, to describe Christ's role, he takes up in 15:45 the word "to make alive" (ζῳοποιοῦν), which he used earlier to contrast all who die in Adam with all (πάντες) who "will be made alive" (ζῳοποιηθήσονται) in Christ (15:22).

[66] Οἱ νεκροὶ ἐγερθήσονται ἄφθαρτοι.

Another tension appears in these passages from 1 Corinthians 15, a tension we also saw in 1 Thess 4:13–18. It again concerns the place of Israel—or the lack of one—in this scenario. As in 1 Thess 4:13–18, Israel and its fate go unmentioned. Again there is no reason to think that Paul excludes Israel. It is still not yet an issue. But one can easily imagine early believers such as the Roman Christians, who probably knew of 1 Corinthians, wondering about Paul's views on such a place or lack of it in his rather universalizing eschatology of Israel, the very group so central to these expectations. Their wonderment would only have increased because of Paul's quotations from Isa 25:8 and Hos 13:14 in 1 Cor 15:54–55. These quotations certainly should include Israel, but Paul does not explicitly mention Israel. Finally, in 1 Cor 15:50, Paul claims that flesh and blood cannot inherit the kingdom of God and that the perishable does not inherit the imperishable. Such language about inheriting or not inheriting the kingdom of God inevitably brings to mind the future fate of Israel, and yet Israel finds no explicit place in 1 Cor 15:50. This too must have been troubling to a Christian community such as that in Rome.

It is doubtful, however, whether the tensions between universality and particularity in 1 Corinthians 15 and the ambiguity about Israel's participation in inheriting the kingdom of God would by themselves have provoked the suspicions of the Roman Christian community. What seems likely is that such suspicions arose among Roman Christians on the basis of passages in Galatians 3–4 or at least on the basis of what they thought Paul's views were in Galatians 3–4. There are numerous parallels between Rom 8:1–17 and Gal 4:4–7. The most obvious have been listed by Wilckens:[67]

Gal 4:4–7	Rom 8:1–17
4: God sending his Son	3: God sending his own Son
5: so that	4: so that
6: we might receive adoption	15: you have received a Spirit of adoption
6: you are sons	14: you are sons of God
6: the Spirit into our hearts	15a: you have received a Spirit
6: crying, "Abba! Father!"	15b: by which we cry, "Abba! Father!"
7: no longer a slave, but a son	15a: not a Spirit of slavery . . . , but a Spirit of adoption
7: if a son, then also an heir	17: if children, then also heirs,
7: through God	17: heirs of God[68]

---

[67] Wilckens, *Römer*, 2:138–39.

[68] Gal 4:4–7   Rom 8:1–17

Gal 4:4–7	Rom 8:1–17
4: ἐξαπέστειλεν ὁ θεὸς τὸν υἱὸν αὐτοῦ	3: ὁ θεὸς τὸν ἑαυτοῦ υἱὸν πέμψας
5: ἵνα	4: ἵνα
6: τὴν υἱοθεσίαν ἀπολάβωμεν	15: ἐλάβετε πνεῦμα υἱοθεσίας
6: ἐστε υἱοί	14: υἱοὶ θεοῦ εἰσιν
6: τὸ πνεῦμα εἰς τὰς καρδίας ἡμῶν	15a: ἐλάβετε πνεῦμα

On the basis of these parallels, some scholars have suggested that a piece of traditional material underlies both passages.[69] Others are more skeptical about any such reconstruction.[70] Whatever the case may be, commentators have failed to notice, for all of the parallels, the starkly contrasting way Paul deals with the issues in the two passages. This study in the next chapter will give a more detailed analysis of these contrasts. For our purposes here, however, what needs to be emphasized is the problematic character of what Paul writes in sections of Galatians 3–4. An understanding of this will help us grasp more specifically why and how Paul reinterprets Gal 4:4–7 in Rom 8:1–17 and why and how the arguments of Romans 8 as a whole are so closely bound up with Romans 9–11.[71]

Paul's purpose in writing Galatians was to dissuade the Galatian believers from being circumcised and observing the Mosaic law as an integral part of their Christian belief and practice. In this context, the sections of Galatians most relevant to an understanding of Romans 8–11 are Gal 3:26–4:11 and 4:21–31. The first is an argument based on an appeal to Christian baptismal traditions; the second is the notoriously difficult allegory of Sarah and Hagar.

The first passage (Gal 3:26–4:11) is an argument based on an appeal to early Christian baptismal traditions (3:26–29). Paul reminds the Gentile Christians of Galatia that it is through faith in Christ Jesus that they are now all sons of God (πάντες . . . υἱοὶ θεοῦ, 3:26). Those who have been baptized into Christ have become sons of God (υἱοὶ θεοῦ). They are now "of Christ" (Χριστοῦ) and have therefore become the "seed of Abraham" and heirs (κληρονόμοι) according to the promise (3:29).

On the basis of these traditions, Paul makes a complicated argument for the parallel situations of Jews and Gentiles both before and after they come to believe in Christ and were baptized (4:1–11). The purpose of the argument is the same as all the other arguments in Galatians: to dissuade the Galatian Christians from being circumcised and observing the Mosaic law. But Paul does this in an odd and bizarre way. He claims that both Jews and Gentiles were in the same position before faith and baptism. Both were equally enslaved to the elemental principles of the universe

---

6: κρᾶζον· ἀββὰ ὁ πατήρ	15b: ἐν ᾧ κράζομεν· ἀββὰ ὁ πατήρ
7: οὐκέτι δοῦλος, ἀλλὰ υἱός	15a: οὐ πνεῦμα δουλείας . . . , ἀλλὰ πμεῦμα υἱοθεσίας
7: εἰ δὲ υἱὸς, καὶ κληρονόμος	17: εἰ δε τέκνα, καὶ κληρονόμοι
7: διὰ θεοῦ	17: κληρονόμοι μὲν θεοῦ

[69] Osten-Sacken (*Römer 8*, 130–31) has suggested the following reconstruction of this piece of traditional material:

ἐξαπέστειλεν ὁ θεὸς τὸν υἱὸν αὐτοῦ,
γενόμενον ἐκ γυναικός,
ἵνα τὴν υἱοθεσίαν ἀπολάβωμεν.
ἐξαπέστειλεν ὁ θεὸς τὸ πνεῦμα τοῦ υἱοῦ αὐτοῦ
εἰς τὰς καρδίας ἡμῶν,
κρᾶζον· ἀββὰ ὁ πατήρ.

[70] E.g., Wilckens, *Römer*, 2:139.

[71] Some but not all of the issues created by Galatians and reinterpreted by Romans 8 are examined here. Another issue, that of the role of the Spirit, is left entirely to the next chapter of this study.

(τὰ στοιχεῖα τοῦ κόσμου).[72] These weak and beggarly elemental principles were by nature no gods. It is only through faith and baptism that Jews and Gentiles alike receive the outpouring of the Spirit and so become both sons and heirs (4:6–7). Consequently, if the Galatian believers now want to be circumcised and observe the Mosaic law, if they want to observe "days, and months, and seasons, and years," they are returning again to the same kind of slavery to the weak and beggarly elemental principles of the universe to which they were enslaved before their conversion (4:8–11).[73]

Paul is arguing that both past and present observance of the Mosaic law by Jews is, in effect, the same as the pagan religious observances by the Galatians before their conversion. The bizarreness of this argument is best illustrated by the comparison that Paul makes in 4:1–5 between those who observe the Mosaic law and those who are "minors." An heir, while still a "minor" (νήπιος), differs not at all from a slave, since he is under guardians and trustees. He does not become an heir until the time set by his father. So too we (ἡμεῖς), when we were minors (ὅτε ἦμεν νήπιοι), were enslaved to "the elemental principles of the universe" (τὰ στοιχεῖα τοῦ κόσμου). Paul uses the first-person-plural "we" (ἡμεῖς) in describing this enslavement. He clearly means by this "we" himself and his fellow Jews, both past and present. Paul then goes on to describe how, in the fullness of time, God sent his Son, born of a woman, born under the law (ὑπὸ νόμον), to redeem those under the law (τοὺς ὑπὸ τὸν νόμον) so that "we" might receive adoption (τὴν υἱοθεσίαν ἀπολάβωμεν). By this "we" he means a more restricted group, himself and fellow Jews who have come to have faith in Christ, have been baptized, and so have become both sons and heirs. Conversely, Jews who have not come to have faith in Christ and have not been baptized remain enslaved to the elemental principles of the universe and so have not become either sons or heirs.

The logic of Paul's argument is that both past and present Jews, by observing the Mosaic law, were enslaved to the elemental principles of the universe. Without faith in Christ and baptism, they cannot become either sons of God or heirs of the promise made to Abraham. The logic of Paul's argument excludes Jews who observe the law, both past and present, from becoming either sons or heirs. Consequently, for the Galatian believers to begin observing the Mosaic law is the same as returning to enslavement to the pagan deities, the "weak and beggarly elemental principles," they

---

[72] The meaning of τὰ στοιχεῖα τοῦ κόσμου is not clear and is the subject of much dispute. Given what Paul wrote in 4:8, which seems to identify these elemental principles of the universe with "beings that are by nature no gods" (τοῖς φύσει μὴ οὖσιν θεοῖς), he seems to be referring to deities of some sort. The vagueness of the phrase may be due to the constraints of Paul's argument. He wants to argue that for the Galatians to observe the Mosaic law is equivalent to returning to the worship of the "weak and beggarly elemental principles" (τὰ ἀσθενῆ καὶ πτωχὰ στοιχεῖα, 4:9); i.e., to the worship of "beings that are by nature no gods." The vagueness of the term "elemental principles" allows it to be applied to both enslavement by observance of the law and the Galatians' previous enslavement to the deities they worshiped before their conversion. See Betz, *Galatians*, 205; Dunn, *Galatians*, 223–26.

[73] The phrase "days, and months, and seasons, and years" is also vague because Paul wants the phrase to apply equally to the Galatians' observance of the Mosaic law and to their religious observances before their conversion.

have previously worshipped. It is crucial to keep in mind that central to the argument Paul makes in this passage in Galatians are words also central to Rom 8:1–17, especially Rom 8:14–17: son(s) (υἱός), referring to believers (Gal 3:26; 4:6, 7[bis]); adoption (υἱοθεσία, Gal 4:5); and heir (κληρονόμος, Gal 3:29; 4:1, 7).

This stark contrast is only deepened by what Paul goes on to write in Gal 4:21–31, the allegory of Hagar and Sarah. This passage is certainly one of the most cryptic and difficult passages in Paul's letters to interpret. Paul begins by contrasting Hagar and her son, Ishmael, and Sarah and her son, Isaac. He then interprets the contrast allegorically (ἀλληγορούμενα) as a contrast between two covenants: one identified with the present Jerusalem and her children (τῶν τέκνων αὐτῆς) (4:25), and the other identified with the Jerusalem above and her children (τέκνα) (4:28, 31). The former are Jews who observe the law, the latter believers in Jesus who have been freed from the law as a yoke of slavery (5:1). As part of the allegory, Paul quotes Gen 21:10:

> Drive out the slave and her son [τὸν υἱόν],
>   for the son of the slave will not inherit [οὐ γὰρ μὴ κληρονομήσει]
>   with the son [μετὰ τοῦ υἱοῦ] of the free woman.

The quotation takes up two key terms from Gal 3:26–4:11, sonship and inheritance. The purpose of Paul's use of the quotation in the allegory is to support his argument that believers in Christ are the true children (τέκνα) and sons (υἱοί) of the free woman Sarah and heirs of the promise to Isaac. They are the ones who will inherit, in contrast to the children of Hagar the slave, the observers of the law.

When one steps back from the intricacies of Gal 3:26–4:11; 4:21–31, the pattern that emerges is that those who observe the law, that is, Jews, are excluded from being either sons of God or heirs of the promises. These designations are reserved for believers in Christ, who has freed them from the law's yoke of slavery to the weak and beggarly elemental spirits. To equate circumcision and observance of the Mosaic law with enslavement to these elemental principles or to exclude Jews as observers of the law from sonship or inheritance, as Paul seems to do in these passages, should strike the reader not simply as odd but bizarre.[74]

Part of the bizarreness is due to the tension in which these passages stand with what Paul writes elsewhere. For example, in Phil 3:4–6 and 2 Cor 11:21–22, Paul is clearly proud of his Jewish heritage, of being part of Israel. Nowhere in his letters does he even intimate that he is no longer a Jew or part of Israel. More specifically, when he describes his own past as an observer of the law, he does so with pride. In Phil 3:5–6, he claims that as to the law he was a Pharisee and as to righteousness under the law he was blameless. Even in Gal 1:14, he says with pride that he "advanced in Judaism beyond many among my people of the same age, for I was far more zealous for the traditions of my ancestors." When he looks at his past, he is ashamed of having persecuted believers in Christ (Gal 1:13; Phil 3:6) but not of having zealously observed the law. In Phil 3:7–11, Paul does claim that, whatever

---

[74] Modern commentators seem not to have been struck by this bizarreness. E.g., see Betz, *Galatians*, 216–17, 238–52; Dunn, *Galatians*, 225–27, 242–59; Matera, *Galatians*, 148–58, 167–79.

gains he had in his zeal for the law, he now counts as loss because of the surpassing value of knowing Christ and being found in him with a righteousness that comes through faith rather than from the law. But in this claim, one good so far surpasses another that the other good pales in comparison. This is very different from seeing the other "good" as equivalent to being in slavery to the weak and beggarly elemental principles of the universe.

Galatians 3:26–4:11 and 4:21–31 even stand in tension with the passage immediately preceding them (3:19–25), where Paul rhetorically asks about the place of the law in relationship to the promises made to Abraham. He argues that the law was added "because of transgressions" (3:19) and that Scripture has confined all things under sin so that "what was promised through faith in Jesus Christ might be given to those who believe" (3:22). The law was meant to serve as a kind of disciplinarian (παιδαγωγός) until Christ came (3:24). Although the law is inferior to the promises because it was ordained through angels by a mediator rather than directly through God (3:19–20), it nevertheless served an important, albeit temporary, purpose.[75] Indeed, Paul emphatically denies that the law is against the promises made to Abraham (3:21). Once again, although the law is inferior to the promises that eventually were to lead to Christ, it is in no way equivalent to enslavement to the evil powers of the universe.

How, then, are we to explain these seemingly bizarre passages in Galatians? Paul's rhetorical strategy in them provides an answer of sorts. The strategy he seems to have adopted in 3:26–4:11 and 4:21–31 (and in 3:6–14) is to bring the Galatian believers to understand that being circumcised and taking up observance of the Mosaic law are equivalent to regressing to the worship of the demonic powers that dominated their lives before their conversion. They are a reenslavement to these forces. Paul hopes that by these arguments his Galatian audience will accept the comparison and reject circumcision and observance of the Mosaic law. But he seems not to have recognized the broader significance or the consequences of the logic of his arguments intended to combat the immediate, acute crisis in Galatia. He seems not to have noticed the extent to which his arguments stand in tension even with some of his own convictions about the place of the law and the importance of Israel, which he expresses elsewhere in his letters and even in other parts of Galatians.

The issues raised by these passages in Galatians contribute to an understanding of why Paul wrote Romans 8–11 and how these chapters form a rhetorical unity. Paul is now faced with the issue that the views expressed in Gal 3:26–4:11 and 4:21–31 seem ultimately to exclude Israel, to make belonging to Israel equivalent to being enslaved to the demonic forces of the universe. Given his own pride in being part of Israel and in observing the law earlier in his life, can this really be the case? Must there not be some misunderstanding of his views, even if this misunderstanding is, in good measure, of his own making? As will be seen below in a closer examination of Rom 8:1–17, Paul significantly revised what he wrote in these passages of Galatians so as not to exclude Israel from either sonship or inheritance.

---

[75] The same view seems to lie behind 2 Cor 3:7–18.

CONCLUSIONS

When one steps back for a moment and takes a broader view, a number of elements converge, all of which contribute to a consistent framework for interpreting what Romans 8–11 is about and what is at stake. If one looks to rhetorical structure as a criterion, Romans 8–11 belongs together. These chapters replicate the rhetorical pattern of the earlier sections of the letter. They also belong together thematically because of the eschatological concerns that span all four chapters.

But the unity is not only rhetorical or thematic; it is also rooted in the complex set of issues Paul was struggling with when he wrote Romans 8–11. Paul is writing to a Roman Christian community whose own eschatological expectations included a central place for Israel. They are suspicious of, and even scandalized by, Paul's views, as expressed in Galatians, that seem ultimately to exclude Israel. Paul is also writing about the ultimate place of Israel in God's mysterious plan. This is a deep and abiding concern to him as a Jew, as a member of Israel. But this concern has been complicated and even put in doubt by some of his own arguments in Galatians, arguments that seem to exclude Israel. This becomes a matter of personal anguish for Paul in a way that no other issue did. Paul's struggles with these issues must have been provoked by the suspicions the Roman Christians have about him. But their suspicions are, in good part, of his making, due to some of his own, in retrospect, ill-considered arguments in Galatians. Paul's arguments in Romans 8–11 represent a struggle not simply with external opponents but with opponents of his own making.

At the same time, his most important ally in this struggle will also be of his own making, the more inclusive and universalistic elements of the eschatology of 1 Corinthians 15. These will provide the framework within which he will place his anguished reflections on the ultimate fate of Israel. If believers' eschatological hopes are to be truly universal, then they must also include a place for Israel. But to do this, Paul has to rethink not only the ultimate place of Israel but also the place of the Gentiles and the relationship of their place to that of Israel. For Paul, the fate of each group becomes so intertwined as to be inseparable. If "all [πᾶς] Israel" is to be ultimately included, as he will argue, then so too must the "fullness [πλήρωμα] of the Gentiles."[76] As the following chapters of this study will show, Paul's struggle over the particular fate of all Israel will paradoxically result in an eschatology that is also the most universal, the fullness of the Gentiles.

---

[76] Rom 11:25–26. See also Rom 11:12, 15, 32, 36.

C H A P T E R   1 0

Eschatology and the
Extent of Sonship

W ITH AN OVERALL SENSE OF HOW AND WHY Romans 8–11 belong together rhetorically and thematically, we can turn to a more detailed analysis of the arguments.[1] The first major section is 8:1–30. For the sake of
clarity, it is worthwhile to recall briefly why this section is a distinct unit within
Romans 8–11. First, the whole passage is expository in nature. This sets it off from
the much more argumentative and controversial style of both what precedes (Romans
6–7) and what follows (8:31–9:36). Second, in its explanatory style, it parallels Rom
1:18–32, 3:21–26, and 5:1–21 and so fits into the larger structural pattern of Romans.
Third, in its use of traditional material and in its lack of arguments based on Scripture, it also parallels 1:18–32, 3:21–26, and 5:1–21. Finally, in its use of traditional
creedal language containing cultic imagery, it especially parallels 3:24–26 and 5:6–9.[2]

For an understanding of what Paul is concerned about in 8:1–30, it is important to emphasize from the start several aspects of his arguments. First, Paul uses a
good deal of traditional material. As he did in 1:18–32, 3:21–26, and 5:1–21, he
draws on material and viewpoints he has in common with his Roman Christian audience. Some of this material he himself also used in earlier letters, especially in
Galatians and 1 Corinthians. In this way he shows how his positions are indeed
based on viewpoints he holds in common with his Roman Christian audience and
with other Christians as well. Second, his interpretation of this material often differs
significantly from parallel material in his letter to the Galatians. This is especially

---

[1] Important studies of Romans 8 include Horst R. Balz, *Heilsvertrauen und Welterfahrung: Strukturen der paulinishcen Eschatologie nach Römer 8, 18–39* (BEvT 59; Munich: Kaiser 1971); Walther Bindemann, *Die Hoffnung der Schöpfung: Röm 8, 17–27 und die Frage einer
Theologie der Befreiung von Mensch und Natur* (Neukirchen-Vluyn: Neukirchener Verlag, 1983);
Osten-Sacken, *Römer 8;* Paulsen, *Überlieferung.*

[2] Although 8:1–30, esp. 8:1–13, takes up themes from Romans 6–7, it does so in the
same way that 3:21–26 and 5:1–21 take up themes from the passages immediately preceding
them. In none of the cases, however, does this mean that these passages should be thought of
structurally as part of the preceding passages.

the case for his interpretations of the role of the Spirit, its contrast with the "flesh," and the meaning of such words as "sons," "children," "adoption," and "heirs." Third, his exposition of eschatology in the second half of Romans 8 rests on views similar to the universalizing tendencies especially of 1 Corinthians 15, mentioned in the previous chapter of this study. Finally, all this contributes to the establishment of an eschatological framework within which Paul can then argue for the final inclusion of "all Israel" in Rom 8:31–11:36; or more accurately, he can argue against those who fear that his views may ultimately exclude Israel. Paul's purpose in 8:1–30 is primarily to show how his eschatology not only does not exclude Jews but can even serve as the basis for their inclusion along with the Gentiles.

The structure of 8:1–30 falls into two main sections: 8:1–17 and 8:18–30. The Spirit plays an important role in both and clearly binds them together.[3] But the emphasis in each section is different. In 8:1–17, the emphasis is on the indwelling of the Spirit, its contrast with the "flesh," and its relationship to those who are "sons," "children," and "heirs." In 8:18–30, the emphasis is on the Spirit's role in a larger, more cosmic eschatological framework. The explanations of the role of the Spirit in 8:1–17 lay the foundation for, and lead to, the broader, more clearly eschatological interpretations of 8:18–30.

One peculiarity of 8:1–30 is that Paul's statement of the subproposition differs from what is found in 1:18–20, 3:21–22c, and 5:1–5. Although he states the subproposition in a preliminary form in 8:1–2, its full statement appears only in 8:11–13. Paul's reinterpretation of Gal 4:4–7 in Rom 8:1–17 has to be so thorough that it is impossible for him to state the subproposition fully until Rom 8:11–13. This sense of struggle on Paul's part and its complexity are, as will be seen, emblematic of the whole of Romans 8–11.

ROMANS 8:1–17: THE SPIRIT AND THE REINTERPRETATION OF ITS ROLE

Paul develops his thought in this section in four steps. Partially taking up the language of Rom 7:25, Rom 8:1–2 contrasts the law of the Spirit of life with the law of sin and death. The former has freed them from the latter, so that in Christ there is no longer any condemnation. This is also the initial statement of the subproposition of this section. Embedded in 8:3 is a creedal formula similar in its cultic language to 3:24–26 and 5:6–9. Romans 8:5–8 contains a second contrast, based on the first, between the Spirit and the flesh. Whereas the Spirit leads to life and peace, the flesh leads to sin and death. The emphasis in the comparison is on the characteristics of the flesh. It is hostile to God; it does not and cannot be obedient to the law of God; it cannot please God. Romans 8:9–13 develops the contrast between the Spirit and the flesh, now with an emphasis on being "in the Spirit" and not "in the flesh." The rhetoric of this passage moves to a climax in 8:11–13. These verses contain a specification of the initial statement of the subproposition:

---

[3] Πνεῦμα appears in 8:2, 4, 5 (bis), 6, 9 (ter), 10, 11 (bis), 13, 14, 15 (bis), 16 (bis), 23, 26 (bis), 27. This is also another reason for thinking of 8:1–30 as a unit.

If the Spirit of him who raised Jesus from the dead dwells in you, he who raised Christ from the dead will give life even to your mortal bodies through his Spirit that dwells in you. So then, brethren, we are debtors, not to the flesh, to live according to the flesh— for if you live according to the flesh, you will surely die; but if by the Spirit you put to death the deeds of the body, you will live.

These verses draw together what Paul has just written about the indwelling Spirit (8:9–10) and its contrast with the flesh (8:5–8), connecting them with their eschatological consequences, either with future life (8:13) and the resurrection of their bodies (8:11) or with death (8:13). This is the basic eschatological conviction underlying all of Romans 8–11. It will be further developed in 8:18–30, which in turn serves as the basis for Paul's claims about the ultimate inclusion of Israel in 8:31–11:36. The final section, 8:14–17, expands on the reality of being led by the Spirit and as a result becoming "sons of God" by "adoption," "children of God," "heirs of God" and "joint heirs with Christ." Most of these concepts have their roots in Jewish eschatological expectations, and so these verses also serve as a transition to the more developed eschatological imagery of 8:18–30.

In 8:1–17, Paul makes elaborate use of the same rhetorical devices he used in 5:1–21, including that of comparison.[4] This time, however, the comparison is between Spirit and flesh. The following table gives a sense of how elaborate the comparison is:

8:1–4:

> The law of the Spirit of life—those who walk according to the Spirit
>
> The law of sin and death—those who walk according to the flesh

8:5–8:

> Spirit—life and peace
>
> Flesh—death—hostility to God—not obedient to the law of God—not able to obey the law of God—not able to please God

8:9–13:

> In the Spirit—the Spirit of God dwells in you—the body is dead because of sin, the spirit is life because of righteousness—the Spirit of the one who raised Jesus from the dead—his Spirit dwelling in you—if by the Spirit you put to death the deeds of the body, you will live
>
> In the flesh—if you live according to the flesh, you will surely die

8:14–17:

> Spirit of adoption by which we cry "Abba! Father!"—sons of God— children of God—heirs of God—joint heirs of Christ
>
> Spirit of slavery to fall back into fear

---

[4] See Aristotle, *Rhet.* 2.23.4–5; *Top.* 2.10; Cicero, *Top.* 23, 68–71; Quintilian, *Inst.* 5.10.86–93, for the different kinds of comparison.

The comparison begins with the initial contrast in 8:1–4 between "the law of the Spirit of life" and "the law of sin and death." The comparison is continued in 8:5–8 with an emphasis on the flesh and in 8:9–13 with an emphasis on the Spirit. Romans 8:14–17 concludes the section with an emphasis on the consequences of the indwelling of the Spirit. This extensive comparison also contributes rhetorically to the unity of the passage.

In making this comparison, Paul also uses a good deal of traditional material and traditional motifs. Although its extent is a matter of dispute, Henning Paulsen lists the traditional elements of this section as follows:[5]

(1) Relatively fixed traditions:

> 8:3: Creedal "sending" formula[6]
>
> 8:3–4: Teleological conclusion from a creedal formula
>
> 8:9: A "sentence of holy law"
>
> 8:11: Creedal formula about the resurrection
>
> 8:15: An acclamation

(2) Traditional motifs:

> 8:5–8: Spirit-flesh antithesis
>
> 8:9, 11: "Indwelling" motif
>
> 8:14: Combination of "Spirit" and "adoption"
>
> 8:15: Motif of "receiving the Spirit"
>
> 8:15: Motif of "crying out"
>
> 8:17: Christological interpretation of glory-sufferings contrast

Although the precise contours of these traditions and traditional motifs are disputed, there can be little doubt that 8:1–17 contains considerable traditional material of various sorts. For our purposes, the significance of this is that, as in 3:21–26 and 5:1–21, Paul is drawing on viewpoints and formulations he thinks he has in common with his Roman Christian audience.

Several elements of this traditional material stand out and are especially important for understanding the purposes for which Paul uses this material. They are contained in 8:3–4, 15–17. Paul already used these elements earlier in Gal 4:4–7. The previous chapter in this study pointed out how problematic the meaning of Gal 4:4–7 is in the larger context of Gal 3:26–4:11; 4:21–31.[7] These parallels between Galatians and Romans help in understanding the extent to which Paul has revised the viewpoints of these sections of Galatians in Rom 8:1–17.

---

[5] Paulsen, *Überlieferung*, 182–83. Paulsen's justification for this is found on pp. 25–106.

[6] The term "creedal," rather than than "kerygmatic," is used here as a more accurate term to describe these formulas.

[7] See above, pp. 268–71.

In comparing Rom 8:1–17 with Gal 4:4–7, it is important to notice again how the parallels between the two span the entire length of Rom 8:1–17.[8] The extensive parallels between these two passages and the fact that the parallels occur in roughly the same order in both passages strongly suggest that behind both of them lies a traditional creedal formula that Paul has commented on. Yet as will become apparent below, he has commented on this formula in very different ways in Galatians and in Romans. At first glance, the parallels between Rom 8:1–17 and Gal 4:4–7 seem to cluster in Rom 8:3–4 (God sending his own son) and in Rom 8:15–17 (the Spirit, sons of God, adoption, slavery, heirs). What comes in between in Rom 8:5–14, however, is a set of comparisons always involving the role of the Spirit. The role of the Spirit is clearly central to both passages (Gal 4:6–7; Rom 8:15). This means that, in all of Rom 8:1–17, Paul is dealing with elements also found in Gal 4:4–7. The extent of attention given to explaining the role of the Spirit in Rom 8:5–14 also indicates how important the proper interpretation of the role of the Spirit is for Paul at this point in Romans. Once one understands the extent of these parallels, one can also begin to see how thoroughly Paul has revised his controversial, seemingly even bizarre, interpretations of this traditional formula in Galatians.

The revisions in Rom 8:1–17, however, go beyond Galatians 4 and extend to other parts of Galatians, especially in the way Paul describes the role of the Spirit. Given the pervasive role of the Spirit in Rom 8:1–17, understanding this role is also the best way to begin to understand what Paul is driving at in this section. Once Paul's view of the Spirit becomes clearer, so too will the specific revisions he makes of his views in Galatians 4.

The most prominent characteristic of the Spirit in Galatians is its contrast to the "flesh" (Gal 5:16–26). Paul exhorts the Galatian Christians to "walk by the Spirit" and not to "gratify the desires of the flesh," for "the flesh desires against the Spirit and the Spirit desires against the flesh; for these are opposed to each other" (5:16–17). Paul then goes on to give lists of vices, the "works of the flesh" (5:19–21), and virtues, the "fruit of the Spirit" (5:22–23). He concludes by exhorting the Galatian Christians that "if we live by the Spirit, let us also follow the Spirit" (5:25). Toward the end of the letter, he points out the results of living either according to the Spirit or according to the flesh: "The one who sows for his own flesh will reap corruption, but the one who sows for the Spirit will reap eternal life" (6:8).

The contrast between Spirit and flesh is also part of Paul's argument in Rom 8:1–17, especially in 8:5–13, and the contrasting results of living according to the Spirit or according to the flesh reappear especially in 8:11–13, 17. But Paul's views in Galatians about the role of the Spirit are significantly revised in Rom 8:1–17. First, in Galatians 5, the Spirit plays the roles of ethical guide and enabler. Paul exhorts his Galatian audience to "walk by the Spirit" (πνεύματι περιπατεῖτε, Gal 5:16), to "be led by the Spirit" (πνεύματι ἄγεσθε, 5:18), and "to follow the Spirit" (πνεύματι καὶ στοιχῶμεν, 5:25). But in Romans 5–7, the section of Romans most concerned with ethical behavior and where one would expect to find

---

[8] See the charts on pp. 267–68. The fact that these parallels to Gal 4:4–7 span all of Rom 8:1–17 is another indication that all of Romans 8 should be taken together instead of linking Rom 8:1–13 with what went before.

the Spirit playing a prominent role, the Spirit plays only a minor role, being mentioned only in Rom 5:5; 7:6. Second, the notions of "walking by the Spirit" and "being led by the Spirit," do reappear, however, but in 8:4, 14. When they reappear in 8:1–17, their meaning has significantly shifted. This is especially so in what the Spirit is contrasted with. In Galatians Paul contrasts the Spirit not simply with the flesh but also with the Mosaic law. In Gal 3:1–5, he first appeals to the Galatian believers' own experience. He asks them how they first received the Spirit. Did they receive it from observance of the law (ἐχ ἔργων νόμου), or did they receive it through hearing in faith (ἐχ ἀκοῆς πίστεως)? The answer, of course, was through hearing in faith. Since the Galatians only recently even considered being circumcised and practicing the Mosaic law, their initial reception of the Spirit had to have been through hearing in faith. In 3:13–14, at the end of his scriptural argument in 3:6–14, Paul concludes that "Christ redeemed us *from the curse of the Law* by becoming a curse for us . . . in order that in Christ Jesus the blessing of Abraham might come to the Gentiles, so that we might receive *the promise of the Spirit through faith.*" Finally, Paul claims in 5:18 that if believers are led by the Spirit, they are not under the law (οὐκ ἐστὲ ὑπὸ νόμον). What is common to all three passages is that the Spirit is, in one way or another, starkly contrasted with the law. The Spirit stands over against not only the flesh but also over against the Mosaic law.

There is, in addition to the contrasts of the Spirit with the flesh and with the law, a third contrast in Galatians, between those who are empowered by the Spirit and those who are circumcised and observe the law. This contrast is found in 5:2–6:

> Now I, Paul, say to you that if you let yourselves be circumcised, Christ will be of no benefit to you. Once again I testify to every man [παντὶ ἀνθρώπῳ] who lets himself be circumcised that he is obliged to obey the entire law. You who want to be made righteous by the law have cut yourselves off from Christ; you have fallen away from grace. For through the Spirit, by faith, we eagerly wait for the hope of righteousness. For in Christ Jesus neither circumcision nor uncircumcision counts for anything; the only thing that counts is faith working through love.

In this passage, Paul is referring specifically to the Gentile Galatians who now want to be circumcised and observe the law, not to Jews. His purpose was to dissuade them from circumcision and observance of the Mosaic law. Yet one would not have to misread the passage by much to conclude that Paul is also referring to Jews. The reason is that the principle Paul enunciates is stated generally, as a principle applying to "every man." In this case, it covers, at least in its essence, not only the Gentile Galatians but also the Jews. A similar and even more telling contrast between those who are empowered by the Spirit and those who observe the Mosaic law appears in 4:8–10, the passage immediately following 4:4–7. Here Paul contrasts those who received the Spirit in their hearts and are no longer slaves but sons and heirs (4:6–7) to the Galatian believers who want to observe the Mosaic law. These Galatian believers, in Paul's view, want again to become slaves to the weak and beggarly elemental principles of the universe (4:8–10). Once again the immediate object of Paul's polemic is Gentile Galatians who now want to be circumcised and obey the Mosaic law. But once again the underlying principle is applicable not only to the Gentile Galatians but to all who are circumcised and observe the Mosaic law, that is, to Jews also.

As one looks at these contrasts, two of them, those between the Spirit and the law and between those who were empowered by the Spirit and those who were circumcised and observed the law, must have been controversial, especially to Roman Christians who saw in such contrasts a rejection of the value of the law. But the controversial nature of these two contrasts may have been even sharper. To contrast the Spirit and those empowered by the Spirit with the law and those who are circumcised and observe the law is to place both the law and those who observe it on the side of the "flesh." Further, if those who do the works of the flesh "will not inherit [οὐ κληρονομήσουσιν] the kingdom of God" (5:21) or reap eternal life but rather corruption (6:8), must not those who observe the law, whether the Gentile Galatians or Jews, be included in this group? The controversial character of these contrasts, then, lies not only in Paul's apparent views about the present situation of those who observe the law but also in his views about their future fate. Such an interpretation of these contrasts could be set aside as implausible, as prescinding far too much from the immediate context and purpose of Galatians. Yet when these contrasts are combined with the controversial passages in Galatians 4 about the apparent exclusion of Jews as "sons" and "heirs" (analyzed in the previous chapter of this study), they form part of a larger pattern in which Jews are apparently excluded not only from the present possession of the Spirit but also from the future salvation of which the Spirit is a pledge. They do not possess the Spirit, and so they can become neither sons of God by adoption nor heirs.

Granted, all of this is in tension with other aspects of Paul's thought, even in Galatians.[9] Granted also, one needs to keep in mind the particular situation in which Paul wrote Galatians. But it is still undeniable that this pattern of interpretation would have troubled the minds of most Roman Christians concerned about the relationship between belief in Christ and the Jewish heritage of which they considered themselves a part. This would have been the case especially for Roman Christian believers who continued to observe the ethical commandments of the Mosaic law. In the end, it also seems to have troubled Paul. This concern emerges in the complex way he revises in Rom 8:1–17 virtually all that he wrote in these passages in Galatians. Although he uses the traditional language found in Gal 4:4–7 as the framework for this revision, the meaning of virtually all the concepts has significantly shifted. This includes particularly a shift in his interpretation of the role of the Spirit. This is because it is through the indwelling of the Spirit that believers become both sons and heirs. Those changes provide the foundation for the rest of Romans 8 and for Romans 9–11.

Romans 8:1–4: Now No Condemnation in Christ Jesus

This section falls into two parts. The first (Rom 8:1–2) takes up language from Romans 5–7 (e.g., κατάκριμα [5:16, 18], νόμος ἁμαρτίας [7:25]) but turns it in a positive direction. There is therefore now no condemnation for those in Christ Jesus because the law of the Spirit of life has freed them from the law of sin

---

[9] Gal 1:15–17; 3:19–25; 5:14; 6:2. See above, pp. 68–70.

and death.[10] These verses provide an immediate response to the situation described so dramatically in 7:7–25. But this should not lead us to think of them as primarily connected with Romans 5–7 or as the conclusion to the arguments in those chapters. Rather, these verses take up elements from Romans 5–7 but move in a different direction, much as 3:21 and 5:1 took up elements from 1:18–3:20 and 3:31–4:25 respectively but also moved in different directions.[11] These verses, then, primarily provide the initial statement of the subproposition for Romans 8–11, which is then specified more clearly in 8:11–13. The second part (8:3–4) offers the grounds for this change from condemnation to freedom from the law of sin and death through the law of the Spirit of life. God, by sending God's own Son, has condemned sin so that the just judgment of the law might be fulfilled in those who walk not according to the flesh but according to the Spirit.

In 8:1–4, Paul is most interested in establishing a set of contrasts that he then develops in 8:5–17. The basic contrast is clearly between the Spirit and the flesh (8:4). This contrast dominates what follows in 8:5–17. Paul uses the word "spirit" (πνεῦμα) in a variety of ways in his letters. Although he sometimes uses the word to mean the human spirit, Paul most often uses it to refer to a divine Spirit, either the Spirit of God or the Spirit of Christ, and so distinct from the human spirit. The same is true here. Of the twenty occurrences of the word in Romans 8, almost all refer to the divine Spirit, and only one (8:16) clearly refers to the human spirit. His use of the word "flesh," however, is more complex and not consistent.[12] Given the basic meaning of the word, it is difficult not to connect it with the material part of human beings. At the same time, Paul often uses the word to refer to that aspect of human existence that turns away from God and sins, but without any specific emphasis on materiality (e.g., Gal 5:16–25). In addition, although the word usually has a negative meaning for Paul, he sometimes uses it in a neutral, descriptive sense.[13] This lack of consistency is due to the fact that Paul's interests are not primarily anthropological but lie elsewhere, particularly in the contrast between Spirit and flesh as shorthand for the contrast between the realm of God's power at work in Christ and the realm of sin and death. For the most part, this is the case in Romans 8, although not completely so, as will be seen in Rom 8:9–13.

In 8:2, Paul first states the contrast as one between "the law of the Spirit of life" and "the law of sin and death." This provides us with an initial clue to how Paul is revising his understanding of the Spirit and to what he is now opposing it. It is in contrast to the way he understood it in Galatians. The contrast here, and in what follows in 8:5–17, is between the Spirit as the source of life and the flesh as the source of sin and death. Unlike Galatians, neither in Rom 8:1–4 nor in Rom 8:5–17 does Paul contrast the Spirit with the Mosaic law or its observance. The Spirit and

---

[10] The reading that the law of the Spirit has freed "you" (σε) rather than "me" (με) is accepted here as the correct one. See above, p. 226, for the justification of this reading.

[11] Romans 8:1 begins with the adverb "now" (νῦν/Νυνί) like 3:21, and with an illative particle (οὖν/ἄρα) like 5:1. Romans 8:1–2 also takes up some of the language of the preceding section, much in the same way as both 3:21–23 and 5:1–2 did.

[12] For the problematic character of Paul's anthropology, see Aune, "Human Nature and Ethics," 298–305.

[13] E.g., Gal 4:13; 1 Cor 5:5; 6:16; 15:39; 2 Cor 7:1; 12:7; Rom 2:28; 4:1; 9:8.

life are on one side of the contrast; the flesh, sin, and death, but not the Mosaic law, are on the other side.

Equally significant is the way Paul sets up the contrast as one between two "laws" (νόμοι), one of the Spirit of life and the other of sin and death. There is considerable dispute about what Paul means by this contrast and about its relationship to "law" at the beginning of 8:3 ("What the law was incapable of in that it was weakened through the flesh"). Since Paul is clearly referring in 8:3 to what he wrote in 7:12–25, "law" in 8:3 must mean the Mosaic law. But the meaning of the two contrasting "laws" in 8:2 is less clear. Some would take them also referring to the Mosaic law, but under different aspects, one as observed in the new era through faith and the power of the Spirit and the other as caught up in the realities of sin and death.[14] Given what Paul has already written in 7:4, 6 about dying to the Mosaic law, however, this interpretation is unlikely. Rather, the genitives in 8:2 ("of the Spirit of life" and "of sin and death") are better taken as appositional and so as two different realities or "principles," the first of which, the Spirit, has freed the Roman Christians from the power of the second, sin and death.[15] Paul is once again playing with various meanings of the word "law," something he has done several times already in Romans.[16]

But connecting the Spirit with νόμος is more than a clever turn of phrase. Unlike what he did in Galatians, Paul not only does not contrast the Spirit with the law; he even describes the Spirit itself as a kind of νόμος. That Paul does this intentionally is shown by his description of the role of the "law" of the Spirit in 8:2 as "freeing" (ἠλευθέρωσεν) the believer from the "law" of sin and death. In Galatians, a central role of the Spirit was also to free the believer, but it was especially to free the believer from the yoke of slavery to the Mosaic law (Gal 5:1, 18). This same intention is manifested in the contrast Paul draws later in Rom 8:7 between the mind-set of the Spirit (τὸ φρόνημα τοῦ πνεύματος) and the mind-set of the flesh (τὸ φρόνημα τῆς σαρκός), which does not and cannot obey "the law of God" (τῷ νόμῳ τοῦ θεοῦ). By implication, the mind-set rooted in the Spirit is obedient to this law. All of this must be intentional on Paul's part.

Through these apparently minor changes, Paul provides his Roman Christian audience with an understanding of the Spirit and its role different from that in Galatians. He no longer sets the Mosaic law in opposition to the Spirit. And although certainly not the Mosaic law as such, even the Spirit itself is a kind of "law." This reconfiguration of the function of the Spirit is also consistent with the ethical views he expresses in Romans 6–7, where the emphasis is on freedom from sin and slavery to God rather than, as it was in Galatians, on freedom from the Mosaic law and on the guidance by the Spirit of those no longer under the Mosaic law.

Once one understands that the fundamental contrast is between the Spirit and life, on the one hand, and the flesh, sin, and death, on the other, the solutions to several other difficult issues in the interpretation of 8:1–4 become clearer. These issues concern the translation and interpretation of 8:3–4. The first difficulty is the rela-

---

[14] So Dunn, *Romans,* 416–17; Wilckens, *Römer,* 2:122–23.

[15] In different ways, Fitzmyer, *Romans,* 482–83; and Byrne, *Romans,* 242.

[16] Rom 2:14, 27; 3:27; 7:21, 23, 25.

tionship of the opening clause ("What the law was incapable of in that it was weak-ened through the flesh") to the rest of 8:3–4.[17] The problem is that the thought of this clause seems to be taken up nowhere else in 8:3–4. A second and closely related difficulty is how to understand the rest of 8:3. Specifically, since the verb "con-demned" (κατέκρινεν) does not complete the thought of the opening clause, does one need to supply a second finite verb such as "accomplished" (ἐποίησεν)? This would smooth out 8:3: "What the law was incapable of in that it was weakened through the flesh, God [has accomplished]: sending his son . . . he condemned sin in the flesh."[18]

The very lack of smoothness, however, suggests that something else is in-volved. In 8:3, Paul is probably quoting part of the traditional creedal formula he used in Gal 4:4–7 and commenting on it in such a way as to make it serve his own purposes in the present context. The presence of this formula is the cause of the awkwardness. Although its extent is difficult to determine, the fragment of the tra-ditional formula in 8:3 probably included the following:

> God sending his own son . . . as a sin-offering
> condemned sin

> ὁ θεὸς τὸν υἱὸν πέμψας . . . περὶ ἁμαρτίας
> κατέκρινεν τὴν ἁμαρτιαν

There are several reasons for suggesting this was the fragmentary formula. First, the nominative absolute at the beginning of 8:3 is clearly Pauline, since it in effect sum-marizes several of his arguments in Romans 7. The awkwardness of the nominative absolute in its present position is due to Paul's attempt to use it to connect the tradi-tional formula that follows to its present context. Second, the phrase "as a sin-offering" (περὶ ἁμαρτίας) is also part of the formula. As Byrne has pointed out, the phrase (τὸ) περὶ (τῆς) ἁμαρτίας often occurs in the LXX as an explanatory comment indi-cating the purpose and effect of rituals prescribed for the expiation of sin.[19] Some-times it even denotes the sacrifice known as the sin offering (e. g., Lev 9:2; 14:31; Ps 39:7 [LXX]). It is also used metaphorically in the fourth Servant Song (Isa 53:10) of the Suffering Servant of God. This last use is especially important because this pas-sage from Isaiah played such an important role in early Christianity's attempts to un-derstand the meaning of Jesus' death on the cross.[20] Given this background, the phrase περὶ ἁμαρτίας probably reflects this cultic sense and means "as a sin-offering" in Rom 8:3. This interpretation is strengthened by the fact that were it taken in a more general sense (e.g., "to deal with sin"), it would become redundant in light of the immediately following clause about God condemning sin.[21] Third, the clause "con-demned sin" (κατέκρινεν τὴν ἁμαρτίαν) is also part of the formula. The formula it-

---

[17] The problem is not strictly one of syntax. The clause is a nominative absolute, and so its syntactical relationship to the rest of 8:3 is loose.

[18] Fitzmyer, *Romans*, 483–84.

[19] Lev 4:3, 14, 28, 35; 5:6, 7, 8, 10, 11, 13; Num 6:16; 7:16; 2 Chr 29:23–24; Ezek 42:13; 43:19, all LXX. Byrne, *Romans*, 236–37, 243.

[20] That Paul is familiar with this interpretation of Jesus' death is clear from Rom 4:25.

[21] Byrne, *Romans*, 243.

self needs a principal verb, and this is provided by "condemned." In addition, since the clause does not provide the expected resumption of thought from the nominative absolute, it is the main reason for the awkwardness of the verse in the first place. Finally, the formula's assertion that God, by sending God's own Son, has "condemned sin" differs from Paul's use of "condemnation" (κατάκριμα) in 8:1, which refers to God's condemnation of sinful human beings rather than of sin itself.

The other phrases in 8:3–4 are probably Paul's interpretative glosses made in order to connect the formula with the present context with its emphasis on the contrast between the Spirit and flesh, sin, and death. This is the case for the final phrase in 8:4 ("for those who walk not according to the flesh but according to the Spirit"), since it serves as the transition to 8:5–8. It is also true for the phrases ἐν ὁμοιώματι σαρκὸς ἁμαρτίας ("in the likeness of sinful flesh") and ἐν τῇ σαρκί ["in the flesh"] in 8:3. The meaning of these two phrases has puzzled interpreters over the years.[22] But if one understands that Paul's purpose in using them is primarily to connect the traditional formula about God's condemnation of sin more closely to the present context with its emphasis on sin's connection with the flesh, then one need not press them too closely for a precise meaning. Their insertion by Paul was meant to be as glosses that join the creedal formula's concern with sin to the present context's connection of sin with the flesh and its contrast with the Spirit. God's Son, being sent "in the likeness of sinful flesh," condemned sin "in the flesh." Finally, the phrase "so that the just requirement [τὸ δικαίωμα] of the law might be fulfilled in us [πληρωθῇ ἐν ἡμῖν]" also seems to be an addition by Paul. One must remember that Paul used the contrast κατάκριμα δικαίωμα, found at the beginning and end of this passage (8:1, 4), earlier in 5:16. The contrast there was between the result of the judgment of Adam (condemnation) and the result of Christ's free gift ("righteousness") and was used primarily for the stylistic reason of the similarity (-μα) of the endings. The same was true of the contrast παράπτωμα δικαίωμα ("trespass"–"righteous act") in 5:18. One suspects something similar is taking place in 8:4. The "just requirement of the law" (δικαίωμα τοῦ νόμου) in 8:4 may serve primarily as the rhetorical counterpoint to the condemnation associated with the flesh, sin, and death in 8:1–2 and mean nothing more specific than what the law would ideally require.[23]

For understanding the function of 8:1–4 in Paul's argument, it is also important to notice that this section, in its use of the traditional creedal formula that contains cultic language, is similar to 3:21–26 and 5:6–11. Both in 8:3–4 and in the two earlier passages, Paul uses traditional material that explains the significance of Christ's death in cultic terms to serve as the basis for his further arguments. This gives additional support to the notion that Paul does this because the Roman Christian community also understood the significance of Christ's death in cultic terms. This view is strengthened by the realization that Paul has substituted the more cultic language of 8:3 for the more controversial and noncultic formula of the parallel in Gal 4:4–5 ("God sent forth his son, born of a woman, born under the law, to redeem those under the law"). Given that the cultic language was probably part of the traditional creedal

---

[22] See Fitzmyer, *Romans*, 485–88, for a discussion of the range of interpretations.

[23] Paul writes in a similar fashion about the "fulfillment" of the law in Gal 5:14 and Rom 13:8–10. See pp. 69–70 and 401–3.

formula rather than his own, Paul in effect replaced his own more controversial formulation in Gal 4:4–5 with the more traditional cultic formulation of Rom 8:3, a formulation he probably shared with his Roman Christian audience.[24]

In this short but complicated passage, Paul has tried to do several things. First, he has reconfigured the contrast of Spirit and flesh in such a way that the Spirit is no longer in opposition to the law as such or to its observers. Rather, the contrast is between the Spirit and life, on the one hand, and flesh, sin, and death, on the other. Second, by characterizing the freedom the Spirit provides as a kind of "law," he not only mutes any contrast between it and the Mosaic law; he also shows that the Spirit is not to be construed as a freedom from "law" in any general sense. Both these purposes contrast with the rhetoric of Galatians 5. Finally, by using the traditional creedal formula and its cultic language as the basis for his arguments and then glossing it to fit into the context of Romans 8, he once again tries to emphasize the common ground that already exists between himself and his Roman Christian audience.

Romans 8:5–8: Contrast of Flesh and Spirit

Paul now develops the contrast between the Spirit and the flesh. He does this in two steps. First, in 8:5–8, he emphasizes the flesh side of the comparison. In 8:5–6, he first contrasts those who live according to the Spirit and have their minds set (φρονοῦσιν) on the things of the Spirit with those who live according to the flesh and have their minds set on the things of the flesh. He then contrasts the results of those two mind-sets (φρονήματα). The mind-set of the flesh leads to death; the mind-set of the Spirit leads to life and peace. In 8:7–8, he then offers reasons for the mind-set of the flesh. It is hostility to God; it is not and cannot be subject to the "law of God." As a result, those who live in the flesh cannot please God. An inclusion (those who live according to the flesh [8:5], those who are in the flesh [8:8]) and the use of φρονέω (8:5) and φρόνημα (8:6, 7) hold this section together rhetorically.

The contrasts between the Spirit and the flesh develop the contrasts begun in 8:1–4. On the one hand, the flesh leads to death; on the other hand, the Spirit leads to life. In explaining why this is so, Paul emphasizes that the flesh is not and cannot be subject to "the law of God" (τῷ νόμῳ τοῦ θεοῦ). Once again, the notion of "law" is part of his explanation. As pointed out above, this "law of God" in 8:7 is not the Mosaic law, but it is nevertheless a kind of law, which the flesh is incapable of obeying—something that, by implication, the Spirit is capable of doing. Once again it is important to notice how the contrasts are developed. The Spirit is contrasted with the flesh and its result, death, but not with the Mosaic law. Indeed, one of the problems with the flesh is that it cannot be obedient to the "law of God." Here the "law of God" is clearly identical with the "law of the Spirit" in 8:2. Again, though clearly not the Mosaic law as such, "law" nevertheless does have a positive meaning. The flesh is not and cannot be "law-abiding" whereas by implication the Spirit can and is.

---

[24] This also suggests that the verb used in the traditional formula was πέμπω (Rom 8:3) rather than ἐξαποστέλλω (Gal 4:4).

Romans 8:9–13: Those in Whom the Spirit Dwells

Paul then continues the contrast between the Spirit and the flesh in 8:9–13. But here the emphasis is on the Spirit and the ultimate results for those in whom the Spirit dwells. In doing so, he directly addresses his audience by using the second person plural (8:9, 11, 12, 13) rather than the third-person description of the flesh in 8:5–8. The structure is similar to the previous section. In 8:9–10, he again contrasts the Spirit, life, and righteousness, on the one hand, with the flesh, death, and sin, on the other. In 8:11–13, he then offers an explanation of the contrast, this time by drawing together the arguments of 8:1–10 and emphasizing their eschatological implications. If the Spirit dwells in them, then God, who raised Jesus from the dead, will also give life even to their mortal bodies. The passage is also held together by an inclusion ("in the Spirit," Rom 8:9, 13). The contrast between the Spirit and the flesh again does not involve a contrast with the law; it is with sin and death.[25]

What Paul seems to be most interested in, however, is using the vocabulary of 8:1–10 and drawing out the eschatological implications of the contrast. In 8:11–13, he claims that if the Spirit of God, who raised Jesus from the dead, dwells in them, then that same God will also give life to their mortal bodies through this same Spirit (8:11). Therefore, if they live according to the flesh, they will certainly die; but if they put to death the deeds of the body, they will live (8:13). Significantly, Paul moves from the present tense to the future tense, from the role of the Spirit in the present to its role in the ultimate resurrection of the dead. He thereby especially points to the eschatological role of the Spirit, a role he will develop further in 8:18–30.

This shift in emphasis toward the eschatological also explains an otherwise puzzling alternation in vocabulary. In 8:1–9, the contrast was consistently between the Spirit and the flesh. In 8:10–11, the contrast becomes one between the Spirit and the body (σῶμα). Then in 8:13, the contrast becomes one between the Spirit and both the flesh and the body. The reason for the shifting between "flesh" (σάρξ) and "body" (σῶμα) is that, in an eschatological context, early Christian belief in resurrection is expressed as a belief in the resurrection of the "body" and not of the "flesh." Thus, in the eschatological context of 8:10–11, Paul needs to adjust his language to reflect this belief.

Within the argument of 8:1–30, 8:11–13 also plays another important role. By taking up the concepts and contrasts of earlier verses, 8:11–13 specifies more clearly the implications of the subproposition expressed in 8:1–2. The ultimate significance of the lack of condemnation for those in Christ (8:1) and of the "law of the Spirit of life" (8:2) is that the Spirit of the God who raised Jesus from the dead will also ultimately give life even to their mortal bodies by raising them from the dead through the power of the Spirit now already dwelling in them. This more specific reformulation of the initial subproposition will then serve as the basis for 8:18–30 and, as we shall see, for 8:31–11:36.

---

[25] In addition, the fluidity of the notion of the Spirit, in that it is described in 8:9 as both the Spirit of God and the Spirit of Christ, should be noted.

Romans 8:14–17: Who Are the Sons and Heirs?

But before he does this, Paul returns in 8:14–17 to the language of Gal 4:6–7 in order to revise it more extensively so that it is in keeping with what he has already written in Rom 8:1–13. These revisions likewise set the stage not only for 8:18–30 but also for 8:31–11:36 on the ultimate fate of Israel. Romans 8:14–17 begins with the statement that those who are led by the Spirit of God are sons (υἱοί) of God. Paul then gives the reason for this in 8:15–16: the reception of the Spirit. Finally, in 8:17, he concludes from this that if we are children, we are also heirs (κληρονόμοι) of God and coheirs (συγκληρονόμοι) with Christ. The passage develops through a concatenation of terms: "led by the Spirit"—"sons of God"—"Spirit of adoption"— "children of God"—"heirs"—"coheirs."

Paul has taken up words and phrases he used earlier in Gal 4:6–7, the most obvious of which are "sons," "Spirit," "Abba, Father," "adoption," and "heirs." Yet he interprets them in a quite different way. Perhaps the best way to grasp the significance of these reinterpretations is to understand what several of these words and phrases would have immediately brought to mind for his Roman Christian audience.

Both the Jewish scriptures and other Jewish literature used several of these words and phrases to describe Israel and its relationship with God. This is most clearly the case with the phrases "sons of God" and "children of God," which, though not very common, were regularly used to refer to Israel.[26] Significantly, contemporary Jewish literature regularly used these phrases to refer, in an eschatological context, to Israel and to Israel's deliverance.[27] In addition, both the Jewish scriptures[28] and other Jewish literature of the period[29] frequently referred to Israel as God's "inheritance," Several of these passages also emphasize that Israel is God's inheritance forever (*Jub.* 22:9–10, 14–15) and that God's wrath would only be temporary (*2 Bar.* 5:1; *L.A.B.* 12:9; 39:7). What all these passages indicate is that words and phrases of this sort would inevitably conjure up in the mind of Paul's Roman Christian audience Israel and its ultimate fate. Yet as pointed out earlier, Paul's use of this language in Gal 4:6–7 within the wider context of Galatians apparently excluded Israel. In Rom 8:14–17, however, the rhetoric moves in a different direction, in such a way that Israel can now be included.

In order to understand how Paul does this, one needs first to realize that the notions of "son" and "heir" have already been reinterpreted by Paul and by early Christianity more broadly. This is indicated by the traditional creedal formula Paul partially quoted in Gal 4:4–7. There Paul wrote that God sent forth God's Son for

---

[26] Exod 4:22–23; Deut 14:1–2; 32:5–6; 31:19–22; Isa 1:2–4; Hos 1:10 (MT); Wis 12:21; 16:10, 21, 26; 18:13; 3 Macc 6:28). The term παῖδες ("children," "servants") is also used in Wis 12:7; 19:6 to refer to Israel.

[27] 1 En. 62:11; *Jub.* 1:24–25; *Pss. Sol.* 17:27; *2 Bar.* 13:9; *As. Mos.* 10:3; *Sib. Or.* 3:702; 5:202; 4QDibHam[a] 3:4–6:3. Several texts make use of roughly equivalent terms (*Jub.* 2:20; *Sib. Or.* 5:68; *4 Ezra* 6:58).

[28] Deut 32:9; 1 Kgs 8:51–53; 2 Kgs 21:14; Ps 33:12; 74:2; Isa 63:17; Jer 10:16; Mic 7:18.

[29] Jdt 13:5; Sir 24:8, 12; *Jub.* 1:19–21; 22:9–10, 14–15; 33:20; *2 Bar.* 5:1; *L.A.B.* 12:9; 21:10; 27:17; 28:2; 39:7; 49:6.

the purpose of redemption so that they might receive "adoption" (υἱοθεσία). God further sent the Spirit of God's Son into those who can now cry out, "Abba, Father." And, if they are now sons (υἱός), they are also heirs (κληρονόμος). Although the concepts of sonship and inheritance were certainly rooted in the Jewish scriptures and in other Jewish literature of the period, the basis for both these realities has been reinterpreted by Paul and other early Christians. It is now rooted in Christ as Son of God and in what has been accomplished especially in his death and resurrection.[30]

What, then, is the relationship between this new way of being sons or heirs and Israel as God's "inheritance" or observant Jews as God's "sons"? In his intensely polemical interpretation of the creedal formula in Galatians, Paul seemingly excluded those who observe the law, that is, Jews, from being sons and heirs. In Rom 8:14–17, however, he takes a quite different view. This becomes clear when one contrasts these verses with Gal 4:4–7. First, negatively, Paul does not mention the Mosaic law in Rom 8:14–17. This is in contrast to Gal 4:4–5, where God sent God's Son, born "under the law," to redeem those "under the law." Galatians 4:4–5 is connected with Paul's wider polemic in Galatians, that the law is a form of slavery in which its observers, or would-be observers, are held (Gal 4:3, 9; 5:1). This omission of any mention of the Mosaic law would not be significant in itself were it not for the second change Paul makes. This second change is connected to the way he writes about the role of the Spirit. In Rom 8:14, he claims that those who are led by the Spirit are sons of God. In 8:15–16 he provides the reason for this:

> For [γάρ] you have not received a spirit of slavery that leads again to fear, but you have received a Spirit of adoption [υἱοθεσίας] by which we cry "Abba, Father." This same Spirit witnesses along with our spirit that we are children [τέκνα] of God.

In continuity with what he has written about the Spirit in 8:1–13, Paul contrasts the reception of the Spirit with a spirit of slavery. The slavery mentioned in 8:15, however, is not slavery to the law but "slavery" to sin and death, the two realities he has constantly set over against the Spirit in this section of Romans. At this point, it becomes apparent why Paul has reconfigured the contrast between Spirit and flesh in 8:1–13. It enables him to describe the eschatologically oriented realities of becoming "sons of God" and "children of God" and consequently "heirs" in such a way that these realities are no longer put in contrast to the law or observers of the law. The result is that Paul no longer precludes the inclusion of Israel, which was, in effect, what he had done in his intensely polemical letter to the Galatians.

It becomes clear what Paul has been trying to do in 8:1–17, both in his use of traditional material and in the revision of what he himself had written earlier. Building on a creedal formula he shares with his Roman Christian audience, Paul subtly

---

[30] The interpretation of the title "Son" or "Son of God" and its background are disputed. This is especially the case for the question of preexistence. Although I think that for Paul it involves a notion of preexistence (esp. in Phil 2:6–11 and even in Rom 1:3–4), what is important for our purposes is that believers become "sons of God" through Christ. See Martin Hengel, *The Son of God: The Origin of Christology and the History of Jewish-Hellenistic Religion* (Philadelphia: Fortress, 1976); and Brendan Byrne, *"Sons of God"—"Seed of Abraham": A Study of the Idea of the Sonship of God of All Christians in Paul against the Jewish Background* (AnBib 83; Rome: Biblical Institute Press, 1979).

reinterprets both the role of the Spirit and concepts of filiation and inheritance so that the ultimate inclusion of Israel is no longer precluded. This standpoint differs significantly from the intense and controversial polemic of Galatians, and it is this difference that makes possible Paul's anguished, but finally positive, reflections on the ultimate fate of Israel in 8:31–11:36. More immediately, however, without such a reinterpretation the inclusive eschatology of 8:18–30 would be impossible.

ROMANS 8:18–30: THE FRAMEWORK OF AN INCLUSIVE ESCHATOLOGY

Once Paul has reinterpreted the role of the Spirit and terms such as "sons of God," "children of God," and "heirs," he can then expand on the eschatological statements of 8:2, 11, 13. That Paul saw 8:18–30 as a development of these eschatological statements is clear from his continued references to the Spirit (8:23, 26–27) as well as to "sons of God" (8:19) and "children of God" (8:21). The structure of the passage falls into three sections: (1) the subjection and groaning for liberation of all creation (κτίσις) (8:18–22); (2) the expectant groaning of all of "us" through the intercession of the Spirit (8:23–28); and (3) the certainty of God's unfolding plan (8:29–30). That sentences beginning with "we know" (οἴδαμεν, 8:22, 28) mark the ends of each of the first two sections indicates rhetorically that this is the structure of the passage.[31]

Before a detailed look at this section, several characteristics of the passage need emphasis. As in 8:1–17, Paul again uses traditional Jewish and early Christian material in 8:18–30. Traditional motifs, though the subject of some dispute among scholars, probably included the following:

8:19–21, 22	Motifs from Jewish apocalyptic literature
8:23	"the firstfruits of the Spirit" (ἀπαρχὴ τοῦ πνεύματος)
8:20, 24–25	The role of hope (ἐλπίς)
8:27	God as the "searcher of hearts" (ὁ δὲ ἐραυνῶν τὰς καρδίας)
8:28	"loving God" (τοῖς ἀγαπῶσιν τὸν θεὸν)

In 8:29–30, Paul may also have made use of a more fixed traditional Christian formula about God foreknowing, calling, justifying, and glorifying—a formula whose original context may have been a baptismal ritual.[32]

Although he uses traditional material of various sorts, Paul again reconfigures it for his own purposes. He does so in several ways. First, the eschatological framework, though not all the specific language, is based especially on the more inclusive

---

[31] For a general view of Paul's eschatology and some of the issues connected with it, see David E. Aune, "Eschatology (Early Christian)," *ABD* 2:602–3.

[32] This is a modified version of the list found in Paulsen, *Überlieferung*, 182–83. Osten-Sacken (*Römer 8*, 96–97) has argued that a traditional Hellenistic Christian text, known to Paul either in writing or orally, lies behind 8:18–27. His arguments, although tempting, remain unconvincing (see Wilckens, *Römer*, 2:150–51).

aspects of 1 Cor 15:20–28, 42–49, 50–57.[33] Second, at crucial points, Paul introduces language that again brings to mind his basic argument that salvation is meant for both Jews and Gentiles. This is especially the case in his use of "all" in Rom 8:22, 28 and his use of "many brethren" in 8:29. Third, Paul also uses language he again takes up in 8:31–11:36 in specifically dealing with the question of the ultimate fate of Israel. This is especially the case in his use of terms in 8:18–30 that are applicable to Israel but are also taken up again in 8:31–11:36: "adoption" (υἱοθεσία, 8:23; 9:4), "purpose" (πρόθεσις, 8:28; 9:11), "foreknow" (προγινώσκω, 8:29; 11:2), "glory" (δόξα, 8:18, 21; 9:4, 23; 11:36), "sons" (υἱοί, 8:19; 9:27), "children" (τέκνα, 8:21; 9:8), "holy" (ἅγιος, 8:27; 11:36), "call" (καλέω, 8:30; 9:7, 12, 24, 25, 26), and the cluster "called"/"elect"/"election" (κλητός/ἐκλεκτός/ἐκλογή, 8:28; 9:11; 11:5, 7, 28). The conjunction of the traditional material in 8:18–30 and Paul's reconfiguration of it into these patterns result in an eschatology that makes for a context within which Paul can then deal more specifically with the fate of Israel in 8:31–11:36.

Romans 8:18–22: The Eager Expectation of Creation

Paul begins with a claim that the sufferings of the present time are not worth comparing with the glory about to be revealed.[34] This claim takes up and expands on 8:17 and establishes the framework for the rest of 8:18–30, which is the contrast between present suffering and future glory. The rest of this section, 8:19–22, is about the present enslavement and the future liberation of "creation." Romans 8:19 begins with a statement about the situation of creation as a whole, that it eagerly awaits the revelation of the "sons of God." Romans 8:20–21 offers a more specific explanation of both creation's present subjection to futility and its future liberation into the glory of the children of God. Finally, in 8:22, Paul concludes with a statement that presumes this explanation is one that would be knowledge common to himself and his Roman audience, that "we know" all creation groans and is in labor until now.

To understand the force of Paul's argument in this section, one has to realize how Paul is making use of traditional apocalyptic images and at the same time reinterpreting them for his own purposes. First, the basic framework of the passage, the contrast between present suffering and future glory, was common in Jewish apocalyptic literature.[35] The contrast was also fairly widespread in early Christianity. Paul himself used the imagery earlier in 2 Cor 4:17, and the same imagery also appears in 1 Pet 4:13; 5:10. A second traditional apocalyptic motif is the connection between the fate of human beings and the fate of "creation," which in Rom 8:19–22 probably refers especially to the nonhuman created world.[36] This motif takes different forms.

---

[33] See above, pp. 265–67.

[34] Paul often connects the suffering of believers with assimilation to the suffering and death of Christ. See 1 Thess 4:13–18; 5:10; Gal 2:19–20; Phil 3:4–11, 20–21; 2 Cor 4:7–14; 6:1–10; 7:3; 13:3–4.

[35] Dan 7:17–27; Wis 2–5; 2 Macc 7; *1 En.* 102–104; *2 Bar.* 15:8.

[36] The meaning of "creation" (ἡ κτίσις) in this context has been disputed over the centuries. See Byrne, *Romans*, 255–56, for a list of the possibilities. See also Fitzmyer, *Romans*, 506–7; Cranfield, *Romans*, 1:414; Wilckens, *Römer*, 2:153; Dunn, *Romans*, 469–70. All these commentators take "creation" to refer to the nonhuman created world.

Sometimes it is explicitly connected with the cursing of the earth because of Adam's transgression in Gen 3:17–19; 5:29.[37] At other times it is connected with the creation of the new heaven and the new earth in Isa 65:17; 66:22.[38] Sometimes it seems to have become a virtually independent motif with little connection to either Genesis or Isaiah.[39] Common to all these texts is that the situation of the nonhuman created world is linked to the situation of human beings, in terms of both disintegration and reintegration or renewal, and that God's future intervention will bring about this renewal. Since Paul has already in Rom 5:12–21 traced the roots of the present situation of sin and death to Adam's transgression, 8:20–21 is closest to the Jewish texts that build on interpretations of the Genesis account, in that the futility to which creation has been unwillingly subjected and the decay to which it is enslaved are the consequences of Adam's transgression.[40] A third traditional apocalyptic motif is the conviction that increased suffering and distress on a cosmic scale will immediately precede the final consummation.[41] A fourth and final traditional apocalyptic motif in this passage is the use, with eschatological overtones, of the image of the birth pangs of a woman in labor.[42]

All four traditional apocalyptic motifs no doubt represent viewpoints Paul and his Roman Christian audience have in common. Yet Paul reconfigures them in several ways, turning them in a direction that serves his own argument. First, he connects them with what he wrote in 8:1–17. The eager longing of creation is for the revelation of the "sons of God" (8:19); creation will be freed into the freedom of the glory of the "children of God" (8:21). Given how Paul in 8:14–17, so as not to exclude Jews, reinterpreted his previous use of these phrases in Galatians, it is significant that the same viewpoint is continued in this section, now in a more clearly eschatological context. The same is true for his description in 8:21 of what creation will be freed from, the slavery to decay, and what it will be freed for, the freedom of the glory of the children of God. "Slavery" is not to the law but to decay (φθορᾶς), similar to the slavery to sin, death, and fear in 8:1, 15. And "freedom" is the freedom of the glory of the sons of God and not, as it was in Gal 5:1, freedom from slavery to the Mosaic law. Both slavery and eschatological freedom are now of a different sort from what they were in Galatians.

Second, Paul revises these motifs into a more inclusive framework similar to sections of 1 Corinthians 15. The best way to understand this is to see them in contrast to the apocalyptic views of which they were traditionally a part. In the apocalyptic texts mentioned above, the situation of creation, both in its disintegration and in its renewal by God, was intimately related to the human situation in its disintegration and renewal by God. It mirrored the latter situation, which included conflict

---

[37] *Jub.* 4:26; *2 Bar.* 56:5–7; *4 Ezra* 7:10–15.

[38] *1 En.* 45:4–5; 91:15–16; *Jub.* 1:29; 23:23–31; *2 Bar.* 31:5–32:6.

[39] *1 En.* 51:3–5; 58:1–6; 61–62; *2 Bar.* 72:1–74:4; *4 Ezra* 7:30–44; 9:19–22; Philo, *Praem.* 88–90; *Sib. Or.* 3:788–795.

[40] See Fitzmyer, *Romans*, 505–8; Byrne, *Romans*, 256–61.

[41] Dan 7:21–22, 25–27; 12:1–3; *4 Ezra* 5:1–13; 6:13–24; 9:1–3; *2 Bar.* 25:2–3; 48:30–41; 70:2–10; *Sib. Or.* 1:62–65; 2:154–173; 3:632–656, 796–806.

[42] Ps 48:6; Isa 13:8; 26:16–17; 66:7–8; Jer 4:31; *1 En.* 62:4; *4 Ezra* 10:6–16; 1QH[a] 3:7–18; 1 Thess 5:3. See also Heraclitus, *All.* 39.14 for Greco-Roman use of this motif.

and was deeply adversarial in nature. Either the Jewish people as a whole or the righteous among them were set over against the unrighteous many, whether Gentiles or unrighteous Jews. For example, the descriptions of the renewal of the created world in *1 En.* 45:4–5; 51:1–5; 58:1–6; 61–62 are part of a larger eschatological scenario of *1 En.* 37–71. The central theme of this section of *1 Enoch* is the reward of the holy ones and the punishment of sinners and the Gentile rulers who have oppressed Israel.[43] Similarly, the descriptions of the renewal of creation in *4 Ezra* 7:10–15, 30–44 and in *2 Bar.* 31:5–32:6; 56:5–7; 72:1–74:4 are part of larger eschatological scenarios in which the righteous will be rewarded and sinners, along with the Gentiles and their rulers, will be punished. The same kind of scenario is the context for the description of the renewal of creation found in the eschatological, though not apocalyptic, *Sib. Or.* 3:788–795. Although in an attenuated form, this adversarial scenario is even reflected in Philo. *Praem.* 169–172.

In Rom 8:18–22, however, the "sons of God" (8:19) and the "children of God" (8:21) are not set over against any other group or groups of human beings from which they will be delivered or against which they will be vindicated. Rather, they will be freed from "slavery to decay" (τῆς δουλείας τῆς φθορᾶς) into the freedom of the glory of the children of God (8:21). Although the use of vocabulary differs somewhat, this outlook is similar to that found in 1 Cor 15:20–28, 42–49, 50–57. There Paul is writing about the eschatological resurrection of the dead. In describing these events, Paul lists in 1 Cor 15:24–26 the enemies over which Christ will triumph, every rule (ἀρχήν), authority (ἐξουσίαν), power (δύναμιν), and finally the last enemy, death (θάνατος). These enemies are not groups of human beings but cosmic powers, the most important of which is death.[44] This same viewpoint is further specified in 1 Cor 15:40–57, which contains a series of contrasts between the present situation of human beings and their future eschatological situation. These verses also contain vocabulary Paul now also uses in Rom 8:18–22. Decay (φθορά) is contrasted with imperishability (ἀφθαρσία), and dishonor (ἀτιμία) is contrasted with glory (δόξα) (1 Cor 15:42–43, 50). Although the pairing in 1 Corinthians differs from that in Rom 8:21, both texts in effect contrast "decay" and "glory," one explicitly and the other implicitly. Finally, both Rom 8:22 and 1 Cor 15:24–28 emphasize that these events involve all of creation. This emphasis on "all" is important for Paul. The word reappears in Rom 8:28, the parallel conclusion to the next section. In addition, it has already been an important word for Paul in Romans, usually pointing to the inclusion of both Jews and Gentiles in God's plan of salvation. Given what Paul will go on to argue in 8:31–11:36, the ultimate inclusion of Israel along with the Gentiles, his use of "all" here is part of the framework he wants to establish, within which he will deal with the issue of the ultimate inclusion of both Jews and Gentiles.

In 8:18–22, Paul, then, has taken up again the basic framework found in 1 Corinthians 15, in which deliverance or vindication is not over human enemies

---

[43] The same is true for *1 En.* 91:15–16, which is part of the much older "Apocalypse of Weeks" (*1 En.* 91:12–17; 93:1–10).

[44] Cf. Rom 8:38 and, in the Pauline tradition, Col 1:16; 2:10–15; Eph 1:21; 3:10; 6:12. See also 1 Pet 3:22; Philo, *Conf.* 171; *Mut.* 59.

but over cosmic powers, particularly those of death and decay. As pointed out in the previous chapter of this study, this shift by Paul in eschatological framework was originally rooted in his convictions about the inclusion of the Gentiles in God's salvific plan. This inclusion almost inevitably provoked a revision of the adversarial categories of traditional Jewish and early Christian eschatology. The Gentiles as a group could no longer be seen as adversaries against whom Israel or the pious of Israel would be vindicated. At the same time, this shift in eschatological framework now comes to serve a further purpose in the context of Romans 8–11. Paul now uses this very inclusiveness as the framework within which he can now struggle with the ultimate inclusion of Israel. Paul now takes up other aspects of this same outlook in 8:23–28.

Romans 8:23–28: Expectations of Those Who Have Received the Spirit

Within this larger eschatological framework, Paul now turns his attention in 8:23–28 to the expectations of those who have received the Spirit. In 8:23, he writes that those who have the firstfruits of the Spirit also groan as they await their adoption, which is the redemption of their bodies. In 8:24–25, he expands on the notion of "awaiting" by emphasizing that "we are saved in hope" and that hope is not in things seen but in things not yet seen but awaited with patience. In 8:26–27, he expands on another element of 8:23, the firstfruits of the Spirit. The role of the Spirit is especially one of intercession in which the Spirit helps them in their weakness, in their lack of understanding of what they should pray for, so they can pray as they ought. Finally, in 8:28, Paul concludes this section with a passage parallel to 8:22, the conclusion of the previous section: "We know that with those who love God, those called according to his purpose, in all things he [God] works for the good."[45]

Although this section is brief, it is remarkably complex, for three reasons. First, Paul once again takes up traditional motifs and transforms them for his own purposes. Second, he again takes up elements from 1 Corinthians 15. Finally and perhaps most significantly, he subtly establishes a particular framework of hope that will lead his audience to the issue of Israel's future with the appropriate mind-set and disposition.

First, several traditional motifs appear in this passage. The image of "firstfruits" in Rom 8:23 comes from Deut 26:1–15, a description of the Israelite ritual in which the firstfruits of the harvest are brought to the temple as an acknowledgment that the whole harvest belongs to God, a *pars pro toto*.[46] Although the image of firstfruits may have been fairly widespread in early Christianity (Jas 1:18; Rev 14:4), the connection of the image with the Spirit may at first seem restricted to Paul, since it is made only here. Yet Paul used a similar phrase, "the pledge [ἀρραβών] of the Spirit," in 2 Cor 1:22; 5:5. If one were to ask where these two phrases would have been at home, the most likely answer would be in connection with baptism, where the Spirit would have first been received. This suggests that Paul derived the

---

[45] It is not clear in the Greek what the subject of the verb "works" is. It could be either "all" (πάντα) or God as the implied subject. Given that the emphasis in 8:28–30 is on what God accomplishes, God is more likely the subject of the clause.

[46] Byrne, *Romans*, 263.

phrase "firstfruits of the Spirit" from early Christian baptismal rituals.[47] A second traditional motif is his characterization of hope in Rom 8:24–25 as an expectation about things unseen (see 2 Cor 4:18; Heb 11:1). A third is that of God as a "searcher of hearts" (1 Sam 16:7; 1 Kgs 8:39; 1 Chr 28:9; Ps 7:9; 17:3; 26:2; 139:1, 3, 23). Finally, the motif of "those who love God" is also traditional.[48]

Paul takes these traditional motifs and weaves them together in such a way as to emphasize the mysterious, incomprehensible character of God's providence. In Rom 8:23, he connects the possession of the Spirit as the firstfruits of what is to come with the expectation of adoption, which he defines, at least partially, as the "redemption of our bodies." By the latter, he clearly means the eschatological resurrection of the dead.[49] In doing this, he takes up themes he has already written about in 8:1–17, but now he places them in a clearly eschatological context. He then expands on each of these two notions, first, in 8:24–25, on expectation as hope, and second, in 8:26–27, on the role of the Spirit in these expectations.[50] In developing these notions, Paul emphasizes their mysterious character. No one hopes for things that are seen; rather, hope is about things that are unseen or not yet seen. The role of the Spirit is to help overcome weakness. One result of this weakness is that we do not know even what we should pray for. Because of this, the Spirit intercedes for us with groans too deep for utterance (στεναγμοῖς ἀλαλήτοις). Only God knows the intention of the Spirit (τὸ φρόνημα τοῦ πνεύματος), that the Spirit intercedes for us.[51] Finally, in 8:28, Paul concludes that, as a result of all this, "we know" that, for those who love God, who are called according to his purpose (κατὰ πρόθεσιν), God works in all things (πάντα) for the good. This verse parallels 8:22 and emphasizes again the notion of "all." "All creation" (πᾶσα κτίσις) of 8:22 finds its parallel in 8:28, in "all things" (πάντα). The result is a combination of confident hope that God will ultimately accomplish for those who love God what has been promised through the possession of the Spirit as firstfruits and the realization that the ways in which God will bring this about go beyond human weakness and surpass human comprehension.

Second, Paul continues, as he did in 8:18–22, to make use of the framework he used in 1 Corinthians 15. He signals this at the beginning of the passage in Rom 8:23 by identifying "sonship" with the "redemption of our body," which refers to the eschatological resurrection of the body, the subject of 1 Corinthians 15. Then, in Rom 8:23–28, those who possess the Spirit as firstfruits and await the redemption of their bodies are not set over against other groups of human beings. Rather, what they hope to be delivered from is their weakness (τῇ ἀσθενείᾳ), in which for the

[47] Paulsen, *Überlieferung*, 120.
[48] Exod 20:6; Deut 5:10; 7:9; Josh 22:5; 1 Kgs 3:3; Neh 1:5; Dan 9:4; CD 19:1; 1QH[a] 16:13; Sir 2:15–16; *Pss. Sol.* 14:1–2; *T. Iss.* 5:1–2; *T. Benj.* 3:1.
[49] This is clearly one of the central points of Paul's arguments in 1 Corinthians 15.
[50] That Paul is intentionally connecting the notions of hope and expectation is clear from 8:25, where he places the two in parallel.
[51] Although the notion of intercession is based on ideas found in the Jewish scriptures (Gen 18:23–33; Exod 8:8, 12, 28–30; Lev 16:21–22; Num 6:23–27; 2 Sam 2:16; 1 Kgs 18:22–40; Tob 12:12; 2 Macc 15:12–16), the attribution of this intercession to the Spirit seems to have been a Pauline novelty. See Fitzmyer, *Romans*, 518.

present the Spirit comes to their aid (8:26). The Spirit stands in contrast to their weakness, a contrast similar to that found in 1 Cor 15:43–46, where the body that was sown in weakness (ἐν ἀσθενείᾳ) will be raised as a "spiritual body" (σῶμα πνευματικόν). Finally, as in Rom 8:22, Paul's insistence in Rom 8:28 that God works in all things (πάντα) for the good echoes his insistence in 1 Cor 15:28 that all things will be ultimately subjected to God, who will then be "all things in every-thing" (πάντα ἐν πᾶσιν). The influence of 1 Corinthians 15 gives to this passage, as it did to Rom 8:18–22, the same inclusive framework. Not only does all of creation long for the revelation of the sons of God; God works in all things for the good of those who love him. Since God's ways are beyond human weakness, they not only surpass human comprehension but do so in a mysteriously inclusive way.

Finally, why does Paul's rhetoric work in this way, and what is his purpose? The answer lies in what it prepares his Roman Christian audience for, in this case the question of the fate of Israel in Rom 8:31–11:36. This is indicated by the fact that two significant terms in 8:23–28 reappear early in 8:31–11:36: "adoption as sons" (υἱοθεσία) of God (8:23) in 9:4 and God's "purpose" (πρόθεσις, 8:28) in 9:11. In both cases their reappearance is connected with Israel. In 9:4, "sonship" is one of the privileges granted to the Israelites, and in 9:11, God's choice of Jacob over Esau is so that "God's purpose in election might persist" (ἵνα ἡ κατὰ ἐκλογὴν πρόθεσις τοῦ θεοῦ μένῃ). This repetition can hardly be accidental. More broadly, Paul's emphases in 8:23–28—on hope as the expectation of things unseen, the convictions that God's ways surpass weak human comprehension, and that God works in all things for the good with those who love him—establish for his Roman Christian audience the kind of mind-set and disposition that would be receptive to his anguished reflections on the ultimate inclusion of Israel, who are his brothers according to the flesh (9:3). This is especially the case since the Roman Christians worried that his previous views in Galatians seemed to point in the opposite direction.

Romans 8:29–30: Those Called and Destined for Glory

Romans 8:29–30 serves as the conclusion of 8:1–30. Formally, they are an example of κλῖμαξ or *gradatio,* that is, a rhetorical figure consisting of a series of clauses in which the last term in one clause become the first term in the next clause.[52]

> For those whom he foreknew, he also predestined
>> to be conformed to the image of his Son,
>>> that he might be the firstborn among many brethren;
>> those whom he predestined, he also called;
>>> those whom he called, he also made righteous;
>>>> and those whom he made righteous, he also glorified.

The structure of this passage is probably traditional, to which Paul adds the clauses "to be conformed to the image of his Son, that he might be the firstborn among many brethren" in 8:29bc. There are several reason for thinking this.

---

[52] See Quintilian, *Inst.* 9.3.54; Demetrius, *Eloc.* 270.

First, the clauses in 8:29bc, which, as shall be seen, contain several Pauline elements, break up the otherwise symmetrical structure of the verses. This suggests that Paul is commenting on an already existing formula.

Second, the use of some of the vocabulary in 8:29–30 differs from Paul's. In the ten other times Paul uses the verb "glorify" (δοξάζω), the object is never a group of human beings. In six of the ten cases, it is God (Gal 1:24; 1 Cor 6:20; 2 Cor 9:13; Rom 1:21; 15:6, 9); in three cases, it is some sort of "ministry," either Paul's own (Rom 11:13) or the "ministry of the Spirit" (2 Cor 3:10 [bis]), or it is even a part of the human body (1 Cor 12:26). Similarly, in Paul's only other use of the verb "predestine" (προορίζω), the object is God's wisdom (1 Cor 2:7). Even Paul's only other use of the verb "foreknow" (προγινώσκω), in Rom 11:2, clearly takes up its use in this verse and so is consistent with its use in 8:29 as traditional.

Third, all of the verbs in 8:29–30 are in the aorist tense, including "glorify" (ἐδόξασεν). Given that in 8:21 Paul writes of the "freedom of the glory [τῆς δόξης] of the children of God" as a future, eschatological event, it is unlikely that he himself would have then used the aorist tense only nine verses later to refer to the same reality.[53]

The basic structure of 8:29–30, then, is probably a piece of traditional material. Although it is conceivable that it was connected with baptism, it is impossible from this distance to describe more closely its original purpose or function. Its appeal for Paul was partially that, as a traditional formula, it was also known to his Roman Christian audience. But its appeal was more than that. The concatenation of the five verbs in these verses ("foreknew"—"predestined"—"called"—"made righteous"—"glorified") admirably expresses for Paul his expansive conviction, found in 8:28, about how God works in all things for the good. All five verbs also would have evoked in Paul's Roman Christian audience images of God's actions found in the Jewish scriptures and in other Jewish literature of the period, particularly images of God's actions on behalf of Israel or on behalf of the righteous in Israel.[54] Given the issues he wants to deal with in 8:31–11:36, such images would be exactly what Paul wants to evoke. That such an evocation is intentional becomes clear when one notes that Paul returns to the first verb in the series ("foreknew" [προέγνω]) in 11:2 ("God has not rejected his people whom he foreknew [προέγνω]"), in the section of 8:31–11:36 where he begins to move directly toward the ultimate inclusion of Israel. The repetition of "foreknew" in 11:2 would inevitably have brought to his Roman Christian audience's minds not only the "foreknew" but also the other four verbs so closely tied to it in 8:29–30.

Paul, however, does not leave this traditional formula untouched. In 8:29, he adds the clauses "to be conformed [συμμόρφους] to the image [τῆς εἰκόνος] of his son, so that he might become the firstborn [πρωτότοκον] among many

---

[53] Some of these reasons are spelled out in greater detail in Paulsen, *Überlieferung*, 156–61; see also Wilckens, *Römer*, 2:251.

[54] "Foreknow" (Heb. ידע ["to know"], often with the connotation of "choose"): Gen 18:19; Ps 1:6; Jer 1:5; Hos 13:5 MT; Amos 3:2; 1QHᵃ 1:7–8; 9:29–30; CD 2:8; "predestine": *As. Mos.* 1:14; 1QS 3:15–16; "call": Hos 1:10; Sir 36:17; *Jub.* 1:25; *L.A.B.* 18:6; *4 Ezra* 6:58; 4QDibHamᵃ 3:4–5; 1QM 3:2; 4:10–11; 1QpHab 10:13; "justify" (usually in the sense of "vindicate"): 1 Kgs 8:32; 2 Chr 6:23; Esth 10:11 (LXX); "glorify": Wis 19:22.

[πολλοῖς] brethren." The addition of these two clauses serves three purposes. First, they explicitly connect this traditional formula with the eschatological event of the resurrection of the dead, which has been a central theme of Romans 8 but was not present in the traditional formula. This is clear from Paul's use of the words σύμμορφος ("conformed to") and εἰκών ("image") elsewhere in his letters. In Phil 3:20–21, Paul writes concerning the resurrection of the dead that believers await (ἀπεκδεχόμεθα) a Savior from heaven, the Lord Jesus Christ, who will transform (μετασχηματίσει) their humble bodies that they may be conformed (σύμμορφον) to his glorious body. In Phil 3:10, Paul connects this process with first being conformed to (συμμορφιζόμενος) Christ's sufferings so that Paul may in this way attain to the resurrection of the dead. In 2 Cor 3:18, Paul describes believers as even now in the process of being transformed (μεταμορφούμεθα) into the image (τὴν αὐτὴν εἰκόνα) of the risen Christ, a process to be completed only at the resurrection of the dead.[55] Finally, in 1 Cor 15:49, Paul claims that "just as we have borne the image of the man of dust [τὴν εἰκόνα τοῦ χοϊκοῦ], we will also bear the image of the man of heaven [τὴν εἰκόνα τοῦ ἐπουρανίου]." Again Paul is referring to the resurrection of the dead. The "man of dust" is Adam, and the "man of heaven" is the risen Christ. This last reference again shows the continuing influence of the framework of 1 Corinthians 15 on this whole section of Romans 8.

This last quotation also points to a second purpose for including these clauses in 8:29, the implicit contrast between Adam and Christ. The use of the word "image" (εἰκών) to refer to Christ in 8:29 inevitably draws the minds of Paul's audience back to Gen 1:26–28, the creation of Adam "in the image" (κατὰ εἰκόνα) of God, and to the contrast between Adam and Christ so prominent in Rom 5:12–21. This contrast is abetted by Paul's reference to Christ as the "firstborn [πρωτότοκος] among many brethren." Although the term "firstborn" may have messianic overtones, alluding as it does to an epithet of the Davidic king (Ps 89:27; see Heb 1:6; Rev 1:5), its use here seems much closer to Paul's similar use of the word "firstfruits" (ἀπαρχή) in 1 Cor 15:20, 23, where he wrote about the relationship between Christ's resurrection and the resurrection of believers.[56] Christ is the "firstfruits of those who have fallen asleep." And just as all die in Adam, so too all will be made alive in Christ, but in a particular order, first Christ as the firstfruits and then at his coming those who belong to Christ.

This contrast between Adam and Christ also leads to the final purpose of Paul's addition to the traditional formula. As pointed out above in the analysis of Romans 5, one reason Paul used the contrast between Adam and Christ in Romans 5 was to emphasize that sin and salvation involved both Jews and Gentiles. That Paul means his Roman Christian audience to make a similar connection here is indicated by his insertion into the traditional formula: "that he [Christ] might be the firstborn among many [πολλοῖς] brethren." In 5:15, 19, Paul contrasted the effects of Adam's trespass with the effects of grace in Christ, the effects of one man's action on "the many" (οἱ πολλοί), whether for ill or for good. In using this term in 5:15, 19, he was building on his immediately prior use of the word "many" (πολλῶν) in

---

[55] In 2 Cor 4:4, Christ is described as the "image of God" (εἰκὼν τοῦ θεοῦ).
[56] For the messianic overtones, see Byrne, *Romans*, 273.

4:17–18, Abraham as the "father of many nations," that is, of Jews and Gentiles. In 8:29, by describing Christ as "the firstborn of many brethren," Paul is pointing again to the reality that what happens in Christ is meant for both Jews and Gentiles.[57]

CONCLUSIONS

As one steps back from the details of this analysis and takes a broader look at 8:1–30, it becomes clear that Paul is primarily interested in articulating an eschatological framework within which he can deal with the issues concerning the Jewish people. Paul's reasons for doing this were of two sorts. First, his Roman Christian audience was understandably suspicious of his previous positions about the status of those who observe the Mosaic law and about the Mosaic law itself, as he expressed them in his letter to the Galatians. His positions, or at least the implications of them, seemed to preclude Jews from becoming "sons of God," "children of God," or "heirs," titles belonging to them in the Jewish scriptures and in other contemporary Jewish literature. Such viewpoints, however unintentionally, also called into question the reliability of God's promises. Second, as will become clearer in the analysis of 8:31–11:36, the issue of the fate of Israel was one that Paul also felt deeply about and came to anguish over. As a result, Paul came to realize that some of his own earlier arguments in Galatians had been ill advised and wrongheaded. This is especially true because these arguments themselves were in tension with some of Paul's other convictions, some in Galatians itself and others elsewhere in his letters, especially in 1 Corinthians 15.

He goes about articulating this eschatological framework in a variety of ways. First, he draws on traditional material and motifs and then expands on them. He thereby hopes his Roman Christian audience will understand that his arguments are based on viewpoints and convictions that he and they hold in common. Second, building on these shared traditions, he significantly revises positions he took earlier in Galatians, positions most Roman Christians find unacceptable. He revises the way he understand the role of the Spirit. The role of the Spirit is no longer one that stands in opposition to the Mosaic law or its observers. The role of the Spirit even becomes more lawlike, a "law of the Spirit." Although the Spirit is not an aid in observing the Mosaic law, it is, nevertheless, an aid in observing the "law of God." The enemies of the Spirit are the flesh, sin, and death, not the law. He also revises the way he understands the significance of terms such as "sons of God," "children of God," "adoption," and "heirs." No longer are these terms interpreted in ways that apparently preclude the inclusion of the Jewish people. The way is opened for the arguments in 8:31–11:36 about the inclusion of Israel. These arguments would have been precluded by the views he seemed to express in Galatians. Third, the eschatological framework Paul establishes in 8:1–30 was deeply influenced by what he

---

[57] This emphasis on the inclusion of both Jews and Gentiles also highlights the fact that Paul's concerns here are communal, that is, concerned with Jews and Gentiles as groups, rather than with individual Jews or Gentiles. Conversely, Paul is not concerned in 8:29–30 with the classical doctrine of divine predestination, in which God ordains individuals for either salvation or damnation. See esp. Byrne, *Romans,* 272.

wrote earlier, especially in 1 Corinthians 15. This framework, with its repeated emphasis on "all things," is expansive and inclusive in character. Though not explicitly dealing with the issue of Israel's fate, it provides the framework within which Paul can deal in new ways with this issue. Paul realizes that the convictions expressed in 1 Corinthians 15 were in tension with the implications of some of what he wrote in Galatians. He uses the more inclusive convictions of 1 Corinthians 15 as a fulcrum to rethink those views. Finally, he also emphasizes the extent to which God's providence or plan surpasses human understanding, whose outcome is sure but whose revelation is not as yet seen and so therefore required hope. This mind-set and disposition are crucial not only for his Roman Christian audience's capacity to understand what is to follow in Rom 8:31–11:36. It is also crucial for Paul himself in his own anguished arguments about the fate of Israel. As will become clear below in the analysis of 8:31–11:36, this issue touched Paul personally in ways that no other issue in Romans did. It is not at all accidental that in 11:25–36, Paul will emphasize how mysterious God's plan is (8:25) that includes "all," Jews and Gentiles alike (11:26, 32), that indeed includes "all things" (8:36).

Perhaps emblematic of 8:1–30 is the impossibility of answering clearly what seems like a simple question. Romans 8:1–30 is filled with first-person-plural references to "we" and to "us."[58] To whom do all of these references refer? At first the answer may seem obvious: the "we" who "walk by the Spirit," who are "sons of God," "children of God," "heirs," who await the "redemption of our bodies," are those who believe in Christ. Yet when one realizes that Paul is writing not simply about the present but also about the future—when one realizes that "sons of God," "children of God," and "heirs" are pointedly not interpreted in such a way as to preclude Israel—then the answer becomes much more mysterious. This mysteriousness emphasized by Paul in 8:18–30 will return at the climax of 8:31–11:36, in 11:11–36. There it will involve more specifically, but no less mysteriously, the interlocking relationship between the ultimate fate of Jews and Gentiles together. In this way, the inclusive tendencies of the eschatology of 1 Corinthians 15 and their origin in Paul's convictions about the fate of the Gentiles will continue to influence Paul's reflections even on the ultimate fate of Israel. This reminds us that although the issue that occasions his anguished reflections and rethinking is certainly the ultimate fate of his fellow Jews, Paul cannot do so without at the same time keeping the fate of the Gentiles also at the front of his mind.

---

[58] Rom 8:4, 9, 10, 11, 12, 15, 16, 17, 18, 23, 24, 25, 26.

CHAPTER 11

Paul's Anguish and the Issue of Israel

R OMANS 8:31–11:36 IS AMONG THE MURKIEST and most controversial passages in all of Paul's letters. One reason for this is the issue of the relationship of this passage (usually thought of as Romans 9–11) to the rest of the letter. Is it a virtually independent unit, or is it an integral part of the letter? If the latter, what is its relationship to the rest of the letter?[1] Chapter 9 of this study argued, on thematic and rhetorical grounds, that 8:31–11:36 is an integral part of Paul's overall argument in Romans and that it follows on 8:1–30. The relationship of 8:31–11:36 to 8:1–30 is analogous to the relationship of 2:1–3:20 to 1:18–32, 3:27–4:25 to 3:21–26, and Romans 6–7 to Romans 5.

Another source of controversy is the character of 8:31–11:36 itself. Almost the whole passage is a complex, interwoven series of arguments based on interpretations of the Jewish scriptures. This was seen earlier in 2:1–3:20 and in 3:27–4:25. But the sheer extent of the scriptural arguments in 8:31–11:36 places it in a class by itself.[2] The length of the passage also points to its complexity. Interpreters' decisions at one point in the argument substantially affect the interpretations of later arguments. A small difference of interpretation at one point becomes a substantial difference further on in the interpretation.

Given these difficulties, four aspects of 8:31–11:36 will be of service in the detailed interpretation of Paul's arguments in the following two chapters: (1) characteristics of the passage itself that point to its unity; (2) the overall structure of the

---

[1] Opinions on the nature of Romans 9–11 and its place in the letter vary extensively. For a review of the positions, see E. Elizabeth Johnson, *The Function of Apocalyptic and Wisdom Traditions in Romans 9–11* (SBLDS 109; Atlanta: Scholars Press, 1989), 110–23. Johnson correctly sides with those who think that Romans 9–11 is integral to the letter. Much of the literature is also reviewed by Hans Hübner, *Gottes Ich und Israel: Zum Schriftgebrauch des Paulus in Römer 9–11* (FRLANT 136; Göttingen: Vandenhoeck & Ruprecht, 1984). For a different but often insightful interpretation of Romans 9–11, see John G. Lodge, *Romans 9–11: A Reader-Response Analysis* (International Studies in Formative Christianity and Judaism 6; Atlanta: Scholars Press, 1996).

[2] Romans 8:31–11:36 contains 99 verses; 2:1–3:20 contains 49; 3:17–4:25 contains 39; and Romans 6–7 contains 48. This passage is twice as long as any of the other three.

passage; (3) the importance of 8:1–30 as the context for understanding 8:31–11:36; and (4) the connections between the beginning of the passage (8:31–39) and its end (11:33–36). The first-person-singular passages in 8:31–11:36 also will be examined at greater length.[3] Understanding how deeply Paul is personally invested in these issues and in what this investment consists will be invaluable for avoiding misinterpretation of a number of Paul's arguments.

IMPORTANT ASPECTS OF ROMANS 8:31–11:36

Several characteristics of 8:31–11:36 point to its unity. They are the same as those found in similarly placed passages earlier in the letter. First is the extensive use of rhetorical questions addressed to an imaginary interlocutor.[4] Second is the use of the phrases "Not at all" (μὴ γένοιτο, 9:14; 11:1, 11) and "What, then, . . . ?" (τί οὖν . . . , 8:31; 9:14; 11:7). The use of these techniques, both of which are common in diatribes, is similar to that found in 2:1–3:20; 3:27–4:25; 6:1–7:25 and sets this passage off from 8:1–30 just as their use similarly sets the other passages off from 1:18–32; 3:21–26; 5:1–21. Third, 8:31–11:36 is characterized by the extensive use and interpretation of scriptural passages.[5] This is similar to the kind of arguments found in 2:1–3:20 and 3:27–4:25 and again sets 8:31–11:36 off from 8:1–30, which contains no scriptural quotations, just as 1:18–32 and 3:21–26 contained no scriptural quotations.[6]

Given these characteristics, the structure of the passage is fairly clear, although a detailed interpretation of how Paul develops his arguments and what their specific purposes are must await the analysis found in chapters 12 and 13 of this study.

A. Transition and introduction (8:31–9:5):

> 1. Transitional passage from 8:1–30 as the beginning of a response to what Paul wrote in 8:1–30 (8:31–39)
>
> 2. Paul's expression of anguish about his fellow Jews and his affirmation of their divine privileges (9:1–5)

B. God's promises have not failed, the choice of Israel, and predictions about the present choice of both Jews and Gentiles (9:6–29)

> 1. God's promises to, and choice of, the patriarchs (9:6–13)
>
> 2. God's justification of Israel's liberation to Moses (9:14–18)
>
> 3. The justification from Scripture of the inclusion of both Jews and Gentiles and the introduction of the notion of a remnant (9:19–29)

---

[3] Rom 8:38–39; 9:1–5; 10:1–4; 11:1–2, 11–14, 25–27.

[4] Rom 8:30, 31, 32, 33, 34, 35; 9:14, 19, 20, 21, 22, 30; 10:8, 14, 15, 19; 11:1, 2, 7, 11.

[5] Rom 8:36; 9:9, 12, 13, 15, 17, 25–26, 27, 29, 33; 10:5, 11, 13, 15, 16, 18, 19, 20, 21; 11:3, 4, 8, 9–10, 26–27, 34–35. This list is conservative in that it does not include the more ambiguous use of Deut 8:17; 9:4; 30:12–14 in Rom 10:6–8.

[6] Rom 5:1–21 also contains no scriptural quotations.

C. The present situation of Israel in relation to the Gentiles as interpreted from the Scriptures under the rubric of a "remnant" (9:30–10:21)

    1. Israel not understanding that Christ is the goal of the law for all who believe, both Jews and Gentiles (9:30–10:13)

    2. Israel at present not responding to the word preached to them, which it has "heard" and "knows" as indicated by the Scriptures; its goal to "make them jealous" (10:14–21)

D. This present "remnant" and the "hardening" of most, as well as their "jealousy," meant to lead to the inclusion of the "fullness of the Gentiles" and finally to the inclusion of "all Israel" (11:1–32)

    1. The present partial hardening of Israel (11:1–10)

    2. Israel's disbelief as only temporary and providential for the inclusion of the Gentiles and as provoking Israel to "jealousy" (11:11–24)

    3. The mystery of the inclusion of all, both "all Israel" and the "fullness of the Gentiles" (11:25–32)

E. Conclusion: Praise of God's incomprehensible wisdom and mercy (11:33–36)

The most obvious characteristic of the structure of 8:31–11:36 is its chronological organization. The framework of Paul's argument in this section is temporal or historical in a way that no other argument in Paul's other letters is. Since it is the longest, most sustained argument in any of his letters, it is difficult to overestimate the importance of this framework. Why this is the case will become clear only in a more detailed analysis of this passage in the next two chapters of this study.

    Several other remarks about this outline are also in order at this point, specifically about the placement of 8:31–39 as the introduction to Romans 9–11 rather than as the conclusion of 8:1–30. The reasons for this are primarily rhetorical. Romans 8:31–39, in 8:31–35, takes up again the repeated use of rhetorical questions.[7] This technique places 8:31–39 with Romans 9–11, where it is also used frequently, and sets these verses off from 8:1–30, where it is not used at all. The change from exposition to rhetorical questions in 8:31–39 parallels similar changes in 2:1–11; 3:27–31; 6:1–14, as seen earlier, from exposition to the use of techniques common in diatribes. In 3:27–31 and 6:1–14, the change is marked, as it is in 8:31–39, by the use of rhetorical questions. Romans 8:31 and 6:1 even begin with the same phrase, "What, then, shall we say . . . ?" (τί οὖν ἐροῦμεν). There are two other reasons for placing 8:31–39 with Romans 9–11. First, the opening question in 8:31, "What, then, shall we say to these things?" (τί οὖν ἐροῦμεν πρὸς ταῦτα), suggests that Paul is beginning something new, a response to what he has written in 8:1–30. Second, the use of the first person singular in 8:38–39 ("For I am convinced that . . . ," πέπεισμαι γὰρ ὅτι . . .) connects this passage with a similar use of the

---

[7] Depending on how one punctuates the passage, there are between seven and nine such questions in 8:31–35. See Dunn, *Romans,* 498–505 (seven); and Fitzmyer, *Romans,* 528–33 (nine).

first person singular in what immediately follows (9:1–5) rather than with 8:1–30. For these reasons, 8:31–11:36 should be seen as a whole.

At the same time, it is important to realize that 8:1–30 remains the context within which 8:31–11:36 must be interpreted. The opening question in 8:31 ("What, then, shall we say to these things?") suggests that 8:31–11:36 responds in some fashion to what is found in 8:1–30 and that 8:1–30 provides the context for Paul's arguments in 8:31–11:36. In addition, Paul carries over some of the significant vocabulary of 8:1–30 into 8:31–11:36 and applies it now to Israel.[8] But such a usage is made possible only on the basis of Paul's reinterpretations of these terms in 8:1–30. They are reinterpretations that, in contrast to their use in Galatians, no longer preclude their application to Israel.

Parallels between the beginning (8:31–39) and the end (11:25–36) of this section also provide an important clue to the interpretation of the complex arguments Paul makes between these two passages. In 8:32, Paul rhetorically asks, "He who did not withhold his own Son, but gave him up for all of us [ὑπὲρ ἡμῶν πάντων], will he not with him also give everything to us [τὰ πάντα ἡμῖν]?" Toward the conclusion of the section, Paul writes that "he [God] has imprisoned all human beings [τοὺς πάντας] in disobedience so that he may have mercy on all human beings [τοὺς πάντας]" (11:32). Then in the concluding doxology of 11:33–36, he writes that "from him [God] and through him and to him are all things [τὰ πάντα]." This use of both the masculine and the neuter plural of "all" (πάντας/πάντα) both at the beginning and at the end of this section must have been intentional on Paul's part.

Whereas in 8:32 the "all," both masculine and neuter, is apparently connected specifically with "us" (ἡμῶν/ἡμῖν) believers, in 11:25–26 it is connected with "the fullness of the Gentiles" and "all Israel" (11:25–26). This indicates that Paul's scriptural arguments between these two passages are meant to show how the "all of us" believers (ἡμῶν πάντων) of 8:32 would in the mystery of God's plan eventually include "all" in a much larger sense, the "fullness of the Gentiles" and "all Israel." All this takes place within the context of the God who gives all things to us with Christ (8:32) and from whom and in whom and to whom are all things (11:36). Given that Paul's arguments between these passages concern especially the status of Israel, any interpretations of these arguments that would seem to preclude the inclusion of Israel must be misinterpretations of what Paul is trying to do. The importance of this will become clearer in the more detailed analysis of Paul's arguments in the next two chapters of this study.

FIRST-PERSON-SINGULAR PASSAGES

Although all these elements provide us with significant guides for the proper context and interpretation of 8:31–11:36, in the end they do not give us an answer to a more basic question. Why does this section make up the longest, most complex,

---

[8] E,g., "adoption" (υἱοθεσία, 8:15, 23; 9:4); "sons of God" (υἱοὶ θεοῦ, 8:14; 9:25–27); "children of God" (τέκνα τοῦ θεοῦ, 8:16–17, 21; 9:7–8); "purpose" (πρόθεσις, 8:28; 9:11); "foreknow" (προγινώσκω, 8:29; 11:2), "call," "calling," "called" (καλέω, κλῆσις, κλητός, 8:28, 30, 9:7, 12, 24–26, 11:29).

and most sustained argument of the whole letter? What did Paul think was at stake in this section, such that he felt compelled to expend so much thought on it? As will be shown in this chapter, the first-person-singular passages in 8:31–11:36 give us significant clues to what Paul's purpose was in writing these chapters and what he thought was at stake. Romans 8:31–11:36 contains six passages that are in the first person singular: 8:38–39; 9:1–5; 10:1–4; 11:1–2; 11:11–14; 11:25–27. Although this concentration of first-person singular passages is significant in itself, these passages are important in interpreting 8:31–11:36 for three other reasons.[9] First, three of the passages (8:38–39; 9:1–5; 11:25–27) come at the beginning and at the climax of this section of Romans. Second, the three other passages (10:1–4; 11:1–2; 11:11–14) are, as shall be seen, placed at crucial points in Paul's argument. Finally, the very first passage (8:38–39) rhetorically sets the context for the whole argument. For these reasons, the first-person singular passages offer important clues for interpreting 8:31–11:36 as a whole. They tell us what is at stake.

Because 9:1–5 and 11:25–27 come toward the beginning and toward the end of 8:31–11:36, an examination of them will offer insights into what the issues were for Paul and what he ultimately wanted to say about them. An examination of three other passages (10:1–4; 11:1–2; 11:11–14) will help clarify how Paul understood the crucial turning points in the arguments that he was making about the issue of Israel's fate.[10] Finally, an examination of the very first passage, 8:38–39, will show how it sets the context for everything that follows. The goal of this analysis is not only to throw light on Paul's arguments but also to show how Paul wanted to portray himself to the Roman Christian community. It will show what Paul personally thought was at stake, both for himself and for his relationship with the Roman Christian community.

Romans 9:1–5 and 11:25–27

Romans 9:1–5 is Paul's anguish-filled claim that he could wish himself accursed and cut off from Christ for the sake of his fellow Jews, his kindred in the flesh. The passage is remarkable in a number of ways, all of which shed light on the meaning of 8:31–11:36. Paul begins by emphasizing the depth and sincerity of his own anguish for his fellow Jews. He claims that he is speaking the truth and not lying and that his conscience bears him witness in the Holy Spirit (9:1). As if to emphasize his truthfulness and sincerity even more, he claims that he would even wish to be accursed and cut off from Christ for the sake of his fellow Jews (9:3).

---

[9] First-person-singular passages are frequent in Paul's letters. Apart from the openings and closings of letters, Paul uses the first person singular in several ways: for emphasis (Gal 4:21–23; 5:2–3, 10–12, 16, 21; 1 Cor 10:14–15); for clarification (Gal 3:2, 17; 4:1; 1 Cor 2:1–3; 3:1–10; 4:6, 9; 5:9–13; 7:1–40; 10:1, 19–20; 11:2–3, 17–19; 12:1–3; 15:1–3, 50–51; Rom 1:16–17; 7:1; 8:18); for apologetic purposes (Gal 1:6–2:21; 1 Cor 9:1–3, 15–27; 15:8–11; 2 Cor 1:15–17; 1:23–2:13; 7:2–16; 11:1–13:10; Phil 4:10–20); for personal appeals (Gal 4:12–20; 1 Cor 1:10–17; 4:3–4, 14–20; Phil 1:3–27; 2:16–18). In each case they serve an important rhetorical purpose.

[10] The demarcation of the first-person-singular passages in Romans 9–11 is indebted to the rhetorical analysis of James W. Aageson, "Scripture and Structure in the Development of the Argument in Romans 9–11," *CBQ* 48 (1986), 286–87.

This insistence is even stronger when contrasted to his conviction that nothing can separate us from the love of God in Christ, expressed in 8:38–39, the immediately preceding verses.

Paul then goes on in 9:4–5 to enumerate the gifts that have been given to his fellow Jews:

> They are Israelites:
> Theirs is the adoption (as sons), the glory, and the covenants,
> the giving of the law, the worship, and the promises;
> theirs are the fathers and from them, according to the flesh, is the Christ.

This elaborate enumeration of the gifts given to the Jews makes clear to Paul's Roman Christian audience how highly he values the privileges his fellow Jews have been given, and this in several ways. He refers to them as "Israelites"; that is, they are members of Israel. Throughout 8:31–11:36, Paul will continue to describe his fellow Jews as "Israel" (9:27, 31; 10:19, 21; 11:7, 25, 26). The emphasis on contemporary Jews as Israel is found only in 8:31–11:36 and nowhere else in Paul's letters.[11] This almost emblematic use of "Israel" highlights the connection of contemporary Jews both with God's gifts and promises of old, gifts and promises that in Paul's mind are irrevocable, and with their final future fate as "all Israel."

Elsewhere in Romans and in his other letters, Paul associates five of the six privileges listed in 9:4 (with the exception of the "giving of the law" [νομοθεσία]) with Christian experience.[12] By thus listing them here as privileges given to the Israelites, Paul emphasizes the extent to which the gifts given to believers are in continuity with those given to the Jews. This enumeration is especially significant in Paul's use of the terms "adoption," "promises," and "covenants" in connection with his fellow Jews. The previous chapter of this study emphasized how Paul's use of the word "adoption" (υἱοθεσία) in 8:15, 23 was such that it did not preclude the inclusion of the Jews and how this differed from his use of the word in Gal 4:5, where Jews did seem to be excluded. Similarly, chapter 5 of this study pointed out that when Paul discussed the promise to Abraham and to his "seed" (σπέρμα) in Romans 4, he took the word as a collective noun (descendants) and so included the Jews among them. This again is in contrast to Gal 3:15–18, where Paul apparently maintained that the promise (ἐπαγγελία) made to Abraham and fulfilled in Christ bypassed the Jewish people entirely. It went directly to Christ, his "offspring" (σπέρματι), and not to the Jews, his "offsprings" (σπέρμασιν). His revisionary interpretations of these two terms in Romans 4 and 8 makes possible their inclusion here in Rom 9:4 as continuing privileges of his fellow Jews.

Paul seems to be making a similar, although not identical, move by his inclusion of the "covenants" among the privileges of his fellow Jews. In 2 Cor 3:6, 14,

---

[11] In 1 Cor 10:18 and 2 Cor 3:7, 13, Paul uses "Israel" to refer to the Israel of history; in Gal 6:16, Paul refers to believers as the "Israel of God"; in Phil 3:5 and 2 Cor 11:22, Paul refers to himself as "the people of Israel" and an "Israelite."

[12] The five are υἱοθεσία (Rom 8:15, 23; Gal 4:5), δόξα (Rom 5:2; 8:18, 21; 9:23; 15:7; 1 Cor 2:7; 2 Cor 3:18; 4:4, 6; Phil 3:21; 1 Thess 2:12), διαθήκη (Rom 11:27; 1 Cor 11:25; 2 Cor 6:1; Gal 3:15, 17; 4:24), λατρεία (Rom 12:1), ἐπαγγελία (Rom 4:13–14, 16, 20; 9:8–9; 15:8; 2 Cor 1:20; 7:1; Gal 3:14–18, 21–22, 29; 4:23, 28).

Paul seemed to contrast negatively the old Mosaic covenant (παλαιὰ διαθήκη) with the new covenant (καινὴ διαθήκη) in Christ. An even more negative contrast of covenants appeared in Gal 4:22–31. In the allegory of Sarah and Hagar, the Jews were associated with the covenant on Sinai and the present Jerusalem, which led to slavery. Believers in Christ, however, were associated with the Jerusalem above, which led to freedom. By contrast, Paul begins his explanation of the situation of the Jewish people here in Romans by claiming in Rom 9:4 that both διαθῆκαι (old and new) are part of God's gifts to the Jews.[13] Given his controversial views about observance of the Mosaic law, especially in Galatians, it is equally significant that Paul also includes the giving of the Mosaic law (νομοθεσία) in this enumeration of Israel's privileges in Rom 9:4. It too is seen as a gift of God to the Jews. This inclusion is made possible by Paul's defense of the Mosaic law in Romans 7, that the law is holy, just, good, and spiritual (7:12, 14, 16).

To highlight this continuity even more, Paul places at the climactic position in the list the fact that "from them, according to the flesh, is the Christ." These gifts are not simply realities of some distant past but include Christ himself. In offering this enumeration, Paul gives no hint that God has withdrawn any of these privileges from the Jews. Rather, the inclusion of "from them, according to the flesh, is the Christ" indicates that the contrary must be the case. The privileges remain valid. If Christ is an integral part of these gifts, then all of the other gifts must also remain valid. Their continuing validity also establishes the root of Paul's anguish over his fellow Jews. How are these still valid gifts to be reconciled with the lack of faith in Christ of most of his fellow Jews? The reconciliation of those two realities is the focus of the rest of Romans 9–11.

Paul ends this passage with a blessing of God (9:5): "God who is over all be blessed for ever. Amen."[14] In its immediate context, Paul's blessing of God refers to the gifts listed in 9:4 that have been given to the Jews. But the blessing serves another, larger purpose. By blessing the God who is over *all*, Paul sets the tone for what follows. The God who is over all can accomplish all things, even the reconciliation of the continuing validity of God's gifts to the Jews and their present lack of faith in Christ, who is the climax of these gifts. That such is Paul's purpose becomes clear when he states in 9:6, "It is not that the word of God has failed."

---

[13] Given the contrast of covenants in 2 Cor 3:6, 14 and Gal 3:15–18 and Paul's use of "new covenant" in 1 Cor 11:25, the most natural way to interpret the "covenants" in Rom 9:4 is "old" and "new." This is especially the case since Christ is included among the privileges given to Israel (Rom 9:4). See Dunn, *Romans*, 527, 534.

[14] The punctuation of 9:5 is much disputed. Some read the doxology as a relative clause whose antecedent is Christ, thus referring to Christ as God (Morris, *Romans*, 349–51; Cranfield, *Romans*, 2:464–70; Bruce M. Metzger, "The Punctuation of Rom 9:5," in *Christ and Spirit in the New Testament* [ed. Barnabas Lindars and S. S. Smalley; London: Cambridge University Press, 1973], 95–112). Others take it as an independent doxology (Dunn, *Romans*, 528–29; Wilkens, *Römer*, 2:189; Käsemann, *Romans*, 259–60). The latter alternative is more likely, since it fits better into Paul's argument in Romans 9–11 that God has confined *all* to disobedience so that he might show mercy to *all* (11:32) as well as into the argument of Romans as a whole (3:29–30; 8:18–37). The phrase "God who is over all" is placed first to emphasize just this point. In addition, it would be very odd indeed, in a context that emphasizes Israel's privileges, to introduce a doxology that would have sounded so controversial to Israel's ears.

From a rhetorical point of view, 9:1–5 introduces the issue of the relationship of God's gifts and the present situation of the Jews. But it also sets the tone for the rest of Romans 9–11, which is an interweaving of deep personal anguish and concern on Paul's part over the fate of his fellow Jews with a confidence that God's gifts are ultimately not in vain. It establishes an ethos of deep personal concern on Paul's part for the fate of his fellow Jews. He emphasizes to his Roman Christian audience that he is personally as concerned about the fate of the Jews and the continuing validity of God's gifts to them as they are.

Romans 11:25–27 comes at the climax (11:25–32) of 8:31–11:36. In these verses Paul sums up and emphasizes his view of the ultimate relationship between Jews and Gentiles, which he has developed especially in 11:1–24. Romans 11:25–27 opens the section and states the point on which Paul then expands in 11:28–32. For Paul, the ultimate "mystery" (μυστήριον) of the relationship between Jews and Gentiles is that, after a partial hardening of Israel until the full complement of the Gentiles has come in, all Israel will also be saved (11:25–26). Israel's partial hardening, then, is part of God's mysterious purpose, the inclusion of the Gentiles. But once the Gentiles have been included, all Israel will also be saved. Paul then quotes from a combination of Isa 59:20–21 and 27:9 as support for this conviction (Rom 11:26–27):

> Out of Zion will come the deliverer;
> he will banish ungodliness from Jacob.
> And this [will be] my covenant with them [Isa 59:20–21],[15]
> when I take away their sins [Isa 27:9].

Romans 11:25–27 serves several purposes and draws on motifs and vocabulary Paul has used elsewhere in Romans as well as in his other letters. Most immediately, it serves as a summary of Paul's explanation of the partial hardening of Israel (11:1–10, esp. 11:7) and its relationship to the inclusion of the Gentiles and Israel's final inclusion (11:11–24).

Romans 11:25–27 also serves several other, larger purposes. First, because it is in the first person singular and comes at the end of 8:31–11:36, it harks back to 9:1–5, Paul's anguished statement about the situation of his fellow Jews and the continuing validity of their gifts and privileges from God. In 11:25–27, Paul now expresses his own deeply held conviction that all Israel will ultimately be saved. The obvious implication is that God's gifts and privileges to Israel are still valid. He makes this implication quite explicit in 11:29 ("For the gifts and the call of God are irrevocable"). All the intervening arguments, then, are meant to establish the claim in 9:6 that "it is not that the word of God has failed."

Second, Paul carefully roots this conviction about the future salvation of Israel in the Jewish scriptures (Isa 59:20–21; 27:9). Paul understands the "deliverer" of Isa 59:20 to be Christ, whose future coming will lead to the inclusion of Israel.[16] These

---

[15] Given that the previous two verbs are in the future tense, the verb to be supplied, at least as far as Paul is concerned, must also be in the future tense.

[16] As Paul understands it, the speaker in Isa 59:20–21; 27:9 is God. The "deliverer," who is referred to in the third person, must be someone other than God. Obviously, for Paul, this means Christ. In addition, the deliverer's future coming refers to Christ's coming in power

quotations are particularly important, since they are the only explicit scriptural references in the final stage of Paul's argument (Rom 11:11–24).[17] They are meant to give scriptural grounding not only for Paul's summary in 11:25–26a but also for the extended metaphor of the cultivated and wild olive trees in 11:17–24. They form part of Paul's continual concern to show how his understanding of the fate of the Jewish people is rooted in the Jewish scriptures and is in continuity with them.[18]

Third, Paul's conviction in 11:26 that "all [πᾶς] Israel will be saved," when seen in conjunction with 11:32, takes us back to earlier sections of Romans explicitly concerned with the relationship of Jews and Gentiles.[19] In 11:32, Paul takes up the πᾶς of "all Israel" (11:26; see also 10:4, 11, 12) when he claims that "God has consigned all [τοὺς πάντας] to disobedience so that he may have mercy upon all [τοὺς πάντας]." This clearly takes up themes of the early parts of Romans where Paul claimed that the gospel was "the power of God for salvation to everyone [παντί] who has faith, to the Jew first and also to the Greek" (1:16), that "all [πάντας], both Jews and Greeks, are under the power of sin" (3:9), that "the whole world [πᾶς ὁ κόσμος] is accountable to God" (3:19), and, most important, "Now the righteousness of God has been manifested apart from the law, although the law and the prophets bear witness to it, the righteousness of God through faith in Jesus Christ for all [πάντας] who believe. For there is no distinction; since all [πάντες] have sinned and fall short of the glory of God" (3:21–23). In this way, Paul's claim early in Romans that Jews and Gentiles were equally sinful is now paralleled by the claim that both Jews and Gentiles will ultimately be equally recipients of God's mercy.[20]

---

rather than to some notion of incarnation. This is clear from Rom 11:15, which connects the inclusion of Israel with the resurrection of the dead.

[17] Given the similar themes in Isaiah 59 and Isaiah 27, the combination of the two texts is understandable. The replacement of the LXX ἕνεκεν Σιών with ἐκ Σιών, however, is more difficult to explain. Berndt Schaller ("ΗΞΕΙ ΕΚ ΣΙΩΝ Ο ΡΥΟΜΕΝΟΣ: Zur Textgestalt von Jes 59:20f in Röm 11:26f.," in *De Septuaginta: Studies in Honour of John William Wevers on His Sixty-Fifth Birthday* [ed. Albert Pietersma and Claude Cox; Mississauga, Ont.: Benben, 1984], 201–6) thinks that lying behind Paul's quotation was a corruption of a translation from εἰς Σιών (MT reads לציון) to ἐκ Σιών (ΕΙΣ and ΕΚ being easy to confuse visually). A more likely explanation, however, is that Paul took the phrase ἐκ Σιών from Isa 2:3 and Ps 14:7; 53:6 (Hübner, *Gottes Ich und Israel*, 115–16). The thematic similarities of all these biblical texts would have been of interest to early Christians, and so Paul may have drawn this quotation from an already existing collection. Since Paul uses the quotation specifically to substantiate his conviction about the future deliverance of Israel, the difference in prepositions is not important.

[18] Paul's identification of the "deliverer" with Christ indicates that he thought that the final salvation of Israel would include Jewish acceptance of Christ, the recognition of Christ as the τέλος of the law (10:4). This makes it impossible to accept the position of Lloyd Gaston and John Gager that, for Paul, Jews are saved by their covenant relationship to God through the law whereas only Gentiles are saved through faith in Christ (Gaston, *Paul and the Torah*; John G. Gager, *The Origins of Anti-Semitism: Attitudes toward Judaism in Pagan and Christian Antiquity* [New York: Oxford University Press, 1985], 193–264, esp. 223–25]). For a critique of Gaston's position, see Johnson, *Function*, 176–205.

[19] Paul contrasts the "remnant" (11:5) with the "rest" (11:7). In 11:11–32, he writes about the fate of the "rest." When the "rest" come in, then all Israel will be saved. By "all Israel," then, Paul means Israel as a whole, as a people, and not "all the remnant" as has been suggested by François Refoulé (". . . *Et ainsi tout Israël sera sauvé*": *Romains 11, 25–32* [LD 117; Paris: Cerf, 1984]).

[20] See also Rom 1:18; 2:9, 10; 3:4; 5:12, 18; 8:22.

Paul's extension, in 11:25–27, 32, of his earlier argument also serves to reinforce that earlier argument and make it seem less controversial. After all, if the argument supports the conviction especially that all Israel will be saved, then its use earlier to claim the equal sinfulness of both Jews and Gentiles becomes more acceptable.

Finally, for Paul, the relationship between Jews and Gentiles is a mystery (μυστήριον, 11:25). By this, Paul does not mean a puzzle but the mystery of God's purpose for the salvation of all humankind, both Jews and Gentiles.[21] Paul used the term μυστήριον in a similar way in 1 Cor 15:51–52 when he wrote about the resurrection of the dead. As in Rom 11:25, Paul wanted to emphasize in 1 Cor 15:51–52 that the final state of the world (there the resurrection of the dead rather than the relationship between Jews and Gentiles) is part of the divine mystery of God's purpose for the salvation for the world. Quite revealingly, in Rom 11:15, Paul connects the "acceptance" of Israel with "life from the dead," the final resurrection of the dead. Paul associates the salvation of both Jews and Gentiles with the final resurrection of the dead; both are integral parts of God's mysterious purpose for salvation. He also used μυστήριον in 1 Cor 2:7, where he claimed that he was imparting to the Corinthian Christians a "mysterious [ἐν μυστηρίῳ] and hidden wisdom of God, which God decreed before the ages for our glorification." Here Paul connected it with God's eternal wisdom, which leads to salvation. He has something very similar in mind in this concluding section of Rom 8:31–11:36 when, in the doxology (11:33–36) that immediately follows his discussion of this mystery (11:25–32), he praises "the depth of the riches and wisdom and knowledge of God" (11:33).[22] In connecting the salvation of "all Israel" with God's mysterious wisdom and the resurrection of the dead, Paul thus rhetorically integrates his viewpoint into broader, widely held Jewish and early Christian views about the ultimate fate of the world.

Romans 11:25–27, then, serves multiple purposes within the immediate argument of Romans 11, within the larger argument of 8:31–11:36, within Romans as a whole, and finally as a reflection of Paul's overall viewpoint on the gospel. In addition, it is not at all accidental that 11:25–27 is in the first person singular, that "I do not want you to be ignorant of this mystery." The use of the first person singular emphasizes Paul's own conviction about, and commitment to, the salvation of his fellow Jews.

Romans 10:1–4; 11:1–2; 11:11–14

Between 9:1–5 and 11:25–27, there are three other passages in the first person singular (10:1–4; 11:1–2; 11:11–14). All three passages come at crucial points in

---

[21] In Rom 11:25 and in 1 Cor 2:7; 15:51, Paul's use of the term "mystery" is indebted to the language of Jewish apocalyptic rather than to the language of mystery cults. See, e.g., *1 En.* 41:1; 46:2; 103:2; 104:10, 12; 106:19; *4 Ezra* 10:38; 12:36–38; 14:5; *2 Bar.* 48:3; 81:4; 1QS 3:23; 4:18; 9:18; 11:3, 5, 19; 1QHᵃ 1:21; 2:13; 4:27–29; 7:27; 11:10; 12:13; 1QpHab 7:5, 8, 14; 1Q27 1:3–4. See also Dunn, *Romans,* 678–79; and Raymond E. Brown, *The Semitic Background of the Term "Mystery" in the New Testament* (FBBS 21; Philadelphia: Fortress, 1968).

[22] Romans 11:33–36 may have originally been a Jewish wisdom hymn that Paul took over and used. It has a number of elements in common with *2 Bar.* 75:1–5; *1 En.* 93:11–14; 1QHᵃ 7:26–33; 10:3–7. See Johnson, *Function,* 164–74.

Paul's argument. All three also offer significant clarifications of Paul's arguments. They also form part of the pattern already seen in 9:1–5 and 11:25–27, where the first person singular rhetorically reinforces Paul's concern for the fate of his fellow Jews.

The first of these passages, 10:1–4, comes close to the beginning of Paul's interpretation of the present situation of the Jewish people (9:30–10:21) and is one of the most difficult passages in Paul to interpret.[23] Paul begins by asserting, in the same kind of language found in 9:1–5, that his heart's desire and prayer to God for his fellow Jews is for their salvation (10:1). He goes on to explain what the problem is: they have zeal for God, and this is something of which he approves, but it is a zeal not "according to knowledge" (κατὰ ἐπίγνωσιν, 10:2). He explains that, by being ignorant of the "righteousness of God" (τὴν τοῦ θεοῦ δικαιοσύνην) and seeking to establish their own righteousness, they did not submit to the righteousness of God (10:3). In 10:4, Paul indicates what this righteousness of God is, which is according to knowledge and of which they are ignorant: "Christ is the τέλος of the law for righteousness [δικαιοσύνην] to every one who believes."

The primary difficulty in interpreting this passage is the ambiguity of τέλος in 10:4, a word with several different but interrelated meanings. Paul himself uses the term elsewhere with a variety of meanings: termination or cessation (2 Cor 2:13); the close or end of the ages (1 Cor 10:11; 15:24); goal or outcome (Rom 6:21, 22; 2 Cor 11:15; Phil 3:19); taxes or revenues (Rom 13:7). He also uses the term adverbially (1 Thess 2:16; 1 Cor 1:8; 2 Cor 2:13). In the interpretation of Rom 10:4, the question specifically is whether the term τέλος implies that with Christ the law has come to an end and ceases to have validity. Does it mean that Christ is the "end" of the law?[24] Or does it mean that Christ is the "goal" or "purpose" of the law?[25] Or does it mean that Christ is the "completion" or "consummation" of the law, that is, a combination of the first two meanings?[26]

An analysis of the context in which the term occurs provides important clues to the proper interpretation of 10:4. A first step is the recognition that 10:1–4 parallels 9:30–33 in several important ways. Indeed, 10:1–4 is an emphatic, more personal restatement of what Paul wrote in 9:30–33. By comparing 10:1–4 with 9:30–33, one can get a clearer sense of what is being said in both passages.[27]

---

[23] For a survey of opinions, see C. Thomas Rhyne, *Faith Establishes the Law* (SBLDS 55; Chico, Calif.: Scholars Press, 1981), 8, 14, 19; and Robert Badenas, *Christ the End of the Law: Romans 10.4 in Pauline Perspective* (JSNTSup 10; Sheffield, England: JSOT Press, 1985), 27–37.

[24] Peter Stuhlmacher, "Das Ende des Gesetzes: Über Ursprung und Ansatz der paulinischen Theologie," *ZTK* 67 (1970): 14–39; Käsemann, *Romans,* 282–83; Hübner, *Gottes Ich und Israel,* 76–94; Heikki Räisänen, "Römer 9–11: Analyse eines gestigen Ringens," *ANRW* 25.4:2907–8; Dunn, *Romans,* 589–91, 596–98.

[25] George E. Howard, "Christ the End of the Law: The Meaning of Romans 10:4ff.," *JBL* 88 (1969): 331–37; Cranfield, *Romans,* 2:515–20; Badenas, *Christ the End;* C. Thomas Rhyne, "*Nomos dikaiosunēs* and the Meaning of Romans 10:4," *CBQ* 47 (1985): 489; Mary A. Getty, "Paul and the Salvation of Israel: A Perspective on Romans 9–11," *CBQ* 50 (1988), 466–68; Johnson, *Function,* 151–59.

[26] Barrett, *Romans,* 198; Wilkens, *Römer,* 2:221–24; Morris, *Romans,* 379–381.

[27] Rhyne notes this parallel but does not develop it ("*Nomos,*" 493).

In 10:3, Paul explains that his fellow Jews have zeal for God but "not according to knowledge." He also contrasts two sorts of "righteousness" (δικαιοσύνη): the righteousness of God, of which they are ignorant, and their own righteousness, which they try to establish. Paul draws a similar contrast in 9:30–32a: Gentiles who do not pursue righteousness have obtained (κατέλαβεν) righteousness, but a righteousness through faith. Israel, however, in pursuing a "law of righteousness" (νόμον δικαιοσύνης), did not attain (οὐκ ἔφθασεν) to that "law" because they did not pursue it through faith but through "works." Paul contrasts pursuing righteousness through faith (ἐκ πίστεως) with pursuing it through observance of the law (ἐξ ἔργων). This contrast parallels the contrast of the righteousness of God versus "their own righteousness" in 10:3.

The metaphor used in 9:30–31 to describe both Gentiles and Israel is also similar to that used in 10:3 to describe Israel. In 9:30–31, Gentiles do not pursue (μὴ διώκοντα) righteousness but nevertheless obtain it whereas Israel does pursue (διώκων) the law of righteousness but does not attain it. His fellow Jews, being ignorant of the righteousness of God, seek (ζητοῦντες) to establish their own righteousness. Israel sought a goal but did not attain it; Gentiles, though not pursuing the goal, did obtain it. Both the basic contrast and the language of 9:30–32a, then, clearly parallel 10:2–3.

Finally, in 9:32b–33, Paul offers a combination of quotations from Isa 28:16 and 8:14 as a scriptural explanation for why Israel failed to attain its goal:[28]

> They [Israel] have stumbled over the stone of stumbling,
>   as it is written:
> "Behold I am laying in Zion a stone of stumbling
>   and a rock of offense;
> and the one who believes [ὁ πιστεύων] in it [ἐπ' αὐτῷ] shall not be put to shame."

Paul interprets "a stone of stumbling and a rock of offense" as Christ, the one in whom the person who has faith will not be put to shame.[29] For those in Zion (i.e., Israel, Paul's fellow Jews), this stone and this rock (Christ) has become a stone of stumbling and a rock of offense. For Paul, the law itself showed what was to happen, that Christ would become a stone of stumbling and a rock of offense for Jews but that no one who had faith in him would be put to shame. Three of these elements (the law, Christ, and

---

[28] The mixture of the two texts is based on the fact that "stone" appears in both of them. First Peter 2:6–8 also combines the two texts (with Ps 118:22 in between). Isaiah 28:16 is also combined with Ps 118:22 in *Barn.* 6.2–4. This suggests that "stone" passages were combined by early Christians into a testimonia collection. Paul's quotation in Rom 9:33 may already witness to such a collection. See Dunn, *Romans*, 584. For a different view, see P. W. Meyer, "Romans 10:4 and the 'End' of the Law," in *The Divine Helmsman* (ed. J. R. Crenshaw and S. Sandmel; New York: KTAV, 1980), 59–78.

[29] Given the way in which these passages seem to have been part of testimonia collected around the term "stone," "stone" probably refers to Christ and not to the law or to the gospel contained in the law as suggested by Barrett and Gaston respectively (Charles K. Barrett, "Rom 9:30–10:21: Fall and Responsibility in Israel," in *Die Israelfrage nach Römer 9–11* [ed. L. de Lorenzi; Rome: Abbey of St. Paul outside the Walls, 1977], 112; Gaston, *Paul and the Torah*, 129). This interpretation is strengthened by the explicit reference to Christ in Rom 10:4.

faith/belief) are also found in 10:4: *Christ* is the τέλος of the *law* for righteousness to everyone who *believes*. Romans 10:4, then, comments on and clarifies 9:32b–33.

The parallelism of viewpoint and language in each of these two passages enlightens the interpretation of the other. It also throws light on the interpretation of the term τέλος in 10:4. But one must be careful about the argument Paul is making in each case. In 9:30–31, he first contrasts Gentiles who do not pursue righteousness (ἔθνη τὰ μὴ διώκοντα δικαιοσύνην) with Israel, which does (Ἰσραὴλ δὲ διώκων). He also contrasts the Gentiles who obtained (κατέλαβεν) it with Israel, which did not attain (οὐκ ἔφθασεν) it. Paul, however, is not contrasting "righteousness" (δικαιοσύνην) in 9:30 with the "law of righteousness" (νόμον δικαιοσύνης) or with the "law" (νόμον) in 9:31. Had Paul meant to contrast these two, he would have written "righteousness" (δικαιοσύνην) in place of the second "law" (νόμον) in 9:31. As the text stands, δικαιοσύνην in 9:30 and νόμον δικαιοσύνης in 9:31 are parallel rather than in contrast to one another. The contrast Paul wants to draw is that Gentiles, although not pursuing righteousness, still obtained it while Israel, although pursuing it, did not attain it. The reason for this is given in 9:32a: Israel pursued it not through faith (οὐκ ἐκ πίστεως) but through observance (ἀλλ' ὡς ἐξ ἔργων).[30]

At first the use of νόμον δικαιοσύνης as a parallel to νόμον alone strikes us as odd. Yet Paul's use of the term νόμος in this context fits well into the pattern of his overall argument in Romans. His argument, in part, is that the law itself points beyond its own observance to righteousness by faith in Christ apart from observance of the law. This was part of Paul's argument in 1:18–3:20 and 3:21–4:25 and is summed up in 3:31, where, in answer to the rhetorical question whether we overthrow the law through faith, he responds, "By no means! On the contrary, we uphold the law [νόμον ἱστάνομεν]."[31] Because righteousness by faith in Christ is embedded in the law itself, Paul can write in 9:31 of a "law of righteousness," not in the sense that one is justified by observance of the law but that the law itself testifies to righteousness by faith in Christ.[32] The quotations from Isa 28:16; 8:14, which immediately follow in Rom 9:33, testify to just such a faith in Christ and Israel's failure to recognize it.

With this in mind, one can understand Paul's point in 10:1–4. He testifies that his fellow Jews do have a zeal for God, a zeal of which he approves, but not a zeal "according to knowledge." Because they are ignorant of the nature of God's righteousness (i.e., through faith in Christ), they continue to seek their own righteousness (i.e., through observance of the law). What they fail to realize is that Christ is the

---

[30] The character of the contrast is also made clear by attending to the grammar of 9:32a. The rhetorical point of 9:32a depends on 9:31. Because of this, one needs to fill out 9:32a on the basis of 9:31: Why (did Israel in pursuing the law of righteousness not attain to the law)? Because (Israel pursued the law of righteousness) not from faith but from works. In other words, had they pursued it from faith and not as if from works, they would have obtained what the Gentiles had obtained, righteousness (9:30).

[31] See also Gal 3:8.

[32] Romans 10:5–8 takes up again the contrast between righteousness through faith and righteousness through observance of the law, the same contrast found in 9:30–32. Both 10:6 and the quotation of Lev 18:5 in Rom 10:5b indicate that the phrase τὴν δικαιοσύνην τὴν ἐκ νόμου in Rom 10:5a refers to righteousness through observance of the law in contrast to righteousness through faith. The contrast is not between righteousness by faith and the law itself.

τέλος of the law for righteousness to everyone who has faith. In the context of 9:30–10:4, it would make little sense to interpret τέλος as "end," for the phrase "for everyone who has faith" (παντὶ τῷ πιστεύοντι) in 10:4 takes up the quotation from the law (Isa 28:16) in Rom 9:33 (ὁ πιστεύων ἐπ' αὐτῷ). If Christ were the "end" or "termination" of the law, then the testimony of the law to Christ would have no weight. The term τέλος, then, in this context most appropriately means "goal" rather than "end." Christ is not the "end" of the law but, as the law itself testifies, its "goal" for the righteousness of everyone who has faith. But it is a righteousness not through observance of the law but through faith.

This interpretation of τέλος is appropriate on the basis not only of Paul's argument but also of the metaphors he uses in 9:30–10:4. He uses metaphors of pursuing (διώκω, 9:30, 31), seeking (ζητέω, 10:3), obtaining (καταλαμβάνω, 9:30), and attaining or reaching (φθάνω, 9:31). This is the language of an athletic contest, and in such a context, one pursues or seeks or obtains or attains a "goal" (τέλος). When Paul uses similar language elsewhere, the same picture emerges. In Phil 3:12–16, several of these terms (διώκω, καταλαμβάνω, φθάνω) appear as part of an extended metaphor of athletic competition in which Paul writes of himself and other Christians as pressing on toward the prize (τὸ βραβεῖον) of the upward call of God in Christ Jesus (Phil 3:14). He uses the same metaphor in 1 Cor 9:24 when he urges the Corinthian Christians to run so as to obtain (καταλάβητε) the prize (τὸ βραβεῖον). When Paul uses this language elsewhere, it is in the context of an athletic contest in which one strives or seeks to obtain a prize. This again indicates that τέλος in Rom 10:4 should also be understood within this same metaphorical context and so means "goal" rather than "end."

Similar metaphorical language is found in Philo.[33] In *Leg.* 3.47–48, Philo describes the mind that seeks God (ζητεῖς θεόν) as going out from itself in its quest for God. Whether this quest (ζητοῦσα) will be successful is not clear, for to many God has not manifested himself and the zeal (σπουδήν) of many has not been successful. Yet seeking noble things, even when it fails of its goal (κἂν τοῦ τέλους ἀτυχῶσι), still brings many good things with it. In this quest the good man, who flees from himself, returns to the knowledge (ἐπίγνωσιν) of the One and thus wins a noble race (δρόμον) and proves the victor in the grandest of contests (ἀγώνισμα). Philo also uses the term τέλος to talk about the goal of the law (*Decal.* 50, 73, 80) as well as of the lawgiver (*Deus* 61, 67). The most elaborate of these passages is *Migr.* 128–143. To follow God is, according to Moses, our goal (τέλος, *Migr.* 131), and we do this by following the divine ordinances. This following of God is "the goal [τέλος] of the way of those who follow the words and injunctions of the law, and march in whatever direction God leads the way" (*Migr.* 143).

Philo's elaborate and extensive use of the same kind of language found in Rom 9:30–10:4 suggests that such metaphorical language about seeking God and the goal

---

[33] The parallels with Philo have been mostly overlooked in the discussion of the meaning of τέλος in Rom 10:4. The exception is Badenas, *Christ the End,* 65–69. Yet even Badenas fails to notice the metaphorical language that Philo uses in connection with τέλος. For a more thorough discussion of the meaning of τέλος in Philo, see Thomas H. Tobin, "Romans 10:4: Christ the Goal of the Law," *SPhA* 3 (1991): 272–80.

of the law was fairly common in Hellenistic Judaism. Paul takes up this language and uses it to explain to his Roman Christian audience how Christ is, on the basis of the testimony of the law itself, the goal of the law. He explains how his fellow Jews, by failing to realize this, are seeking to establish their own righteousness, one based on observance rather than on faith. Whereas most of his fellow Jews would have found this argument unconvincing, it is significant that Paul was nevertheless trying to explain to Roman Christians the failure of his fellow Jews to believe in Christ in a language and in categories that were common in Hellenistic Judaism.

More important for our immediate purpose, by casting this passage in the first person singular, Paul again emphasizes his own concern for the salvation of his fellow Jews. He also emphasizes his conviction that although righteousness is now by faith in Christ rather than by observance of the Mosaic law, Christ and righteousness through faith in him are also the goal of that same law. Paul personally testifies to their "zeal for God" and understands this zeal as something positive. True, it is without proper knowledge; but this does not make their zealousness something unworthy of praise.

The next section where the first person singular appears is 11:1–2a. Once again it comes at a crucial point in Paul's argument. He begins by asking a rhetorical question that expects a negative answer: "I ask then, has God rejected his people? Certainly not!" (11:1a). He then uses himself as an example of the fact that God has not repudiated his people. He himself is an Israelite, a descendant of Abraham, a member of the tribe of Benjamin (11:1b). In 11:2a, he then restates his conviction that God has not repudiated his people, whom God "foreknew" (προέγνω).

This short section serves several purposes. First, it gives Paul another chance to emphasize his membership in the Jewish people, his own Jewishness, and so his concern for his fellow Jews. Second, he reemphasizes his conviction that God has not rejected his people, whom God foreknew. Both these elements take up two themes that were prominent at the beginning of Romans 9: (1) Paul's concern for his fellow Jews (9:2–4) and (2) his conviction that the "word of God," which here means God's promises to the Jewish people, has not failed (9:6). Third, Paul's claim that God has not rejected the people whom God "foreknew" harks back to 8:28–30 and places the fate of the Jewish people within his larger conviction that God ultimately works all things for the good with those who love God, for those whom God "foreknew" (προέγνω) and predestined to be conformed to the image of God's Son.

But this section also serves two, more structural purposes within Paul's argument. First, it comes after 10:14–21, in which Paul has explained why his fellow Jews have no excuse for not recognizing the gospel, for the gospel has been preached to them (10:14–18). Through quotations from Deut 32:21 and Isa 65:1, he even suggests that they should have known through the Jewish scriptures themselves that the preaching of the gospel to the Gentiles was meant to make them "jealous" (Rom 10:19–20). Romans 11:1–2 serves to restate that, in spite of this, God has still not rejected the Jewish people, a people whom God foreknew.

The second and more important purpose is that 11:1–2a creates the context within which the argument in 11:2b–10 is to be understood. In 11:2b–10, Paul argues, on the precedent of an episode from the Elijah story (1 Kgs 19:10, 14, 18), that "at the present time" (ἐν τῷ νῦν καιρῷ) a chosen "remnant" (λεῖμα) of the

Jewish people remains, a remnant that includes Jewish Christians like himself (Rom 11:2b–6). In contrast, the rest (οἱ λοιποί) have been hardened (Rom 11:7). To make this point, Paul appeals to Deut 29:4, which describes how God has given the "rest" a spirit of stupor, eyes that would not see and ears that would not hear, and he appeals to Ps 69:22–23, which describe eyes that are darkened (Rom 11:8–10).[34] Romans 11:1–2a places these passages, however, in a context that significantly tempers their seeming harshness. In spite of their harshness, God has still not rejected his people, whom he foreknew. The context created by 11:1–2a serves to emphasize Paul's words in 11:5, that "at the present time" there is but a remnant, and the phrase in 11:8 from Deut 29:4, that their eyes do not see and their ears do not hear "to this very day." Because God has not rejected his people, both Rom 11:5 and 11:8 suggest that there *will* be a time when there *will* be more than a remnant and when their eyes *will* see and their ears *will* hear.[35] Romans 11:1–2a, then, serves to reaffirm to Paul's Roman Christian audience his concern for his fellow Jews and thus places both 10:14–21 and 11:2b–10 in a much different light.

Like the first-person-singular passages in 10:1–4 and 11:1–2, the third passage (11:11–14) also comes at a crucial point in Paul's argument. In 11:1–10, Paul wrote about the present situation of his fellow Jews, that for the present only a "remnant" remain and the "rest" have been hardened. In 11:11–32, Paul turns to the ultimate fate of "the rest." Romans 11:11–14 is the opening section of Paul's argument about the fate of the "rest." He begins with a rhetorical question, "So I ask, have they stumbled so as to fall?" and immediately answers, "By no means" (μὴ γένοιτο). He then offers a reason for claiming that they have not "fallen": "For through their trespass salvation has come to the Gentiles, so as to make them jealous" (11:11). On this basis, Paul draws a conclusion in the form of an argument from the lesser to the greater *(a minore ad maius):* "And if their trespass means riches for the world, and their failure riches for the Gentiles, how much more [πόσῳ μᾶλλον] will their fullness [πλήρωμα] mean?" (11:12). Paul even places his own ministry in this context (11:13–14): "I am speaking to you Gentiles. In as much then as I am an apostle of the Gentiles, I magnify my ministry so that somehow I might make them jealous and save some of them."

This passage serves several important purposes in the development of the final part of Paul's argument. First, he begins by restating in different words what he said at the beginning of his argument in 9:6 ("It is not that the word of God has failed"). Most of his fellow Jews at the present time have stumbled, but they have not fallen. He once again reminds his Roman Christian audience of his underlying conviction about the fate of his fellow Jews.

---

[34] The phrase πνεῦμα κατανύξεως in 11:8 comes from Isa 29:10. The combination of these two verses may point to an early collection of scriptural quotations that sought to explain why Jews, for the most part, did not come to believe in the gospel, especially since the section from which Isa 29:10 comes was used by early Christians in this way (Isa 28:16 [Rom 9:33; 1 Pet 2:6]; 29:13 [Mark 7:6–7 par.]; 29:14 [1 Cor 1:19]; and 28:11 [1 Cor 14:21]). See B. Lindars, *New Testament Apologetic* (London: SCM, 1961), 164; Dunn, *Romans,* 641. In addition, given the final goal of Paul's argument (Rom 11:11–32), the phrase διὰ παντός from Ps 69:23 must mean "continually" rather than "forever" (C. E. B. Cranfield, *Romans,* 2:552; and "The Significance of διὰ παντός in Romans 11:10," *SE* 2 [1964]: 546–50).

[35] Cranfield, *Romans,* 2:548–52.

Second, with this in mind, he states in 11:11b–12 his own conviction about their ultimate fate. Their trespass (παραπτώματι) (here meaning their failure to have faith in the gospel) has led to the salvation of the Gentiles so as to make them jealous (εἰς τὸ παραζηλῶσαι). He takes up here the phrase "to make jealous" from the quotation of Deut 32:21 in Rom 10:19 ("I will make you jealous [παραζηλώσω] by a nation that is no nation; by a senseless nation I will make you angry"). In this way he recalls the scriptural point that he made there, that the Jewish scriptures attest to the failure of his fellow Jews. But in 11:12, he goes beyond that through the use of the argument from the lesser to the greater: If their trespass and their failure have brought riches to the world and in particular to the Gentiles, then how much more must their fullness mean? The language of 11:12 looks forward to 11:25–32, the conclusion of Paul's argument. Romans 11:33 and 11:25 take up "riches" (πλοῦτος) and "fullness" (πλήρωμα) again respectively. In other words, the trespass or failure of his fellow Jews is part of a larger plan or mystery that will ultimately lead to the salvation of all Israel (11:26).

Third, in 11:13–14, Paul places his own work as an apostle to the Gentiles within this context. Paul claims that he magnifies his own ministry to the Gentiles that he may make his fellow Jews jealous and so save "some of them" (τινὰς ἐξ αὐτῶν). Paul speaks frequently in his letters of the fact that he is an apostle and, on the basis of Gal 1:1, 16; 2:7–10, especially to the Gentiles.[36] But only in this passage does he also connect this apostolate with a hope for the salvation of some of his fellow Jews. At first reading, Rom 11:13–14 appears to be out of place. Since Paul seems to be writing about his apostolate as a *present* activity for the salvation of *some* of his fellow Jews, one would expect to find this passage earlier in his argument, in 11:1–6, where he describes the present remnant of Jews like himself who have believed in the gospel. Yet by placing this first-person description of his own ministry at this point, Paul connects it with the ultimate salvation of "all Israel" rather than with the present, small "remnant." Rhetorically, this emphasizes for Paul's audience his conviction about, and his commitment to, the ultimate salvation of all of his fellow kinsmen. His immediate role may concern the salvation of only "some of them," but this immediate role is embedded in a larger plan that will ultimately lead to the salvation of all Israel.

This also helps to explain why Paul addresses 11:13–14 (as well as 11:17–24) to "you Gentiles," that is, in the second person plural. Paul is making use of apostrophe. He is not directly addressing a particular group in the Roman Christian community. Rather, he has a different rhetorical purpose in mind. In this case, it is to portray himself as a Jew, one of whose concerns in preaching the gospel to "you Gentiles" is to make his fellow Jews jealous and so lead to their salvation. By addressing the Roman Christians this way, Paul emphasizes his identity as a Jew; and by placing his apostolate to the Gentiles in the framework of seeking the salvation of his fellow Jews, he shows that there is no conflict between his mission to the Gentiles and his concern for his fellow Jews. Consequently, Paul's apostolate to "you Gentiles," because it is also an apostolate on behalf of the Jews, should not raise

---

[36] Rom 1:1; 1 Cor 1:1; 4:9; 9:1–2; 15:9; 2 Cor 1:1; 11:5; 12:11–12; Gal 1:1, 17; 1 Thess 2:6.

concerns among Roman Christians about his commitment to his fellow Jews or to the promises made by God to them in the Jewish scriptures.

Romans 8:38–39

It may seem odd that the last first-person-singular passage to be analyzed is the first to occur in 8:31–11:36. But the role the passage plays in Paul's argument in this section, especially in the transition from 8:1–30 to 8:31–11:36, is best treated here. In 8:38–39, Paul insists on his personal conviction (πέπεισμαι) that nothing "will be able [δυνήσεται] to separate us from the love of God in Christ Jesus our Lord." He uses the rhetorical topic of enumeration (*congeries*, συναθροισμός) to list in highly charged fashion all of the things that will be unable to separate us from the love of God:[37]

> neither death nor life,
> neither angels nor rulers,
> neither things present nor things to come
> neither powers nor height nor depth,
> nor any other created thing.

The list is made up mostly of contrasting pairs (death/life, things present/things to come, height/depth), broken up by the presence of "powers" (δυνάμεις) in the fourth contrast (neither height nor depth). Paul has used some of these pairs elsewhere in his letters: death/life in Phil 1:20; 1 Cor 3:22, and things present/things to come in 1 Cor 3:22. The introduction of "powers" into the fourth pair may be due to Paul's use of this word in a similar context in 1 Cor 15:24. All of this suggests that the present list itself is of Paul's own making, even though two of the contrasting pairs (death/life and things present/things to come) are so obvious as to have been commonplace. The rhetorical effect of this list is to press home to his Roman Christian audience Paul's conviction that nothing in creation, whether now or in the future, can separate us from the love of God. Because the content of Paul's conviction, however, is in the future tense (nothing "will be able"), the emphasis is especially on the future.

These two verses are also part of the larger section of Rom 8:31–39, which contain Paul's initial response ("What are we to say about these things?" in 8:31) to the inclusive eschatology of 8:1–30. Through a series of seven rhetorical questions in 8:31–35, Paul insists that, because of what God has accomplished in Christ's death and resurrection (8:32, 34), no one can separate us from the love of Christ (8:35) and in all these things we are more than conquerors through him who loves us (8:37). Paul thereby emphasizes again the notion of "all." Because God gave up his Son for "all of us" (ὑπὲρ ἡμῶν πάντων), how will God not with him give us "all things" (τὰ πάντα, 8:32)? In "all these things" (ἐν τούτοις πᾶσιν) we are more than conquerors through him who loves us (8:37). Finally, 8:31–37, like 8:38–39, is put in the future tense (8:32, 33, 35).

In all these ways Paul takes up the inclusive eschatology of 8:1–30 (see esp. 8:22, 28–29). Paul then expresses this as his own deeply held personal conviction

---

[37] See Quintilian, *Inst.* 8.4.26–27, for this figure.

in 8:38–39, that nothing will be able to separate us from the love of God. This rhetoric also looks forward to the end of Romans 11, where Paul insists in the final first-person-singular passage that "this mystery" (11:25) of which he writes, the entrance of the "fullness of the Gentiles" and then the salvation of "all Israel" (11:25–26), shows that God has not only imprisoned "all," both Jews and Gentiles, in disobedience but has also had mercy on "all," again both Jews and Gentiles (11:32), for "from him and through him and to him are all things" (11:36). What occurs between in Romans 9–11—his anguished reflections on the past, present, and ultimate fate of his fellow Jews—Paul situates rhetorically within the context of his own personal conviction about nothing being able to separate us from the love of God in Christ Jesus.

CONCLUSIONS

Several patterns emerge from this analysis of the first-person-singular passages in 8:31–11:36. These patterns are interrelated and throw light both on the nature of Paul's arguments in this section of Romans and on the reasons he involves himself so personally in these arguments.

First, Paul goes out of his way to emphasize personally his conviction that God's gifts and promises to Israel are irrevocable. He does this explicitly in 11:1–2, 11–14, 25–26. But it is implicit also in his enumeration of God's gifts to Israel (9:4–5) and in 8:38–39, which emphasizes that nothing in creation can ultimately withstand God's purpose.

Second, Paul goes out of his way to emphasize his own membership in Israel, his own identity as a Jew. In 9:3, he expresses his anguish for his brethren, his kindred in the flesh. In 11:1, he describes himself explicitly as an Israelite, a term that identifies him as one to whom the gifts mentioned in 9:4 have been given. He even describes the purpose of his apostolate to the Gentiles as making his kindred jealous in order to save some of them (11:14). Only here, in all of his letters, does he insist that even his apostolate to the Gentiles is on behalf of his fellow Jews.

Third, Paul carefully connects both the present hardening of part of Israel and Israel's ultimate salvation with quotations from the Jewish scriptures. Romans 10:1–4 is a personal clarification of 9:30–33, which ends with quotations from Isa 28:16; 8:14. These quotations are meant to explain Israel's present failure to believe in Christ. Quotations from Isa 59:20; 27:9 in Rom 11:26–27 serve to validate Paul's conviction that the hardening of part of Israel will last only until the fullness of the Gentiles has been included and then all Israel will be saved. In addition, Paul roots both Christ and the promises in the Jewish scriptures. In 9:1–5, he describes both Christ and the gifts, which he elsewhere associates with believers, as realities that form part of the God's gifts to Israel. In 10:4, he describes Christ as the goal to which the law itself points.

None of this, of course, takes away from Paul's criticism of his fellow Jews' failure to believe in the gospel, nor does it compromise his conviction that salvation is now through Christ apart from observance of the Mosaic law. But it does place both his criticism and his conviction within a context that emphasizes the continuing validity of God's gifts and promises to the Jewish people in the Jewish scriptures and their ultimate salvation. In 8:31–11:36, Paul consciously and insistently portrays himself as someone whose belief in Christ is in continuity with the Jewish scriptures and whose mission to the Gentiles has not lessened his concern for his fellow Jews or his conviction about their ultimate salvation.

No doubt most of his fellow Jews would have found, and did find, this portrait unconvincing. No doubt also many of them would have thought, and did think, of him as an apostate. But Paul's arguments were directly intended neither for Jews nor against Jews but for the Roman Christian community. As we have seen before, this community was suspicious of Paul on this issue because, at least by implication, his views about "adoption," becoming "sons of God," "children of God," or "heirs" as expressed in Galatians seemed to exclude Jews. In 8:1–11:36, he is trying to demonstrate that this is not the case. His references to his own Jewish identity and his expressions of his own personal concern for the fate of his fellow Jews serve rhetorically to establish an ethos within which Paul makes his arguments.

Yet there is also something more going on here. Paul explicitly referred to his Jewish identity at two other points in his letters, in Phil 3:4–6 and in 2 Cor 11:21–22. In both cases he was clearly proud of it.

> If anyone else has reason to be confident in the flesh, I have more: circumcised on the eighth day, of the people of Israel, of the tribe of Benjamin, a Hebrew born of Hebrews; as to the law a Pharisee; as to zeal, a persecutor of the church; as to righteousness under the law, blameless. (Phil 3:4–6)

> But whatever anyone dares to boast of—I am speaking as a fool—I also dare to boast of that. Are they Hebrews? So am I. Are they Israelites? So am I. Are they the seed of Abraham? So am I. (2 Cor 11:21–22)

At the same time, both these affirmations occur within very polemical contexts aimed at Jewish Christians of two different sorts. Philippians 3:4–6 seems aimed against the potential but not immediate danger from Jewish Christians, probably from Palestine, who would have the members of the Philippian Christian community be circumcised and observe the Mosaic law.[38] Second Corinthians 11:22 seems aimed again at a group of probably Hellenistic Jewish Christians, like Paul himself, who have challenged Paul's authority, although not on the grounds of circumcision and observance of the Mosaic law, as in Galatia, but on the grounds of their superior eloquence, their "letters of recommendation," and their power to work wonders.[39] In both cases Paul emphasizes his own Jewish credentials in order to argue against the viewpoints of other Jewish Christians. In one case, in Phil 3:4–6, Paul even claims that, proud as he is of his Jewish identity, it too fades into insignificance when compared with the sur-

---

[38] See Murphy-O'Connor, *Paul: A Critical Life*, 228–30. Murphy-O'Connor plausibly suggests that the Judaizing threat at Philippi is potential rather than actual. Paul may be writing to preempt the plans of the Judaizers who had previously come to Galatia but who now planned to move on to Philippi. This would account for the rhetoric of Phil 3:2–4:1, which does not seem to be aimed at some group already present at Philippi.

[39] Clarifying the position of Paul's opponents in 2 Corinthians 10–13 has been notoriously difficult. The issues between them and Paul, however, seem to have concerned the questions of circumcision or observance of the Mosaic law. For a treatment of the different possibilities, see Martin, *2 Corinthians*, xl–lii; and Furnish, *II Corinthians*, 48–54.

passing value of coming to know Christ and the righteousness that comes through faith in Christ (Phil 3:7–10). In both cases, his Jewish identity serves as the basis for advocacy against the viewpoints of other Jewish Christians. In the course of Rom 8:1–11:36, however, the situation is very different. Paul, on the basis of his Jewish identity, now becomes an advocate for "all Israel," which here means the ultimate inclusion of "all Israel." This is the first time in his letters that he has taken this role, and the first-person singular passages in these chapters emphasize how important the role has now become for him.

It is also the first time in his letters that he explicitly thinks through the issue of the ultimate fate of his fellow non-Christian Jews. Even the texts from Galatians that seemed to exclude his fellow Jews from "adoption" and from being included as "sons of God," "children of God," and "heirs" were about the present and not explicitly about the future. They were of eschatological importance only by implication. Explicitly eschatological texts such as 1 Thess 4:13–5:11 and 1 Corinthians 15, however, made no mention of Jews, even though the images were rooted in Jewish apocalyptic expectations.[40]

All of this strongly suggests that in Rom 8:1–11:36 Paul is thinking through the issue of the ultimate fate of his fellow Jews for the first time. The suspicions aroused in Roman Christians about the implications of his polemics in Galatians seem to have struck a responsive chord in Paul himself. This chord was his own Jewish identity, which he never ceased to claim. But what of the implications of his polemic in Galatians? If these implications were indeed true, then what of God's promises to Israel? If these promises have failed, then what is there of which to be proud? Given the extent and complexity of Paul's arguments in Rom 8:1–11:36, this issue seems to have engaged Paul in a way that virtually no other issue did and led him to rethink much of what he wrote in Galatians. It even forced him to rethink what had, by his own account in Gal 1:15–16, marked him from the very moment of his call, his apostleship to the Gentiles. In Rom 11:13–14, Paul comes to describe even this as something done for the sake of Israel, in order to make his fellow Jews jealous and thus save some of them. With a fuller awareness of the extent of Paul's personal engagement in this issue, we can now turn an analysis of the arguments themselves.

---

[40] The only possible exception is 1 Thess 2:14–16, which there is reason to think is a later interpolation. Even should it be authentic, it has no discernible effect on Paul's eschatological viewpoints, even in 1 Thess 4:13–5:11.

CHAPTER 12

Christ, Jews, and Gentiles

*P*AUL'S ARGUMENT IN ROM 8:31–11:36 is clearly the longest, most complex, and most sustained argument not only in Romans but in all of his letters. As pointed out in the previous three chapters of this study, it is also one of the most difficult and controversial passages to interpret. Several initial comments about this passage will be helpful before a more detailed analysis of the particular arguments.

The passage is filled with rhetorical figures commonly found in diatribes: rhetorical questions, apostrophe, dialogue with imaginary interlocutors, personification, and speech-in-character.[1] On the one hand, this means that there is an argumentative tone to the whole passage: Paul is trying to answer objections, whether correct of not, raised against his views. On the other hand, the argument is, for the most part, indirect. The imaginary interlocutors, for example, do not directly represent the views of his audience; they are straw men whose views are not identical with those of his audience. Nevertheless, behind these imaginary interlocutors, lie real issues and objections. The use of the diatribe again allows Paul to deal with these real issues and objections without, however, directly attacking the members of his Roman Christian audience.

As argued in chapters 9–11 of this study, some of the underlying objections to Paul by the Roman Christians concerned the views he apparently expressed in Galatians about the place, or lack of it, for the Jewish people. One of the central concerns of Paul's arguments in Rom 8:31–11:36 is to overcome these suspicions. But Paul does not deal with the issue of the place of the Jewish people in isolation. The context of his argument, which he established in 8:1–30, is broader than that. So too will be his arguments in 8:31–11:36. Paul will interpret the issue of the place of the Jewish people within a broader context by insisting on the interconnection of the present situation of the Jewish people and their fate with that of the Gentiles in the "mystery" (11:25) of God's overall plan. This insistence complicates the issue,

---

[1] Rhetorical questions (8:31–35; 9:14, 20–23, 30, 32; 10:8, 14–19; 11:1–4, 7, 11); apostrophe (9:20–29; 11:13–16, 17–24); dialogue (9:19–20; 11:13–24); personification (11:17–24); speech-in-character (10:6–8; 11:19).

but it needs to be kept constantly in mind in order to understand what Paul is struggling to argue in this passage.

Another reason for the complexity of Paul's arguments is that they are largely scriptural. We need to be reminded about the hermeneutical perspective or prism through which these scriptural texts are interpreted, lest we misunderstand what their intended force is. Paul, his fellow Jews, early Christians in general, and his Roman Christian audience in particular all shared the common conviction that what was contained in the Scriptures was immediately relevant for their own contemporary situation (see 4:23–24; 1 Cor 9:10). They differed, however, about how it was relevant. To take an extreme example, Philo's perspective on the contemporary relevance of Scripture was very different from that found in the scriptural interpretations from Qumran.[2] Nevertheless, they all were firmly convinced that the Scriptures were immediately relevant. All early Christians, including Paul and his Roman Christian audience, were convinced that central to this relevance were the ways in which the Scriptures shed light on the events of Christ's life, death, resurrection, and continued significance in the present and in the future. All early Christians read and interpreted the Scriptures from this perspective. In his scriptural interpretations, Paul assumes the existence of this perspective of immediate relevance and supposes that he shares it with his Roman Christian audience.

The structure of Paul's scriptural arguments in Rom 8:31–11:36 is basically chronological. Romans 9:6–29 deals primarily with the past, 9:30–10:21 primarily with the present, and 11:1–36 primarily with the future.[3] This temporally or historically oriented structure is not, however, a matter of convenience. Rather, it is due to Paul's convictions concerning the Jewish people, that "the word of God has not failed" (9:6) and that "the gifts and the call of God are irrevocable" (11:29). Paul struggles to interpret the Scriptures in order to understand what is for him and other early Christians the anomalous situation that the vast majority of his fellow Jews do not have faith in Christ but a growing number of Gentiles do. Given God's irrevocable promises to Israel in the Scriptures, how could this be? Have these promises failed? He struggles to understand this by placing it in the larger context of God's past dealings with Israel. He also tries to show how both Israel's present situation and its future inclusion as well as the present and future situation of the Gentiles are all in reality consistent with Israel's past as it is found in the Scriptures. Paul's arguments are chronological because his scriptural interpretations are intended to make some sense of events past, present, and hoped for. This chronological perspective is also consistent with Paul's more temporal and historically oriented arguments throughout Romans. What in Galatians had been contrasting *principles* become in Romans different historical *stages* in God's dealings with humankind.

---

[2] For Philo, see Tobin, *Creation of Man.* For Qumran, see Maurya P. Horgan, *Pesharim: Qumran Interpretations of Biblical Books* (CBQMS 8; Washington, D.C.: Catholic Biblical Association of America, 1979); Devorah Dimant, "Pesharim, Qumran," *ABD* 5:244–51; Lawrence H. Shiffman, *Reclaiming the Dead Sea Scrolls: The History of Judaism, the Background of Christianity, the Lost Library of Qumran* (Philadelphia: Jewish Publication Society, 1994), 211–22.

[3] For a more detailed outline, see above, pp. 300–301.

This is especially true of Rom 8:31–11:36. The passage cannot be understood without constantly keeping this different orientation in mind.

It is also crucial to keep in mind that, in 8:31–11:36, Paul is concerned with the relationship of Jews and Gentiles and their ultimate fates as groups and not as individuals. This is consistent with his concerns throughout Romans, but it is especially important to keep it in mind in interpreting 8:31–11:36. Any interpretation of this passage that moves to the level of Jews and Gentiles as individuals simply misconstrues what Paul is concerned with. His concerns are about two groups, Jews and Gentiles.

Finally, it is also important to be sensitive to the points in Paul's arguments where he assumes that there is agreement between himself and his Roman Christian audience and where he moves beyond these areas of agreement to demonstrate how his more controversial viewpoints are actually in continuity with the areas of agreement between them and himself. This is crucial because Paul's arguments both here and earlier in Romans emphasize real continuity amid seeming controversy. Without constant awareness of this, one risks misinterpreting Paul's arguments and misjudging their intended force. Now for the arguments themselves.

ROMANS 8:31–9:5: TRANSITION AND INTRODUCTION

Although we have looked at the first-person-singular parts of this passage (8:38–39; 9:1–5) in the previous chapter, more needs to be said about its structure, its relationship to 8:1–30, and its function in the scriptural arguments that follow. The passage serves both as a transition from 8:1–30 to what follows and as an introduction to the specific issue Paul feels compelled to deal with in the rest of Romans 9–11, the ultimate fate of "all Israel." The passage falls into two main sections: 8:31–39, which serves primarily as a response to 8:1–30, and 9:1–5, which establishes Paul's own personal anguish over the present situation of Israel.

Paul opens the first section with the question in 8:31, "What shall we say about these things?" It then continues with other questions in 8:31b–34, all of which are rooted in images of the law court—images of accusation (8:31b, 33, 34), defense (8:31b, 33), and acquittal (8:32, 33).[4] The next part of the passage (8:35–39), which states personal convictions based on 8:31–34, is held together by an *inclusio* about not being separated from the love of God/Christ (8:35, 39). Within this *inclusio*, Paul has two lists of things unable to separate us from the love of God or Christ, first a list of afflictions (a *peristaseis* catalogue) in 8:35–37 and then a list of cosmic realities (8:38–39).[5]

---

[4] Ἐγκαλέω ("accuse"); δικαιόω ("vindicate"); κατακρίνω ("condemn"); ἐντυγχάνω ("appeal to," "petition").

[5] Lists of tribulations, afflictions, or difficult circumstances (περιστάσεις) were a common topos in Stoic literature, Jewish apocalyptic literature, and writers such as Plutarch and Josephus. Paul uses similar lists in 1 Cor 4:10–13; 2 Cor 4:7–12; 6:4–10; 11:23–27; 12:10. See Robert Hodgson, "Paul the Apostle and First Century Tribulation Lists," *ZNW* 74 (1983): 59–80.

In the second section (9:1–5), Paul insists on his own personal anguish over the present situation of Israel. It begins in 9:1–2 with an expression of his great sorrow and then continues in 9:3–5a with the specification of what this sorrow is. Paul claims that he would even wish himself to be cut off from Christ for the sake of his fellow Jews, to whom belongs a whole series of privileges from God. He then ends this section in 9:5b with a doxology: "God who is above all things be blessed forever. Amen."[6]

Romans 8:31–39: Nothing Can Separate Us from the Love of God

The resumption of the use of rhetorical questions in 8:31–35 is formally the same as that seen in 3:27 and 6:1 and functionally similar to the use of apostrophe in 2:1. All indicate that Paul is beginning sections of the letter dealing with objections or difficulties raised by the Roman Christian community against his views or at least against what they saw as implications of his views. In 8:31–39 is a series of questions (8:31 [bis], 32, 33, 34, 35 [bis]). The first in 8:31 ("What shall we say about these things?") is the most important from a formal point of view because it indicates that Paul sees what follows as a response to, or as conclusions based on, 8:1–30.

As mentioned above, 8:31b–34 is filled with the vocabulary of the law courts. Here this vocabulary is part of an eschatological judgment scene in which God is the judge (8:31, 33, 34) and Christ is the one who sits at the right hand of God as intercessor (8:34). The basic imagery of such a scene is familiar from Jewish literature of this period.[7] In 8:32, 34, Paul also uses phrases taken from traditional Christian creedal formulas to bring out what has already become the traditional role of Christ in this kind of judgment scene.[8] Paul's use of future tenses at crucial points in the passage (8:32, 33, 35, 39) also emphasize the eschatological nature of the imagery.

The way Paul uses this traditional imagery is consistent with the way he used similar imagery in 8:1–30. He does this in three ways. First, given the use of eschatological imagery in both Judaism and early Christianity during this period, the imagery of an eschatological judgment scene is the appropriate climax of the process described in 8:1–30. The longings of both creation (8:19–22) and believers for the revelation of the sons of God (8:19, 21, 23) are brought to completion in just such a scene. Second, as in 8:1–30, this eschatological judgment scene, unlike most other such scenes in either Jewish or early Christian literature, does not set believers over against some other group of human beings. Rather, the scene is painted in entirely positive colors. There is no one to bring a charge against God's elect (8:33) or to condemn them (8:34). On the contrary, Christ, who is seated at the right hand of

---

[6] For the justification for taking 9:5b as an independent doxology to God rather than as a clause dependent on Χριστός in 9:5a, see above, p. 305, n. 14.

[7] E.g., Dan 12:1–3; *Jub.* 23:27–31; *1 En.* 104; *4 Ezra* 7:26–44. See George W. E. Nickelsburg, *Resurrection, Immortality, and Eternal Life in Intertestamental Judaism* (HTS 26; Cambridge: Harvard University Press, 1972).

[8] The phrases "who did not spare his own son but gave him up for us" (8:32) and "who sits at the right hand of God and who intercedes for us" (8:34) were probably originally parts of creedal formulas. See Byrne, *Romans,* 279–80; Fitzmyer, *Romans,* 533; Dunn, *Romans,* 500–504.

God, intercedes for them (8:34). This positive tone is further emphasized by Paul's continuing use of "all." God did not spare God's own Son but gave him up for "all of us" (ἡμῶν πάντων, 8:32), the "all" being an addition by Paul to the traditional creedal formula that Christ was given up "for us."[9] Because of this, will God not also give us "all things" (τὰ πάντα) with Christ (8:32)? Third, as he did in 8:1–30, Paul uses a term, this time in 8:33, "God's elect" (ἐκλεκτῶν θεοῦ), whose meaning is deeply embedded in Jewish self-understanding.[10] When one sees this in conjunction with Paul's use of "all" in this same passage, it becomes clear that Paul is describing this judgment scene in a way that intimates the inclusion not only of the Gentiles but also of his fellow Jews, which is what is at issue for Paul in this part of the letter.

Paul develops the same sense of inclusiveness and the same absence of opposing groups of human beings in 8:35–39. As mentioned above, this section is marked off by an *inclusio* about nothing being able to separate us from the love of God (8:35, 39). The section is dominated by two lists or catalogues, one a *peristaseis* catalogue of afflictions (8:35b) and the other a catalogue of cosmic forces (8:38–39), neither of which will be able to separate believers from the love of God. Paul's use of the rhetorical figure of enumeration (*congeries*, συναθροισμός) in both these catalogues adds emphasis to them.[11] It is also significant that once again the list of afflictions does not single out any specific group of human beings as responsible for these afflictions. Rather, Paul's emphasis is on the reality that "in all these" (ἐν τούτοις πᾶσιν) afflictions we are more than victorious because of the God who loves us (8:37). In addition, the list of cosmic forces in 8:38–39 expands on the afflictions in such a way as to emphasize that nothing at all in creation can stand in the way of the love of God. The importance of this last element for Paul is indicated by his expression of it as something of which he is personally convinced (πέπεισμαι, 8:38). Both the inclusive character of the eschatology and the lack of any mention of groups of human opponents in 8:31–39 also reflect the similar eschatological convictions Paul expressed in 1 Cor 15:24–28, 51–55. These convictions, found in 1 Corinthians 15 and reaffirmed in Rom 8:31–39, serve as one of the foundation stones for his arguments in Romans 9–11.

Romans 9:1–5: Paul's Personal Anguish over His Fellow Jews

In 9:1–5, the tone changes and becomes a very personal expression of Paul's sorrow and anguish over the present situation of his fellow Jews. Although this passage has been analyzed in the previous chapter, several additional points need to be made about its function within 8:1–11:36 as a whole. The sudden change in tone from what immediately precedes it at first seems jarring. All of a sudden, in 9:1–5, Paul expresses a personal anguish quite different from the confidence he has expressed in 8:31–39. This seemingly sudden change in tone, however, becomes understandable once one sees it as following on Paul's reinterpretations in 8:1–30 of his

[9] Dunn, *Romans*, 500–501.

[10] 1 Chr 16:13; Ps 89:3; 105:6; Isa 42:1 (LXX); 43:20; 45:4; 65:9, 15, 22; Sir 46:1; 47:22; Wis 3:9; 4:15; *Jub.* 1:29; *1 En.* 1:3, 8; 5:7–8; 25:5; 40:5; 41:2; 48:1; 51:5; 93:2; *Sib. Or.* 3:69; 1QS 8:6; CD 4:3–4; 1QM 12:1; 1QpHab 10:13. Dunn, *Romans*, 502, rightly emphasizes this.

[11] See Quintilian, *Inst.* 8.4.26–27.

own earlier, quite controversial views in Galatians. His insistence in 9:1–5 that he is telling the truth and not lying about his anguish for his fellow Jews makes much more sense when seen in the context of 8:1–30. There he tried to reinterpret basic concepts such as "adoption" and becoming "sons" of God, "children" of God, and "heirs" in such a way as ultimately not to exclude his fellow Jews, as he seemingly did in Galatians. It also makes much more sense when seen in the more immediate context of 8:31–9:5. This very personal expression in 9:1–5 immediately follows on the similarly personal expression of confidence in 8:38–39 that nothing will be able to separate us from the love of God. These two personal expressions represent the tensive polarities that dominate the rest of Romans 9–11. In these arguments, Paul struggles to integrate his own convictions about the inclusiveness of God's love, specifically the inclusion of the Gentiles, on the one hand, with the promises and privileges made to Israel, on the other, specifically an Israel that unexpectedly seems not to accept this inclusiveness. Both are deeply held convictions on Paul's part, but how are they to be reconciled?

This polarity and, at the same time, Paul's confidence that God will overcome it are perhaps best expressed by the doxology in 9:5b, with which Paul concludes this expression of anguish: "God who is over all [ἐπὶ πάντων] be blessed for ever." Similar kinds of doxology are common in both the Jewish scriptures and in early Christianity.[12] What is important for our purposes is that only in this doxology is God referred to as "over all." That Paul intends to emphasize this addition is clear from the fact that he reverses the traditional form of the doxology by placing the phrase "the God who is over all" before "blessed" rather than after it.[13] This addition by Paul is especially significant when set against the common characterization of God in these doxologies as the God "of Israel" or the God "of our fathers."[14] By placing this doxology immediately after his list of the privileges granted by God to Israel, Paul emphasizes several things. First, in the immediate context of 9:1–5, he places these privileges granted to Israel within the larger context of God's inclusiveness, which includes the Gentiles. Second, he connects the end of this section with its beginning (8:32), where he wrote that God gave up his Son "for all of us" (ὑπὲρ ἡμῶν πάντων) and that God will grant "all things" (τὰ πάντα) to us with him, and with the conclusion of the catalogue of afflictions (8:37), where he claims that "in all these" (ἐν τούτοις πᾶσιν) afflictions they are more than conquerors through the one who loves them.

The function of 8:31–9:5, then, is to provide the immediate framework for the scriptural arguments to follow. In keeping with the views he expressed in

---

[12] For early Christianity, see Luke 1:68; Eph 1:3; 1 Pet 1:3. Similar formulations also appear elsewhere in Paul (2 Cor 1:3; 11:31; Rom 1:25).

[13] One of the objections to 9:5b being a doxology has been that it reverses the standard order of traditional doxologies. Paul's addition of "over all" and his desire to emphasize it explains why 9:5b is most plausibly taken as a doxology even though the standard order is reversed. For a discussion of the issue, see Metzger, *Textual Commentary*, 459–62.

[14] E.g., the God "of Israel" (1 Sam 25:32; 1 Kgs 1:48; 8:15; 1 Chr 29:10; 2 Chr 2:11; 6:4; Pss 40:14; 105:48; Tob [Codex Sinaiticus] 13:18; *Odes Sol.* 9:18), the God "of our fathers" (Ezra 7:27; Dan [LXX] 3:26, 52; *Odes Sol.* 7:26; 8:52; 14:34). Similar formulations are found in Gen 9:26; 24:27; 1 Macc 4:30; 2 Macc 11:17; 3 Macc 7:23.

1 Corinthians 15, Paul insists that nothing can separate us from the love of God, not even the present situation of his fellow Jews. At the same time, this present situation is a matter of deep personal concern for Paul, which should put to rest the suspicions of Roman Christians who think that the matter is otherwise. In effect, he brings to bear what he wrote in Rom 8:1–30 on the ultimate fate of Israel. He does so in such a way that both his deeply held convictions about the inclusion of the Gentiles and the promises made to Israel serve as the basis for his arguments in what follows about the ultimate fate of "all Israel."

ROMANS 9:6–29: GOD'S PROMISES HAVE NOT FAILED—THE CHOICE OF ISRAEL AND THE GENTILES

The first stage of Paul's scriptural argument begins with Abraham and his "seed" (9:7–9), continues through Isaac and Jacob (9:10–13), goes on to Moses (9:14–18), and concludes with interpretations of Scripture that point to the present situation of Israel and the Gentiles (9:19–29). This leads into the next stage (9:30–10:21) of the argument. Paul has structured 9:6–29 rhetorically around an opening principle, that the word of God has not failed (9:6a), followed by one question about whether there is injustice on God's part (9:14) and a second question about why God still finds fault (9:19). Together they mark the stages in the argument. To understand its force and direction, it is important to locate where Paul moves beyond interpretations he shares with his Roman Christian audience to interpretations that break new ground both for him and his audience.

Romans 9:6–13: God's Promises to Israel Have Not Failed (Abraham, Isaac, and Jacob)

Paul begins in 9:6a with what amounts to a statement of principle, that "it is not that the word of God has failed."[15] By the "word of God" he clearly means the Jewish scriptures, particularly where the various promises and privileges granted to Israel listed in 9:4–5 are found, including that of being the ones from whom the Christ comes. No matter how it may appear, it is not the case that God's promises and privileges to Israel found in the Scriptures have failed. Paul derived this principle from the Scriptures themselves (Josh 21:45; 23:14; 2 Kgs 10:10), and it is clearly one he shares with his Roman Christian audience. It also becomes the rubric under which he means his scriptural arguments to be seen, not only in Rom 9:6–29 but also in the whole of Romans 9–11.

He then follows this in 9:6b with a second statement ("For [γάρ] not all those from Israel [πάντες οἱ ἐξ Ἰσραήλ] are Israel"), meant in some fashion to specify and justify the principle expressed in 9:6a. How Paul means the second statement to specify or justify the first, however, is not obvious. Is the point that the word of God has not failed because the word of God itself shows that not all Israelites truly be-

---

[15] The opening phrase (Οὐχ οἷον δὲ ὅτι) is a combination of the Hellenistic οὐχ οἷον ("by no means") and οὐχ ὅτι ("not as if"). It expresses a strong denial. See BDAG 701.

long to Israel? In this case 9:6b would have a restrictive sense.[16] Or does 9:6b mean that the word of God shows that "Israel" is not restricted only to the lineal descendants of Jacob/Israel, the Jews, but also includes others, the Gentiles? In this interpretation the statement is expansive rather than restrictive.[17] Given that the direction of Paul's arguments in Romans 9–11 is to include both "all Israel" (11:26) and the "full number of the Gentiles" (11:25), one is tempted to opt for the expansive interpretation. Yet opting for either may be asking too much of Paul's statement. The statement itself sounds almost proverbial, meaning nothing more specific than that "not all Israelites are the real thing." This interpretation has two advantages. First, it reflects the fact that Paul never returns to this statement in the rest of Romans 9–11 whereas he does return to 9:6a in 11:1, 24. Second, after the statement about Israel in 9:6b, Paul immediately turns to the specific cases of Abraham and Isaac, both of whom lived before Jacob/Israel, in such a way as seems to follow immediately on 9:6a. This too suggests that 9:6b should be taken in the general, proverbial sense that "not all Israelites are the real thing." Its meaning should not be pressed beyond that.

Paul then turns to the interpretation of parts of the scriptural accounts of God's choice of the offspring of the patriarchs, first of Abraham's son Isaac (9:7–9) and then of Isaac's son Jacob (9:10–13). He begins in 9:7 by asserting that not "all 'children' are the 'seed of Abraham.'"[18] He then quotes Gen 21:12, "in the line of Isaac shall 'seed' be called into being for you." Paul goes on to explain more specifically in Rom 9:8–9 what this means. It is not the "children of the flesh" who are the "children of God"; rather, it is the "children of the promise" who are reckoned as "seed." To show that this is so, he quotes God's promise to Abraham in Gen 18:10, 14: "At the appointed time I shall come [ἐλεύσομαι], and Sarah will have [ἔσται] a son," both verbs being in the future tense, thus showing that what God says is by way of a promise.

Paul's argument in this passage is more complex than it first appears, especially when seen against the background of Romans 4 and 8 and the controversies connected with them. In 9:7, Paul begins by distinguishing between "children" (τέκνα) of Abraham and "seed" (σπέρμα) of Abraham. "Children" is the broader category, "seed," the narrower. He justifies the distinction by quoting Gen 21:12: "In Isaac shall your seed be called." He interprets this to mean that although both Ishmael and Isaac are "children" of Abraham, only Isaac and his descendants are also the "seed" of Abraham. He then goes on in Rom 9:8 to explain this further (τοῦτ' ἔστιν . . .) by

---

16 So Byrne, *Romans* 293; Cranfield, *Romans*, 2:472–73; Wilckens, *Römer*, 2:191–92; Fitzmyer, *Romans*, 559–60.

17 So, it seems, Dunn, *Romans*, 539–40.

18 In 9:7a, the subject of the clause must be "all 'children'" (πάντες τέκνα). This is the only way that Paul's use of the quotation from Gen 21:12 in Rom 9:7b and his interpretation of it in Rom 9:8 make any sense. The generic category is πάντες τέκνα. This is divided into two more specific categories: (1) σπέρμα Ἀβραάμ, which is identical with τέκνα τοῦ θεοῦ . . . τέκνα τῆς ἐπαγγελίας, and (2) τὰ τέκνα τῆς σαρκός. Paul's point is that not all members of the generic category are members of the first specific category. This is the interpretation of Dunn, *Romans*, 540. Others take σπέρμα Ἀβραάμ as the subject (Byrne, *Romans*, 293; Wilckens, *Römer*, 2:191–93; Fitzmyer, *Romans*, 560; Cranfield, *Romans*, 2:473–74).

distinguishing between two kinds of "children," "children of the flesh" (τέκνα τῆς σαρκός) and "children of God" (τέκνα τοῦ θεοῦ). Only the latter are also "children of the promise" (τέκνα τῆς ἐπαγγελίας) and can be reckoned (λογίζεται) as "seed." He justifies the identification of "children of the promise" with "seed" by quoting a combination of Gen 18:10 and 14, in which God promises to Abraham that he will return at the appointed time and Sarah will have a son, Isaac. When combined with Gen 21:12 cited a verse earlier, this means that Isaac, who is the son of the promise (18:10, 14), is also the one through whom "seed" will be called forth for Abraham (21:12).

What is not justified in the immediate context of Paul's exegetical argument in Rom 9:8, however, is the identification of "children of the promise" with "children of God." In many ways such an identification must have been obvious both for Paul and for his Roman Christian audience. It was through Isaac's descendants that the Jewish people traced their identity as "children of God." Yet because of the controversies swirling around Paul's interpretation of terms such as "seed," "children of God," and "promise" in Galatians 3–4, one has to remember that it is obvious only because of Paul's reinterpretations of the meanings of "seed" in Rom 4:13, 16, 18 and of "children of God" in 8:16, 17, 21. It is these reinterpretations that allow for the inclusion of the Jewish people. At the same time, by beginning with Abraham and once again connecting Abraham's "seed" with the "promise," Paul is also implicitly recalling to his Roman Christian audience's mind that these terms ultimately refer to not only Jews but also Gentiles.

In 9:10–13, Paul moves to the next generation, to Rebecca and Isaac and their sons Esau and Jacob. Paul points out that God chose the younger Jacob over the elder Esau even before they were born. He uses two scriptural quotations in support of this, one from Gen 25:23, that the elder will serve the younger, the other from Mal 1:2–3, that God "loved" Jacob but "hated" Esau. Once again Paul's arguments are more subtle than they appear at first. In Rom 9:11–12, he comments on the circumstances of this choice and its purpose:

> while they were not yet born and had not yet done anything either good or evil,
> so that [ἵνα] God's purpose in election [ἡ κατ᾽ ἐκλογὴν πρόθεσις] might persist,
> not because of deeds [οὐκ ἐξ ἔργων]
> but because of the one who calls [ἐκ τοῦ καλοῦντος]

Paul draws on a significant detail in the story of the birth of Esau and Jacob in Gen 25:19–26: God chose the younger Jacob over the elder Esau before either of them were even born and before either of them had done anything, either good or evil, to deserve God's choice. Paul then offers an explanation for this apparently puzzling action on God's part. God did it so that his purpose in election would continue not because of deeds but because of God's call. This explanation is strikingly similar to Paul's interpretation in Rom 4:1–6 of Abraham's call in Genesis 15. In both cases God's choice was not the result of what either Jacob or Abraham had done (ἐξ ἔργων) but, rather, preceded it. This second example of Esau and Jacob strengthens the force of the example of God's choice of Isaac by way of a promise in Rom 9:7–9, so that all three patriarchs—Abraham, Isaac, and Jacob—are implicated in God's mysterious choices before doing anything to deserve it: Abraham by faith, Isaac by promise, and Jacob by God's choice before his birth.

Why does Paul think all this happened in this way? So that God's purpose in election might persist. The phrase Paul uses, "God's purpose in election" (ἡ κατ' ἐκλογὴν πρόθεσις τοῦ θεοῦ), clearly echoes phrases he used earlier in 8:28, 33. In 8:28, Paul wrote that "we know that for those who love God, for *those called according to his purpose* [τοῖς κατὰ πρόθεσιν κλητοῖς], he works all things with them for good; in 8:33, he rhetorically asked, "who will bring a charge *against God's elect* [κατὰ ἐκλεκτῶν θεοῦ]?" In using similar phrases both in 9:11 and in 8:28, 33, Paul is rhetorically weaving together God's choice of Israel with the broader, mysterious purposes of God that he has already emphasized at the end of Romans 8.

Why does Paul highlight these particular aspects of the stories of the Jewish patriarchs? Perhaps the best way to answer this question is to ask a different question first. Would he have expected his Roman Christian audience to have agreed with him about the important and positive value of God's choices of Abraham, Isaac, and Jacob? The answer is clearly yes. The basic framework of Paul's interpretation of the positive significance of the patriarchal narratives was something he and his Roman Christian audience had in common. At the same time, Paul interprets these narratives in such a way as to prepare his audience for the explanations he will offer of the present and future situations of both Jews and Gentiles. These patriarchal narratives serve as precedents about God's choice apart from deeds and in keeping with his promises, both of which eventually lead to the inclusion of the Gentiles. Turning it around, God's word has not failed partially because the inclusion of both Jews and Gentiles is rooted in the way God chooses, beginning even with the patriarchs. From a more strictly rhetorical point of view, this is also part of an argument based on previous judgments in similar cases, a type of argument Paul used earlier, in 1:18–3:20.[19]

Finally, in order to understand the movement of Paul's argument, it is important to note that the second scriptural quotation—from Mal 1:2–3, the idea that God "loved Jacob" but "hated Esau"—plays no real role in Paul's interpretation in Rom 9:11–12. Its role is solely to provoke the rhetorical question in 9:14 about whether this implies some injustice on God's part and so to move the argument one step further.

Romans 9:14–18: God Is Not Unjust in His Choices (Moses and Pharaoh)

Romans 9:14–18 and the following section (9:19–29) begin with rhetorical questions. They are similar in content and sequence to earlier rhetorical questions in 3:5–6 and 3:7–8 respectively. Both 9:14 and 3:5–6 begin with questions about whether God is unjust in dealings with human beings. Romans 9:19 and 3:7–8 begin with similar questions about why God continues to find fault with anyone (9:19) and the other about why anyone is still judged by God as a sinner (3:7). These similarities are not accidental. Both sets of questions reflect underlying objections by the Roman Christians about what they suspect are the implications of Paul's views about righteousness as a gift of God apart from observance of the

---

[19] See above, pp. 107–8; and *Rhet. Her.* 2.19; Quintilian, *Inst.* 5.11.36–44.

Mosaic law. As pointed out in the analysis of Romans 5–7, these suspicions concern issues of moral conduct. If righteousness is a gift of God apart from observance of the Mosaic law, does moral conduct not become irrelevant, and would not God be "unjust" in judging or condemning such conduct? Paul argued in Romans 5–7 that these suspicions are groundless, that indeed quite the opposite is true. Another aspect of this issue concerns the continuing relevance of the scriptural accounts of God's choice, starting with the patriarchs, of "Israel." Are not Paul's convictions about righteousness as a gift apart from observance of the Mosaic law now granted to Gentiles so unprecedented in terms of these scriptural accounts that they are at variance with the "word of God"? Are not God's gifts and privileges to Israel now left to one side? Do they not become irrelevant, and does Israel itself not become irrelevant? Issues such as these affect the way Paul interprets the Scriptures in both 9:14–18 and 9:19–29.

Romans 9:14–18 begins with the question, which expects a negative answer, about whether there is injustice on God's part. Paul's reply is, "Certainly not!" (μὴ γένοιτο). He follows this with two quotations from Scripture, Exod 33:19 in Rom 9:15 and Exod 9:16 in Rom 9:17. Each of the quotations is followed by a conclusion (ἄρα οὖν), one in 9:16 and the other in 9:18, drawn from the respective quotation from Exodus.

The initial question and Paul's strong denial in 9:14 about the possibility of injustice on God's part are occasioned by the scriptural quotation in 9:13 from Mal 1:2–3, that God "loved Jacob" but "hated Esau." Paul certainly would have shared such a denial of injustice on God's part with his Roman Christian audience. But he then goes on to quote two passages from Scripture to support the denial. Does he do this to convince his audience that God is not unjust? This is unlikely. Rather, the two quotations are meant to show how it is that God is not unjust or, more positively, how God is not only just but generous. The first quotation, in Rom 9:15, is taken from Exod 33:19:

> I will have mercy on whom I have mercy,
> and I will have compassion on whom I have compassion.

The context of this sentence in Exodus is important. It occurs in one of the scenes in which Moses intercedes with God on behalf of Israel after the Israelites have constructed and worshipped the golden calf (Exod 32:1–6). By right, God would be justified in destroying the Israelites. But through Moses' intercession, God relents and shows mercy. In his dealings with Israel, he is not only not unjust; he is more than just. He is generous and merciful. In harmony with this context, Paul concludes that "so then it is not a matter of willing or achieving but of God showing mercy" (Rom 9:16).[20] God's mercy to Israel during the Exodus did not depend on what the people of Israel did, just as it did not depend on what Abraham, Isaac, or Jacob had done. The second quotation, in Rom 9:17, comes from Exod 9:16, God's words to Pharaoh:[21]

---

[20] Something like ἐστί has to be understood as the main verb of the sentence. It is not clear what the subject of the sentence is; it may be ἡ κατ' ἐκλογὴν πρόθεσις in Rom 9:11.

[21] Paul has made several changes in this quotation in comparison with the LXX. For a detailed discussion of these changes, see Cranfield, *Romans*, 2:485–88.

For this very purpose I have raised you up,
   so that I may show my power in you
   and so that my name may be proclaimed in all the earth.

After this quotation Paul once again draws a conclusion, this time one that pithily sums up both quotations (Exod 33:19 and 9:16), that God "has mercy on whomever he wills and he hardens whomever he wills" (Rom 9:18). The latter phrase refers to the frequent motif in Exodus that Pharaoh refused to let the Israelites go because God had "hardened his heart."[22] But Paul is not interested in the hardening of Pharaoh's heart itself. Rather, he is interested in God's purpose in doing so. This is the point of quoting Exod 9:16. By God's showing forth his power in Pharaoh, God's name will be proclaimed in "all the earth" (ἐν πάσῃ τῇ γῇ). This is what is important for the development of Paul's argument. He quotes this particular text from the scriptural account of the exodus because in it God himself proclaims that in the exodus there is already an element or intimation of universality.

Through these two quotations, then, Paul highlights two further aspects of God's dealings with Israel, God's mercy to Israel even though Israel has been unfaithful and God's wider, more universal purpose in delivering Israel from the power of Pharaoh. The first aspect provides an additional precedent similar to those in Rom 9:6–13; the second introduces another kind of precedent—the broader scope of God's purposes in dealing with Israel— that will be developed explicitly in 9:19–29.

Romans 9:19–29: The Example of the Potter and Its Application to God's Richness to Both Jews and Gentiles

Until this point, the framework of Paul's arguments has been traditional viewpoints he has in common with his Roman Christian audience. Certainly he has highlighted or emphasized particular aspects of the stories of the patriarchs and the exodus that are most important to him because they provide him with precedents for his later arguments. Nevertheless, the traditional framework provided by the foundational events of the history of Israel remains. In 9:19–29, however, the character of his arguments changes. Although this section contains a variety of traditional elements shared by Paul and his audience, he puts them in the service of a different and enlarged framework, which will then serve as the basis for his arguments in both 9:30–10:21 and 11:1–32. This shift in framework also explains why Paul's arguments in this passage become more elaborate.

From a rhetorical perspective, the passage is constructed as a dialogue between Paul and an imaginary interlocutor. More specifically, it is structured around six questions, the first two of which (9:19) are the objections of the imaginary interlocutor whereas the following four (9:20–24) provide Paul's response.[23] In 9:19, the

---

[22] Exod 4:21; 7:3, 22; 8:15; 9:12, 35; 10:1, 20, 27; 11:10; 13:15; 14:4, 8, 17.

[23] Though technically a dialogue, after the imaginary interlocutor's two questions, the rest of the section effectively becomes an apostrophe. This explains why the identity of the imaginary interlocutor remains unclear. In 9:20, he is addressed as ὦ ἄνθρωπε. Paul has used this form of address before, in 2:1, 3, where at first it seems to refer to a hypocritical Gentile

imaginary interlocutor asks, "why then does he [God] still find fault, for who can resist his will?" Paul responds in several steps. In 9:20–21, he responds by asking several questions in return: Who are you, a mere human being, to answer back to God? Will something that has been made say to its maker, "Why did you make me thus?" Does the potter not have the right over the clay, to make out of the same lump one vessel for a noble use and another for a menial use? In 9:22–24, Paul applies the metaphor of the potter and the vessels to what God has a right to do. Specifically, he applies it to God's call of those not only from among Jews but also from among Gentiles. In 9:25–29, he supports his claims in 9:22–24 with scriptural quotations from Hosea about Gentiles (9:25–26) and from Isaiah about Jews (9:27–29). It is important to realize that in Greek all of 9:22–26 form one complex argument and that the scriptural quotations from Isaiah in 9:27–29, though syntactically new sentences, follow immediately on the quotations from Hosea in 9:25–26. Romans 9:22–29 is in reality one complex and interrelated argument.

Like the questions that opened 9:14, the ones that open 9:19 are provoked by what immediately precedes. In the case of 9:19, it is 9:18 that provokes the interlocutor's questions: "Therefore he [God] has mercy on whomever he wills and he hardens whomever he wills." The interlocutor's questions are to the effect that if this is so, then why does God continue to find fault, since no one can resist his will? The second question echoes both Job 9:4 and especially Wis 12:12; both texts will prove helpful in understanding Paul's responses. As in Rom 9:14, the questions in 9:19 imply there is some injustice on God's part. In one way, the questions simply serve as the occasion for Paul's response in 9:20–21, since neither Paul nor his audience would have allowed for any injustice on God's part. But in another way, given Paul's arguments in 9:23–29 about God's call not only of Jews but also of Gentiles, the questions again reflect the Roman Christians' concerns about Paul's earlier views about the situation of his fellow Jews. Does Paul think that God has "hardened" his fellow Jews the way he hardened Pharaoh's heart?

Paul's initial response to these questions in 9:20–21 comes in the form of three further questions, the second of which expects a negative answer and third a positive answer:

> On the contrary, who are you, a mere human being, to argue with God?
> Will what is molded say to its molder, "Why have you made me thus?"
> Or does the potter not have the right over the clay,
>   to make from the same lump one vessel for a noble use
>   and another for a menial use?

Paul does not in fact quote any passage from Scripture to support his response. But he makes use of several images common enough in the Jewish scriptures and in other contemporary Jewish literature. The first response, about the impossibility of a mere human being arguing with God, echoes views found in Job, particularly Job 9:1–4 on

---

but, as one reads further, it comes to apply to any hypocrite, either Jew or Gentile. The same vagueness seems to be the case in 9:19–20. The interlocutor serves only to raise the questions Paul wants to deal with.

the impossibility of contending with God or answering him back.[24] This connects Paul's first response with the imaginary interlocutor's second question. The second and third responses (Rom 9:20b–21) invoke images of God as a potter and human beings as vessels God can mold for different purposes. These images ultimately have their starting point in the second account of the creation of man in Gen 2:7, where God molds man from the dust of the earth. But they also came to be used to defend God's doing as God thought best. The best examples are found in Isa 29:16 and 45:9:[25]

Shall you not be regarded as the potter's clay [ὁ πηλὸς τοῦ κεραμέως]?
Shall the thing molded [τὸ πλάσμα] say to its molder [τῷ πλάσαντι],
   "You did not mold me";
or what is made [τὸ ποίημα] say to its maker [τῷ ποιήσαντι],
   "You did not make me skillfully"? (29:16)

Woe to him who strives with his maker,
   earthen vessels with the potter!
Does the clay say to the one who fashions it, "What are you making"?
   or "Your work has no handles"? (45:9)

The immediate context of both verses (Isa 29:9–16; 45:9–19) is a defense of God's ways of working in the events of human history, especially in the events of the history of Israel. The point of the images is not that God has the right to be arbitrary but that God's ways are mysterious and beyond the capacity of human beings to comprehend. When similar images were used elsewhere in Jewish literature of this period, they were also used in the context of defending God's mysterious ways of acting.[26] The images Paul draws on, then, in Rom 9:20–21 to defend God's ways of acting as mysterious and beyond human comprehension were already quite traditional. This stage in Paul's response is a commonplace and shared by his Roman Christian audience. Paul quite rightly expects them readily to agree that human beings certainly cannot argue with God and that God certainly does have the right to do what God wants with regard to human beings. This does not mean, however, that God is arbitrary or unjust. The expected agreement also establishes a basic principle, a common ground, upon which Paul builds the next stage of his response.

    This second stage, which in effect extends from 9:22 through 9:29, is complex. The argument itself is found in 9:22–24, which Paul then supports by scriptural quotations in 9:25–29.

---

[24]"Then Job answered: 'Indeed I know that this is so;
   but how can a mortal be just before God?
If one wished to contend with him,
   one could not answer him once in a thousand.
He is wise in heart, and mighty in strength—
   who has resisted him, and succeeded?' "

[25]To highlight the similar vocabulary, the translation of Isa 29:16 is from the LXX. The translation of Isa 45:9 is from the MT, although the translation of the first half of the verse is uncertain. This difficulty is also reflected in the LXX translation.

[26]Jer 18:1–12; Sir 33:10–13; *T. Naph.* 2:2–4; 1QS 11:22; 1QHa 1:21; 3:20–24; 4:28–29; 11:3; 12:26.

But what if [εἰ δέ] God, willing [θέλων] to show [ἐνδείξασθαι] his wrath and to make known his power [τὸ δυνατόν], has endured with much patience vessels of wrath made for destruction, even so that [καὶ ἵνα] he might make known the riches of his glory for the vessels of mercy, which he had prepared beforehand for glory [προητοίμασεν εἰς δόξαν], us whom he also called [ἐκάλεσεν] not only from among Jews but also from among Gentiles? (9:22–24)

These three verses together form one complex and very rhetorical question.[27] They are meant to follow on the principle enunciated in 9:20–21, that God's ways are mysterious and beyond the capacity of human beings to comprehend. From the opening words of the passage ("But what if . . ."), these verses seem at first to be a hypothetical question about God's mysterious ways of dealing with human beings. Still, in spite of their grammatical form as a question, Paul intends these verses to be more than a question: Paul expects his audience to agree that God would indeed be in the right were God to do these things. Paul then uses the scriptural quotations in 9:25–27 to carry the argument one step further by showing that God has foretold that God would indeed accomplish all these things, specifically by including not only Jews but also Gentiles among the "vessels of mercy."

What is perhaps most remarkable about this argument is the extent to which Paul draws on concepts and vocabulary he has just used in 9:14–18, 20–21 as well as earlier in Romans 8 and 9:1–13. Paul begins in 9:22 by asking what if God "wills" to "show" his wrath and to make known "his power." This takes up Paul's quotation of Exod 9:16 in Rom 9:17–18 about God's raising up Pharaoh to "show my power" as well as his conclusion from this that God has mercy on whom God "wills" and hardens whom God "wills." In 9:22–23, Paul distinguishes between "vessels of wrath" and "vessels of mercy." This distinction takes up the similar distinction in 9:21 between a "vessel intended for noble use" and a "vessel intended for menial use." In addition, "vessels of mercy" harks back to Paul's quotation of Exod 33:19, in which God "has mercy" on sinful Israel. This intentional reuse of vocabulary, however, extends beyond the immediately preceding section. In Rom 9:23, God making known the richness of his "glory" to the vessels of mercy whom God prepared beforehand for "glory" harks back to 9:4, where "glory" was one of the privileges given to Israel. It also harks back to 8:18, 21, where believers await God's "glory" about to be revealed to them when creation itself will also be freed into the "glory" of the children of God. Finally, in 9:23–24, Paul describes these vessels of mercy as ones that God "prepared *beforehand* for glory" (προητοίμασεν εἰς δόξαν) and ones whom "he called" (ἐκάλεσεν) not only from among Jews but also from among Gentiles. Both of these expressions hark back to 8:29–30, to those whom God "*fore*knew" (προέγνω), "*pre*destined" (προώρισεν), "called" (ἐκάλεσεν), and "glorified" (ἐδόξασεν).

The thickness of cross-references in such a small compass is almost cento-like. Its purpose and function in these verses, however, is not a matter of literary ornamentation but central to the argument Paul is making. Perhaps the best way to grasp

---

[27] The καὶ ἵνα in 9:23 should be translated "even so that" because καί has no preceding coordinate clause that would allow it to be translated as "and" [see Deut 8:18; 9:5; 1 Esd 4:50; Isa 40:20; Rev 18:17 as parallels]. In addition, the sentence continues to the end in Rom 9:24, which is an appositive relative clause dependent on ἐπισκευὴ ἐλέους in 9:23.

this argument is to look more closely at the notion of God's activity of "bearing with much patience" (ἤνεγκεν ἐν μολλῇ μακροθυμίᾳ) in 9:22. Paul has referred to God's patience once before, in 2:4, where he pointed out that God's kindness, forbearance, and patience (μακροθυμίας) are meant to lead the sinner to repentance. More broadly, the notion of God being patient is a common motif in the Jewish scriptures.[28] Divine patience is often associated also with other attributes of God, particularly God as showing compassion (οἰκτίρμων) and mercy (ἐλεήμων) and as abounding in mercy (πολυέλεος).[29]

But the notion of God's patience or forbearance also became part of a larger discussion in Jewish literature about God's ways of punishing or delaying the punishment of sinners, the discussion of which Paul is aware, as indicated in 2:4. Two such discussions are found in Sir 5:1–8 and 2 Macc 6:12–17. In Sir 5:1–8, the author advises his reader not to delay repentance, for, although God is slow to anger, the day of calamity will come and will come suddenly. In a direct address to the reader in 2 Macc 6:12–17, the author explains that God punishes Israel immediately for its sins instead of delaying, as God does with the other nations. God does this out of mercy for Israel because God does not want to have to take greater vengeance on them later when their sins have been built up.

The most extensive and most apposite discussion of the issue, however, occurs in Wis 12:3–18.[30] This section is part of the author's description of the events of Israel's exodus from Egypt. The author first describes the sins of the Canaanites that justify God's transfer of the land from them to Israel as a "worthy colony of the servants of God" (12:3–7). He then describes God's forbearance even in these circumstances, how God sent wasps upon the Canaanites to lead them to repentance even though God knew that they were thoroughly evil (12:8–11). On the basis on this example, the author of Wisdom is moved to reflect more generally on the way God judges human beings (12:12–18). The beginning of this reflection (12:12) is similar to Rom 9:19: "For who will say, 'what have you done?' or will resist your judgment?" He then goes on to point out that God has no rival whose care is for all people or to whom one could appeal when punished (Wis 12:13–14). God is righteous (δίκαιος), and it is alien to his power (τῆς σῆς δυνάμεως) to punish those who do not deserve it (12:15–16). God punishes those who doubt his power (δυνάμεως) and who are insolent, but otherwise God judges with mildness (ἐν ἐπιεικείᾳ) and shows great restraint (μετὰ πολλῆς φειδοῦς) (12:17–18).

Like Wis 12:3–18, the discussion in Rom 9:22–24 concerns the subjects of God's wrath, God's forbearance, and God's power. These are all set within the context of God's justice. Paul is clearly aware of this discussion within Judaism during this period. He makes use of it here, but he puts it to a different purpose. For Paul, God's patience is also meant to serve a different and larger purpose, expressed in

---

[28] The verb "to be patient" (μακροθυμέω) is used in Sir 18:11 to refer to God. The adjective "patient" (μακρόθυμος) is used a number of times in the LXX as an attribute of God (Exod 34:6; Num 14:18; 2 Esd 19:17; Ps 7:12; 85:15; 102:8; 144:8; Jonah 4:2; Dan [Theodotian] 4:27; Joel 2:13; Nah 1:3; 2 Macc 6:14; *Odes Sol.* 12:7; Wis 15:1; Sir 5:4).

[29] These three attributes of God are found along with "patient" in the LXX of Exod 34:6; 2 Esd 19:17; Ps 85:15; 102:8; 144:8; Jonah 4:2; Joel 2:13.

[30] See Johnson, *Function*, 110–75.

Rom 9:23–24: "even so that [καὶ ἵνα] he might make known the riches of his glory for the vessels of mercy, which he had prepared beforehand for glory, us whom he also called not only from among Jews but also from among Gentiles." This is the point in the argument where Paul moves beyond the traditional discussions of the issue of God's patience and forbearance to claim an additional reason for this patience and forbearance, the inclusion not only of Jews but also of Gentiles as vessels of mercy. Notice especially how Paul once again puts this in terms of the both-and pattern we have already seen in 4:1–15, where both Jews and Gentiles are included within the promises made to Abraham. When seen in the context of his reinterpretations of Galatians in Rom 8:1–30 and of his interpretation of the choice of the patriarchs and of the events of the exodus in 9:6–13, 14–18, the inclusion of Gentiles is not a choice by God against Israel but an expansion or widening of God's mercy that additionally includes Gentiles.

Once we are aware of both the extent of the cross-references in these verses and Paul's use and development of the kinds of discussion reflected in Wis 12:3–18, the force of his argument becomes clearer. It is based on the principle he enunciated in Rom 9:20–21, that God has the right to do what God thinks best. Paul's argument in 9:22–24 is that God would also be just if God, though willing to show his wrath and make known his power, much as God did in the exodus and the choice of the patriarchs, showed forbearance *even so that* God might make known his richness not only to Jews but also to Gentiles. The force of the cross-references and his use of the motif of God's patience is that this new development is indeed in continuity with the ways God has previously dealt with Israel. What is new is that this now includes not only Jews but also Gentiles. Put another way, Paul's purpose is to give such plausibility to his apparently hypothetical question in 9:22–24 that his Roman Christian audience will be convinced by the scriptural quotations he uses in 9:25–29 to show that the hypothetical question is indeed really the case.

Finally, Paul concludes this stage of his argument with quotations from the prophets Hosea (Hos 2:25[23]; 2:1[1:10]) and Isaiah (Isa 10:22–23; 1:9). These quotations are meant to show that God has indeed said he would call "vessels of mercy" not only from among Jews but also from among Gentiles. To understand what Paul means by using these quotations, one must remember that Paul, like many of his Jewish contemporaries, believed that the Scriptures had a direct meaning for his own day.[31] Even so, what Paul's specific intention is in quoting these passages from Scripture, particularly the verses from Hosea, is not completely clear.

Perhaps the best way to get it is to begin with what is clear. First, Paul uses the quotations from Hosea to refer to Gentiles, and the two quotations from Isaiah to refer to Israel. It is clear that as Paul uses them, these quotations have two different references (Gentiles and Jews). In the immediately preceding verse (Rom 9:24) and in the immediately following verses (9:30–31), the discussion is about both Israel and the Gentiles. Additionally, in 9:27, Paul indicates that he is moving from a scriptural quotation from Hosea about Gentiles to two quotations from Isaiah about Israel.

---

[31] See 1 Cor 9:9–10; 10:6; Rom 4:23–24.

Second, Paul takes the quotations to refer to his own time, to the present situation of the Gentiles and Israel, his fellow Jews. The verbs in Hos 2:23; 1:10 and Isa 10:22–23 are in the future tense, and the quotation from Isa 1:9 is introduced by the clause "and as Isaiah predicted [προείρηκεν]."[32] On the one hand, Paul thinks that these quotations refer to a time later than either Hosea or Isaiah. On the other hand, given what follows in Rom 9:30–10:21, which clearly refers to the situation of Gentiles and Jews in Paul's own day, he is using the quotations not as references to some final situation of either Gentiles or Jews but as references to their present situation. He then develops this in 9:30–10:21.

Third, in describing the present situation of the Gentiles, Paul, by quoting Hos 2:23; 1:10 out of order so that God's "calling" forms an inclusion at the beginning and the end of the quotation, emphasizes that they too are now "called" by God. He also substitutes the verb "I will call" (καλέσω) at the beginning of the quotation for "I will say" (ἐρῶ), found in the LXX. This emphasizes the connection of the present calling of the Gentiles with Paul's convictions about God's mysterious plan of foreknowing, predestining, *calling*, and so forth, in Rom 8:29–30. It also emphasizes how the present situation of the Gentiles of being "called" is in continuity with God's "calling" of the patriarchs in 9:7, 12. God's calling of the Gentiles is of a piece with the way he has already dealt with Israel.

Fourth, in the quoting of Isa 10:22–23 and 1:9 in Rom 9:27–29 to elucidate the present situation of Israel, the crucial notion is that "the remnant will be preserved" (τὸ ὑπόλειμμα σωθήσεται). To understand properly Paul's point in quoting these two passages from Isaiah, one has to realize that he is using the term "remnant" positively.[33] He makes this clear by citing Isa 1:9 in addition to the quotation from Isa 10:22–23. Were God not gracious in preserving a remnant, Israel would become as desolate as Sodom and Gomorrah. This is important because it affects the interpretation of Rom 9:30–10:21 and is consistent with Paul's equally positive interpretation of "remnant" found in 11:1–10, where he takes up this language again.

There are two problems with Paul's use of these quotations. First, only the citation of Isa 1:9 in Rom 9:29 is verbatim from the LXX. The quotations from Hosea and from Isaiah 10:22–23 vary in a number of ways from the LXX.[34] For the most part, these deviations do not change the meaning of the quotations, although it is not clear why Paul made them. The second and more significant problem concerns Paul's use of Hos 2:23; 1:10 to refer to Gentiles. In the context of Hosea 2, these

---

[32] In Rom 9:25, καλέσω; 9:26, ἔσται, κληθήσονται; 9:27, σωθήσεται; 9:28, ποιήσει.

[33] The language of "remnant" is used positively in Gen 45:7; 2 Kgs 19:31; Mic 4:7; 5:7–8; Ezra 9:8, 13; 1 Macc 3:25; CD 1:4–5; 1QM 13:8; 14:8–9; 1QH[a] 6:8, but negatively in 2 Kgs 21:14; Isa 14:22, 30; Ezek 8:10; 1QS 4:14; 5:13; CD 2:6; 1QM 1:6; 4:2; 14:5; 1QH[a] 6:32; 7:22.

[34] The quotation of Hos 2:23 differs from the LXX in the following ways: (1) the order of the two halves of the verse is reversed; (2) instead of ἐρῶ, Paul writes καλέσω; and (3) forms of ἀγαπάω replace forms of ἐλεέω. In the quotation of Hos 1:10, καὶ αὐτοί before υἱοί is omitted. The quotation of Isa 10:22–23 differs from the LXX in the following ways: (1) Paul quotes the passage in a somewhat abbreviated form, and (2) he writes ὑπόλειμμα instead of κατάλειμμα, ὁ κύριος instead of ὁ θεός, ἐπὶ τῆς γῆς instead of ἐν τῇ οἰκουμένῃ ὅλῃ, and ὁ ἀριθμὸς τῶν υἱῶν Ἰσραήλ instead of ὁ λαὸς Ἰσραήλ.

references are to the northern kingdom of Israel just prior to its destruction by the Assyrians, and not to the Gentiles. It is difficult to imagine that Paul was simply unaware that Hosea 2 originally referred to the northern kingdom of Israel.[35] What seems more likely is that Paul took these verses, which originally referred to a future restoration of the northern kingdom, which had rejected the Davidic monarchy, practiced idolatry, and so, in a sense, was no longer God's "people" or God's "sons," as pointing to God's future call of the Gentiles: to God's future calling of a people who were "not my people" but who now become "my people" and "sons of the living God."[36]

Once one understands the style and the content of the arguments in Rom 9:19–29, the rhetorical form of the argumentation also becomes clearer. The argumentation in this section is implicitly another example of the argument from the greater to the lesser (a maiore ad minus). In 9:20–21, the proper answers to the rhetorical questions are that God, in dealings with human beings, has the right to do what God thinks best, whatever that "best" is. In 9:22–29, the proper answer to the rhetorical question in 9:22–24 and its supporting scriptural quotations in 9:25–29 is that God therefore is also in the right when God foretells that he will call vessels of mercy not only from among Jews but also from among Gentiles. The logic of the argument is that if God can do whatever God thinks best (the "greater"), God can also, more specifically, show mercy not only to Jews but also to Gentiles (the "lesser").

The very elaborateness of the argumentation in 9:19–29 also raises a further question. What was controversial for his Roman Christian audience that would have led Paul to offer this quite elaborate justification for God's inclusion not only of Jews but also of Gentiles? The answer lies first of all in Paul's use of the two quotations from Isaiah (Isa 10:22–23; 1:9) in Rom 9:27–29, both of which are used to point to a remnant of Israel in the present time. Although Paul understands this remnant positively, as a result of God's graciousness, it is nevertheless a remnant of Israel, not all Israel. Second, the answer emerges clearly in 9:30–10:21 that the reason for only a remnant of Israel remaining in the present is the present failure of most of Israel, most Jews, to understand that righteousness is by faith in Christ apart from observance of the Mosaic law and for Jews and Gentiles alike. When these two elements are taken together, the rhetorical elaborateness of 9:19–29 becomes more comprehensible. It is meant to provide the foundation, in the form of various precedents provided by God's ways of acting toward Israel in the past as are found in the Scriptures, for interpreting the present puzzling situation of Israel in relation to the Gentiles. Paul is trying to situate this quite puzzling situation within the larger context of God's dealings with Israel as they are revealed in the Scriptures.

---

[35] Paul even quotes the phrase "the number of the sons of Israel" from Hos 1:10 in the opening part of the quotation from Isa 10:22–23.

[36] This interpretation is closest to the one offered by Dunn, *Romans*, 575. It is also worth noting that 1 Pet 2:10 also interprets Hos 1:10 as applying to the Gentiles. In addition, the form of the quotation in 1 Pet 2:10 also reflects the same reversal of the two halves of the verse as is found in Rom 9:25. This is another indication of the influence of Pauline theology on the next generation of the Roman Christian community, of which the author of 1 Peter was probably a member.

Conclusions

As one looks back over this section, it is important to remember that all of it falls under the rubric found in 9:6, that God's word has not failed. This word includes the various privileges granted to Israel found in the Scriptures and mentioned in 9:4–5. As Paul interprets the history of the patriarchs and the exodus in these Scriptures, he selects and emphasizes aspects of the accounts that are crucial for his purposes, in particular God's call of the patriarchs by means of promise, in keeping with God's own purposes of election rather than on the basis of their deeds, and God's merciful choice of Israel in the exodus so that God's name would be proclaimed in all the earth. On the basis of these precedents of promise, call, and mercy, Paul claims that God's ways are such as to exceed the capacity of human beings to comprehend them, so that human beings have no standing on the basis of which to challenge God's ways. Up to this point Paul's arguments probably would have evoked the general agreement of his Roman Christian audience. But in 9:19–29, Paul pushes the argument a step further, by arguing *a maiore ad minus,* that God would be acting in ways consistent with God's actions toward Israel in the past should God eventually include not only Jews but also Gentiles in his mysterious plans. Paul then quotes the passages from Hosea and Isaiah that he reckons point to the present situation, in which this has come to pass. The present situation, then, in which only a remnant of Israel remains, is not one in which God's word even to Israel has failed. This word is still valid, even as it now increasingly includes Gentiles. Paul can now turn in the next section to offer a more detailed interpretation of what this present situation is and why it is the way it is.

ROMANS 9:30–10:21: THE PRESENT SITUATION OF JEWS IN RELATION TO THE GENTILES

In Rom 9:30–10:21, Paul tries to explain the present situation of his fellow Jews, the vast majority of whom have not come to have faith in Christ. To understand Paul's arguments, it is again important to keep in mind the issues that make up their context. As seen above in the analysis of Romans 8, Paul reinterpreted concepts such as "adoption," "sons of God," "children of God," and "heirs" so that they no longer precluded, even by implication, the inclusion of Jews. This was meant to allay the suspicions of the Roman Christians about what he had written in Galatians 3–4, which seemed to preclude, at least by implication, the inclusion of his fellow Jews. Similarly, in Romans 7, Paul defended the goodness of the Mosaic law, again to allay Roman Christian suspicions that his views of the Mosaic law in Galatians were such that the law and its observance were flawed from the beginning. Finally and more immediately, the general principle within which Paul argues in Rom 9:30–10:21 is still that "it is not that the word of God has failed" (9:6). These make up the rhetorical constraints within which he argues. This means that Paul's interpretation of the present situation of his fellow Jews must be such that their ultimate inclusion as "vessels of mercy" must again be kept in mind, that their present situation is consistent with what is said about them in God's word in the Scriptures, and that the Mosaic law itself must not be made the cause of the problem.

For understanding Paul's interpretation of the present situation of his fellow Jews, it is also important to realize that these constraints are not simply the result of Roman Christian suspicions. The first-person-singular passage in 10:1–4 is a reminder that this issue is also of great personal concern and anguish for Paul. Roman Christian suspicions are not so much the cause for Paul's reflections as their occasion. That is, Paul's interpretations, in 9:30–10:21, of the present situation of his fellow Jews have no parallels in his other letters. It is conceivable that Paul is only now writing down what he has long thought. But given what he wrote in Galatians, it is more likely that Rom 9:30–10:21 is the result of Paul's seriously thinking through for the first time the place of his fellow Jews in God's mysterious providence. Though occasioned by Roman Christian suspicions, they are not simply mirrorlike responses to them. This point is perhaps best illustrated, as will be seen, by Paul's conviction, expressed again in this section, that righteousness is now through faith in Christ for Jews and Gentiles alike and apart from observance of the Mosaic law. This final constraint within which Paul argues is neither caused nor occasioned by the suspicions of the Roman Christian community but arises from his own most deeply held convictions about righteousness through faith in Christ being apart from observance of the Mosaic law and meant for Jews and Gentiles alike.

These convictions also account for something that at first appears as an odd omission in 9:30–10:21. In quoting Isa 10:22–23 and 1:9 in Rom 9:27–29, Paul was particularly interested in the notion of a remnant of Israel (τὸ ὑπόλειμμα [9:27]; ἐγκατέλιπεν [9:29]). But he does not take up this particular concept again until the beginning of Romans 11 (ὑπελείφθην [11:3]; κατέλιπον [11:4]; λεῖμμα [11:4]). As far as the image of a remnant of Israel is concerned, one would be tempted to jump immediately from 9:29 to 11:1 and simply bypass 9:30–10:21. This apparently odd fact highlights something crucial for any real understanding of what Paul is driving at in 9:30–10:21. The arguments in this section are about why in the present only a remnant of Israel remain faithful. The reasons Paul will give are connected with Israel's failure to recognize that righteousness is now through faith in Christ apart from observance of the Mosaic law and equally available for both Jews and Gentiles. The Scriptures witness to all this. What comes to the fore in 9:30–10:21 is Paul's concern to connect the explanation of the present situation of most of Israel with their failure to recognize the elements central to Paul's own interpretation of the gospel, the righteousness of both Jews and Gentiles by faith apart from observance of the Mosaic law. Paul's struggle to understand the present situation of his fellow Jews takes place within the context of his larger, perduring convictions about the meaning of the gospel. This deeply affects the way he approaches the present situation of Israel and its relation to the Gentiles, and it will serve as the foundation for how he will struggle to interpret the final situation of Israel and its relation to the Gentiles in 11:1–32. One cannot be thought of apart from the other. The two are inextricably intertwined.

A detailed analysis of 9:30–10:21 is now possible. Paul develops his arguments in two basic steps. First, in 9:30–10:13, he argues that the present situation of Israel in relationship to the Gentiles is due not to Israel's zealousness for the law (which is commendable) but to its failure to understand that Christ is really the goal of the law for all who believe, both Jews and Gentiles. It is a goal pointed to by the Scriptures. Second, in 10:14–21, Israel's present situation cannot be excused by the fact that it has not "heard" or "known," since Scripture itself again points to its present situation and the reason for it.

Romans 9:30–10:13: Jews, Gentiles, and Christ as the Goal of the Law

In Rom 9:30–10:13, Paul attempts to explain the present situation of his fellow Jews in relation to the Gentiles within the context of Scripture. In 9:30–10:4, he states that Israel's failure is that it did not recognize that Christ is the goal of the law for righteousness to everyone who believes (10:4). In 10:5–13, he offers additional scriptural grounds for this conclusion, more specifically, that this righteousness for all who believe is apart from observance of the Mosaic law.

As the previous chapter of this study has already commented on several critical issues connected with the interpretation of 9:30–10:4, they will not be fully reviewed here.[37] Briefly, however, 9:30–33 and 10:1–4 are best understood as parallel arguments, the second of which restates the first in a much more personal way that emphasizes Paul's own concern for his fellow Jews. Paul's argument is that, at present, Gentiles who were not seeking righteousness have obtained it whereas Israel, which was pursuing it, did not attain it because Israel was pursuing it through observance of the law rather than through faith in Christ. In this, they ended up pursuing their own righteousness rather than God's righteousness because, though zealous for God, they did not understand that Christ was indeed the goal of the law for everyone who has faith. According to Paul, that such would happen was indicated by Isa 28:16; 8:14, where God foretold that he would put in Zion a stumbling block (i.e., Christ) but that anyone who believes in him would not be put to shame.

Several additional points about Rom 9:30–10:13, particularly about its role in Paul's larger argument, are important. First, Paul is describing what the *present* situation of Israel is. This is clear from the way he begins this section in 9:30: "What, then, shall we say?" This is meant to cue his audience in to the fact that what follows is a response to 9:19–29, which ends by pointing to what the present situation of Israel would be. In addition, in 10:4, Christ is the goal of the law, and in 9:33, Christ is understood as the stumbling block in Zion mentioned in Isa 28:16; 8:14. This can only refer to the present situation of Israel, that is, Israel's situation in the wake of Christ. Put another way, Paul is not—and this needs to be emphasized—referring to Israel's situation prior to Christ but to Israel's situation in the wake of Christ. There is a temporal orientation to the argument.

Second, when Paul writes in Rom 9:31–32 that Israel, in pursuing the law about righteousness, did not attain to it because it pursued it not from faith but on the basis of observance, he is not stating a general, timeless principle. Rather, he is referring to Israel's present failure to recognize Christ as the goal of the law, in whom there is righteousness for everyone who has faith. Paul is not disparaging past attempts by Israel to observe the Mosaic law. This differs from the stance he took in

---

[37] See above, pp. 309–13; and Tobin, "Romans 10:4."

Gal 3:6–14, where the contrast between observance of the law and faith was general and timeless, where those who rely on observance of the law are under a curse (3:10) and those who live by faith are contrasted with those who live by observing the commandments of the law (3:12). The lack of such views about the Mosaic law in Rom 9:30–10:4 is significant and consistent with Paul's defense of the law in Romans 7.

Third, it is important to understand the role played by Paul's quotation of Isa 28:16; 8:14 in Rom 9:33:

> Behold I am laying in Zion a stone of stumbling
>   and a rock of offense;
> and he who believes [ὁ πιστεύων] in him [ἐπ' αὐτῷ] will not be put to shame.

Paul's quotation is a conflation of Isa (LXX) 28:16 and 8:14. The image of God placing the stone in Zion and the promise that he who believes or trusts in it will not be put to shame come, although not verbatim, from Isa 28:16. The stone of stumbling and the rock of offense come, again not verbatim, from Isa 8:14. The grounds for the conflation are that (1) both texts refer to a "stone" and (2) both texts refer, in the LXX but not in the MT, to someone believing or trusting. This is another example of the use of the hermeneutical technique that in rabbinic literature came to be called *gᵉzērāh šāwāh* ("comparison of equals" or "equal ordinance").[38] One suspects that Paul did not conflate the texts himself but is using them as already conflated. This is because there is evidence that early Christians had collected scriptural texts about a "stone" and identified this stone with Christ, specifically in Isa 28:16; 8:14; and Ps 118:22.[39]

Paul has three basic purposes in using this conflated quotation. First, given the identification of the stone with Christ, Paul uses the passage to show that God foretold that Christ would be a stumbling block to his fellow Jews. The present situation of the Jews, then, is one that God himself foretold in the Scriptures would happen. Second, God also foretold that whoever believes or trusts in this stone will not be put to shame. The proper response to the presence of this stone, therefore, is faith in Christ. Romans 10:4 sums up these two purposes: "Christ is the goal of the law for righteousness for everyone who believes." Third, Paul also uses the quotation as the starting point for his interpretations of the present relationship between Jews and Gentiles in 10:5–13. This is indicated especially by his return to the last part of the quotation of Isa 28:16 in Rom 10:11, that the one who believes in him will not be put to shame. Romans 10:5–13 further specifies this by arguing that this faith in Christ is apart from observance of the law (10:5–10) and is meant to include both Jews and Gentiles (10:11–13). Israel's present failure to understand this is, at once, both a failure to recognize the gospel, the "word of faith that we preach" (10:8), and a failure to recognize that God foretold this in the Scriptures in Isa 28:16.

Paul writes Rom 10:5–13 as a further specification and justification of his argument in 9:30–10:4, especially the statement in 10:4 that Christ is the goal of the law for righteousness to everyone who believes. This is indicated by his use of "for" (γάρ) to introduce 10:5. What follows gives reasons to support 10:4. More specifi-

---

[38] See Strack and Stemberger, *Introduction to the Talmud and Midrash*, 21.

[39] See Matt 21:42–44; Mark 12:10–11; Luke 20:17–18; Eph 2:20; 1 Pet 2:6–8; *Barn.* 6:2–4. For a more detailed analysis, see Dunn, *Romans*, 583–85; Cranfield, *Romans*, 2:511–12.

cally, these verses give reasons for the latter half of 10:4, "for righteousness to every-one who has faith." This helps us to understand the structure of these verses. Romans 10:5–10 explains how this righteousness (δικαιοσύνην) is based on faith (ἐκ πίστεως) rather than on observance of the law (ἐκ τοῦ νόμου). In 10:11–13, Paul then explains how this righteousness is available to everyone who has faith (πᾶς ὁ πιστεύων), no distinction being made between Jew and Greek (οὐ γάρ ἐστιν διαστολὴ Ἰουδαίου τε καὶ ῞Ελληνος). Both explanations include the inter-pretation of Scripture.

In 10:5–10, Paul contrasts what Moses wrote about righteousness based on the law in Lev 18:5, that the man who observes the commandments will live in them (Rom 10:5), with what "righteousness based on faith" says; Paul apparently uses passages from Deuteronomy, especially Deut 30:12–14 (Rom 10:6–10).[40] The crucial point Paul wants to make by using this language is found in Rom 10:8, where he interprets the phrase "the word is near to you, in your mouth and in your heart" to refer to "the word of faith which we preach."

Considerable dispute reigns about how this passage works. There are really three main issues. First, how does one understand the odd opening phrase of 10:6, that "the righteousness based on faith speaks thus," which seems to be followed by passages from Deuteronomy originally spoken by Moses in his role as God's spokes-man? Second, and this is related to the first issue, Paul's use of the combination of texts from Deuteronomy is quite loose, both in the way he cites them and especially in the way he seems to use them to refer to the "word of faith" that he preaches rather than to their original referent, which is clearly the commandments of the law. Why this seemingly very odd interpretation? Third, granted that there is some sort of contrast between Rom 10:5 and 10:6–10, between what Moses writes and what "the righteousness based on faith" says, what more specifically is the contrast, espe-cially given the first two issues?

The best place to start is with the first issue, the apparently odd way Paul be-gins 10:6, with "the righteousness based on faith" speaking, which is followed appar-ently by loose quotations from Deuteronomy, particularly from Deut 30:12–14. From a rhetorical perspective, "the righteousness based on faith" is a personification.[41] It is another example of the rhetorical technique speech-in-character (prosopo-poeia), which was seen earlier in 7:7–25. But this time the speaker is not a human being, as was the case in 7:7–25, but a virtue—in this case, righteousness. This use of speech-in-character in connection with virtues and vices is a rhetorical technique again found in popular philosophical discourse of the period and one that Paul now employs in 10:6–8.[42] It is part of the diatribe style Paul's Roman Christian audience would have been familiar with, and so they would have understood his use of it here. In 10:6–8, "the righteousness based on faith" speaks the lines based on Deut 8:17; 9:4; 30:12–14, which Paul then comments on in the clauses beginning with "that is" (τοῦτ᾽ ἔστιν) in 10:6–8.

---

[40] The δέ probably has adversative rather than simply copulative force in Rom 10:6.

[41] Both Fitzmyer (*Romans*, 589) and Cranfield (*Romans*, 2:522) point this out.

[42] Hermogenes, *Prog.* 9.4–6; *Rhet. Her.* 4.66; Cicero, *Inv.* 1.99–100; Quintilian, *Inst.* 9.2.31.

Once one realizes how Paul is using this rhetorical technique again, the second issue, the purpose of the rather paraphrastic way he cites the passages from Deuteronomy, becomes more understandable.[43] He is not really quoting Deuteronomy but loosely using its language and placing it in the mouth of "righteousness based on faith."[44] This obviates the need to justify in detail the changes Paul makes to the text of Deuteronomy. He uses the language of these passages from Deuteronomy in such a way that they can more easily refer to Christ and to faith.[45] It also obviates the need to offer any inevitably complicated explanation about how Paul came to quote passages from Deuteronomy originally spoken by Moses as if they were spoken by "righteousness based on faith."

It is also important to understand that Paul was not alone in using Deut 30:12–14 so loosely. Passages from Bar 3:29–30 and Philo, both of which make use of Deut 30:12–14, are instructive. Baruch 3:29–30 is part of a larger poem (Bar 3:9–4:3) in praise of wisdom and exhorting Israel to observe the commandments and seek for wisdom:

> Who has gone up into heaven [ἀνέβη εἰς τὸν οὐρανόν] and taken her,
>   and brought her down from the clouds?
> Who has gone over the sea [διέβη πέραν τῆς θαλάσσας] and found her,
>   and will buy her for pure gold?

The pseudonymous author of Baruch was clearly using Deut 30:12–14 but was not actually quoting it.[46] In addition, although the author goes on in Bar 4:1 to identify wisdom with the law (ὁ νόμος) and the commandments (τῶν προσταγμάτων), the antecedent of "her" in both verses is "wisdom" (φρόνησιν, Bar 3:28) rather than "the commandment" (ἡ ἐντολή), as it is in Deut 30:11.[47] The author of Baruch used Deut 30:12–14 quite freely by adapting both its language and even its referent for his own purposes.

Philo uses Deut 30:12–14 in six passages (*Post.* 83–88; *Mut.* 236–238; *Praem.* 79–81; *Somn.* 2.180; *Spec.* 1.301; *Virt.* 183–184). In none of these passages is Philo

---

[43] Deut 30:12–14:

	Rom 10:6–8
τίς ἀναβήσεται ἡμων	τίς ἀναβήσεται
εἰς τὸν οὐρανόν . . . ;	εἰς τὸν οὐρανόν; . . .
τίς διαπεράσει ἡμῖν εἰς	τίς καταβήσεται εἰς
τὸ πέραν τῆς θαλᾶσσης . . . ;	τὴν ἄβυσσον; . . .
ἔστιν σου ἐγγύς τὸ ῥῆμα	ἐγγύς σου τὸ ῥῆμά ἐστιν
σφόδρα ἐν τῷ στόματί σου	ἐν τῷ στόματί σου
καὶ ἐν τῇ καρδίᾳ σου	καὶ ἐν τῇ καρδίᾳ σου

[44] Recently Badenas, *Christ the End*, 125–26, has also taken this position.

[45] The most obvious change is from "Who will go over for us to the other side of the sea?" (Deut 30:13) to "Who will go down into the abyss?" in Rom 10:7. A similar interpretation of Deut 30:13 is found in *Tg. Neof.* Deut 30:13. Given the probably late date of *Targum Neofiti*, however, there is no reason to think that Paul was aware of such an interpretation. See Fitzmyer, *Romans*, 590–91.

[46] Baruch was composed originally in Hebrew, but the Hebrew text is no longer extant. The most important translation is the Greek found in the LXX. Baruch was probably composed in Palestine between 200 and 60 B.C.

[47] In this poem the two terms for "wisdom," φρόνησις (Bar 3:9, 14, 28) and σοφία (Bar 3:12, 23), are used interchangeably.

concerned about quoting Deut 30:12–14 verbatim. His only interest in the actual language of these verses is connected with Deut 30:14, where he is consistently careful to indicate that the "word" is "in your mouth and in your heart and in your hands." But he does this only so that he can then interpret these phrases allegorically to refer to "words" (λόγοις), "plans" (βουλαῖς), and "actions" (πράξεσι).[48] More important for our purposes, he is not interested in connecting any of this with what the "word" in Deut 30:14 refers to, "this commandment" in Deut 30:11. He is certainly aware this is the referent (*Praem.* 79–81), but for Philo what is near at hand, if one only orders one's words, plans, and actions properly, is really "the good" (τἀγαθόν) (*Post.* 84; *Mut.* 236; *Praem.* 80; *Somn.* 2.180). In *Praem.* 81, Philo even connects all this with "wisdom" (σοφία) and "prudence" (φρόνησις), using the same words as did the author of Baruch.

These passages from Baruch and Philo indicate that Jewish writers during this period used Deut 30:12–14 quite freely to emphasize that the capacity to acquire central religious realities such as "the good" or "wisdom" was not an impossible task but was "near at hand" and within the reach of all. Paul uses Deut 30:12–14 in a similar way. He is not interested in quoting the passage verbatim or in its original referent. Rather, he is interested in using it to emphasize the nearness of a central religious reality, in his case the nearness of the "word of faith." One should not overlook, however, the important difference between Paul and both Baruch and Philo. Baruch and Philo still connect the passage, in some fashion, with the Mosaic law and its observance, but Paul does not. Yet at the same time, one cannot ignore the fact that all three authors use the passage quite loosely for their own purposes.

But the purposes to which Paul puts this Deuteronomistic language call for more specification. This leads to the third issue, the real character of the contrast between Rom 10:5 and 10:6–10. Since Paul is not quoting the language of Deuteronomy, it is unlikely that this language itself bears the weight of the argument he is trying to make. Where this weight lies emerges from an examination of how Paul develops his point in Rom 10:6–10. Personified "righteousness based on faith" speaks three times (10:6a, 7a, 8a). Paul then comments, in his own voice, on each of these utterances (10:6b, 7b, 8b), each comment being introduced by "that is" (τοῦτ' ἔστιν), and then adds a fuller explanation of his point in 10:9–10, again in his own voice, introduced by "because" (ὅτι).[49] Both the comments and the final explanation emphasize that righteousness and salvation are not far away as if one has to bring Christ down from heaven or raise him from the dead. Rather, they are near at hand in confessing with one's mouth that "Jesus is Lord" and in believing in one's heart that "God raised him from the dead." Both of these phrases are clearly part of early Christian creedal formulas. Although they may have been widely used in early Christian worship, their most obvious place would have been in the context of baptism, as

---

[48] The words Philo uses in these allegorical triads vary somewhat, but the underlying character of the triads is the same. The triad listed above is from Philo, *Post.* 83–88, Philo's most extended use of Deut 30:12–14. The same triad is found in *Virt.* 183–184. Other triads are λόγοις, βουλαῖς, ἔργοις in *Mut.* 236–238; and λόγῳ, διανοίᾳ, and πράξεσιν in *Praem.* 79–81 and *Somn.* 2.180.

[49] It is unclear whether ὅτι in 10:9 is causal or simply declarative. The former seems more likely, since 10:9–10 gives a reason 10:6–8 is the case.

baptismal confessions or acclamations. Paul is appealing to the baptismal practices and traditions that he and his Roman Christian audience have in common.[50] The point of this appeal is to show how their own experience is such that their own righteousness and salvation are the direct results of their faith and their confession of this faith in baptism.

Part of this appeal includes also noticing what is not involved. Baptism as the confession of faith that "Jesus is Lord" and that "God raised him from the dead" does not entail observance of the Mosaic law, and so this faith, together with the righteousness and salvation connected with it, is apart from such observance. This aspect of Paul's appeal is more than implicit, and it leads us directly to the interpretation of the contrast between 10:6–10 and 10:5. In 10:5, Paul points out how Moses writes about the character of "righteousness based on the law" in Lev 18:5, that "the one who observes them [i.e. the commandments of the law] will live in them." He then contrasts this with what the "righteousness based on faith" says in Rom 10:6–10 about the nearness of faith and its confession in baptism. That Paul intends this as a contrast is clear. But it is important to understand what the contrast is and what it is not. It is not a contrast between "writing" and "speaking," since the change from one to the other is due to Paul's use of speech-in-character in 10:6–8.[51] The contrast is, rather, primarily a temporal one, between the past observance of the law, of which Moses writes (10:5), and the present confession of faith in Jesus as Lord and as raised by God from the dead (10:6–10). The point of the contrast is not between right and wrong but between past and present. Paul is not claiming through the contrast that observance of the Mosaic law in the past was wrong. In continuity with 9:30–10:4, he is describing the present situation, in which righteousness and salvation are through faith in the Lord Jesus, whom God raised from the dead, rather than, as in the past, through observance of the law.

Paul thereby once again revises a viewpoint he expressed in Galatians. The contrast with this previous viewpoint is crucial for understanding what Paul is doing in this section of Romans. In Rom 10:5, Paul quotes Lev 18:5, that "the man who observes them will live in them." This is observance of the commandments of the law. Paul also quoted this passage in Gal 3:12. As is the case with Rom 10:5–10, Paul used the quotation from Leviticus as part of a larger contrast (Gal 3:10–12), where he set Lev 18:5 in contrast with Hab 2:4: "The just man will live by faith." In addition, just before the quotation from Habakkuk, he also claimed that all who live on the basis of observance of the law are under a curse (Gal 3:10) and that it is clear that no one is justified before God by the law (3:11). Although the proper interpretation of this passage from Galatians is difficult, the contrast Paul made between observance of the law and faith concerned two very different and opposed ways of being religious. In Rom 10:5, Paul once again quotes Lev 18:5 as part of a larger but significantly different contrast. To begin with, he does not use Hab 2:4 here.[52] In addition, by using the literary technique of speech-in-character, by having

---

[50] Paul also did this in 6:1–14. See above, pp. 192–97.

[51] Nor is it a contrast between the "letter" and the "Spirit" in 2 Cor 3:6.

[52] Paul does quote Hab 2:4 in the statement of the proposition in Rom 1:17. As seen earlier, Paul used this quotation in the proposition as a general scriptural support for his asser-

"righteousness based on faith" use the language of Deut 30:12–14 to elucidate the present situation of faith in Christ, Paul has shifted the contrast to a temporal one. This significantly changes the contrast. It is no longer a fundamental contrast between conflicting ways of being religious, one under a curse and the other not. Rather, the difference is between two eras or periods of time. In this way, Paul uses Rom 10:5–10 to support his argument that the *present* situation of his fellow Jews is due to their failure to recognize that this new era has dawned, that Christ is the goal of the law for everyone who *has faith* (10:4).

Why does Paul so significantly shift and soften this contrast between observance of the law and faith? The reason is once again connected with the overall issue Paul is struggling with in Romans 8–11. If the contrast between observance of the law and faith was as fundamental as he apparently made it out to be in Gal 3:10–12, if those under the law were also under a curse and incapable of being justified before God, did this not imply that there was something fundamentally wrong with the law from the very beginning? If so, how could the giving of the law ever have been a privilege for Israel to receive, as Paul claimed it was in Rom 9:4? If the word of God was not to fail, then the contrast between observance of the law and faith could not be as fundamental as Paul seemed to imply in Gal 3:10–12. By turning the contrast into a temporal one, as he does in Rom 10:5–10, Paul hopes to preserve this "word of God." This word, as he has argued up to this point, has indeed not failed because the word itself points to a time when righteousness will be through faith in the Lord Jesus apart from observance of the law.

But this righteousness is not only through faith apart from observance of the law; it is also for *"everyone* who believes" (Rom 10:4). It is this part of 10:4 that Paul takes up in 10:11–13. In 10:11, he first repeats the last line of the quotation from Isa 28:16 he used in Rom 9:33, introducing it with "for scripture says." But he adds "everyone" (πᾶς) at the beginning of the quotation, thus indicating the part of 10:4 he wants to emphasize. He then offers an explanation in 10:12 that takes up this addition, that "there is no distinction [διαστολὴ] between Jew and Greek, for the same Lord is Lord of all [πάντων], bestowing his riches [πλουτῶν] on all who call upon him [πάντας τοὺς ἐπικαλουμένους αὐτόν]." In 10:13, using the words "all" and "call upon" from the previous verse and "saved" (σωθήσῃ, σωτηρίαν) from 10:9–10 as hooks, he then quotes Joel 3:5 (LXX), that "everyone [πᾶς] who calls upon [ἐπικαλέσηται) the name of the Lord will be saved [σωθήσεται]."

Clearly, Paul's emphasis in these verses is on "all," all who have faith, God as the God of all and bestowing riches on all who call upon the name of the Lord. The explanation Paul offers in Rom 10:12, between the two scriptural quotations, is thick with the themes central to his arguments in Romans, that there is no distinction between Jew and Greek (3:22), that God is the God of all (3:29), that is, of Jews and Greeks alike (2:9–11; 3:9, 29; 4:16–17), and that God is generous to all who have faith (3:22; 4:11–12). In addition, the quotations from Isa 28:16 (LXX)

---

tion about the character of the gospel. Regarding the interpretation of Rom 10:5–10, in quoting Hab 2:4 in Rom 1:16–17, Paul does not set it over against the law or its observance, as he did in Gal 3:10–12. As with his quotation of Lev 18:5 in Rom 10:5, Paul's use of Hab 2:4 in Rom 1:17 is much less polemical than was his use of it in Gal 3:10–12.

and Joel 3:5 (LXX) are almost verbatim.[53] Given Paul's quotation of Isa 28:16 earlier in Rom 9:33, he clearly understands his addition of "everyone" (πᾶς), at the beginning of the quotation of the same line of Scripture, in 10:11 as an interpretation rather than as part of the quotation itself. This explains why he then goes on to quote Joel 3:5, which does contain the word "everyone" (πᾶς), in Rom 10:13. He uses the quotation from Joel to justify his reading of Isaiah as including the notion of "everyone." The real change in interpretation is the referent of the two quotations. As in the interpretation of the initial quotation of Isa 28:16 in Rom 9:33, Paul takes the "one who has faith in him [ἐπ' αὐτῷ]" as referring to Christ. This means that he also takes the referent of "all who call upon *him*" in Rom 10:12 and "everyone who calls upon the *name of the Lord*" in the quotation of Joel 3:5 in Rom 9:13 to be Christ. One suspects Paul's justification for this is that if the referent in Isa 28:16 is to Christ, then the similar language of Joel 3:5 must indicate the same referent.

Stepping back from the details of Paul's argumentation, the function of the arguments in Rom 9:30–10:13 becomes clearer. This section represents Paul's attempt to interpret, or to reinterpret, the present situation of Israel, his fellow Jews, and the reasons for this situation. His argument is that his fellow Jews, though zealous for God, have failed to recognize Christ as the goal of the law itself and that the Scriptures themselves point to the present reality of righteousness for all, Jews and Gentiles alike, through faith in Christ apart from observance of the law. He has thereby placed in a very different framework a number of things he wrote earlier in Galatians. Although the contrast between righteousness based on observance of the law and righteousness based on faith in Galatians was fundamental and from the beginning, in this new framework the contrast between the two types of righteousness is a temporal one, the change from the former to the latter being brought about by Christ being raised from the dead. This change enables Paul to integrate Israel and its privileges into a larger pattern of interpretation that would have been virtually impossible had he maintained the stark contrasts of Galatians. At the same time, this larger pattern of interpretation inextricably intertwines the present situation of Israel with that of the Gentiles in that Israel's present situation is rooted in its failure to understand the centrality of faith apart from observance of the Mosaic law for all who believe, Jews and Gentiles alike.

Romans 10:14–21: God's Promises and the Present Responses of Israel and the Gentiles

The emphasis in Rom 9:30–10:13 was on what Israel is ignorant of, that the Scriptures themselves point to a time when God would include not only Jews but also Gentiles through faith in what was accomplished by God through Christ apart from observance of the Mosaic law. In 10:14–21, Paul is still dealing with the issue of the present situation of Israel but from a different perspective. Are there reasons that would excuse Israel's present ignorance? For example, are there reasons Israel

---

[53] The quotation of Joel 3:5 (LXX) is verbatim; in the quotation of Isa 28:16, καται-σχυνθῇ (aorist subjunctive) is changed to καταισχυνθήσεται (future indicative) with no change in meaning.

does not "know" these things or did not even "hear" of these things? The answers to these questions are important, for, should the answers be affirmative, the question of God's fairness or arbitrariness once again becomes real. More specifically, should Israel have no way of "hearing" or "knowing" through the Scriptures of God's eventual inclusion of the Gentiles through faith in Christ apart from observance of the law, then either the truth of Paul's own gospel is thrown into doubt or the "word of God" is thrown into doubt. In this sense, the "word of God" would have failed. It is to this aspect of the issue that Paul turns in 10:14–21.

Romans 10:14–21 is structured around a series of questions. It begins in 10:14–15a with four questions. The questions are interlocking and are another example of the rhetorical figure of κλῖμαξ or *gradatio*, where the last term of one clause becomes the first term of the next clause. This was seen before in 8:29–30. In 10:15b–17, Paul quotes Isa 52:7 and 53:1 to show that two of the terms mentioned in Rom 10:14–15 are interrelated, how faith depends on hearing—hearing the word about Christ. Paul structures the rest of the passage around two further questions: (1) did they (i.e., Israel) not hear (10:18a), and (2) did Israel not know (10:19a)? The expected answer to both questions is that Israel did hear and that Israel did know. Paul's responses to both questions is by means of quotations from Scripture, the response to the first through Ps 19:5 (Rom 10:18b) and that to the second through one quotation from Deut 32:21 and a second from Isa 65:1–2 (Rom 10:19b–21).

As with other rhetorical questions in Romans, the function of the four interlocking questions in 10:14–15a is to lead into Paul's responses. Paul begins the series of questions by taking up the word "call upon" (ἐπικαλέσηται) in the quotation of Joel 3:5 (LXX) in Rom 9:13:

> How then are they to call upon [ἐπικαλέσωνται] him
>   in whom they have not believed [ἐπίστευσαν]?
> And how are they to believe in him
>   of whom they have not heard [ἤκουσαν]?
> And how are they to hear
>   without someone preaching [κηρύσσοντος]?
> And how will they preach
>   unless they are sent out [ἀποσταλῶσιν]?

Although the four questions are in the form of an interlocking parallelism, not all the questions are equally important for Paul. In the light of what follows, Paul is primarily interested in the conjunction of hearing and preaching. This is indicated by the way the questions are formulated. The subjects of the first three activities (calling upon, believing, and hearing) are Paul's fellow Jews, Israel. The subjects of the last two activities (preaching and being sent) are preachers of the gospel. Paul's interest is primarily in the conjunction of hearing, the last activity of the first set, and preaching, the first activity of the second set. The lack of a foundation for such a conjunction in Scripture would provide an excuse for Israel's lack of faith.

Paul begins his response to these questions with two quotations from Isaiah. The first is from Isa 52:7: "How beautiful [or timely] are the feet of those who announce [εὐαγγελιζομένων] good news." The freedom with which he cites the quotation suggests that his interest in it is rather general. His interest in the quotation is partially due to the obvious relationship of the word εὐαγγελιζομένων to εὐαγγέλιον ("good news," "gospel") in the next verse (Rom 10:16) and partially because, on this basis, it grounds in a general way both the activities of preaching and being sent in Scripture. It functions primarily to set the stage for what follows.[54] Paul then immediately points out in the next verse that "not all have heeded [ὑπήκουσαν]" the good news or gospel (τῷ εὐαγγελίῳ). He quotes Isa 53:1 to support this, "Lord, who has believed [ἐπίστευσεν] our report [τῇ ἀκοῇ]?" From this he draws the conclusion (ἄρα) that faith (ἡ πίστις) comes from hearing (ἐξ ἀκοῆς) and hearing (ἡ ἀκοή) is through the word (ῥήματος) about Christ.

The dense sprinkling of Greek in the previous paragraph is necessary because the rhetorical effect of these verses depends so much on wordplay. The verb "to heed" (ὑπακούω) is a compound of the verb "to hear" (ἀκούω); and ἡ ἀκοή (from the same root as "to hear") means both "report" and "hearing." Paul's uses these two closely related verses from Isa 52:7 and 53:1 much less as an argument than as a clever way of presenting the issue. The issue is that in order to believe or have faith, one must first hear either the good news announced at the time of Isaiah or, in this case, the gospel about Christ. Paul's quotation of the verses refers to both situations, but his primary interest is pointing out the obvious, that believing depends on hearing.

With this in mind, Paul then asks in Rom 10:18, "Did they not hear?" The "they" refers to his fellow Jews, Israel. His reply is that they did hear, and he quotes Ps 19:5 to show this:

Their voice has gone out to all the earth
and their words to the ends of the world.

In the present context, Paul's purpose in quoting this verse is ambivalent. On the one hand, it could mean that since the voice and words of those preaching the gospel have gone out to the whole earth, Jews too must have heard it. On the other hand, it could also mean that their voice and words have gone out to all the earth, that is, to both Jews and Gentiles. The point of the quotation would then be to show again how the Scriptures themselves point toward the eventual inclusion not only of Jews but also of Gentiles. Because this appears in the Scriptures, Jews would have "heard" this already. Based on what follows in Rom 10:19–21 about Jews and Gentiles, one is tempted to opt for the latter interpretation. But given Paul's use of wordplay already in the passage, he may well have been happy with the quotation's ambivalence.[55]

Paul then reformulates the question in a somewhat different form in 10:19a, "Did Israel not know [ἔγνω]?" The reformulation is stylistic rather than substantive, intended as a variation to avoid repetition. Paul's answer is that Israel did know, and he offers two scriptural quotations to support this, one from Moses in Deut 32:21 and the other, in two parts, from Isa 65:1–2. Both quotations refer to both Jews and Gentiles. In the first quotation from Deut 32:21, God says,

---

[54] The quotation is quite loose from Isa 52:7, which reads, πάρειμι ὡς ὥρα ἐπὶ τῶν ὀρέων, ὡς πόδες εὐαγγελιζομένου ἀκοὴν εἰρήνης, ὡς εὐαγγελιζόμενος ἀγαθά.

[55] In the original context of Psalm 19, the "voice" and the "words" are those of the heavens and the firmament, who tell the glory of God and proclaim his handiwork (Ps 19:1). Later in Psalm 19, the psalmist goes on to describe the law of God as perfect and sure.

I will make you jealous [παραζηλώσω] over what is not a nation [οὐκ ἔθνει],
over a foolish nation [ἔθνει] I will make you angry [παροργιῶ].[56]

Paul takes the word ἔθνει to refer to Gentiles, which is fair enough in this context in Deuteronomy. Since both verbs are in the future tense, Paul also takes the quotation to refer to the future from the perspective of Moses, that is, to the present situation of the relationship of Jews and Gentiles. God foretells that in the future God will make Israel jealous and angry by means of the Gentiles. In the original context of Deut 32:21, this is because Israel provoked God with their idols. Paul, however, does not quote this part of the verse. Rather, he uses the verse at this point in his argument to set the stage for his own explanation in Rom 11:11–24 for why God made Israel jealous. At this point, all that Paul wants to claim is that God will make Israel jealous and that this jealousy will be connected with the Gentiles.

Paul follows this with a quotation of Isa 65:1–2, again referring to both Jews and Gentiles:

I [God] have been found by those who did not seek me [μὴ ζητοῦσιν],
I have shown myself to those who did not ask for me.
All day long I have held out my hands to a disobedient and defiant people [λαόν].

In the context of Isaiah 65, both verses refer to Israel. Paul, however, takes the first to refer to the Gentiles and only the second to refer to Israel. He clearly indicates this by his introduction of the second verse with "but he [Isaiah] says about Israel." Paul's justification for this distinction probably lies in the notion that "those who did not seek me" and "those who did not ask for me" more appropriately apply to Gentiles. This interpretation echoes and is supported by Rom 9:30, which is about Gentiles who were not seeking righteousness but who obtained it. Conversely, the term "people" (λαόν) more appropriately applies to Israel. Given the distinction, the quotation of Isa 65:1–2 then lends support to Deut 32:21.

Something more needs to be said, however, about Paul's use of these two quotations because they come at the end of a major part of his argument and because they lead into the next major section (Rom 11:1–32). By using these two quotations, what is it Paul claims that Israel should know on the basis of the Scriptures? It comes to two things: (1) God foretold that God would be found by Gentiles, that is, by those who had not sought him, and (2) by this means, God would make Israel jealous. This sums up much of the argument of 9:30–10:21 in the sense that Israel's present situation in relation to the Gentiles is rooted in, and foretold by, the Scriptures. For this reason, Israel has no excuse for not knowing this. Once again, it is not that God's word has failed. Rather, Israel has failed by not understanding what is found in that word. At the same time, these two quotations also point toward the next stage of Paul's argument in Romans 11. The quotation from Deut 32:21 introduces for the first time the notion of Israel's "jealousy." In Rom 11:11–14, Paul will take up this notion again and show how it will ultimately work not only to the Gentiles' but also to Israel's benefit. In addition, the quotation from Isa 65:2, that God has held out his hands even to a

---

[56] The only change Paul made in the citation is to change "them" (αὐτούς) in the LXX to "you" (ὑμᾶς). This makes the citation a bit more vivid.

disobedient and defiant people (λαόν), Israel, leads immediately to Paul's denial in Rom 11:1 that God has rejected his people (τὸν λαὸν αὐτοῦ).

Conclusions

As one looks at Paul's arguments in 9:30–10:21, several important patterns emerge. First, his explanations of the present situation of Israel are very much in keeping with the arguments he has been making in Romans up to this point. Nearly all of the major themes are present: (1) what God accomplishes in Christ is in keeping with the Scriptures; (2) what is accomplished is righteousness; (3) what is accomplished is for Jews and Gentiles alike; and (4) all of this happens through faith apart from observance of the Mosaic law.

Second, there are two recurring patterns in Paul's use of Scripture in this section. He consistently uses it to show either (1) that Israel's present situation is rooted in its failure to recognize that the Scriptures themselves point to the four themes mentioned above or (2) that Israel's present failure itself was foretold in the Scriptures. These two patterns are closely related for Paul. This interrelationship can best be seen by asking these questions: If the four major themes mentioned above are found in the Scriptures, why at present does Israel, the vast majority of Paul's fellow Jews, not recognize them? Does not such a lack of recognition count against Paul's claim that these four themes are present in the Scriptures? If Israel's failure to recognize them, however, was itself foretold in the Scriptures, then Israel's lack of recognition of them does not count against their presence in the Scriptures. Indeed, it even strengthens their presence, since the lack of recognition of them by Israel is itself also foretold in the Scriptures. This interrelationship is also important for Paul because his anguished attempt to understand both the present situation of his fellow Jews and their ultimate inclusion must remain within the context of his basic convictions about righteousness through faith in Christ apart from observance of the Mosaic law not only for Gentiles but also for Jews. In reality, Paul's personal anguish is in great part caused by his insistence that the two, his concern for his fellow Jews and his convictions about the inclusion of the Gentiles, are not only reconcilable but intertwined.

Third, Paul places his interpretation of the present situation of Israel within a framework that differs significantly from that found in Galatians. The fundamental contrast between the Mosaic law and its observance, on the one hand, and faith, on the other hand, is recast in temporally and historically oriented categories in Rom 9:30–10:21. Faith, in contrast to observance of the law in the past, characterizes the *present* situation brought about by what God has accomplished in Christ. This contrast is not less important for Paul, but its nature has been significantly changed and limited by being placed within a temporal framework. This recasting also fits into Paul's larger argument. It builds on the pattern of God's dealings with human beings, found in 9:6–29 but especially in 9:24–29, where Paul cites passages from Hosea and Isaiah to support his claim that in the Scriptures God tells of his future calling of "us" not only from among Jews but also from among Gentiles. In 9:30–10:21, Paul then interprets how he understands the present situation in the light of those texts. In terms of Paul's larger argument about the ultimate fate of Israel, the temporal character of Paul's interpretation in 9:30–10:21 also allows for the temporary character of Israel's present situation. This makes way for what he argues in 11:1–32.

CHAPTER 13

All Israel and the
Full Number of the Gentiles

OMANS 11:1–32 IS THE CLIMAX OF PAUL'S ARGUMENT; in it he brings to
bear directly on the issue of the ultimate fate of Israel concepts and vocabulary he used earlier. Just as the emphasis in 9:6–29 was on Israel's past and
in 9:30–10:21 it was on the present situation of Israel, the emphasis in 11:1–32 is on
the future fate of Israel. As he did in the earlier sections of the argument, Paul structures this section by his use of rhetorical questions. The first is in 11:1, "I ask, then,
God has not rejected his people, has he?"; the second is in 11:11, "I ask, then, they
have not stumbled so as [ἵνα] to fall, have they?"[1] In each case, Paul's answer is,
"Certainly not" (μὴ γένοιτο). The third and final part of this section is introduced
by "For I do not want you to be ignorant, brethren" in 11:25, a phrase he has used
elsewhere to introduce important arguments or parts of arguments.[2] The clearly
parallel structure of two questions and two initial responses in 11:1 and 11:11 indicates that Paul sees each of these sections as a rhetorical unity. In addition, Paul
clearly understands 11:25–32 as the final explanation (γάρ, 11:25) that brings together the arguments of both 11:1–10 and 11:11–24.

Several characteristics of this passage must be kept in mind. First, Paul takes up
again concepts he used earlier in his arguments in 8:1–10:21. The most prominent of
these are "remnant" and "jealousy." Paul concluded 9:6–29 with the concept of a "remnant" (τὸ ὑπόλειμμα) of Israel being saved and of God "leaving" (ἐγκατέλιπεν) Israel seed. Both concepts were supported by quotations from Isa 10:22–23; 1:9 in Rom
9:27–29. Similarly he concluded 9:30–10:21 with the concept of God foretelling that
God would make Israel jealous (παραζηλώσω) by means of what was not a nation
(10:19). This was also supported by a scriptural quotation, this time from Deut 32:21.
Paul takes up the first in Rom 11:1–10 and the second in 11:11–24. But he also
takes up other concepts from earlier parts of his arguments: "know beforehand"

---

[1] In Hellenistic Greek, ἵνα can be used to introduce not only final clauses but also consecutive clauses. It is not clear which is meant in this verse. See Zerwick, *Biblical Greek,* §§351–53.
[2] E.g., 1 Thess 4:13; 1 Cor 10:1; 12:1.

(προγινώσκω, 11:2; 8:29); "election" (ἐκλογή, 11:5, 7, 28; 9:11); "call" (κλῆσις) and "to call" (καλέω) in 8:30; 9:7, 12, 24, 25, 26); "gifts" (χαρίσματα, 11:29; see 9:4–5); "mercy" (ἔλεος, 11:31; 9:23); "be merciful" (ἐλεέω, 11:30, 31, 32; 9:15, 18); "all" (πᾶς) referring to both Jews and Gentiles (11:26, 32; 8:32; 10:4, 11, 12, 13); and contrasts with "deeds" (ἔργα, 11:6; 9:12, 32). All these parallels with earlier parts of Romans 8–11 collectively show the extent to which Paul sees his arguments in 11:1–32 as cumulative. They depend in large part for their persuasiveness on the patterns he has already established in 8:1–10:21.

Second, the perspective in 11:1–32 changes. In 9:30–10:21, the emphasis was on Israel's present failure to understand what is contained in the Scriptures about Christ as the goal of the law for righteousness for all, Jews and Gentiles, who have faith apart from observance of the Mosaic law. In 11:1–32, the emphasis is on how all of this serves a larger divine purpose for the inclusion of the "full number of the Gentiles" and ultimately the inclusion of "all Israel." This helps to explain why especially 11:1–10 seems at first to repeat parts of 9:30–10:21. There is repetition, but Paul changes the perspective. Whereas 9:30–10:21 emphasized present Israel's failure to understand, 11:1–10 emphasizes that even this failure is part of a larger plan in which God does not reject his people (11:1).

Third, in 11:1–32, there comes a point where Paul no longer uses quotations from Scripture as part of his argument. Whereas 11:1–10 contains four quotations from Scripture (1 Kgs 19:10, 14, 18; Deut 29:3; Ps 69:23–24), Rom 11:11–24 contains none, and 11:25–32 contains only one (Isa 59:20–21; 27:9 in Rom 11:26–27). Given the frequency with which Paul used scriptural quotations in the earlier sections of Romans 8–11 and their centrality in his arguments, this sudden lack of quotations is certainly surprising. But it is also more than that. As shall be seen, it provides us with important clues to Paul's struggle to interpret Israel's fate within the context of his convictions about the parallel fate of the Gentiles.

Finally, it is worth recalling once again that Paul's overarching concerns in Romans 8–11 are the present situation of his fellow Jews and their future fate. These concerns were occasioned by the suspicions of his Roman Christian audience that some of his views, at least by implication, seemed to leave no place for Israel or its future. If this were true, then the privileges God granted to Israel have come to nothing, and God's "word" as it is found in the Scriptures has failed. But Paul's concerns in 11:1–32 will also extend beyond the ultimate inclusion of "all Israel" (11:26) to the inclusion of the *"full number* of the Gentiles" (τὸ πλήρωμα τῶν ἐθνῶν, 11:25), something Paul has never written about before. His concern for the ultimate inclusion of "all Israel" will significantly affect the way he also comes to understand the place of the Gentiles in God's providential plan for the world. His struggle to understand the place of Israel will lead him to broaden even his earlier convictions about the Gentiles.

ROMANS 11:1–10: ISRAEL'S PRESENT HARDENING IS PARTIAL

Paul begins in 11:1a with the rhetorical question that serves to introduce 11:1b–10: whether God has rejected his people. Paul immediately gives the answer, "Certainly not." He first offers himself as an example of how God has not rejected his people (11:1b) and then restates the question as an assertion that indeed God has not rejected his people and adds, "whom he foreknew" (11:2a).[3] In 11:2b–4, he expands on this by offering a scriptural example, again introduced by a question. The example is the precedent provided by the dialogue between God and the prophet Elijah in 1 Kgs 19:10–18. Elijah complains to God that his fellow Jews have killed the prophets and demolished God's altars, that he alone is left (ὑπελείφθην μόνος), and that they are seeking to kill even him. Paul introduces God's response with a third question about what the Scriptures say. God responds by telling Elijah that God has left (κατέλιπον) for himself seven thousand who have not bowed the knee to Baal. Paul then begins to apply this precedent to the present time in Rom 11:5–6. A remnant (λεῖμμα) also remains in the present time "according to the election of grace" (κατ᾽ ἐκλογὴν χάριτος) and so no longer (οὐκέτι) on the basis of observance of the Mosaic law (ἐξ ἔργων). Beginning with a fourth question, Paul expands on this in 11:7–10, emphasizing the present situation of "the rest" (οἱ λοιποί). They have been "hardened" (ἐπωρώθησαν). In support of this, he quotes Deut 29:3 (LXX) and Ps 68:23–24 (LXX). Both these texts mention, among other things, the eyes of the Jewish people being blinded.

The opening question in Rom 11:1a and the question in 11:11a opening the next section state the situation of Israel in its sharpest terms. After immediately dismissing the possibility of God rejecting Israel, Paul's first response is to appeal to his own identity as a Jew: "I myself am an Israelite, from the seed of Abraham, of the tribe of Benjamin." Chapter 11 of this study argued that this appeal serves several purposes. It gives Paul another chance to emphasize his membership in the Jewish people and his concern for his fellow Jews. It also reemphasizes his own conviction that God has not rejected God's people, even in the face of the fact that Paul's fellow Jews have no excuse for not recognizing the gospel that has been preached to them (10:14–21). Finally, it creates the context for 11:2b–10, so that these verses must be interpreted in the light of Paul's conviction that God has not rejected Israel.

Three other aspects of Paul's initial response also need to be highlighted. The first concerns the logic of the response. The issue at stake is whether God has rejected his people (τὸν λαὸν αὐτοῦ). Paul's response is, "Certainly not." What are the grounds for his response? The underlying logic of the response is that because Paul is certainly a member of this "people" and God has not rejected Paul, God therefore has not rejected his people. As is often the case with rhetorical enthymemes, what is obvious in the enthymeme is suppressed—in this case, that God has not rejected Paul. The second aspect is that Paul's ultimate concern is with the fate of God's "people" and not simply of a "remnant." How this is the case will not become clear until 11:11–24. But Paul's posing the question the way he does in 11:1–2 establishes what the real issue is for what follows in Romans 11. The third aspect is that, in restating the question as an assertion in 11:2, he adds the clause "whom he foreknew" (ὃν προέγνω). This harks back to 8:29–30 and so includes Israel within Paul's broader conviction that God works all things for the good with those who love him, for those whom God "foreknew" and predestined to be conformed to the image of his Son. The fate of Israel is part of this larger purpose.

---

[3] For a fuller discussion of these verses, see above, pp. 313–14.

Paul now turns in 11:2b–4 to the scriptural precedent of Elijah's encounter with God on Mount Horeb in 1 Kgs 19:9–18. Paul's interest centers on the exchange between God and Elijah. Elijah appeals to God against Israel, that it has killed the prophets and thrown down God's altars and that he alone is left and it is now trying to kill him (1 Kgs 19:10, 14 in Rom 11:3). God responds that God has left for himself seven thousand men who have not worshiped Baal (1 Kgs 19:18 in Rom 11:4).[4] As becomes clear in Rom 11:5, what especially draws Paul's attention is the use of verbs compounded from λείπω ("leave"). Elijah claims to "be left" (ὑπελείφθην) alone; God responds that he "has left" (κατέλιπον) seven thousand men who have not worshiped Baal. Paul uses this passage to take up the concept of "remnant" (τὸ ὑπόλειμμα) he introduced but did not develop in Rom 9:27, where he quoted Isa 10:22–23, that a "remnant" would be saved. But what was introduced in Rom 9:27 as a kind of *insinuatio* now becomes a central element in Paul's struggle to understand Israel's present situation in relation to its ultimate fate.

It is important to notice how Paul quotes both Elijah's appeal and God's response. For the application, in Rom 11:5–10, of the encounter as a precedent for the present, Paul need only quote God's response about "leaving" seven thousand men. But by also quoting Elijah's claim that he "alone is left," Paul contrasts Elijah's viewpoint with God's, which is much more generous than Elijah's. Paul's introduction of God's response in 11:4 ("But [ἀλλά] what does [God's] oracle say to him?") indicates that the contrast is intentional. Paul does not explicitly refer to this contrast in what follows, but the contrast of God's generous response with Elijah's rather cramped appeal contributes to its tone.

In 11:5–10, Paul uses God's response to Elijah as a scriptural precedent for understanding what is happening also in the present situation (καὶ ἐν τῷ νῦν καιρῷ) of Israel. As in the time of Elijah, there is also a "remnant" (λεῖμμα) in the present (11:5). By "remnant" here, Paul means Jewish Christians. On the other hand, "the others" (οἱ δὲ λοιποί), by which Paul means the rest of his fellows Jews, have been "hardened" (ἐπωρώθησαν, 11:7). To clarify the latter claim, Paul then quotes Deut 29:4 and Ps 69:23–24 (Rom 11:8–10).

Once again Paul's argument is more subtle than it at first appears. He characterizes this remnant represented by Jewish Christians in Rom 11:5 as "according to the election of grace" (κατ᾽ ἐκλογὴν χάριτος). He goes on in the next verse to clarify what this means: "If it is by grace [χάριτι], it is no longer [οὐκέτι] based on works [ἐξ ἔργων]; otherwise grace would no longer be grace." The present situation of Jewish Christians is based on God's gift and not on their observance of the law. This contrast between "grace" and "works" is consistent with what Paul has been arguing all along. Righteousness through faith is a gift of God and is apart from observance of the law for Jews and Gentiles alike. At the same time, it is also consistent with his arguments in 9:30–10:21, where he intentionally restricted his explanations to the *present* situation of Israel. So too here this "election by grace" is what prevails in the present time (11:5). No longer is it through observance of the

---

[4]In quoting 1 Kgs 19:10, 14, 18, Paul abbreviates a bit but does not alter the sense. In the quotation from 1 Kgs 19:18, Paul's use of κατέλιπον instead of καταλείψεις, found in the LXX, agrees with the MT, which has הִשְׁאַרְתִּי.

law (11:16). Perhaps most important, Paul's use of the phrase "according to the election of grace" reminds his audience of what he wrote in 9:11, where he described how God chose Jacob over Esau even before their birth "so that God's purpose according to election [ἡ κατ' ἐκλογὴν πρόθεσις τοῦ θεοῦ] might stand." Similarly, as in 11:6, the choice of Jacob was also based not on "works" (ἐξ ἔργων) but on God's calling (9:12). In this way, Paul folds God's present election of the "remnant" of Jewish Christians into God's larger purposes for Israel. And this larger purpose is consistent with God's treatment of Israel in the past. As will be seen, Paul uses the term "election" again in 11:28 in connection with the eventual inclusion of "all Israel."

In 11:7, Paul then carries the argument a step farther by asking, "What then?" His answer is, "What Israel sought [ἐπιζητεῖ], it did not obtain [ἐπέτυχεν]. The elect [ἡ δὲ ἐκλογή] obtained [ἐπέτυχεν] it." This viewpoint, though not the exact vocabulary, is very close to 9:30–32, where Paul, describing Israel's present situation, contrasted the Gentiles who did not pursue righteousness but who obtained (κατέλαβεν) it with Israel, which had pursued the law about righteousness but had not attained (οὐκ ἔφθασεν) it. The reason he gave for Israel's failure in 9:32 was that the pursuit was not based on faith (οὐκ ἐκ πίστεως) but on observance (ἀλλ' ὡς ἐξ ἔργων), whereas for the Gentiles it was based on faith apart from observance of the law (see 10:5–13). The contrast between Israel and the Gentiles in 9:30–32 is thus parallel to that between Israel and the remnant in 11:6–7. The present inclusion of the remnant of Jewish Christians is basically on the same terms as was the inclusion of the Gentiles in 9:30–32.

Finally, when Paul turns to the present situation of "the rest," the vast majority of his fellow Jews, his claim is that "they were hardened" (11:7). Given the context, the hardening is brought about in some fashion by God. Apart from 2 Cor 3:14, this is the only time in his letters Paul uses πωρόω, and his use of it here is obviously part of his struggle to clarify the meaning of the present situation of most of his fellow Jews. In 11:8–10, he then gives two scriptural quotations to clarify what this hardening is:

> God gave them a spirit of torpor,
> eyes that they should not see
> and ears that they should not hear,
> down to this very day [Deut 29:4].
> Let their table become a snare and a net,
> and a trap and a retribution for them;
> let their eyes be darkened so they do not see,
> and bend their backs continually [Ps 68:23–24 (LXX)].

Deuteronomy 29:4 is part of Moses' farewell speech to the Israelites (Deut 29:1–30:20) and refers to the Israelites' lack of understanding during the exodus and the forty years of wandering in the desert down to the very day of Moses' speech.[5] In accordance

---

[5] Although the basic meaning is preserved, Paul cites Deut 29:4 quite freely. He changes the first line ("And the Lord God did not give you a heart to understand" [LXX]) to "God gave them a spirit of torpor [πνεῦμα κατανύξεως]," the last phrase coming from Isa 29:10. He also

with the view of Scripture shared by Paul and his audience, Paul takes the phrase "down to this very day" to refer to his own day and so to the present situation of Israel. The second quotation, from Ps 68:23–24 (LXX), was, for both Jews and early Christians, spoken by David (Rom 11:9). Paul connects this quotation with that from Deut 29:4 because both refer to eyes that do not see (ὀφθαλμοὶ/ὀφθαλμοὺς τοῦ μὴ βλέπειν).

Paul's reason for using these two quotations is less than obvious at first. After all, ἐπωρώθησαν does not appear in either quotation. Indeed, πωρόω ("harden") appears only once in the LXX (Job 17:7). Had Paul wanted to, he could have used another Greek verb with virtually the same meaning (σκληρύνω), which appears thirty-nine times in the LXX. In addition, he could have chosen any number of scriptural passages that used this verb or words from the same root to describe Israel's present "hardened" situation.[6] But he does neither. There are probably two reasons for this. This first is that σκληρύνω is so closely connected in the exodus with God's hardening of Pharaoh's heart.[7] Paul himself already used this verb in Rom 9:18 to describe what God had done to Pharaoh. Whatever God's present hardening of Israel is, for Paul it is not like that. Second, Paul uses Deut 29:4 and Ps 68:23–24 (LXX) because of what is common to both, God giving Israel eyes that do not see. Israel's hardening consists of not seeing, not recognizing what it should. In this way, Paul's purpose in using these two texts is very much of a piece with his description of Israel's failure in Rom 10:1–4, where he commends Israel for its zeal but claims that this zeal is "not according to knowledge" (οὐ κατ᾽ ἐπίγνωσιν) and that because of this Israel is "ignorant" (ἀγνοοῦντες) of God's righteousness and has failed to understand that Christ is the goal of the law for righteousness for everyone who believes. In both instances, then, what is at issue is Israel's failure to see, to recognize, to understand. What is new in 11:7–10 is that this hardening of Israel, understood as a failure to see or comprehend, is attributed to God himself rather than simply to Israel's own failure. This difference emphasizes that, in Paul's mind, the present hardened situation of most of his fellow Jews is part of a larger divine plan and serves a larger divine purpose. Paul then turns to what this larger purpose is in 11:11–24, 25–32.

ROMANS 11:11–24: ISRAEL'S DISBELIEF, THE ENTRY OF THE GENTILES, AND THE SALVATION OF ISRAEL

Romans 11:11–24 is at once crucial to Paul's argument and yet, in comparison with the earlier arguments in 8:31–11:10, quite odd. The passage is crucial because it is here that Paul argues for the ultimate inclusion of Israel as a whole and not

---

changes "you" (ὑμῖν) in the first line to "them" (αὐτοῖς). These changes then necessitate introducing negatives into the second and third lines to maintain their force. The reason for these changes is not clear. One possible reason is the desire to allude to Isa 29:10 by using the phrase "a spirit of torpor."

[6] E.g., σκληροκαρδία (Deut 10:16; Jer 4:4), σκληροκάρδιοι (Ezek 3:7), σκληρός (Deut 31:27; 1 Kgs 12:13; 2 Chr 10:13; Isa 8:12; Bar 2:33), σκληρότης (Deut 9:27; Isa 4:6; 28:27), σκληροτράχηλος (Exod 33:3, 5; 34:9; Deut 9:6, 13; Bar 2:30).

[7] Exod 4:21; 7:3, 22; 8:15; 9:12, 35; 10:1, 20, 27; 11:10; 14:4, 8, 17.

simply as a "remnant." This is the goal to which all his arguments are leading. At the same time, given the extent to which Paul has used Scripture in his arguments up to this point, it is extremely odd that he uses no scriptural quotations at all in the whole passage. What is one to make of this? How is it that Paul could think of this passage as being somehow persuasive to his Roman Christian audience? Perhaps the best way to understand this puzzling fact is to look first at the structure of the passage and then the way the arguments as they now stand work. We can then return to our initial question in a more nuanced way.

In 11:11, Paul begins, as he did in 11:1, with a rhetorical question that expects a negative answer: "I ask, therefore, they have not stumbled (ἔπταισαν) so as to fall (ἵνα πέσωσιν), have they?" The images of stumbling and falling hark back to Paul's use, in 9:33, of texts from Isaiah about God placing in Zion a "stone of stumbling" and a "rock of offense." "They" in the question are "the rest" of 11:7–10, most of his fellow Jews. He immediately answers, "Certainly not," and goes on to explain that by their trespass (τῷ αὐτῶν παραπτώματι) salvation has come to the Gentiles in order to "make them jealous" (εἰς τὸ παραζηλῶσαι αὐτούς). This answer takes up the quotation from Deut 32:21 that Paul used in Rom 10:19, that God will make Israel jealous (παραζηλώσω) with what is not a nation, the Gentiles. In 11:12, he expands on this by using an argument of comparison, specifically an argument "from the lesser to the greater" *(a minore ad maius).* The force of the argument is that if their failure has such marvelous consequences, the salvation of the Gentiles, how much more marvelous will the consequences of their inclusion be.

In 11:13–14, another first-person-singular passage, Paul then addresses "you Gentiles" (ὑμῖν . . . τοῖς ἔθνεσιν) in an apostrophe and claims that even his own ministry as an "apostle of the Gentiles" is directed at somehow (πως) making his fellow Jews jealous (παραζηλώσω) and saving some of them.[8] In 11:15–16, he takes up again, though not formally, the same comparative argument from the lesser to the greater he just used in 11:12. If their "loss" (ἡ ἀποβολή) means reconciliation of the world, what will their "acquisition" (ἡ πρόσλημψις) mean but life from the dead (ζωὴ ἐκ νεκρῶν)?[9] Likewise, if the dough offered as firstfruits is holy, so too is the whole lump; and if the root is holy, so too are the branches.

This comparison of root and branches leads to an extended comparison in 11:17–24 about the relationship between Jews and Gentiles, in which Jews are compared to branches of a cultivated olive tree that have been cut off and Gentiles are compared to branches of a wild olive tree that have been grafted on to the cultivated olive tree. This comparison is again in the form of an apostrophe, a direct address in the second person singular to a representative Gentile, exhorting him not to boast of being "grafted" on to the cultivated olive tree in place of Jews.[10] This comparison

---

[8] The identity of "you Gentiles" in this address will become clearer a little later in this analysis. It is not the Gentile members of the Roman Christian community.

[9] It is difficult to translate accurately either ἡ ἀποβολή or ἡ πρόσλημψις in this context. The pairing of the two suggests the image of "loss" and "gain" or "acquisition" of property or possessions rather than "rejection" and then "acceptance." See LSJ, s.v. ἀποβολή and πρόσλημψις.

[10] As an apostrophe, it is not addressed directly to the ethnically Gentile members of his Roman Christian audience. The significance of this will be made clearer below.

reaches its climax in 11:24, where Paul uses another comparative argument. As in 11:12, this argument is based on a comparison, only this time "from the greater to the lesser" *(a maiore ad minus)*. If God can accomplish the more difficult task of "grafting on," contrary to nature, the Gentiles, who are by nature not part of the cultivated olive tree, how much more is God able to accomplish the easier task of "grafting on" again the Jews, who are by nature part of the cultivated olive tree.

In interpreting the present situation and future fate of most of his fellow Jews, the "rest," it is crucial always to keep in mind the overarching conviction within which Paul works: God has not rejected his people (11:1), and more immediately, they have stumbled but not so as to fall (11:11). Under these rubrics Paul now reintroduces the notion of God making them "jealous," an image he first introduced in 10:19 with the quotation from Deut 32:21. Just as he took up again the notion of a remnant in Rom 11:3–6 from the concluding section of 9:6–29, so now he takes up the notion of jealousy from the concluding section of 9:30–10:21. Whereas Paul earlier used the notion of a remnant to interpret the situation of Jewish Christians, he now uses the notion of jealousy to interpret the present situation and future fate of the "rest."

It is not immediately clear why Paul uses this image of God provoking the rest to jealousy. It becomes clearer, however, when one looks more closely at 11:11–15 and keeps in mind Paul's earlier quotation of Deut 32:21 in Rom 10:19. As Paul used the quotation there, he took it to refer to a future time, his own time, when God would make Israel jealous and provoke it to anger by means of what was not a nation (οὐκ ἔθνει) and by a senseless nation (ἔθνει ἀσυνέτῳ). Paul obviously understood this "nation" as the Gentiles. Paul takes up this connection between Israel's jealousy and the Gentiles again in Rom 11:11 and tries to clarify it. By Israel's "trespass," salvation (ἡ σωτηρία) has come to the Gentiles (τοῖς ἔθνεσιν). Paul certainly means here the salvation through faith in Christ he mentions in the proposition of the letter (1:16, 17) and more proximately in 10:9–13, a faith apart from observance of the Mosaic law. The trespass of the majority of his fellow Jews is their present failure, described earlier in 9:30–10:21, to recognize Christ as the goal of the law for righteousness for everyone who has faith apart from observance of the Mosaic law.

In offering this interpretation of Israel's present failure, Paul provides us with the first example in earliest Christianity to connect the mission to the Gentiles and its comparative success to the lack of success in preaching the gospel among Jews.[11] But unlike some later examples in early Christianity of this connection, salvation for the Gentiles serves a further purpose for Paul, to make his fellow Jews jealous. In turn, what is the purpose of this jealousy? In the context of Deuteronomy 32, it would eventually give way to God's vindication of his people Israel (Deut 32:36). In keeping with this, Paul clarifies the purpose of this jealousy in Rom 11:13–14 when he describes even his own ministry as an apostle of the Gentiles as, in some way (πως), meant to make his fellow Jews jealous (παραζηλώσω) and so save some of them (σώσω τινὰς αὐτῶν). As is clear from 11:26, this ministry is only a part of a

---

[11] This is especially prominent in Acts (13:44–48; 14:1–7; 17:1–9; 18:1–10; 19:8–10; 28:23–29).

larger purpose that will ultimately lead to the salvation of "all Israel." Given the larger context of Paul's argument in Romans as a whole, specifically his interpretation of Israel's failure in 9:30–10:21, this "salvation" will in some way include the recognition and acceptance of Christ as the goal of the law for righteousness for everyone who has faith, both Jews and Gentiles.

The Deut 32:21 motif of God making Israel jealous is not found elsewhere in the Scriptures or elsewhere in Judaism during this period.[12] This suggests something crucial for understanding what Paul intends in using it. His employment of this isolated motif is the result of his own rather anguished search for a scriptural foundation or a scriptural category that would allow him to interpret the present failure of his fellow Jews in a way that could lead to their eventual inclusion, indeed the inclusion of "all Israel" in God's mysterious plan. Although they do not now understand, their jealousy of what the Gentiles have received will finally lead them to receive it also.

That this is his ultimate purpose becomes clear through his explicit use of the two arguments of comparison in Rom 11:12 and 11:24. Coming at the beginning and at the end of the passage, they form an *inclusio* and so provide significant clues for what Paul intends in the arguments of the passage. To understand what Paul means in 11:12, it is important to be aware of the universalizing tone of the argument:

> If their trespass [τὸ παράπτωμα αὐτων] means riches for the world [πλοῦτος κόσμου],
> and their loss [τὸ ἥττημα αὐτῶν] riches for the Gentiles [πλοῦτος ἐθνῶν],
> how much more [πόσῳ μᾶλλον] will their full number [τὸ πλήρωμα αὐτῶν] mean.[13]

Following as it does on 11:11, where the salvation or deliverance of the Gentiles is mentioned, the point of this comparison is between the significance of the salvation of the Gentiles (riches for the Gentiles) and the salvation of the Jews (their full number). But the mention of the Gentiles comes only in the second line of the protasis. What Paul first mentions is "riches for the world." For him, the salvation of the Gentiles occurs within a larger, quite literally "cosmic" context. If the salvation of the Gentiles is this significant, how much more significant must the eventual inclusion of Israel be. At first, one wonders what in particular Paul has in mind by using this comparison. It becomes clearer in 11:15: "If their loss [ἡ ἀποβολὴ αὐτῶν]

---

[12] Sirach 50:25–26 contains an allusion to the phrase "not a nation" of Deut 32:21 but not to the notion of jealousy. The reverse of this motif, of Israel provoking God to jealousy or anger, is more common (1 Kgs 14:22; Ps 77:58; Isa 65:3; *T. Levi* 3:10; *T. Zeb.* 9:9; *T. Ash.* 2:6).

[13] Paul uses πλήρωμα six time in his letters (Gal 4:4; 1 Cor 10:26; Rom 11:12, 25; 13:10; 15:29). Only Rom 11:12 and 11:25 are relevant for our purposes. Given the similar contexts of both of these occurrences, they most likely have the same meaning in both verses. Most commentators agree that the meaning of the word in 11:25 is clearly "full number." The same is probably the case for 11:12. The case for translating the word as "full number" is also strengthened by the immediate context of 11:12, where the imagery is that of commercial gain and loss. The notion of "full number" would make perfect sense in that context. See also above, p. 359, n. 9. For discussions of the issue, see Dunn, *Romans*, 654–55, 679–80; Cranfield, *Romans*, 2:557–58, 575–76; Byrne, *Romans*, 345, 354; Fitzmyer, *Romans*, 611, 621–22; Wilckens, *Römer*, 2:243, 254–55.

means reconciliation for the world [καταλλαγὴ κόσμου], what will their acquisition [ἡ πρόσλημψις] mean but life from the dead [ζωὴ ἐκ νεκρῶν]?" The protasis and apodosis of 11:15 parallel and clarify the protasis and apodosis of 11:12. For Paul, if Israel's "loss" means the reconciliation of the world, then Israel's ultimate inclusion means something even greater, the resurrection of the dead.

Paul has used the language of "reconciliation" (καταλλαγή) twice before (2 Cor 5:18–21; Rom 5:10–11), and his previous uses of it are helpful in understanding what he is doing here. Second Corinthians 5:18–20 is part of a larger exhortation by Paul to reconciliation, to be reconciled to God (5:11–6:10). In 5:19, Paul seems to quote a fragment of a traditional confessional formula: "In Christ God was reconciling [ἦν . . . καταλλάσσων] the world [κόσμον] to himself, not counting their trespasses [τὰ παραπτώματα] against them."[14] Introducing the formula, Paul wrote in 5:18 that "all things [τὰ πάντα] are from God who reconciles [καταλλάξαντος] us to himself through Christ and gives us the ministry of reconciliation." What is important for our purposes is that both the fragmentary formula ("God was reconciling the world") and Paul's introduction to it ("all things are from God") emphasize the universal significance of what God is accomplishing. When Paul uses this language of reconciliation in Rom 5:10–11, it is again within a universalizing context in which the universal consequences of Adam's trespass are set over against the universal consequences of Christ's death.[15] And so, when Paul uses the phrase yet again in 11:15 about the "reconciliation of the world," he is drawing on an image already shared with, and familiar to, his Roman Christian audience. But in 11:15, he uses this shared viewpoint as the basis for an argument *a minore ad maius* about the significance of the ultimate inclusion of his fellow Jews. If their "loss" means the reconciliation of the world, what can their "acquisition" mean except the resurrection of the dead? On the one hand, Paul's claim about the significance of the ultimate inclusion of the Jews would have come as a welcome relief for a community suspicious about those views of Paul that seem so universal but also apparently leave no place for the inclusion of the Jews. On the other hand, Paul makes this claim without in any way surrendering his more universalizing convictions about the inclusion of the Gentiles.

Paul again uses a comparative argument at the end of this section, in 11:24. This time, however, the argument moves in the opposite direction, from the greater to the lesser *(a maiore ad minus):*

> For if you [σύ] were cut from an olive tree that is wild by nature [κατὰ φύσιν]
>   and grafted contrary to nature [παρὰ φύσιν] into a cultivated one,
> how much more [πόσῳ μᾶλλον] will these, the natural branches [οἱ κατὰ φύσιν]
>   be grafted back into their own olive stock?

If God can accomplish the greater and more difficult task of "grafting," contrary to nature, the Gentiles on to the cultivated olive branch, how much easier will it be for God to accomplish the easier task of "grafting" the Jews back on to the olive tree to which they belong by nature.

---

14 See above, pp. 163–65.
15 See above, pp. 163–65; and Dunn, *Romans,* 657–58.

Coming at the beginning and at the end of this passage, these two comparative arguments provide the framework for Paul's other arguments and so serve as guides for their interpretation. Paul wants to claim that if the present "loss" of most of his fellow Jews means the reconciliation of the world, their inclusion must be even more significant—indeed, the resurrection of the dead. In addition, if God can accomplish the more difficult task of the inclusion of the Gentiles, how much easier will it be for God ultimately to include the Jews. In these two arguments, then, Paul emphasizes both the significance of the inclusion of the Jews and the comparative ease with which God can accomplish it. Both these arguments would have been important and welcome to Roman Christians suspicious about the implications of Paul's earlier views.

A similar concern marks the way Paul portrays himself in 11:13–24. In 11:13, he writes, "I am speaking to you Gentiles." In effect, he continues this apostrophe all the way through 11:24. In 11:17–24, he changes from the second person plural of 11:11 to the second person singular, but the object of the apostrophe remains the same—Gentiles. Paul changes to the second person singular because of the extended metaphor of the olive trees in 11:17–24, in which he addresses the personified "branch" of the wild olive tree grafted on to the cultivated olive tree. At the same time, it is clear from 11:13–14 that, in describing the purpose of his ministry to the Gentiles as trying to make "my flesh" (μου τὴν σάρκα)—his fellow Jews—jealous, he is portraying himself as a Jew. Paul is intentionally portraying himself, then, as a Jew addressing Gentiles in this whole section.

It is important to keep in mind who these Gentiles are whom he portrays himself as addressing—and who they are not. Given the way Paul uses the metaphor of the olive tree in 11:17–24, one is certainly tempted to think of them as Gentile believers. In a certain sense, this is true. But given the strongly eschatological character of the passage that immediately follows (11:25–32), the identity of the Gentiles whom Paul is addressing needs to be understood rather broadly, as not only present Gentile believers but all Gentiles who now believe or who will believe. Consequently, Paul is not directly addressing the Gentile members of the Roman community in 11:13–24. As seen again and again in the course of Romans, Paul's addressees are imaginary opponents to whose questions and objections he is replying. There is no reason to think Paul uses the rhetorical conventions of the diatribe any differently here.[16] In addition, as also seen repeatedly in Romans, it is not that the members of the Roman Christian community who are ethnically Gentile are indifferent to, or boast over, the situation of the Jews. On the contrary, they are concerned about Paul's seeming indifference toward the fate of his fellow Jews. In their eyes, although Jewish, he is too identified with the Gentiles and their salvation and too little concerned about his fellow Jews. In addressing these Gentiles in 11:13–24, Paul's rhetorical purpose is to emphasize his own Jewish identity and concern for his fellow Jews over against possible Gentile indifference or arrogance toward the fate of Jews, an indifference or arrogance his Roman Christian audience suspects Paul of fostering, even if unintentionally.

---

[16] Paul also uses metaphorical indirection in 1 Cor 12:12–31.

That this is Paul's purpose becomes very clear when he describes his own work as an apostle of the Gentiles in 11:13–14. As pointed out in chapter 11 of this study, this is the only point in his letters where Paul claims that the purpose of his ministry to the Gentiles is somehow to make his fellow Jews (literally, his "flesh") jealous and so save some of them.[17] Even his commitment to the Gentiles, which might appear to some as indifference to the fate of his fellow Jews, is really intended to show concern for his fellow Jews. Because Paul gives no hint of this understanding of his ministry in his other letters, one can only think that, for Paul, this is a new understanding of the relationship between the fate of his fellow Jews and the purpose of his own ministry. In rethinking and revising his own earlier views on this issue, however misunderstood he may have been by the Roman Christians, he was also compelled to rethink the purpose of the ministry to which he had been committed for the previous two decades. This is another indication of how deeply this issue came to affect him personally.

The close connection between the issue of the fate of his fellow Jews and his own identity as an apostle emerges in a small compass in the parallel structure of 11:11–12 and 13–15. Romans 11:11–12, Paul's initial response to the question of his fellow Jews stumbling so as to fall, begins with a statement that, by the Jews' trespass, salvation has come to the Gentiles in order to make them jealous. It is then followed by a conditional sentence (11:12): if their trespass or loss means riches for the world and the Gentiles (protasis), then their full inclusion must mean something much more (apodosis). This same structure is repeated in 11:13–15 at the much more personal level of Paul's own ministry. In 11:13, Paul claims that his ministry to the Gentiles is meant somehow to make his fellow Jews jealous and so save some of them. It too is followed by a conditional sentence (11:14–15): if their loss means the reconciliation of the world (protasis), what will their acquisition mean but life from the dead (apodosis)? Romans 11:13–15 replicates at the personal level of Paul's ministry the general process described in 11:11–12. Just as, by its trespass, salvation has come to the Gentiles to make Israel jealous, so too Paul's own ministry to the Gentiles is meant to make his fellow Jews jealous. Similarly, just as the "full number" of the Jews will be of more significance even than their trespass or loss in bringing riches to the world and the Gentiles, so too their acquisition will mean life from the dead, something beyond even the reconciliation of the world that their loss makes way for. Paul now locates his own ministry as one element, however small, within the larger divine plan ultimately leading not only to the inclusion of the Gentiles but, even more significantly, to the inclusion of his fellow Jews.

This portrayal by Paul of himself as a Jew addressing Gentiles continues, after a transition in 11:16, in the extended comparison of Gentiles and Jews to the grafting of a branch from a wild olive tree on to a cultivated olive tree in 11:17–24.[18] In this extended comparison, Paul warns a representative Gentile, as a wild olive branch grafted by God on to the cultivated olive tree of Israel, not to boast over those Jews who, as branches of the cultivated olive tree of Israel, have been cut off (11:17–18). They were cut off because of their lack of faith, but the Gentile has

---

[17] See above, pp. 314–16.
[18] For an example of this practice, see Columella, *Rust.* 5.9.16.

been grafted on because of his faith, and so the Gentile should be appropriately fearful and not think so highly of himself (11:19–20). After all, God can both cut the Gentile off should he not remain faithful and graft Jews on again who do not remain unfaithful (11:21–23). Indeed, if the Gentile has been grafted, contrary to nature, on to the cultivated olive tree, how much easier will it be for God to graft on again the Jews, who are by nature part of the cultivated olive tree of Israel (11:24).

In his portrayal of himself as a Jew exhorting an imaginary Gentile believer, Paul also draws on what he has emphasized earlier in Romans, particularly the contrast between boasting and faith. Paul has condemned boasting several times earlier in the letter. In 2:17, 23, he condemned the Jew who boasted of being a Jew but who did not observe the law. In 3:27, boasting is excluded because righteousness is through faith in Christ and not by observance of the law. This was then illustrated by the example of Abraham, who had no basis for boasting (4:2) because he was justified by his faith in God rather than by circumcision. Common to all of these condemnations of boasting is that they involved Jews in one way or another. In addition, in both 3:27 and 4:2, Paul excluded boasting, on the grounds that righteousness is through faith. In 11:17, 20, 23, boasting is again excluded on the grounds of faith, but this time explicitly referring to Gentiles. Just as boasting by Jews on the grounds of observing the law was excluded, so too is boasting by Gentiles on the grounds of their present situation in comparison with the majority of Jews. In both cases, boasting is excluded for the same reason, because of faith. In this way, Paul demonstrates that, as a Jew, he condemns Gentile boasting as much as Jewish boasting, especially when this boasting is at the expense of Jews.

But Paul's purpose in using the metaphor of the olive tree is not only to emphasize his own identity as a Jew concerned about his fellow Jews. He also uses it to clarify by example the present relationship between Jews and Gentiles and their ultimate fates. In a broad sense, Paul's metaphor of Israel as an olive tree echoes Hos 14:6, where Israel is likened to an olive tree, and Jer 11:16–17, where God calls the Jewish nation a green olive tree, which, however, God will set fire to and destroy because of the idolatry of both Israel and Judah. Yet neither of these metaphors is nearly as elaborate as Paul's, and neither includes the image of cutting off branches, which is central to Paul's use of the metaphor.

One needs to look elsewhere to situate Paul's use of this metaphor within the Judaism of his own time. A comparison of 11:17–24 with the concluding section of Philo's *De praemiis et poenis* (162–171) suggests that Paul took over and altered for his own purposes a plant metaphor more widely known in Judaism and used as part of an explanation of God's disciplining and restoration of Israel.

This section of *De praemiis et poenis* contains Philo's reinterpretation of more widely held Jewish eschatological expectations, which, at least as they appear in *Praem.* 163–171, are rooted in the Deut 30:1–10 paradigm of Israel returning to God and God consequently gathering and restoring Israel.[19] Philo begins by claiming that if Jews accept their present misfortunes not as leading to their destruction but as a warning to change their lives for the better (163), they will be set free by their Gentile captors and return to their own land (164–165). In this process of

---

[19] For a fuller discussion of this issue in Philo, see Tobin, "Philo and the Sibyl."

conversion and reconciliation with God, they will be helped by three advocates: God's clemency and kindness, which prefers forgiveness to punishment; the holiness of the founders of their race (166); and their own reformation (167). When they arrive home, they will experience unheard-of prosperity (168). Everything will be reversed, and God will turn the curses against their enemies (Gentiles) who rejoiced over Jewish misfortunes (169) and did not understand that their good fortune was not for their own sake but as a lesson to the Jews who had subverted the institutions of their fathers and as a medicine to save them from destruction (170). Their enemies will realize that their own misconduct was in reality against those of a high lineage (171). Philo then concludes the treatise with this passage (172):

> For just as when the stalks are cut away, if the roots are not destroyed, new shoots sprout which supersede the old stumps, so too in souls, if a tiny seed is left of those qualities that lead to virtue, though other things have been stripped away, nothing less than the most valuable and worthwhile things for human life spring forth from that tiny seed, through which cities are settled and manned with good citizens and nations grow into a great population. (Colson, LCL)

In this final passage, Philo has clearly taken a plant metaphor used to explain God's disciplining and restoration of the Jewish people and turned it into part of his own allegory of the soul. In order to do this in his interpretation, he has even had to change the metaphor itself, from a plant metaphor to a seed metaphor. This means, however, that he has not constructed the plant metaphor itself but has reinterpreted an already existing metaphor for his own purposes.

To a lesser extent, this is also true of *Praem.* 163–172 as a whole. Philo has significantly toned down more clearly apocalyptic viewpoints and images.[20] But what is still visible, even with Philo's reinterpretations, is an interpretation of the present difficulties of the Jewish people based on their own misconduct and an expectation that the Jewish people will ultimately repent of this misconduct and, through God's intervention, return to their own land and great prosperity. Their enemies, the Gentiles who rejoiced at Jewish misfortune, however, will be punished because they did not recognize that God's punishment was intended as a lesson and a medicine to save them rather than destroy them. The plant metaphor, with its description of cutting back the stalks so that new shoots could sprout, is an integral part of this explanation.

Once one realizes this, one can see the extent to which Paul is using and reinterpreting the same kind of metaphor to deal with the same kind of issue. Paul is doing the same kind of thing as Philo, but in a different way. Behind both Philo and Paul lay similar explanatory frameworks that tried to deal with both the present misfortune and the future restoration of the Jewish people and with the present good fortune and future punishment of the Gentiles who gloated over Jewish misfortune. Likewise, the explanatory framework behind both Paul and Philo saw present Jewish misfortune as part of a larger plan meant by God to lead them to repentance and restoration. Unlike Philo, Paul does not reinterpret the plant metaphor as an allegory of the individual soul. For Paul, the metaphor remains social or public instead of becoming individualized as in Philo.

---

[20] Ibid., 94–103.

But Paul significantly realigns the metaphor. Although he clearly retains the condemnation of Gentile gloating over Jewish misfortune, he now grafts the Gentiles on to the plant, the olive tree, of Israel. Similarly, although Paul still clearly uses the metaphor to clarify Israel's present misfortune and ultimate restoration, he also connects it with the grafting on of new shoots, the inclusion of the Gentiles. More specifically, within the larger framework of Rom 11:11–24, Paul explains the present misfortune of Israel as part of a larger divine plan in which Israel's misconduct leads to the inclusion of the Gentiles, which, in turn, is meant to make them jealous and ultimately lead to their restoration.

One can now see more clearly why Paul has used and reinterpreted this metaphor. He has taken a Jewish metaphor shared with the Roman Christian community, a metaphor meant to clarify not only—and, in a sense, not primarily—present Jewish misfortune but also, and especially, final Jewish restoration. This remains a central purpose of the metaphor for Paul. He then introduces into this framework, however, the inclusion of the Gentiles as part of this larger plan, but a part still leading to the restoration of Israel. Paul's use and reinterpretation of the metaphor, then, are very similar to what he has done throughout Romans. He has taken what he has in common with his Roman Christian audience and tries to show how his own central convictions are in continuity with, or at least compatible with, those shared viewpoints and convictions. His central convictions about the inclusion of the Gentiles do not preclude the ultimate inclusion of Israel. In reality, the Gentiles' inclusion is part of a larger divine plan culminating in Israel's inclusion.

In 11:11–24, Paul has tried to show his Roman Christian audience several points. First, he wants to insist that his own convictions are such that the ultimate inclusion of Israel is of the greatest importance, indeed even more important than the inclusion of the Gentiles. Second, the inclusion of the Gentiles is integrally part of a larger divine plan leading to the inclusion of Israel. Third, he even sees the purpose of his own ministry as an apostle to the Gentiles as in some way contributing to this ultimate inclusion. Fourth, as part of this ministry, he can even portray himself as warning Gentile believers not to boast over Israel's present misfortune.

Finally, at this point we return to the question asked at the beginning of this section: Given the intensely scriptural character of Paul's arguments in 8:31–11:10, why are there suddenly no quotations from scripture in 11:11–24? In a sense, the answer is now obvious. It is because there are no quotations in scripture that interpret Israel's present situation and future restoration in such a close and intertwined fashion with the inclusion of the Gentiles. But the obviousness of the answer also reveals two crucial aspects of what Paul is driving at in 11:11–24 and in 8:1–11:36 as a whole.

First, although his arguments in 11:11–24 are not themselves scriptural, their persuasiveness depends on them being understood as conclusions based on prior arguments that were scriptural. If God's promises in Scripture to Israel have not failed, if God also promised in Scripture, in ways consistent with God's call of Israel, also to call Gentiles "my people" who were not "my people" and to save all, both Jews and Gentiles, on the basis of faith in Christ, and if God also foretold in Scripture that God would leave a remnant in Israel and would make Israel jealous by means of these Gentiles and their faith in Christ, then Israel's present situation as a remnant must be part of a larger divine plan by means of which the Gentiles can be saved and through whose salvation, by making Israel jealous, Israel will also ultimately be restored and included. In this way, the persuasive power of 11:11–24 lies in being understood by Paul's audience as conclusions based on premises provided by the scriptural arguments of the previous section, 8:31–11:10.

Second, the lack of scriptural quotations in 11:11–24 also suggests something crucial about the process Paul has engaged in as part of his struggle with the issue of the present situation and future fate of his fellow Jews. There were no ready, easy answers in Scripture to which Paul could appeal. Rather, he had to struggle as he never had to before, both to maintain his own central convictions about the inclusion of the Gentiles through faith in Christ apart from observance of the law and to overcome the suspicions of the Roman Christians that his inclusive views seemed to preclude the inclusion of his fellow Jews. This struggle was intensified even further because, in facing up to the objections of the Roman Christian community, he had to seriously reconsider a number of his own earlier ways of thinking. Paul brings the results of this struggle to final expression in 11:25–32.

ROMANS 11:25–32: THE MYSTERY OF ISRAEL AND THE GENTILES

Although 11:25–32 express the conclusions of Paul's struggle to understand in new ways the present situation and ultimate fate of his fellow Jews, of "all Israel," within the context of God's promises to Israel in the Scriptures (9:1–11:24), they also do considerably more than that. Paul's concerns about his fellow Jews and his rethinking of their place in the light of God's promises in the Scriptures also lead him also to formulate the place of the Gentiles in a new way. This should not be surprising, since Paul's arguments in 9:1–11:24 already interwove the present and the future situation of his fellow Jews with the present and future situation of the Gentiles. In addition, Paul's consideration of these issues took place within the larger, universalizing context of 8:1–30, 31–39 as well as within the even larger context of Paul's arguments in 1:16–7:25, which often emphasized his conviction that God's mercy now extends to all, both Jews and Gentiles. Yet his final formulation in 11:25–32, especially as it relates to the Gentiles, goes beyond what he wrote about the Gentiles in any of his other letters and even beyond what he has explicitly written about them up to this point in Romans.

Romans 11:25–32 falls into two parts. In 11:25–27, Paul directly addresses his Roman Christian audience and sums up what his arguments lead to: all of this is a "mystery" (μυστήριον). A "hardening" has come upon part of Israel until the full number of the Gentiles has entered and thus "all Israel" is saved. To support the latter claim, Paul cites in 11:26b–27 a combination of Isa 59:20–21 and 27:9, the first scriptural quotation since Rom 11:8–10. He then further specifies the meaning of this mystery in 11:28–32 through two similarly structured formulations, in which two closely related statements are then followed by a reason. In 11:28–29, he writes that, regarding the gospel, most of his fellow Jews are enemies for "your" sake but, regarding God's election, they are beloved because of the "fathers." The reason for this is that God's gifts and call are irrevocable. In 11:30–32, the two statements are in the form of a comparison that reformulates 11:25–26a in more temporal terms. Just as "you" were once disobedient to God but now have received mercy because of "their" disobedience, so too "they" have now been disobedient in the interests of mercy to "you" in order that they also may presently receive mercy. Paul again offers a reason for this: God has imprisoned all in disobedience in order that God may have mercy on all.

What are the antecedents of the pronouns "they" and "you" (plural) that occur frequently in the passage?[21] These antecedents are important for understanding the perspective of the passage. Paul introduces 11:25–32 with "I do not want you to be ignorant, brothers." Paul has used this introductory clause elsewhere in his letters (1 Thess 4:13; 1 Cor 10:1; 12:1; 2 Cor 1:8; Rom 1:13). In all cases, he is directly addressing his audience, the Christian community to which he is writing. The same is true in Rom 11:25. This means that the "brothers" whom he is directly addressing are the Roman Christians, both Gentile and Jewish. The "you" (plural) in 11:25, then, should not be confused with the "you" (plural and singular) of the imaginary Gentile interlocutor(s) of 11:13–24. The "you" of 11:25 includes both Gentile Christians and Jewish Christians, although the majority of Roman Christians were ethnically Gentile rather than Jewish. The "they" in this passage, on the other hand, refers to the part of Israel that has been "hardened" for a time (11:25). The distinction, then, between "you" and "they" is not between Gentile Christians and Jews but between both Gentile and Jewish Christians, on the one hand, and the rest of Israel that has been temporarily hardened, on the other hand.

With this in mind, we can look more closely at how the passage works. Paul begins by emphasizing that he does not want the Roman Christians to be ignorant of "this mystery" (τὸ μυστήριον τοῦτο). When Paul has used this introductory phrase elsewhere in his letters—about not wanting his audience to be ignorant of something—in all cases it was a way to emphasize the importance of what was to follow. The same is true here. He wants to emphasize the importance of "this mystery" that he is about to describe and clarify in 11:25–32.

In characterizing what he is about to say as a "mystery," Paul uses a word whose meanings were rich and complex both in contemporary Judaism and in the larger Greco-Roman world. The word μυστήρια ("mysteries"), predominantly in the plural, referred to the secret rituals and teachings of the initiation ceremonies that were part of various cults in the Greco-Roman world, the most famous being those at Eleusis. The word also took on a more metaphorical meaning, referring to secret or esoteric knowledge, often associated with philosophy. In Jewish literature, the word (both singular and plural) appears in the LXX translation of Daniel 2, where it translates the Aramaic word *rāz*, which was itself probably a Persian loan word.[22] In Daniel 2, it means secret knowledge revealed by God about what will happen at the end of days (Dan 2:28). The word *rāz* also appears in other Palestinian Jewish literature of the period.[23] There too it often refers to secret knowledge

---

[21] "You" (plural) or its equivalent: ὑμᾶς, ἦτε, ἑαυτοῖς (11:25); δι' ὑμᾶς (11:28); ὑμεῖς ἠπειθήσατε, ἠλεήθητε (11:30); τῷ ὑμετέρῳ ἐλέει (11:31); "they" or its equivalent: αὐτῶν (11:30); τούτων (11:30); οὗτοι ἠπείθησαν, αὐτοὶ ἐλεηθῶσιν (11:31).

[22] Dan 2:18, 19, 22, 28, 30, 47.

[23] *1 En.* 16:3; 41:1; 46:2; 103:2; 104:10, 12–13; 106:19 (=4QEnoch[c] 5.2.26); *4 Ezra* 10:38; 12:36–39; *2 Bar.* 48:3; 81:4; 1QS 3:23; 4:18; 9:18; 11:3–5; 1QH[a] 2:13; 4:27–28; 7:27;

revealed by God.[24] This secret knowledge, however, is more often than not eschato-logical in nature. It is connected with what will happen at the end of the age or the end of the world. These eschatological events often include God reversing a present situation of distress or affliction. In this way, the secret knowledge God reveals about the future is greatly at variance with the present situation and so is counterintuitive when viewed from the perspective of the present. Although there is an overlap in Greek and Jewish literature in terms of secret or esoteric knowledge, the meaning of the word μυστήριον as used by Greek writers and its meaning as used to translate *rāz* by Palestinian Jewish writers differ significantly. The use by Greek writers lacks the eschatological, counterintuitive emphasis found in Palestinian Jewish writers. Hellenistic Jewish writers, however, such as the author of Wisdom of Solomon and Philo, use the word μυστήρια in ways close to those of Greek writers. Although the author of Wisdom uses the word once to refer the secret purposes of God (Wis 2:22) in a way similar to its use in Palestinian Jewish literature, elsewhere in Wis-dom he uses it to refer disparagingly to pagan initiation rituals (14:15, 23) or to the secret knowledge associated with wisdom (6:22). The same is also true of Philo. Al-though he uses the word disparagingly about Greek mystery initiations (*Spec.* 1.319; 3.40), he usually employs it metaphorically to refer to Judaism as a kind of truly philosophical initiation into the mystery of God (*Leg.* 1.104; 3.3, 71, 100; *Cher.* 48, 49; *Sacr.* 60, 62; *Deus* 61; *Contempl.* 25).[25]

Paul's use of the word in his letters spans these meanings. Apart from Rom 11:25, Paul uses the term six times, all in 1 Corinthians. In three instances (1 Cor 4:1; 13:2; 14:2), he uses the word in the plural and means by it something close to a Christian version of the esoteric knowledge of God to which Wisdom and Philo refer. In the other three instances (1 Cor 2:1, 7; 15:51), Paul uses the word in the singular and means by it God's hidden plan that is now revealed and that is espe-cially concerned with the final state of the world. His use of the word in these three instances is much closer to the way the word was used in Daniel and the other Pal-estinian Jewish texts mentioned above. This is especially the case for 1 Cor 15:51, the text closest in meaning to Rom 11:25: "I tell you a mystery [μυστήριον]. We will not all die, but we will all be changed," at the resurrection of the dead. Both this passage and Rom 11:25 emphasize the eschatological significance of the mystery. Both passages also emphasize some sort of reversal: in the case of 1 Cor 15:51, the reality that although not all will die, all will be changed; in the case of Rom 11:25, that all Israel will be saved, but only in connection with the unexpected intermediate step of the salvation of the Gentiles.

How does Paul describe the content of this mystery in Rom 11:25b–27? He characterizes this mystery in the following way:

11:10; 12:13; 1QpHab 7:1–5, 8–14; 1Q27 (1QMyst) 1:3–4. Although *2 Baruch* and *4 Ezra* are not extant in either Hebrew or Aramaic, the word *rāz* almost certainly is the word lying behind the translations of these texts.

[24] Sometimes the word refers simply to secrets or secret information (Sir 22:22; 27:16, 17, 21; Tob 12:7, 11; Jdt 2:2; 2 Macc 13:21).

[25] Josephus almost always uses the term to refer disparagingly to initiation cults (*Ag. Ap.* 2.189; 266; *Ant.* 19.30, 71, 104). He does, however, use it once to refer positively to the meal of the Essenes (*J.W.* 2.133).

> A hardening [πώρωσις] in part [ἀπὸ μέρους] has come upon Israel
>   until [ἄχρις οὖ] the full number [τὸ πλήρωμα] of the Gentiles comes in,
> and thus [καὶ οὕτως] all Israel [πᾶς Ἰσραήλ] will be saved,
> as it is written,
>   "The deliverer [ὁ ῥυόμενος] will come from Zion [ἐκ Σιών],
>   he will banish godless deeds from Jacob.
>   And this will be my covenant with them [Isa 59:20–21]
>   when I take away their sins [Isa 27:9]."

There are several difficulties in this passage—one of translation and several of interpretation. The difficulty of translation concerns the prepositional phrase ἀπὸ μέρους. Should it be taken with "hardening," thus meaning "a partial hardening"? Or should be it taken with "Israel," thus meaning "a part of Israel"? Given the placement of the phrase immediately after "hardening," the former seems more likely, although the latter cannot be excluded. The difference in meaning, however, is not significant once one understands that Paul is referring back to "the rest" (οἱ λοιποί) of Israel mentioned in Rom 11:8–10. What is more important is the interpretation of the phrases "and thus [καὶ οὕτως] the full number of the Gentiles [τὸ πλήρωμα τῶν ἐθνῶν] comes in" and "all Israel" (πᾶς Ἰσραήλ). Finally, the interpretation of the quotation from Isaiah is also important for understanding how Paul views all Israel's salvation.

First, to understand this passage and what follows in 11:28–32 correctly, one must take seriously that Paul wrote, "and thus [καὶ οὕτως] all Israel will be saved," and not "and then [καὶ τότε] all Israel will be saved." Whereas, in 11:11–24, Paul clearly thinks of all Israel's salvation coming after that of the Gentiles, the point he is making here is not only a temporal one. Rather, Paul wants to emphasize the dependence or even the causal nexus between the two. The partial hardening of Israel and the entry of the full number of the Gentiles are the way through which all Israel will be saved. Although there is a temporal sequence, this is not the real "mystery." The real mystery of God's plan is a paradoxical relationship: all Israel's salvation depends on the entry of the full number of the Gentiles. This way of understanding the ultimate fate of all Israel, of his fellow Jews, which was obviously arrived at after much reflection and anguish, is crucial for Paul. It enables him to maintain his own deepest convictions about the salvation of the Gentiles in such a way as to include his fellow Jews, indeed "all Israel."

The extent of this paradoxical relationship between all Israel and the "full number of the Gentiles" is perhaps best seen in conjunction with Paul's use of the image of the full number of the Gentiles "coming in" (εἰσέλθη) in 11:25. There has been considerable dispute about what Paul thinks the full number of the Gentiles is coming into. Is it the kingdom of God, or is it the community of salvation? Given what Paul writes in the next verse about all Israel being "saved" (σωθήσεται), it certainly entails salvation for the full number of the Gentiles. One can probably be no more specific than this. But the image of the Gentiles "coming in" would bring to the minds of his Roman Christian audience the eschatological image of Gentiles streaming to the temple in Jerusalem in Isa 2:2–3:[26]

---

[26] The LXX version is given here.

> In the last days the mountain of the Lord will be manifest
>   and the house of God on the mountain tops,
> and it will be exalted above the hills;
> all the nations [πάντα τὰ ἔθνη] will stream to it.
> And many nations [ἔθνη πολλά] will come and say,
>   "Come, let us go up to the mountain of the Lord,
>   and to the house of the God of Jacob,
> that he may announce his way and that we may walk in it."
> For out of Zion [ἐκ Σιών] will go forth the law,
> and the word of the Lord from Jerusalem.

In one way or another, this text from Isaiah has influenced other biblical texts as well as other Jewish texts of the period.[27] In the text from Isaiah, the Gentiles stream to a restored and exalted Jerusalem and its temple. The Gentiles now can participate in the privileges first granted to Israel. But Paul reverses this scenario. All Israel will ultimately participate in the privileges received by the full number of the Gentiles, who must enter first.[28] The paradox lies, however, not so much in the reversal itself as in the paradoxical reality that, in God's mysterious plan, the entry of the Gentiles is both the result of Israel's failure and the condition or cause for all Israel's final inclusion. This highlights even further Paul's attempt not only to include all Israel but to do so in such a way as to tie all Israel's inclusion to that of the Gentiles.

Interpretation of the phrases "the full number [τὸ πλήρωμα] of the Gentiles" and "all [πᾶς] Israel" is also central for understanding Rom 11:25–27. They stand in parallel to each other and in contrast to "in part" (ἀπὸ μέρους) of the preceding verse. In addition, Paul also used the word πλήρωμα in 11:12 in connection with the ultimate inclusion of his fellow Jews. There have been different interpretations of the meaning of the phrase "all Israel."[29] Perhaps the best place to begin to understand the meaning of the phrase is to note the obvious, that the phrase appears very frequently in the Jewish scriptures, approximately 150 times, and it always designates historic, ethnic Israel as a whole.[30] It is in this sense that Paul seems to be using the phrase here, since it includes both the "remnant" (11:5) and "the rest" (11:7). This corporate sense of the phrase is very much in keeping with Paul's concerns throughout Romans about the relationship between two groups of people, Jews and Gentiles, and how this relationship has been changed through the death and resurrection of Christ. Paul's use of the phrase "all Israel," however, does not necessarily include every individual Israelite. Or more precisely, his concern is not with the fate of any individual Israelite but with Israel as a whole, as a group.[31]

---

[27] Isa 56:6–7; 60:3–14; Mic 4:1–2; Zech 14:16–17; Tob 13:11; 14:6–7; *Pss. Sol.* 17:31, 34; *2 Bar.* 68:5; *T. Benj.* 9:2; *Sib. Or.* 3:772.

[28] Byrne, *Romans*, 349–50, especially emphasizes this reversal.

[29] The four main interpretations are listed by Cranfield (*Romans*, 2:576–77): (1) all the elect, both Jews and Gentiles; (2) all the elect of the nation Israel; (3) the whole nation Israel, including every individual member; and (4) the nation Israel as a whole but not necessarily including every individual member. For some of the patristic interpretations, see Fitzmyer, *Romans*, 623–24.

[30] Fitzmyer, *Romans*, 623.

[31] See 1 Kgs 12:1; 2 Chr 12:1; Dan 9:11.

Given this understanding of the phrase "all Israel," the meaning of the parallel phrase "the full number [τὸ πλήρωμα] of the Gentiles" also becomes clearer. Paul means the Gentiles as a whole, as a group, although again not necessarily every individual Gentile. This interpretation is also in keeping with his earlier use of phrase "their full number" (τὸ πλήρωμα αὐτῶν) in 11:12 as synonymous with "all Israel" in 11:26. The phrase "the full number of the Gentiles" is parallel in meaning to "all Israel." Just as "all Israel" as a whole will be saved, so too will the "full number of the Gentiles" as a whole be saved.

What is perhaps less obvious is how this formulation represents not only a development in Paul's struggle over the fate of his fellow Jews but also a development in the way he thinks about the ultimate fate of the Gentiles. Throughout his career as a missionary, Paul has seen his role as preaching especially to the Gentiles. This was the case from the point of his call or conversion onward (Gal 1:15–17), and he reaffirmed it in Rom 11:13–14. As pointed out in chapter 10 of this study, this was one impetus for the rather universalizing eschatology found in parts of 1 Corinthians 15 and in Romans 8.[32] Yet in neither of these passages did he mention the inclusion of "the full number" of the Gentiles. Both passages allow for such an inclusion, and this is especially true of Rom 8:1–30, which provides the framework for 8:31–11:36. But neither passage actually discusses such an inclusion. Rather, the inclusion of the "full number" of the Gentiles in Rom 11:25–26 is the result of Paul's struggle to understand how "all Israel" could be included. One of Paul's central convictions in Romans is the equality of both Jews and Gentiles, both in sinfulness (1:18; 2:8–9; 3:9, 19–20; 5:12–21; 11:32) and in salvation (1:16; 2:7, 10; 3:21–26; 4:11–12, 16–17; 5:12–21; 9:24–26; 10:5–13; 11:32). There is no distinction (3:22; 10:12), and God is impartial (2:11). Consequently, if "all Israel" is ultimately to be saved, then the same must be true for "the full number of the Gentiles." In this way, Paul's concerns about the fate of his fellow Jews as a whole also lead him to a significant reformulation of his views about the fate of the Gentiles as a whole, a reformulation that is more "fully" universal even regarding the Gentiles.

Finally, Paul's quotation from Isaiah in Rom 11:26–27 is a combination of Isa 59:20–21 and 27:9. There are several reasons Paul felt free to combine the two quotations.[33] First, both quotations are spoken by God. Second, both refer to a future event. Third, both have parallel formulations ("And this will be my covenant with them" [Isa 59:21]; "and this is the blessing for him" [Isa 27:9]). And finally, both refer to God's removing sins or godless deeds from Jacob, from Israel.[34]

Paul intends the combination to serve as scriptural support for his immediately preceding claim about the ultimate salvation of "all Israel." From Paul's

---

[32] See above, pp. 288–97.

[33] The full LXX version of Isa 27:9 reads, "Therefore the lawlessness of Jacob will be removed, and this is the blessing for him [Jacob], when I take away his sin."

[34] In quoting this combination of Isa 59:20–21 and 27:9, Paul makes several changes in the LXX text. In the line from Isa 27:9, he has changed both "his" (αὐτοῦ) and "sin" (ἁμαρτίαν) to plurals. The reason for this is that both "them" (αὐτοῖς) and "godless deeds" (ἀσεβείας) in Isa 59:20–21 are plural. He has also changed "for the sake of Zion" (ἕνεκεν Σιών) in Isa 59:20 to "from Zion" (ἐκ Σιών). The reason for this change is less clear; it does not affect the way Paul uses the passage. It is probably due to the influence of Isa 2:3 ("from Zion"), mentioned above.

perspective, it does this in several ways. First, he interprets the quotation as referring to future events, since the two verbs in Rom 11:26 are in the future tense. Second, "the deliverer" (ὁ ῥυόμενος) (referred to in the third person) who will come from Zion is other than the speaker of the quotation (referred to in the first person), who is God. Given this differentiation, Paul certainly takes this deliverer to be Christ. This is supported by 1 Thess 1:10, where Paul referred to Jesus as "the one who delivers [τὸν ῥυόμενον] us from the wrath to come." Third, this deliverer will take away the godless deeds of Jacob, of Israel, and God will remove their sins. For Paul, the reference to Jacob/Israel is not to a remnant or to a part of Israel but simply to Israel, to Israel as a whole. Finally, although a bit less clearly, Paul probably takes this quotation from Isaiah as a reference neither to Jesus' earthly life nor to his death and resurrection but to his future coming. This is indicated by the beginning of Rom 9:26, where Paul refers to "all Israel" being saved as a future event (σωθήσεται), and by his connection of Israel's "acquisition" (ἡ πρόσλημψις) in 11:15 with the resurrection of the dead (ζωὴ ἐκ νεκρῶν).

Paul's employment of this quotation as well as his reasons for doing so also serve to answer a larger question, one raised in recent years, about the place of Christ in 11:1–32. The question arises because Christ is not explicitly mentioned in all of 11:1–32. Rather, it is God himself who is the central figure. Does this mean that Paul sees the final, eschatological salvation of all Israel as something occurring apart from Christ? More broadly, does this mean that while the salvation of the Gentiles is based on faith in Christ, the ultimate inclusion of all Israel will take place apart from Christ and will still be based on observance of the law?[35] Paul's use of the quotation from Isa 59:20–21; 27:9 indicates that this is not the case, for Paul connects the salvation of all Israel with the future coming of "the deliverer," whom Paul identifies with Christ. In addition, Paul's interpretation of Israel's present situation in Rom 9:30–10:21 is based on its present failure to recognize Christ as the goal of the law for everyone who has faith in Christ, both Jews and Gentiles. Finally, given Paul's insistence throughout Romans on the significance of Christ for both Jews and Gentiles and on the equality of Jews and Gentiles in both sin and salvation, it is almost impossible to imagine that he could think of Israel's ultimate salvation as somehow apart from Christ.

Paul certainly connects the ultimate salvation of Israel with Christ, just as he does the salvation of the Gentiles. It is important, however, to realize how vague he is about the way all of this is to take place. These eschatological events will involve Christ; they will include the resurrection from the dead; they will bring about the entry of both "the full number of the Gentiles" and "all Israel." But beyond this, Paul is remarkably vague about how all these things will come about. This is due, in part, to the fact that all of 8:1–11:36 represents the results of Paul's intense struggle to understand in new ways both the inclusion of his fellow Jews, all Israel, and the full number of the Gentiles. These chapters represent the farthest reach of Paul's thought at this point. In part, however, this vagueness is also of a piece with his earlier strenuous refusal in 1 Cor 15:35–57 to specify how the dead will be raised. Paul

---

[35] E.g., this is the position, with some variations, taken by Gager, *Origins of Anti-Semitism*, 261–64; and Gaston, *Paul and the Torah*, 135–50.

has deep convictions and hopes about the future and about the universal extent of God's mercy in Christ, but he has no descriptions of it to offer. In Rom 11:25 as in 1 Cor 15:51, this remains a mystery.

In the second half of this passage (Rom 11:28–32), Paul continues to emphasize and specify the intertwined relationship between the full number of the Gentiles and all Israel. In doing so, however, he also recapitulates the central points he has made in these chapters and, more broadly, in the letter thus far. In 11:28–29, he offers a contrast, both sides of which concentrate on the situation of Israel, and then a justification for the contrast:

> ²⁸As regards the gospel they are enemies
>   on account of you [δι' ὑμᾶς],
> but as regards the election they are beloved
>   on account of the fathers [διὰ τοὺς πατέρας].
> ²⁹For the gifts and the call of God are irrevocable.

Each member of one side of the contrast is parallel to a member of the other side: "gospel"/"election"; "enemies"/"beloved"; "on account of you"/"on account of the fathers." The contrast partially restates what Paul wrote in 11:25–26, that Israel's hardening as regards the gospel has taken place on account of, or for the sake of, "you," the Gentiles and the Jewish Christians. But these verses also specify what Paul wrote in 11:25–26. They do so by emphasizing what he wrote toward the beginning of his arguments. Specifically, regarding the election, the Jews remain beloved on account of the fathers. Paul is clearly referring back to the "fathers" who represent one of the privileges granted to Israel in 9:5 and particularly to God's choice of the patriarchs in 9:6–13.[36] Paul then gives a reason for their remaining beloved, a reason that emphasizes the status of Israel: God's gifts and call (κλῆσις) are irrevocable. Paul thus restates his claim in 9:6 that the word of God has not failed and his claims in 8:28–30 that all things work for good for those called according to God's purpose (τοῖς κατὰ πρόθεσιν κλητοῖς), for those whom God called (ἐκάλεσεν) and whom God would also make righteous and glorify. What has changed, however, from these earlier claims is that in between Paul has argued that the way God's word has not failed must be understood through the mystery of the interrelationship by which of Israel's partial hardening makes possible the inclusion of the Gentiles, which in turn makes possible the inclusion of all Israel.

This same conviction about the causal nexus between the fate of Israel and that of the Gentiles is also found in 11:30–32, here with an emphasis on the temporal interlocking of their fates:

> For just as you were once [ποτε] disobedient to God,
>   but now [νῦν] you have been shown mercy because of their disobedience
>   [τῇ τούτων ἀπειθείᾳ];
> so too they have now [νῦν] been disobedient in the interests of mercy to you
>   [τῷ ὑμετέρῳ ἐλέει],

---

[36] There is no reason to think that Paul has in mind here any notion of the "merits" of the fathers or any sort of intercession by them before God.

so that they also may presently [νῦν][37] be shown mercy.
For God has imprisoned all [τοὺς πάντας] in disobedience
so that he might show mercy to all [τοὺς πάντας].

Although this comparison is more elaborately temporal in perspective, the emphasis is still on the causal nexus of what is described. Once again, it is important to keep in mind that the "you" in this passage refers to both Gentile and Jewish Christians, even though the majority would be Gentiles, whereas the "they" refers to "the rest" (οἱ λοιποί) of Israel. The cause for mercy now being shown to the formerly disobedient Gentile and Jewish Christians is the present disobedience of the rest of Israel.[38] So too the purpose of the present disobedience of the rest of Israel in the interests of Gentile and Jewish Christians is so that they too might presently be shown mercy.[39] Paul then states the purpose for all this: God has imprisoned all in disobedience so that God might show mercy to all, both Jews and Gentiles. By concluding in this way, Paul emphasizes the conviction that has dominated the arguments throughout the letter, beginning with his statement of the proposition in 1:16, that the gospel is the power of God for everyone who has faith (παντὶ τῷ πιστεύοντι), the Jew first and then the Greek.[40] The reason given in 11:32 is structurally parallel to the reason given in 11:29. These two reasons, taken together, restate the two convictions underlying Paul's arguments in these chapters. One conviction is the irrevocable character of God's promises and the privileges granted to Israel (11:29). The second is the conviction about the inclusion of all in God's mercy, both Jews and Gentiles, the conviction that serves as the context within which Paul struggled over the issue of the inclusion of all Israel (11:32).

A phrase in Rom 11:25, "so that you may not be wise [φρόνιμοι] in your own estimation," which is part of Paul's direct address to the members of the Roman Christian community (ἀδελφοί), draws us back to the specific situation of the letter, to the Roman Christian community's concerns and suspicions that he was addressing. One of Paul's primary goals has been to show the Roman Christians that he is not indifferent to the ultimate fate of his fellow Jews and that his views do not exclude his fellow Jews, even by implication. Rather, he is deeply concerned about both their present situation and their ultimate salvation. Indeed, "all Israel" will ultimately be saved, and so their suspicions are groundless. At the same time, however, the Roman Christians should be aware of "this mystery" lest they think themselves too wise, that the salvation of Israel is tied to the salvation of the full number of the Gentiles. Their suspicions that his commitment to the Gentiles and salvation apart from observance of the law has led him to ignore his fellow Jews is profoundly wrong. Rather, "lest they be wise in their own estimation," the Roman Christians

---

[37] On text-critical grounds, it is difficult to make a decision about the presence or the absence of the second νῦν in 11:31. Both internal and external evidence is fairly evenly divided. Its presence, however, is the more difficult reading. Its translation in 11:31, given the larger context of 11:25–32, which refers to the future, must be something like "presently," which is its meaning when used with a future tense.

[38] The phrase τῇ τούτων ἀπειθείᾳ is best taken as a dative of cause (BDF §196).

[39] The phrase τῷ ὑμετέρῳ ἐλέει is a dative of advantage.

[40] See also 2:9–11; 3:9, 19–20, 22–23; 4:11, 16; 5:12–21; 8:28–30, 32, 37; 9:25–26; 10:11–12.

need to realize that it is really Paul's commitment to the Gentiles and their salvation that, in reality, leads to the ultimate salvation of his fellow Jews. He is reminding them that their suspicions of him are not nearly as wise as they might have thought.

ROMANS 11:33–36: CONCLUDING PRAISE AND DOXOLOGY OF GOD

Paul concludes in 11:33–36 with praise of God and God's mysterious ways. This brings to a fitting rhetorical conclusion not only Paul's arguments in 8:1–11:32 but indeed those from 1:16–11:32. Triads dominate the structure of this rhetorically elaborate passage. It opens in 11:33 with three exclamations about how mysterious and exceeding human comprehension God's actions are. Within the first exclamation are three attributes of God (richness, wisdom, and knowledge). In 11:34–35, three rhetorical questions follow that take up in reverse order the three attributes of God mentioned in 11:33a and quote (Isa 40:13) or paraphrase (Job 41:3) passages from Scripture. This section concludes in 11:36 with three prepositional phrases (that all things are *from* God, *through* God, and *to* God) and a doxology.

For our purposes, two aspects of this section are especially important. The first is the world that this rhetoric would have conjured up for Paul's Roman Christian audience: the world of Jewish literature, which combines both apocalyptic revelation and wisdom. It is the world reflected in such texts as *2 Bar.* 14:1–10; 75:1–5; *1 En.* 93:11–14; 1QH^a 7:26–32. Like Rom 11:33, three of the texts begin with statements about God's deeds (*2 Bar.* 14:1–7; *1 En.* 93:1–10; 1QH^a 7:26–27). All four of them, like Rom 11:34–35, contain a series of rhetorical questions emphasizing how utterly impossible it is for human beings to understand the actions of God (*2 Bar.* 14:8–10; 75:1–5; *1 En.* 93:11–14; 1QH^a 7:28). In addition, *2 Bar.* 14:8–10 contains vocabulary very similar to Rom 11:33–34 (judgment, way, path, counsel, wisdom).

Perhaps the most enlightening passage for understanding Rom 11:33–36, however, is 1QH^a 15:26–32:

> I give you [thanks, Lord,]
> because you have taught me your truth,
> you have made me know your wonderful mysteries [*rāzê*],
> your kindness with [sinful] men,
> your bountiful compassion with the depraved of heart.
> Who is like you, Lord, among the gods?
> Who is like your truth?
> Who, before you, is just when judged?
> No spirit can reply to your reproach,
> no one can stand up against your anger.
> All the sons of your truth
> you take to forgiveness in your presence,
> you purify them from their sins
> by the greatness of your goodness,
> and in your bountiful mercy,
> to make them stand in your presence,
> for ever and ever.
> For you are an eternal God

and all your paths remain from eternity to eternity.
And there is no one apart from you.
What is empty man, owner of futility,
to understand your wondrous deeds?[41]

Like Rom 11:34–35, this passage contains three questions about the impossibility of any human being understanding God (1QH^a 15:28). It also contains three statements about the exalted character of God (15:31–32), similar to the three exclamations in Rom 11:33. But most important for our purposes is the fact that all of this is placed in the context of the speaker's thanksgiving for God's revelation to him of God's wonderful "mysteries" (*rāzê*, 15:27). As seen earlier, the Hebrew term for "mystery" *(rāz)* is the equivalent of the Greek word μυστήριον, used by Paul in Rom 11:25. Romans 11:33–36, like this hymn from Qumran, is a response to God's mysterious plan.

The reason for looking at these texts, especially the one from Qumran, is that Paul's Roman Christian audience probably would have perceived the language of Rom 11:33–36 as of a piece with such texts. His Roman Christian audience would have found in this praise of God's unsearchable ways something familiar, something characteristically Jewish. In concluding his struggle to understand the certain yet deeply paradoxical salvation of Israel as dependent on the salvation of the Gentiles, Paul expresses himself in a way that is certainly elaborate yet familiar to the minds and sensibilities of his audience. In the end, this mystery of God's actions is ultimately very Jewish.

The second important aspect of Rom 11:33–36 is the extent to which it resumes some of the language, style, and thought of 8:1–30, 31–39. When understood against the background of Galatians, one of the central purposes of Rom 8:1–30 was to reinterpret notions such as "son," "sonship," and "heir" in such a way as to allow for the inclusion of the Jewish people. But another purpose was to place the possibility of such an inclusion within a larger eschatological context. In this concluding hymn and doxology, Paul takes up several aspects of these earlier passages. First, there is the matter of style. Romans 8:28–30 and 38–39 were marked by the rather elaborate use of parallel sentence structures—straightforward parallelism in 8:38–39 and a stairstep parallelism in 8:28–30. Not since these verses has Paul used such highly rhetorical parallelism as is found in 11:33–36, with three parallel exclamations followed by three parallel questions. Second, Paul also takes up some of the significant vocabulary of 8:28–30, 31–39. In 11:33, he exclaims about the depths of the knowledge (γνώσεως) of God. This takes up 8:29, where Paul wrote that God would make righteous and glorify those whom he "foreknew" (προέγνω). It is God's foreknowledge that sets all in motion, and it is now this knowledge Paul praises at the end. In 11:36, Paul emphasizes that "all things" (τὰ πάντα) are from God and through God and for God. This echoes both Paul's claim in 8:28, that God works "all things" (πάντα) for the good with those who love him, and his claim in 8:32, that God will grant "all things" (τὰ πάντα) with Christ.

Most important, however, is the mind-set of 8:1–30, 31–39 that Paul resumes in 11:33–36. The earlier discussions of 8:18–30 and 8:31–39 pointed out how Paul

---

[41] The translation is from Florintino García Martínez, *The Dead Sea Scrolls Translated: The Qumran Texts in English* (2d ed.; Leiden: Brill, 1996), 344–45.

emphasized an eschatology that was bound up with God's mysterious actions, which worked in "all things" and far exceeded human comprehension. Paul is convinced that God's working in all things will ultimately succeed and that nothing in all of creation can separate "us" from the love of God (8:28, 39). This expressed the basic framework of his convictions. But who this "us" is and how God works "all things" for the good was left undefined. In 11:36, he returns to this claim that "all things" are from God and through God and for God. But in between Paul has struggled, in the face of the suspicions of the Roman Christians about him, to show how this "us" ultimately includes not only the full number of the Gentiles but also all Israel. In God's mysterious plan, both Israel's present failure and its future salvation are inextricably intertwined with the salvation of the Gentiles. In this way, Paul can restate with renewed confidence in 11:36 his previous, undefined conviction about God working all things for the good in 8:28 because in 8:31–11:32 he has struggled to comprehend, if only in part, how the "us" could include both the full number of the Gentiles and all Israel.

CONCLUSIONS

Romans 8–11 forms the longest and most complex argument not only in Romans but also in any of Paul's letters. At this point we need to step back from its details and take a broader perspective. It has become clearer how and why Romans 8–11 forms an articulated whole. Romans 8:1–30 provides the necessary foundation for Paul's more controversial interpretations in 8:31–11:36 of the relationship between the present situation and future inclusion of "all Israel" and the present situation and future inclusion of the "fullness of the Gentiles." Without the inclusive eschatology of 8:1–30 and especially Paul's reinterpretation of the notions of "sons of God," "children of God," and "heirs" in such a way as to allow for the inclusion of his fellow Jews, the arguments of 8:31–11:36 would have been impossible. It is no accident that Paul takes up again the rhetorical style of 8:28–30, 31–39 in 11:25–32, 33–36. What comes between these passages is the articulation and specification of the implications of 8:1–30.

More broadly, one can reread 1:16–7:25 and notice how in different ways these chapters build toward Romans 8–11. It cannot be accidental that Paul placed his longest and by far most complex argument at this point in the letter. Romans 1:16–7:25 is certainly not simply prefatory to Romans 8–11, but establishing what is found in these earlier chapters is in some ways necessary for dealing with the issues of Romans 8–11. Paul first needed to establish the equal, though not identical, sinfulness of Jews and Gentiles (1:18–3:20). Second, he needed to persuade his Roman Christian audience that righteousness, which is now through faith apart from observance of the Mosaic law for both Jews and Gentiles, in reality upholds rather than nullifies that law (3:21–4:25). Third, he needed to show how this righteousness apart from observance of the law does not lead inevitably to moral confusion and disarray but in baptism provides the capacity to live morally in ways beyond what the Mosaic law could provide, however good the law is and however holy its commandments (Romans 5–7). Without these foundations, the arguments of Romans 8–11 about

Israel's present failure to recognize all these things and the intertwining of the fate of "all Israel" with that of the "fullness of the Gentiles" would make little or no sense.

Given the frequency of first-person passages in 8:31–11:36, the issues of the present situation of Israel and its future fate are clearly issues of deep personal concern for Paul in ways none of the previous issues were. But these are issues not only for Paul but also for his Roman Christian audience. The Roman Christians, however, understand these issues in different terms, and more important, they suspect that Paul is somehow indifferent to them. He even seems to them, on the basis of what he wrote in Galatians, to exclude, at least by implication, the majority of his fellow Jews from sonship and so from the inheritance promised Israel in the Scriptures. Paul seems to have been stung by these suspicions on the part of the Roman Christians that, as an "apostle of the Gentiles," he is indifferent to the present situation and future fate of his fellow Jews. Yet from the ways Paul argues in Romans 8–11, especially in the ways he significantly revises his previous views in Galatians, he has become painfully aware that the suspicions of the Roman Christians are not without foundation, that some of his own earlier arguments, made in the heat of his controversies with the Galatians, did seem to exclude his fellow Jews from the promises and privileges made by God to them in the Scriptures.

The difficulties of interpreting Romans 8–11 are due in part to the fact that Paul himself is rethinking these issues for the first time. This is similar to the difficulties of interpreting Romans 7, which also represents new thinking on Paul's part, there about the place of the Mosaic law, both its goodness and holiness and yet its temporary character. But the difficulties are also due to Paul's insistence on remaining faithful to his deeply held convictions about salvation now for all, Jews and Gentiles alike, through faith in Christ and apart from observance of the Mosaic law. For Paul, the present situation and future fate of his fellow Jews cannot be understood apart from these convictions. Indeed, the two must be intertwined. Because of this, Paul's rethinking of the issues concerning Israel also forces him to rethink how he understands the present situation and future fate of the Gentiles. For him, the two cannot be separated. Israel's present situation is due to its failure to recognize from the Scriptures that righteousness is now through faith rather than by observance of the Mosaic law and that it is meant for Jews and Gentiles alike. In addition, Israel's present failure is part of a larger, mysterious plan, again indicated in the Scriptures, through which the gospel is preached to the Gentiles. Conversely, the ultimate inclusion of "all Israel" is closely connected with the ultimate inclusion of the "full number of the Gentiles." Indeed, Paul's firm hope for the inclusion of all Israel leads him to a new conviction about the inclusion of the full number of the Gentiles, a conviction that is rooted in the universalizing parts of the eschatology of 1 Corinthians 15 but emerges with clarity only in Rom 11:11–32. The salvation of all Israel cannot but be paralleled by the salvation of the full number of the Gentiles.

These arguments also serve an additional purpose. If Israel's present failure is in not recognizing in the Scriptures that righteousness is now through faith apart from observance of the Mosaic law, then this failure also strengthens Paul's argument about righteousness through faith apart from the Mosaic law earlier in the letter. This is especially important in the face of most Roman Christians' continuing observance of the ethical commandments of the law. Paul's interpretations of the perduring validity of the promises and privileges granted to Israel are meant both to allay the Roman Christians' suspicions that he is indifferent to Israel's fate and to persuade them that concerns about Israel must also be part of a broader perspective recognizing that righteousness is now apart from observance of the Mosaic law for both Jews and Gentiles and that all this is in continuity with God's unfailing word in the Scriptures.

Romans 8–11 also brings to the fore the extent to which Paul has recast in more temporally or historically oriented categories the ways in which he thinks about all these issues. Paul certainly has a perspective on events in Israel's past in his other letters (e.g., the importance of the promises to Abraham and the fact that the law came 450 years later in his letter to the Galatians; his interpretation of the events of the wilderness generation in 1 Cor 10:1–13). He also has an eschatological perspective on the future in his other letters (1 Thess 4:13–5:11; 1 Corinthians 15). Still, in Romans, especially in 8:31–11:36, this historical perspective becomes more elaborate and central in his thinking. In Galatians, the contrast between righteousness through faith and righteousness through observance of the Mosaic law was primarily a contrast between different principles or ways of being religious. Those who observe the law are under a curse; those who have faith receive the blessings promised to Abraham (Gal 3:6–14). In Rom 8:31–11:36, however, the contrast between righteousness through observance of the Mosaic law and righteousness through faith becomes a temporal one, between a past defined by observance of the law and a present defined by the events of Christ's death and resurrection and accepted by faith apart from observance of the law.

There are several reasons for this much more temporally or historically oriented perspective. First, it enables Paul to emphasize elements of continuity with the past, especially with Israel's past (e.g., God's choice of the patriarchs in Rom 9:6–13). Second, it enables him to understand the Mosaic law and its purpose in such a way that although its observance in the present is no longer necessary, the law itself is still something that is good and holy. In the same way, Israel's observance of the law in the past is no longer a problem. Rather, it is Israel's present failure to recognize that Christ is the goal of the law and that righteousness is now through faith apart from observance of the law. Finally, this more historically oriented perspective enables Paul to see most of Israel's present situation as temporally demarcated and so not permanent but temporary and leading, in God's mysterious plan, to final reconciliation.

Finally, there is the way Paul interprets Israel's history and the promises and privileges granted to it as reflected in the Scriptures. Although one can read through Romans and see Israel's history and the promises and privileges granted to it in a way that is thoroughly Jewish, the patterns of accentuation in Paul's interpretations are nevertheless different. He accentuates elements such as promise, mercy, call, faith, and Gentiles. All of these are certainly present in the Scriptures. But for Jewish writers roughly contemporary with Paul, writers as varied as Philo, Josephus, and the authors of the sectarian works found at Qumran, the central core of the Scriptures was the figure of Moses and the law given by God through him to Israel.[42] Although Moses and

---

[42] See E. P. Sanders, *Paul and Palestinian Judaism: A Comparison of Patterns of Religion* (Philadelphia: Fortress, 1977); *Jewish Law from Jesus to the Mishnah: Five Studies* (Philadelphia:

the Mosaic law are present in Romans and the law is understood as something holy and good, neither plays a prominent role in Paul's interpretation of Israel's history in 9:6–29. For Paul, the Jewish scriptures are and always remain God's "word," God's "oracles." But at the same time, Paul has significantly shifted the focus, the patterns of accentuation, in his interpretation of what is central in these scriptures, what is of perduring value. No doubt Paul sees this as being thoroughly Jewish and deeply faithful to Israel and Israel's God. The persuasiveness of his arguments to the Roman Christian community depends on it. At the same time, however, his own experience of the risen Christ (as well as the experience of other, although not all, early Christians) has compelled him to interpret Israel's history, its law, and its scriptures in a very different way. One can certainly argue, and with a good deal of merit, that there is no one correct way to interpret the Scriptures. Nevertheless, one must also recognize that Paul's interpretations of them significantly differ from those of most of his Jewish contemporaries. This does not mean one is right and the other wrong. But it is important to realize how different they are and the extent to which these differences affected the very different histories of Judaism and Christianity in the following centuries.

Trinity Press International, 1990). Although the situation of first-century Judaism is more complicated than Sanders allows for, the Mosaic law and its observance are nevertheless a central part of God's covenant with Israel.

CHAPTER 14

Issues of Christian Living: Love, Harmony, Accommodation, and the Greater Good

*T*HIS BOOK HAS ARGUED THAT PAUL IN ROMANS is trying to explain to the Roman Christians, in ways that would be both intelligible and persuasive to them, his central but controversial convictions about the equal status of Jews and Gentiles, righteousness by faith apart from observance of the law, and the ultimate place of the Jewish people in God's larger providence. In doing so, he also substantially revises some of his earlier and, in retrospect, ill-considered arguments in Galatians and, to a far lesser extent, in 1 Corinthians. He tries to overcome their deep misgivings and suspicions about him without surrendering his basic convictions about the character of the gospel. In Romans 5–7, he also tries to show that his views about how believers should live their lives does not lead, however unintentionally, to ethical confusion and disarray. Grace is incompatible with sin, for in baptism believers have died to sin. In 12:1–15:7, Paul returns to this issue but turns from explanation and defense to an exhortation to ethical practice.

Only in 15:8–13, after the exhortation in 12:1–15:7, does Paul conclude his overall argument. This means that he clearly intends his Roman Christian audience to take 12:1–15:7 as an integral part of the overall argument, which extends from 1:16 through 15:13.[1]

This is also Paul's first opportunity to present more specifically his views on ethical practice in his own words to the Roman Christian community. The Roman Christians have already heard about what they think are Paul's ethical perspectives and have been deeply suspicious of them. Paul already tried to deal with some of these basic suspicions in Romans 5–7. But he was primarily concerned there with broad ethical dispositions. In 12:1–15:7, he turns more explicitly and specifically to ethical practice and, in an extended fashion, to exhortation. In 12:1–15:7, Paul becomes much more practical.

---

[1] This is also true of Gal 5:1–6:10, where Paul's exhortation is also integral to his argument in Gal 2:15–4:25.

It is not simply the contents of his ethical exhortation, however, that are important for Paul. Equally important is the portrait he presents of himself in 12:1–15:7. In ancient rhetorical terms, Paul is concerned not simply about the arguments themselves (the *logos*) but also about the character (the *ēthos*) of the person presenting them.[2] For the Roman Christians, Paul does not simply hold controversial ethical views. He himself is controversial and a cause of division. For this reason, his ethical exhortation in 12:1–15:7 is no less about who he is and what his character is than about what he is exhorting the Roman Christians to. One of Paul's goals in 12:1–15:7 is to show that he is not the sower of dissension and division but an advocate of love, harmony, accommodation, and the common good of the whole community.

In this same vein, one should not assume that all that Paul writes in 12:1–15:7 is directed against specific problems in the Roman Christian community. Certainly Paul's emphasis on harmony, accommodation, and the common good in 12:1–21 prepares his audience for his attempt to reconcile the "strong" and the "weak" of the community in 14:1–15:7. But much of what he writes in 12:1–21 is less about problems in the Roman Christian community than about displaying a vision of ethical practice that both he and his Roman Christian audience would have in common.

Especially 12:1–21, the first part of Paul's exhortation, is deeply indebted to traditional Jewish wisdom instructions. Paul quite consciously couches his ethical exhortation in modes of thought that are recognizably and traditionally Jewish. They would be intelligible, familiar, and, so he hopes, persuasive to his Roman Christian audience. Couching this exhortation in terms of traditional Jewish wisdom instructions, however, also serves a further and more important purpose. These instructions were usually structured collections of proverbs and maxims that, however, seldom appealed to the commandments or prohibitions of the Mosaic law. Indeed, their contents were seldom specifically Jewish. This must have appealed to Paul, since they represent a recognizably Jewish type of exhortation that does not involve recourse to the law. This means that he can, without appealing to observance of the Mosaic law, describe with specificity how believers, both Jewish and Gentile, are to live ethical lives.

Paul's ethical exhortation, however, is also more than an adaption and reworking of Jewish wisdom instructions. At crucial points in the exhortation, he also appeals to viewpoints he grounds explicitly in Christ. The most obvious is his description of believers as forming one body in Christ in 12:3–8. But he also appeals to Christ and his example in 13:14; 14:8–9, 15, 18; 15:1–6. Some of these appeals, as we shall see, are similar to, and grounded in, the arguments he made earlier in Romans 5–7.

Paul also draws heavily in this exhortation on what he wrote earlier in 1 Corinthians 8–10, 12, 13. But he does not simply repeat what he wrote there. We need to be sensitive, however, to what changes he makes and why he makes them. It is not simply that the context of the Roman Christian community differs from the com-

---

[2] See Aristotle, *Rhet.* 1.2.4–6; 2.1.1–7; Cicero, *De or.* 2.178–216, 310–312; Quintilian, *Inst.* 6.2.8–9. See also Anderson, *Glossary of Greek Rhetorical Terms*, 61–63.

munity at Corinth. Rather, he also makes these changes because his own thinking about ethical practice has also changed.

The seeming generality of much of 12:1–15:7 has led some interpreters to challenge even the specificity of 13:1–7, on submission to secular authority, and 14:1–15:7, on the divisions between the "strong" and the "weak." As seen earlier, the latter controversy plays a central role in the larger discussion about what Paul and the Roman Christian community knew about each other.[3] Yet as shall be seen, the whole of 12:1–15:7, and not simply 13:1–7 and 14:1–15:7, reflects a knowledge of the Roman Christian community and its deep misgivings about Paul.

THE STRUCTURE OF ROMANS 12:1–15:7

The structure of 12:1–15:7 is looser than those of the previous sections of the letter. The structure in general, however, is still fairly clear.

Part I: The values of love, unity, and harmony both inside and outside the community (12:1–13:14)

    A. Paul's wisdom instruction (12:1–21)

        1. Programmatic statement of the basis for Christian living (12:1–2)

        2. Descriptive section on the Christian community as one body in Christ (12:3–8)

        3. Prescriptive section on the theme of love (ἀγάπη) (12:9–21)

    B. Submission to secular authorities and the payment of taxes (13:1–7)

    C. Love of neighbor, the law, and the demands of baptism (13:8–14)

        1. Love of neighbor as the fulfillment of the law (13:8–10)

        2. Christian conduct in the light of the approaching end (13:11–14)

Part II: The issue of reconciling the weak and the strong (14:1–15:7)

    A. The challenge of the weak (14:1–12)

    B. The responsibility of the strong (14:13–23)

    C. Christ as exemplar (15:1–7)

The exhortation clearly falls into two parts. With the exception of 13:1–7, on submission to secular authorities and the payment of taxes, the first part is more general. The topics include the Christian community as one body in Christ (12:3–8), the centrality of love (12:9–21), love of neighbor as the fulfillment of the law (13:8–10), and behaving in an orderly way (εὐσχημόνως) in light of the approaching end (13:11–14). The second part of the exhortation is much more specific. In 14:1–15:7, Paul is concerned about resolving tensions between the strong

---

[3] See above, pp. 70–76.

and the weak members of the Roman Christian community. The tensions are over the continuing observance of certain Jewish dietary laws (14:2–3, 6, 14–17, 20–21, 23) and probably the Jewish Sabbath (14:5–6) by some members of the Roman Christian community (the "weak"). The two parts, however, are inseparable. The first part serves as the basis for the resolution of the tensions between the strong and the weak in the second part. Conversely, the second part shows how Paul is concretely the advocate of the values of love and harmony advocated in the first part.

ROMANS 12:1–21: PAUL'S WISDOM INSTRUCTION ON CHRISTIAN ETHICS

Paul begins his exhortation with what can best be described as a wisdom instruction on Christian ethics in 12:1–21. He develops it in three stages.[4] In the first stage (12:1–2), Paul exhorts his Roman Christian audience to present their bodies as a living sacrifice, holy and acceptable to God. He exhorts them not to be conformed to this world but to be transformed so that they may discern the will of God. The second stage (12:3–8) is primarily descriptive. He begins with a maxim about the importance of not thinking too highly of oneself but of thinking in appropriately moderate terms. The metaphor of the human body dominates the rest of the section. Just as the human body is one but has different members that perform different functions, so too believers form one body in Christ and are individually members of this body. Because of this, different members of the body have different functions. The third and final stage (12:9–21) is primarily prescriptive; in it the central theme is love. Love must be without pretense, hating what is evil and holding fast to what is good. Love brings with it a whole series of obligations, which Paul lists in 12:11–13. He concludes the section (12:14–21) with a series of maxims about how believers are to behave toward each other and toward those outside the community. Paul sees all these maxims as specifications of loving without pretense.

Romans 12:1–21 bears structural resemblances to several other Jewish wisdom instructions. The most important are Prov 3:11–35 (LXX), Sir 6:18–37, Ps.-Phoc. 70–96, and *T. Naph.* 2:2–3.5.[5] As in Romans 12, all four begin with a programmatic statement (Prov 3:11–12; Sir 6:18–19; Ps.-Phoc. 70; *T. Naph.* 2:2–5). In each case, this is then followed by a descriptive section (Prov 3:13–20; Sir 6:20–22; Ps.-Phoc. 71–75; *T. Naph.* 2:6–8). Finally, all four texts conclude with a prescriptive section (Prov 3:21–35; Sir 6:23–35; Ps.-Phoc. 76–96; *T. Naph.* 2:9–3.5). These three sections function in much the same way in Romans 12 and in these four Jewish wisdom instructions. The opening section states the overall point of the instruction. The descriptive section then develops this overall point in more detail and serves as the basis of the prescriptive section that follows. Paul is clearly using a type of instruction that is familiar within Judaism and would be familiar to the Roman Christians. At the same time, the similarities are not such as to show that Paul is literally

---

[4] This analysis of 12:1–21 is heavily indebted to Walter T. Wilson, *Love without Pretense: Romans 12.9–21 and Hellenistic-Jewish Wisdom Literature* (WUNT 46; Tübingen: Mohr, 1991).

[5] For a more detailed analysis of these similarities, see ibid., 95–126.

dependent on any of these four texts.[6] Rather, he is aware of, and is a participant in, the broad tradition of Jewish wisdom instruction.

Romans 12:1–2: The Basis of Christian Living

Paul begins with a programmatic statement in which he exhorts his Roman Christian audience to offer their bodies as a living sacrifice, holy and pleasing to God. This is their rational worship, that is, a worship proper to the mind. He then calls on them not to be conformed to this present age but to be transformed through a renewal of their minds. In this way, they will be able to discern the will of God, what is good and holy and perfect.

Paul intends these verses to be foundational for ethical practice. But in what sense are they a foundation, and why does Paul settle on this foundation? Perhaps the best way to get at these questions is to note what Paul does not appeal to as foundational. He does not appeal to the Mosaic law. The reason for this is obvious enough. For Paul, believers, whether Jewish or Gentile, are no longer obligated to observe the law.[7] But neither does he appeal to what he himself appealed to as foundational in his earlier letters, the guidance of the Spirit. In Galatians, Paul exhorted believers to "walk by the Spirit" (Gal 5:16) and to "live by the Spirit" (Gal 5:25). He also described the catalogue of virtues in Gal 5:22–24 as the "fruit of the Spirit." Although he shifted the emphasis, Paul also gave a central role to the Spirit in 1 Corinthians 12. He saw the role of the Spirit there especially as the force that unified the community. In describing the different charisms given to believers, Paul emphasized the role of the Spirit as the unifying force working in all the different charisms for the good of the whole community (1 Cor 12:4–11). In addition, believers form one body because they have all been baptized in the one Spirit and have all drunk of that same Spirit (1 Cor 12:13). That Paul does not appeal in Rom 12:1–2 to the Spirit as foundational for ethics is especially noteworthy. In Rom 12:3–8, which immediately follows this passage, Paul draws heavily on what he wrote in 1 Corinthians 12 about the community as the body of Christ, whose different charisms are meant to be exercised for the good of the whole. But in Rom 12:3–8, unlike in 1 Corinthians 12, he nowhere mentions the Spirit. Paul's omission, then, of any mention of the Spirit as foundational for ethical practice must have been intentional. Indeed, Paul mentions the Spirit only twice in all of Rom 12:1–15:7. In 12:11, he lists "aglow with the Spirit" as only one of ten obligations specifying what characterizes sincere love. In 14:17, he claims that the kingdom of God does not consist of food and drink but of righteousness, peace, and joy in the Holy Spirit. The Spirit, then, plays no role in 12:1–2 and only a very minor role in the rest of Paul's exhortation in 12:1–15:7.

The fact that Paul uses neither the law nor the Spirit as foundational for ethical practice is emblematic. On the one hand, by not appealing to the law or its observance, Paul remains faithful to his fundamental conviction that believers are no

---

[6] Ibid., 147–48.

[7] In Rom 13:8–10, Paul will claim that the one who loves his or her neighbor has "fulfilled" the law and that love itself is the "fulfillment" of the law. As will be seen later in this chapter, Paul clearly means by this something different from observance of the law.

longer obliged to observe it. On the other hand, by not appealing to the Spirit, Paul again seems to recognize the legitimacy of the Roman Christians' concerns not only about what he wrote in Galatians but also about the situation that developed in the Corinthian Christian community. In the light of both his own convictions and their concerns, what, then, does Paul now take as foundational for believers' ethical practice? In Rom 12:1–2, he formulates a basis for ethical practice that is recognizably Jewish and takes into consideration the legitimate concerns of the Roman Christians. At the same time, he is unwilling to surrender his own basic convictions that believers are no longer obliged to observe the Mosaic law.

Paul goes about this in three ways. First, he takes up material from his arguments about the incompatibility of grace and sin in Romans 5–7. It is crucial to see 12:1–2 against the background of Paul's description in Romans 5–7 of what believers' ethical dispositions should be. The most obvious connection is with 6:13, 16–19. In 12:1, Paul exhorts his Roman Christian audience to offer (παραστῆναι) their bodies as a living sacrifice that is holy and pleasing to God. This exhortation clearly takes up the language of 6:13, 16–19. In 6:13, Paul exhorts the Roman Christians not to offer (παριστάνετε) their members as weapons or instruments of wickedness to sin but to offer (παραστήσατε) themselves and their members as weapons or instruments to God. In 6:16, he writes that they are slaves to the one to whom they offer (παριστάνετε) themselves in obedience. Finally, in 6:19, he exhorts them so that just as they offered (παρεστάνετε) their members as slaves through uncleanness for lawlessness, so now they should offer (παραστήσατε) their members as slaves to righteousness for sanctification. In 12:1, Paul clearly takes up this language of offering. By playing on the meaning of the verb "to offer" (παρίστημι), however, Paul changes from a military metaphor (6:13) and a metaphor of slavery (6:16, 19) to a cultic metaphor. By their conduct, believers are to offer themselves as a "living sacrifice" to God. This sacrifice is their rational worship. In applying cultic language to ethical conduct, Paul is part of a wider trend both in Judaism and in the wider Greco-Roman world.[8] In this sense, he is appealing to a way of thinking about ethics that is probably both familiar and persuasive to his Roman Christian audience. More specifically, however, Paul also seems to be drawing a parallel between believers' ethical conduct as a sacrifice of rational worship, on the one hand, and the death of Jesus as a sacrifice found in 3:24–26, 5:6–11, and 8:3, on the other. In the latter passages, Christ's death brings about the forgiveness of sin. By implication, believers' offering of themselves as a living sacrifice to God must reflect this same victory over sin.

---

[8] For the metaphorical use of sacrificial language, see Ps 50:14, 23; 51:16–17; 141:2; Prov 16:6; Isa 1:11–17; Mic 6:6–8; Sir 35:1; Tob 4:10–11; 1QS 9:3–5; *2 En.* 45:3; *Let. Aris.* 234; Josephus, *Ant.* 6.147–150; Philo, *Plant.* 126; *Spec.* 1.277, 287. For the Greco-Roman world, see Plato, *Leg.* 716D; Xenophon, *Mem.* 1.3.3; *Anab.* 5.7.32; Isocrates, *Ad Nic.* 20; Epictetus, *Diatr.* 1.19.25. As already seen in the discussion of 3:24–26 earlier, the issue of sacrifice and its interpretation and reinterpretation in the ancient world is very complicated. One should avoid the use of vague terminology such as "spiritualization." See Hans Dieter Betz, "Christian Ethics according to Romans 12:1–2," in *Witness and Existence: Essays in Honor of Schubert M. Ogden* (ed. Philip E. Devenish and George L. Goodwin; Chicago: University of Chicago Press, 1989), 63–64.

Second, Paul emphasizes that believers are not to be conformed to this age but should be transformed through a renewal (ἀνακαινώσει) of their minds. The word Paul uses for "renewal" (ἀνακαίνωσις) is not found in Greek literature prior to Paul. He may have coined it. He is harking back here to his exhortation in 6:4 that just as Christ was raised from the dead, so too believers should walk in a "newness" (καινότητι) of life that comes to them through their baptism. Their conduct must be very different from that of the present age. Paul wants to emphasize this difference in the face of the Roman Christians' suspicion that, without observance of the ethical commandments of the law, believers' conduct risks falling to the same level as that of their Greco-Roman neighbors. Believers' conduct must differ from that of this age, but the difference is not due to observance of the law. It is due, rather, to the transformation of their minds that is rooted in the newness of life through the baptism they all share.

Third, Paul emphasizes in 12:2 that the purpose of all this is to be able to discern (δοκιμάζειν) the "will of God" (θέλημα τοῦ θεοῦ). In emphasizing the importance of the will of God, Paul is obviously drawing on a viewpoint embedded in Judaism and in the Jewish scriptures.[9] It is also something that is important to Paul himself. In his previous letters, Paul used the phrase to characterize both his own calling (1 Cor 1:1; 2 Cor 1:1) and how believers are to live (1 Thess 4:3; 5:18; 2 Cor 8:5). In Rom 1:10 and 15:32, he uses the phrase when he expresses his hope that through the will of God he might be speeded on his way to Rome to visit the Roman Christian community and be refreshed by them. Finally, in the apostrophe in 2:18, Paul addresses the Jew who claims to know God's will and to be able to discern (δοκιμάζεις) what is important because he is instructed from the law. He rhetorically asks why this person teaches others to act according to the law but does not observe it himself. By emphasizing in 12:2 that the goal is the discernment of the will of God, he is at once appealing to something that is characteristically Jewish and that both he and his Roman Christian audience share. At the same time, however, Paul does not specify the "will of God" he is referring to as the Mosaic law. Rather, in contrast to 2:18, he specifies it as "what is good and pleasing and perfect." By this he certainly means what is good, pleasing, and perfect before God rather than any general philosophical notion of the good, the pleasing, or the perfect. At the same time, however, he does not connect it with observance of the law.

In 12:1–2, then, Paul reformulates part of what he now takes to be foundational for ethical practice. He carefully expresses this foundation in terms that are characteristically Jewish and would be familiar and persuasive to his Roman Christian audience. The ethical practice of believers should be radically different from that of their Greco-Roman neighbors. Paul also takes seriously both the Roman Christians' suspicions and misgivings about his earlier emphasis on the Spirit and his own experience of the ethical issues the Corinthian Christians presented him with. The imagery of 12:1–2 is that of offering one's body as a sacrifice to God and of submission to God's will rather than of being empowered by the Spirit. He does

---

⁹ 1 Esd 8:16; 9:9; Ps (LXX) 29:8; 39:9; 102:21; 142:10; Jer 9:23 (LXX); Dan 4:35 (Theodotion); Mal 1:10; 1 Macc 3:60; 2 Macc 1:3; 4 Macc 18:16; Sir 43:16; *Pss. Sol.* 7:3; Philo, *Leg.* 3.197.

this, however, in a way that does not compromise his own basic convictions that believers are no longer obligated to observe the Mosaic law. Rather, they must discern the will of God.

Romans 12:3–8: Descriptive Section—the Christian Community as One Body in Christ

Paul then moves on to a section, 12:3–8, that is largely descriptive in character. He begins with an introductory statement (12:3a) followed by a maxim (12:3b), which he then interprets for the present context (12:3c). Paul bids everyone by the grace given to him (12:3a) not to think too highly (of themselves) beyond what they ought to think but to think with moderation (12:3b).[10] In the present context, this means that everyone should think according to the measure of faith God has measured to each (12:3c). Paul then offers a comparison he used before in 1 Cor 12:12–14, 27–30. Just as we have many members in one body (Rom 12:4a) and not all the members have the same function (12:4b), so too all of us are one body in Christ and individually members of one another (12:5). We have different gifts according to the grace given to us (12:6a). Paul then lists seven different gifts: prophecy, service, teaching, exhortation, sharing, giving aid (or patronage), and acts of mercy (12:6b–8).[11]

The purpose of this descriptive section is to present a model for ethical behavior that further specifies the programmatic statement in 12:1–2 and in turn serves as the basis for the prescriptive section that follows (12:9–21).[12] In this it is similar to the descriptive sections in Prov 3:13–30; Sir 6:20–22; Ps.-Phoc. 71–75; *T. Naph.* 2:2–8. In Paul's case, the model is that of "one body in Christ." It is meant to establish and reinforce the social and religious identity of believers. It is also meant to serve as a way of establishing criteria for ethical priorities and responsibilities in the community.[13]

The maxim with which Paul begins this section is a call to exercise the virtue of moderation. Moderation or self-control (σωφροσύνη) was an important virtue in Greek philosophy.[14] It also played a role in Greek gnomic and sapiential literature.[15] More proximately, it often appeared as a virtue in Jewish literature of the Greco-Roman period.[16] Even as Paul makes use of this maxim, however, he also specifies it for the present context. He puts it in an explicitly religious context. To think moderately means to think according to the measure of faith (μέτρον πίστεως) God has measured (ἐμέρισεν) to each member of the community. Paul's emphasis at this

---

[10] It is impossible to reproduce in English Paul's wordplay between ὑπερφρονεῖν, φρονεῖν, and σωφρονεῖν in the maxim. See 1 Cor 4:6.

[11] This basically follows the structure suggested by Wilson, *Love without Pretense*, 126–48.

[12] Ibid., 93.

[13] Ibid., 139–40.

[14] Plato, *Resp.* 430a–432a, 435b, 442c; *Phaedr.* 237e–238a; Aristotle, *Eth. nic.* 1.13; 2.7; 3.8; Zeno, in Plutarch, *Stoic. rep.* 7; *SVF* 1:374; 3:256, 262.

[15] Pseudo-Diogenes, *Ep.* 22; Pseudo-Socrates, *Ep.* 34.3; Menander, *Monostichoi* 1.

[16] Wis 8:7; 9:11; *T. Jos.* 4:2; 6:7; 9:2; 10:2–3; Ps.-Phoc. 76; 4 Macc 1:30–35; Philo, *Leg.* 1.69–76; *Mut.* 225; *Ios.* 40; *Spec.* 3.51; *Prob.* 67, 70, 159; Josephus, *Ag. Ap.* 2.195.

point seems to be on the "measure of faith" less as a matter of more-or-less than as the appropriate order and limits God has set for different members of the community.

Paul then turns again to a comparison of the community and its members to the human body and its members. The comparison of the "body politic" to the human body was well known in the Greco-Roman world.[17] It also appears in the Jewish writers Josephus and Philo.[18] The purpose of the comparison was almost invariably to advocate the values of unity and harmony in a political community and to show how damaging disorder and strife could be to it. It emphasized the common good over the good of any individual. It also emphasized that the unity of the body politic is an articulated one. Different members perform different functions.

Paul puts the comparison basically to the same purposes. He emphasizes the articulated unity of the Christian community. The community forms one body, but the members of the community have different functions. In addition, the seven functions Paul lists in Rom 12:6–8 are all orientated toward the common good of the community rather than toward any individual's good. Paul also qualifies each function in such a way that individual members should be aware of their limits and not encroach on other members' functions. Prophecy should be exercised according to the proportion of faith; service, by serving; teaching, by teaching; and so forth. Paul implies that there must be a proper and harmonious order among these functions.

There are, however, two crucial differences in the way Paul uses the comparison. These differences make the "body" that the community forms something far beyond the usual body politic. First, the unity of the community is due to the fact that together they form one body "in Christ." Christ is an active and central reality within the life of the community. The basis for the solidarity and harmony of the community is not primarily social but religious, in the sense that the community is rooted in its forming one body "in Christ." Second, in keeping with this first difference, the different functions the individual members exercise in the community are different gifts (χαρίσματα) that are according to the divine grace (κατὰ τὴν χάριν) given to each of them.

As mentioned above, this is not the first time Paul has made use of the comparison of the community and its members to the human body and its members. Paul used it earlier in a much more elaborate way in 1 Cor 12:4–31. There he emphasized some of the same things as in Rom 12:3–8. Just as the human body is one and has many members, the same is true of the community (1 Cor 12:12–13, 27). Just as in the human body different members have different functions, the same is true of the community (12:14–30). In addition, these various functions are gifts (12:4) and are meant to be used for the common good (τὸ σύμφερον) (12:7). Finally, these functions are to be exercised in an orderly and harmonious way (12:27–30).

There are, however, significant differences between the two passages. These differences are important because they reflect some of the ways Paul has rethought

---

[17] Plato, *Resp.* 462c–d; Xenophon, *Mem.* 2.3.18; Livy, *Urbe cond.* 2.32.7–2.33.1; Cicero, *Off.* 3.5.21–23; Seneca, *Ira* 2.31.7; Epictetus, *Diatr.* 2.10.4–5; Plutarch, *Arat.* 23.5; Dio Chrysostom, *Or.* 33.16, 44; 39.5; 40.21; 41.9; 50.3–4; Aelius Aristides, *Or.* 17.9; 23.31; 24.18, 38–39; 26.43.

[18] Josephus, *J.W.* 4.406–407; 5.277–279; Philo, *Spec.* 3.131.

and revised how he understands the character of the Christian community, its articulated unity, and the importance of proper order and harmony in the community.
First, and emblematic of these differences, is the list of gifts Paul mentions in Rom
12:3–8. With the exceptions of prophecy and teaching, they have nothing in common with the gifts listed in 1 Cor 12:4–11, 28–30. The list in Rom 12:3–8 contains
none of the more extraordinary gifts, such as healings and miracles (1 Cor 12:9–10)
and tongues and their interpretation (1 Cor 12:10, 28). The gifts Paul lists in Rom
12:6–8 are acts of generous but ordinary service to the community.

Second and consistent with this, the Spirit plays no role and is not even mentioned in Rom 12:3–8. This is very different from what Paul wrote in 1 Corinthians
12. All the gifts Paul mentioned in 1 Cor 12:7–11 were given by the Spirit. Indeed,
he referred to these gifts themselves as "spiritual gifts" (τῶν πνευματικῶν) (12:1).
In addition, the one body that the community formed was because all its members
were baptized in the one Spirit (ἐν ἑνὶ πνεύματι) and all had drunk of the one
Spirit (ἓν πνεῦμα, 12:13). In Rom 12:3–8, however, the Spirit plays neither of these
roles. It is certainly true that in Rom 12:3–8 these different gifts are given to members of the community according to the grace given them and so are gifts given by
God.[19] But Paul does not mention the Spirit as the giver of these gifts. In addition,
when Paul describes the community as "one body," he does not mention the Spirit as
the cause of its becoming one body.

Third, Paul describes the "one body" that the community forms rather differently in Rom 12:3–8 than he did in 1 Cor 12:12–13, 27. There, through baptism in
the one Spirit, the members of the community became the "body of Christ" (σῶμα
Χριστοῦ) and individually members of it. As seen earlier, this body they formed was
through baptism into the risen body of Christ.[20] But in Rom 12:5, they become
"one body in Christ" (ἓν σῶμα . . . ἐν Χριστῷ) and individually members of one
another. The two images are quite different. The image in 1 Cor 12:12–13, 27 is one
in which the community and its members become part of, or are integrated into, the
risen body of Christ. But this is not the case in Rom 12:3–8. The community and its
members do form one body, but it does not entail an integration into the risen body
of Christ. Rather, they form one body that is "in Christ" (ἐν Χριστῷ). Paul uses the
phrase "in Christ" or "in Christ Jesus" about fifty-seven times in his letters, and it is
clearly important for him.[21] Sometimes he uses it in a more objective sense, where it
refers to what has happened or will happen "in Christ."[22] At other times he uses it
more subjectively, to refer to the experience of believers who are "in Christ."[23] As

---

[19] In Rom 12:6, believers have different gifts according to the grace given (δοθεῖσαν) to
them. The use of the passive participle implies that God is the giver.

[20] See above, pp. 200–208.

[21] 1 Thess 1:1; 2:14; 4:16; 5:18; Gal 1:22; 2:4, 17; 3:14, 26, 28; 5:6; 1 Cor 1:2, 4, 10; 3:1;
4:10, 15 (bis), 17; 15:18, 19, 22, 31; 16:24; 2 Cor 2:14, 17; 3:14; 5:17, 19; 12:2, 19; Phil 1:1, 13,
26; 2:1, 5; 3:3, 14; 4:7, 19, 21; Rom 3:24; 6:11, 23; 8:1, 2, 39; 9:1; 12:5; 15:17; 16:3, 7, 9, 10;
Phlm 8, 10, 23.

[22] E.g., 1 Thess 5:18; Gal 2:17; 3:14; 5:6; 1 Cor 1:4; 15:22; 2 Cor 3:14; 5:19; Phil 2:5;
4:19; Rom 3:24; 6:23; 8:2, 39. The breakdown in these three categories follows James D. G.
Dunn, *The Theology of Paul the Apostle* (Grand Rapids: Eerdmans, 1998), 396–401.

[23] E.g., Gal 1:22; 2:4; 3:28; 1 Cor 1:2, 30; 15:18; 2 Cor 5:17; Rom 6:11; 8:1; 12:5; 16:3.

believers, they now exist in the realm of Christ's power. Finally, Paul uses it where he is writing of his own activity or is exhorting believers to accept a certain attitude or course of action.[24] None of these uses, however, involve or imply an image of Christ's "body" that believers become part of or into which they are integrated. The context of the phrase in Rom 12:5 indicates that it is an example of the more subjective use. It refers to the community's experience of unity through its existential participation in the new reality brought about by Christ. But in the way Paul describes this unity in Rom 12:3–8, it is the community that forms "one body." In contrast, in 1 Cor 12:12–13, 27, the "one body" is the risen body of Christ, into which believers have been integrated through their baptism in the one Spirit.

Because of these changes, Paul gives relatively more weight to the community as an ordered and harmonious whole. Missing is the earlier emphasis on the role of the Spirit and the community as composed of members of the risen body of Christ. Both these omissions are consistent with what Paul did earlier in Romans 5–7. There too the Spirit played no role as ethical guide. Nor were believers baptized into the risen body of Christ. Rather, they were baptized into his death and so into a death to sin (Rom 6:1–14). In both cases, these omissions serve similar purposes. The omission of the role of the Spirit removes one of the causes for the religious "enthusiasm" and excess that Paul encountered in the Corinthian community and that also so troubled his Roman Christian audience. It is certainly true that Paul has already emphasized in 1 Corinthians 12 that the Spirit was meant to be a unifying force in the community, which created harmony rather than dissension. But in Romans 12, as in Romans 5–7, he goes even further and omits altogether any mention of the Spirit. Paul seems to have come to the conclusion that thinking of the Spirit as an ethical guide has made for confusion and dissension rather than order and harmony. In addition, Paul's rethinking of the image of the community members as one body in Christ rather than as members of the risen body of Christ removes any notion that members of the community are already "raised," already immortal, and so free from ordinary ethical constraints. This too is in keeping with Romans 6. Believers are not already raised. This is still something in the future. But now they are baptized into the death of Christ, through which they are to be freed from sin and become slaves to God and to righteousness. In 12:3–8, the unity of the community is still centered "in Christ." But harmony and order have come much more to the fore in the model for ethical behavior that Paul presents and that serves as the basis for the prescriptive section that follows.

Romans 12:9–21: Prescriptive Section—the Theme of Love and Social Responsibilities

Romans 12:9–21 is largely prescriptive in character. Paul begins in 12:9a with the theme that love should be "without pretense" (ἀνυπόκριτος). He follows this with a protreptic maxim exhorting believers to hate what is evil and cling to what is good (12:9b). He then lists ten obligations following from this (12:10–13). Finally, he concludes with a series of maxims and two scriptural quotations to support the

---

[24] E.g., 1 Cor 4:15, 17; 16:24; 2 Cor 2:17; 12:19; Rom 9:1; Phlm 20.

maxims (12:14–21).[25] Paul's purpose is to illustrate and specify the kinds of conduct required of believers on the basis of the ethical principle enunciated in 12:1–2 and the model of one body in Christ described in 12:3–8.[26] Romans 12:9–21 is similar in purpose to the parallel sections in Prov 3:21–35; Sir 6:23–37; Ps.-Phoc. 76–95, and *T. Naph.* 2:9–3.5.[27]

Just as in Rom 12:3–8 Paul drew on what he wrote in 1 Corinthians 12, so in Rom 12:9–21 he draws on what he wrote in 1 Corinthians 13. Love (ἀγάπη) is the preeminent virtue in both Rom 12:9–21 and 1 Corinthians 13. In other ways, however, the two passages are quite different. First Corinthians 13 is a hymn in praise of love. In Rom 12:9–21, however, love serves as the overarching virtue, which is then specified by the ten obligations listed in 12:10–13 and in the maxims and proof texts in 12:14–21. The word ἀγάπη appears infrequently in non-Christian Greek literature.[28] It appears nineteen times in the LXX but usually with the meaning of sexual love or the love of a married couple.[29] It does, however, appear in Wis 3:9; 6:17–18 with a meaning as something characteristic of those who have faith in God and pursue wisdom. Early Christians accorded it a more prominent place and gave it much more significance as an overarching virtue than had previously been the case.[30] This gives Rom 12:9–21 a character that is distinctively Christian.

The moral qualities that love includes, however, in 12:9–21 are often similar to those embraced by the outside world and, more specifically, by the Jewish wisdom tradition. What Paul writes in 12:9–21 is similar to Prov 3:11–35, Sir 6:18–37, and *T. Naph.* 2:2–3.5. Paul often seems to be echoing and reworking traditional Jewish material in this section.[31] In this sense, the section again would have had a familiar ring to it in the ears of his Roman Christian audience. In addition, he also seems to rework material he himself previously used. This is especially the case for his re-working of material he first used in 1 Thessalonians 5.[32]

The obligations Paul lists in Rom 12:10–13 and the kinds of action he calls for in 12:14–21 are not a random collection.[33] They are, for the most part, either directly or indirectly social in orientation, either toward other members of the community or toward the outside world. Paul especially emphasizes harmony within the community through acting with compassion and humility. Community members should be of one mind with one another (12:16), show love toward one another

---

[25] This follows the overall structure suggested by Wilson, *Love without Pretense*, 149–99. This structure is also followed by most other commentators.

[26] Ibid., 142.

[27] Ibid., 143.

[28] See BDAG 6–7. The verb ἀγαπάω, however, appears much more often.

[29] 2 Kgdms 13:15; Song 2:4, 5, 7; 3:5, 10; 5:8; 7:7; 8:4, 6, 7; Jer 2:2.

[30] This follows the explanation of Wilson, *Love without Pretense*, 150–51. The word ἀγάπη appears 19 times in the LXX, as mentioned, and 146 times in the NT.

[31] Ibid., 145–46.

[32] Rom 12:9bc//1 Thess 5:21b–22; Rom 12:11b//1 Thess 5:19; Rom 12:12a//1 Thess 5:16; Rom 12:12c//1 Thess 5:17; Rom 12:17a//1 Thess 5:15a; Rom 12:18b//1 Thess 5:13b. See Wilson, *Love without Pretense*, 159.

[33] Wilson, ibid., 172–76, argues that 12:14–21 is in a ring construction. The beginning (12:14) and the end (12:21) are certainly parallel to each other, but it is much more difficult to see how what comes between these two verses forms a ring construction.

(12:10), contribute to relieving each other's needs, and practice hospitality (12:12). They should also rejoice with those who rejoice and grieve with those who grieve (12:15). In addition, they should do all of these things with humility, showing each other respect (12:10) and not being arrogant but associating with the lowly (12:16). Even virtues that at first seem more individually oriented, such as hope, patience in tribulation, and perseverance in prayer (12:12), indirectly have important social consequences for building up the community. Paul also emphasizes the importance of harmonious relations with the outside world. He does this by calling on believers to be at peace with all human beings (12:17–18). More specifically, he calls on them to be nonviolent and not to retaliate against those who have wronged them (12:17, 19–21). Vengeance should be left to God. For their part, they should give food and drink to an enemy who is in need. Paul especially emphasizes leaving vengeance to God and caring for enemies, since he devotes all of 12:17–21 to these points and quotes two verses from Scripture (Deut 32:35; Prov 25:21–22) for support.

Paul's specification of believers' moral obligations and responsibilities in Rom 12:9–21, with its emphasis on harmony and social solidarity, is of a piece with 12:3–8. Since he draws on the wider tradition of Jewish wisdom instructions, the values Paul calls for in this exhortation would be both familiar and persuasive to his Roman Christian audience. But it is also important to understand Paul's *ēthos*, how he presents himself in this passage. He is not someone who foments divisions but someone who encourages harmony and good order within the community. Equally important is how he does this. He reworks and develops the traditions of Jewish wisdom instructions, but he does not appeal to the ethical commandments of the law or their observance. Finally, his emphasis on peaceful relations and nonretaliation toward outsiders leads naturally into 13:1–7, where he deals with the more specific issue of believers's relationship to civil authority and the payment of taxes.

ROMANS 13:1–7: SUBMISSION TO SECULAR AUTHORITIES AND THE PAYMENT OF TAXES

Romans 13:1–7 is the first place in 12:1–15:7 where Paul seems to become more specific in his exhortation. He first exhorts everyone (πᾶσα ψυχή) to be subject to the governing authorities (13:1–5) and then directly addresses the Roman Christians and exhorts them to pay the various taxes demanded of them (13:6–7). Paul begins with a general exhortation that everyone should be subject to the "governing authorities" (ἐξουσίαις ὑπερεχούσαις, 13:1a). By the term "governing authorities," Paul here means civil authorities, specifically the authorities of the Roman Empire.[34] In 13:1b–2, he offers a rationale for this subjection: There is no authority except that which has been established by God; as a result, anyone who opposes this authority opposes what God has appointed. In 13:3–4, he then explains the role of

---

[34] Given the context of 13:1–7, Paul clearly means by "governing authorities" the various offices that make up the Roman civil government and not, as Oscar Cullmann (*The State in the New Testament* [New York: Scribners, 1956], 50–70, 94–114) once suggested, either the angelic powers behind the state or the government of the state and the angelic powers together.

rulers in commending good conduct and punishing evil conduct. If you (singular) do not want to fear this authority, then do good. But if you (singular) do evil, then fear the authority because he does not carry the sword for nothing.[35] In this respect, governing authority is a servant of God and an avenger for wrath to the evildoer. In 13:5, Paul returns to his opening point, that it is necessary to be subject to these governing authorities. Because of the rationale he has provided in 13:1b–4, this subjection should not be only out of fear of punishment but also a matter of conscience. In 13:6–7, Paul then applies this to the more specific issue of paying different taxes. He exhorts them, now in the second person plural, to render to everyone their due, to pay tribute to those to whom tribute (φόρον) is due and tax (τέλος) to whom tax is due. This is because the governing authorities are God's ministers as they engage in this activity. Paul seems to be distinguishing here between two kinds of taxes. Tribute (φόρος) refers to direct taxes, such as property or poll taxes. Tax (τέλος) refers to indirect taxes, such as tolls or sales taxes.[36] Finally, he concludes on a more general note that believers are to show fear to whom fear is due and honor to whom honor is due.

Paul's use of the second-person-singular form of address to an imaginary interlocutor in 13:3–4 and his use of the rhetorical question in 13:3 are familiar techniques from the diatribe. Paul is thus only indirectly addressing his Roman Christian audience in 13:1–5. His change to the second-person-plural form of address in 13:6–7, however, indicates that it is especially in these two verses that Paul now directly addresses his Roman Christian audience. Because of their directness and specificity, these verses probably also point to the immediate purpose of the exhortation, the payment of the various taxes levied by the Roman government.

At first reading, the presence of this passage may seem odd. Paul does not specifically discuss the issue of the relationship of believers to civil authorities anywhere else in his letters.[37] In addition, the passage contains no obvious christological elements, a lack that also seems odd given Paul's usual approach to issues.[38] This has led some interpreters to claim that the passage is a later interpolation into the letter and reflects viewpoints from the end of the first century A.D. such as are found also in 1 Pet 2:13–17, 1 Tim 2:1–4, and Titus 4:1–3.[39] Although clearly distinct, Rom 13:1–7 does exhibit connections both with what precedes and what follows. It is a continuation of the theme of conduct toward outsiders in 12:17–18, especially the command as far as possible to be at peace with all human beings in 12:18. There are also verbal links both with what precedes and with what follows. The most obvious

---

[35] The "sword" Paul mentions in 13:4 is clearly a reference to capital punishment. Exercise of this level of punishment was limited to the Roman authorities themselves. Nanos's attempt (*Romans*, 310–14) to take it as a reference to synagogue authorities is unconvincing. The same must be said for his arguments that 13:1–7 is an exhortation for Roman Christians to remain obedient to Jewish synagogue authorities (pp. 289–336).

[36] Fitzmyer, *Romans*, 669–70.

[37] In Phil 3:20, Paul uses the word πολίτευμα ("commonwealth"), but the context is clearly not about the relationship of believers to the civil authorities. The commonwealth of believers is in heaven.

[38] This and other issues are discussed by Cranfield, *Romans*, 2:651–55.

[39] See, e.g., Walter Schmithals, *Der Römerbrief als historisches Problem* (SNT 9; Gütersloh: Mohn, 1975), 185–97.

is the contrast between "good" (ἀγαθόν) and "evil" (κακόν), which runs through this entire section of the letter (12:2, 9, 17, 21; 13:3a, 3c, 4a, 4d; 13:10). Other verbal links are also present.[40] There is no convincing reason, then, to think that Paul did not compose this passage and place it where he did.

The similarities of Rom 13:1–7 to 1 Pet 2:13–17, 1 Tim 2:1–4, and Titus 4:1–3 contribute to our understanding of the thought world of which all four texts are a part and of the specific purpose of Paul's argument in Rom 13:1–7. Although the most extensive parallels are with 1 Pet 2:13–17, all four texts share common elements: (1) subjection to civil authorities (Rom 13:1, 5; 1 Pet 2:13; Titus 3:1); (2) religious reason for subjection (Rom 13:1–7; 1 Pet 2:14); (3) the authorities' role in praise and punishment (Rom 13:3–4; 1 Pet 2:14); (4) the contrast between good conduct and evil conduct (Rom 13:3–4; 1 Pet 2:14–16; Titus 3:1–2); and (5) the duty to honor the authorities (Rom 13:7; 1 Pet 2:17).[41] It is important to keep in mind that all these attitudes believers should have refer to non-Christian rulers. The extent of these parallels suggests that Paul's view of the relationship of believers to civil authority was a fairly widely held one among early Christians. As the book of Revelation shows, it was not the only one; but it certainly was not peculiar to Paul.

Indeed, it was not even peculiar to early Christians. The same basic viewpoint toward Gentile rulers is also found in Jewish literature and was common among Jews living in the Greco-Roman world. This viewpoint contained two aspects. The first was that these rulers received their power to rule from God. A number of biblical texts affirm this viewpoint. One of the clearest examples is Prov 8:15–16:

> By me [God] kings reign, and rulers decree what is just;
> by me princes rule, and nobles govern the earth.

Other examples include Jer 27:5–7 (34:5–7 [LXX]); Isa 45:1–3; Dan 2:21, 36–38; 4:17; Sir 10:4. A number of Hellenistic Jewish texts reflect the same basic attitude (*Let. Aris.* 224; Wis 6:3; Josephus, *J.W.* 2.140; *Ant.* 15.374; *Ag. Ap.* 2.76–77).[42] The second aspect was that these rulers ought to be held in honor. Because of this, for example, Jews should offer prayers and sacrifices to God on behalf of their Gentile rulers. Examples of this are again found both in biblical texts (Jer 29:7 [36:7 (LXX)]; Ezra 6:10; 1 Macc 7:33) and in Hellenistic Jewish texts (*Let. Aris.* 45; Philo, *Legat.* 157; Josephus, *J.W.* 2.197; *Ag. Ap.* 2.76–77). Perhaps the most instructive text for our purposes, because of both its content and its proximity in time and place, is from Josephus's *Against Apion*.

> He [Moses] did not, however, forbid that worthy men should be paid homage through other honors secondary to that paid to God; with such honors we do glorify the

---

[40] Other verbal links are ὀργή (12:19; 13:4, 5), ἀποδιδόναι (12:17; 13:7), ἐκδικοῦντες (12:19), ἔκδικος (13:4), προσκαρτεροῦντες (12:12; 13:6), τὰς ὀφειλάς (13:7), μηδὲν ὀφείλετε (13:8). See Byrne, *Romans*, 386; Wilckens, *Römer*, 3:30–31.

[41] Similar views are also found in *1 Clem.* 60:2–61:2.

[42] See also a fragment of Philo, the text and translation of which are found in Erwin R. Goodenough, *The Politics of Philo Judaeus: Theory and Practice* (New Haven: Yale University Press, 1938), 99: "in his material substance (οὐσίᾳ) the king is just the same as any man, but in the authority [τῇ ἐξουσίᾳ] of his rank he is like the God of all."

emperors and the Roman people. For them we offer perpetual sacrifices; and not only do we perform these ceremonies daily, at the expense of the whole Jewish community, but, while we offer no other victims in our corporate capacity, even for the (imperial) family, we jointly accord to the emperors alone this signal honor which we pay to no other individual. (*Ag. Ap.* 2.76–77)[43]

Josephus claims that Jews hold the emperor and the Roman people in such honor as is second only to that paid to God. The Jewish people offer daily sacrifices in the Jerusalem temple on behalf of the emperor and the Roman people. Although the last part of the Latin translation is somewhat obscure, Josephus also seems to be claiming that these sacrifices were offered especially on behalf of the emperor and were offered on behalf of no other individual. In any case, these various biblical and Hellenistic Jewish texts show that the basic attitudes toward Gentile rulers concerning the source of their authority and the honor due them expressed by Paul in Rom 13:1–7 as well as by 1 Pet 2:13–17, 1 Tim 2:1–4, and Titus 3:1–3 were common not only to early Christians but also to Jews, especially those living in the Greco-Roman world. It was a viewpoint both Paul and his Roman Christian readers would have shared.

This common viewpoint, however, was neither an elaborate set of principles nor an elaborated theory of political power. There was nothing absolute about either political power or submission to it. Rather, it was a religiously grounded attitude on the part of a minority group in the Roman empire toward the overwhelming reality of Roman power. It also included a recognition of the value of the relative social and political stability Roman power provided. There were still good rulers and bad ones, and God would punish the bad ones. Josephus provides a good illustration of this attitude. He tells the story about a meeting between an Essene, Manaemus (Menahem), and Herod the Great when Herod was still a boy. Manaemus once greeted Herod as "king of the Jews." Herod, puzzled by the greeting, reminded Manaemus that he was only a private citizen. Manaemus, however, slapped him on the backside and said to him,

You will be king and you will rule the realm happily, for you have been found worthy of this by God. . . . For the best attitude for you to take would be to love justice and piety toward God and mildness toward your citizens. But I know that you will not be such a person, since I understand the whole situation. Now you will be singled out for such good fortune as no other man has had, and you will enjoy eternal glory, but you will forget piety and justice. This, however, cannot escape the notice of God, and at the close of your life His wrath will show that He is mindful of these things. (Josephus, *Ant.* 15.374–76 [Marcus, LCL])

The vignette illustrates well the viewpoint that although rulers receive their power from God, this power is not absolute. God punishes rulers who misuse their power. Other Jewish texts make much the same point (Jer 27:5–7 [34:5–7 (LXX)]; Dan 2:21;

[43]This section of *Against Apion* is preserved only in a sixth-century Latin translation commissioned by Cassiodorus: *Aliis autem honoribus post deum colendos non prohibuit viros bonos, quibus nos et imperatores et populum Romanorum dignitatibus ampliamus. Facimus autem pro eis continua sacrificia et non solum cotidianis diebus ex impensa communi omnium Iudaeorum talia celebramus, verum cum nullas alias hostias ex communi neque pro filiis [?] peragamus, solis imperatoribus hunc honorem praecipuum pariter exhibemus, quem hominum nulli persolvimus.*

Wis 6:1–3; *Let. Aris.* 224; Josephus, *J.W.* 2.197; *1 En.* 46:5; *2 Bar.* 82:9). There is no reason to think that Paul's attitude was any different in this matter.[44]

Why does Paul include this exhortation in his letter to the Roman Christians? What does he hope to achieve in writing it, and is there some situation in Rome that led him to write it? As one reads Rom 13:1–7, one is left with two quite different impressions. On the one hand, what is specific in the passage is Paul's exhortation to the Roman Christians to pay their taxes. This is the specific point Paul wants to make in the passage. On the other hand, he devotes relatively little space to it. It is mentioned only toward the end, in 13:6–7. Indeed, the whole exhortation in 13:1–7 is relatively brief, at least in comparison with what follows in 14:1–15:7, on the controversy over the observance of Jewish dietary laws. These two different impressions leave the reader with the sense that although Paul is interested in exhorting Roman Christians to be subject to the Roman authorities and specifically to pay the Roman taxes, he does not perceive that the issue is either immediate or critical. Rather, he seems to be addressing a more chronic, neuralgic point, the issue of taxes, which was always in danger of becoming a matter of acute and critical importance. The Roman Christians were paying their taxes, but they also found these taxes onerous. What Paul seems to be doing is exhorting them to continue to pay their taxes on the basis of their shared views about subjection to, and honor of, the governing authorities, in this case the Roman authorities.

This interpretation of Paul's purpose fits well into what we know about the problem of taxation in Rome in the middle of the first century A.D. The Roman writer Tacitus provides a valuable description of the problem in Rome in 58 during the earlier part of the emperor Nero's reign:

> In the same year, as a result of repeated entreaties from the people, which complained of the excesses of the tax farmers, Nero hesitated whether he ought not to decree the abolition of all indirect taxes [*vectigalia*] and present this as the noblest of gifts to the human race. His impulse, however, after much preliminary praise of his magnanimity, was checked by the senators who pointed out that the dissolution of the empire was certain if the income on which the state subsisted were to be curtailed: "For, the moment the duties on imports were removed, the logical sequel would be a demand for the abolition of the direct taxes [*tributorum*]." (Tacitus, *Ann.* 13.50 [Jackson, LCL])[45]

According to Tacitus (*Ann.* 13.51), Nero accepted their self-serving but prudent advice. He did not abolish the indirect taxes, but he did introduce a number of reforms intended to make the collection of taxes fairer and the prosecution of the excesses of the tax farmers easier.[46] What is valuable for our purposes is that Tacitus provides us

---

[44]Unfortunately, Rom 13:1–7 has been turned into the basis for various theories of absolute submission to political power. This is certainly a misuse of the passage. For the use of this passage in later periods, see Wilckens, *Römer*, 3:43–66.

[45]*Eodem anno crebris populi flagitationibus immodestiam publicanorum arguentis dubitavit Nero an cuncta vectigalia omitti iuberet idque pulcherrimum donum generi mortalium daret. Sed impetum eius, multum prius laudata magnitudine animi, attinuere senatores, dissolutionem imperii docendo, si fructus quibus res publica sustineretur deminuerentur: quippe sublatis portoriis sequens ut tributorum abolitio expostularetur.*

[46]This episode comes from the early part of Nero's reign (54–68). Nero's excesses came later in his reign.

with a window into the situation in Rome about a year after Paul wrote his letter to the Roman Christians. There were chronic complaints from the inhabitants of Rome especially about various indirect taxes and their rapacious collection by the tax farmers. In addition, the senators' argument that Nero's abolition of indirect taxes would inevitably lead to a demand for the abolition of direct taxes suggests that the Roman populace also saw as excessive the direct taxes levied by the Roman government. These are the two kinds of taxes that Paul mentions in Rom 13:7: direct taxes (φόρος, *tributa*) and indirect taxes (τέλος, *vectigalia*). One can easily imagine Paul urging the Roman Christians in these circumstances to continue to show restraint. They should continue to pay their taxes. Paul may also have thought that this was also called for given the fact that only about eight years earlier the previous emperor, Claudius, had expelled some Jews and Jewish Christians from Rome for causing disturbances. Among them were Paul's friends and associates Priscilla and Aquila. Under these circumstances, the Christians in Rome were particularly vulnerable and had no need to repeat what had happened.

A final element that may have been lurking in the background and may have been on Paul's mind in writing this exhortation to the Roman Christians was the eschatological expectations they may also have had about the final vindication of Israel. This study, in discussing earlier the apocalyptic expectations of the Romans Christians, pointed to a text from Josephus (*Ant.* 10.210) in which he reticently referred to Dan 2:44–45 about the "hidden things that are to come."[47] This passage described how God would set up a kingdom that would last forever and would crush all other kingdoms. In the context of Daniel, this eternal kingdom was obviously Israel. However reluctantly, Josephus attested to eschatological expectations about the Jewish people that were yet to be fulfilled. As also argued earlier in this study, these expectations for the vindication of Israel were probably shared by the Roman Christians. For them, as much as for the Roman Jewish community, eschatological expectations probably included not only a place for corporate Israel and its vindication but also for the crushing of all other kingdoms. Such expectations of eschatological vindication may also have contributed to an underlying sense of dissatisfaction with, and unrest toward, Roman authority on the part of the Roman Christian community and may have manifested itself specifically in a question by some Roman Christians of whether to continue to pay various Roman taxes. This reality may also have been in the back of Paul's mind and formed an underlying reason for his exhortation to the Roman Christians to continue to pay their taxes and be subject to Roman authority.

ROMANS 13:8–14: LOVE OF NEIGHBOR, THE LAW, AND THE DEMANDS OF BAPTISM

In Rom 13:8, Paul returns to the theme of love, which was also central to 12:9–21. He connects it somewhat artificially with 13:1–7 by using the verb "owe" (ὀφείλετε) as a catchword with the corresponding noun "debts" (ὀφειλάς) in 13:7.

---

[47] See above, pp. 261–62.

Although 13:8–14 is relatively short, Paul places it at the end of the more general section of his exhortation. This means that it is important for him. Indeed, both 13:8–10 and 13:11–14 touch on issues that have been crucial for Paul in Romans. In both passages he emphasizes that his ethical convictions about believers no longer being obligated to observe the Mosaic law are rooted in traditional views they share. They also do not lead to ethical disarray. On the contrary, they lead to a well-ordered life.

Romans 13:8–10: Love of Neighbor and the Fulfillment of the Law

Paul's concern in 13:8–10 is with the relationship of love to observance of the Mosaic law. His initial claim is that the one who loves his neighbor has "fulfilled" (πεπλήρωκεν) the law.[48] Paul gives his reason for this in 13:9: The particular commandments not to commit adultery, to murder, to steal, to covet, or any other commandment (Exod 20:13–15, 17; Deut 5:17–19, 21) are summed up (ἀνακεφαλαιοῦται) in the one commandment to love one's neighbor as oneself (Lev 19:18).[49] This means that love does no wrong to a neighbor. He concludes from this that love is the fulfillment (πλήρωμα) of the law (Rom 13:10).

Much in this passage would have been familiar to Paul's Roman Christian audience from the Judaism he and they shared. The negative form of the Golden Rule (do not do harm to a neighbor) appears in Zech 8:17; Sir 10:6; *Let. Aris.* 168, 207; *Jos. Asen.* 23:12; *Tg. Yer. I* to Lev 19:18; *b. Šabb.* 31a. Allusions to Lev 19:18 also appear frequently in Jewish literature.[50] Although neither the negative form of the Golden Rule nor the allusions to Lev 19:18 were used in this literature as an organizing principle for ethics, there are two exceptions. The first is *b. Šabb.* 31a, where the early-first-century rabbi Hillel tells a would-be proselyte, "What is hateful to you, do not do to your fellow human being. This is the entire law, all of it; the rest is commentary. Go and study!"[51] The second is in *Sipra* to Lev 19:18. There the early-second-century rabbi Akiba claims that Lev 19:18 is the "greatest general principle in the law."[52] Although both texts are found in much later documents and so must be treated with a certain skepticism, they nevertheless indicate at least that such viewpoints were not out of place in early Judaism.

Granted this common background, Paul's argument in Rom 13:8–10 and the purposes to which he puts it are more complicated. Romans 13:8–10 clearly echoes Gal 5:14, where Paul wrote in his exhortation to the Galatian believers that "the

---

[48] Most commentators correctly take the Greek word ἕτερον ("other"/"neighbor") with the preceding verb, "love," rather than with the following word, "law." Paul uses the word as equivalent to "neighbor" in Gal 6:4; 1 Cor 6:1; 10:24, 29; 14:17. See Fitzmyer, *Romans*, 678.

[49] Paul cites the commandments in an order different from that found in the Hebrew or in most LXX MSS of Exod 20:13–17 and Deut 5:17–21. The order, however, seems to reflect one that is common in the Jewish Diaspora (Deut 5:17 [LXX-B]; Nash Papyrus; Philo, *Decal.* 36, 51, 121–153, 168–174; *Spec.* 3.8, 83; 4.2, 79; Luke 18:20; Jas 2:11; Clement of Alexandria, *Strom.* 6.16).

[50] Sir 13:15; *Jub.* 7:20; 20:2; 36:4, 8; *T. Reu.* 6:9; *T. Iss.* 5:2; *T. Gad* 4:2; *T. Benj.* 3:3–4; Philo, *Spec.* 4.186; 1QS 5:25; 8:2; *Sipra* on Lev 19:18.

[51] "This is the entire law, all of it" (הִיא כל התורה כולה).

[52] "This is the greatest general principle in the law" (זה כלל גדול בתורה).

whole law is fulfilled [πεπλήρωται] in one word, 'You shall love your neighbor as yourself.'" Chapter 2 of this study has argued, on linguistic grounds and on the basis of the overall argument of Paul's exhortation in Gal 5:1–6:10, that he clearly did not mean by "fulfilling" the law the same thing as its observance.[53] Rather, he was claiming that believers, by being guided by the Spirit and loving one another through the practice of virtue, were equivalently carrying out what had been central to the Mosaic law. They were fulfilling the law, but they were not, as such, observing it. Paul is making a similar point in Rom 13:8–10. Like Gal 5:14, Rom 13:8–10 is part of a larger exhortation (12:1–13:14) in which Paul is urging believers to practice a series of virtues, all of which fall under the general principle of love. For Paul, the practice of these virtues, which are rooted in, and derived from, love of neighbor, represent the "fulfillment" of the law but not its observance. They are an alternative to observance. In this sense, Paul's use of the negative form of the Golden Rule and of Lev 19:18 differs significantly from the sayings of Hillel and Akiba. For them, Lev 19:18 and the negative form of the Golden Rule were ways of summarizing observance of the law and not an alternative to it. For Paul, they are just such an alternative.

There are, however, also two important differences between Gal 5:14 and Rom 13:8–10. The first is that, in Gal 5:1–6:10, the Spirit played a central role as a guide to proper ethical behavior. Galatians 5:14 was followed almost immediately by Paul's lists of vices and virtues, in which he exhorted the Galatians to "walk by the Spirit" and not to gratify the desire of the flesh (Gal 5:16–26). But Paul makes no such appeal in Rom 12:1–13:14. The reason for this is Paul's recognition that his earlier emphasis on the role of the Spirit led to the kind of ethical problems reflected in 1 Corinthians, the reports of which came to be of great concern to the Roman Christians.

The second difference is how Paul in Rom 13:8–10 expands on what he wrote in Gal 5:14. The first expansion is a list of commandments in Rom 13:9, from the second half of the Decalogue, against adultery, murder, stealing, coveting, together with "any other commandment." At first this expansion may seem innocuous. But why, in comparison with Gal 5:14, which contains no such list of commandments, does he do this? The reason is that it makes much more explicit than Gal 5:14 the kinds of things love does not permit the believer to do. Paul's second addition in Rom 13:10 is similar: "Love does no wrong to a neighbor." Both these expansions seem to be making the same point. The love to which Paul is exhorting the Roman Christians is one that equivalently "fulfills" the commandments of the law against these various vices even though believers are not as such observing the law.

At first this may seem a distinction without a difference. But this is obviously not the case in Paul's mind. On the one hand, he continues to insist on his long-standing conviction that believers are no longer obligated to observe the Mosaic law. Their ethic practice is now rooted in their love of neighbor; it is no longer rooted in the Mosaic law or its observance. On the other hand, their orderly practice of love of neighbor, specified in the list of obligations and responsibilities in Romans 12, certainly means that believers do not commit adultery, murder, steal, or covet. It is the

---

[53] See above, pp. 69–70.

latter that Paul emphasizes more fully in 13:8–10 than in Gal 5:14. This, combined with Paul's omission of any mention of the role of the Spirit, indicates that once again he is trying to maintain his own basic convictions but at the same time take into account the legitimate concerns of the Roman Christians about earlier expressions of his views.

Romans 13:11–14: The Nearness of the End and Living Orderly Lives

In 13:11–14, Paul concludes this part of his exhortation with eschatologically oriented admonitions. He seems less interested here in eschatology itself than in the motivation that an eschatological orientation provides for present ethical behavior. Now is the time for believers to awake from sleep. This is because their salvation is nearer now than when they first believed. Believers are to put off the deeds of darkness and put on the armor of light. They are to live in an orderly way (εὐσχημόνως), put on the Lord Jesus Christ, and not make provision for the flesh so as to gratify its desires.

Paul here again seems to be drawing heavily on traditional material taken from early Christian baptismal liturgies.[54] The first section of traditional material is in 13:11–12. Given the parallelism of the lines and the rhythmic nature of the prose, it was probably part of an early Christian baptismal hymn:

> It is the hour for you to awake from sleep; . . .
> The night is far gone, the day is near at hand;
> Let us cast off the works of darkness;
> Let us put on the armor of light.

The second section of traditional material is in 13:13–14. This was perhaps part of a baptismal catachesis:

> As in the day, let us walk becomingly, not in reveling and drunkenness, not in debauchery and licentiousness, not in quarreling and jealousy. But put on the Lord Jesus Christ, and make no provision for the flesh, to gratify its desires.

There are two primary reasons to suggest that both these passages were traditional in character. First, in 13:11c, Paul seems to be commenting on 13:11b ("It is the hour for you to awake from sleep") by adding after the first line that this is so because salvation is nearer now than when they began to believe. The purpose of the commend seems to be to apply the hymn to the present situation. He offers a reason for thinking that the present is also the hour for believers to awake from sleep: "now our salvation is nearer than when we began to believe." For Paul, the phrase "It is the hour for you to awake from sleep" is first connected with the time when they first believed. The most likely context for this is the ritual of baptism. In commenting on it, he wants to maintain that this baptismal hymn is equally appropriate for their present situation. The second reason, which strengthens the first, is that the imagery of "taking off" and "putting on"

---

[54] Schlier, *Römerbrief,* 395–96, proposes this view. For a fuller explanation, see Wilckens, *Römer,* 3:74–75.

used in both blocks of material was connected especially with the ritual of baptism (Gal 3:27; 1 Cor 12:11–12; Eph 4:24) in early Christianity.

Why, then, does Paul use this material at the end of this section of his exhortation? There are several reasons. First is the attraction of the traditional character of the language and imagery itself. Paul is able to end this part of the exhortation with convictions based on traditional material whose viewpoints he and his Roman Christian audience have in common. Second, the material intimately connects baptism with ethical behavior. The Roman Christians' ethical practice is now rooted in what Paul wrote about baptism in Romans 6. It is rooted in their common baptism into the death of Christ, by which they also died to sin. Through baptism, believers were freed from sin and became slaves to God in righteousness. Both in Romans 6 and in 12:1–2, Paul already emphasized that the ethical consequences of baptism are meant to be transformative. The traditional baptismal material in 13:11–14 is also full of images of transformation.[55] Third, the connection between baptism and its ethical consequences is made without reference to the law or its observance. In this sense, this traditional baptismal material supports Paul's claim to root ethics in baptism and its consequences rather than in observance of the Mosaic law. Finally, the phrase used in the baptismal catechesis to characterize believers' conduct is "to walk in an orderly way" (εὐσχημόνως περιπατήσωμεν). This phrase both echoes and contrasts with Gal 5:16, where Paul exhorted the Galatians to "walk by the Spirit" (πνεύματι περιπατεῖτε). The difference between the two phrases is emblematic of the change in approach Paul takes toward issues of ethics in Romans when compared with Galatians. It supports Paul's insistence both in Rom 12:1–21 and earlier in Romans 5–7 that his views about righteousness apart from the law do not lead, however unintentionally, to ethical confusion and disarray but to a well-ordered life both for individuals and for the community.

ROMANS 14:1–15:7: RECONCILING THE WEAK AND THE STRONG

In the second part of his exhortation (14:1–15:7) Paul turns to a specific set of issues that have been causing divisions in the Roman Christian community.[56] Paul deals with these issues in ways consistent with his overall emphasis on harmony, love, and the common good of the community in 12:1–13:14. The issues that divide the community concern two different areas of Jewish observance: dietary laws and Sabbath observance.[57] The former seem to have been by far the more contentious of the two issues. Paul mentions the latter only in 14:5–6. How these two areas of Jewish observance divided the community requires some clarification.

Regarding probably the less contentious issue, Sabbath observance, Paul in 14:5–6a writes about divisions in the observance of "days":

---

[55] For the background of the images in 3:11–14, see Dunn, *Romans*, 786–87.

[56] The discussion here is especially indebted to Barclay, "'Do We Undermine the Law?'" See also Mark Reasoner, *The Strong and the Weak: Romans 14.1–15.13 in Context* (SNTSMS 103; Cambridge: Cambridge University Press, 1999).

[57] See Reasoner, *Strong and the Weak*, 1–23; and Cranfield, *Romans*, 2:690–95, for different opinions on what the issues were.

One person regards one day as more important than another [ἡμέραν παρ' ἡμέραν]; yet another regards every day as the same [πᾶσαν ἡμέραν]. Let each one be fully convinced of this in his own mind: One who observes a day observes it for the Lord.

Although it is possible that Paul also includes the observance of various Jewish feasts, the primary reference is most naturally to the observance of the Jewish Sabbath, in which six days of the week are distinguished from the seventh.[58] Evidently some Roman Christians felt bound to observe various laws for the Sabbath. Paul gives us no hint of what specifically these were. Indeed, he brings this issue up very briefly only at this point and never returns to it in the rest of 14:1–15:7. Given the brevity with which he treats it, it is difficult to imagine he saw it as a major problem. Such observance, whatever it may have been, must not have significantly disrupted the unity of the Roman Christian community. In addition, he seems to offer nothing explicit about how to deal with the issue other than a brief exhortation in 14:6a that each one's observance should be based on real conviction and that the day should be observed "for the Lord." This suggests that the Sabbath observances Paul has in mind are probably things such as the Sabbath rest or lighting Sabbath candles rather than, for example, continued participation in Sabbath services at Roman Jewish synagogues. The former observances, though perhaps puzzling to other Roman Christians, would not have caused any real disruption in the community. The latter, however, would have raised the issue of divided loyalties and almost certainly would have been a major cause of tension and division in the Roman Christian community.[59]

The really divisive issue in the Roman Christian community is the issue of Jewish dietary laws. Some members of the community confidently eat anything while others eat vegetables (14:2). Paul argues that if members of the community are harmed because of the food other members eat, then the latter are no longer acting in keeping with love (14:15). He urges them not to let what they eat bring ruin on one for whom Christ died (14:15) or to destroy the work of God (14:20). The kingdom of God is not a matter of food and drink (14:17). It is good not to eat meat or to drink wine or to do anything that makes a member of the community stumble, for the one who doubts is condemned if he eats (14:21–22). The primary object of these scruples is the issue of eating meat. A secondary object is the issue of drinking wine (14:17, 21). Paul brings this up, however, rather late in this section. Some scholars think he may have mentioned it for purposes of rhetorical completeness rather than because it was an actual issue for some Roman Christians.[60] The parallels

---

[58] See Fitzmyer, *Romans*, 690; and Dunn, *Romans*, 803–6.

[59] This disagrees with Barclay, "'Do We Undermine the Law?'" 296–99, 303–8. Barclay thinks that some Roman Christians "may have been anxious to maintain their place in the Jewish community even if they met opposition in that context" (p. 299). This would have led them to continue to participate in the life of some of the Jewish synagogues of Rome. There are two problems with this approach. First, as mentioned above, it would have created divided loyalties and been a major source of division in the Roman Christian community. Second, there is no evidence in the rest of Romans for any connection between the Roman Christian community and the Roman Jewish community. In fact, the disturbances in 49 mentioned by Suetonius, which led to Tiberius expelling some Jews and Christians from Rome, suggests the opposite.

[60] This is the opinion of Byrne, *Romans*, 422; and Cranfield, *Romans*, 2:725.

cited below, however, suggest that this too may have been a real, if secondary, issue for some Roman Christians.

The divisions in the Roman Christian community concern religious scruples about consuming certain foods—specifically, eating meat and drinking wine. It is also clear that these scruples are rooted in judgments about what is clean (καθαρά) versus what is unclean (κοινόν) (14:14, 20).[61] This contrast between clean and unclean means that their scruples are connected with the observance of the Jewish dietary laws. In this respect, their religious scruples differ from those of some Corinthian Christians who also were concerned with eating meat (1 Corinthians 8–10). In the latter case, Paul did not use the categories of clean and unclean in dealing with the issue. The reason was that the Corinthians' scruples were not about the observance of Jewish dietary laws but about the propriety of eating meat that had previously been offered to the gods in the city's temples.[62] When Paul uses the contrasting terms "clean" and "unclean" in 14:14, 20, however, he must be referring to scruples rooted in the interpretation and observance of the Jewish dietary laws.

What is at first puzzling about the scruples of the Roman Christians is that the Mosaic law does not prohibit either eating meat or drinking wine, nor does it call for vegetarianism. Obviously, the Mosaic law prohibited eating pork. Since this was one of the more popular meats in Rome, Jewish abstinence from pork was widely noticed and ridiculed by the Romans.[63] There is also evidence, however, that some Jews, especially some Jews living in the Diaspora, did refrain from eating meat and drinking wine in some situations. These situations were primarily those in which Jews were worried about the status of food prepared by Gentiles (e.g., Jdt 10:5; 12:1–2; Add Esth 14:17; see 2 Macc 5:27).[64] The closest parallel is Dan 1:8–16, in which Daniel and his companions persuade their Gentile jailer to allow them to eat only vegetables and to drink only water rather than defile themselves by eating what the king has ordered put before them. The parallel closest in time and place, however, comes from Josephus. In *Life* 13–16, Josephus describes a trip he made to Rome in A.D. 61 as a young man to obtain the release of some imprisoned Jewish priests whom Felix, the procurator of Judaea, had sent to Rome on trumped-up charges. Josephus was edified by the fact that "even in affliction, they had not forgotten the pious practice of religion and nourished themselves on figs and nuts" (*Life* 14) rather than on other food their jailers provided to them.

The basis for such scruples is not difficult to find. Both meat and wine were subject to special regulations in Jewish law. Animals had to be slaughtered and pre-

---

[61] The word κοινόν, which literally means "common," is here translated "unclean." Greek-speaking Jews used it as a technical term for what was ritually unclean (1 Macc 1:47, 62; Mark 7:2, 5; Acts 10:14, 28; 11:8; cf. Josephus, *Ant.* 11.346).

[62] The parallels between 14:1–15:7 and 1 Corinthians 8–10 will be considered in more detail on pp. 412–14.

[63] Macrobius, *Sat.* 2.4.1; Philo, *Legat.* 361; Petronius, frg. 37 (*GLAJJ* 1:195); Juvenal, *Sat.* 6.160; 14.98–99; Tacitus, *Hist.* 5.4.2.

[64] This should be distinguished from refraining from certain foods and alcoholic drink for ascetic reasons, such as Philo describes in *Contempl.* 37 about the Therapeutae (a diet of bread and water) or that Eusebius (quoting Hegesippus) describes in *Hist. eccl.* 2.23.5 about the practice of James the Just (drinking no wine or strong drink and eating no meat). There is no hint of ascetic motivation in Rom 14:1–15:7.

pared in specific ways, and wine was subject to issues of uncleanness when passing through the hands of Gentiles.[65] Obtaining products that were ritually clean would have been more difficult in the Diaspora than in Palestine itself. But over time, settled Jewish communities must have established regular means of doing so. In the examples given above, however, the real problem was not that Jews could not obtain such products through established channels but that Gentiles were serving these products to them. The examples from Daniel and Josephus are about Jews who were in prison and were being served food by Gentile authorities. To avoid eating food that was almost certainly ritually unclean, they confined their diet to vegetables and water in one case and to figs and nuts in the other. These were products for which ritual cleanness would not have been an issue.

These examples also provide clues about the context of the divisions in the Roman Christian community. The issue Paul is dealing with was probably not about what different Roman Christians ate or drank in their own flats or houses. That would have been a private matter and not something that would have divided the community. Rather, the issue was about what they ate or drank when they were together. It was an issue of commensality.[66] When Roman Christian communities came together for meals and to celebrate the Eucharist, the situation in the minds of some, the "weak," was analogous to the situation of ritually unclean food and drink being served by Gentiles. Some, the weak, thought that what was provided at these community functions should be ritually clean. Others, the "strong," thought this was unnecessary, probably because for them "nothing is unclean" (14:14) and "all is clean" (14:20). From the way he writes to them, however, Paul seems to be assuming that the two groups are still coming together on a regular basis. The weak have not withdrawn from these gatherings.[67] Rather, they feel obliged to refrain from eating the meat and drinking the wine served at them. These divisions, however, still threaten the unity of the community, threaten to turn these gatherings into occasions of ever greater discord or even make them impossible.

The next question concerns the makeup of these divisions. What are the different sides of the argument? Who are the weak, and who are the strong? Given the arguments so far in this study, the divisions are not simply between Jewish Christians and Gentile Christians. Rather, the division over the observance of the Jewish dietary laws at gatherings of the community cut across the distinction between Jewish Christians and Gentile Christians. Both are on both sides of the argument. Paul himself provides evidence for this. The terms Paul uses to characterize the two

---

[65] For the proper preparation of meat, especially the draining of all blood from the meat, see Lev 3:17; 7:26–27; 17:10–14; cf. Acts 15:20, 29. For issues connected with wine, see *m. ʿAbod. Zar.* 2:3–4; 4:10–5:12; *t. ʿAbod. Zar.* 7:1–17; *y. ʿAbod. Zar.* 4:8–5:15, 44a–45b; *b. ʿAbod. Zar.* 55a–76b. The references to rabbinic literature are obviously later, but they probably give a fair sense of the issues concerning the status of wine that was in any way connected with Gentiles.

[66] Barclay, " 'Do We Undermine the Law?' " 291, emphasizes this point.

[67] Paul's opening exhortation in 14:1 strengthens this view. The Roman Christians should accept the one weak in conviction and "not for disputes over opinions." The situation imagined by Paul seems to be one in which the two groups are still gathering together but the strong are disputing with the weak over observance of Jewish food regulations. Paul is exhorting them to stop such disputes.

groups are the "weak" and the "strong." He never gives any hint that the divisions run along ethnic lines, that is, Jews versus Gentiles. Since the issue of the relationship between Jews and Gentiles is central to the whole letter, its absence in this section of the letter is significant. The division between the strong and the weak must be something other than that between Jewish Christians and Gentile Christians.

The first two chapters of this study offered what seems the most plausible explanation for the origins, organization, and makeup of the Roman Christian community. In the late 30s or early 40s of the first century, Jewish believers in Jesus from Jerusalem or Palestine came to Rome. There they won over to belief in Jesus as the Christ some Roman Jews and some sympathetic Gentiles associated with the Jewish community. This took place still within the Roman Jewish community. By the end of the 40s, however, serious conflict developed within the Jewish community over belief in Jesus and led to the expulsion of both Jewish and Gentile believers in Jesus from the Jewish community. From that point on, the Roman Christian community was separate from the Roman Jewish community. By the time of Paul's letter, the majority of Roman Christians were probably ethnically Gentile, although many of the Gentiles Christians had been originally associated with Jewish synagogues.

There was, however, a continuity of beliefs and practices between the majority of Roman Christians, whether ethnically Jewish or Gentile, and the beliefs and practices of the Roman Jewish community from which they had been expelled. This continuity was rooted first of all in Jewish monotheism. In addition, it included an emphasis on the superiority of the Mosaic law, especially its ethical aspects, over what they saw as the degrading ethical practices of the Greco-Roman world. This would have been true of the majority of the Roman Christian community. For a minority of the community, however, the continuity also included observance of the Sabbath (and perhaps other festivals) and especially observance of some of the dietary laws. They would have made up a second group within the community. A third group, consisting of Priscilla and Aquila and the other Roman Christians associated with Paul, was probably the smallest of the three. All three groups would have included both Jewish Christians and Gentile Christians. In the controversy over what kinds of food and drink should be served at the community gatherings, the first and the third groups would have been on one side of the argument, and the second group would have been on the other. The majority of Roman Christians, then, whether ethnically Jewish or Gentile, would not have been concerned about the ritual purity of the food and drink served at these gatherings.

The delineation of these groups in the Roman Christian community also clarifies two other aspects of the conflict. The first is the origin of the designation of the two groups as the "strong" and the "weak." At the beginning of the section, Paul exhorts the Roman Christians to accept "the person weak in conviction" (τὸν δὲ ἀσθενοῦντα τῇ πίστει, 14:1) and in the next verse refers to "the weak person" (ὁ δὲ ἀσθενῶν, 14:2) who eats only vegetables at community gatherings. It seems rather odd for Paul to begin an exhortation to accept this group by characterizing its members negatively as "weak" or "weak in conviction."[68] It makes more sense if Paul

---

[68] The word πίστις must be translated here "conviction" or "confidence" rather than "faith" or "trust." This is in keeping with Paul's use of the Greek verb πιστεύω in 14:2, where it

is using a term here that one group has already been using to characterize and show contempt for the other group.[69] This is strengthened by Paul's exhortation in 14:2, which he repeats in 14:10 as rhetorical questions. Whereas Paul exhorts the one who does not eat not to judge or condemn the one who does, he exhorts the one who eats not to despise (μὴ ἐξουθενείτω, 14:2) the one who does not. The latter gives credence to the notion that "weak" was a term of opprobrium used first by those who had no scruples about eating to show contempt for those who did. Paul's designation of the other group as the "strong," however, probably worked a bit differently. He uses this term only toward the end of the exhortation, in 15:1: "We who are strong [οἱ δυνατοί] ought to support the weaknesses [τὰ ἀσθενήματα] of the powerless [τῶν ἀδυνάτων] and not please ourselves." Paul intentionally associates himself with the strong, but he does so with a sense of irony, almost sarcasm. If we are truly strong or powerful, then we ought to be able to support or bear the weaknesses of the powerless and weak. This suggests that the term was not one that the strong used to refer to themselves but one Paul chose to use in referring to them. He used it ironically, almost sarcastically, to get them to see things in a different and more responsive light.

The second aspect of the conflict concerns the power relationship between the two groups. The two terms "strong" and "weak" seem to describe not simply degrees of convictions but also the relative power or standing of the two groups in the community. At the very beginning of the exhortation, in 14:1, Paul calls upon Roman Christians to receive or accept (προσλαμβάνεσθε) the one weak in conviction and not for the purpose of disputes over opinions (μὴ εἰς διακρίσεις διαλογισμῶν). The words Paul uses, that the strong should accept or receive the weak, indicate that the strong are the ones in control. In addition, Paul exhorts them not to do this for the purpose of carrying on more disputes over the issue. His point seems to be that the strong should not continue to try to browbeat the weak into submission. Again, toward the end of the exhortation, in 15:1, Paul contrasts the groups by using the two Greek words δυνατοί and ἀδύνατος. These two words mean not only strong versus weak in terms of capacity or power. They also are used to contrast people of importance or social standing versus those of no importance or social standing.[70]

---

must mean "to be confident that" or "to believe that" one can eat anything. The weak person here is not fundamentally lacking in faith but is not confident or convinced that he or she should not be concerned about observing the food regulations of the Mosaic law. See Fitzmyer, *Romans*, 688–89. The word has the same meaning in 14:22–24.

[69] Paul also used words for "weak" in 1 Cor 8:7–13 to describe the Corinthian Christians who worried about the propriety of eating meat that may have been first offered to idols: ἀσθενής (8:7, 9, 10) and ἀσθενῶν (8:11, 12). Other Corinthian Christians who were convinced they had every right (ἐξουσία) to eat anything may have first used these words to show contempt for those who had such worries, and Paul then may have made use of them for his own purposes. Certainly the Corinthian Christians who had no worries about what they ate had first used the word "right" to justify their actions (8:9; cf. 9:3, 5, 6, 12, 18).

[70] See LSJ and BDAG, s.v. δυνατός, ἀδύνατος. Reasoner, *Strong and the Weak*, also emphasizes this aspect of the relationship between these two groups. But he also exaggerates the importance of the contrast and subsumes too many elements into the contrasts he draws between the strong and the weak. E.g., the evidence Reasoner (pp. 102–38) presents that the abstinence of the weak was connected with some sort of eclectic asceticism is not convincing.

Once again this suggests that those who are convinced that they can eat everything, the strong, are also those who have the upper hand and are in control in the community. They probably include most of those who have any social standing or wealth in the community.

With this social geography in mind, we can now turn in a more systematic way to how Paul deals with the conflict. He begins his exhortation in 14:1 with a programmatic statement, that the Roman Christians should receive (προσλαμ-βάνεσθε) the person weak in conviction, but not for quarrels about opinions.[71] He also ends the exhortation in 15:7 with a similar thought, that they should receive (προσλαμβάνεσθε) one another. The first section of the exhortation is 14:1–12. The major theme of this section is the need for the two groups to respect one another. He expresses this by a series of parallel formulations:

> One is confident he can eat anything,
> but the weak man eats vegetables.
> Let the one who eats not despise the one who doesn't eat,
> but let the who doesn't eat not judge the one who eats. (14:2–3)

> One esteems one day as better than another,
> while another esteems all days alike.
> Let each one be fully convinced in his own mind. (14:5)

> Also the one who eats does so for the Lord—indeed he gives thanks to God,
> and the one who does not eat does so for the Lord, and he gives thanks to God. (14:6)

> Who are you to judge your brother?
> Or you, who are you to despise your brother? (14:10)

Paul emphasizes through the use of these parallel sentences that because the two groups are similarly situated, they should show respect for each other. He urges the strong not to despise the weak and the weak not to pass judgment on the strong. After all, both groups do what they do for the Lord and, indeed, give thanks to God. Between these parallel formulations, Paul offers a series of reasons, introduced by γάρ ("for"), for acting this way. God has received both him who eats and him who does not (14:3). God is able to make stand both him who eats and him who does not (14:4). In 14:7–9 and 14:10–12, Paul presents two slightly more elaborate reasons for showing this mutual respect. In 14:7–9, he argues that none of us lives or dies for himself or herself. Rather, all of us belong to the Lord, for Christ died and rose in order that he might be Lord of all, both the living and the dead. Supported by a quotation from Isa 49:18; 45:23 (LXX), Paul argues in Rom 14:10–12 that they should neither despise nor pass judgment on one another because all will stand before the judgment seat of God and each will have to render an account of himself or herself. In giving both of these more elaborate reasons, Paul is appealing to central beliefs that both groups share in common and that should ground their respect for one other.

Up until this point in the exhortation, Paul is writing nothing that would be controversial. Both groups would understand and accept, perhaps grudgingly, that

---

[71] As becomes clear in 14:1–15:7, the burden for avoiding such quarrels lies with the strong.

what Paul is writing to them is true. On the basis of their shared beliefs, they owe each other respect. But although mutual respect has to ground any solution to their divisions, it is not in itself a solution. Granted a mutual respect, how are they to conduct themselves when the community comes together? More specifically, what foods can be served and what not? It takes more than mutual respect to solve the issue.

On the basis of this mutual respect, Paul turns in 14:13–23 to offer a more specific solution. He begins by urging that believers should no longer judge one another and then goes on to argue that believers should not place stumbling blocks in the way of other believers. More specifically, if serving food and drink that some believers think is unclean becomes such a stumbling block, then such food and drink should not be served at community gatherings. The good of these believers is more important than maintaining the admittedly correct principle that "nothing is unclean" and "everything is clean." The passage itself is in the form of a ring construction:

A. Judging properly (13ab)

  B. Not placing a stumbling block or hindrance for a brother (13c)

    C. Nothing is unclean except for one who thinks it is (14)

      D. Do not let a brother be injured by what you eat (15)

        E. Explanation of the characteristics of the kingdom of God (16–19)

      D'. Do not destroy a work of God because of food (20a)

    C'. Everything is clean, but eating becomes evil for one who eats as a result of being made to stumble (20bc)

  B'. Responsibility not to eat or drink or do anything that makes a brother stumble (21)

A'. Judging with confidence versus judging with doubts (22–23)[72]

There is a logic to the way Paul rhetorically develops his argument. He begins with two basic principles: (1) one ought not to create difficulties for other believers (14:13c), and (2) nothing is unclean of itself except for the person who thinks it is unclean (14:14). He then applies these principles. If a fellow believer is injured because of what you eat (principle 2), you are not acting in keeping with love (principle 1). Therefore, do not let what you eat destroy one for whom Christ died (14:15). In 14:16–19, Paul roots the logic of his argument in an enumeration of central characteristics of the kingdom of God. The kingdom of God does not consist of food and drink. Rather, it consists of righteousness, peace, and joy in the Holy Spirit. Therefore, we ought to pursue what leads to peace and to building one another up. These are the values that should serve as criteria for how believers should act. On this basis, Paul then reverses the order of his original argument in 14:20–23. One must not destroy a work of God because of what one eats (14:20a). Everything is clean, but it becomes evil for one who has been made to stumble (14:20bc) (principle 2). Therefore, it is good not to eat meat or drink wine or do anything that makes a fellow believer stumble (14:21) (principle 1). The strong should keep the conviction they have that

---

[72] This structure is basically that suggested by Dunn, *Romans*, 816.

all things are clean between themselves and God. But they should not impose it on other, weaker members of the community. Happy is the person of conviction who does not condemn himself by what he eats, for the one who has doubts about eating is condemned because he doesn't eat on the basis of conviction (14:22–23).[73]

In making this argument, Paul has implicitly identified himself with those who think that "nothing is unclean in itself" (14:14) and that "everything is clean" (14:20). At the beginning of the final section of the exhortation (15:1–7), he makes this identification explicit: "We the strong ought to bear the weaknesses of the powerless and not please ourselves." In using the first person plural, he places the burden of supporting the weak not only on the strong's shoulders but also on his own. He continues to use the first person plural in the following verses (15:2–4) as he invokes the example of Christ and quotes from the Scriptures. Each of us should seek to please his neighbor for the neighbor's good, for the neighbor's edification. This is as Christ did. He then quotes Ps 68:10 (LXX): "The reproaches of those who reproached you fell on me." These words, he claims, were written for our instruction.[74] He then concludes the whole exhortation with a prayer that God will grant them to live in harmony so as to praise God together (15:5–6), and a final exhortation for them to accept (προσλαμβάνεσθε) one another as Christ has accepted (προσελάβετο) them (15:7). Once again he draws a parallel between Christ's conduct and their own. This final exhortation both takes his hearers back to the opening words in 14:1 about accepting (προσλαμβάνεσθε) the "weak" and leads into his concluding summary in 15:8–13 of all of 1:16–15:7.

Like much of what Paul wrote in 12:1–13:14, this section is also heavily influenced by what he wrote earlier in 1 Corinthians. In the case of Rom 14:1–15:7, there are numerous parallels with 1 Corinthians 8–10. First, like the Roman Christians, the Corinthian Christians were divided over the propriety of eating certain foods. Some of them were convinced they had the right to eat anything they wanted to, even meat previously offered to idols. Others' consciences, however, were offended by this practice. The latter, who were until recently accustomed to worshiping idols, risked thinking that they were somehow still eating food offered to these Greco-Roman gods. In this way, their weak consciences would be defiled (1 Cor 8:7–13). Second, the terminology Paul uses in 1 Corinthians 8–10 is often similar to what he uses in Rom 14:1–15:7: (1) words connected with "weakness" in Rom 14:1, 2; 15:1 and 1 Cor 8:7, 9, 10, 11, 12; (2) the necessity of not putting a hindrance in the way of fellow believers in Rom 14:13, 20, 21 and 1 Cor 8:9, 13; 10:32; (3) the use of the verb "to please" (ἀρέσκω) in Rom 15:1, 2 and 1 Cor 10:33; and (4) the

---

[73] It is impossible to translate into English the wordplay in 14:22–23 on κρίνω ("judge," "condemn"), διακρίνω ("doubt," "waver"), and κατακρίνω ("condemn"). Given the context of these two verses, it is also best to translate πίστις as "conviction." This translation clarifies the meaning of the last part of 14:23: whatever does not proceed from conviction (ἐκ πίστεως) is sin. Paul is making a point about the state of the believer's conscience. He is not making a broader theological claim that every act not based on faith is sinful. We should be careful not to turn a maxim into a principle. One certainly has to keep in mind the resonances of "faith" and "trust" the word inevitably has in Paul, but one cannot treat the word as if it did not have a range of meanings on which Paul played.

[74] See Rom 4:23–25; 1 Cor 9:9–10; 10:11.

references to edification in Rom 14:19; 15:2 and 1 Cor 8:1; 10:23.[75] Finally, the structure of Paul's solution to the issue in 1 Corinthians 8–10 is similar in significant ways to what he uses in Rom 14:1–15:7. Paul identified his own convictions on the issue of eating meat previously offered to idols basically with those who thought that eating such meat should not be a problem (1 Cor 8:6).[76] This is similar to his identification with the strong in Rom 14:1–15:7, who thought that everything is clean (Rom 14:14, 20). He also insisted on the necessity of respecting fellow believers' consciences (1 Cor 8:9–12). In Rom 14:1–15:7, he insists on respecting fellow believers' convictions about the observance of certain Jewish dietary laws. Finally, he insisted on the obligation to refrain from exercising what would otherwise be a right (1 Cor 8:13; 9:12; 10:33) if the exercise of that right would harm the faith of fellow believers. In both cases, this meant not eating certain kinds of foods because of the offense it would cause to fellow believers.

The differences between the two passages, however, are as important as the similarities. There are two significant differences. The first concerns the nature of the disputes themselves. The division in the Roman Christian community is over observance of Jewish dietary laws at community gatherings. It is an issue of commensality. The division in the Corinthian Christian community, however, was not over observance of Jewish dietary laws, nor did it concern conduct at community gatherings. The division at Corinth was over the propriety of eating meat from the marketplace, at a banquet in a pagan temple, or at a banquet at a non-Christians' home. None of these instances involved community gatherings or commensality. Nor was the dispute about the observance of Jewish dietary laws. Paul never mentioned the distinction between clean and unclean in 1 Corinthians 8–10. Rather, the dispute was directly over the consumption of meat that may have previously been offered to idols (εἰδωλόθοτα). The question of Jewish dietary laws simply did not enter into the picture.

The second difference concerns Paul's relationship to each of the two communities. Paul saw himself as the founder of the Corinthian Christian community. As a result, he thought he was in a position of some authority in the community, and he expected that the Corinthian Christians would take seriously what he wrote.[77] Paul is in no such position, however, in relation to the Roman Christian community. He did not found it, nor is he in any position of authority over it. As seen in this study, large segments of the Roman Christian community in fact are deeply suspicious of some of his central convictions. His relationship to these two communities, then, is

---

[75] A more detailed list of these parallels is found in Cranfield, *Romans*, 2:691–92.

[76] I say "basically" because in 1 Corinthians 8–10 Paul addresses three different situations. The first is that of Christians eating meat as part of a banquet in a temple (8:10). This Paul rejects as wrong, although he gives different reasons for this in 8:11–13 and 10:14–22. The second is that of eating meat purchased at the market. Paul thinks this can be done without any problems of conscience (10:25–26). The final situation concerns Christians invited to a banquet at a non-Christian's home. They should eat what is served to them except when a fellow Christian shows concern that the meat being served may have been previously offered to idols. In this case, the Christian should refrain from eating the meat, not, however, because it may have been offered to idols but because of the weakness of the other Christian's conscience (10:27–30).

[77] See esp. 1 Cor 5:1–8; 7:25; 9:1–27.

414 PAUL'S RHETORIC IN ITS CONTEXTS

fundamentally different. From a rhetorical perspective, Paul had an *ēthos* or an antecedent credibility with the Corinthian Christians that he does not have with the Roman Christians.

These two differences are valuable for understanding what Paul intends in Rom 14:1–15:7 and what seems, at first glance, to be counterintuitive. In both 1 Corinthians and Romans, Paul takes the side of one group, the weaker group, although his substantive position in each case agrees with the other, stronger group. He does this because of his concern for the integrity of the consciences and religious sensitivities of the weaker group. In both cases, he also takes a risk by urging the stronger party to cede the exercise of a right or a conviction because of the sensitivities of the weaker party. But the risk he takes is far greater in the case of the Roman Christian community. He already had credibility and a good measure of authority with the Corinthian Christians. In 1 Corinthians, he could even use his own behavior as an example of how he was urging the Corinthian Christians to behave (1 Corinthians 9). But he has no such credibility with the Roman Christians. Quite the opposite is the case. The risk Paul is willing to take with the Roman Christians is a measure of his commitment to an articulated harmony within the Christian community, a harmony that acknowledges the obligation to take into consideration the moral sensitivities of weaker members of the community.

The seriousness of Paul's commitment in this regard emerges especially when one recalls that the issue at stake is the obligation that some members of the Roman Christian community feel to observe the Jewish dietary laws and the problem of commensality it creates. One of the most important of Paul's earlier controversies was with Peter at Antioch over the observance of just such Jewish dietary laws at Christian community gatherings (Gal 2:11–14). When Peter came to Antioch in the autumn of 48, he at first ate with the largely Gentile Christian community there without any concern for observing the Jewish dietary laws. But when some Jewish Christians connected with James came to Antioch from Jerusalem, Peter and the other Jewish Christians, including Barnabas, withdrew from commensality with the rest of the community over observance of the Jewish dietary laws. At this point, Paul rebuked Peter publicly. He accused him of being a hypocrite for refusing to eat with the rest of the community only after the arrival of the Jewish Christians from around James and for trying, in effect, to force the Gentile Christians of Antioch to observe the Jewish dietary laws as the price for maintaining commensality. Certainly Paul thought that something crucial was at stake in his dispute with Peter at Antioch, that is, the agreement that had been reached earlier in Jerusalem between himself and the largely Gentile Christian community of Antioch, on the one hand, and the Jewish Christian leaders of Jerusalem, on the other (Gal 2:1–10).[78] Paul now saw this agreement unraveling before his very eyes.

Paul does not think that this is at stake in the case of the dispute in the Roman Christian community. Were it the case, he certainly would react differently, especially since his viewpoint did not prevail in the dispute with Peter at Antioch.[79] Yet it is still remarkable, given the significance of his earlier controversy with Peter,

---

[78] See above, pp. 59–61.
[79] See above, pp. 61–62.

that he reacts as he does in this controversy between these two groups of Roman Christians. He urges the stronger group to accommodate the religious sensitivities of the weaker group over observance of these Jewish dietary laws at community gatherings. It is the starkest example in all of Rom 12:1–15:7 of how important a value the articulated unity and harmony of the Christian community has become for Paul. He is even willing to risk alienating the goodwill and support of the larger part of the Roman Christian community, which he so desperately wants, in order to preserve the religious sensitivities of a minority of the Roman Christian community with whose views he disagrees.

CONCLUSIONS

At the end of his exhortation, what does Paul hope the Roman Christians will be persuaded of? Certainly he hopes he has persuaded them that, as believers, their minds should be transformed so that they can discern what the will of God is for them. He also hopes they will be persuaded that harmony, unity, love, and proper order are central values for themselves and their community. Together they form one body in Christ. Because of this, they should be in harmony with one another and at peace, as far as possible, with the outside world. On the basis of these values, they should also accommodate themselves to the sensitivities and scruples of the weak among them. They are to place the common good above their individual goods to such an extent that they will even be willing to refrain from exercising a legitimate right when the exercise of that right would do damage to a minority in their midst. If they do all these things, they will do no harm to their neighbor. Indeed, they will be loving their neighbor as themselves. Such a love, in reality, fulfills the Mosaic law even though it does not entail observing it. Their lives as believers are rooted in their baptism into the death of Christ and in their freedom from sin and slavery to God in righteousness rather than in their observance of the law.

Surely the Roman Christians would have readily agreed with much of what Paul is exhorting them to. Paul is reminding them of much they already know and believe in. Exhortations are often of this sort. But what of the things that Paul does have to persuade them of? Even here what is different and controversial he tries to root in beliefs and convictions they all share. Paul certainly continues to argue that believers are no longer obligated to observe the law. But the alternative way of living to which he urges them is carefully rooted by him in proverbs and maxims of the Jewish wisdom tradition and in the baptism that they share and that formed them into one body in Christ. The same is true of Paul's exhortation for the strong to accommodate themselves to the sensitivities of the weak. All believers belong to Christ. One therefore should not, because of food, cause the ruin of one for whom Christ died. In both cases, Paul hopes they will be persuaded that what seems different or controversial is in reality embedded in what they have in common and is the logical consequence of it.

But there is another way of posing the question, and it is equally important. At the end of his exhortation, what does Paul hope the Roman Christians will think of him? He certainly presents himself as someone who is an advocate of peace and, as far as possible, accommodation and not the cause of dissension and disunity. This is obviously the case for the way in which he urges the strong to accommodate themselves to the scruples of the weak. But it is also true of the exhortation as a whole. Paul presents himself as someone for whom love, harmony, unity, and proper order are central values. Their misgivings about him as a cause of disunity and disruption are misplaced.

But what of Paul himself? In what ways does this exhortation represent changes in his own views? Perhaps the most important change is that Paul seems much more aware of the importance of harmony and proper order within the community and of the disruptive potential of some of the points he previously emphasized. This is especially the case for his previous emphasis on the role of the Spirit as an ethical guide. He emphasized this role of the Spirit in Galatians. But he came to see in the problems of the Corinthian community how this emphasis could go very much awry. As a result, in Rom 12:1–15:7, he directly emphasizes the values of love and their resultant harmony, unity, and proper order and is very reticent even to mention the Spirit. A second change is that Paul seems more willing to accommodate himself to the sensitivities and even scruples of those believers with whom he disagrees. He learned the importance of this in dealing with the issue of eating meat offered to idols at Corinth and now applies it to the analogous issue of observing Jewish dietary laws at the community gatherings of the Roman Christian community.

Yet such accommodations are possible for Paul only when they do not touch his bedrock convictions. In his exhortation in Rom 12:1–15:7, Paul still maintains that believers, whether of Jewish or Gentile origin, are no longer obligated to observe the Mosaic law. Their ethical practice is rooted in their baptism and their love for their neighbor and not in observance of the law. What they do in reality fulfills the purpose of the law. But it is an alternative to the law and not simply a alternate way of describing its observance. Paradoxically, this is true even of his exhortation to the Roman Christians to accommodate themselves to the scruples of the weak. His advocacy of harmony and unity through placing the common good above the exercise of an otherwise legitimate right places him in opposition to the conduct of the strong. Accommodation of the strong to the scruples of the weak for the sake of harmony and unity is not an accommodation to the strong. Paul is taking a risk in advocating such an accommodation. But it is a risk he is willing to take for the sake of a deeper and broader unity. He has become convinced of the importance of such a unity through his experience with the Corinthian community. In the end, Paul's exhortation in Rom 12:1–15:7 is of a piece with the rest of his argument in Romans and displays all of the complexity of that larger argument.

Concluding Observations

*T*HIS CHAPTER IS NOT A SUMMARY OF THIS STUDY'S arguments, which by now should be clear enough. Rather, it contains several concluding observations about the character of the arguments and about what they reveal about Paul and what is central to his own arguments. These observations will be suggestive and sketchy rather than systematic and detailed.

Most of the arguments in this study are based on analyses and interpretations of Romans itself, of other letters of Paul, and of various Greco-Roman, Jewish, and early Christian texts. The cogency of these arguments depends on the cogency of these analyses and interpretations. But it is also clear that the arguments are rooted in several more speculative positions. These positions influenced how Romans and, for that matter, many of the other texts have been analyzed and interpreted here. They concern primarily the contexts within which and the purposes for which Paul wrote his letter to the Christian community of Rome.

Broadly speaking, the contexts within which Paul wrote Romans are the situation of the Roman Christian community, Paul's own situation, and the relation between the two. Regarding the Roman Christian community, this study argued that Roman believers in Jesus had originally been part of the Roman Jewish community. The Roman Jewish community also had a number of Gentile sympathizers associate with it. Even after their expulsion from the Roman Jewish community in the late 40s of the first century, these Christian believers (both Jewish and Gentile) continued to see their faith in Jesus as the Christ within the context of Jewish belief and practice and as still part of Judaism. More specifically, this meant they saw their commitment to Jewish monotheism and their continued observance of the ethical commandments of the Mosaic law as a way of living clearly superior to that found among their Greco-Roman neighbors.

Regarding Paul's own situation, the study argued that it was rooted first of all in his own experience of the risen Jesus, which he described, however briefly, in Gal 1:15–17, Phil 3:7–11, and 1 Cor 9:1; 15:8. This experience convinced him that righteousness before God was now through faith in Christ but apart from observance of the Mosaic law. In addition, this righteousness through faith in Christ was intended equally for Jews and Gentiles. But Paul's situation was also deeply influenced especially by his controversy with the Galatian Christians. In addition to their faith in Christ, some of them sought also to be circumcised and to observe the Mosaic law. The bitterness of this controversy led Paul to contrast starkly faith in Christ with observance of the law. Among other things, Paul argued that observance of the law was slavery to the elemental principles of the universe and was no different from the situation of Gentiles who worshiped these same elemental principles. Righteousness was possible only to those who had faith in Christ and lived virtuous lives through the guidance of the Spirit. Jews who continued to be circumcised and to observe the Mosaic law were ultimately excluded from the sonship and inheritance promised to them by God. In fact, righteousness had never really been through circumcision and observance of the law.

Finally, regarding the relation between the two, this study argued that these convictions on Paul's part were known to the Roman Christian community through the mediation of the Christians whom Paul mentioned in Rom 16:3–16. The Roman Christians found the views expressed by Paul in Galatians deeply troubling. These views called into question the value of the Mosaic law and the validity of the promises made by God in the Jewish scriptures. In addition, the Roman Christians saw the Corinthian Christian community's moral confusion, which is reflected in 1 Corinthians, as resulting from Paul's abrogation of observance of the ethical commandments of the law and his emphasis on the role of the Spirit as a guide to moral conduct.

In turn, Paul was aware of their views of him, and this awareness deeply influenced why and how he wrote Romans. At one level, Paul's purpose in writing Romans is clear. He wants to visit Rome on his way to preach the gospel in Spain. He hopes to be received favorably by the Roman Christians and, more important, to be supported by them in his missionary effort in Spain. In itself, however, such a purpose would not have demanded a letter as long and complex as Romans. At another level, then, Paul's purpose in writing Romans is much more complex. He needs to overcome their suspicions, distrust, and even hostility toward him. This requires Paul to rethink and to revise significantly some of his earlier views, especially views expressed in his letter to the Galatian Christians. Paul tries to do this in ways that are both understandable and persuasive to the Roman Christians, especially by appealing to beliefs that he and they have in common. But in doing this, he also wants to maintain what he still regards as his own deepest convictions about the gospel he preaches and to persuade the Roman Christians of the truth of these convictions.

All of these arguments about the interpretation of Romans contain an element of speculation. This is especially the case for the interpretations of the situation of the Roman Christian community, their knowledge of, and reaction to, Paul's controversial views, and Paul's purposes in writing Romans. It seems, however, that such speculation is not only justified but even necessary. Paul's letter to the Roman Christian community was written to a specific community at a specific point in Paul's career as a missionary. Much of the letter is clearly argumentative in tone; Paul is trying to persuade the Roman Christians of something. In addition, at points Romans is clearly a revision and even a reversal of views Paul argued so strenuously in Galatians. In short, there is every reason to think that Romans is an occasional letter. It is not a treatise aimed at providing a systematic account of the gospel Paul preached.

If Romans is an occasional letter, if it arises out of a particular situation and is addressed to a particular situation, then any interpreter must try to understand as best he or she can this situation in as much complexity as possible. Obviously, this is not easy to do, especially when we have only Paul's side of the argument. At the same time, it is not utterly impossible. It demands that the interpreter read between the lines, that the interpreter look at whatever other evidence is available that might throw even an indirect light on the particular situation and its complexity. More broadly, it demands a certain willingness to use one's imagination to offer a plausible reconstruction of the situation against which and within which one can then interpret Romans. In the end, the criterion for judging the success or failure of such an effort must be the extent to which such a reconstruction explains in a plausible way all of the evidence that we do have. The only alternative to such a reconstruction is to read Romans apart from any particular context. This inevitably leads to misconstruing the issues Paul was concerned about and what his purposes were in writing Romans. It also leads to a reading of Romans that is once again caught up in the web of the Reformation debates. This can hardly be a responsible way to interpret Romans.

What does this study reveal about Paul and his arguments? It is clear at a number of points in Romans that Paul's thought has changed when compared with parallel passages in his other letters. For example, in Gal 3:15–18, Paul argued that, in the promises made by God in Genesis to Abraham "and to his seed," the word "seed" referred to Christ. Paul's justification for this interpretation was that the word "seed" is in the singular and not in the plural. This interpretation seemed to exclude the Jews between Abraham and Christ from being the "seed of Abraham." In Rom 4:13–17, however, Paul goes out of his way to interpret the word "seed" not as a singular but as a collective noun. "Seed" includes both Jews and Gentiles, so that Abraham would be called "the father of many nations" (Rom 4:17). Jews are no longer excluded but included.

To take a broader example, in Gal 5:1–6:10, Paul argued that believers are to live their lives guided by the Spirit. This guidance would enable them to practice the appropriate virtues and avoid the contrary vices. Believers have been called to freedom, and they should not submit themselves again to the yoke of slavery. Paul means by this "yoke of slavery" observance of the Mosaic law. The governing ethical values in Gal 5:1–6:10 are freedom and guidance by the Spirit, and Paul starkly contrasts them to the yoke of slavery represented by observance of the Mosaic law. When one turns to Romans 5–7, however, a quite different picture emerges. These chapters, like Gal 5:1–6:10, are primarily concerned with ethical behavior. But Paul's emphases in Romans 5–7 are very different. First of all, the Spirit plays virtually no role in the way Paul describes how believers are to live ethical lives. Second, freedom from the law is no longer a central ethical value. Rather, it is slavery to God. As Paul conceives of how believers are to live ethical lives in Romans 5–7, the issue is not slavery to the law versus the freedom that comes from guidance by the Spirit, as it was it Gal 5:1–6:10, but slavery to sin versus a slavery to God that leads to righteousness. The issue now is not slavery versus freedom but to what or to whom one is a slave: to sin or to God? Although Paul continues to contrast slavery with freedom (Rom 6:15–23), the contrast works in a very different way. He no longer contrasts freedom with the law and its observance. Believers are freed, through baptism, from sin and so have become slaves to righteousness. When they were once slaves of sin, they were free in regard to righteousness. Now that they have been freed from sin, they have become slaves of God.

In both examples, Paul has changed his views in light of objections to them made by the Roman Christians. This is certainly true as far as it goes. But Paul is doing something much more than simply responding to specific objections and changing his views on the basis of them. In the course of Romans, Paul also significantly reconfigures or shifts some of his fundamental categories. In Galatians Paul made most of his arguments through the use of stark and virtually irreconcilable contrasts. Paul's arguments in Gal 3:1–4:31 consistently and unfavorably contrasted the Mosaic law and its observance with faith in Christ (3:1–5, 6–14; 4:12–20), with the promise to Abraham (3:15–18), or with baptism (3:26–4:11). The reception of the Spirit, righteousness, sonship, and inheritance all come through faith and baptism and not through the law or its observance. The logic of most (although not all) of Paul's arguments in Galatians were such that it is nearly impossible to see how the Mosaic law or its observance could ever have been something ordained by God. Much of this is due to the starkly contrasting character of Paul's arguments in Galatians. In Romans, however, the framework of Paul's arguments is very different. Paul puts his arguments in a much more historically oriented framework. This very different framework allows him to maintain his own basic convictions that righteousness is *now* through faith in Christ apart from observance of the law and intended equally for both Jews and Gentiles. But it also allows him to do so without denigrating the past value of the Mosaic law and its observance and without calling into question the ultimate truth and trustworthiness of God's promises in the past to Israel.

Again to take several examples. In Rom 3:21–26, at the beginning of the second stage of his argument, Paul explains how it is that "now [Νυνί] the righteousness of God has been manifested apart from the law" (3:21). Paul sets this *present* manifestation of God's righteousness in the death of Jesus over against the *prior* situation of both Jews and Gentiles as groups, which he described in 1:18–3:20. At the end of the passage, Paul again emphasizes the temporal character of this reality. All that has happened through Christ's death was "to prove that in the present time [ἐν τῷ νῦν καιρῷ] that he himself [God] is righteous and makes righteous him who has faith in Jesus" (3:26).

What is true on a smaller scale of 3:21–26 is also true of larger sections of Romans. In Romans 9–11, Paul deals with the situation of Israel. Although it is the most complex and difficult section of the letter, the basic outline of Paul's argument is clearly temporal. Romans 9:6–29 deals with God's promises to Israel in the past; 9:30–10:21 deals with the present situation of Israel's partial hardening; and 11:1–36 deals with Israel's ultimate inclusion along with the Gentiles in salvation. The same temporal structure is also true at an even larger scale in 1:16–11:36 as a whole. After Paul's statement in 1:16–17 of his basic thesis, 1:18–3:20 deals with the equal sinfulness of both Jews and Gentiles *before* Christ. Though for very different reasons, both Jew and Gentiles have equally fallen short of the glory of God. Romans 3:21–4:25 concerns what has *now* happened in Christ and how this affects

Jews and Gentiles together. Both Jews and Gentiles are now made righteous by God through faith in Christ and apart from observance of the Mosaic law. All of this, Paul maintains, actually upholds rather than annuls the law. In Romans 5–7, Paul then turns to how believers, Jewish and Gentile alike, are now to live their lives because they have died with Christ in baptism. Although they are no longer under the obligation to observe the law, they are nevertheless to live lives in which they are freed from sin and so live to God in righteousness. Finally, in Romans 8–11, Paul turns to the future, to issues of eschatology. Here he argues for the intertwined fate of both Jews and Gentiles, in which the inclusion of the "fullness of the Gentiles" in salvation must ultimately lead also to the inclusion of "all Israel." Paul argues that this intertwined fate is the proper way to understand the meaning of the Jewish scriptures and the promises of God to Israel found in them.

In various sorts of ways, this much more historically oriented framework enables Paul to take seriously the objections raised by the Roman Christians about his views of the law, about ethics, and about his seeming exclusion of Israel from God's promises. But it also points to something more than this. It points to the extent to which Paul not only has revised his positions on particular issues but has also reconfigured the very framework of his thought. He has not simply revised the particular positions he took in Galatians. He has also rejected the starkly contrasting framework in which he put them in Galatians, and he has rethought his positions in a very different, historically oriented framework. This historically oriented framework allows Paul to reinterpret the past in the light of a new, present reality without being forced to reject the value or importance of past realities.

All of the changes Paul made to particular positions as well as the substantial rethinking he did about the framework of his thought might lead one to think that Paul is primarily agreeing in Romans with the criticisms of the Roman Christians and adjusting his positions and his overall framework accordingly. But this is clearly not the case. Although Paul does come to see a number of his previous positions as deeply flawed, his letter to the Roman Christians is something very different from a concession speech. Most of Romans is argumentative. Paul still means to persuade the Roman Christian community of the truth of his basic convictions about the nature of the gospel that he preaches and of which he is not ashamed. Basically these convictions are the same ones that have guided his missionary efforts from the beginning: (1) salvation is now through faith in Christ; (2) it is apart from observance of the Mosaic law; and (3) it is meant for Jews and Gentiles equally. In Romans Paul is trying to persuade the Roman Christians of the truth of these three basic convictions. What distinguishes Romans from Galatians is not the centrality of these three convictions but the framework Paul now places them in and the kinds of arguments he uses to support them. Romans represents Paul's attempt to rethink and reaffirm these convictions on the basis of arguments that take seriously the objections of the Roman Christians, that are based on beliefs they have in common, and that would have been, at least in Paul's mind, persuasive to them.

This mode of argumentation marks all four major steps in Paul's arguments in 1:16–11:36. In 1:18–3:20, Paul argues that both Jews and Gentiles as groups have been equally sinful. This argument is important for Paul because it prepares the ground for his argument in the next section, that righteousness through faith in

Christ is both apart from observance of the law and intended for Jews and Gentiles equally. At the same time, however, his arguments are intended to take seriously the objections of the Roman Christians, that the value of the Mosaic law as something ordained by God is destroyed by his claims in Galatians that no one is made righteous through observance of the law (Gal 2:16) or that observance of the law is submitting to a yoke of slavery (Gal 4:31). And so Paul draws on both Hellenistic Jewish critiques of pagan religiosity and on the scriptural conception of God's impartiality, in which Jews and Gentiles are both to be judged on the basis of their conduct. Both of these conceptions Paul shares with the Roman Christians. The reasons Jews and Gentiles as groups are equally sinful are different: Gentiles, because they have not recognized the one true God, have worshipped idols, and so have fallen into moral depravity; and Jews, because they have not lived up to their claims by observing the Mosaic law. For this reason, the problem is not the law itself but Jews' failure as a group to observe it. In this way, Paul is able to maintain the equal sinfulness of Jews and Gentiles as groups but in a way that meets the Roman Christians' objection that Paul has brought into doubt the value of the law itself.

In Rom 3:21–4:25, Paul then argues that righteousness now comes through faith in Jesus Christ, is apart from observance of the Mosaic law, and is intended for all who have faith, Jews and Gentiles equally. These are Paul's three basic convictions. Paul tries to persuade the Roman Christians of their truth, however, on the basis of early Christian creedal traditions he and the Roman Christians have in common and on the basis of the example, found in the Jewish scriptures, of God's promises to Abraham about becoming the "father of many nations." These promises were made to Abraham in response to his faith and were before and apart from any deeds on Abraham's part. Paul claims that both these creedal traditions and the scriptural example of Abraham support his convictions about the meaning of the gospel and uphold the truth of the law.

In Romans 5–7, Paul turns to issues of ethics. His arguments here are meant to show that he is convinced of the incompatibility of sin and righteousness no less than the Roman Christians are. Paul's arguments in Romans 5–7 are meant to counter the Roman Christians' objections that his views expressed in Galatians, that believers are to live lives pleasing to God by being guided by the Spirit but free of observance of the law, lead to the kind of ethical disintegration found among the Corinthian Christians. As in the previous section, Paul tries to persuade the Roman Christians by appealing to traditions he shares with them. These traditions are about the significance of the death of Christ, the significance of baptism, and the consequences of both for how believers are to live lives pleasing to God. Even though believers are no longer under the law but under grace, they are nevertheless freed from sin by dying with Christ in baptism in order to become slaves to God in righteousness. Paul does all of this, however, without appealing to the law or its observance as a basis for believers' conduct. At the same time, however, Paul goes out of his way in Romans 7 to praise the holiness of the law and its demands. The problem is not with the law itself but with the inability of human beings to observe it.

Finally, in Romans 8–11, Paul turns to issues of eschatology. Here above all, Paul takes seriously the objections of the Roman Christians that in Galatians he excluded Jews from sonship and from the inheritance promised to them by God in the

Scriptures. Paul's arguments in Romans 8–11 are meant to show that "Israel," Jews as a group, will not be excluded from God's promises of sonship and inheritance. Rather, in the end, both "the fullness of the Gentiles" and "all Israel" will be included in God's mysterious plan of salvation. But again Paul makes this argument in a way that reaffirms basic convictions that righteousness is now on the basis of faith in Christ, apart from the observance of the law, and intended for Jews and Gentiles equally. In light of this, Paul interprets Israel's present partial "hardening" as due to its failure to recognize these three central realities. This hardening, however, is both temporary and providential in the sense that through Israel's hardening the gospel has come to the Gentiles. But once the "fullness of the Gentiles" has come in, so too will "all Israel" be included.

Romans, then, represents at the same time both a substantial change in Paul's thought and a basic continuity of his central convictions. In the attempt to understand this very complex reality, it might be helpful to ask one final question: What was it that drove Paul to argue the way he did in Romans? Was there something that lay behind or suffused all of Paul's argument in Romans? Here one needs to turn again to Romans 8–11. These chapters are clearly the most complex and difficult in all of Paul's letters. Reading them, one has the impression of listening in as Paul thinks through, and struggles with, something that has become for him a matter of deep and troubling personal concern. Because of this, Romans 8–11 provides us with clues to understanding much about the letter as a whole.

Romans 8–11 is where Paul himself seems most obviously invested. This is apparent from the number of first-person-singular passages in these chapters (8:38–39; 9:1–5; 10:1–4; 11:1–2, 11–14, 25–27). But this personal involvement is also of a very specific sort. It is the involvement of Paul as a Jew and the anguish he feels over the situation of his fellow Jews. In 9:3, Paul claims that he would wish even to be accursed and cut off from Christ for the sake of his fellow Jews. In 11:13–14, Paul even claims that the purpose of his work as an apostle to the Gentiles is in order to make his fellow Jews jealous and thus save some of them. Put in a different way, Romans 8–11 is the anguished reflection of Paul as a Jew over the fate of Israel. Of the sixteen times Paul uses the word "Israel" in his letters, eleven occur in Romans 9–11.[1] None of the other five appearances of "Israel" outside Romans occurs in an eschatological context. The eschatological fate of Israel, that is, of the Jewish people as a whole, clearly became an issue for Paul only in Romans.

But why did it become an issue for Paul only in Romans? The answer is clear enough: because the Roman Christians were appalled by what Paul wrote in Galatians, where he seemed to exclude Jews from the sonship and inheritance promised to them by God in the Scriptures. Yet in Romans 8–11, it is more than an issue for Paul. It is a matter of personal anguish. In large part, Paul's anguish comes from his realization that the issue of Israel's eschatological fate is largely of his own making. It comes from his realization that the ill-considered logic of some of his arguments in Galatians did indeed exclude the Jewish people as a whole from the sonship and inheritance promised to them by God in the Scriptures.

---

[1] These eleven occurrences are in Rom 9:6 (bis), 27 (bis), 31; 10:19, 21; 11:2, 7, 25, 26. The other five are in 1 Cor 10:18; 2 Cor 3:7, 13; Gal 6:16; Phil 3:5.

At the same time, however, the basic resource that Paul uses in his attempt to rethink significantly the issue of the eschatological fate of the Jewish people as a whole is also of his own making. This is the universalizing eschatology, found especially in 1 Corinthians, in which every rule and every authority would ultimately be subjected to God so that God might be all things to all. It is this universalizing eschatological framework that serves as the basis for Paul's struggle in Romans 8–11 to rethink what he wrote in Galatians in such a way that "all Israel" would ultimately be included along with the "fullness of the Gentiles."

But in Romans 8–11, Paul is concerned with more than the situation and ultimate fate of Israel. He is also concerned with the relationship of these to his own basic convictions about the centrality of faith in Jesus and about a righteousness, apart from observance of the Mosaic law, that is for Jews and Gentiles equally. Paul's struggle in Romans 8–11 is to maintain these convictions and at the same time restore Israel to its place as an object of God's promises. Indeed, much of the density and complexity of Roman 8–11 is due to Paul's insistence on maintaining these basic convictions and reconciling them with the ultimate inclusion of "all Israel" in God's mysterious plan of salvation of Jews and Gentiles alike. Paul does this through a complex reinterpretation of the Jewish scriptures, in which he tries to show how the inclusion of the Gentiles was always part of God's mysterious plan and that this mysterious plan will also lead ultimately to the inclusion of "all Israel." Israel's present partial hardening is due to its failure to recognize that righteousness is now through faith in Christ but apart from observance of the law and is now intended for Jews and Gentiles alike. In this mysterious plan, even Israel's present partial hardening plays another important role. It is what allows the gospel to go to the Gentiles in the first place. But once the "fullness of the Gentiles" comes in, so too will "all Israel" be included.

Finally, the complex struggle reflected in Romans 8–11 is also a perspective that throws light on Paul's arguments earlier in Romans. In a sense, Romans 8–11 is emblematic of Paul's struggle in all of Romans to reconcile and integrate his basic convictions—that righteousness is now through faith in Christ but apart from observance of the law and is intended for both Jews and Gentiles equally—with his own renewed convictions about the trustworthiness of the promises made by God to Israel in the Jewish scriptures. Paul's arguments in Romans consistently reflect his attempt to show how his basic convictions, whether about the equal sinfulness of Jews and Gentiles, or about righteousness through faith in Christ now intended for Jews and Gentiles alike, or about how believers are to live lives pleasing to God apart from observance of the Mosaic law, are all reconcilable with and indeed in continuity with the Jewish scriptures, Jewish tradition, and Jewish hopes.

The extent to which Paul's arguments were successful is another question that goes well beyond the scope of this study, which was meant to produce a much clearer understanding of the complexity of Paul's purposes and arguments in Romans and the contexts within which Paul wrote Romans. The reader, it is hoped, has obtained a better sense of the almost dramatic character of the letter, of the ways in which Paul struggled to rethink in very significant ways the meaning of his own basic religious convictions and the complex and changing relationship of these convictions to his own sense of himself as a believing and committed Jew.

Appendix: Outline of Romans

Address and Greeting (1:1–7)

Thanksgiving (1:8–10)

Paul's Desire to Come to Rome and His Attempt to Gain the Goodwill of the Roman Christians *(Captatio Benevolentiae)* **(1:11–15)**

Proposition (Statement of Thesis) (1:16–17): The gospel is the power of God for salvation to every one who has faith, to the Jew first and also the Greek. For in it the righteousness of God is revealed through faith for faith.

I. The Sinfulness of Both Gentiles and Jews (1:18–3:20): The issue is the equal sinfulness of the two groups, Jews and Gentiles, on the basis of scriptural and traditional Jewish viewpoints.

   A. Subproposition: The wrath of God is being revealed against *all* who sin, for what can be known of God is plain to them (1:18–20)

   B. Exposition of the theme of God's impartial judgment on *all* immorality, especially a description of Gentile idolatry and moral depravity (1:21–32)

   C. Defense and proofs of the controversial position of the equal sinfulness of Jews and Gentiles (2:1–3:18)

      1. Apostrophe to someone who hypocritically condemns immorality and yet acts immorally, which leads to the conclusion of the impartiality of God's judgment (2:1–11)

      2. The impartiality of God and its consequences (2:12–29)

         a. Comparison of the impartial judgment of those under the law and those not under the law (2:12–16)

         b. Apostrophe addressed to a Jew who hypocritically boasts of knowledge of the law and yet does what is condemned by the law (2:17–29)

      3. Objections and replies about the value of being a Jew and God's faithfulness in the face of human unfaithfulness (3:1–18)

D. Conclusion: The whole world (i.e., Jews and Gentiles as groups) is held accountable to God (3:19–20)

II. Righteousness Now apart from the Law but Confirmed by the Law in the Example of Abraham (3:21–4:25): The issue here is that although righteousness through faith for both Jews and Gentiles now takes place apart from observance of the law, it is witnessed to by the law, e.g., in the example and paradigm of Abraham. The law is thus upheld.

A. Subproposition: The righteousness of God revealed through faith in Jesus Christ apart from the law for all who believe, witnessed to by the law and the prophets (3:21–22c)

B. Exposition of the theme through the use of fragments of an accepted creedal formula of redemption through Jesus' death as an atoning sacrifice (3:22d–26)

C. Defense and proof of the controversial position that righteousness for both Jews and Gentiles through faith apart from observance of the law upholds the law rather than nullifies it (3:27–4:25)

1. Rhetorical questions and replies claiming that this position upholds the law (3:27–31)

2. Proof through the use of the example or paradigm of Abraham, which emphasizes the significance of the promise to Abraham for both Jews and Gentiles (4:1–22)

a. Abraham's faith was reckoned to him as righteousness (4:1–8)

b. Abraham's righteousness was prior to his circumcision so that he could be the father of both the circumcised and the uncircumcised (4:9–12)

c. The promise comes through faith and not through the law to all Abraham's "seed," not only to Jews but also to Gentiles; but if it comes through the law, then God's promise is rendered void (4:13–17a)

d. Abraham had faith in God's promise even if it concerned God's giving life to the dead (4:17b–22)

D. Conclusion: Connection with 3:21–31 through the application of the example of Abraham to those who have faith that God raised Jesus from the dead (4:23–25)

III. Salvation through God's Free Gift and Its Relationship to Christian Living, Sin, and the Law (5:1–7:25): The issue is how this viewpoint about righteousness apart from the law and its observance is incompatible with sin.

A. Subproposition: As Christians made righteous by faith, let us have peace with God through this grace in which we now stand, and let us boast even of our afflictions and of the virtues that the love of God poured out into our hearts through the Spirit produces in us (5:1–5)

B. Exposition about the significance of Christ's death and the comparison and contrast of Christ and Adam, free gift and trespass, showing the utter incompatibility between grace and sin (5:6–21)

    1. The significance of Christ's death for believers, building on traditional creedal formulas (5:6–11)

    2. Comparison and contrast of Christ and Adam, bringing out the incompatibility of grace and sin (5:12–21)

        a. Adam's sin (5:12–14)

        b. Comparison and contrast with Christ (5:15–21)

C. Defense and proofs of the controversial aspects of Paul's views on Christian living and the value of the law (6:1–7:25)

    1. Baptism and ethics (6:1–23)

        a. The reinterpretation of baptism (6:1–14)

            (1) Rhetorical questions about continuing in sin (6:1–2)

            (2) Baptism into the death of Christ (6:3–4)

            (3) Dying to sin and living to God in Christ Jesus (6:5–11)

            (4) Let not sin reign but offer yourselves to God (6:12–14)

        b. Freed from sin, we are now slaves to righteousness (6:15– 23)

            (1) Slaves either to sin or to righteousness (6:15–19)

            (2) The consequences (6:20–23)

    2. A defense of the holiness of the law that sits over against the weakness of human beings. This defense also shows what the law cannot do (7:1–23)

        a. Freedom from the law through the death of Christ, compared with marriage law (7:1–6)

        b. Rhetorical question/prosopopoeia: Is the law sin? No, but sin used the law (7:7–12)

        c. Rhetorical question/prosopopoeia: Did the law bring about death? No, the law is good but human beings are weak (7:13–23)

D. Conclusion: Thanks be to God through Jesus Christ that with my mind I now serve the law of God (7:24–25)

IV. Eschatology and the Place of the Jewish People (8:1–11:36): The issue of eschatology and the possible exclusion of the Jews is the one to which Paul has given the most thought, sometimes in great anguish.

A. Exposition of the Christian life and confident hope in its eschatological outcome that does not preclude the inclusion of the Jewish people (8:1– 30)

1. The Spirit and the reinterpretation of its role (8:1–17)

    a. God, in sending Christ in the likeness of sinful flesh, has condemned sin in the flesh, something impossible for the law. So the just requirement of the law is fulfilled in Christians who walk according to the Spirit rather than according to the flesh (8:1–4)

    b. The contrast between flesh and Spirit (8:5–8)

    c. The ultimate results for those in whom the Spirit dwells (8:9–13)

    d. Through the Spirit, believers become sons/children and heirs destined for glory (8:14–17)

2. The framework of an inclusive eschatology (8:18–30)

    a. Creation itself and Christians groan in travail, awaiting the revelation of the sons of God, the resurrection of the body (8:18–22)

    b. The expectations of those who have received the Spirit (8:23–28)

    c. Those called and destined for glory (8:29–30)

B. Anguished defense/reflections on the ultimate incorporation of the Jewish people (8:31–11:36)

1. Transition and introduction (8:31–9:5)

    a. Paul's rhetorical conviction that nothing can separate us from the love of God (8:31–39)

    b. Paul's personal anguish over his fellow Jews (9:1–5)

2. God's promises have not failed: God's choice of Israel and God's extension of it to the Gentiles (9:6–29)

    a. God's promises to Israel have not failed (Abraham, Isaac, Jacob) (9:6–13)

    b. God is not unjust in his choices (Moses and Pharaoh) (9:14–18)

    c. The example of the potter and its application to God's richness to both Jews and Gentiles (9:19–29)

3. The present situation of Jews in relation to the Gentiles (9:30–10:21)

    a. Jews, Gentiles, and Christ as the goal of the law, and scriptural proof of faith being near at hand for both Jews and Gentiles (9:30–10:13)

    b. God's promises and the present responses of Israel and the Gentiles (10:14–21)

4. God's plan and the future final salvation of Israel and the Gentiles (11:1–32)

    a. Israel's present hardening is partial (11:1–10)

b. Israel's disbelief is temporary and providential in that it allows for the entry of the Gentiles, after which Israel will be saved (11:11–24)

c. The mystery of God's plan: Both Israel and the Gentiles will be saved (11:25–32)

5. Concluding praise and doxology of God (11:33–36)

V. Issues of Christian Living: Love, Harmony, Accommodation, and the Greater Good (12:1–15:7)

A. Paul's wisdom instruction on Christian ethics (12:1–21)

1. The basis of Christian living (12:1–2)

2. Descriptive section: The Christian community as one body in Christ (12:3–8)

3. Prescriptive section: The theme of love and social responsibilities (12:9–21)

B. Submission to secular authorities and the payment of taxes (13:1–7)

C. Love of neighbor, the law, and the demands of baptism (13:8–14)

1. Love of neighbor and the fulfillment of the law (13:8–10)

2. The nearness of the end and living orderly lives (13:11–14)

D. Reconciling the weak and the strong (14:1–15:7)

VI. Concluding summary of 1:16–15:7: God's mercy and faithfulness for both Jews and Gentiles (15:8–13)

VII. Paul's Plans, Coming Task, and Request for Prayers (15:14–33)

A. Paul's explanation of his missionary principle of preaching to the Gentiles to whom no one has yet preached (15:14–21)

B. His visit to Rome and Spain and the collection for the poor of Jerusalem (15:22–33)

1. Trip to Rome and Spain (15:22–24)

2. Collection for the poor of Jerusalem (15:25–27)

3. Trip to Rome and Spain (15:28–29)

4. Collection for the poor of Jerusalem and request for prayers that the collection will be acceptable in Jerusalem (15:30–32)

5. Blessing (15:33)

VIII. Letter Conclusion: Letter of Recommendation for Phoebe and Greetings to Roman Christians (16:1–27)

A. Recommendation for Phoebe, a minister of Cenchreae (16:1–2)

B. Paul's greetings to various persons in Rome (16:3–16)

C. Paul's admonition about false teachers; his concluding blessing (16:17–20)

D. Greetings from Paul's companions and the scribe Tertius (16:21–23)

E. Final blessing (16:24)

[F. Concluding doxology (16:25–27)]

For an explanation the complex history of the text of Romans, see Harry Y. Gamble, Jr., *The Textual History of the Letter to the Romans: A Study in Textual and Literary Criticism* (Studies and Documents 42; Grand Rapids: Eerdmans, 1977).

Bibliography

TRANSLATIONS OF ANCIENT AUTHORS

Aristotle. *The "Art" of Rhetoric.* Translated by John Henry Freese. Loeb Classical Library. Cambridge: Harvard University Press, 1967.

Augustine. *The City of God against the Pagans.* Translated by G. E. McCracken, W. M. Green, et al. 7 vols. Loeb Classical Library. Cambridge: Harvard University Press, 1957–72.

Dio Cassius. *Roman History.* Translated by Earnest Cary. 9 vols. Loeb Classical Library. Cambridge: Harvard University Press, 1955–61.

Epictetus. *The Discourses as Reported by Arrian, the Manual, and Fragments.* Translated by W. A. Oldfather. 2 vols. Loeb Classical Library. Cambridge: Harvard University Press, 1925–28.

Epictetus. *Discourses, Book I.* Translated by Robert F. Dobbin. Oxford: Clarendon, 1998.

Euripides. *Euripides.* Translated by A. W. Way. 4 vols. Loeb Classical Library. 1912. Repr., Cambridge: Harvard University Press, 1971.

Galen. *On the Doctrines of Hippocrates and Plato.* Edited and translated by Phillip De Lacy. 3 vols. Corpus Medicorum Graecorum 5.4.1.2. Berlin: Akademie, 1980–1984.

García Martínez, Florentino, ed. *The Dead Sea Scrolls Translated: The Qumran Texts in English.* 2d ed. Leiden: Brill, 1996.

Horace. *Horace.* Translated by C. E. Bennett and H. Rushton Fairclough. 2 vols. Loeb Classical Library. Cambridge: Harvard University Press, 1927–29.

Josephus, Flavius. *Josephus.* Translated by H. St. Thackeray, R. Marcus, A. Wikgren, et al. 10 vols. Loeb Classical Library, Cambridge: Harvard University Press, 1926–65.

Juvenal. *Juvenal and Persius.* Translated by G. G. Ramsay. Loeb Classical Library. Cambridge: Harvard University Press, 1928.

Livy. *Livy.* Translated by B. O. Foster, F. G. Moore, E. T. Sage, et al. 14 vols. Loeb Classical Library. Cambridge: Harvard University Press, 1919–59.

Ovid. *Metamorphoses.* Translated by Frank Justus Miller. 2 vols. Cambridge: Harvard University Press, 1921.

Philo of Alexandria. *Philo*. Translated by F. H. Colson, G. H. Whitaker, and R. Marcus. 10 vols. And 2 supplementary vols. Loeb Classical Library. Cambridge: Harvard University Press, 1922–62.

Plutarch. *Plutarch's Lives*. Translated by Bernadotte Perrin. 11 vols. Loeb Classical Library. Cambridge: Harvard University Press, 1914–26.

Quintilian. *Institutio Oratoria*. Translated by H. E. Butler. 4 vols. Loeb Classical Library. Cambridge: Harvard University Press. 1920–22.

Rhetorica ad Herennium. Translated by Harry Caplan. Loeb Classical Library. Cambridge: Harvard University Press, 1954.

Seneca. *Ad Lucilium Epistulae Morales*. Translated by Richard M. Gummere. 3 vols. Loeb Classical Library. Cambridge: Harvard University Press, 1917–25.

Seneca. *Moral Essays*. Translated by John W. Basore. 3 vols. Loeb Classical Library. Cambridge: Harvard University Press, 1928–35.

Seneca. *Tragedies*. Translated by Frank Justus Miller. 2 vols. Loeb Classical Library. Cambridge: Harvard University Press, 1960–61.

Stern, Menachem. *Greek and Latin Authors on Jews and Judaism*. 3 vols. Jerusalem: Israel Academy of Sciences and Humanities, 1976–1984.

Suetonius. Translated by J. C. Rolfe. 2 vols. Loeb Classical Library. Cambridge: Harvard University Press, 1970.

Tacitus, Cornelius. *The Histories and the Annals*. Translated by Clifford Moore and John Jackson. 4 vols. Loeb Classical Library. Cambridge: Harvard University Press, 1925–37.

COMMENTARIES ON ROMANS

Barrett, C. K. *The Epistle to the Romans*. New York: Harper & Row, 1957.

Bruce, F. F. *The Epistle of Paul to the Romans: An Introduction and Commentary*. 5th ed. Tyndale New Testament Commentaries 6. Grand Rapids: Eerdmans, 1985.

Byrne, Brendan. *Romans*. Sacra pagina 6. Collegeville, Minn.: Liturgical Press, 1996.

Cranfield, C. E. B. *A Critical and Exegetical Commentary on the Epistle to the Romans*. 6th ed. 2 vols. International Critical Commentary. Edinburgh: T&T Clark, 1975–1979.

Dodd, C. H. *The Epistle of Paul to the Romans*. Moffatt New Testament Commentary 6. London: Fontana, 1959.

Dunn, James D. G. *Romans*. 2 vols. Word Biblical Commentaries 38A, 38B. Dallas: Word, 1988.

Fitzmyer, Joseph A. *Romans: A New Translation with Introduction and Commentary*. Anchor Bible 33. New York: Doubleday, 1993.

Käsemann, Ernst. *Commentary on Romans*. Edited and translated by Geoffrey W. Bromiley. Grand Rapids: Eerdmans, 1980.

Knox, John. "The Epistle to the Romans." Pages 353–668 in *Acts, Romans*. Vol. 9 of *The Interpreter's Bible*. 12 vols. New York: Abingdon, 1954.

Moo, Douglas J. *The Epistle to the Romans*. New International Commentary on the New Testament. Grand Rapids: Eerdmans, 1996.

Morris, Leon. *The Epistle to the Romans.* Pillar New Testament Commentary. Grand Rapids: Eerdmans, 1988.

Sanday, William, and Arthur C. Headlam. *A Critical and Exegetical Commentary on the Epistle to the Romans.* 5th ed. International Critical Commentary. Edinburgh: T&T Clark, 1902.

Schlier, Heinrich. *Der Römerbrief: Kommentar.* Herders theologischer Kommentar zum Neuen Testament 6. Freiburg im Breisgau: Herder, 1977.

Schmithals, Walter, *Der Römerbrief: Ein Kommentar.* Gütersloh: Mohn, 1988.

Schreiner, Thomas R. *Romans.* Baker Exegetical Commentary on the New Testament 6. Grand Rapids: Baker, 1998.

Stuhlmacher, Peter. *Paul's Letter to the Romans: A Commentary.* Louisville: Westminster John Knox, 1994.

Wilckens, Ulrich. *Der Brief an die Römer.* 3 vols. Evangelisch-katholischer Kommentar zum Neuen Testament 6. Zurich: Benziger, 1978–1982.

BOOKS AND ARTICLES

Aageson, James W. "Scripture and Structure in the Development of the Argument in Romans 9–11." *Catholic Biblical Quarterly* 48 (1986): 265–89.

Anderson, R. Dean. *Glossary of Greek Rhetorical Terms Connected to Methods of Argumentation, Figures, and Tropes from Anaximenes to Quintilian.* Louvain: Peeters, 2000.

Attridge, Harold W. *The Epistle to the Hebrews.* Hermeneia. Philadelphia: Fortress, 1989.

———. *The Interpretation of Biblical History in the "Antiquitates judaicae" of Flavius Josephus.* Harvard Dissertations in Religion 7. Missoula, Mont.: Scholars Press, 1976.

———. "Josephus and His Works." Pages 185–232 in *Jewish Writings of the Second Temple Period: Apocrypha, Pseudepigrapha, Qumran, Sectarian Writings, Philo, Josephus.* Edited by Michael E. Stern. Compendia rerum iudaicarum ad Novum Testamentum 2.2. Philadelphia: Fortress, 1984.

Aune, David E. "Eschatology (Early Christian)." Pages 594–609 in vol. 2 of *Anchor Bible Dictionary.* Edited by D. N. Freedman. 6 vols. New York: Doubleday, 1992.

———. "Human Nature and Ethics in Hellenistic Philosophical Traditions and Paul: Some Issues and Problems." Pages 291–312 in *Paul in His Hellenistic Context.* Edited by Troels Engberg-Pedersen. Minneapolis: Fortress, 1995.

Badenas, Robert. *Christ the End of the Law: Romans 10.4 in Pauline Perspective.* Journal for the Study of the New Testament: Supplement Series 10. Sheffield, England: JSOT Press, 1985.

Balz, Horst R. *Heilsvertrauen und Welterfahrung: Strukturen der paulinischen Eschatologie nach Römer 8, 18–39.* Beiträge zur evangelischen Theologie 59. Munich: Kaiser, 1971.

Barclay, John M. G. "'Do We Undermine the Law?': A Study of Romans 14.1–15.6." Pages 287–308 in *Paul and the Mosaic Law: The Third Durham-Tübingen Symposium on Earliest Christianity and Judaism.* Edited by James D. G. Dunn. Grand Rapids: Eerdmans, 2001.

———. *Obeying the Truth: A Study of Paul's Ethics in Galatians.* Studies of the New Testament and Its World. Edinburgh: T&T Clark, 1988.

Barrett, Charles K. *From First Adam to Last: A Study in Pauline Theology.* New York: Charles Scribner's Sons, 1962.

———. "Rom 9:30–10:21: Fall and Responsibility in Israel." Pages 99–121 in *Die Israelfrage nach Römer 9–11.* Edited by L. de Lorenzi. Rome: Abbey of St. Paul outside the Walls, 1977.

Bassler, Jouette M. *Divine Impartiality: Paul and a Theological Axiom.* Society of Biblical Literature Dissertation Series 59. Chico, Calif.: Scholars Press, 1982.

Beard, Mary, John North, and Simon Price. *Religions of Rome.* 2 vols. Cambridge: Cambridge University Press, 1998.

Beare, Francis W. *St. Paul and His Letters.* Nashville: Abingdon, 1962.

Betz, Hans Dieter. "Christian Ethics according to Romans 12:1–2." Pages 55–72 in *Witness and Existence: Essays in Honor of Schubert M. Ogden.* Edited by Philip E. Devenish and George L. Goodwin. Chicago: University of Chicago Press, 1989.

———. *Galatians: A Commentary on Paul's Letter to the Churches in Galatia.* Hermeneia. Philadelphia: Fortress, 1979.

———. *2 Corinthians 8 and 9: A Commentary on Two Administrative Letters of the Apostle Paul.* Hermeneia. Philadelphia: Fortress, 1985.

———. "Transferring a Ritual: Paul's Interpretation of Baptism in Romans 6." Pages 84–118 in *Paul in His Hellenistic Context.* Edited by Troels Engberg-Pedersen. Minneapolis: Fortress, 1995.

Bickerman, Elias J. *Chronology of the Ancient World.* 2d ed. Ithaca, N.Y.: Cornell University Press, 1980.

Bindemann, Walther. *Die Hoffnung der Schöpfung: Röm 8, 17–27 und die Frage einer Theologie der Befreiung von Mensch und Natur.* Neukirchen-Vluyn: Neukirchener Verlag, 1983.

Borgen, Peder. *Philo, John, and Paul: New Perspectives on Judaism and Early Christianity.* Brown Judaic Studies 131. Atlanta: Scholars Press, 1987.

Brandenburger, Egon. *Adam und Christus: Exegetisch-religionsgeschichtliche Untersuchung zu Röm. 5, 12–21 (1. Kor. 15).* Wissenshaftliche Monographien zum Alten und Neuen Testament 7. Neukirchen-Vluyn: Neukirchener Verlag, 1962.

Brändle, Rudolf, and Ekkehard W. Stegemann. "The Formation of the First 'Christian Congregations' in Rome in the Context of the Jewish Congregations." Pages 117–27 in *Judaism and Christianity in First-Century Rome.* Edited by Karl P. Donfried and Peter Richardson. Grand Rapids: Eerdmans, 1998.

Breytenbach, Cilliers. *Versöhnung: Eine Studie zur paulinischen Soteriologie.* Wissenshaftliche Monographien zum Alten und Neuen Testament 60. Neukirchen-Vluyn: Neukirchener Verlag, 1989.

———. "Versöhnung, Stellvertretung, und Sühne: Semantische und traditionsgeschichtliche Bemerkungen am Beispiel der paulinischen Breife." *New Testament Studies* 39 (1993): 59–79.

Brooten, Bernadette J. *Love between Women: Early Christian Responses to Female Homoeroticism.* Chicago: University of Chicago Press, 1996.

Brown, Raymond E. *The Semitic Background of the Term "Mystery" in the New Testament.* Facet Books, Biblical Series 21. Philadelphia: Fortress, 1968.

Brown, Raymond E., and John P. Meier. *Antioch and Rome: New Testament Cradles of Catholic Christianity.* New York: Paulist, 1983.

Bultmann, Rudolf. *History of the Synoptic Tradition.* 2d ed. New York: Harper & Row, 1963.

———. *Theology of the New Testament.* 2 vols. New York: Scribner, 1951–1955.

Burgess, Theodore C. *Epideictic Literature.* Chicago: University of Chicago Press, 1902.

Burkert, Walter. *Ancient Mystery Cults.* Carl Newell Jackson Lectures. Cambridge: Harvard University Press, 1987.

Burridge, Richard A. *What Are the Gospels? A Comparison with Graeco-Roman Biography.* New Testament Studies 70. Cambridge: Cambridge University Press, 1992.

Butts, James M. "The *Progymnasmata* of Theon: A New Text with Translation and Commentary." Ph.D. diss., Claremont Graduate School, 1987.

Byrne, Brendan. *"Sons of God"—"Seed of Abraham": A Study of the Idea of the Sonship of God of All Christians in Paul against the Jewish Background.* Analecta biblica 83. Rome: Biblical Institute Press, 1979.

Carroll, John T., and Joel B. Green. *The Death of Jesus in Early Christianity.* Peabody, Mass.: Hendrickson, 1995.

Cohen, Shaye J. D. *The Beginnings of Jewishness: Boundaries, Varieties, Uncertainties.* Berkeley, Calif.: University of California Press, 1999.

Cohn, L. "An Apocryphal Work Ascribed to Philo of Alexandria." *Jewish Quarterly Review* 10 (1898): 277–332.

Collins, John J. "The Development of the Sibylline Tradition." *ANRW* 20.1:421–59. Part 2, *Principat,* 20.1. Edited by Wolfgang Haase. New York: de Gruyter, 1987.

———. "The Genre Apocalypse in Hellenistic Judaism." Pages 531–48 in *Apocalypticism in the Mediterranean World and the Near East.* Edited by David Hellholm. 2d ed. Tübingen: Mohr (Siebeck), 1989.

———. *The Scepter and the Star: The Messiahs of the Dead Sea Scrolls and Other Ancient Literature.* Anchor Bible Reference Library. New York: Doubleday, 1995.

———. *The Sibylline Oracles of Egyptian Judaism.* Society of Biblical Literature Dissertation Series 13. Missoula, Mont.: Scholars Press, 1974.

Collins, Raymond F. *First Corinthians.* Sacra pagina 7. Collegeville, Minn.: Liturgical Press, 1999.

Conzelmann, Hans. *1 Corinthians: A Commentary on the First Epistle to the Corinthians.* Hermeneia. Philadelphia: Fortress, 1975.

Corrington, Gail Paterson. "The Defense of the Body and the Discourse of Appetite: Continence and Control in the Greco-Roman World." Pages 65–74 in vol. 1 of *Discursive Formations, Ascetic Piety, and the Interpretation of Early Christian Literature.* Edited by Vincent L. Wimbush. 2 vols. *Semeia* 57–58. Atlanta: Scholars Press, 1992.

Cranfield, C. E. B. "The Significance of διὰ παντός in Romans 11:10." *SE* 2 (1964): 546–50.

Cullmann, Oscar. *The State in the New Testament.* New York: Scribner's, 1956.

Dahl, Nils A. "Romans 3:9: Text and Meaning." Pages 184–204 in *Paul and Paulinism: Essays in Honour of C. K. Barrett.* Edited by M. D. Hooker and S. G. Wilson. London: SPCK, 1982.

Davies, William D. *Paul and Rabbinic Judaism: Some Rabbinic Elements in Pauline Theology.* 4th ed. Philadelphia: Fortress, 1980.

Dimant, Devorah. "Pesharim, Qumran." Pages 244–51 in vol. 5 of *Anchor Bible Dictionary.* Edited by D. N. Freedman. 6 vols. New York: Doubleday, 1992

Donfried, Karl P. "False Presuppositions in the Study of Romans." Pages 102–24 in *The Romans Debate.* Edited by Karl P. Donfried. Rev. and expanded ed. Peabody, Mass.: Hendrickson, 1991.

Donfried, Karl P., and Peter Richardson, eds. *Judaism and Christianity in First-Century Rome.* Grand Rapids: Eerdmans, 1998.

Dunn, James D. G. *The Epistle to the Galatians.* Black's New Testament Commentaries. Peabody, Mass.: Hendrickson, 1993.

———, ed. *Paul and the Mosaic Law: The Third Durham-Tübingen Symposium on Earliest Christianity and Judaism.* Grand Rapids: Eerdmans, 2001.

———, *The Theology of Paul the Apostle.* Grand Rapids: Eerdmans, 1998.

Engberg-Pedersen, Troels. *Paul and the Stoics.* Louisville: Westminster John Knox, 2000.

Fee, Gordon. *Paul's Letter to the Philippians.* New International Commentary on the New Testament. Grand Rapids: Eerdmans, 1995.

Feldman, Louis H. *Jew and Gentile in the Ancient World: Attitudes and Interactions from Alexander to Justinian.* Princeton, N.J.: Princeton University Press, 1993.

Fischer, Ulrich. *Eschatologie und Jenseitserwartung im hellenistischen Diasporajudentum.* Beihefte zur Zeitschrift für die neutestamentliche Wissenschaft 44. Berlin: de Gruyter, 1978.

Fitzmyer, Joseph A. *The Acts of the Apostles: A New Translation with Introduction and Commentary.* Anchor Bible 31. New York: Doubleday, 1997.

———. "The Consecutive Meaning of ἐφ' ᾧ in Romans 5.12." *New Testament Studies* 39 (1993): 321–39.

———. "Crucifixion in Ancient Palestine, Qumran Literature, and the New Testament." Pages 125–46 in *To Advance the Gospel: New Testament Studies.* New York: Crossroad, 1981.

———. "The Letter to the Galatians." Pages 780–90 in *The New Jerome Biblical Commentary.* Edited by Raymond E. Brown, Joseph A. Fitzmyer, and Roland E. Murphy. Englewood Cliffs, N.J.: Prentice Hall, 1990.

———. *Paul and His Theology: A Brief Sketch.* 2d ed. Englewood Cliffs, N.J.: Prentice Hall, 1987.

Fowler, Alastair. *Kinds of Literature: An Introduction to the Theory of Genres and Modes.* Cambridge: Harvard University Press, 1982.

Furnish, Victor Paul. *II Corinthians.* Anchor Bible 32A. Garden City, N.Y.: Doubleday, 1984.

Gager, John G. *The Origins of Anti-Semitism: Attitudes toward Judaism in Pagan and Christian Antiquity.* New York: Oxford University Press, 1985.

———. *Reinventing Paul.* Oxford: Oxford University Press, 2000.

Gamble, Harry Y., Jr. *The Textual History of the Letter to the Romans: A Study in Textual and Literary Criticism.* Studies and Documents 42. Grand Rapids: Eerdmans, 1977.

García Martínez, Florentino, ed. *The Dead Sea Scrolls Translated: The Qumran Texts in English.* 2d ed. Leiden: Brill, 1996.

Gaston, Lloyd. *Paul and the Torah.* Vancouver: University of British Columbia Press, 1987.

Georgi, Dieter. *The Opponents of Paul in Second Corinthians.* Philadelphia: Fortress, 1986.

———. *Remembering the Poor: The History of Paul's Collection for Jerusalem.* Nashville: Abingdon, 1992.

Getty, Mary A. "Paul and the Salvation of Israel: A Perspective on Romans 9–11." *Catholic Biblical Quarterly* 50 (1988): 456–69.

Goldstein, Jonathan A. *1 Maccabees.* Anchor Bible 41. Garden City, N.Y.: Doubleday, 1976.

Goodenough, Erwin R. *The Politics of Philo Judaeus: Theory and Practice.* New Haven: Yale University Press, 1938.

Goodman, Martin. *Mission and Conversion: Proselytizing in the Religious History of the Roman Empire.* Oxford: Clarendon, 1994.

Gundry, Robert H. "The Moral Frustration of Paul before His Conversion: Sexual Lust in Romans 7:7–25." Pages 228–45 in *Pauline Studies: Essays Presented to Professor F. F. Bruce on His 70th Birthday.* Edited by Donald A. Hagner and Murray J. Harris. Grand Rapids: Eerdmans, 1980.

Hägg, Tomas. *The Novel in Antiquity.* Berkeley, Calif.: University of California Press, 1983.

Hay, David, and E. Elizabeth Johnson, eds. *Romans.* Vol. 4 of *Pauline Theology.* SBLSym 54. Atlanta: Scholars Press, 1997.

Hays, Richard B. *The Faith of Jesus Christ.* Society of Biblical Literature Dissertation Series 56. Chico, Calif.: Scholars Press, 1983.

———. "Have We Found Abraham to Be Our Forefather according to the Flesh?" *Novum Testamentum* 16 (1985): 76–98.

Hecht, Richard D. "The Exegetical Contexts of Philo's Interpretation of Circumcision." Pages 51–79 in *Nourished with Peace: Studies in Hellenistic Judaism in Memory of Samuel Sandmel.* Edited by Frederick E. Greenspahn, Earle Hilgert, and Burton L. Mack. Homage Series 9. Chico, Calif.: Scholars Press, 1984.

Hengel, Martin. *The Atonement: The Origins of the Doctrine in the New Testament.* Philadelphia: Fortress, 1981.

———. *Judaism and Hellenism: Studies in Their Encounter in Palestine during the Early Hellenistic Period.* 2 vols. Philadelphia: Fortress, 1974.

———. *The Pre-Christian Paul.* Philadelphia: Trinity Press International, 1991.

———. *The Son of God: The Origin of Christology and the History of Jewish-Hellenistic Religion.* Philadelphia: Fortress, 1976.

Henten, Jan Willem van. *The Maccabean Martyrs as Saviours of the Jewish People: A Study of 2 and 4 Maccabees.* Supplements to the Journal for the Study of Judaism 57. New York: Brill, 1997.

———, ed. *Die Entstehung der jüdischen Martyrologie.* Leiden: Brill, 1989.

Hodgson, Robert. "Paul the Apostle and First Century Tribulation Lists." *Zeitschrift für die neutestamentliche Wissenschaft und die Kunde der älteren Kirche* 74 (1983): 59–80.

Hooker, Morna D. *Not Ashamed of the Gospel: New Testament Interpretations of the Death of Jesus.* Grand Rapids: Eerdmans, 1995.

Horgan, Maurya P. *Pesharim: Qumran Interpretations of Biblical Books.* Catholic Biblical Quarterly Monograph Series 8. Washington, D.C.: Catholic Biblical Association of America, 1979.

Hollander, Harm W., and Marinus de Jonge. *The Testaments of the Twelve Patriarchs: A Commentary.* Studia in Veteris Testamenti pseudepigraphica 8. Leiden: Brill, 1985.

Howard, George E. "Christ the End of the Law: The Meaning of Romans 10:4ff." *Journal of Biblical Literature* 88 (1969): 331–37.

Hübner, Hans. *Gottes Ich und Israel: Zum Schriftgebrauch des Paulus in Römer 9–11.* Forschungen zur Religion und Literatur des Alten und Neuen Testaments 136. Göttingen: Vandenhoeck & Ruprecht, 1984.

Jacobson, Howard. *A Commentary on Pseudo-Philo's "Liber antiquitatum biblicarum."* 2 vols. Arbeiten zur Geschichte des Spätjudentums und Urchristentums 31. Leiden: Brill, 1996.

Jervell, Jacob. *Imago Dei: Gen 1, 26 f. im Spätjudentum, in der Gnosis, und in den paulinischen Briefen.* Forschungen zur Religion und Literatur des Alten und Neuen Testaments 58. Göttingen: Vandenhoeck & Ruprecht, 1960.

Jewett, Robert. *A Chronology of Paul's Life.* Philadelphia: Fortress, 1979.

Johnson, E. Elizabeth. *The Function of Apocalyptic and Wisdom Traditions in Romans 9–11.* Society of Biblical Literature Dissertation Series 109. Atlanta: Scholars Press, 1989.

Jonge, Marinus de. *The Testaments of the Twelve Patriarchs: A Study of Their Text, Composition, and Origin.* Assen: Van Gorcum, 1953.

Karris, Robert J. "The Occasion of Romans: A Response to Prof. Donfried." Pages 125–27 in *The Romans Debate.* Edited by Karl P. Donfried. Rev. and expanded ed. Peabody, Mass.: Hendrickson, 1991.

———. "Romans 14:1–15:6 and the Occasion of Romans." Pages 65–84 in *The Romans Debate.* Edited by Karl P. Donfried. Rev. and expanded ed. Peabody, Mass.: Hendrickson, 1991.

Kennedy, George A. *Classical Rhetoric and Its Christian and Secular Tradition from Ancient to Modern Times.* Chapel Hill: University of North Carolina Press, 1980.

———. *New Testament Interpretation through Rhetorical Criticism.* Chapel Hill: University of North Carolina Press, 1984.

Kent, John Harvey. *The Inscriptions, 1926–1950.* Corinth: Results of Excavations Conducted by the American School of Classical Studies at Athens 8.3. Princeton, N.J.: American School of Classical Studies at Athens, 1966.

Kirby, J. T. "The Syntax of Romans 5:12: A Rhetorical Approach." *New Testament Studies* 33 (1987): 283–86.

Klauck, Hans-Josef. *1. Korintherbrief.* Neue Echter Bibel 7. Würzburg: Echter, 1984.

Klijn, A. Frederik J. "1 Thessalonians 4.13–18 and Its Background in Apocalyptic Literature." Pages 67–73 in *Paul and Paulinism: Essays in Honour of C. K. Barrett.* Edited by M. D. Hooker and S. G. Wilson. London: SPCK, 1982.

Kloppenborg, John S. "An Analysis of the Pre-Pauline Formula in 1 Cor 15:3b–5 in the Light of Some Recent Literature." *Catholic Biblical Quarterly* 40 (1978): 351–67.

———. "The Sayings Gospel Q and the Quest of the Historical Jesus." *Harvard Theological Review* 89 (1996): 307–44.

Kloppenborg, John S., and S. G. Wilson, eds. *Voluntary Associations in the Graeco-Roman World.* London: Routledge, 1996.

Koester, Helmut. *History and Literature of Early Christianity.* Vol. 2 of *Introduction to the New Testament.* New York: de Gruyter, 1982.

———. "ΝΟΜΟΣ ΦΥΣΕΩΣ: The Concept of Natural Law in Greek Thought." Pages 521–41 in *Religions in Antiquity: Essays in Memory of Erwin Ramsdell Goodenough.* Edited by Jacob Neusner. Supplements to Numen 14. Leiden: Brill, 1968.

Kustas, George L. *Diatribe in Ancient Rhetorical Theory.* Berkeley, Calif.: Center for Hermeneutical Studies, 1976.

Lambrecht, Jan. *The Wretched "I" and Its Liberation: Paul in Romans 7 and 8.* Louvain Theological and Pastoral Monographs 14. Louvain: Peeters, 1992.

Lampe, Peter. *Die stadrömischen Christen in den ersten beiden Jahrhunderten: Untersuchungen zur Sozialgeschichte.* 2d ed. Wissenschaftliche Untersuchungen zum Neuen Testament 18. Tübingen: Mohr, 1989.

Lane, William L. "Social Perspectives on Roman Christianity during the Formative Years from Nero to Nerva: Romans, Hebrews, *1 Clement.*" Pages 196–244 in *Judaism and Christianity in First-Century Rome.* Edited by Karl P. Donfried and Peter Richardson. Grand Rapids: Eerdmans, 1998.

Lausberg, Heinrich. *Handbook of Literary Rhetoric: A Foundation for Literary Study.* Edited by David E. Orton and R. Dean Anderson. Translated by Matthew T. Bliss, Annemiek Jansen, and David E. Orton. Leiden: Brill, 1998.

Leon, Harry J. *The Jews of Ancient Rome.* Rev. ed. Peabody, Mass.: Hendrickson, 1995.

Levison, John R. *Portraits of Adam in Early Judaism: From Sirach to 2 Baruch.* Journal for the Study of the Pseudepigrapha: Supplement Series 1. Sheffield, England: JSOT Press, 1988.

———. *Texts in Transition: The Greek "Life of Adam and Eve."* Society of Biblical Literature Early Judaism and Its Literature 16. Atlanta: Society of Biblical Literature, 2000.

Lindars, B. *New Testament Apologetic.* London: SCM, 1961.

Lodge, John G. *Romans 9–11: A Reader-Response Analysis.* International Studies in Formative Christianity and Judaism 6. Atlanta: Scholars Press, 1996.

Long, A. A. *Hellenistic Philosophy.* 2d ed. London: Duckworth, 1986.

Long, A. A., and D. N. Sedley. *The Hellenistic Philosophers.* 2 vols. Cambridge: Cambridge University Press, 1987.

Luz, Ulrich. *Matthew 1–7: A Continental Commentary.* Minneapolis: Fortress, 1992.

Malherbe, Abraham J. *Ancient Epistolary Theorists.* Society of Biblical Literature Sources for Biblical Study 19. Atlanta: Scholars Press, 1988.

———. *The Cynic Epistles: A Study Edition.* Society of Biblical Literature Sources for Biblical Study 12. Missoula, Mont.: Scholars Press, 1977.

———. "*Mē genoito* in the Diatribe and Paul." Pages 25–33 in *Paul and the Popular Philosophers.* Minneapolis: Fortress, 1989.

———. *Social Aspects of Early Christianity.* 2d ed. Philadelphia: Fortress, 1983.

Martin, Dale B. *The Corinthian Body.* New Haven: Yale University Press, 1995.

Martin, Ralph P. *2 Corinthians.* Word Biblical Commentaries 40. Waco, Tex.: Word, 1986.

Matera, Frank J. *Galatians.* Sacra pagina 9. Collegeville, Minn.: Liturgical Press, 1992.

Martyn, J. Louis. *Galatians: A New Translation with Introduction and Commentary.* Anchor Bible 33A. New York: Doubleday, 1997.

McKnight, Scot. *A Light among the Gentiles: Jewish Missionary Activity in the Second Temple Period.* Minneapolis: Fortress, 1991.

Mendelson, Alan. *Philo's Jewish Identity.* Brown Judaic Studies 161. Atlanta: Scholars Press, 1988.

Metzger, Bruce M. "The Punctuation of Rom 9:5." Pages 95–112 in *Christ and Spirit in the New Testament.* Edited by Barnabas Lindars and S. S. Smalley. London: Cambridge University Press, 1973.

———. *A Textual Commentary on the Greek New Testament.* 2d ed. New York: United Bible Societies, 1994.

Meyer, P. W. "Romans 10:4 and the 'End' of the Law." Pages 59–78 in *The Divine Helmsman.* Edited by J. R. Crenshaw and S. Sandmel. New York: KTAV, 1980.

Mitchell, Margaret M. *The Heavenly Trumpet: John Chrysostom and the Art of Pauline Interpretation.* Louisville: Westminster John Knox, 2002.

———. *Paul and the Rhetoric of Reconciliation: An Exegetical Investigation of the Language and Composition of 1 Corinthians.* Louisville: Westminster John Knox, 1991.

Mitchell, Stephen. *Anatolia: Land, Men, and Gods in Asia Minor.* 2 vols. Oxford: Clarendon, 1993.

Murphy, Frederick J. *Pseudo-Philo: Rewriting the Bible.* New York: Oxford University Press, 1993.

Murphy-O'Connor, Jerome. *Paul: A Critical Life.* Oxford: Clarendon, 1996.

Nanos, Mark D. *The Mystery of Romans: The Jewish Context of Paul's Letter.* Minneapolis: Fortress, 1996.

Nickelsburg, George W. E. "Eschatology (Early Jewish)." Pages 579–94 in vol. 2 of *Anchor Bible Dictionary.* Edited by D. N. Freedman. 6 vols. New York: Doubleday, 1992.

———. *Resurrection, Immortality, and Eternal Life in Intertestamental Judaism.* Harvard Theological Studies 26. Cambridge: Harvard University Press, 1972.

Nickle, Keith F. *The Collection: A Study in Paul's Strategy.* Studies in Biblical Theology 48. Naperville, Ill.: Allenson, 1966.

Nikiprowetzky, Valentin. *La troisième Sibylle.* Paris: Mouton, 1970.

Nilsson, Martin P. *Geschichte der griechischen Religion.* 2 vols. 3d ed. Munich: Beck, 1967–1974.

Noy, David. *Foreigners at Rome: Citizens and Strangers.* London: Duckworth, 2000.

———. *Jewish Inscriptions of Western Europe.* 2 vols. Cambridge: Cambridge University Press, 1993–1995.

Nussbaum, Martha C. *The Therapy of Desire: Theory and Practice in Hellenistic Ethics.* Princeton, N.J.: Princeton University Press, 1994.

Osten-Sacken, Peter von der. *Römer 8 als Beispiel paulinischer Soterologie.* Forschungen zur Religion und Literatur des Alten und Neuen Testaments 112. Göttingen: Vandenhoeck & Ruprecht, 1975.

Paulsen, Henning. *Überlieferung und Auslegung in Römer 8.* Wissenshaftliche Monographien zum Alten und Neuen Testament 43. Neukirchen-Vluyn: Neukirchener Verlag, 1974.

Pearson, Birger. "1 Thessalonians 2:13–16: A Deutero-Pauline Interpolation." *Harvard Theological Review* 64 (1971): 79–91.

Penna, R. "Les Juifs à Rome au temps de l'apôtre Paul." *New Testament Studies* 28 (1982): 321–47.

Peters, Francis E. *Greek Philosophical Terms: A Historical Lexicon.* New York: New York University Press, 1967.

Poland, Franz. *Geschichte der griechischen Vereinswesens.* 1909. Repr., Leipzig: Zentral-Antiquariat der Deutschen Demokratischen Republik, 1967.

Porter, Stanley E. "Paul of Tarsus and His Letters." Pages 533–85 in *Handbook of Classical Rhetoric in the Hellenistic Period (330 BC–AD 400).* Edited by Stanley E. Porter. Leiden: Brill, 1997.

Pseudo-Philo. *Les Antiquités bibliques.* Edited by Daniel J. Harrington et al. 2 vols. Sources chrétiennes 229, 230. Paris: Cerf, 1976.

Rabello, A. M. "The Legal Condition of the Jews in the Roman Empire." *ANRW* 13:662–762. Part 2, *Principat,* 13. Edited by Hildegard Temporini. New York: de Gruyter, 1980.

Räisänen, Heikki. *Paul and the Law.* Philadelphia: Fortress, 1986.

———. "Römer 9–11: Analyse eines geistigen Ringens." *ANRW* 25.4:2891–2939. Part 2, *Principat,* 25.4. Edited by Wolfgang Haase. New York: de Gruyter, 1987.

Reardon, B. P. *Collected Ancient Greek Novels.* Berkeley, Calif.: University of California Press, 1989.

———. *The Form of Greek Romance.* Princeton, N.J.: Princeton University Press, 1991.

Reasoner, Mark. *The Strong and the Weak: Romans 14.1–15.13 in Context.* New Testament Studies 103. Cambridge: Cambridge University Press, 1999.

Refoulé, François. *". . . Et ainsi tout Israël sera sauvé": Romains 11, 25–32.* Lectio divina 117. Paris: Cerf, 1984.

Rhyne, C. Thomas. *Faith Establishes the Law.* Society of Biblical Literature Dissertation Series 55. Chico, Calif.: Scholars Press, 1981.

———. *"Nomos dikaiosynēs* and the Meaning of Romans 10:4." *Catholic Biblical Quarterly* 47 (1985): 486–99.

Richard, Earl J. *First and Second Thessalonians.* Sacra pagina 11. Collegeville, Minn.: Liturgical Press, 1995.

Richardson, Peter. "Augustan-Era Synagogues in Rome." Pages 17–29 in *Judaism and Christianity in First-Century Rome.* Edited by Karl P. Donfried and Peter Richardson. Grand Rapids: Eerdmans, 1998.

Riesner, Rainer. *Paul's Early Period: Chronology, Mission Strategy, Theology.* Grand Rapids: Eerdmans, 1998.

Saldarini, Anthony J. *Pharisees, Scribes, and Sadducees in Palestinian Society: A Sociological Approach.* Wilmington, Del.: Michael Glazier, 1988.

Sanders, E. P. *Jewish Law from Jesus to the Mishnah: Five Studies.* Philadelphia: Trinity Press International, 1990.

———. *Paul and Palestinian Judaism: A Comparison of Patterns of Religion.* Philadelphia: Fortress, 1977.

Schaller, Berndt. "ΗΞΕΙ ΕΚ ΣΙΩΝ Ο ΡΥΟΜΕΝΟΣ: Zur Textgestalt von Jes 59:20f. in Röm 11:26f." Pages 201–6 in *De Septuaginta: Studies in Honour of John William*

Wevers on His Sixty-Fifth Birthday. Edited by Albert Pietersma and Claude Cox. Mississauga, Ont.: Benben, 1984.

Schiffman, Lawrence H. *Reclaiming the Dead Sea Scrolls: The History of Judaism, the Background of Christianity, the Lost Library of Qumran.* Philadelphia: Jewish Publication Society, 1994.

Schmeller, Thomas. *Paulus und die "Diatribe": Eine Vergleichende Stilinterpretation.* Neutestamentliche Abhandlungen. Neue Folge 19. Münster: Aschendorff, 1987.

Schmithals, Walter. *Der Römerbrief als historisches Problem.* Studien zum Neuen Testament 9. Gütersloh: Mohn, 1975.

Schrage, Wolfgang. *Der erste Brief an die Korinther.* 4 vols. EKKNT; Zurich: Benziger, 1991–2001.

Schürer, Emil. *The History of the Jewish People in the Age of Jesus Christ (175 B.C.–A.D. 135).* Revised and edited by Geza Vermes, Fergus Millar, and Martin Goodman. 3 vols. in 4. Edinburgh: T&T Clark, 1973–1987.

Scott, James M. "Paul's Use of Deuteronomic Tradition." *Journal of Biblical Literature* 112 (1993): 651–57.

Scroggs, Robin. *The Last Adam: A Study in Pauline Anthropology.* Philadelphia: Fortress, 1966.

Seeley, David. *The Noble Death: Graeco-Roman Martyrology and Paul's Concept of Salvation.* Journal for the Study of the New Testament: Supplement Series 28. Sheffield, England: Sheffield Academic Press, 1990.

Segal, Alan. *Paul the Convert: The Apostolate and Apostasy of Saul the Pharisee.* New Haven: Yale University Press, 1990.

Selb, Walter. "Διαθήκη im Neuen Testament: Randbemerkungen eines Juristen zu einem Theologenstreit." *Journal of Jewish Studies* 25 (1974): 183–96.

Sharpe, J. L. *Prolegomena to the Establishment of the Critical Text of the Greek Apocalypse of Moses.* Ph.D. diss., Duke University, 1969. Ann Arbor, Mich: University Microfilms, 1969.

Skehan, Patrick W., and Alexander A. Di Lella. *The Wisdom of Ben Sira.* Anchor Bible 39. New York: Doubleday, 1987.

Smyth, Herbert Weir. *Greek Grammar.* Rev. ed. Cambridge: Harvard University Press, 1956.

Stendahl, Krister. *Paul among Jews and Gentiles.* Philadelphia: Fortress, 1976.

Sterling, Gregory E. "'Wisdom among the Perfect': Creation Traditions in Alexandrian Judaism and Corinthian Christianity." *Novum Testamentum* 37 (1995): 355–84.

Stern, Menahem. *Greek and Latin Authors on Jews and Judaism.* 3 vols. Jerusalem: Israel Academy of Sciences and Humanities, 1976–1984.

Stone, Michael Edward. *Fourth Ezra.* Hermeneia. Minneapolis: Fortress, 1990.

Stowers, Stanley K. *The Diatribe and Paul's Letter to the Romans.* Society of Biblical Literature Dissertation Series 57. Chico, Calif.: Scholars Press, 1981.

———. *Letter Writing in Greco-Roman Antiquity.* Library of Early Christianity 5. Philadelphia: Westminster, 1986.

———. "Paul's Dialogue with a Fellow Jew in Romans 3:1–9." *Catholic Biblical Quarterly* 46 (1984): 707–22.

————. *A Rereading of Romans: Justice, Jews, and Gentiles.* New Haven: Yale University Press, 1994.

————. "Romans 7.7–25 as a Speech-in-Character (προσωποποιία)." Pages 180–202 in *Paul in His Hellenistic Context.* Edited by Troels Engberg-Pedersen. Minneapolis: Fortress, 1995.

Strack, Hermann L., and Günter Stemberger. *Introduction to the Talmud and Midrash.* Edinburgh: T&T Clark, 1991.

Stuhlmacher, Peter. "Das Ende des Gesetzes: Über Ursprung und Ansatz der paulinischen Theologie." *Zeitschrift für Theologie und Kirche* 67 (1970): 14–39.

Swetnam, James. "The Curious Crux at Romans 4,12." *Biblica* 61 (1980): 110–15.

Thrall, Margaret E. *A Critical and Exegetical Commentary on the Second Epistle to the Corinthians.* 2 vols. International Critical Commentary. Edinburgh: T&T Clark, 1994–2000.

Tobin, Thomas H. *The Creation of Man: Philo and the History of Interpretation.* Catholic Biblical Quarterly Monograph Series 14. Washington, D.C.: Catholic Biblical Association of America, 1983.

————. "Philo and the Sibyl: Interpreting Philo's Eschatology." *Studia philonica Annual* 9 (1997): 84–103.

————. "Romans 10:4: Christ the Goal of the Law." *Studia philonica Annual* 3 (1991): 272–80.

————. *The Spirituality of Paul.* Message of Biblical Spirituality 12. Wilmington, Del.: Michael Glazier, 1987.

Tomson, Peter J. *Paul and the Jewish Law: Halakha in the Letters of the Apostle to the Gentiles.* Compendia rerum iudaicarum ad Novum Testamentum 3.1. Minneapolis: Fortress, 1990.

Wagner, Günther. *Pauline Baptism and the Pagan Mysteries: The Problem of the Pauline Doctrine of Baptism in Romans VI.1–11.* Edinburgh: Oliver & Boyd, 1967.

Walters, James C. "Romans, Jews, and Christians: The Impact of the Romans on Jewish/Christian Relations in First-Century Rome." Pages 175–95 in *Judaism and Christianity in First-Century Rome.* Edited by Karl P. Donfried and Peter Richardson. Grand Rapids: Eerdmans, 1998.

Waltzing, Jean Pierre. *Étude historique sur les corporations professionnelles chez les Romains depuis les origins jusqu'à la chute de l'Empire d'Occident.* 4 vols. 1895–1900. Repr., Bologna: Forni, 1968.

Weber, Heinrich. *De Senecae philosophi dicendi genere Bioneo.* Marburg: F. Soemmering, 1895.

Wengst, Klaus. *Christologische Formeln und Lieder des Urchristentums.* Studien zum Neuen Testament 7. Gütersloh: Mohn, 1972.

White, John L. *Light from Ancient Letters.* Foundations and Facets. Philadelphia: Fortress, 1986.

————. "Saint Paul and the Apostolic Letter Tradition." *Catholic Biblical Quarterly* 45 (1983): 433–44.

White, L. Michael. "Synagogue and Society in Imperial Ostia: Archaeological and Epigraphic Evidence." Pages 30–68 in *Judaism and Christianity in First-Century Rome.* Edited by Karl P. Donfried and Peter Richardson. Grand Rapids: Eerdmans, 1998.

Williams, Sam K. *Jesus' Death as Saving Event: The Background and Origin of a Concept.* Harvard Dissertations in Religion 2. Missoula, Mont.: Scholars Press, 1975.

Wilson, Walter T. *Love without Pretense: Romans 12.9–21 and Hellenistic-Jewish Wisdom Literature.* Wissenschaftliche Untersuchungen zum Neuen Testament 46. Tübingen: Mohr, 1991.

Winston, David. *The Wisdom of Solomon.* Anchor Bible 43. Garden City, N.Y.: Doubleday, 1979.

Wuellner, Wilhelm. "Paul's Rhetoric of Argumentation in Romans: An Alternative to the Donfried-Karris Debate over Romans." Pages 128–46 in *The Romans Debate.* Edited by Karl P. Donfried. Rev. and expanded ed. Peabody, Mass.: Hendrickson, 1991.

Yaron, Reuven. *Gifts in Contemplation of Death in Jewish and Roman Law.* Oxford: Clarendon, 1960.

Zerwick, Max. *Biblical Greek: Illustrated by Examples.* Translated by Joseph Smith. Scripta Pontificii Instituti Biblici 114. Rome: Pontifical Biblical Institute, 1963.

Ziebarth, Erich. *Das griechische Vereinswesen.* Stuttgart: S. Hirtzel, 1896.

Index of Modern Authors

Aageson, J., 303n10
Andersen, R. D., 259n37
Anderson, R., 84n15, 110n14, 384n2
Attridge, H., 28n49, 140n42, 168n27
Aune, D., 229n30, 262n49, 280n12, 288n31

Badenas, R., 309n23, 309n25, 312n33, 344n44
Balz, H., 273n1
Barclay, J., 41n90, 155n1, 404n56, 405n59, 407n66
Barrett, C. K., 167n23, 178n50, 309n26, 310n29
Bassler, J., 106n4, 112n19, 114n23
Beard, M., 25n39, 27n46
Beare, F., 252n1
Betz, H. D., 50n7, 51n9, 61n26, 62n29, 63n31, 64n34, 66n40, 67n41, 69n46, 96n59, 122n49, 127n2, 128n4, 128n5, 133n14, 133n15, 198n17, 199n18, 200n23, 200n24, 211n42, 269n72, 270n74, 388n8
Bickerman, E., 26n41
Bindemann, W., 273n1
Bogaert, P., 174n42, 175n43
Borgen, P., 116n32
Brandenburger, E., 167n23
Brandle, R., and W. Stegemann, 34n70
Breytenbach, C., 139n40, 164n17, 165n19
Brooten, B., 109n9
Brown, R., 308n21
Brown, R., and J. P. Meier, 23n30, 40n88, 99n73
Bultmann, R., 40n87, 252n1
Burgess, T., 118n40
Burkert, W., 204n33
Burridge, R., 89n27, 90n32
Butts, J., 227n20

Byrne, B., 1n1, 109, 114n25, 119n42, 135n17, 164n16, 164n17, 177n49, 178n52, 179n56, 193n5, 194n9, 195n11, 197n14, 197n15, 224n10, 237n55, 243n59, 253n13, 253n15, 254n20, 281n15, 282, 287n30, 289n36, 290n40, 292n46, 296n56, 297n57, 323n8, 327n16, 327n18, 361n13, 372n28, 397n40, 405n60

Carroll, J., and J. Green, 137n26
Cohen, S., 30n58, 33n68, 61n25
Cohn, L., 174n42
Collins, J., 171n31, 256n27, 257n30, 258n32, 258n33, 259n37, 260n39, n41
Collins, R., 74n59, 75n60, 75n63, 176n48, 190n2, 201n27, 202n28, 205n36, 206n37, 265n59
Conzelmann, H., 176n48, 265n59
Corrington, G., 26n43
Cranfield, C. E. B., 1n1, 114n25, 121n46, 136n24, 152n64, 161n9, 177n49, 179n56, 197n14, 208n39, 221n3, 224n10, 225n15, 237n55, 243n59, 252, 253n13, 253n16, 254n18, 254n19, 289n36, 305n14, 309n25, 314n34, 314n35, 327n16, 327n18, 330n21, 342n39, 343n41, 361n13, 372n29, 396n38, 404n57, 405n60, 413n75
Cullmann, O., 395n34

Dahl, N., 121n47
Davies, W. D., 167n23
Di Lella, A., 168n26
Dimant, D., 321n2
Dobbin, R., 92, 94n54, 94n55
Dodd, C. H., 251–52
Donfried, K., 71n51

Dunn, J., 1n1, 55n16, 61n26, 62n28, 62n29, 66n40, 67n41, 68n44, 69n46, 71n55, 72n56, 81–83, 114n25, 117n36, 120n46, 121n47, 133n14, 133n15, 146n52, 147n56, 177n49, 179n56, 211n42, 224n10, 237n55, 243n59, 246n67, 252, 253n13, 253n16, 253n17, 254n19, 254n21, 255n22, 246n67, 269n72, 270n74, 281n14, 289n36, 301n7, 305n13, 305n14, 308n21, 309n24, 310n28, 314n34, 323n8, 324n9, 324n10, 327n17, 327n18, 338n36, 342n39, 361n13, 362n15, 392n22, 404n55, 405n58, 411n72

Engberg-Pedersen, T., 84n14, 229n31

Fee, G., 133n16
Feldman, L., 23n32, 32n64
Fischer, U., 257n29, 259n36, 260n45, 261n46
Fitzmyer, J., 1n1, 17, 48n1, 48n5, 51n10, 53n11, 59n23, 59n24, 62n28, 71n55, 72n56, 81–83, 114n25, 128n3, 132n13, 136n21, 137n25, 137n27, 143n47, 157n4, 158n6, 161n9, 177n49, 178, 178n51, 178n52, 194n9, 195n11, 197n14, 209n40, 214n46, 224n11, 237n55, 243n59, 252, 253n13, 253n15, 254n20, 254n21, 281n15, 283n22, 289n36, 290n40, 293n51, 301n7, 323n8, 327n16, 327n18, 343n41, 344n45, 361n13, 372n29, 372n30, 396n36, 405n58, 409n68
Fowler, A., 89n27
Furnish, V., 163n15, 164n18, 318n39

Gager, J., 4n3, 55n17, 307n18, 374n35
Gamble, H., 79n1
García Martínez, F., 377–78
Gaston, L., 4n3, 307n18, 310n29, 374n35
Gaylord, H. E., Jr., 259n36
Georgi, D., 24n32, 50n7, 71n50
Getty, M., 309n25
Goldstein, J., 17
Goodenough, E., 397n42
Goodman, M., 24n32

Hägg, T., 90n31
Harrington, D., 174n42, 175n43
Hay, D., and E. Johnson, 132n11
Hays, R., 132n11, 146n52
Hecht, R., 116n32
Hengel, M., 137n30, 138n32, 227n28, 287n30
Henten, J., 138n35

Hodgson, R., 322n5
Hollander H., and M. Jonge, 258n31
Hooker, M., 137n26
Horgan, M., 321n2
Howard, G., 309n25
Hübner, H., 299n1, 307n17, 309n24

Jacobson, H., 174n42
Jervell, J., 167n23
Jewett, R., 48n5
Johnson, E., 299n1, 307n18, 308n22, 309n25, 309n27, 335n30
Johnson, M., 173, 174n41
Jonge, M., 258n31

Karris, R., 71n51
Käsemann, E., 121n46, 305n14, 309n24
Kee, 258n31
Kennedy, G., 63n31, 63n32, 64n34, 67n42, 96n59, 98n65, 107n5
Kent, J., 48n1
Kirby, J. T., 178n50
Klauck, H., 176n48, 264n58
Klijn, A. F., 173n34, 263n53
Kloppenborg, J., 205n36, 262n48
Kloppenborg, J., and S. G. Wilson, 22
Koester, H., 54n13, 115n27
Kustas, G., 91n35

Lambrecht, J., 225n15
Lampe, P., 37n77, 38n81, 39n84, 71n55, 72n56
Lane, W., 34n70, 39n84
Lausberg, H., 84n15, 118n40, 178n55
Leon, H., 17, 22n25, 23n28, 23n29
Levison, J., 167n22, 167n24, 173n35
Lindars, B., 314n34
Lodge, J., 299n1
Long, A. A., 229n29
Long, A. A., and D. N. Sedley, 229n29
Luz, U., 70n48

Malherbe, A., 89n29 , 96n60, 96n61, 96n62, 118n39, 227n28
Martin, D., 205n35, 264n57
Martin, R., 164n18, 318n39
Martyn, J. L., 62n28, 62n29, 63n30, 66n41, 69n46, 122n49, 133n14, 156n1, 211n42
Matera, F., 62n28, 62n29, 66n40, 66n41, 69n46, 133n14, 156n1, 211n42, 270n74
McKnight, S., 24n32
Mendelson, A., 115n30, 116n32
Metzger, B., 146n52, 158n6, 173n34, 226n17, 245n66, 305n14, 325n13
Meyer, P. W., 310n28

Mitchell, M., 76n65, 83n13, 96n59
Mitchell, S., 62n27
Moo, D., 1n1
Morris, L., 1n1, 121n46, 157n4, 237n55, 253n13, 305n14, 309n26
Murphy, F., 175n43
Murphy-O'Connor, J., 48n5, 58n22, 59n23, 62n27, 62n28, 62n29, 63n30, 71n53, 72n57, 80n4, 81n4, 84n14, 227n28, 262n50, 318n38

Nanos, M., 36n74, 396n35
Nickelsburg, G. W. E., 257n27, 323n7
Nickle, K., 50n7
Nikiprowetzky, V., 258n32
Nilsson, M., 25n39, 26n41
Noy, D., 17n4, 71n54
Nussbaum, M., 26n43, 229n29

Osten-Sacken, P., 254n21, 273n1, 288n32

Paulsen, H., 254n21, 273n1, 276, 288n32, 293n47, 295n53
Pearson, B., 263n54
Penna, R., 23n28
Pennington, A., 259n37
Peters, F., 231n39
Poland, F., 22
Porter, S., 83n13

Rabello, A. M., 21n21
Räisänen, H., 243n61, 309n24
Reardon, B. P., 90n31
Reasoner, M., 404n56, 404n57, 409n70
Refoulé, F., 307n19
Rhyne, C., 309n23, 309n25
Richard, E., 80n4, 262n50, 263n51, 263n52, 263n54, 264n55
Richardson, P., 22, 40n86
Riesner, R., 59n23

Saldarini, A., 53n12
Sanday, W., and A. Headlam, 119n42, 237n55, 252n1
Sanders, E. P., 260n43, 260n44, 381n42, 382n42
Schaller, B., 307n17
Schlier, H., 1n1, 403n54
Schmeller, T., 91n35
Schmithals, W., 1n1, 396n39
Schrage, W., 74n59, 75n60, 75n63, 176n48, 190n2, 201n27, 202n28, 205n36, 206n37
Schreiner, T., 1n1, 82n10
Schürer, E., 17, 21n21, 23n30, 23n32, 31n59, 32n64, 53n12, 258n32

Scott, J., 263n54
Scroggs, R., 167n23, 178n50
Seeley, D., 139n40
Segal, A., 55n15
Selb, W., 128n5
Sharpe, J. L., 173n38
Shiffman, H., 321n2
Smyth, H., 178n50, 224n12
Stendahl, K., 4n2, 55n15, 226, 252n2
Sterling, G., 176n47
Stone, M., 172n33, 173n34
Stowers, S., 80n2, 91, 96, 117n35, 118n39, 119n41, 119n43, 120n44, 120n45, 121n46, 226n18, 227n20, 232n41
Strack, H., and G. Stemberger, 127n2, 161n11, 342n38
Stuhlmacher, P., 157n4, 253n13, 309n24
Swetnam, J., 149n58

Thrall, M., 51n9, 71n50, 163n15, 164n18
Tobin, T., 55n15, 169n28, 171n30, 176n47, 259n35, 312n33, 321n2, 341n37, 365n19, 366n20
Tomson, P., 214n45

Wagner, G., 204n33
Walters, J., 34n70
Waltzing, J., 22
Weber, H., 93n44
Wengst, K., 139n40
White, J., 80n2, 80n3
White, L., 22n25, 40n86
Whittaker, M., 173
Wilckens, U., 1n1, 81–83, 114n25, 121n46, 135n17, 137n27, 161n9, 177n49, 179n56, 193n6, 198n16, 221n3, 224n10, 237n55, 241n57, 243n59, 252–53, 253n13, 253n15, 254n21, 267, 268n70, 281n14, 288n32, 289n36, 295n53, 305n14, 309n26, 327n16, 327n18, 361n13, 397n40, 399n44, 403n54
Williams, S., 139n40
Wilson, W., 386n4, 386n5, 387n6, 390n11, 390n12, 390n13, 394n25, 394n26, 394n27, 394n30, 394n31, 394n32, 394n33
Wintermute, O., 171n32
Wuellner, W., 71n51

Yaron, R., 128n5

Zerwick, M., 214n46, 353n1
Ziebarth, E., 22

Index of Primary Sources

HEBREW BIBLE / OLD TESTAMENT

Genesis
1–3   167, 168, 169, 171
3   167, 170, 171, 175
1:26–28   168, 296
1:27   176
2:7   176, 333
2:16–17   180
2:17   170
3:1–6   180
3:14–19   169
3:17   180
3:17–19   290
3:19   168
3:22   170
5:29   290
9:26   325n14
12–50   180
12:3   65n36, 100n66, 127, 128
12:7   2, 65n39, 101
13:5   2, 65n39
13:15   128
15   328
15:5–6   100n66
15:6   65n36, 127, 145, 146n51, 146n54, 147, 148, 149
17:1–8   150n60
17:4–6   149n60
17:5   100n66
17:6   150n60
17:7   2, 65n39
17:10–11   100n66, 148
17:11–22   150n60
17:15–21   151
17:17   128

18:10   327–328
18:14   327–328
18:18   100n66, 127
18:19   295n54
18:23–33   293n51
19:30   150n60
21:10   270
21:12   327–328, 327n18
22   146n54
22:15–18   150n60
22:18   128, 215
24:7   2, 65n39, 128
24:27   325n14
25:1–6   150n60
25:12–15   150n60
25:19–26   328
25:23   328
26:5   69n47, 215
39:7–12   231n37
45:7   337n33

Exodus
4:21   331n22, 358n7
4:22–23   286n26
7:3   331n22, 358n7
7:22   331n22, 358n7
8:8   293n51
8:12   293n51
8:15   331n22, 358n7
8:28–30   293n51
9:12   331n22, 358n7
9:16   330–331, 334
9:35   331n22, 358n7
10:1   331n22, 358n7
10:20   331n22, 358n7
10:27   331n22, 358n7
11:10   331n22, 358n7
12:17   69n47
13:10   69n47

13:15   331n22
14:4   331n22, 358n7
14:8   331n22, 358n7
14:17   331n22, 358n7
20:6   293n48
20:13–15   401
20:13–17 (LXX)   401n49
20:17   85, 190, 220, 220n2, 228–229, 256, 401
20:27   7
22:21   116n32
25:17–22   135n17
33:3   258n6
33:5   258n6
33:19   330–331, 334
34:6 (LXX)   335n28, 335n29
34:9   258n6

Leviticus
3:17   407n65
4:3 (LXX)   282n19
4:14 (LXX)   282 n19
4:28 (LXX)   282 n19
4:35 (LXX)   282 n19
5:6 (LXX)   282 n19
5:7 (LXX)   282n19
5:8 (LXX)   282n19
5:10 (LXX)   282n19
5:11 (LXX)   282n19
5:13 (LXX)   282n19
7:26–27   407n65
9:2   282
11:29   57
14:31   282
16   135n17
16:21–22   293n51
17:10–14   407n65
18:5   65n36, 127, 311n32, 343, 346

19:18   69, 156, 211, 401, 402
19:37   69n47
22:31   69n47
26:14   215
26:15   69n47
26:18   215
26:21   215
26:27   215
30:10–15   220n2

Numbers
5:30   69n47
6:16 (LXX)   282n19
6:23–27   293n51
7:16 (LXX)   282n19
14:18 (LXX)   335n28
15:22   69n47
15:40   69n47
19:19   69n47
21   182
22:31   69n47
24:7 (LXX)   261
24:17 (LXX)   261
25   181

Deuteronomy
4:2   69n47
4:40   69n47
5:10   293n48
5:17 (LXX-B)   401n49
5:17–19   401
5:17–21 (LXX)   401n49
5:18   7, 85, 190, 220,
   228–229, 256
5:21   401
5:29   69n47
6:4   143, 144
6:17   69n47
6:25   69n47
7:9   69n47, 293n48
7:11   69n47
8:2   69n47
8:6   69n47
8:11   69n47
8:17   300n5, 343
8:18   334n27
9:4   300n5, 343
9:5   334n27
9:6   258n6
9:13   258n6
9:27   258n6
10:13   69n47
10:16   258n6
10:17   111
11:8   69n47

13:19   69n47
14:1–2   286n26
15:5   69n47
16:12   69n47
17:19   69n47
19:9   69n47
20:11   215n48
21:10   129
21:23   65, 65n36, 127–128
24:1   220n2
26:1–15   292
26:4   58
26:14   215
26:17   215
26:18   69n47
27:1   69n47
27:10   69n47
27:26   65, 65n36, 65n38,
   105, 127–128
28:1   69n47
28:15   69n47
28:45   69n47
29:1–30:20   357
29:3   354, 355
29:4   314, 356, 357, 358
30:1–7   259
30:1–10   365
30:2   215
30:8   69n47
30:10   69n47
30:11   344
30:12–14   300n5, 343,
   344–345, 347
30:13   344n45
31:19–22   286n26
31:27   258n6
32   360
32:5–6   286n26
32:9   286n28
32:21   313, 315, 349–351,
   353, 359–361
32:35   395
32:36   360

Joshua
17:13   215n48
21:45   326
22:3   69n47
22:5   69n47, 293n48
23:14   326
24:30   216n49

Judges
2:7   216n49
2:8   216n49

2:17   215
2:20   215
10:16   216n49

1 Samuel
7:4   216n49
12:20   216n49
12:23   216n49
16:7   293
20:8   216n49
23:11   216n49
25:32   325n14

2 Samuel
2:16   293n51
7:5   216n49
7:8   216n49
7:20   216n49
11:4   216
13:15 (LXX)   394n29
23:13–17   231n38

1 Kings
1:48   325n14
3:3   293n48
8:15   325n14
8:32   295n54
8:39   293
8:51–53   286n28
12:1   372n31
12:13   258n6
14:22   361n12
18:22–40   293n51
19:9–18   356
19:10   313, 354, 356
19:10–18   355
19:14   313, 354
19:18   313, 354, 356

2 Kings
10:10   326
10:23   216n49
19:31   337n33
21:14   286n28, 337n33
22:36   215n48

1 Chronicles
17:7   216n49
22:12   69n47
28:9   293
29:10   325n14
29:19   69n47

2 Chronicles
2:11   325n14
6:4   325n14

6:23 295n54
6:41 200
10:13 258n6
11:15–19 231n38
12:1 372n31
14:3 69n47
16:13 324n10
29:5 216
29:16 216
29:23–24 (LXX) 282n19
30:8 216n49
33:16 216n49
34:33 216n49

Ezra
6:10 397
7:26 69n47
7:27 325n14
9:8 337n33
9:13 337n33

Nehemiah
1:5 293n48
1:9 69n47
9:34 69n47
10:29 69n47

Esther
10:11 (LXX) 295n54

Job
9:1–4 332
9:4 332
17:7 (LXX) 358
29:14 200
41:3 377

Psalms
1:6 295n54
2:11 (LXX) 216n49
5:10 121
7:9 293
7:12 (LXX) 335n28
9:9 137n28
10:7 121
14:1–3 121
14:7 307n17
17:3 293
19 350n55
19:1 350n55
19:5 349–350
21:31 (LXX) 216n49
26:2 293
29:8 (LXX) 389n9
32:1 148

32:1–2 146–147
32:11 147n57
33:12 286n28
34:26 (LXX) 200
35:28 137n27
36:2 121
36:7 137n27
39:7 (LXX) 282
39:9 (LXX) 389n9
40:9–10 137n29
40:14 325n14
48:6 290n42
50 (LXX) 119
50:6 (LXX) 119
50:14 388n8
50:23 388n8
51:16 137n27
51:16–17 388n8
53:2–4 121
53:6 307n17
59:7–8 121
62:12 111, 112
68:10 (LXX) 412
68:23–24 (LXX) 355, 357,
  358
69:22–23 314
69:23 314n34
69:23–24 354, 356
74:2 286n28
77:58 361n12
85:4 (LXX) 216n49
85:15 (LXX) 335n28,
  335n29
89:3 324n10
89:27 296
96:13 137n28
98:2 137n28
99:2 (LXX) 216n49
101:23 (LXX) 216n49
102:8 (LXX) 335n28,
  335n29
102:21 (LXX) 389n9
103:17 137n27
105:6 324n10
105:48 325n14
106:31 181n60
112:9 137n27
115:2 (LXX) 119
118:22 310n28, 342
118:65 (LXX) 216n49
122:2 (LXX) 216n49
131:9 (LXX) 200
133:1 (LXX) 216n49
134:1 (LXX) 216n49
139:1 293

139:3 293
139:23 293
141:2 388n8
142:10 (LXX) 389n9
143:1–2 122
143:2 100
144:8 (LXX) 335n28,
  335n29

Proverbs
3:11–35 (LXX) 386
3:13–30 390
3:21–35 394
4:3 215n48
6:24 (LXX) 220n2
6:29 (LXX) 220n2
8:15–16 397
13:1 215n48
16:6 388n8
16:10 137n27
21:28 215n48
24:12 111, 112
25:21–22 395

Ecclesiastes
7:20 121, 121n48

Song of Songs
2:4 (LXX) 394n29
2:5 (LXX) 394n29
2:7 (LXX) 394n29
3:5 (LXX) 394n29
3:10 (LXX) 394n29
5:8 (LXX) 394n29
7:7 (LXX) 394n29
8:4 (LXX) 394n29
8:6 (LXX) 394n29
8:7 (LXX) 394n29

Isaiah
1:2–4 286n26
1:9 336–338, 340, 353
1:11–17 388n8
2:2–3 (LXX) 371–372
2:3 307n17, 373n34
2:12 111n15
3:13 137n28
4:6 258n6
8:12 258n6
8:14 310, 311, 317, 341,
  342
10:22–23 336–338, 340,
  353, 356
13:6 111n15
13:8 290n42

14:22   337n33
14:30   337n33
24:21   111n15
25:8   266, 267
26:16–17   290n42
27   307
27:9   306, 317, 354, 368,
   371, 373, 373n33, 374
28:11   314n34
28:16   310, 311, 312,
   314n34, 317, 341, 342,
   347–348
28:27   258n6
29:9–16   333
29:10   314n34, 357n5
29:13   314n34
29:14   314n34
29:16   333
40:13   377
40:20   334n27
42:1 (LXX)   324n10
43:20   324n10
45:1–3   397
45:4   324n10
45:9   333
45:9–19   333
45:23 (LXX)   410
46:13   137n27
49:1   54
49:5–6   54
49:18 (LXX)   410
51:5   137n29
51:6   137n29
51:8   137n29
52:5 (LXX)   116
52:7   349–350
52:13–53:12   152n65
53:1   349–350
53:10   282
56:1   137n29
56:6–7   372n27
59   307
59:16   137n27
59:17   200
59:20   306, 317
59:20–21   306, 354, 368,
   371, 374
59:21   373
60:3–14   372n27
61:10   137n29, 200
63:17   286n28
65   351
65:1   313
65:1–2   349–351
65:2   351

65:3   361n12
65:9   324n10
65:12   215
65:15   324n10
65:17   290
65:22   324n10
66:4   215
66:7–8   290n42
66:22   290

Jeremiah
1:5   54, 295n54
2:2 (LXX)   394n29
4:4   258n6
4:31   290n42
9:23 (LXX)   389n9
10:16   286n28
11:16–17   365
12:1   137n28
13:10   215
13:13   215
13:25   215
16:12   215
18:1–12   333n26
27:5–7   397, 398
29:7   397
34:5–7 (LXX)   397, 398
36:7 (LXX)   397
46:10   111n15

Ezekiel
3:7   258n6
7:7   111n15
8:10   337n33
30:3   111n15
36:20   116n31
42:13 (LXX)   282n19
43:19 (LXX)   282n19

Daniel
1:8–16   406
2 (LXX)   369
2:18 (LXX)   369n22
2:19 (LXX)   369n22
2:21   397, 398
2:22 (LXX)   369n22
2:28 (LXX)   369
2:30 (LXX)   369n22
2:36–38   397
2:44–45   261, 400
2:47 (LXX)   369n22
3:26 (LXX)   325n14
3:29   215
3:52 (LXX)   325n14
3:85   216n49

4:17   397
4:27 (Theodotian)   335n28
4:35 (Theodotian)   389n9
7:10   181n60
7:13–14   263n53
7:17–27   289n35
7:19–27   257n28
7:21–22   290n41
7:25–27   290n41
8:23–25   257n28
9:4   293n48
9:11   372n31
12:1–2   263n53
12:1–3   257n28, 265,
   290n41, 323n7
12:2   265

Hosea
1:10   286n26, 295n54
2   337–338
2:1   336–338
2:25   336–338
4:1–2   137n28
12:3   137n28
13:5   295n54
13:14   266, 267
14:6   365

Joel
2:1–2   111n15
2:13 (LXX)   335n28, 335n29
3:5 (LXX)   347, 349

Amos
3:2   295n54
5:18   111n15

Jonah
1:9   216n49
4:2 (LXX)   335n28, 335n29

Micah
4:1–2   372n27
4:7   337n33
5:7–8   337n33
6:6–8   388n8
6:12   137n28
7:18   286n28

Nahum
1:3 (LXX)   335n28

Habakkuk
2:4   65n36, 104, 105, 127,
   346

Zephaniah
1:7 111n15
1:15 111n15
1:18 111n15
2:2–3 111n15

Zechariah
3:3–5 200
8:17 401
14:16–17 372n27

Malachi
1:2–3 328–330
1:10 389n9

**NEW TESTAMENT
(EXCEPT ROMANS)***

Matthew
in toto 250
5:17 69n48
5:17–20 69n48, 250n70
21:42–44 342n39
28:19 199

Mark
7:2 406n61
7:5 406n61
11:22 132n12
12:10–11 342n39

Luke
1:68 325n12
18:20 401n49
20:17–18 342n39

Acts
3:15 152n64
3:16 132n12
4:10 152n64
8:3 53n13
9:1 53n13
9:11 53
10:2 32n64
10:14 406n61
10:22 32n64
10:28 406n61
10:35 32n64
11:8 406n61
11:25–26 59

13–14 59
13:1–3 59
13:16 32n64
13:26 32n64
13:43 32n64
13:44–48 360n11
13:50 32n64
14:1–7 360n11
14:26–28 59
15:1 59
15:1–35 59
15:20 407n65
15:29 407n65
16:6 62
16:14 32n64
17:1–9 360n11
17:4 32n64
17:17 32n64
18:1–2 20
18:1–3 36, 37
18:1–10 360n11
18:2 20–21, 44
18:7 32n64
18:16 199
18:18–19 72
18:23 62
18:24–28 203n31
19:1 203n31
19:5 199
19:8–10 360n11
19:22 48n2
20:1–6 48
20:4 48n4
21:39 53
22:3 53, 84n14
26:9–12 53n13
26:10 53n13
26:11 53n13
28:23–29 360n11

1 Corinthians
in toto 74–76, 162, 192,
    214, 247, 248, 254, 273,
    326, 402, 418
1–4 75, 204
1:1 49, 71n52, 315n36, 389
1:2 39n82, 392n21, 392n23
1:4 392n21, 392n22
1:7–8 264n55
1:8 111n15, 309
1:9 132

1:10 392n21
1:10–17 201, 202, 203,
    303n9
1:12 202, 202n28
1:13 163n14, 199, 203
1:13–17 202
1:14 47, 72
1:15 202
1:18–4:21 189n2
1:30 136, 392n23
1:31 144n49
2:1 370
2:1–3 303n9
2:6–9 265
2:7 295, 304n12, 308, 370
3:1 242n58, 392n21
3:1–9 202n28, 203n29
3:1–10 303n9
3:3 194n7
3:13 264n55
3:22 202n28, 316
4:1 370
4:2 132
4:3–4 303n9
4:5 264n55
4:6 303n9, 390n10
4:9 303n9, 315n36
4:10 392n21
4:10–13 322n5
4:14–20 303n9
4:15 392n21, 393n24
4:17 132, 166n21, 392n21,
    393n24
5 204
5:1–8 413n77
5:1–13 75, 189n2
5:2 75n60
5:5 111n15, 280n13
5:6 75n60
5:9–13 303n9
6:1 401n48
6:1–11 75
6:2 264n55
6:12–14 75n60
6:12–20 189n2
6:14 152n64
6:16 280n13
6:18 135
6:20 295
7 204
7:1–40 75, 189n2, 303n9

---

*This index does not include entries for Romans. The table of contents should be sufficient for finding references to this letter.

7:5   136
7:17   194n7
7:25   132, 413n77
7:25–35   264n55
8–9   212
8–10   75, 204, 212, 214n45,
   216, 384, 406, 406n62,
   412–413, 413n76
8:1   75, 413
8:1–11:1   189n2
8:4   75
8:6   413
8:7   409n69, 412
8:7–13   409n69, 412
8:9   213n44, 409n69, 412
8:9–12   413
8:10   409n69, 412, 413n76
8:10–12   213
8:11   163n14, 409n69, 412
8:11–13   413n76
8:12   409n69, 412
8:13   412, 413
9   212, 414
9:1   5, 8, 54, 75, 212, 417
9:1–2   315n36
9:1–3   303n9
9:1–27   413n77
9:3   409n69
9:4   213n44
9:5   213n44, 409n69
9:6   213n44, 409n69
9:8–11   58
9:9–10   152, 336n31,
   412n74
9:10   152, 321
9:11   242n58
9:12   213n44, 409n69, 413
9:15   144n49
9:15–27   303n9
9:18   213n44, 409n69
9:19   75, 212
9:21   114n22
9:24   312
10:1   303n9, 353n2, 369
10:1–2   201
10:1–4   203
10:1–13   381
10:6   181, 182, 229n32,
   336n31
10:11   152, 182, 309,
   412n74
10:13   132
10:14–15   136, 303n9
10:14–22   413n76
10:18   304n11, 423n1

10:19–20   303n9
10:24   401n48
10:25–26   413n76
10:26   361n13
10:27–30   413n76
10:29   401n48
10:32   412
10:33   412, 413
11:1–16   75
11:2–3   303n9
11:2–16   201n26
11:2–14:40   189n2, 201
11:10   166n21
11:17–19   303n9
11:17–34   75
11:25   304n12, 305n13
11:26   264n55
11:30   166n21
12   384, 387, 393, 394
12–14   75, 204, 212, 216,
   217, 249n69
12:1   353n2, 369, 392
12:1–3   303n9
12:1–14:40   201
12:4   391
12:4–11   387, 392
12:4–31   391
12:7   391
12:7–11   392
12:9–10   392
12:10   392
12:11–12   404
12:12   201
12:12–13   11, 75, 201, 203,
   212, 222, 391–393
12:12–31   201, 202, 203,
   363n16
12:13   201, 387, 392
12:14–30   391
12:26   295
12:27   391–393
12:27–30   391
12:28   392
12:28–30   392
13   384, 394
13:2   370
13:13   159
14:2   370
14:17   401n48
15   13, 75, 204, 205,
   205n35, 251, 264, 266,
   272, 290, 291, 292, 293,
   319, 373, 381
15:1–3   303n9
15:1–11   205, 264

15:1–28   205
15:1–34   205
15:3   163, 207
15:3–5   176, 193, 205,
   206–207
15:4a   207
15:4b   207
15:8   417
15:8–9   5, 8, 54
15:8–11   303n9
15:9   53, 315n36
15:10   141
15:11   206
15:12   206
15:12–19   206, 264
15:13   206
15:15   152n64, 206
15:16   206
15:18   392n21, 392n23
15:19   392n21
15:20   176, 296
15:20–28   176, 177, 206,
   264, 265, 265n63, 266,
   289, 291
15:21   182
15:21–22   167, 175, 176,
   176n48, 177, 182–183,
   265
15:22   180, 266n65,
   392n21, 392n22
15:23   176, 206, 265, 296
15:23–28   176
15:24   309, 316
15:24–26   265, 291
15:24–27   206
15:24–28   291, 324
15:28   294
15:29   201
15:31   144n49, 392n21
15:35–49   205, 205n35
15:35–57   374
15:39   280n13
15:40–57   291
15:42–43   291
15:42–49   176, 266, 289,
   291
15:43–46   294
15:44–45   242n58
15:45   266n65
15:45–49   167, 175
15:47–49   266
15:49   296
15:50   267, 291
15:50–51   303n9
15:50–57   266, 289, 291

15:51   370, 375
15:51–52   266, 308
15:51–55   324
15:52   266
15:54–55   267
15:57   266
16:1   68
16:1–4   50, 60, 68
16:12   202
16:19   72
16:24   392n21, 393n24

2 Corinthians
1:1   39n82 49, 71n52, 162,
   315n36, 389
1:3   325n12
1:4   160
1:6   160
1:8   160, 369
1:8–10   72
1:9–10   264n55
1:12   144n49
1:14   111n15, 144n49,
   264n55
1:15–17   303n9
1:18   132
1:20   304n12
1:22   292
1:23–2:13   303n9
2:1   48n5
2:4   160
2:9   160
2:13   309
2:14   392n21
2:15   265n63
2:15–16   264n55
2:17   392n21, 393n24
3:6   304, 305n13, 346n51
3:7   304n11, 423n1
3:7–18   271n75
3:10   295
3:13   304n11, 423n1
3:14   304, 305n13, 357,
   392n21, 392n22
3:18   296, 304n12
4:1   166n21
4:2   194n7
4:3–4   264n55, 265n63
4:4   296n55, 304n12
4:6   304n12
4:7–12   322n5
4:7–14   289n34
4:7–16   207n38
4:14   152n64, 207, 264n55
4:17   160, 289

4:18   293
5:5   292
5:7   194n7
5:10   264n55, 265n63
5:11–6:10   362
5:12   136, 144n49
5:14–15   139, 163, 163n14,
   164
5:17   392n21, 392n23
5:18   362
5:18–19   139
5:18–20   362
5:18–21   164, 362
5:19   362, 392n21, 392n22
5:19a   164
6:1   304n12
6:1–10   207n38, 289n34
6:4   160
6:4–10   160, 322n5
6:5   72
6:7   196n13
6:15   132
7:1   280n13, 304n12
7:2–16   303n9
7:3   207, 207n38, 289n34
7:4   144n49, 160
7:13   144n49, 166n21
8–9   51, 60
8:1–5   51
8:1–24   51
8:2   160
8:4   51
8:5   389
8:8   51
8:9   51
8:13   160
8:13–14   51
8:24   51, 144n49
9:1–2   51
9:1–5   51
9:1–15   51
9:2   144n49
9:3   144n49
9:5   51, 184n64
9:7   51
9:11–12   51
9:13   51, 160, 295
10–13   318n39
10:1   196n13
10:2   194n7
11:1–13:10   303n9
11:5   315n36
11:7   136n22
11:10   144n49
11:15   309

11:21–22   270, 318
11:22   304n11, 318
11:23   72
11:23–27   322n5
11:31   325n12
12:2   392n21
12:7   280n13
12:7–10   160
12:10   322n5
12:11–12   315n36
12:12   160
12:18   194n7
12:19   392n21, 393n24
12:21   48n5
13:3   16
13:3–4   207n38, 289n34
13:10   166n21
13:12   48n5
13:14   48n5

Galatians
in toto   2, 87, 219, 248, 254,
   256, 272, 273, 277, 287,
   305, 325, 348, 380, 418,
   422
1:1   49, 64, 315, 315n36
1:1–2   71n52
1:2   39n82
1:4   264n55, 265n63
1:6   64, 141
1:6–2:21   303n9
1:7   62
1:9   62
1:11   62
1:11–2:14   62, 63
1:13   53, 270
1:13–17   55, 250
1:14   68, 87, 270
1:15   141
1:15–16   5, 8, 319
1:15–17   54, 55, 56, 279n9,
   417
1:16   64, 315
1:17   56, 58, 315n36
1:18   58
1:18–19   64
1:19–20   59
1:21   59
1:22   392n21, 392n23
1:23   53
1:24   295
2:1   64
2:1–10   50, 59, 60, 64, 211,
   414
2:1–14   5

2:2   64
2:4   211, 392n21, 392n23
2:6   64
2:6–9   60
2:7–10   315
2:9   64, 141
2:10   50
2:11–14   15, 60–61, 414
2:14   61
2:15–16   104, 132–134
2:15–21   64–65, 104
2:15–4:25   383n1
2:15–4:31   63, 64, 67
2:16   100, 104, 122, 132, 133, 422
2:17   392n21, 392n22
2:19   207
2:19–20   207n38, 289n34
2:20   132, 133
2:21   104, 136n22, 141, 163n14
3–4   251, 256, 267–268, 328, 339
3:1–5   62, 65, 278, 420
3:1–4:31   9, 65, 127, 210, 420
3:2   202, 303n9
3:6   147
3:6–9   128, 149
3:6–14   5, 65, 100, 105, 127–129, 145, 147, 152, 271, 278, 342, 381, 420
3:6–29   133
3:7–10   147
3:7–12   147
3:8   311n31
3:9   132
3:10   105, 147, 156, 219, 249, 342
3:10–12   128, 346–347
3:10–13   127, 128
3:10–14   221
3:11   105, 346
3:12   105, 342, 346
3:13   219
3:13–14   278
3:14   127, 128, 128n4, 392n21, 392n22
3:14–18   304n12
3:15   62, 304n12
3:15–18   2, 5, 65, 100, 127, 128, 304, 419, 420
3:16   101, 128
3:17   303n9, 304n12
3:17–18   128

3:18   129
3:19   271
3:19–20   271
3:19–25   68, 87, 130, 190, 249, 271, 279n9
3:21   271
3:21–22   304n12
3:22   132, 133, 271
3:23   190
3:24   271
3:26   199, 268, 270, 392n21
3:26–28   11, 198–200, 203
3:26–29   201, 268
3:26–4:11   12, 66, 105, 268, 270–271, 420
3:27   199, 200, 200n24, 201, 404
3:27–28   199, 201
3:28   66, 199, 200, 201, 201n26, 392n21, 392n23
3:29   268, 270, 304n12
4   254, 277, 279
4:1   221, 270, 303n9
4:1–5   269
4:1–11   211, 221, 268
4:3   212, 221, 287
4:4   361n13
4:4–5   221, 283–284, 287
4:4–6   212
4:4–7   13, 267–268, 274, 276–277, 278, 279, 282, 286, 287
4:5   190, 221, 270, 304, 304n12
4:6   270
4:6–7   269, 278, 286
4:7   221, 270
4:7–8   221
4:8   269n72
4:8–9   212
4:8–10   129, 278
4:8–11   265, 269
4:9   157, 190, 218, 219, 249, 269n72, 287
4:10   64n33
4:12   62
4:12–20   66, 303n9, 420
4:13   62, 280n13
4:17   62
4:21   129, 212
4:21–23   66, 303n9
4:21–31   5, 66, 105, 127, 129, 211, 212, 268, 270–271
4:22   212

4:22–31   305
4:23   212, 304n12
4:24   212, 304n12
4:25   212, 270
4:26   212
4:28   62, 270, 304n12
4:29–30   129
4:30   212
4:31   129, 212, 270, 422
5   159, 212, 216, 217, 247, 248, 249, 277, 284
5:1   11, 67, 69, 87, 129, 156, 189, 210, 212, 218, 270, 281, 289, 290
5:1–26   202
5:1–6:10   5, 11, 63, 67, 69–70, 80, 101, 155, 189, 204n32, 210–211, 383n1, 402, 419
5:2   64n33, 65n38
5:2–3   303n9
5:2–5   159
5:2–6   218
5:4   69, 141
5:5   156n2, 159
5:5–6   67
5:6   156, 392n21, 392n22
5:7–12   67
5:10   62
5:10–12   303n9
5:11   62
5:13   62, 67, 156, 189, 211, 212
5:14   69–70, 156, 211, 217, 279n9, 283n23, 401, 402
5:16   156, 156n2, 189, 194n7, 202, 211, 229n32, 277, 303n9, 387, 404
5:16–17   277
5:16–25   280
5:16–26   277, 402
5:17   156, 156n2, 229n32, 230
5:17–18   67
5:18   69, 156n2, 189, 210, 211, 277, 278, 281
5:19–21   189, 211, 277
5:19–23   67, 156
5:21   265n63, 279, 303n9
5:22   67, 156, 156n2
5:22–23   69, 189, 211, 277
5:22–24   387
5:23   211
5:24   223n6, 229n32, 229n33

5:24–25   189
5:25   67, 156, 156n2, 211, 277, 387
6:1   62, 156n2
6:1–10   67, 155n1
6:2   69–70, 87, 211, 265n63, 279n9
6:4   144n49, 401n48
6:8   156n2, 277, 279
6:9–10   265n63
6:10   184n65
6:12–13   62
6:13   64n33
6:16   304n11, 423n1
6:16–26   11
6:18   62, 202
6:25   202

Ephesians
1:3   325n12
1:21   291n44
2:20   342n39
3:10   291n44
4:24   404
6:12   291n44

Philippians
1:1   39n82, 71n52, 392n21
1:1–2   81n4
1:3–27   303n9
1:3–3:1   81n4
1:6   111n15, 264n55
1:7   72
1:10   111n15, 264n55
1:12   72
1:13   392n21
1:14   72
1:17   72
1:17–2:18   80, 81n4
1:20   316
1:23   229n32
1:26   144n49, 392n21
1:27   132n12
1:28   265n63
2:1   392n21
2:5   392n21, 392n22
2:6–11   175n46, 287n30
2:8   215
2:12   215
2:15   265n63
2:15–16   264n55
2:16   111n15, 144n49
2:16–18   303n9
2:22   160
3:2–11   55, 87, 250

3:2–4:1   318n38
3:2–4:3   81n4
3:3   144n49, 392n21
3:3–11   5, 8
3:4–6   270, 318
3:4–11   207n38, 289n34
3:5   53, 304n11, 423n1
3:5–6   53, 56, 270
3:6   53, 270
3:7   56
3:7–10   319
3:7–11   56, 65, 270, 417
3:9   132, 133
3:10   229n33, 296
3:10–11   207, 264n55
3:12–16   312
3:14   312, 392n21
3:17   181, 194n7
3:19   309
3:20   396n37
3:20–21   207n38, 264n55, 289n34, 296
3:21   207, 304n12
4:4–9   81n4, 249n69
4:7   392n21
4:10–14   249n69
4:10–20   81n4, 303n9
4:19   392n21, 392n22
4:21   392n21
4:21–23   81n4

Colossians
1:16   291n44
2:10–15   291n44
2:12   132n12

1 Thessalonians
in toto   262–264
1:1   39n82, 71n52, 392n21
1:1–2:12   80n4, 262n50
1:3   159–160
1:6   160
1:7   181
1:9   209, 264n57
1:9–10   263n51, 265n63
1:10   263, 374
2:6   315n36
2:12   194n7, 304n12
2:12–4:2   80n4
2:13   166n21
2:13–4:2   262n50
2:14   392n21
2:14–16   263n54, 319n40
2:16   309
2:17   229n32

2:19   144n49, 263, 264n55
3:3   160
3:5   166n21
3:7   160, 166n21
3:13   263, 264n55
4   251
4:1   194n7
4:1–2   80, 80n4
4:3   389
4:3–5:28   80n4, 262n50
4:5   229n32, 229n33
4:12   194n7
4:13   353n2, 369
4:13–15   264
4:13–18   207n38, 264, 267, 289n34
4:13–5:11   319, 381
4:14   207
4:15   263
4:16   392n21
4:16–17   263, 264
4:17   207, 263n52, 264n55
5   394
5:1–11   264n55, 265n63
5:2   111n15, 263
5:3   290n42
5:4   263
5:6   184n65
5:8   159, 200
5:10   163n14, 207, 207n38, 289n34
5:12–22   80, 80n4
5:12–24   249n69
5:18   389, 392n21, 392n22
5:23   263, 264n55
5:24   132

2 Thessalonians
2:13   132n12

1 Timothy
2:1–4   396–398

2 Timothy
4:10   68n44
4:20   48n2

Titus
4:1–3   396–398

Philemon
1   71n52
8   392n21
10   392n21
15   166n21

20   393n24
23   392n21

Hebrews
1:6   296
11:1   293
13:24   140n42

James
1:15   178n55
1:18   292
2:1   132n12
2:11   401n49

1 Peter
1:1   68n44
1:3   325n12
1:21   152n64
2:6–8   310n28, 342n39
2:10   338n36
2:13–17   396–398
3:18   163n14
3:22   291n44
4:13   289
5:10   289

Revelation
1:5   296
14:12   132n12
14:14   292
18:17   334n27

**APOCRYPHA AND
SEPTUAGINT**

Baruch
2:30   358n6
2:33   358n6
3:9–4:3   344
3:28   344
3:29–30   344
4:1   344

1 Esdras
1:47   216
4:50   334n27
8:16   389n9
9:9   389n9

2 Esdras
19:17   335n28, 335n29

Additions to Esther
14:17   406

Judith
2:2   370n24
10:5   406
12:1–2   406
13:5   286n29

1 Maccabees
1:47   406n61
1:62   406n61
2:52   146n54, 181n60
3:25   337n33
3:60   389n9
4:30   325n14
7:33   397
8:17–32   17
12:1–4   17
12:6   150n60
12:21   150n60
13:48   69n47
14:24   17
15:15–24   17

2 Maccabees
in toto   230
1:2   146n54
1:3   389n9
5:9   150n60
5:27   406
6:12–17   335
6:14   335n28
7   138, 289n35
11:17   325n14
13:21   370n24
14:37–46   138
15:12–16   293n51

3 Maccabees
6:3   129n6
6:28   286n26
7:23   325n14

4 Maccabees
1:12–13   230
1:15–17   231
1:30–35   390n16
1:35   231
2:1–6   231
2:4–6   231
2:16   231
2:18   231
3:6–18   231
3:11   231
3:17   231
6:27–29   138
6:33   231

7:4   231
13:2   231
13:7   231
17:20–22   138
18:16   389n9

Sirach
2:1   216n49
2:15–16   293n48
4:15   215
5:1–8   335
5:4   335n28
6:18–37   386
6:20–22   390
6:23–37   394
9:9   220n2
10:4   397
10:6   401
13:15   401n50
14:17   168n25
15:14   168n25
17:1–4   168
17:1–24   168n25
17:30–32   168n25
18:7–14   168n25
18:11   335n28
22:22   370n24
24:8   286n29
24:12   286n29
24:22   215
24:28   168n25
27:16   370n24
27:17   370n24
27:21   370n24
33:7–13   168n25
33:10–13   333n26
35:1   388n8
36:17   295n54
40:1   168n25
40:11   168n25
43:16   389n9
44:19   146n54, 149n60
44:20   145n53
44:21   129n6, 149n60
46:1   324n10
47:22   324n10
50:25–26   361n12

Susanna
1:62 (Theodotian)   69n47

Tobit
3:5   69n47
4:10–11   388n8
12:7   370n24

12:11   370n24
12:12   293n51
13:11   372n27
13:18   325n14
14:6–7   372n27

Wisdom of Solomon
2–5   289n35
2:22   370
2:23–24   168n25
2:24   179n57
3:8   260n44
3:9   324n10, 394
4:15   324n10
6:1–3   399
6:3   397
6:17–18   394
6:22   370
7:1–6   168n25
8:7   390n16
9:1–3   168n25
12:3–7   335
12:3–18   335, 336
12:7   286n26
12:8–11   335
12:12   332
12:12–18   335
12:13–14   335
12:15–16   335
12:17–18   335
12:21   286n26
13–15   109, 260n42
13:1–9   109n10
13:1–15:17   43n95
13:10–14:11   109n11
14:12–31   109n11
14:15   370
14:23   370
14:26   109n12
15:1   335n28
15:11   168n25
16:10   286n26
16:21   286n26
16:26   286n26
18:13   286n26
19:6   286n26
19:22   295n54

OLD TESTAMENT PSEUDEPIGRAPHA

Apocalypse of Abraham
in toto   151n62
20:5   129n6

Apocalypse of Moses
in toto   173
8:2   174
13:5   174
14:2   174, 180
19:3   174n40
28:4   174n40
30:1   174
32   174n39

Assumption of Moses
1:14   295n54
10:3   286n27

2 Baruch
5:1   286, 286n29
13:8–12   257n28
13:9   286n27
14:1–10   377
15:8   289n35
19:1–8   257n28
21:4   151n63
24:1   181n60
25:2–3   290n41
30:1–2   257n28
30:1–3   263n53
31:5–32:6   290n38, 291
48:3   308n21, 369n23
48:8   151n63
48:30–41   290n41
48:42   180
48:45–47   114n24
51:3–6   257n28
54:13–19   173
54:15   180
56:5–7   290n37, 291
57:1–2   145n53
68:5   372n27
70:2–10   290n41
72:1–73:7   257n28
72:1–74:4   290n39, 291
75:1–5   308n22, 377
77:1–10   257n28
78:4   149n59
78:7   257n28
81:4   308n21, 369n23
82:9   399
83:1–85:13   257n28

3 Baruch
in toto   259

4 Baruch
4:10   149n59

1 Enoch
1:1–9   257n28
1:3   324n10
1:8   324n10
5:1–10   257n28
5:7–8   324n10
5:45–57   257n28
5:91–104   257n28
16:3   369n23
25:5   324n10
37–71   291
40:5   324n10
41:1   308n21, 369n23
41:2   324n10
45:1–46:8   263n53
45:2–6   111n15
45:4–5   290n38, 291
46:2   308n21, 369n23
46:5   399
48:1   324n10
48:2–10   263n53
51:1–5   263n53, 291
51:3–5   290n39
51:5   324n10
58:1–6   290n39, 291
61–62   290n39, 291
61:8–13   263n53
62:4   290n42
62:7–16   263n53
62:11   286n27
69:26–29   263n53
71:15–17   263n53
91:12–17   291n43
91:15–16   290n38, 291n43
93:1–10   291n43
93:2   324n10
93:11–14   308n22, 377
102–104   289n35
103:2   308n21, 369n23
104   323n7
104:7   181n60
104:10   308n21, 369n23
104:12   308n21
104:12–13   369n23
106:19   308n21, 369n23

2 Enoch
in toto   259, 260
2:2   260n40
5:10   260n40
5:17–18   260n40
10:22   260n40
10:31   260n40
11:37   259n38
13:28   260n40

13:35   260n40
13:44   259n38
13:48   259n38
13:51   260n40
13:59   259n38
13:71   259n38
17:2   260n40
17:4–6   259n38
22:2   260n40
45:3   388n8
65:6–11   259n38

4 Ezra
3:7–10   172
3:15   129n6
3:21   180
3:21–22   172
3:21–27   172
3:26   172
5:1–3   290n41
6:1–28   257n28
6:11–28   263n53
6:13–24   290n41
6:17–24   111n15
6:58   286n27, 295n54
7:10–15   290n37, 291
7:26–44   323n7
7:28–61   257n28
7:30–44   290n39, 291
7:102   111n15
7:118–121   172
9:1–3   290n41
9:19–22   290n39
9:26–10:59   257n28
10:6–16   290n42
10:38   308n21, 369n23
12:31–34   263n53
12:31–39   257n28
12:36–38   308n21
12:36–39   369n23
13:21–56   257n28
14:5   308n21

Joseph and Aseneth
23:12   401

Jubilees
1:19–21   286n29
1:24–25   286n27
1:25   295n54
1:29   290n38, 324n10
2:13–4:6   171
2:20   286n27
3:8–14   171
3:26–31   171

3:27   171
4:26   290n37
4:29–30   171
5:12–19   114n24
7:20   401n50
11:14–23:7   146n53, 151n62
11:18–24   150n60
12–46   180n59
12:23   149n60
12:24   129n6
13:4   129n6
13:19–21   129n6
14:5   129n6
14:7   129n6
14:13   129n6
14:18   129n6
15:6   150n60
15:9–10   129n6
15:19   129n6
16:17–20   129n6
16:26   129n6
16:28   129n6
18:15–16   129n6
19:21–25   129n6
20:2   401n50
20:11–13   150n60
21:22   129n6
21:25   129n6
22:9–10   286, 286n29
22:14–15   286, 286n29
23:23–31   290n38
23:27–31   323n7
30:17   181n60
33:20   286n29
36:4   401n50
36:8   401n50

Letter of Aristeas
in toto   25
45   397
128–171   67n43
128–172   43n95
130–171   156n3
132–141   109n11
143–152   57
144   57
152   109n11, 109n12
162–166   57, 58
168   401
187–300   156n3
207   401
224   397, 399
234   388n8

Liber antiquitatum biblicarum (Pseudo-Philo)
6:1–8:14   151n62
11:1–3   114n24
11:1–5   257n28
12:9   286, 286n29
13:8   180
13:8–10   174–75, 179
18:5   129n6
18:6   295n54
19:12–13   257n28
21:10   286n29
23:4   149n59
23:5   129n6, 146n54
23:7   150n60
23:13   257n28
27:17   286n29
28:2   286n29
32:1   149n59
39:7   286, 286n29
49:6   286n29

Life of Adam and Eve
in toto   173
34:2   174
34:3   174
44:4   174n39]

Odes of Solomon
7:26   325n14
8:52   325n14
9:18   325n14
12:7   335n28
14:34   325n14

Pseudo-Phocylides
3   57n21, 109n12
6   57n21
8   57n21
14   57n21
15   57n21
18   57n21
22–30   57n21
70–96   386
71–75   390
76   390n16
76–95   394
84–85   57n21
99   57n21
100–101   57n21
109   57n21
109–192   109n11
177–183   57n21
184   57n21
185   57n21

186   57n21
190–192   43n95, 57n21, 109n12
198   57n21
213–214   43n95, 57n21, 109n11, 109n12
220–222   57n21
225–226   57n21

Psalms of Solomon
7:1–10   257n28
7:3   389n9
8:22   216
8:23–24   257n28
9:9   129n6
9:9–10   149n59
14:1–2   293n48
15:12–13   111n15
17:21–46   257n28
17:26   263n53
17:27   286n27
17:31   372n27
17:32   263n53
17:34   372n27
18:1–9   257n28
18:3   129n6

Sibylline Oracles
1–2   171
1:22–86   171
1:40–45   171
1:50–54   171
1:62–65   290n41
2:154–173   290n41
3   259
3:8–45   109
3:15–23   109n10
3:29–35   109n11
3:29–45   43n95
3:36–45   109n11
3:49   259n34
3:69   324n10
3:184–187   43n95, 109, 109n12
3:191–195   259n34
3:286–294   259n34
3:594–600   43n95, 109, 109n12
3:632–656   290n41
3:652–656   259n34
3:660–701   259, 265n60
3:702   286n27
3:702–709   258
3:764   43n95, 109, 109n12
3:772   372n27

3:788–795   290n39, 291
3:796–806   290n41
5   259, 261n47
5:68   286n27
5:108   259n34
5:155   259n34
5:179–237   259, 265n60
5:202   286n27
5:248–255   258
5:256   259n34
5:414   259n34

fragments
1–3   109
1:3–17   109n10
1:18–21   109n11
1:19   109n11
1:23–25   109n11
1:32–35   109n10
3:3–14   109n10
3:19   109n11
3:21–33   109n11

Testament of Abraham
in toto   151n62, 259, 260
2:6   129n6
8:7 (recension A)   129n6
13:5–6 (recension A)   260

Testament of Moses
3:9   129n6

Testaments of the Twelve Patriarchs
in toto   258

Testament of Asher
2:6   361n12

Testament of Benjamin
3:1   293n48
3:3–4   401n50
9:2   258, 372n27
11:4   181n60

Testament of Gad
4:2   401n50

Testament of Issachar
5:1–2   293n48
5:2   401n50

Testament of Joseph
4:2   390n16
6:7   390n16

9:2   390n16
10:2–3   390n16

Testament of Judah
22:1–3   258
25:5   258

Testament of Levi
3:10   361n12

Testament of Naphtali
2:2–4   333n26
2:2–8   390
2:2–3:5   386
2:9–3:5   394

Testament of Reuben
6:9   401n50

Testament of Simeon
7:2   258

Testament of Zebulun
9:9   361n12

DEAD SEA SCROLLS

1QapGen *(Genesis Apocryphon)*
18–22   151n62
21:10   129n6
21:12   129n6

1QH[a] *(Hodayot or Thanksgiving Hymns*[a]*)*
1:7–8   295n54
1:21   308n21, 333n26
2:13   308n21, 369n23
3:7–18   290n42
3:20–24   333n26
4:27–28   369n23
4:27–29   308n21
4:28–29   333n26
6:8   337n33
6:32   337n33
7:22   337n33
7:26–32   377
7:26–33   308n22
7:27   308n21, 369n23
9:29–30   295n54
10:3–7   308n22
11:3   333n26
11:10   308n21, 370n23
12:13   308n21, 370n23

12:26   333n26
15:26–32   377
15:28   378
15:31–32   378
16:13   293n48

1QpHab *(Pesher Habakkuk)*
7:1–5   370n23
7:5   308n21
7:8   308n21
7:8–14   370n23
7:14   308n21
10:13   295n54, 324n10

1QM *(Milḥamah* or *War Scroll)*
1:6   337n33
3:2   295n54
4:2   337n33
4:10–11   295n54
12:1   324n10
12:2–8   257n28
13:8   337n33
14:5   337n33
14:8–9   337n33

1QS *(Serek Hayaḥad* or *Rule of the Community)*
1:6   175n45
3:15–16   295n54
3:23   308n21, 369n23
4:14   337n33
4:16–25   257n28
4:18   308n21, 369n23
5:13   337n33
5:25   401n50
8:2   401n50
8:6   324n10
9:3–5   388n8
9:18   308n21, 369n23
11:3   308n21
11:3–5   369n23
11:5   308n21
11:19   308n21
11:22   333n26

CD (Cairo Genizah copy of the *Damascus Document*)
1:4–5   337n33
2:6   337n33
2:8   295n54
2:16   175n45
4:3–4   324n10
19:1   293n48

1Q27
1:3–4   308n21, 370n23

4QDibHam^a *(Words of the Luminaries^a)*
3:4–6:3   286n27
3:4–5   295n54

4QEnoch^c
5:2:26   369n23

4Q169 (4QpNah *Pesher Nahum)*
fragments 3–4, column 1, lines7–8   128n3

4Q285 *(Sefer ha-Milḥamah)*
257n28

11Q19 (11QT^a *Temple Scroll^a)*
66:11–13   128n3

PHILO

De Abrahamo
in toto   151n62
5   115n29
135–136   109n11
135–137   109n12
249   115n27
275–276   115n29, 146n53

De aeternitate mundi
59   115n27

De agricultura
31   115n27
66   115n27

De cherubim
48   370
49   370

De confusione linguarum
40–41   175n46
62–63   175n46
146–147   175n46
171   291n44

De decalogo
in toto   57n19, 67n43, 156n3
1   115n29

2–9   115n30
36   401n49
50   312
51   401n49
73   312
80   312
121–153   401n49
142   232
142–153   231
146   232
149   232
168–174   401n49
173–174   231

Quod Deus sit immutabilis
4   146n54
61   312, 370
67   312

De ebrietate
37–38   115n28
141–142   115n26

De fuga et inventione
110   200n22

De Iosepho
29   115n27
40   390n16

Legatio ad Gaium
in toto   20n16
155   18, 23
156   22n25
156–158   18
157   397
159–160   19n15
159–161   19
361   406n63

Legum allegoriae I, II, III
1.69–76   390n16
1.104   370
2–3   169
2.71–108   170n29
3.1–253   170n29
3.3   370
3.36   109n11
3.47–48   312
3.71   370
3.100   370
3.167–168   115n28
3.197   389n9
3.203   129n6
3.228   146n54

17.71   370
17.100   370

De migratione Abrahami
43–44   146n54
89–94   117n33
92   116n32
128–143   312
131   312
132   146n54
143   312

De mutatione nominum
59   291n44
181–187   146n54
201–202   146n54
225   390n16
236–238   344–345

De opificio mundi
1–3   29
3   115n26
65–88   169
69–88   176n47
129–130   176n47
134–147   176n47
134–170a   169, 170
151–152   170
152   170
154   170
154–155   170
156   170
157   170
157–166   170
165   171
167–170a   170
171   115n27

De plantatione
126   388n8

De posteritate Caini
83–88   344–345
185   115n27

De praemiis et poenis
in toto   259
49   146n54
79   265n61
79–81   344–345
88–90   290n39
91–97   265n61
95   261n47
108   115n27
127–162   259

162–171   365
163–171   365–366
164   259
165   259
168   259
169–170   259, 265n61
169–172   291
171   259

Quis rerum divinarum heres sit
8   129n6
14   146n54
26   183n63
86   129n6
90–93   146n54
96–99   146n54
313–314   129n6

Quod omnis probus liber sit
30   115n27
37   115n27
67   390n16
70   390n16
159   390n16

Quaestiones et solutiones in Exodum I, II
2.2   116

Quaestiones et solutiones in Genesis
1.4–57   169
1.31–57   170
3.2   146n54
3.54   150n60
3.56   146n54
3.58   146n54
4.17   146n54

De sacrificiis Abelis et Caini
60   370
62   370

De sobrietate
25   115n30

De somniis I, II
1.93–94   58
1.102   243n61
2.174–175   115n28
2.180   344–345
2.223   115n28

De specialibus legibus I, II, III, IV
in toto   57n19, 156n3
1.202   115n28
1.277   388n8
1.287   388n8
1.301   344–345
1.305   116n32
1.306   115n28
1.319   370
2.13   115n28
2.197   243n61
3.32   115n27
3.37–42   109n11, 109n12
3.40   370
3.51   390n16
3.131   391n18
3.189   115n27
4.79–82   232
4.79–131   231
4.84–85   232
4.92–94   232
4.96   243n61
4.100–125   232
4.123   232
4.149–150   115n29
4.186   401n50

De virtutibus
in toto   67n43
183–184   344–345
194   115n29

De vita contemplativa
25   370
37   406n64
59   115n27
59–62   109n11

De vita Mosis
1.162   115n29
2.4   115n29
2.13   115n30
2.14   115n28
2.48   115n26
2.81   115n27
2.245   115n27

JOSEPHUS

Against Apion
1.169–171   32n67
1.190–192   109
1.225   109

1.239   32n65, 109
1.244   109
1.249   109
1.254   109
1.304–311   32n65
2.66   109
2.76–77   397–398
2.81   109
2.86   109
2.89–111   32n65
2.121–124   32n65
2.128–129   109
2.137   33n69
2.137–142   32n67
2.139   109
2.145   29, 29n55
2.145–178   30
2.145–219   27
2.145–286   27, 28, 29, 32,
    43, 45, 105
2.145–296   156n3
2.146   27
2.150   29
2.151–168   29
2.154–156   27
2.164–167   27, 105
2.164–219   57
2.168   27
2.168–174   105
2.169–174   29
2.170–171   27
2.174   27
2.175–178   29n54
2.179–183   27
2.189   29n54, 370n25
2.190–192   27, 105
2.190–219   105
2.195   390n16
2.199   29
2.199–203   29n56, 109
2.199–211   27
2.199–214   29n55
2.204   29n54
2.206–208   109
2.209–210   32
2.214   27
2.215   29n56
2.220–224   29n54
2.220–225   105
2.220–278   27, 29
2.225–231   29n54
2.225–235   29n55
2.232–249   105
2.234   27
2.236   30

2.236–238   29n53
2.243–247   29n57
2.250–254   29n55
2.251–289   67n43
2.254   30
2.256–257   27
2.257   27
2.258   30
2.266   370n25
2.270   30
2.271–278   29n54, 105
2.273   29n55
2.273–275   29n56, 29n57,
    109n12
2.276   29n56
2.281–284   27

Jewish Antiquities
1.1–26   89n30
1.14   168n27, 169
1.20   168n27, 169
1.25   57
1.32–72   168
1.40   168
1.46   169
1.60–66   169
1.68–69   169
1.72   169
1.151–256   151n62
1.167–168   150n60
1.191–193   150n60
1.205–206   150n60
1.220–221   150n60
1.230   243n61
1.235   150n60
1.238–241   150n60
1.315   243n61
2.257   150n60
3.259–260   57
5.54   183n63
6.147–150   388n8
10.210   261, 265n62, 400
11.169   149n59
11.346   406n61
12.226   150n60
14.110   32n64
14.127–139   18n10
14.185–267   21n21
14.195   32n64
14.215–216   22
14.255   149n59
15.157   243n61
15.183–218   18n10
15.374   397
15.374–376   398

16.160–178   21n21
17.299–303   23n31
18.81–84   19
18.81–85   31n61
18.257–309   20n16
19   31n61
19:16   132n12
19.30   370n25
19.71   370n25
19.104   370n25
20.195   31n61

Jewish War
1.1–30   89n30
1.3   28n50
1.11   243n61
1.187–194   18n10
1.386–397   18n10
1.431–434   18n10
2.80–83   23n31
2.90   243n61
2.133   370n25
2.140   397
2.184–203   20n16
2.197   397, 399
4.406–407   391n18
5.20   243n61
5.277–279   391n18
5.380   147
6.239   243n61
6.288–315   260
6.312–314   260, 265n62
6.346   243n61
6.353   243n61

The Life
13–16   406
14   406
422–430   28n51
424–425   28n51
428–429   28n51

**RABBINIC
LITERATURE**

Mishnah

ᶜAbodah Zarah
2:3–4   407n65
4:10–5:12   407n65

Qiddušin
1:1   220n1

Tosefta

ʿAbodah Zarah
7:1–17   407n65

Sanhedrin
7.11   127n2

Sotah
6.6   129n8

Babylonian Talmud

ʿAbodah Zarah
55a–76b   407n65

Niddah
61b   220n1

Šabbat
30a   220n1
31a   401

Jerusalem Talmud

ʿAbodah Zarah
4:8–5:15, 44a–45b   407n65

Targums and Midrashim

Targum Neofiti
Deut 30:13   344n45

Targum Yerusalmi
Lev 19:18   401

Targum Pseudo-Jonathan
Gen 22.1   129n8

Genesis Rabbah
53.11   129n8

Sipra
Lev 19:18   401, 401n50

APOSTOLIC FATHERS

Barnabas
6:2–4   310n28, 342n39

1 Clement
Introduction   40n85
5–6   35
60:2–61:2   397n41

Diognetus
11.6   132n12

Ignatius, *To the Romans*
Introduction   40n85

OTHER ANCIENT CHRISTIAN WRITERS

Ambrosiaster

Commentarius in Epistulam ad Romanos
4–7   34n71

Clement of Alexandria

Stromata
6.16   401n49

Eusebius

Historia ecclesiastica
2.23.5   406n64
5.25.5–7   35n72

Orosius

Adversus Paganos
7.6.15   20n18

GREEK AND LATIN WRITERS

Aelius Aristides

Orationes
17.9   391n17
23.31   391n17
24.18   391n17
24.38–39   391n17
26.43   391n17

Aeschylus

Septem contra Thebas
224   178n55

Appian

Historia Romana
1.2   243n61

Apuleius

Metamorphoses
11.1–26   75n64
11.13–15   204n34
11.21–23   204n34
11.24   200
11.25   204n34

Aristotle

Ethica nichomachea
1.13   390n14
2.7   390n14
3.5–21   230n36
3.8   390n14
3.10–12   230n34

Rhetorica
1.2.4–6   384n2
1.2.13   112n20, 146n55
2.22.1–3   112n20, 146n55
2.23.4–5   161n10, 275n4
2.23.12   108n7
3.13.4–5   86n24

Topica
2.10   161n10, 275n4

Arrian

Epistulae
2   92

Artapanus

Fragment 1
apud Eusebius, *Praeparatio evangelica*
9.18.1   150n60

Athenaeus

Deipnosophistae
2.49d   178n53
12.53   200n23

Cicero

In Catilinam
3.9.21   107n6

De oratore
2.178–216   384n2
2.310–312   384n2
3.205   227n19

Pro Flacco
28.66   18
28.67–68   18n9

De inventione rhetorica
1.19   86n24
1.41.77   112n20, 146n55
1.53.101   107n6
1.99–100   227n19, 227n24, 343n42

Pro Ligario
6.19   107n6

De officiis
3.5.21–23   391n17

Orato ad M. Brutum
85   227n19
138   227n19

Partitiones oratoriae
53   227n19
57   227n19

Topica
23   161n10, 275n4
45   227n19
68–71   161n10, 275n4

Columella

De re rustica
5.9.16   364

Demetrius

De elocutione
265–266   227n19, 227n25
270   160n8, 294n52

Demosthenes

In Aristogionem ii
23   137n30

In Midiam
172   183n63

Dio Cassius

Historia Romana
57.18.5   19
59.19.1–2   178n53
59.20.3   178n53

60.6.6   20–21, 22
61.33.8   178n53
63.28.5   178n53
67.4.6   178n53
67.14.1–2   31n61
73.18.1   178n53

Dio Chrysostom

Orationes
33.16   391n17
33.44   391n17
39.5   391n17
40.21   391n17
41.9   391n17
50.3–4   391n17

Diodorus Siculus:

Biblioteca historica
1.1.1–14.7   89n30
3.73.6   183n63

Diogenes Laertius

Diogenes Laertus, *De clavorum philosophorum vitis*
7.173.1–5   178n53
10.127–128   230n34
10.149   230n36

Pseudo-Diogenes

Epistle
22   390n15

Dionysius of Halicarnassus

Antiquitates romanae
7.37.2   135n18

Epictetus

Diatribae (Dissertationes)
1.2.1   94n53
1.2.5–7   94n53
1.3.3–6   244n65
1.4.1–4   94n53
1.4.18–21   94n53
1.4.28–29   227n26
1.6   95
1.6.1–3   94n53
1.6.13–22   94n53
1.6.40   94n53, 95

1.9.12–15   227n26
1.11   93, 97n63
1.12.1–4   94n53
1.12.7   94n53
1.12.17   94n53
1.12.28   244n65
1.13   93, 97n63
1.14   97n63
1.15   97n63, 97n64
1.19.25   388n8
1.26.1   243
1.26.5–7   227n26
1.27.1–4   94n53
1.27.7   94n53
1.28.5–9   233n46, 234n49
1.28.8   234n48
2   92
2.1   95
2.1.2–3   94n53
2.1.6–7   94n53
2.1.10–14   94n53
2.1.29   94n53
2.1.40   94n53
2.4   97n63, 97n64
2.10.1–3   94n53
2.10.4–5   391n17
2.10.5–6   94n53
2.11.1–2   94n53
2.11.13   94n53
2.11.23–25   94n53
2.16.47   230n36
2.17.18   244n65
2.17.18–19   233
2.17.21   233
2.18.8–9   230n36
2.24   93, 97n63
2.25   92
2.26.1   234
2.26.1–7   233n46
2.26.4   234
3.1   93, 97n63, 97n64
3.4   93, 97n63, 97n64
3.4.22–24   94n53
3.4.84–87   94n53
3.5   93, 97n63
3.7   93, 97n63
3.9   93, 97n63, 97n64
3.13.4   244n65
3.14.1–3   94n53
3.14.9–12   94n53
3.17.6   243
3.22   93, 97n63
3.24   93, 95
3.24.68–70   227n26
4.1   93, 95

4.1.147   234n47
4.6   93, 97n63
4.7   93
4.8.2   121n47

Pseudo-Eupolemus
apud Eusebius, *Praeparatio
   evangelica*
9.17.3–4   150n60
9.17.8   150n60

Euripides

Andromache
1200   244n65

Hecuba
342–378   137n31
432–437   137n31

Hippolytus
875   244n65

Iphigenia aulidensis
536   244n65

Medea
in toto   232, 242
1077b–1080   233, 241

Phoenissae
911–1018   137n31
1090–1092   137n31
1335   244n65
1346   244n65
1599   244n65

Galen

*De placitis Hippocratis et
   Platonis*
3.3.13   233n44
3.3.13–18   234n50
3.4.23–27   233n45, 234n50
4.2.10–18   230n36
4.2.27   234n50
4.6.20   233n44
4.6.20–21   234

Heraclitus

*Allegoriae (Quaestiones
   homericae)*
39.14   290n42

Epistulae
4   96n62
7   96n62
9   96n62

Hermogenes

Progymnasmata
2.19–22   235n53
9.1–43   227n19
9.4–6   227n24, 343n42
9.13–17   227n23
9.28–35   227n25
9.37–41   238
9.42–43   227n27

Herodotus

Historiae
1.1   89n30
7.220   138n34

Homer

Iliad
15:495–498   137n30

Horace

Carmina
3.2.13   137n30

Sermones
1.4.139–43   24
1.9.60–78   24
1.9.68–72   26
1.9.69–70   33n69

Isocrates

Ad Nicoclem
20   388n8

Juvenal

Satirae
3.296   22n25
6.160   406n63
14.96   26
14.96–102   31–32
14.96–106   24, 33n69
14.97   25
14.98–99   26, 406n63
14.99   31
14.103–104   26, 32
14.105–106   26

Livy

Ab urbe condita libri
praef.   89n30
2.32.7–2.33.1   391n17
8.9.10   138
10.28.12–13   138n33

Macrobius

Saturnalia
2.4.1   406n63

Martial

Epigrammata
7.30.5   33n69
7.35   33n69
7.55.4–8   33n69
7.82   33n69
11.94   33n69

Menander

Monostichoi
1   390n15

Nepos

Pelopidas
1.1   89n30

Ovid

Metamorphoses
7.18   244n65
7.19–21   234

Persius

Satirae
5.184   33n69

Petronius

Satyricon
68.8   33n69
frg. 37   406n63

Phalaris

Epistulae
81.1   135n18

Plato

Apologia
32a   137n30

Leges
716D   388n8

Phaedrus
237e–238a   390n14

Res publica
430a–432a   390n14
435b   390n14
442c   390n14
462c-d   391n17

Symposium
179b   137n30

Plutarch

Alexander
1.1–3   89n30

Aratus
23.5   391n17
44.4.1   178n53

Cicero
7.6.5   31n61

Cimon
8.6.4   178n53

De curiositate
552E.4–6   178n53

De Iside et Osiride
3 (352B)   200

Pelopidas
20–21   137n31, 138
21.4   138n34

De Stoicorum repugnantiis
7   390n14

Polybius

Historiae
1.1.1–1.2.8   89n30
1.31.6   183n63
2.18.10   243n61

Quintilian

Institutio oratoria
1.8.3   277n19
3.8.10–12   63n32
3.8.49–51   227n27
3.8.49–54   277n19
3.9.1   86n24
4.1.28   227n19, 227n22,
   227n25
4.1.42–48   110n13
4.1.63–70   110n14
4.1.69   227n19, 227n22
4.4.1–5.28   64n34
4.4.4   64n34
5.1.1   65n35
5.2.1–5   108n7
5.10.86–93   161n10, 275n4
5.11.3   118n40
5.11.5   118n40
5.11.36–37   107
5.11.36–44   107n6, 329n19
5.11.42   107
5.11.43   107n6
5.13   118n38
5.14.24–26   112n20,
   146n55
6.1.3   227n19
6.1.25–27   227n19, 227n25
6.2.8–9   384n2
8.4.26–27   316, 324n11
9.2.14–15   118n40
9.2.29–30   227n25, 236n54
9.2.29–39   227n19
9.2.31   227n24, 343n42
9.2.36–37   227
9.3.54   160n8, 294n52
9.3.89   178n55
11.1.39–40   227n27
11.1.39–41   227n19

Rhetorica ad Herennium
1.4   86n24
2.13.19   107
2.19   329n19
2.30.48   107n6
2.48   107
4.33   118n40
4.66   227n19, 227n24,
   343n42

Rutilius Lupus

*De figures sententiarum et
   elocutionis*
2.6   178n55

Sallust

Bellum Catalinae
1.1–4.5   89n30

Seneca

Epistulae morales
108.22   26

De Ira
2.31.7   391n17

De superstitione
apud Augustine, *De civitate
   Dei*
6.11   24n33, 24n34, 26n40

Medea
952   235
991   235

Troades
193–202   137n31

Pseudo-Socrates

Epistle
34.3   390n15

Sophocles

Ajax
981   244n65

Antigone
1211   244n65

Oedipus coloneus
753   244n65
847   244n65
1338   244n65
1401   244n65

Philoctetes
744   244n65
1360   178n55

Stobaeus

Eclogae
2.88.4   230n36
2.89.4–90.6   230n36
2.90.7   230n34

Strabo

Geographica
16.1.37   33n69
16.4.9   33n69
17.2.5   33n69

Suetonius

Divus Claudius
25.4   16–17, 20, 34

Domitianus
12.2   33n69

Divus Julius
42.3   22n23

Tiberius
36   19, 31

Tacitus

Agricola
1   89n30

Annales
2.85.4   19n12
13.50   399
13.51   399
15.42   35
15.43   35
15.44   34, 35

Historiae
5.2.1–3   25
5.3–4   25
5.4.2   406n63
5.5.1   27, 32
5.5.1–2   26

5.5.1–3   26–27
5.5.2   24, 25, 26, 31, 33n69
5.5.4   25, 27
5.13.1–2   260–261
5.13.3   27

Theon of Alexandria

Progymnasmata
2.94.17   235n53
2.96.11   235n53
2.115.11–117.6   227n27
2.115.11–118.5   227n19
2.115.14–19   227n23
2.117.6–32   227n25
2.118.12–14   227
2.123.22   235n53

Thucydides

Historiae
1.1–2   89n30
2.43.1–2   137n30

Tibullus

Carmina
1.3.18   26n41

Valerius Maximus

*Factorum et Dictorum
   Memorabilia*
1.3.3   17–18, 24

Xenophon

Anabasis
5.7.32   388n8

Memorabilia
1.3.3   388n8
2.13.18   391n17

Oeconomicus
5.17   178

INSCRIPTIONS

*Jewish Inscriptions of
Western Europe*
2:2   22n27
2:33   22n27
2:62   31n59
2:96   22n27
2:100   22n27
2:130   22n27
2:163   22n27
2:167   22n27
2:169   22n27
2:170   22n27
2:189   22n27
2:194   22n27
2:218   31n59
2:224   31n59
2:292   22n27
2:392   31n59
2:489   31n59
2:491   31n59
2:542   22n27
2:547   22n27
2:549   22n27
2:562   22n27
2:577   22n27
2:578   22n27
2:579   22n27
2:602   22n25